# Architecture Competitions
## and the Production of
## Culture, Quality and Knowledge
### *An International Inquiry*

Published in 2015 by
**Potential Architecture Books**
T2 - 511 Place d'Armes
Montreal (Quebec), Canada
H2Y 2W7
www.potentialarchitecturebooks.com

Library and Archives Canada Cataloguing in Publication

**Architecture competitions and the production of culture, quality and knowledge : an international inquiry** / edited by Jean-Pierre Chupin, Carmela Cucuzzella, Bechara Helal.

Includes bibliographical references and index.
ISBN 978-0-9921317-0-8 (bound)

     1. Architecture--Competitions. I. Chupin, Jean-Pierre, 1960-, editor II. Cucuzzella, Carmela, 1962-, editor III. Helal, Bechara, 1973-, editor

NA2335.A73 2015     720'.79     C2015-900227-3

Keywords : International competitions, Architectural judgment, Design thinking, Digital archiving (databases), Architectural publications, Architectural experimentation

Art direction and graphic design : Catherine Bisaillon
Infography : Tiphaine Abenia, Claude Bédard, Ange Sauvage

Typeset in FF Din

# Architecture Competitions
## and the Production of
## Culture, Quality and Knowledge
### *An International Inquiry*

**Edited by**
Jean-Pierre Chupin
Carmela Cucuzzella
Bechara Helal

POTENTIAL
ARCHITECTURE
BOOKS

# Contents

# A World of Potentialities

Competitions as Producers
of Culture, Quality and Knowledge

# 278

Average number of competitors per major international competitions between 1945 and 2000.

___

## Ratio of international competitions between 2007 and 2010
*Compared with rank in Human Development Index (HDI) as provided by the United Nations Development Programme in 2014*

**86% in Germany** (HDI = 6)
**86% in The Netherlands** (HDI = 4)
**46% in the United Kingdom** (HDI = 14)
**37% in Canada** (HDI = 8)
**35% in Sweden** (HDI = 12)
**6% in Brazil** (HDI = 79)

**21%** of all competitions organized in Canada between 1945 and 2010 have been open internationally with:
    **46%** for ideas competitions
    **54%** for projects competitions

**45%** of international competitions in Canada are organised for urban design issues.

___

## Main conferences organized in the field of competitions research since 2000
### 2008 (Stockholm)
KTH Royal Institute of Technology: "Conference on Architectural Competitions"
### 2010 (Copenhagen)
Copenhaguen Business School: "Constructions Matter. Managing Complexities, Decisions and Actions in the Building Process"
### 2012 (Montréal)
Université de Montréal: "International Competitions and Architectural Quality in the Planetary Age"
### 2012 (Helsinki)
Aalto University: "Fourth International Conference on Architectural Competitions"
### 2014 (Delft)
Technical University Delft: "Conditions for Architect-Client Interactions"

## Main links to databases on competitions
**Germany**
www.wettbewerbe-aktuell.de
**USA**
www.competitions.org
**Canada**
www.ccc.umontreal.ca/index.php
**France**
www.archi.fr/MIQCP/rubrique.php
**Switzerland**
www.konkurado.ch
**Brazil**
www.concursosdeprojeto.org

For a comprehensive inventory on competitions websites : http://www.crc.umontreal.ca/index.php

As gathered by the Research Chair on Competitions and Contemporary Practices in Architecture at Université de Montréal.

# A World of Potentialities

**Competitions as Producers of Culture, Quality and Knowledge**

**Jean-Pierre Chupin**, Ph.D.
Director of the Research Chair on Competitions and
Contemporary Practices in Architecture
Université de Montréal
Canada

**Carmela Cucuzzella,** Ph.D.
Design and Computation Arts, Concordia University
Canada

**Bechara Helal**, Ph.D. candidate
School of Architecture, Université de Montréal
Canada

*"Competitions are driven by the desire to go beyond what already exists — unthought-of architecture — whereas commissions are mostly demand-driven and often by those of the market. We could say that competitions are to everyday architecture what competitive sport is to everyday fitness training. Competitive sports break existing human boundaries and set records for bodily capacities. Similarly, architectural competitions are invitations to make conceptual leaps and to open new frames, speeds and scales through which we perceive space and time."* [1]

Farshid Moussavi

## ▬ The competition : a historical utopia?

This book comprises a series of 22 case studies by renowned experts and new scholars in the field of architecture competition research. In 2015, it constitutes the most comprehensive survey of the dynamics behind the definition, organizing, judging, archiving and publishing of architectural, landscape and urban design competitions in the world. These richly documented contributions revolve around a few questions that can be summarized in a two-fold critical interrogation: How can design competitions — these historical democratic devices, both praised and dreaded by designers — be considered laboratories for the production of environmental design quality, and, ultimately, for the renewing of culture and knowledge ?

The rather long history of competitions in architecture does not prevent numerous designers of being critical of the outcomes of such a process of identifying the best project and/or the best team for a specific given architectural situation. Such criticism can be found for example in the paradoxical stance adopted by Shohei Shigematsu, a partner at the Office for Metropolitan Architecture, director of the New York office of OMA, and the linchpin of some of the agency's most celebrated projects. Answering our question regarding the importance of international competitions vis-à-vis the improvement of architectural quality, Mr. Shigematsu stated that it is necessary to regularly question whether the competition becomes an abuse of power, more than a form of transparency. [1] Without summarizing Shigematsu's demonstration, backed by a decade of experience in design competitions, suffice it to say that, according to him, there seems to be no future — for OMA and most "shortlisted" offices — other than participating in design competitions.

One could wonder what is at stake in this apparent contradictory stance on competitions by "Mr. Competitions" himself, as he is often nicknamed by OMA associates, including its notorious founder, Rem Koolhaas.

Farshid Moussavi, principal of FMA in London, adopts the same paradoxical approach to competitions. While acknowledging her participation in an impressive 218 competitions over a span of 20 years (1993-2013) and openly stating that competitions should be regarded as a locus of "creative leaps" [2], Mrs. Moussavi still remains somehow critical of the competition process. Drawing a parallel between competitions in sports and in architecture, she underlines a major difference by pointing out that, in architecture, "losing can have less to do with your performance than with the theatre of unpredictability within which competitions unfold." [3]

For most authors gathered in the international inquiry that is the present publication, i.e. from a more objective and scientifically removed viewpoint on competitions, this "theatre of unpredictability" depicted by both Moussavi and Shigematsu does not look as dramatic as architects emotionally feel. Although most designers will always remain ambivalent with regards to the question of competitions, it appears that they often also agree on the virtues of a principle of emulation offering a terrain for exploration and renewal much needed by all agencies on a regular basis, if only to stimulate team work. This point being made, what do competitions bring concretely to society as a whole ? The hypothesis behind this collective book says

that every design competition can be seen as an opportunity for design research, inside and outside design studios or, as we would like to point in these introductory remarks, **every competition remains a world of possibilities : an intermediary space-time locus for the search for excellence in architecture. In some ways, competition projects function like utopias.**

It is not certain, however, that viewing competitions as fertile spaces for utopian experimentation will be received with serenity by competition organizers, developers and many institutional clients — or even more so, private ones — particularly in our current risk society. Even the history of this competitive practice still needs to be written properly. Some of the more knowledgeable amongst the proponents of competitions will evoke a timeless practice in terms of transparency and equity, while others will pinpoint the origins of this practice with the holding of mythical competitions like the one for the reconstruction of the Parthenon in ancient Greece or, more symbolically for the building of Architecture as a autonomous discipline, the famous competition for the "solving" of the Florence's Dome in the mid 15th Century, brilliantly won by Filippo Brunelleschi **[Fig.1]**. More sceptical commentators could trace back a legendary origin of modern competitions to the infamous cooptation practices of the late 20th Century École des Beaux-Arts, using this link to prove the obsolescence of competitions in supposedly transparent educational contexts. All these standpoints remain partial views. In fact, despite a handful of notable ancient competitions, organized sometimes at the initiative of a prince, at other times controlled by the Academies — or both as was the case for the façade of the Louvre under the regime of Louis XIV — it would be more accurate to historically link the beginning of the contemporary political and democratic use of competitions to the concerns in the wake of the French Revolution, as "public order" becomes a matter of "public welfare". It is precisely at that time that the often frightening "National Convention", exceedingly concerned with "liberté, égalité et fraternité", dictates the recourse to a procedure supposedly equitable and transparent in order for "revolutionary projects" to be designed at the crossroads of aesthetics and ethics. This understanding is borrowed from art historian Werner Szambien's study *Les projets de l'an II : Concours d'architecture de la période révolutionnaire (1986)*, detailing the remarkable competitions held during the revolutionary period (DATES). [4] Szambien catalogued no less than 480 projects submitted to 25 different competitions in the spring of 1794 alone. More specifically, 207 projects for architectural programs have been designed through a total of 352 drawings and 12 models **[Fig.2]**. Projects spanned the spectrum from realistic to utopian but all were revolutionary: triumphal arches, covered arenas, temples of equality and other public buildings. Interestingly, these projects were submitted to not just one jury, as is the practice nowadays, but to *two* grand juries. The first jury — a general Beaux-Arts jury - comprised 51 individuals who judged the overall quality for all Beaux-Arts disciplines, while the second jury of 40 members — comprised of artists, politicians and scientists — was called upon to discuss architectural qualities and to judge the projects for the specific competition. Extraordinarily, such a judgement process was set against the backdrop of a globalizing aesthetics of fine arts, where the same jury assumed the coherence of the politics: a sort of council of the wise for the quality of public space. Highlighting the unusual character of these numbers, Szambien ironically adds: "Before judging, the two juries endeavoured to establish their criteria in a realm of abstraction, a remarkable effort of which juries do not seem capable nowadays".[5]

**Fig. 1**
Florence Cathedral. Typical view of the Dome built by Filipo Bruneleschi after he won the historical 1418 structural design competition against Lorenzo Ghiberti. Photo Marcus Obal 2008.

## —— The competition: judging between ignorance and scheming?

The French Revolution marked modern history with its demise of powerful monarchies and churches, and the rise of democracy — a social, cultural, as well as a religious crisis that profoundly modified the role of architects and artists who, until that time, had to pay due respect to their patrons — or what was referred to as their protectors. Like many revolutionary changes, the recourse to competitions had been brewing for some time. Remarkably, Quatremère de Quincy promptly includes the word "competition" in his *Encyclopédie méthodique*. In hindsight, one could say that he first established the field of research on architectural competitions when he calls for an "institution of public competitions" in order, "to preserve the artists from the humiliation of the ignorant pride of their protectors"[6]. Quatremère de Quincy's theory of competition as a device articulated around a judgement procedure is of an outstanding finesse, as is seen in the following excerpt, which summarizes with a touch of paradoxical humour, what can still be referred to nowadays as the dilemma of judgment:

**Fig. 2**
An example of unbuilt project designed in the renewal of competitions during the French Revolution. Monument of Freedom, Weight and Measures. A figure of Freedom, brandishing a downwards-pointing spear, coming out of a Bastille. Circa 1791. Anonymous author.

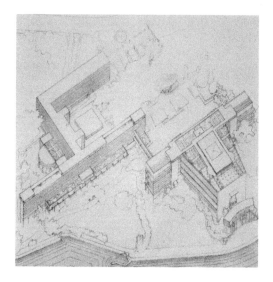

**Fig. 3**
The famous runner-up project by Le Corbusier for the
Palais des Nations competition in 1927
(© Fondation Le Corbusier).

**Fig. 4**
Winning project for the Musée National des Beaux-
Arts du Québec (Québec, 2009) by OMA/Provencher
Roy et Associés, architectes.

*The competition's main purpose is to remove from the
ignoramus the choice of the artists who are responsible
for public works and to prevent that scheming does not
usurp the work due to talent. Therefore, on the one hand
artists should not be able to plot, and on the other, the
ignoramuses must not be able to choose: but if artists
judge, or appoint themselves as judges, then intrigue
reappears, and if they do not judge themselves, or do not
appoint their own judges, then we can see that ignorance
influences the order of things again*[7].

Following this revolutionary origin, the history of the
democratization of design competitions in the 19th Century
will somewhat be linked to the rise of both Beaux-Arts
academicism and scientific positivism. The present introduction is not the appropriate place for a comprehensive
historical survey but a specific competition, organized some
125 years later, should nevertheless be mentioned here in
order to further investigate the paradoxes of this so-called
"theatre of unpredictability": the competition for the Palace
of Nations in Geneva in 1927. Often regarded as the ultimate clash of neoclassicism and modern architecture, this
regrettable competition falls under the category of historical
errors in terms of a theory of architectural judgment, and
even more so because this competition called for the design of a building symbolizing the union of all people after
the First World War. The fact that the jury awarded the top
prize to Nemot and Flegenheimer's extremely conventional
project — built but nevertheless absent from any of the 20th
Century historical surveys on architecture — is already
a sign of major disciplinary controversy. Furthermore,
because the jury was unable to realize a true convergence
of ethics and aesthetics, it also resolutely overlooked the
modern projects of Le Corbusier, Hannes Meyer and even
Richard Neutra. It is now well known that Le Corbusier, in an
opportunistic and ambitious move, turned his loss — and his
project — into a symbol of modern architecture's struggle
against academicism. His has become a perfect example
of "potential architecture" since it is a historical fact that
the built laureate of the Palace of Nations remains in the
shadow of Le Corbusier's unbuilt proposal **[Fig.3]**. This
competition was supposed to demonstrate exemplary global
democracy, in keeping with the mission of the League of
Nations (predecessor to the United Nations). Despite the
fact that the jury was mainly composed of architects, it
demonstrated both ignorance and conspiracy. It took forty
years for the Swiss Society of Architects and Engineers to

recover from this controversial competition. At the dawn of the 1960s, another important competition in Geneva for a similarly great organization, the *World Health Organization* ended with the first prize being awarded to another Swiss architect, the first of an important architectural lineage: Jean Tschumi. If this competition, in a way, healed the wounds of Swiss architecture competitions, the 1927 competition of the Palace of Nations still remains the symbol of a crisis of judgement in the 20th Century.

## Six scholars on the problematic of judging architectural quality

In all fields of environmental design, judging has a long disciplinary tradition. There is hardly any design that is not complemented by a judging process, be it in schools, in professional offices, or even in this peculiar judging machine called the architectural competition. In fact, judgment in design cannot be easily separated from design itself. Although common in the everyday practice, judgement has been little theorized. When asked to give a theoretical model of judgement, one might quickly fall short of diagrams. Six scholars have been asked to reflect on the problematic of judging architectural quality through competitions.

Noting that our **risk society** imposes its own rules and an increasing power of **expertise** over creative enterprises, and drawing cases from the Canadian context, **Cucuzzella** considers current environmental injunctions and questions the role of norms and certifications on the redefinition of quality as it obviously impacts the judgement process itself. She concludes by wondering "if [the competition format] should not be reformulated by taking into account the space for exploration and innovation and the search for quality" rather than resorting to the *power* of environmental certifications given that "the design proposals and the jury deliberation cannot be aptly accomplished through the "efficient" use of quantitative methods that rely on abstract and fragmented models of the world".

Through this bold and simple question, " How is architectural quality judged?", **Crossman,** attempts an inquiry on the effective role of **judgement criteria** in the jury process. She identifies two conflicting poles following a series of Canadian cases: " an *elimination-style judgement procedure* which results when judges comment on the problematic aspects of a project, and a *selective judgement procedure* where judges comment on the ideas as well as the efficient and innovative solutions of a project" **[Fig.4]**.

In a study on Swiss housing competitions organised between 1997 and 2010, **Katsakou** identifies a paradoxical tension between **quality and iconicity** and argues that "the procedural framework of architectural competitions can strengthen the demand for iconic architectural projects, even in sectors of the construction activity like the residential, where similar concepts were, until recently, less frequent".

Also studying mainly the Swiss context, **Silberberger** provides a short narrative essay that want to demonstrate why "the **honourable mention** is to be considered an integral part of the architectural competition". He concludes in identifying three processes of translation and transformation and suggests that it is the honourable mention that: "allows for full-blown iteration leaps throughout the whole sequence of an architectural competition".

For the French architectural critic and theoretician **Fromonot**, competitions must be seen as "**urban generators**". She shows how a careful analysis of the various competitions for Les Halles in Paris — but most particularly the competitions organized between 2002 and 2004 — allow for a deeper criticism of what she calls "compositional" urbanism. Here the competition is not so much understood as a judgement process as it is read as a generator of doctrines and principles that need to be further theorised by scholarly research **[Fig.5]**.

Finally, for American design strategist, competitions organizer and architecture critic **Sirefman**, competitions do not exist in cultural vacuums: The country within which an architecture competition takes place, be it a public or private venture, informs the rules, regulations, procedures, protocols, process, input and outcome of that competition" **[Fig.6]**. American's culture of "free choice" has led to a plethora of ways in which to select an architect therefore making design competitions the exception rather than the rule.

## Eight Scholars on internationality and competitions in a multipolar world

This section underlines some contradictions and issues related to the differences between national and international competitions as an interest in the latter can logically be seen, on one hand, as an indicator of an "opening to the world" and, on the other hand, potential instruments of multicultural politics. Is there a new definition of international competitions in a multipolar world differing from the bipolar one of post World War II as exemplified by the

**Fig. 5**
Les Halles competition (Paris, 2004). Runner-up project by team Rem Koolhaas (OMA with XDGA and One Architects): model (Photo Benoît Grimbert — SEM Paris-Centre).

history of the *Union Internationale des Architectes* from the 1950s to the 1970s? Eight scholars have been asked to reflect on international competitions.

Analyzing the situation in **Switzerland**, **Van Wezemael** and **Silberberger** emphasize the necessity to question the actual international opening of the already well-established Helvetic competition culture. Even though Switzerland signed the World Trade Organization Agreement in 1996, "the organization of public construction markets according to international free trade agreement does not generate international competitions!" For both authors, it remains clear that a competition would operate at its best when generating discursive space for architectural projects.

In their analysis of three case studies from the **Belgian regions** of Brussels, Wallonia and Flanders, **Vanderburgh** and **Menon** question the capacity of international competitions to tackle local issues. They show that, in order to get the most from competitions, organizers must familiarize themselves to a certain point with the definition of both means and ends or what the authors metaphorically call the "finger" (i.e. the jury) and the "moon" (i.e. the project).

**France** remains the country in which the greatest number of competitions has been organized in the last decades and where research on competitions is still rather weak. In a careful reconstruction of the eventful history of the 1982 *Tête Défense Competitions* (Paris), **Lenne** very carefully demonstrates how a competition can serve as a communication tool and how the culture of various actors — starting with the President of the Republic himself — can influence both the competition decisions and the resulting built project.

The **Nordic countries** (Denmark, Norway, Sweden) have long used architectural competitions in order to harmonize advanced social and cultural principles with the organizational forms of residential care homes. **Andersson**, an expert on competitions in this region, has surveyed 77 competitions organized between 2000 and 2012 for residential care homes. He concludes that a competition is never a guarantee of successful projects, since there is always the danger of counterproductive tensions between socio-political ideas and international findings on architectural devices for ageing well.

**Greece** is perhaps the country in which the history of competitions comprises the oldest examples and, at times, the most paradoxical ones. **Paisiou** has closely studied the four competitions for the New Acropolis Museum organized between 1976 and 2000 and she shows how international and European regulations literally "landed" on the Greek construction scene, by explaining that "architectural competition may be thought of as an organizational platform derived from local issues and constraints, which frame the urban projects conforming to international regulations and economic rules".

In the **Canadian context**, competitions are still — and strangely — not as common a democratic device as they can be, when compared to many European countries. **Chupin** reflects on more than two decades of international competitions (1988-2012) and identifies a series of **four political reasons** for opening a competition at the international level. On some instances, concludes Chupin : "an international opening does not so much mean to be open to the world, as it means to open the world to your own market" **[Fig.7 to 11]**.

## ▬ Six experts and scholars on the archiving of competition projects and the preservation of potential knowledge

If potential architecture can be defined as elements within a project that can re-emerge in other projects long before they are realized, then the phenomenon includes transfers of ideas, solutions, aesthetic or technical figures, from project to project by different — or even the same — architects. It is a complex and scarcely researched phenomenon, since a project can have one of several outcomes : a) it can be built, b) it will never be built, or c) it will be renewed while being built (in other words preparing its eventual construction within another project). However, unbuilt architecture can sometimes be as influential as built projects. One could think, for example, of Adolf Loos' design for the Chicago Tribune competition in 1922, Le Corbusier's Palace of Nations project in 1927, or more recently Rem Koolhaas' and OMA's Parc de la Villette proposoal in 1982, all of which have become modern paradigms of this potential architecture phenomenon. Farshid Moussavi summarizes this phenomenon with convergent historical examples :

*There are then the countless ground-breaking yet competition-losing entries that – like NASA's space exploration positively influencing everyday life – go on to inspire other projects. In 1921 a more conservative design triumphed over Mies van der Rohe's skyscraper proposal for Berlin's Friedrichstrasse. But his depiction of a glacial skyscraper contained the unprecedented idea that a steel skeleton could free the exterior walls from their loadbearing function. His vision of a glass curtain wall has gone on to inspire legions of architects all over the world.*

*Similarly, OMA's unrealised proposal for the site of two Yokohama markets in 1992 envisioned a 24-hour destination that reframed the whole idea of a master plan away from definitions of fixed space into space that remains continuously active by changing use over time. The space-time section invented by OMA for this project inspired the work of countless other architects.* [8]

The production of knowledge presupposes a research environment convergent on paradigmatic scientific models. The experts gathered in this section all reflect on both the epistemological and methodological conditions of knowledge production through competitions : from experimentation to digital culture, they point to the current need for the building of ambitious documentary databases of competition projects.

While considering the common understanding of "competitions as laboratories", **Helal** develops a systematic criticism of the so-called **experimental nature** of design competitions. Looking at competitions through the lens of a theory of experimentation, he proposes a clarification of the multiple forms of experimentation in and outside design thinking (artistic, scientific... architectural). As he puts it, after an examination of the famous Parc de la Villette competitions of 1976 and 1982 : "used to their full extent, architecture competitions can be experimental in the sense that they will have an impact on the future of the discipline through the construction of knowledge".

**Chupin**'s presentation of the **Canadian Competitions Catalogue**, a unique scientific database first launched in 2006 and totally revised and reprogrammed in 2014, allows for a reappraisal of digital libraries of projects not only as depository but more importantly as **collective legacies**. Chupin concludes with an appeal to develop and connect multiple libraries of competition projects, at an international level, as a form of recognition of the inherent value of the numerous instances of unbuilt architecture, which should be seen as a true reservoir of knowledge and ideas.

The team led by **Strebel** presents an ambitious prototype for a **Swiss competition database named** *Konkurado* and the multiple issues related to the various stakeholders. Their work is "based on a user-centered approach which aims at studying and improving work cooperation between people and information technology". Although

**Fig. 6**
Winning project for the Orchestre Symphonique de Montréal
competition (Montréal, 2002) by De Architekten Cie./Aedifica
inc./Les architectes Tétreault Parent Languedoc et associés.
Building cancelled.

**Fig. 7**
Runner-up project for Orchestre Symphonique de
Montréal (Montréal, 2002) by Saucier et Perrotte,
architectes (Saucier+Perrotte) /Menkès Shooner
Dagenais, architectes 2002.

**Fig. 8**
Runner-up project for Orchestre Symphonique de Montréal
(Montréal, 2002) by Bernard Tschumi Architecte 2002.

**Fig. 9**
Runner-up project for Orchestre
Symphonique de Montréal (Montréal,
2002) by Alsop Architects Ltd. 2002.

**Fig. 11**
Runner-up project for Orchestre Symphonique de
Montréal (Montréal, 2002) by Behnisch, Behnisch &
Partners with Architects Alliance 2002.

**Fig. 10**
Runner-up project for Orchestre Symphonique de Montréal
(Montréal, 2002) by Emilio Ambasz & Associates Inc. 2002.

this kind of database is still in an exploratory phase, they can already identify the main risks regarding a system in which competition organizers and participants upload their own information.

Finally, for **Sobreira**, operating in the **Brazilian context**, the so-called digital revolution has a real impact on the promotion, diffusion and judgement of architectural competitions. Presenting some experiences related to online disseminations of competitions and their role in the democratization and dissemination of architectural competitions in Brazil, his reflection brings together editorial, academic and professional perspectives.

### ▬ Four chief editors concerned with publishing competition and one sociologist on the production of "culture" between shadows and spectacles.

Are competitions true vehicles for the critical debate on architectural quality in an international landscape of media ?

Founder of ***wettbewerbe aktuell*** in 1971, and perhaps the longest engaged of all experts gathered in this international inquiry, **Hoffmann-Kuhnt**'s views are grounded in more than 40 years of experience on archiving and disseminating competition results in Germany **[Fig.12]**. While recognizing that a large portion of the media is primarily interested in completed projects, he advocates that competitions ought to be recognized in a more significant way, as impetus for German building culture :

> *An important question remains as to what the future holds for architecture in the digital age, and how we can bring architectural quality closer to the public. One possibility is that those of us in the media can stimulate the debate about architectural quality with ongoing suitable online and print publications. On the other hand, one has to show tenders and clients that competitions lead to the best solution for their building projects, and that they may also contribute to positive public relations.*

As experienced as Hoffmann-Kuhnt in the field of competition archiving and publishing, **Collyer** provides precious views on competitions both in the USA and in the world, which need to be considered carefully. Founder of ***Competitions*** magazine, Collyer evaluates the role of architecture competitions both in the age of globalization and in the age of information technologies. He concludes

**Fig. 12**
Cover of German journal WA
(wettbewerbe aktuell). February 2010

**Fig. 13**
Cover of French journal d'a
(D'architectures). Special issue on
competitions, # 216, April 2013.

**Fig. 14**
The "Water cube". Built for the 2008 Beijing Olympic the swimming
pool was designed by architects PTW and engineers Ove Arup and
Partners (Competition 2003). *Photo C. Cucuzzella.*

with a call for a greater responsibility: "Media coverage of competitions is a snapshot of the state of architecture, and society. It may even indicate a consensus — or lack there-of — concerning new approaches to solving urban issues in these changing times. Analyzing the selection process and encouraging those involved discussing their priorities when ranking the entries is certainly beneficial for the profession and adds to an ongoing dialogue about design. This is where media shoulders its greatest responsibility".

As chief editor of the French journal *d'architecture*, **Caille** adopts what is probably the most critical view of the current problematic dissemination of projects in a society dominated by communication devices and proced-ures **[Fig.13]**. In this global context of media competition, it is less surprising to witness the evolution of a new branch of architects rightly nicknamed "starchitects", who literally live on competitions in the world, producing projects sometimes at the expense of regional identity and cultural diversity. As Caille concludes: "It is… necessary to face the fact that the international quality of architecture has now been almost entirely overshadowed by that of *starchitects*".

Considering a less glamorous Canadian context of national and international competitions, **Chodikoff**, former chief editor of *Canadian Architect*, now executive director of Architecture Canada, discusses:

*The critical significance of carefully structuring a design competition so that the desired outcome can best rep-resent the goals of the client while ensuring the highest calibre of design excellence possible.*

Finally, **Violeau**, from a strictly **sociological standpoint**, looks at the peculiar conditions of young teams of laureates in the aftermath of competitions, and evaluates what he calls the "advantages and constraints of two French trade-marks", namely: *EUROPAN (France)*, the French branch of the largest competition organiser in Europe, and the *Nouveaux Albums des Jeunes Architectes* dedicated to the promotion of new talents. Reviewing closely a series of case studies of French competitions and their winners, he critically wonders if national prizes should not be con-sidered effectively as governmental devices: i.e. a system established to control the profession through rewards.

## ▬ Design competitions and their multiple outcomes outside the realms of building industries

Why should all the projects of a design competition be disseminated? The question remains an important one when considering the current state of architectural prac-tices and publications, as architects are often reluctant to disseminate architecture at the design stage and, oddly enough, the competition phenomenon is always threatened by its spectacular nature. There is a tendency to display and recognize only winning projects, with a limited run for public exhibitions that in no way give all submitted proj-ects any long-term visibility. In our era of communication agents, most public organizers seem to be more and more concerned with controlling the message. This ill situation reinforces the dispersion of documents and ideas, para-doxically supporting the depreciation of "architecture as project". Even though winners are always clearly indicated, some organizers seem overtly worried with the principle of an equal representation of all submissions, asking for a relative downplaying — if not absolute elimination — of those not chosen by the jury. This "aesthetic cleansing" remains a troubling attitude. It brings the question of the valorizing of architecture as project: the very cognitive and creative device at the center of professional competence. At the same time, as many designers often recognize, ideas and concepts are meant to travel, as do built and unbuilt projects. From this point of view, both built and unbuilt projects have equal value within the production of culture, quality and knowledge.

The study of design competitions in the fields of archi-tectural, urban and landscape design therefore reveals not only the paradoxical tensions underlying these disciplines of the built environment. It also reveals some of the ways projects participate in the structuring of culture: either in *a physical and material way*, by building the heritage of tomorrow, but also in *an intellectual and immaterial way*, by building knowledge and culture **[Fig.14]**. These two methods, one concrete, the other virtual, converge within "edification", a grand ancient idea that perhaps needs to be reactivated in our present state of relativism.

However numerous the studies and inquiries gathered in the present book, there is still too little research done on the competition phenomenon, in stark contrast to the plethora of richly illustrated monographs. This might ex-plain in part why, in recent years, teams on both sides of the Atlantic Ocean are using the competition as a field of

**Fig. 15**
Winning project for Absolute Design Ideas Competition
(Mississauga, 2005) by MAD office (Yansong Ma, Shen
Huihui, Yosuke Hayano, Dang Qun, Shen Jun).

**Fig. 16**
Grande Arche in the main axis of *La Défense*
quarters. Competition project by Johan Otto von
Spreckelsen and Erik Reitzel, built project by Paul
Andreu (competition in 1982). Photo Loïse Lenne.

**Fig. 17**
The Parthenon as seen from the New Acropolis
Museum, competition project won by Tschumi
Architects in 2000, built in 2008. Photo JPC 2009.

study and inquiry of contemporary practices in architecture, landscape design and urban planning. Indeed, as we have attempted to demonstrate through this survey, more and more researchers have decided to devote themselves to the study of competitions. Be they in Sweden, Denmark, Belgium, France, Canada, Germany, the USA, Finland, Brazil, Switzerland or the Netherlands, they study whether the competition is an effective manager of architectural quality and an efficient and reliable instrument of policy procurement.

## ▬ Final cut on a world heritage

**Adamczyk**, relying on his long experience in teaching, researching, dissemination and criticism of contemporary architecture — whether through competitions or not — presents in his concluding text, facetiously titled "Final Cut", what he calls a "remarkable cross-section of architectural tendencies". Adamczyk here reflects on the theme of architectural **representation** to show how competition studies allow for a transcultural and transhistorical approach of disciplinary issues and indeed a renewal of knowledge in the fields of environmental design.

Quality, culture, and knowledge: it is on these three productive roles of design competitions that this international inquiry finds its conclusion. Beyond this longitudinal section, the constitution of competition databases, ideally compatible and interconnected, appears to be the next step for this research field to prove its relevance. But these "libraries of projects" should not only be meant to preserve the frustrated memory of what some architects consider to be "lost projects". This web of databases should be meant to transform the understanding of the multiple roles of competitions and projects for both the profession and the discipline. Such a production of knowledge, useful if architects actively participate in the digital age's knowledge society, will not be confined to academia or to some obscure professional archives. If the competition situation promotes research and experimentation, our hypothesis is that the qualitative judgment procedure at the heart of it will continue to contribute to the building of meaningful public spaces **[Fig.15] [Fig.16] [Fig.17]**. Like any true world heritage, the archival and sharing of competition projects will then nourish the debates with the values and orientations of our societies, and lead to the intensification of reflexive practices and cultural mediations within future architectural, urban and landscape design projects. In other words, through competitions, one can see the edification of our future heritage.

## ▬ Notes

[1] Moussavi, F. , "Viewpoints : Farshid Moussavi on Competitions : 'Creative leaps in the arena of architectural competitions' ", *The Architectural Review*, January 31st 2013.

[2] Shohei Shigematsu communicated this view during his keynote lecture at the "International Competitions and Architectural Quality in the Planetary Age," an international symposium on the subject of architecture competitions which took place at the Université de Montréal on March 16th and 17th, 2012. This symposium – organized jointly by the Research Chair on Competitions and Contemporary Practices in Architecture and by the Laboratoire d'Étude de l'Architecture Potentielle – is where most of the texts presented in this book were first proposed. For a video recording of Shohei Shigematsu's lecture, see *www.crc.umontreal.ca/ index.php?id=141*

[3] Moussavi, F. "Viewpoints", 2013.

[4] Id.

[5] Szambien, W.,, *Les projets de l'an II : concours d'architecture de la période révolutionnaire*, Paris, École nationale supérieure des beaux-arts, 1986. p. 3.

[6] Id., p.XXX

[7] The term "institution of public competitions" belongs to Quatremère de Quincy.

[8] Quatremère de Quincy, A. C., *Encyclopédie méthodique : Dictionnaire d'architecture (3 volumes)*, vol. 2, Paris, Panckoucke, 1788 - 1801 - 1820. p. 38

[9] Moussavi, F. "Viewpoints", 2013

## ▬ References

**Moussavi,** Farshid, "Viewpoints : Farshid Moussavi on Competitions : "Creative leaps in the arena of architectural competitions"", *The Architectural Review*, January 31st 2013. (*www.architectural-review.com/comment-and-opinion/farshid-moussavi* Last accessed, November 15th, 2014)

**Quatremère de Quincy,** Antoine C., *Encyclopédie méthodique : Dictionnaire d'architecture (3 vol.)*, Paris, Panckoucke, 1788 – 1801.

**Szambien,** Werner, *Les projets de l'an II : concours d'architecture de la période révolutionnaire*, Paris, ENSBA' 1986.

## Section 1
# Organizing Architectural Democracy

## Switzerland

- International boundary
- ★ National capital
- Railroad
- Expressway
- Road

0    20    40 Kilometers
0    20    40 Miles

Lambert Conformal Conic Projection, SP 46N/48N

**FRANCE**

**GERMANY**

**ITALY**

**AUSTRI**

**LIECHTENSTEIN**

Strasbourg
Nürtingen
Offenburg
Tübingen
Reutlingen
Ulm
Sélestat
Balingen
Colmar
Biberach
Villingen-Schwenningen
Freiburg
Tuttlingen
Memminge
Kaufb
Mulhouse
Ravensburg
Kempten
Lure
Singen
Schaffhausen
Konstanz
Friedrichshafen
Vesoul
Belfort
Lörrach
Kreuzlingen
Montbéliard
Delle
Basel
Frauenfeld
Bregenz
Porrentruy
Liestal
Baden
Winterthur
Wil
Sankt Gallen
Dornbirn
Besançon
Delémont
Aarau
Zürich
Herisau
Appenzell
Feldkirch
La Chaux-de-Fonds
Biel
Solothurn
Olten
Zürichsee
Vaduz
Bludenz
La
Morteau
Burgdorf
Zug
Niederurnen
Le Locle
Lucerne
Schwyz
Glarus
AUSTI
Neuchâtel
Langnau
Sarnen
Stans
Lake of Lucerne
Glarus
Pontarlier
Lac de Neuchâtel
**Bern**
Altdorf
Linthal
Chur
Davos
Champagnole
Fribourg
Thun
Brienzer See
Andermatt
Thusis
Scuol (Schuls)
Vallorbe
Spiez
Interlaken
Thuner See
Saint Moritz
Morges
Lausanne
Gletsch
Bormio
Nyon
Vevey
Montreux
Chiavenna
Evian
Aigle
Sierre
Brig
Bellinzona
Sondrio
Tirano
Thonon
Monthey
Sion
Locarno
Saint-Julien
Cluses
Martigny-Ville
Lugano
Lecco
Annecy
Omegna
Bergamo
Aix-les-Bains
Saint-Gervais
Aosta
Saint-Vincent
Varese
Como
Albertville
Bourg-Saint-Maurice
Treviglio
Chambéry
Biella
Busto Arsizio
Monza
**ITALY**
Ivrea

# 1.1. We Have Never Been 'Swiss'

## Some Reflections on Helvetic Competition Culture

**Joris Van Wezemael**, Ph.D.
Department of Architecture, ETH Zürich
Switzerland

**Jan M. Silberberger**, Ph.D.
ETH Wohnforum — ETH CASE, Department of
Architecture, ETH Zürich
Switzerland

In Switzerland, the competition was both the midwife and the baby of an emerging national construction market, a consolidating architectural scene, an emerging architectural style and a distinct character of the architect that has become associated with a Swiss identity. However, what is referred to as 'Swiss' has been an amalgam from the very beginning as, for instance, the Beaux-Arts and the Semper schools competed in Switzerland. Before this background we state that 'we have never been Swiss' and use this perspective in order to explore the feature of internationality in competitions. In a first section we recall the historical breakup of the Beaux-Arts school's monopoly in Western Switzerland. Then we discuss the contemporary situation and state that, with regard to internationality, the competition tends to be viewed primordially in its role as a procurement instrument that is bound to WTO regulations. In fact, a large share of competitions in Switzerland is juridically speaking 'international' in kind — but only few processes use this attribute to flag its project and to stand out of the crowd. Here we highlight the competition's ability to transform construction and design projects into public discourse. These reflections allow us to reconsider how 'internationality' can perform and be performed in architectural competitions.

**Cover**
Shaded Relief Map of Switzerland.
Courtesy of *The General Libraries,
The University of Texas at Austin*.

In the paper at hand we will question the aspect of internationality with regard to Swiss architectural competitions. In other words, we will ask : What does this internationality produce ? What are its effects ? When and why do Swiss authorities put forward the aspect of internationality when conducting an architectural competition ?

In order to trace these questions we will at first orient towards the beginning of the architectural competition in Switzerland. By summoning up Viollet-le-Duc's work in the late 19th century we will describe the emergence of Swiss architectural competitions as a struggle between two different 'foreign' schools : the 'French' teaching of the École nationale supérieure des Beaux-Arts in Paris on the one side and the 'German' teaching of the Polytechnicum in Zurich ruled by Gottfried Semper and his disciples on the other side. Referring to Viollet-le-Duc we will introduce a historical trajectory that is crucial for understanding the emergence of architectural competitions as devices to perform meaning.

Subsequently we will address this capability of performing meaning by introducing two rather different research works : Van Wezemael et al.'s study on a series of architectural competitions between 1885 and 1899 regarding Swiss Federal Post Offices [1] and Sorkin's study on the World Trade Center Design Competition. [2]

Then we will briefly address the WTO Agreement on Government Procurement (GPA), which Switzerland signed in January 1996 with regard to the internationality of the field of participating architecture offices.

Finally, against this background, we will examine four recent respectively ongoing international competitions — the "Basel Kunstmuseum Burghof Extension", the "Métamorphose Prés-de-Vidy" in Lausanne, the "Erneuerung Kunstmuseum St.Gallen" and the "Ersatzneubau Wohnsiedlung Tièchestrasse" in Zurich — and put forward some hypotheses on what internationality in Swiss architectural competitions is about today.

## ▬ The Birth of the Architectural Competition in Switzerland

In his "Histoire d'un hôtel de ville et d'une cathédrale," [3] Viollet-le-Duc imagined the small town "Clusy", assumed to be thriving under the reign of Philippe-Auguste, through which he established a kind of 'heterotopy' [4] *avant la lettre*, which enabled him to use an imaginary location in a historical narrative to give credibility to a place where the average regulator of a competition would ideally display its effects. Armand Brulhart provided a perfect

synthesis of this in the introduction to his article "L'institution du concours à Genève" [5] but did not consider the problematic repercussions that would highlight how Viollet-le-Duc made use of this parable to reflect on the general and contemporary scope of architectural competitions as construction instruments both of a society as such and of its representation. The narrative space opened up by Viollet-le-Duc enabled him to draw a complete picture of the protagonists, of what was at stake for them, and of the structures within which they were going to interact. Since the objective of the authorities and the cathedral chapter of Clusy was to compare the offers, to evaluate them and to reach a common ground on which a decision would be possible, they simply tried to find that solution which was the most advantageous from every point of view. Since this concerned the construction of a cathedral, which the author openly regarded as a public building of general interest, a "works council" made up in equal parts of "members of the chapter" and of burghers was set up. This council constituted the principal for the building. After it had collected information about the state of the art in the kingdom and identified the architects capable of satisfying the proposed requirements, the council agreed that it would be of interest to organise a competition. The panel of judges was mixed : it consisted of professionals — "a master carpenter, two master masons, two stone-masons and sculptors" — as well as members of the council and burghers of the town. This combination reveals something that was of central significance in Viollet-le-Duc's approach and indicates that for him, there was no purely architectural solution to the construction problem at hand. The procedure was not anonymous, and the authors "were invited to explain their projects". They were even offered an opportunity to "discuss them among themselves". Viollet-le-Duc's rational utopia integrated interpersonal dimensions and human passions and imbued the procedure with the qualities of a court of arbitration. "It goes without saying that these discussions were tempestuous at times. The impassive judges let the rivals speak, convinced that common sense would finally prevail in every free discussion". We are very much inclined to translate this passage into contemporary words and to say that Viollet-le-Duc described the conditions of an optimal solution which, for this highly specific and complex type of work, would be a "competition that architects are invited to join at the end of a selective process".

The link between Viollet-le-Duc and Switzerland can be seen in relation with the *heterotopy* of Clusy. Frey [6] has shown that on the building site of the Cathedral of

Lausanne, Viollet-le-Duc had encountered a completely novel situation that was almost ideal and was reminiscent of that which he displayed in his imaginary town in "L'histoire d'un hôtel de ville et d'une cathédrale". The political landscape of the Swiss Confederation under the sway of the 1874 Constitution and that of the Canton of Vaud under the regime of the liberal "radicals" presented itself to him in an unprecedented light. The restoration of Lausanne Cathedral took place without any Catholic clergy and without a diocesan architect. Instead, the authority in charge was a lay government, which regarded its cathedral church, in which Protestant services were held, as a national monument, as a public good. The analogy with Clusy is obvious. In this respect, the Canton of Vaud and the Swiss Confederation turned out to be an ideal field for the regulated conduct of an architectural competition — even more so if we turn to contemplating what Viollet-le-Duc called "solemn competitions", namely those leading up to the construction of the public buildings of the State.

At this point we would like to orient towards the ultimate basis of architectural competitions. This ultimate basis appears in the somewhat disenchanted reservations that Viollet-le-Duc formulated with regard to the institution of the competition in general and with regard to that organised for the reconstruction of the Paris City Hall in 1873. He concluded his criticism with a remark of general scope, which is of interest in this context. Viollet-le-Duc wrote that if we speak of competitions, we speak of competitors and judges, and if we speak of competitors, we speak of teaching; if we want serious competitions, we need serious competitors; and if we want serious competitors, we need serious teaching.[7]

Now, it is obvious that this question of teaching weighed heavily on the field of architectural competitions in Switzerland during the last third of the 19th century and the early 20th century. Owing to its nature and origin, the institution of competitions was culturally linked with the French teaching of the École Nationale Supérieure des Beaux-Arts in Paris. As such, it clearly instituted itself, for the duration of the period under consideration, as an authority for the validation and promotion of a guild that was skilfully brilliant in a competition system that was governed by rules it had drawn up itself and whose contents and proposals it judged itself. According to Frey,[8] in certain cantons of French-speaking Switzerland, where architects coming from the "Beaux-Arts" constituted a strong predominance, this phenomenon is evident and almost hegemonic. *Only in international competitions and in some competitions of a national scope was their hegemony breached for the benefit of their only possible challenger:* the Polytechnicum in Zurich, over which ruled the figure of Gottfried Semper and his disciples.

To conclude on a questioning and critical note, we would again like to refer to Viollet-le-Duc and borrow from him a global appraisal that is remarkably concise and pertinent: he considered that "it is in the nature of assemblies to prefer the invention of an unknown value to the recognition of an existing and rival value, and if this unknown value is worthless, so much the better, since it will take its brilliance from the choice that has brought it to light".[9] It sets the margins of debate in the possible options within a procedure. This is why in Geneva, it was not before 1908 that Zurich's Gustave Gull took part in the competition for the International Reformation Monument and that the Beaux-Arts' monopoly, which had completely dominated public construction in French-speaking Switzerland, was finally broken.

## ▬ Architectural competitions as devices to perform meaning

In their paper "Mattering the Res Publica,"[10] Van Wezemael et al. have addressed the role of the institution of architectural competitions in the field of construction policy in the young Swiss Confederation. By analysing the jury reports of a series of ten competitions within 14 years (1885-1899) all considering post office buildings they elaborated how this "continuum" of competitions — or to be more precise: the continuum of the respective jury sessions — contributed to sharpen evaluation and assessment criteria regarding the quality of architecture (not only with regard to post offices) and urban design. In this way Van Wezemael et al. showed how the setup of a regulative device generated a new "objectivity" with regard to construction-related trades and architectural style. At the same time Van Wezemael et al. elaborate how the series of post office competitions achieved a manifestation of the young federal state in a political situation that objected to direct intervention and was deeply sceptical with regard to central state in general. In their paper they describe the architectural competition as a form of distributed agency enabling the new founded Swiss republic to transcribe its ideals and objectives into its built environment.

Whereas Van Wezemael et al. do not claim that the architectural competition in Switzerland was invented in a strategic manner, Sorkin[11] suggests that running an architectural competition concerning the site of the World Trade Center was nothing else but a strategic decision. Sorkin points out that every relevant issue had been decided "behind the scenes, without formal accountability" [12] long before the competition was announced, which resulted in a competition brief so narrow that only a limited number of minor decisions remained to be taken by the competing architecture offices and — in consequence — in competition entries varying only with regard to the shape of their exterior form. According to Sorkin, the Post World Trade Center Design Competition can be regarded as a device to "sell" the client's request to the public. For him, running the architectural competition, that is, promising the opportunity to develop, discuss and maybe even realise extraordinary propositions for "Ground Zero" (without making good on that promise) allowed for realizing a rather dull project targeting mainly profitable office space on a site that has been (and still is) so much the centre of attention and has been attracting such a diversity of architectural propositions.

## ▬▬ The WTO Government Procurement Agreement (GPA)

Van Wezemael et al. [13] describe that all entries in an architectural competition together define a space of possibilities, which the jury in its assessment sessions has to explore. Obviously, this possibility space in exceptional competitions, that is, in competitions which generate a certain media coverage especially with regard to the non-trade press is co-constituted by Swiss and international projects. Hence, "Swissness" can become a unique characteristic, a unique selling proposition only in the face of non-Swissness: what it means to 'be Swiss' can only be elaborated, rated and displayed in an international 'space of possibilities'.

According to the WTO [14] "(i)n most countries the government, and the agencies it controls, are together the biggest purchasers of goods of all kinds, ranging from basic commodities to high-technology equipment. At the same time, the political pressure to favor domestic suppliers over their foreign competitors can be very strong". Again, referring to the WTO "(a)n Agreement on Government Procurement was first negotiated during the Tokyo Round and entered into force on 1 January 1981". The WTO defines the purpose of the Agreement on Government Procurement as "to open up as much of this business as possible to international competition. It is designed to make laws, regulations, procedures and practices regarding government procurement

more transparent and to ensure they do not protect domestic products or suppliers, or discriminate against foreign products or suppliers".

In January 1996 Switzerland signed the WTO Agreement on Government Procurement. (As its name implies the GPA does not apply to private clients organizing an architectural competition.) Without going into detail we would now like to explicate the implications of the GPA on Swiss architectural competitions regarding the aspect of internationality. Currently there is a threshold value in Swiss public procurement of 350000 CHF regarding costs for conducting the competition including price sums for the competing architecture offices. In case this threshold value is exceeded international bids have to be called for. According to various project managers at building authorities such as the "Amt für Hochbauten" in Zurich, the "Hochbau- und Planungsamt" in Basel and the "Service d'Architecture" in Lausanne there is a rule of thumb: as soon as the value of the planned construction reaches 4 to 5 million CHF the threshold value will most likely be exceeded. This means that, in practice, for every housing competition of an average size (let us say of 20 apartments) there has to be an international bidding.

## ▬▬ Findings of case studies, the international 'hedge'

In this section we will orient towards three recent respectively ongoing international competitions in Switzerland: the "Basel Kunstmuseum Burghof Extension" (completed in 2010), the "Métamorphose Prés-de-Vidy" in Lausanne (ongoing), the "Erneuerung Kunstmuseum St.Gallen" (completed in 2012) and the "Ersatzneubau Wohnsiedlung Tièchestrasse" (completed in 2010) in Zurich. We studied the competitions in Basel and Zurich by means of a participatory observation, that is, we attended sessions during the preparation of the competition as well as jury sessions and observed the respective project managers at their desks. For the competitions in Lausanne and St.Gallen we did a detailed analysis of the documents the competition produced as well as a series of interviews with the respective project managers.

In what follows we will compare the field of applicants on the prequalification level and the field of selected offices of these four competitions. Two of these competitions consider an extension or a renovation respectively of a exhibition hall for fine arts, one the construction of a mixed

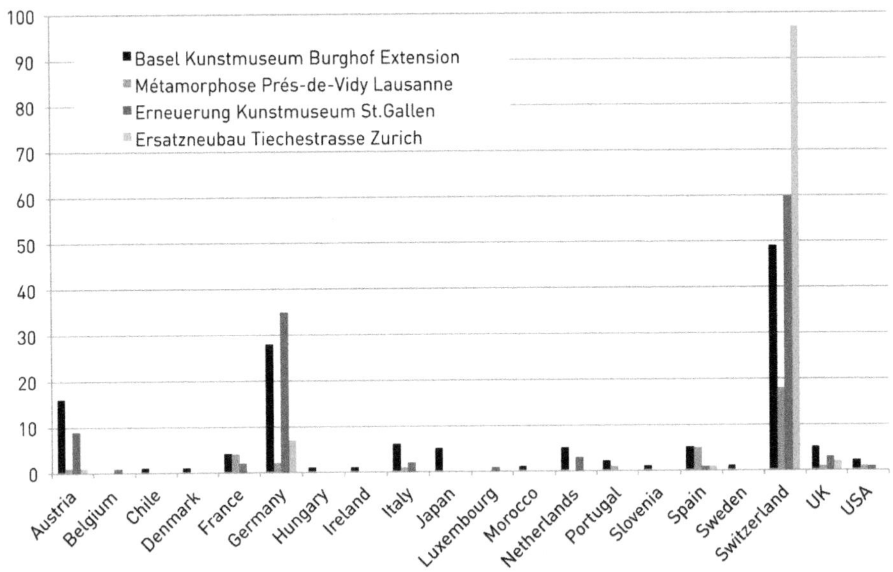

**Fig. 1**
Number of applicants by country for "Prequalification"

| | Basel Kunstmuseum Burghof Extension | | Métamorphose Prés-de-Vidy Lausanne | | Erneuerung Kunstmuseum St.Gallen | | Ersatzneubau Tiechestrasse Zurich | |
|---|---|---|---|---|---|---|---|---|
| **Total** | **134** | **100%** | **34** | **100%** | **118** | **100%** | **108** | **100%** |
| Austria | 16 | 11.9% | 1 | 2.9% | 9 | 7.6% | 1 | 0.9% |
| Belgium | | | | | 1 | 0.8% | | |
| Chile | 1 | 0.7% | | | | | | |
| Denmark | 1 | 0.7% | | | | | | |
| France | 4 | 3.0% | 4 | 11.8% | 2 | 1.7% | | |
| Germany | 28 | 20.9% | 2 | 5.9% | 35 | 29.7% | 7 | 6.5% |
| Hungary | 1 | 0.7% | | | | | | |
| Ireland | 1 | 0.7% | | | | | | |
| Italy | 6 | 4.5% | 1 | 2.9% | 2 | 1.7% | | |
| Japan | 5 | 3.7% | | | | | | |
| Luxembourg | | | | | 1 | 0.8% | | |
| Morocco | 1 | 0.7% | | | | | | |
| Netherlands | 5 | 3.7% | | | 3 | 2.5% | | |
| Portugal | 2 | 1.5% | 1 | 2.9% | | | | |
| Slovenia | 1 | 0.7% | | | | | | |
| Spain | 5 | 3.7% | 5 | 14.7% | 1 | 0.8% | 1 | 0.9% |
| Sweden | 1 | 0.7% | | | | | | |
| Switzerland | 49 | 36.6% | 18 | 52.9% | 60 | 50.8% | 97 | 89.8% |
| UK | 5 | 3.7% | 1 | 2.9% | 3 | 2.5% | 2 | 1.9% |
| USA | 2 | 1.5% | 1 | 2.9% | 1 | 0.8% | | |

use town quarter (various sports facilities and housing) in Lausanne and one the construction of a housing complex (which comprises of about 100 apartments) in Zurich. On the basis of this comparison and by referring back to what has been said in section 3 we will finally put forward some hypotheses on what internationality in Swiss architectural competitions is about today. **[Fig. 1 to 4]**

When comparing these figures one may notice several things : For instance, that there is a significantly high percentage of offices based in Spain selected for the competition in Lausanne. This however can be explained by the fact that there was a well-respected Spanish architect within the board of jurors, which encouraged five offices to apply out of which four were selected. Or, one may notice that Swiss architecture offices are the largest group applying on the "prequalification" level and being selected for the competition in all four cases. Or, that the percentage of Swiss architecture offices increases in all cases as the competition advances. While on the "prequalification" level 36.6 % (Basel), 52.9 % (Lausanne), 50.8 % (St.Gallen) and 89.8 % (Zurich) of the applicants were offices from Switzerland, 58.3 % (Basel), 56.3 % (Lausanne), 53.3 % (St.Gallen) and 91.7 % (Zurich) of the offices selected to develop projects are based in Switzerland. Which slightly indicates why the prequalification level is considered to be problematic with respect to the Government Procurement Agreement (GPA). Yet, this discussion is not in the focus of the paper at hand.

Instead of focussing on the relation between prequalification and competition figures (36.6 %/58.3 %, 52.9 %/56.3 %, 50.8 %/53.3 % and 89.8 %/91.7 %) we would like to draw the attention to the striking difference between the first three competitions — where we can say that roughly 50 % of the applying and 55 % of the selected offices are based in Switzerland — and the last competition, where roughly 90 % of the applying and selected offices are based in Switzerland. How can we explain this significant difference? Especially when taking into account that the competition in Zurich concerned a highly attractive inner-city site and the organiser was a highly reputable building authority?

At this point we can refer to Schmiedeknecht who introduces a distinction between "routine" and "exceptional" competitions.[15] Routine competitions, according to Schmiedeknecht, concern "everyday" or "ordinary" projects, projects, which are not considered "to be particularly glamorous", where it is usually more important "to fulfil functional requirements" than "to find spectacular formal solutions".[16] Exceptional competitions on the other hand

"are perceived to be the place where the avant-garde can show their credentials."[17] Schmiedeknecht further relates exceptional competitions to "signature buildings designed as one-off spectacles,"[18] which attract an international field of participating architecture offices as well as media coverage, especially with regard to the non-trade press.

Against this background we can assign the competitions "Basel Kunstmuseum Burghof Extension", "Métamorphose Prés-de-Vidy" in Lausanne and "Erneuerung Kunstmuseum St.Gallen" to the exceptional type and the "Ersatzneubau Wohnsiedlung Tièchestrasse" in Zurich to the routine type. As outlined in section 4, all four competitions are open to international participants. Yet, only the exceptional type activated an international field of participants (see figures above). Referring to De Landa,[19] we can argue that these exceptional competitions used the internationality of its participants as an expressive component, that is, as a resource to affect, as a resource to fuel the visibility of the project, to promote it (sometimes the link to financial aspects is more obvious as in the case of the "Métamorphose Prés-de-Vidy" in Lausanne, sometimes not).

▬▬▬

In this article we trace 'internationality' through important periods of the evolution of the Swiss competition. We identify some key characteristics of competitions such as their ability to fold together different fields (economic, legal, academic, professional, etc) or their ability to transform material resources into expressive ones. With regard to internationality we can learn that the reconfiguration of the 'local' and the 'global' concerning the flux and nexus of practices, routines, styles or regulations has generated a scene that was coined 'national' in the 19th Century, but also, that the often referred to 'neoliberal' regime of the WTO since the late 20th Century does not produce reconfigurations as such — rather it has to be called upon. The organization of public construction markets according to international free trade agreements does not generate international competitions. Rather, internationality of competitions is actively and consciously being used to hedge the visibility of a project, to legitimate cost and to sell a design to the public. This does not have to be (judged) as negative as in Sorkin's reading of the competition for Ground Zero; we may also argue that a competition works at its best when generating discursive space for architectural projects. With other words, there's a this line between Viollet-le-Duc's

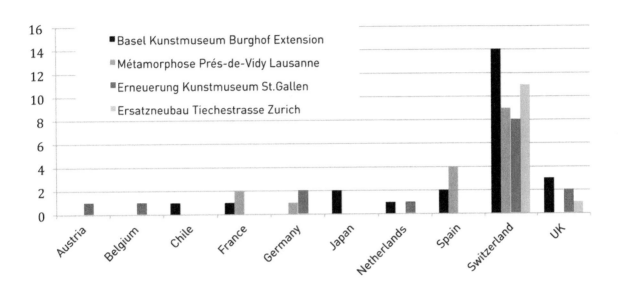

| | Basel Kunstmuseum Burghof Extension | | Métamorphose Prés-de-Vidy Lausanne | | Erneuerung Kunstmuseum St.Gallen | | Ersatzneubau Tiechestrasse Zurich | |
|---|---|---|---|---|---|---|---|---|
| **Total** | **24** | **100%** | **16** | **100%** | **15** | **100%** | **12** | **100%** |
| Austria | | | | | 1 | 6.7% | | |
| Belgium | | | | | 1 | 6.7% | | |
| Chile | 1 | 4.2% | | | | | | |
| France | 1 | 4.2% | 2 | 12.5% | | | | |
| Germany | | | 1 | 6.3% | 2 | 13.3% | | |
| Japen | 2 | 8.3% | | | | | | |
| Netherlands | 1 | 4.2% | | | 1 | 6.7% | | |
| Spain | 2 | 8.3% | 4 | 25% | | | | |
| Switzerland | 14 | 58.3% | 9 | 56.3% | 8 | 53.3% | 11 | 91.7% |
| UK | 3 | 12.5% | | | 2 | 13.3% | 1 | 8.3% |

**Fig. 2**
Number of selected offices by country

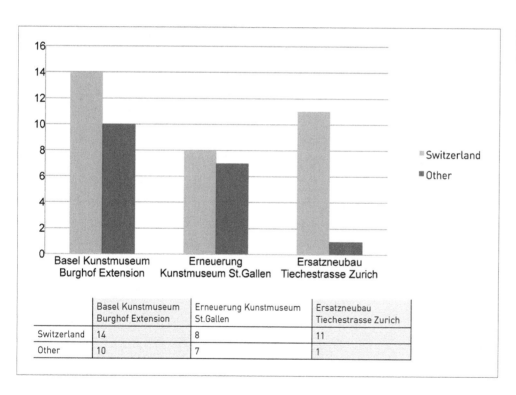

**Fig. 3**
Number of Swiss and other
applicants for "Prequalification"

| | Basel Kunstmuseum Burghof Extension | Erneuerung Kunstmuseum St.Gallen | Ersatzneubau Tiechestrasse Zurich |
|---|---|---|---|
| Switzerland | 49 | 60 | 97 |
| Other | 85 | 58 | 11 |

**Fig. 4**
Number of Swiss and other
selected offices

| | Basel Kunstmuseum Burghof Extension | Erneuerung Kunstmuseum St.Gallen | Ersatzneubau Tiechestrasse Zurich |
|---|---|---|---|
| Switzerland | 14 | 8 | 11 |
| Other | 10 | 7 | 1 |

statement that the value "will take its brilliance from the choice that has brought it to light" [20] in the sense of aiming at good processes for good architecture at the one hand, and Sorkin's notion that a competition also works brilliantly as a Trojan Horse that promises the opportunity to develop and discuss extraordinary propositions for a historical site and to sell a dull project, at the other. Thus, the ability of competitions to perform meaning must be seen as such as strong resource that its use may be perverted, the abuse being a mock of a democratic process and the mere selling of the (most profitable) idea to a public that is taken for a fool.

### ▬ Notes

[1] Joris E. Van Wezemael et al., "'Mattering' the Res Publica: The Architectural Competitions for the Swiss Federal Post Offices in the Late 19th Century as a Foucauldian Dispositif," *disP-The Planning Review* 47, no. 184 (2011).

[2] Michael Sorkin, *Democracy Degree Zero*, ed. Österreichische Gesellschaft für Architektur, Wettbewerb! Competition! (Wien: ÖGFA., 2005).

[3] Eugène-Emmanuel Viollet-le-Duc, *Histoire d'un Hôtel de ville et dune cathédrale* (Paris: J. Hetzel, 1874).

[4] A concept coined by Michel Foucault on the occasion of a lecture given in 1967, which was published under the title of "Des espaces autres" in Architecture, mouvement, continuité, No. 5, in 1984.

[5] Armand Brulhart, "L'institution du concours à Genève," in *Concours d'architecture et d'urbanisme en Suisse Romande: Histoire et actualité*, ed. Armand Brulhart, Pierre Frey, and Ivan Kolecek (Lausanne: Payot, 1995).

[6] Pierre Frey, "Form, Struktur, Umwelt. Viollet-Le-Duc in Lausanne: Drei Untertitel Für Ein Vermächtnis," in *Das Prinzip Rekonstruktion*, ed. Uta Hassler and Winfried Nerdinger (Zürich: vdf Hochschulverlag, 2010).

[7] Eugène-Emmanuel Viollet-le-Duc, *Entretiens sur l'architecture* (Paris: A. Morel, 1863).

[8] Pierre Frey, "Alphonse Laverrière, l'entrée en lice d'un protagoniste," in *Concours d'architecture et d'urbanisme en Suisse romande: histoire et actualité*, ed. Armand Brulhart, Pierre Frey, and Ivan Kolecek (Lausanne: Payot, 1995).

[9] Viollet-le-Duc, *Entretiens sur l'architecture*, p.408 in the French 1977 Mardaga reedition.

[10] Van Wezemael et al., "'Mattering' the Res Publica: The Architectural Competitions for the Swiss Federal Post Offices in the Late 19th Century as a Foucauldian Dispositif."

[11] Sorkin, *Democracy Degree Zero*.

[12] Id., p.108.

[13] Van Wezemael et al., "'Mattering' the Res Publica: The Architectural Competitions for the Swiss Federal Post Offices in the Late 19th Century as a Foucauldian Dispositif."

[14] The following statements are quoted from the WTO internet site *http://www.wto.org/english/tratop_e/gproc_e/gp_gpa_e.htm*

[15] Torsten Schmiedeknecht, "Routine and Exceptional Competition Practice in Germany as Published in wettbewerbe aktuell," in *The Architectural Competition: Research Inquiries and Experiences*, ed. Magnus Rönn, Reza Kazemian, and Jonas E. Andersson (Stockholm: Axl Books, 2010).

[16] Id., p.155.

[17] Ibid.

[18] Ibid., p.176.

[19] Manuel de landa, *A New Philosophy of Society: Assemblage Theory and Social Complexity* (London: Continuum, 2006).

[20] Viollet-le-Duc, *Entretiens dur l'architecture*, p. 408 in the French 1977 Mardaga reedition.

### ▬ References

**Brulhart**, Armand. «L'Institution du concours à Genève.» In *Concours d'architecture et d'urbanisme en Suisse romande: histoire et actualité*, edited by Armand Brulhart, Pierre Frey and Ivan Kolecek, 37-47. Lausanne: Payot, 1995.

**De Landa**, Manuel. *A New Philosophy of Society: Assemblage Theory and Social Complexity*. London: Continuum, 2006.

**Foucault**, Michel. «Des espaces autres.» *Architecture, Mouvement, Continuité*, no. 5 (1984 1984): 46-49.

**Frey**, Pierre. «Alphonse Laverrière, l'entrée en lice d'un protagoniste.» In *Concours d'architecture et d'urbanisme en Suisse romande: histoire et actualité*, edited by Armand Brulhart, Pierre Frey and Ivan Kolecek, 61-74. Lausanne: Payot, 1995.

**Frey**, Pierre. «Form, Struktur, Umwelt. Viollet-Le-Duc in Lausanne: Drei Untertitel Für Ein Vermächtnis.» In *Das Prinzip Rekonstruktion*, edited by Uta Hassler and Winfried Nerdinger, 154-67. Zürich: vdf Hochschulverlag, 2010.

**Schmiedeknecht**, Torsten. «Routine and Exceptional Competition Practice in Germany as Published in wettbewerbe aktuell.» In *The Architectural Competition: Research Inquiries and Experiences*, edited by Magnus Rönn, Reza Kazemian and Jonas E. Andersson, 152-77. Stockholm: Axl Books, 2010.

**Sorkin**, Michael. *Democracy Degree Zero*. Wettbewerb! Competition! edited by Österreichische Gesellschaft für Architektur Wien: ÖGFA., 2005.

**Van Wezemael**, Joris E., Jan M. **Silberberger**, Sofia **Paisiou**, and Pierre **Frey**. «'Mattering' the Res Publica: The Architectural Competitions for the Swiss Federal Post Offices in the Late 19th Century as a Foucauldian Dispositif.» *disP-The Planning Review* 47, no. 184 (2011): 52-59.

**Viollet-le-Duc**, Eugène-Emmanuel. *Entretiens sur l'architecture*. Paris: A. Morel, 1863.

**Viollet-le-Duc**, Eugène-Emmanuel. *Histoire d'un hôtel de ville et d'une cathédrale*. Paris: J. Hetzel, 1874.

# 1.2. The Finger and the Moon

## Belgian Competitions in Their Representational Context

**David Vanderburgh**, Ph.D.
University of Louvain
Belgium

**Carlo Menon**, Architect
The Bartlett School of Architecture
United Kingdom

The way in which the majority of architectural competitions are conducted in Belgium is far from homogeneous, since each of the numerous public authorities is free to define its own procedures. In this paper we seek to better understand how architectural competitions are conducted in Belgium. Three case studies at different scales, each coming from one of the three Belgian regions — Brussels, Wallonia and Flanders — are studied. Each competition is presented via a specific facet: the brief, the competition entries, and the jury's judgement. We have chosen not to limit our empirical field to "exemplary" competitions since it is often easier to understand a machine when it breaks down. Some considerations on the relationships between architectural competitions and the practice of architecture, emphasizing the representational context in which projects are carried out, will be discussed.

**Cover**
"The Fight Between Carnival and Lent" (excerpt). Pieter Bruegel, 1559. Oil-on-panel 118x164 cm, Kunsthistorisches Museum Vienna.
*Source: Directmedia Publishing*

Public architectural competitions, in Belgium as elsewhere, offer a visible opportunity for architects to contribute to the common good, and for public authorities to contribute to the betterment of architecture. Of course, as a well-known literature has established,[1] the dynamics of real competitions are more complex and the results often ambiguous. Indeed, some architects and political figures argue strongly against competitions. It is nonetheless important to find a theoretical middle ground between idealization and debunking, in which competitions can be evaluated for their capacity to inform us about the process of design, and perhaps about how best to foster good quality public architecture. We contend that in this context, the word "competition" must be seen in a very broad sense, as characterizing not only the relationship between explicit competitors, but also between and among all parties and even among different means or modes of representation.[2]

An old saying has it that, while the savant points at the moon, the idiot looks at the savant's finger. In the case studies that follow, we try to cultivate what might be called an "idiot savant" approach, in which we consider both means and ends of representation — both finger and moon — as equally important. Moreover, we hope to show that the representational context, including the specific representational "work" performed by competitors and organizers, is fundamentally important to the outcomes of design and competition processes.

The article is structured in three main parts:
First, we briefly explain how most architectural competitions are conducted in Belgium. It is a faithful portrait of Belgian politics: each of the numerous and intersecting public authorities is to a great extent autonomous in determining the rules for announcing and organizing competitions.

Second, we show three case studies at different scales: an art centre in Liège, a public square in Antwerp and a master plan for the European Quarter in Brussels. Each case study comes from one of the three Belgian regions (Wallonia, Flanders and Brussels) and is presented via a specific facet of the competition: the brief, the proposals, and the jury's judgment. We choose moreover not to present only "exemplary" competitions, in order to allow deeper insight into the subject; it is often easier to understand the working of a machine when it breaks down.

Third, we return to some more general considerations on the relationships between architectural competitions and the practice of architecture, emphasizing the representational context in which projects are carried out.

Competitions often raise questions of identity, whether urban, cultural, or institutional. The question asked for the session in which this paper was first presented — "Can international competitions tackle local issues?" — is indeed relevant to the Belgian context. Our study seems to conclude that indeed they can, but not always in a straightforward way: local, European, global knowledge intertwine and react in a back-and-forth movement affecting the brief, the proposals and even the work of the jury.

## ▄▄▄ Competitions in Belgium
### Belgium as a European country

Currently, design teams for public buildings or spaces in Belgium must be designated through a public tender process, but not necessarily an architectural competition. There is nonetheless a general tendency among the various authorities that organize public building, to institutionalize the practice of architectural competitions. For the last ten years, the tendency seems to be on the rise, although the situation isn't yet stable.

This political vector can be considered as the resultant of several forces: European policies defining new rules in public tenders for intellectual and creative services; good examples from neighbouring countries like France, Germany and Holland; and the pressure of the architecture community, demanding quality, transparency and equal opportunity in the selection of designers.

Architectural competitions as a means to award public contracts were first defined legally in 1993, with a new law on public tenders that became operational in 1997. The latter is a direct translation of European directives, in a collective effort to standardize procedures and to foster the mobility of merchandise, services and enterprises within the European market. Among other modes of selection, the Belgian law explicitly considers the architectural competition as a privileged way to designate architects. Other procedures, close to, if not entirely equivalent to the classic competition, also allow public authorities to ask for architectural proposals and to compare them in order to choose a winning design team, to whom a contract will be awarded. In this article we will use the term "architectural competition" within this broader definition: a competition brief, several proposals, a jury, a winner.[3]

The law of 1993 can be considered as a milestone in the study of architectural competitions in Belgium, as before this law, public authorities were entirely free to designate an architect without any sort of competition, whether architectural or economic. And even when there was a competition, such as for the Brussels Courthouse in 1860, respect for procedures was relatively weak. What has remained in Belgian collective memory is the fact that a monumental building (the largest built in the nineteenth century) was in the end realized by one of the erstwhile jury members, following moreover a massive expropriation of property in one of the most vulnerable areas of the city: since then, in that quarter of Brussels, the word "architect" is an insult, meaning someone who is at once powerful and egotistical.[4]

## The Privatization of the Public

Not everything is going in the right direction. Even today, some major public commissions are awarded without proceeding via public tender: Santiago Calatrava was recently commissioned for the train station in Mons, for instance, on the strength of his recent construction of the train station in Liège. A similar commission happened with the Midi Station in Brussels, awarded without competition to Jean Nouvel. This can be explained by the fact that the owner of the stations is a private corporation (the Belgian train company, recently "privatized" while retaining many aspects of a state monopoly), which is not subject to the laws regarding public tenders.

These somewhat shocking examples could serve as a warning. More and more today, the economic condition of European countries, and in particular the rigid injunctions to reduce national debt imposed by the European Central Bank, push public authorities to appoint private partners to accomplish public missions. Through these public-private partnerships (PPP), or "design, build & finance" processes, or through other initiatives such as the privatization of communication, energy, and maintenance services, governments transfer the competence of clearly public domains into the hands of the private sector — a well-known practice in North America and the UK. It is important to consider this situation *also* in architectural terms, as these phenomena are increasingly present across all sectors. In the future, the political and architectural questions regarding public space may no longer be negotiated within the framework of the democratic tools that we consider legitimate today.

## International?

Another ambiguity that results from belonging to the collective European superpower is that the Union promotes internal exchanges among its members but also protects its borders.

Architecture in Europe is thus subject to this double-edged condition of inclusiveness and exclusiveness. Despite a certain idea of a Planetary Age of circulation of ideas and information, it is quite rare to see extra-European firms able to act freely on the European territory. On the one hand, every tender in which the fees are expected to be more than 200.000 euros is submitted to the legal obligation of European-level publicity, which means that any European firm can participate in the competition. Any significant project will obviously exceed this threshold. On the other hand, the European market limits the participation of other counties: Australian, Indian or Brazilian firms have to open an office in Europe in order to get access to European tenders.[5]

There is only one way to organize a truly international competition for a public building in Europe: to go through the International Union of Architects (UIA), appointed by UNESCO to accredit competitions according to its "Standard regulations for international competitions in architecture and town planning" adopted in 1956 and revised in 1978.

## European?

Of course, European publication does not necessarily guarantee participation of practices from other European countries, whether in Belgium or elsewhere. If, in a strict sense, nearly every competition is "international" because French, Italians, Lithuanian or Greek architects can apply, few competitions really show significant participation of foreign architects: most participants in Belgian competitions are Belgian, whether French- or Flemish-speaking, or if "foreign," they are likely French or Dutch, i.e. from the country's closest and most influential neighbours.

It seems difficult to speak of a "European architecture" that would be any more cohesive than previous periods in European modernity. Aside from a few star architects, European architects are still linked to their territories and few of them are credible as competitors in other parts of Europe or beyond... Even if public tender procedures are common, building regulations and practices are far from standardized across Europe, and this constitutes a major obstacle to any effective mobility.[6]

## Multiple Procedures in Belgium

To explain some of the specific aspects of architectural competitions in Belgium, the first thing to say is that there is an almost surreal multitude of public authorities who deal with public space or public buildings, and who use different procedures. UIA-approved international competitions are very rare. There are no common structures or rules like the MIQCP in France or the (late) CABE in the United Kingdom, for instance. This is a consequence of the fragmentation of power in such a small country, where six main federated authorities share the power, in addition to many other different local authorities. This is quite complex, and we can only briefly summarize the main lines of the principal organizers of architectural competitions.[7]

## Flanders: the *Open Oproep* procedure

Among the various Belgian authorities, Flanders has a long experience in public tenders for architects, the so-called *Open Oproep* ("Open Call"): all public authorities in Flanders, such as municipalities, water companies, social housing institutions, and so on, may follow a common procedure organized by the "Master Architect" of the Flemish Regional Government (*Vlaams Bouwmeester*), a specialized service of twenty people who help public clients to organize the competition. The head of the service is appointed every five years through a call open to practicing architects of the private sector.

In order to concentrate attention and efforts by the architects, the Master Architect issues a list of forthcoming architectural competitions twice a year — around twenty projects. Architects send a portfolio and choose the competitions they're interested in, and wait to be called. The minimum requirement is that they have at least one realized project in their portfolio.

For every competition, the Master Architect team selects ten architects who are suitable for the project, among which several foreign practices; he then discusses the list with the local authorities (for example a school director) and they agree on a shortlist of five who receive all the documents and form a design team. Teams are then invited to two question-and-answer sessions with the client and the future users of the building, as well as other stakeholders, in order to refine the information of the brief and to better understand the client's requirements. Proposals are submitted to a committee composed of the Master Architect, the client, the future users and one independent architect. Teams can attend all of the other teams' presentations, but the discussions as well as the jury's deliberations are private. The procedure is anonymous until the shortlisted architects meet the jury (in any case, anonymity is quite difficult to maintain in such a small country).

The brief is generally rather open. As for the documents to be submitted, what is required is more a presentation of intentions, with a first-sketch proposal, than a full preliminary design. This is because in most cases the design will have to be substantially modified during the necessary discussion with the client — something that is legally impossible to organize during the tender — and it would be a loss of time to push the design further.

It is important to note that every team receives the same amount of money to cover the costs of their participation. Compensation is rather low in comparison to France or Germany: between 3.250 euros and 25.000 euros (calculated approximately at 1 % of the building costs to be divided among the number of participants), with an average of around 6.000 euros per competitor and per project. Unlike in France, for example, Belgian architects can't live off the income from unsuccessful competitions.

## Procedures in Wallonia and Brussels

Procedures in Wallonia and Brussels are similar enough to be treated together, but we will begin by sketching out their specific circumstances.

The second major region of Belgium, Wallonia, has yet to define common regulations for the organization of architectural competitions. The most relevant authority, called the Architecture Unit of the Wallonia-Brussels Federation,[8] resembles that of the Flemish Master Architect, but doesn't have the political mandate to impose its preferred procedures on all the various local authorities of the region. The third important actor of the federal state, the Brussels region, covers the territory of the capital of Belgium (one million inhabitants, a tenth of the total population) and, of course, of Europe. In terms of the organization of architectural competitions, procedures in Brussels are about halfway between those of Flanders and Wallonia. On the one hand, like Flanders, it recently appointed a Master Architect administration (six staff members), which is meant to co-ordinate all other public authorities within its territory and to define its procedures. But on the other hand, such a new institution has little authority to lead local powers, so that the situation in Brussels is still fragmented.[9]

Both the Architecture Unit of the Wallonia-Brussels Federation and the Master Architect of the Brussels Region propose a negotiated procedure in two stages. Once the announcement is published in the Belgian and European official journals, architects form a complete design team and submit a prequalification file with a cover letter and relevant references, built or unbuilt. There are no restrictions regarding minimum cash flow or size of the practice. [10]

A jury is formed by representatives of the public authority, the future users and three independent architects and professors in schools of architecture. This jury shortlists five design teams, which receive all the documents necessary to produce a proposal.

Aside from these initial differences, the procedure is similar to the Flemish one:

- Shortlisted teams visit the site and participate in a question-and-answer session with the future users and the public authority.
- Their entry is made up of a sketch design proposal and a cursory analysis of the project context (landscape, stability, technical systems).
- In a one-day session, the jury attends oral presentations by all five competitors, and then designates the winning team. The whole session is private.
- All teams receive the same amount of money to cover the costs of the procedure, and the winner obtains the contract.

Despite a certain diversity due to the political, cultural and linguistic context, the three "Master Architect" authorities of Flanders, Wallonia and Brussels get along quite well and often exchange ideas and experiences on architectural competitions. They also discuss general and future problems, such as how to preserve architectural quality within the economic context of the aforementioned public-private partnerships.

### ▬ Case Studies

We have chosen our three case studies in order to take account of the diversity of factors that are at stake: regional identity, scale, program, and representational context. Concerning this last factor, a full analysis would take more space than we have here. But we've found that some elements in that context seem to dominate in each particular situation; rather than trying to draw a systematic comparison among them, we have chosen to emphasize particular aspects of each. This should provide at once an overview of architectural competitions in Belgium and a kind of answer to the question of our conference session, as to whether international competitions might (or might not) be helpful in tackling local issues.

The three case studies are:

1. CIAC International Centre for Art and Culture, Liège, Wallonia
   *Competition for building and surroundings*
   *Representational context: the design proposals (in particular the oral presentation)*
2. Rue de la Loi, Brussels
   *Competition for town planning*
   *Representational context: the jury*
3. Theaterplein, Antwerp, Flanders
   *Competition for urban design*
   *Representational context: the brief and the competition rules*

### ▬ CIAC, Liège

For the "Design of an International Centre for Art and Culture" (CIAC) in Liège (2009-present, now under construction), we focus on how international firms responded to a programme that raised some very local issues while affirming aspirations for "star" architecture and urban branding (the so-called Bilbao Effect). This problematic architectural competition somehow led to the selection of a good project: the rhetorical skills and political posture of the winning team, Rudy Ricciotti (France) together with Cabinet p.HD, a local practice, convinced the jury to make a responsible, context-sensitive choice.

**The Competition Context: Great Expectations**
It is rare in Wallonia to have the opportunity to build projects costing more than 10M euros, especially for cultural buildings. [11] It's even rarer to attract broad international interest for a competition: in this case almost half of the participating teams included foreign firms.

In recent years, the city of Liège has pursued an aggressive strategy of touristic development and renewal of its centre via high-profile, high-budget projects, beginning with the previously-mentioned construction of the TGV station by Calatrava, [12] the urban renewal of the boulevard opposite and of the banks of the Meuse river, and a new shopping and leisure centre called Médiacité (with a mall designed by Ron Arad). For the creation of the CIAC, situated on an island in the middle of the river and facing the new train station **[Fig. 1]**, the aim was to appeal to large numbers of "city-trotters," to punctuate the promenade between these two attractions. [13]

**Fig. 1**
The competition site.
*Copyright : Microsoft and Blom*

The project is intended to follow in the line of other cultural centres appearing in middle-sized European cities, such as the Pompidou Centre branch recently built in Metz by Shigeru Ban, or the Museum an de Stroom in Antwerp by Neutelings-Riedrich Architects.[14] Such free-standing, iconic buildings constitute a tourist attraction in themselves, intended to be worth the trip quite independently from the content of the exhibition.

To ensure that only big practices could participate, the public authority had established a minimum threshold of 1,5M euros income or cash flow as a prequalification crite-rion. As a result, few of the younger, more creative offices that usually participate in competitions applied ; those that did were obliged to associate with others in order to boost their financial profile.

It is worth noting that these latter, in their letters of motivation, were the only ones who explicitly underlined the importance of taking a step back from the seductive idea of a "Bilbao" in Liège, keeping this model at a critical distance. None were retained for the second stage of the competition. Instead, the jury was quite efficient in short listing five well-known practices among the twenty-eight applications submitted. Four out of these five were foreign offices, in some cases associated with a local partner.[15]

**The Programme : Generic *and* Local Issues**

Architecturally speaking, the programme was simple and familiar. The site, on the other hand, is quite exception-al. The public authority recognized its potential, and the competition brief stated the importance of preserving and implementing the relationships between two existing build-ings and their surroundings. The brief was rather open : participants could choose what to do with the two existing buildings without demolishing them, and also had the free-dom to build a new one in order to fill out the programme. The collections of the current Museum of Modern and Contemporary Art would be transferred elsewhere, leaving the space empty for temporary exhibitions. A major exhibi-tion and a smaller one would take place simultaneously, in addition to a space dedicated to local artists or artists in residence, and with all the usual facilities : restaurant, cafeteria, bookshop.

Such a competition was a perfect opportunity for design teams to express their sensibility and posture: freedom of space, a beautiful spot in the middle of a city park, a few constraints but not a *tabula rasa*.

## A Responsible Decision

Even though, from the beginning, the public authority seemed more engaged in a process of *city branding* leading toward an iconic building, surprisingly it was the turn of the competing architects to take more responsibility towards the site and the existing buildings **[Fig. 2 to 7]**. With one or two exceptions (for example, Jakob & Macfarlane / B612's and Kengo Kuma's entries) and via different approaches, indeed, the design teams took a clear, contextual position, trying to reveal, to adjust or to meet the brief with a rather modest amount of new architecture. One might even say that these proposals are local and international at the same time, both exotic and appropriate.

After the oral presentation of the five design proposals to the jury, on May 25, 2010, the winning proposal by Rudy Ricciotti and his team was judged to be the most convincing. The interventions proposed in the existing buildings and their surroundings were elegant, respectful, and flexible with regard to the programme. But why did the jury, of which around half the members weren't architects, go back on its initial spectacular expectations and vote for the project that made the least "noise" possible? We believe that the reason for this change of tack is to be found in the speech more than in the drawings: it was the winners' presentation that made the members of the jury take another attitude toward the competition and evaluate the projects more in terms of architectural quality than the aforementioned touristic logic.

The presentation was introduced by Rita Occhiuto, a local landscape designer and professor. She told the story of the artificial island, of the splendour of the initial project, when the city of Liège hosted the international World's Fair in 1905, and the technical skills of the local industry of steel and concrete were at their peak. Both the park and the building, although eclectic and romantic in their appearances, were built with very modern technologies. She explained why this design should be revealed and not dismantled through the new Art Centre.

Then the local architect associated with Rudy Ricciotti, Paul Hautecler (Cabinet p.HD), did almost the same thing, telling the jury why and how the existing building should be adapted for contemporary exhibitions while being restored.

Finally, it was Rudy Ricciotti who addressed the jury more directly, talking about a "sense of guilt" that the design team felt towards the site. In a later interview he stated,

*"I consider that I have fulfilled my political responsibility toward this island: first, to preserve the site; second, not to take it hostage [to contemporary culture and tourism]; third, to allow culture to have a civic and responsible posture; fourth, to open the building like a big cinematographic window towards the popular district on the other bank of the Meuse river."* And, even more explicitly: *"Maybe the people in Liège wanted a spectacular building... Bad luck, they ended up with a reactionary architect like me. The architects sitting in the jury protected the city from the risk of wrecking the city yet again with a 'bombastic' building."*[16]

## Can International Competitions Tackle Local Issues?

It is clear that the local members of the design team set the broad outlines of the winning scheme.[17] Rudy Ricciotti scrupulously followed these premises, in the area defined by them and in the same logic, while intelligently "heating up" the rhetoric. Would a project like this have been selected by the jury, if no international architect had proposed or 'sponsored' it?

Our feeling is that this project was rather like some of those envisioned by the local architects, which were rejected in the first stage of the competition. But a collaboration of this sort got the project's "foot in the door" and allowed it to be considered. From then on, it was first the rhetorical skills of the designers that drew the jury's attention, and *then* the quality of the project that led to its victory.

**Fig. 2**
Liège-based Atelier d'architecture Pierre Hebbelinck — Pierre de
Wit proposed a 'white cube' in symbiosis with the existing building.

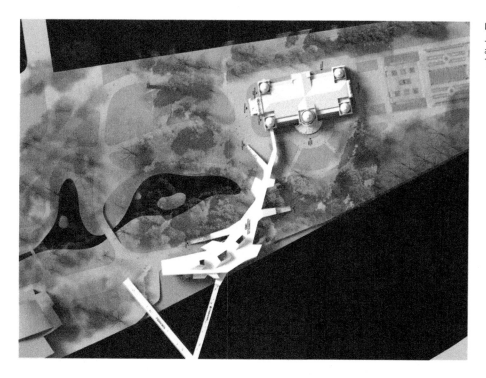

**Fig. 3**
Jakob + Macfarlane / B612 :
autonomous architecture as
'flotsam'.

**Fig. 4**
Kengo Kuma : a peaceful site
where contemporary architecture
dominates the existing.

**Fig. 5**
Dominique Perrault Architecture:
the new programme is fitted in a
circular basement.

**Fig. 6**
The winning project by Rudy
Ricciotti and Cabinet p.HD :
"almost nothing".

**Fig. 7**
The winning project, south facade.

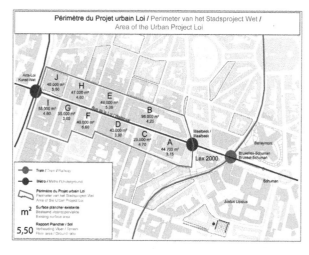

**Fig. 8**
The competition site, linking the
European Institutions with the city
centre.

## ▬▬ Rue de la Loi, Brussels

For the "Definition of a new urban form for the Rue de la Loi" (2008 – 2012), a major street in the European Quarter of Brussels, our emphasis is on questions of critical judgment; in particular on the mental confusion in the jury provoked by some of the competition images and models, and the way in which, instead, less explicit documents helped the winner to succeed **[Fig.8]**.

The brief required doubling density and public space along the street and environs, while at the same time conveying a more democratic image of European institutions. For once, the competition raised local expectations, calling for an idea of urban form, something very rare in Brussels — especially when it concerns European institutions, whose establishment in the city has always followed a sort of "hide and seek" logic. But after meeting each team twice, the committee opted for the lighter touch of a relatively vague proposal by French architect Christian de Portzamparc.

And yet, this choice must have been thoroughly deliberated by the jury: after the first presentation, they were unable to agree on a ranking and they decided to invite the five shortlisted teams a second time, two months later, asking them to explain further some aspects of their projects. [18] In the context of an urban-scale project, it may have been too difficult to distinguish the formal aspects from the strategic ones, urban outlines from architectural proposals, projections from visions.

### Urban-Scale Competitions

Urban-scale competitions are more difficult to approach than architectural ones, and it would be worthwhile to explore this field further, focusing on its specificities. Should urban competitions be different in form, means of expression, and jury procedures, from architectural competitions? Taking our sources from articles written at the time and recent interviews of some of the participating architects made for the purposes of this paper, [19] we consider that the proposals weren't fully understood by all the members of the jury. Notably, in our opinion, the proposals that were considered as "radical" seem to be the most feasible.

Briefly, the competition consisted in proposing a new urban form for the Rue de la Loi and its immediate surroundings. The winner would establish a master plan including publicly commissioned projects (for which the architects would be chosen through separate competitions) and the so-called natural market interplay of private property owners that had defined the district thus far. There were three proposed axes of development:

- to double the density of an important boulevard linking the European Parliament and institutions to the city centre of Brussels;
- to make it a mixed-use neighbourhood instead of the mono-functional, office-oriented district it is today;
- to improve the public image of the European institutions in Brussels, which in the current collective consciousness are considered too bureaucratic and self-centred.

It is interesting to compare three of the proposals from the point of view of the aforementioned radicality/feasibility dialectic **[Fig.9] [Fig.10] [Fig.11]**. Coincidentally, they represent the production of three generations of OMA/Rem Koolhaas and its descendants: OMA itself, associated with Nicolas Firket (a former OMA partner, in his thirties, now established in Brussels); Xaveer De Geyter, also based in Brussels, who worked at OMA in its "golden age"; and the young Belgian star-architect Julien De Smedt (founder of Plot in Denmark and ex-associate of BIG), associated with Secchi-Viganò.

The team led by JDS and Secchi-Viganò proposed to work on every parcel in the district, according to a "cursor" or gradation of architectural freedom: from small interventions in existing buildings to a *tabula rasa*. The aim was to create more public space for pedestrians, with diagonal paths and small "plazas" in the interior of every block.

Their project would have required quite some time to become effective, and the hypothesis of the cursor could lead to unpredictable results, uncertainties due to the freedom of initiative under the law and the pressure of the market. In the end, perhaps only a few of these interventions would become part of the new look of the Rue de la Loi — far from the image promoted in the competition panels!

The jury, however, was greatly influenced in its judgement by the images, which led it to imagine the proposition as a unitary act of architecture — as if the team had intended to demolish and rebuild the whole district by themselves, thereby reducing urbanism to architecture.

This was clearly not among the team's intentions; their design process was based more on diagrams and probability than on a final urban form imposed on the district. In an interview, Julien De Smedt admitted that he had decided to push the imageability of the proposal beyond the schemes and diagrams elaborated together with Secchi-Viganò, in order to overcome — in his words — "the reluctance of Southern-European urbanism to use form as a design tool."

Both OMA/NFA and XDGA proposed instead to intervene only on parcels that were already held by the European Community. We can consider that their proposition of clearly identifiable European buildings (the porticos of OMA/NFA or the crossroads of towers of XDGA) proceeded simultaneously from two angles of attack. On the one hand, the analysis of the existing was processed through the notion of "dirty realism":[20] waiting for building sites to become available would compromise the possibility of ever building a true urban form, as urbanism in Brussels is very difficult to control and the stakeholders and property-owners quite numerous. On the other hand, the demand to concretely build an image for Europe in Brussels was approached and then determined in the proposals through morphological studies, basically working with models.

Considering the documents entered for the competition, both proposals were quickly assimilated by the jury (unlike the proposal by JDS/Secchi-Viganò) and both of them frightened it: most members worried that such a concentration of programme wouldn't benefit the image of European institutions, as the tall buildings would be considered by the population as overwhelming.

OMA/NFA's "porticos" were considered as totalitarian by Eastern European members of the jury, whereas the image that the design team sought to communicate — possibly ironically, as if they knew their proposal might be misunderstood — was that of the Greek colonnade that unifies and shelters.

Xaveer De Geyter Architects chose to concentrate programme elements at the intersection between two different sectors of the European district, creating an event at a multi-modal node where European high-rise buildings could emerge. The construction site would be easy to manage, without expropriation. This proposal, although elegant and straightforward, was apparently too extreme to be accepted by the jury.

### Aiming for the Middle Ground

Christian de Portzamparc was lucky or clever enough to make a proposal less radical than the ones by OMA or XDGA, less diluted than Fletcher Priest and WIT's, and less extravagant than JDS's **[Fig. 12]**. Theoretically speaking, his proposal could be appropriated by any member of the jury who could project his or her own preoccupations onto the drawing, whether looking for high-rise buildings or trying to avoid them (something that OMA and XDGA decided not to hide, but on the contrary to promote), or a sustainable eco-district, a clean boulevard for those pedestrians that

**Fig. 9**
OMA/NFA project: the "portico"
as a European archetypal form
that can accommodate the new
programme in its entirety.

**Fig. 10**
Xaveer De Geyter Architects: all
the programme is concentrated at
a single crossroads, implicating
multi-modal exchange and high-rise
buildings.

**Fig. 11**
JDS Julien De Smet / Studio Associato Secchi-Viganò: interventions at
different levels (cursor), while opening up public space at the street level.

**Fig. 12**
Agence Christian de Portzamparc : an "open street"
punctuated with "pocket parks" and shops for
pedestrians ; taller European buildings direct the
concert of private initiative.

**Fig. 13**
The square facing the Theatre before (east view) and
after the project (west view) © Microsoft and Blom.

hate the scruffiness and dirt of most Brussels outdoor
spaces : in other words, a consensual project. Working by
exclusion, the jury took no risks in selecting the project by
de Portzamparc.

Most of the issues at stake in the launching of this
competition, which had sought to emancipate Brussels by
truly defining its urban form through the shaping of public
space, were thus sidelined. As the president of the jury
lamented afterward, "What's the point of organizing an
international competition if it means selecting a project that
promises no more than the natural process of densification
of the current European district ?" [21]

## ▬ *Theaterplein*, Antwerp

This third case study presents a winning proposal that
has already been built. It is the result of an *Open Oproep*
procedure launched by the City of Antwerp in collaboration
with the Flemish Master Architect in 2004, and completed
in 2009. The winning team was led by the Italian firm Studio
Associato Secchi-Viganò, along with local architect Dirk
Jaspaert.

The scale of the project called for in the competition
brief, entitled "Development of the Theater Square and its
surroundings," is smaller than that of our previous case. It
is on the borderline between urbanism and architecture : [22] a
defined urban space, the square in front of the city theatre,
to be redesigned mostly using architectural and urban
design tools rather than planning methods **[Fig.13]**. In
this case, we could consider the brief as the "finger" (as a
medium of representation), and the design proposals as the
"moon," since these latter constitute the public authorities'
goal in organizing the competition : we found that the brief
helped significantly to orient the competitors' positions and
proposals, in both explicit and implicit ways.

### The Competition

The brief called for the renovation of a square in the city centre, but without fixing precise goals or criteria. Competing
teams were expected to reinvent the urbanity and the identity of the square. We reproduce here a fairly extensive
extract of the text, in order to give an idea of its explicit
openness to a variety of solutions :

**Fig. 14**
A model of the winning project by
Studio Associato Secchi-Vigano
and Dirk Jaspaert.

**Fig. 15**
The project as built.
*Photo Teresa Cos*

*The Theatre Square is in very poor condition and is considered as being of low quality. The open space is too broad, with no obvious limits. It is only used on weekends, as a market space. The surroundings of the Theatre Square have a lot of potential. The Bird Market and the surrounding tourist attractions such as the Rubens House, the Bourlaschouwburg, the Botanical Gardens, the Royal Palace, and several adjacent theaters give the square a strategic position. The malls are just a stone's throw away and are part of the pedestrian path to the old town. This strategic location is a unique opportunity to make this area a square with different uses at different times. A responsible, sustainable and functional reconstruction of the Theatre Square is required, including the adjacent public domain.* [23]

This rather open problem statement was preceded by a poem, "Agoraphobia" by Tom Lanoye, a celebrated local writer, which opens with a call for action : "For the Theatre Square/cradle of the Bird Market,/anxiously awaiting renovation…" But, as the subtle conclusion of the poem implies, such action should not necessarily mean filling up the empty space :"…For my essence — /the void — I am/myself most afraid". Deliberately ambiguous, this last stanza allows, without imposing, the interpretation of the void as something to protect rather than to, as it were, avoid.

In our opinion, while leaving complete freedom to design teams, the public authority was able via this poem to orient the project. The winning team best interpreted the spirit of the programme, giving an answer to the void without filling it, and liberating a project that couldn't be defined otherwise — certainly not, for example, by a more constrained or constraining brief **[Fig.14] [Fig.15]**.

**European Identity**

This competition and its resulting realization can be considered as an excellent exercise in democracy. The canopy that covers part of the square structures the space without influencing its unpredictable uses. It allows a new perception of the existing buildings that give onto the square, whether remarkable or regrettable ; it even draws little attention to the new interventions. This notion of democracy is also relevant when we speak of the competition organizers, who decided not to be too present (via the brief) in order to let the competitors summon their own preoccupations and sensibilities. This trust they put in the private operators led to five very different and personal approaches.

This freedom is also evident in the choice of documents that competitors could submit. At the time, the Flemish Master Architect left this choice open, considering that competing teams should be allowed to decide for themselves. This is no longer the case : it has since been decided to limit the format and number of documents to be submitted, in order to limit speculation on the best means to employ for the competition. Time will tell whether this measure is fruitful.

▬

The Belgian context is indeed diverse with respect to the administrative management of architectural competitions, and so the answers that we might give to the overarching question of international competitions vs. local issues are correspondingly varied. Provisionally, we might conclude that, *when circumstances are right*, the international dimension can indeed be helpful for resolving local questions. In two of our three examples — CIAC and *Theaterplein* — this seems to have been the case. But we shrink from such a cautious conclusion, which amounts to saying that with luck, everything will turn out all right…

We'd prefer to turn the question on its head, and ask : "When is it useful to call upon international firms in order to resolve local questions ?" Rephrasing the question allows us to remind ourselves that in any architectural project there is always a local dimension, whereas there may or may not be an international one. And, furthermore, as our examples show, the "international" contribution can intervene at very different levels in the process. In the CIAC example, for instance, the success of the winning entry appears to turn on the personal contribution of an international "star," adopting a position that many sensible local architects would have taken up. On a quite different level, the *Theaterplein* competition benefited from its openness to the international dimension in the sense that "outsiders" might be better able to perceive the generic issues at stake than locals, who might be too likely to engage in naïve contextualism. It's worth underlining that an open competition for open space with an open brief has a certain appealing coherence.

However, as we've already intimated, our "successful" examples may in the end be less informative than the one that, for the moment, appears to have "broken down". Our Brussels example ends, to paraphrase the President of the jury (and T.S. Eliot) "not with a bang but a whimper." Why ? It seems that the critical judgment of the jury, but also of the competitors, was distorted in the matter of the means and modes of representation. The general context — Brussels as European capital, with a notably contentious history of urban and political representation — was of no help to anyone. From a purely architectural point of view, the only entry answering to the explicit *and implicit* problems at stake in the project was local: Xaveer De Geyter based his proposal on his intimate knowledge of the city. But once one includes the impact of issues like European political representation in the jury's judgment, it seems in retrospect that the only possible outcome was what is known here as a *"compromis à la belge"*: in other words a solution that leaves everyone equally unhappy.

Our conviction is that, in order to get the most from the study of competitions, we must get used to a certain breadth of definition of both means and ends — of the finger and of the moon. When it comes down to real situations, it becomes clear that only broad or "deflationist" definitions allow us to take full account of what may be at stake.

As concerns the "finger" or representation, the epistemologist Mario Suarez[24] assigns great importance to the judgment of an assembly of competent experts — a jury, in other terms — in order to establish criteria for effective representation. These criteria are inevitably contingent. This would explain the diversity of "winning" (or "losing") representational modes in the competitions studied here. In the imagination of architects, it is often the drawings and renderings that convince the jury. But in reality, a competent jury will base its judgment on the entire ensemble of elements presented: drawings, texts, models, and oral presentations. As we've seen in the case of the CIAC competition, it was most probably the latter that "won" the competition. And in the case of the Brussels competition, it is more likely that the drawings of the vanquished contenders "lost" them the competition, rather than that those of the winning team "won" it. When we turn our attention to the "moon," to the project in and for itself, it appears to us that among the decisions made by a competent jury, it is just as much a question of arbitrating among competing modes of representation as it is of selecting the best project. Arguably, then, the most contingent or situation-dependent of judgements is also a theoretical *prise de position* in a quite fundamental sense. Each competition re-establishes the pecking order among competing modes of representation, from politics to geometry and back again.

## Notes

[1] See, among (many) others, Hélène Lipstadt, ed., *The Experimental Tradition. Essays on Architectural Competitions* (Princeton: Princeton Architectural Press, 1989); Elisabeth Tostrup, *Architecture and Rhetoric: Text and Design in Architectural Competitions, Oslo 1939-1997* (London: Andreas Papadakis Publishers, 1999); Magnus Rönn, Reza Kazemian, Jonas E. Andersson, eds., *The Architectural Competition: Research Inquiries and Experiences* (Stockholm: Axl Books, 2010).

[2] This idea has been developed further in our article "Who — or What — «Wins» an Architectural Competition? A Model and a Case Study", *FORMakademisk*, vol. 7, no. 1 *Architectural competitions II* (2014). Available online: *https://journals.hioa.no/index.php/formakademisk/article/view/822*

[3] Law of 23/12/1993 concerning public tenders for construction, supplies and services; architectural competitions are defined at the article n°20; two 'Royal Acts' (8/01/1996 and 26/9/1996) specify the application rules of this law. Since then, two new laws have been published on 15 and 16/6/2006 following the European Directive 2004/18/CE, but they became effective only in 2013 (Royal Acts of 15/07/2011 and 14/01/2013, operational since July 2013). This gap between Belgian and European legislations will remain, as in the meantime the 2004 European Directive on public procurement was replaced in 2014 (2014/24/UE).

[4] See Pierre Loze et. al., *Le Palais de justice de Bruxelles: monument XIXe* (Brussels: Atelier Volkaer, 1983).

[5] According to specific agreements, certain countries may participate in European tenders: Iceland, Liechtenstein, Norway, Canada, Korea, the United States, Israel, Japan and Switzerland (Royal Act of 8/01/1996, art. 79).

[6] There are nonetheless some forces pushing toward European unity. For instance, the Erasmus student exchange program between universities allows students to experience up to one year abroad, usually in another European country. The Europan program of competitions for young architects is another good way to foster young architects' mobility and the exchange of ideas throughout Europe. The journal *A10*, published in the Netherlands, shows completed buildings from the distant parts of Europe in a neutral, horizontal way.

[7] It is worth noting here that there are still some public procedures that don't require architects to produce an architectural proposal in order to be awarded a contract. Instead, they base selection on competitive bids on the level of professional fees, so that the chosen architect will work for minimum fees. These are, in fact, not architectural competitions in any real sense of the term.

[8] One of the authors of the present article worked for several years in this service, composed of six staff members.

[9] Following the designation of the Brussels Master Architect, several cities in Wallonia opened up a debate to nominate one. As of the present, Charleroi has appointed a "Charleroi *Bouwmeester*" (2013), a team of 4 people.

[10] This rule and the amount of the indemnities are often opposed by the local project owner: another consequence of the lack of political coherence throughout all levels of the Belgian administration.

[11] In this case, the building costs are estimated at 16M euros, funded by several institutional partners, among which the European Regional Development Fund.

[12] For the record, it cost 312M euros, three times the expected price (www.eurogare.be).

[13] A first benchmarking predicted attracting to Liège, through this project, 600,000 visitors every year. This estimation was later reduced to a more realistic but still optimistic 300,000.

[14] Good reviews of these projects can be found in *Criticat* no. 7 (Françoise Fromonot, Jacqueline Trichard: "Metz, ville générique", March 2011), and in *OASE* no. 81, with a double review of the MAS project by Christophe Van Gerrewey and Maarten Delbeke (June 2010).

<sup></sup>[15] International candidates with local partners (those shortlisted are underlined): 1. Jakob + Macfarlane/B612 Associates; 2. Agence Rudy Ricciotti/Cabinet p.HD; 3. Dominique Perrault Architecture; 4. Kengo Kuma & Associates Europe; 5. Grimshaw Architects; 6. JDS Architects (Julien de Smedt); 7. Atelier Christian de Portzamparc/Artau; 8. Bodin & Associés/Pierre Sauveur; 9. Wilmotte & Associés; 10. Gae Aulenti Architetti Associati/NJDA Architecture; 11. Coldefy & Associés Architectes Urbanistes (CAAU); 12. Josep Llinas Architecte/Baumans Deffet; 13. Robbrecht en Daem Architecten/Bureau d'études Dethier; 14. Odile Decq Benoit Cornette Architectes Urbanistes. Local candidates: 15. Atelier d'architecture Pierre Hebbelinck; 16. Matador/Alain Richard/Laurent Ney/Secchi-Viganò; 17. Bureau Vers plus de bien être (V+)/Fantastic; 18. Bureau d'Architecture Emile Verhaegen; 19. Atelier de l'Arbre d'Or; 20. INCA/Steinmetz De Meyer; 21. Archi+I/BURO II; 22. CERAU/BAG/TEMPORA; 23. Polaris Architects; 24. Hasevoets/Hors-Champs/Confino/Noé-Martin Architectes; 25. Atelier d'architecture de Genval/Atelier du Sart Tilman; 26. Anorak/Bureau Bas Smets; 27. SumProject/K2A4; 28. AUPA/n! studio.

[16] Interview with Carlo Menon and Lino Polegato for the art magazine *Fluxnews* no. 55, (April-June 2011): 28-29. Some excerpts of the interview can be viewed online: fluxnews.skyrock.com

[17] Interview with Paul Hautecler and Rita Occhiuto on 29/02/2012.

[18] The oral presentation and the possibility to engage in discussion with the competitors is allowed by the "negotiated procedure," which is a fundamental principle of "good competitions" in the three regions of Belgium. The promoters of the project were the Region of Brussels and the European Commission. The jury was thus composed of twelve members: two representatives of the Brussels Region, two from the European Commission and two from the City of Brussels, plus six international experts chosen via the "permanent representations" at the European Union.

[19] Sources: the official catalogue of the exhibition that followed the competition, including the five entries (www.adt-ato.be). Audrey Contesse, "Loi de consensus", *A+* no. 217 (April 2009): 8-12, with an interview of Olivier Bastin, president of the jury and outgoing 'Master Architect' of the Brussels Region. Interviews of Julien De Smedt (6/01/2012), Nicolas Firket (7/01/2012), and Sara Noel Costa de Araujo for XDGA (7/03/2012).

[20] One can understand that the three entries were based on the conviction, clearly exposed by Rem Koolhaas since his study on the European institutions (since 2001), that Brussels and Europe needed a form, a hardware, instead of being just a lightweight hub, without built consistency, distributing power to the various parts of Europe, which was rather the position of intellectuals such as Umberto Eco. See *Brussels, Capital of Europe*, Final Report of the Group of Policy Advisers of the European Commission, 2001, ec.europa.eu/dgs/policy_advisers/archives/publications/docs/brussels_capital.pdf

[21] Contesse, "Loi de consensus", 12.

[22] Articles on this project: Hans Ibelings, *Designing for the public* (Amsterdam: SUN architecture Publishers/Flemish Government Architect, 2009), 98-101; Roemer Van Toorn, "The Ultimate Value of *Beinahe Nichts*", in *The Specific and the Singular: Architecture in Flanders* (Antwerp: Flemish Architecture Institute, 2010): 119-125; Géry Leloutre and Hubert Lionnez, "Rationalité minimum", interview of Bernardo Secchi and Paola Viganò, *A+* no. 197 (December 2005): 36-45.

[23] Excerpt of the competition brief, translated by the authors.

[24] Mauricio Suárez, «An Inferential Conception of Scientific Representation», *Philosophy of Science*, Vol. 71, No. 5 (2004): 767-779.

## ▬ References

**Commission, Group of Policy Advisers of the European**. "Brussels, Capital of Europe. Final Report." 2001.

**Ibelings**, Hans. Designing for the Public: Flemish Government Architect 1999-2009. Amsterdam: SUN Architecture Publishers, 2009.

**Leloutre**, Géry, and Hubert **Lionnez**. "Rationalité Minimum, Interview of Bernardo Secchi and Paola Vigano." A+, no. December 2005–197 (2005): 36-45.

**Lipstadt**, Hélène, Barry **Bergdoll**, and **Architectural League of New York**. The Experimental Tradition : Essays on Competitions in Architecture. New York, N.Y. : Princeton Architectural Press, 1989.

**Loze**, Pierre et. al. Le Palais De Justice De Bruxelles: Monument Xixe Brussels: Atelier Volkaer, 1983.

**Menon**, Carlo. "Projet du CIAC. Rencontre avec Rudy Ricciotti." Fluxnews, no. April – June 55 (2011): 28-29.

**Rönn**, Magnus, Reza **Kazemian**, and Jonas E. **Andersson**. The Architectural Competition: Research Inquiries and Experiences Stockholm: Axl Books, 2010.

**Suarez**, Mauricio. "An Inferential Conception of Scientific Representation." Philosophy of Science 71, no. 5 (2004): 767-79.

**Tostrup**, Elisabeth, and **Arkitekthøgskolen i Oslo**. Architecture and Rhetoric : Text and Design in Architectural Competitions, Oslo, 1939-90. Oslo: Oslo School of Architecture, 1996.

**Van Toorn**, Roemer. "The Ultimate Value of Beinahe Nichts." In Architecture in Flanders, edited by Flemish Architecture Institute. Antwerp : Flemish Architecture Institute, 2010.

# 1.3. The President's Choice

**An Eventful History of the 1982 Tête Défense Competition**

**Loïse Lenne**, Ph.D. student in architecture
University Paris-Est
France

When he became President of France in 1981, François Mitterrand, an architecturally inclined politician, started the *Grands Travaux* (Great Projects) — a policy that intended to leave an imprint on the country as a result of planning of several important buildings. One such building was programmed at La Défense, on a site that had already been the object of many projects. Recalling the history of the competition that led to Johann Otto von Spreckelsen's *Grande Arche* (1982-1989), we will study the roles of the various people who participated in the project, chosen by a jury as well as by Mitterrand himself, before analyzing how the competition served as a communication tool. Then, by comparing it with another competition that took place in London at the same period (Lloyd's building, Richard Rogers partnership, 1977-1986), we will explain how the program, its formulation, and above all, how the culture of the various actors influence a decision and the built result. In conclusion, we will illustrate how these buildings may be considered as events, which may be divided into two separate categories; that is, historical and spatial — terms that we will define.

**Cover**
The Grande Arche in its 2014 context viewed from Hotel Melia under construction.
*Photo: Loïse Lenne.*

## An eventful history of the competition for the *Tête Défense*

When he became President of France in 1981, François Mitterrand, an architecturally inclined politician, started the *Grands Travaux* (Great Projects) — a policy that intended to leave an imprint on the country as a result of the planning of several important buildings. The *Parc de la Villette* and the Orsay Museum had been launched by his predecessor, Valéry Giscard d'Estaing, and were finished during Mitterrand's presidency. In contrast the project chosen for the *Tête Défense* was deemed to lack ambition and was thus abandoned. A new competition was launched in 1982 with a new program (two ministries and an "International Center of Communication"), and a new intent to make itself visible from the historical axis of Paris, which goes west from the Louvre.

In 1983 a Danish architect, unknown in France, became the winner of this prestigious international competition. In 1989, Johann Otto von Spreckelsen's *Grande Arche de la Défense* **[Fig.1]** was about to be one of the most appreciated projects of Mitterrand's *Grands Travaux*. To this day the building is considered a success as "the work is part of the Great Monuments in the capital city [...] which make France's reputation".[1]

"Take a photograph and remove the Arch: there's no unity to La Défense without it".[2] The building is often described in terms of unity, as if the solution had been obvious in a competition that was itself exemplary. However, the history of the project shows that the one quality of the competition as a tool is in fact that it allows a story to be told in retrospect, and one that has invariably been rewritten. Making a definitive choice was not so simple, and Mitterrand's controversial role in the process deserves some clarification.

Comparing the competition with another great competition that took place in the eighties and which led to the building of the Lloyd's (Richard Rogers partnership, 1977-1986), we will highlight the fact that the competition process is an extremely cultural affair. The participant's habits greatly influence the built result, which in both cases was considered to be a "major event" — an expression we will question at the end of this article.

## The Competition (as a) Result

The *Grande Arche* competition should be considered in conjunction with the history of La Défense. The potential of the whole site of La Défense, which is the extension of the *Axe royal* (Royal Axis) of Paris, was already noted at the beginning of the twentieth century.[3] Public and private projects, as well as competitions, were frequent until the architects Robert Camelot, Jean de Mailly, and Bernard Zehrfuss were hired to design a master plan for the area. In 1958 the public organization *Établissement public pour l'aménagement de la région de la Défense* (EPAD; Public Agency for the Development of La Défense) was created in order to oversee the project. This was a voluntary act for the planning of the area, whose control was given to the EPAD beyond the city limits.[4]

The plan was typical of above-ground planning: symmetrical and centered, including office and housing buildings, each of their own individual form **[Fig.2]**. In this highly ordered context built inside a pear-shaped circular boulevard, the building of the CNIT (*Centre des nouvelles industries et technologies* / Center of New Industries and Technologies) and its symmetrical site on the other side of the axis became a focal point. Bernard Zehrfuss suggested that the building on the second site be composed of four towers up to 200 meters high. This project opened the way for a number of other projects because it transgressed the original regulated plans: "Consistency, calm, symmetry, a few subtly-dosed discrepancies, and a final climax in the form of a unique "event" [...]: a very high tower, or rather four towers [...]".[5] Along with the CNIT and the pear shape of the square, the project for these towers moved La Défense's centre of gravity over to the west, almost to what was soon to be known as the *Tête Défense*[6] — the highest point of the square, comprising a third point of a triangle formed by the two previously mentioned sites **[Fig.3]**.

When the general plan was decided, it became possible to focus on the individual projects. In 1969 Ieoh Ming Pei was commissioned by the developer Jean-Paul Aaron to design a building on the site of Zehrfuss' unbuilt towers. The architect proposed twin towers on the *Tête Défense* instead:[7] soon, all eyes would turn to this site. This project forced the EPAD to investigate the central question of the *Tête Défense*, and it asked Émile Aillaud to come up with a project as well. Even though he too closed off the axis, he proposed two low-rise buildings with reflecting walls. Both projects proposed terms and ideas that created a debate that would last for over twenty years — to close or to open?

**Fig. 1a**
(from left) J.O. von Spreckelsen, his translator,
François Mitterrand, and Robert Lion, facing a model
of the Grande Arche (c1983).
*Copyright: Defacto*

**Fig. 1b**
The Grande Arche in the royal axis (from Neuilly), in its context of 2013.
*Photography: LL.*

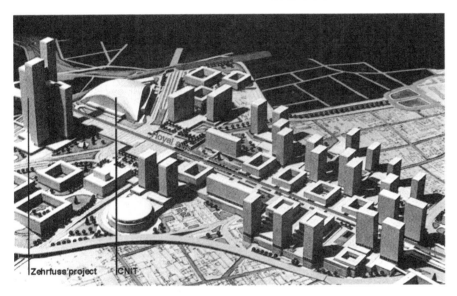

**Fig. 2**
Model of the project for La Défense,
around 1964.
*Copyright: Defacto*

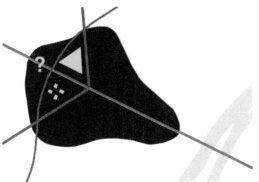

**Fig.3**
Schematic plan of La Défense as
planned in 1964. The roads mark
out three sites : one for the CNIT,
already built, one for the towers of
Zehrfuss, and a third one on the
Royal Axis (in red).
*Document: LL*

To reflect the axis ? What shape should it take ? How high should it be ? The question of the building's visibility from the *Arc de Triomphe* was central. In the end the only question not asked was of the program itself, when in fact placing office buildings on an axis that Parisians considered to belong to everyone could cause a larger problem.

When the two projects were revealed in 1971 controversy ensued, and even more so in 1972 when Parisians suddenly saw the under construction *Tour Gan* appear in the royal axis : "To disfigure [...] the horizon, where, for all the patriotic souls, the red sun of the Austerlitz battle set, seemed unforgivable".[8] The French media covered this "scandal" for the summer, and in September the French government announced that Aillaud's project was postponed. This time the EPAD organized a consultation and not a direct command. President Georges Pompidou had just completed the competition for the Beaubourg Centre (which was renamed after Pompidou following his death) ; it was a known fact that the choice of the jury was not his own. Nonetheless, the competition rules forced him to follow though with the winning project, and this experience made him less inclined to organize another open competition. A limited competition was finally organized, of which Aillaud was supposedly again the likely winner ;[9] however nothing came of it.

The EPAD decreased its consultations on the site, which remained internal until 1980, when a nationwide competition was launched. Jean Willerval — whom the mayor of Paris Jacques Chirac had just asked to build his project for *Les Halles* — came out the front-runner with his project, in the form of a compromise. He used the idea of reflecting the axis without closing it off completely, and a non-symmetrical building that nevertheless resided on a set-on-axis composition. Moreover, as stipulated by the rules, the building was to be 35-meters high in order to "avoid seeing it through the opening of the *Arc de Triomphe* from any point whatsoever of the Louvre to the *Étoile* section of the main axis".[10] The project was suspected of being the choice of President Valéry Giscard d'Estaing and not the result of the competition itself.[11]

The project could have continued its journey until completion, but Jean-Paul Lacaze,[12] director of the EPAD, "found it preferable to wait"[13] because of the upcoming presidential election : the question of the *Tête Défense* was becoming political.

In fact, François Mitterrand came into office in May 1981 and launched his policy of the *Grands Travaux* (Great Projects), which, with the exception of the Louvre pyramid, would all spring from competitions. Mitterrand's interest in architecture went far beyond his desire to put his personal imprint on the country, though this too was an important criterion. Richard Rogers, who was a member of the jury for the *Tête Défense* competition, still recalls how impressed he was by Mitterrand's sense of space, interest in the project, and wide knowledge of Paris.[14]

At first, the projects were managed at the Paris region level, and Robert Lion, one of the right-hand men of the President, in charge of the *Grands Travaux* remembers : "[...]fun times. On the table were the Opera project, the *Cité des Sciences* (Science Museum), and [...] the Center of Communication. [...] And all that was done with a map of Paris that we turned in all directions — What will be done at La Villette ? What's for the Bastille ? What about La Défense ? What will be further out ?".[15] With Lion's help, Mitterrand quickly decided to set aside Willerval's project in favor of a "more ambitious and significant" one.[16] The new president was also soon to be accused of abusing his power.

The problem of the function of the only one of the *Grands Travaux* in the suburbs, but, more than that, of the *Tête Défense*, was finally decided on, and a *Centre International de la Communication* (CIC ; International Center of Communication) as well as two Ministries[17] were planned for the occupation of the site. All these incidents in the course of the project had made the *Tête Défense* an important stake, a "prestigious site".[18] As there had already been several competitions, something somewhat bigger had to be organized, at least to prove that this time the winning project was going to be completed. An international competition was thus launched.

## ▬ A Great Competition

Because of the importance of this competition, measures were taken accordingly. The competition's organization directly involved the president and the general director of the EPAD. A very large amount of money (2 million francs[19]) was set aside for the participants, even though only the prize-winners and honorable mentions received compensation. An outside organization, the International Union of Architects (UIA), was called upon for guidance. It seems that this was done more to add yet another token of quality, and maybe again to reassure the architects who were tired of taking part in one competition after another for the same site, than to actually take advantage of the organization's expertise. For example, its role is never quoted in any of the articles about the project in the newspaper *Le Monde*.

For Joseph Belmont, newly-nominated president of the EPAD, nothing was impossible : "'a 1000-meter-high tower, why not ? [...].' In his opinion, there were two possible ways of proceeding : having the French President choose directly or organizing an open competition of an international dimension, which seemed to him to be the best solution [...]. "The French," he explained, "have built entire cities [...]. But they no longer know how to create monumental architecture". [20] The choice of the international criteria was thus not a consequence of the blessing from the UIA. On the contrary, it was made the by teams in place, and for some, even, it was undoubtedly made by President Mitterrand's team itself. [21] As for the fact that competition was anonymous, it's a rule for all French competitions.

The brief that the nearly 900 candidates received was a large box containing several files, blueprints, and tracing paper for the rendering which had to be of a specific format, layout, scale and number of documents. The level of detail given was very high, thanks to the amount of analyses available internally at the EPAD and to the dozens of already-designed projects.

The analysis by the technical commission was undertaken afterwards in consequence. Seven pages detailed every aspect of the projects — shape, position, access, and surface area, and the general "technical and economic feasibility". [22] The amount of work was considerable — each team of analysts was composed of specialists who devoted two to three hours to each project. [23]

The jury chosen was international and prestigious, composed of foreign architects, including Richard Meier and Richard Rogers ; of French architects, including Bernard Zehrfuss ; of prominent foreign figures, including the architecture critic Ada Louise Huxtable ; and of prominent French figures. [24] This jury met a first time in October to go over the stakes, and decided that its president should be Robert Lion, who immediately took charge. As a former member of the French Ministry of Equipment, he had already studied the question and had "vigorously taken a stand against the 'mediocrity' of Giscard's choice [the Willerval project], a low-rise building, which made it impossible to see the 'small head' (*Tête*) of La Défense [...]". [25] His stand had brought him to be called upon by Mitterrand when he was elected President ; he in fact had become one of the "President's four right-hand men" directly involved in the *Grands Travaux*.

The EPAD then welcomed the jury for a week in April to review the projects, on the forty-fourth floor of the Fiat Tower, recently bought by Framatome, who lent the space. [26] Other places in La Défense had been considered, but the specially refurbished apartment of the former CEO made the prestige of the operation more pointedly clear. [27] The analyses by the technical commission and the deliberations by the jury took several weeks ; nowadays, it is very difficult to spend that much time on these, but it was a prerequisite for the *Grands Travaux*.

## ▬ Program Versus "Landmark"
The program reveals several key points : in particular, the history of the axis, the urban plan, and the "problem of the *Tête Défense*" ; all of which were described in detail in the beginning of the program, giving a clear idea of the challenge ahead. The axis was clearly the main issue : "Of all these axes, none is more important, richer in historic symbols, dearer to the hearts of Parisians, more spectacular for the visitor, than the greater western axis [...]". The "planning data" stated the demands for "monumental and expressive" projects slightly more precisely. [28]

The question of whether to close off or open the axis remained unanswered, but it was specified at one point that, historically, it was supposed to stay open ("The historical axis could thus continue on freely."). Yet, at that point, it was considered "appropriate to end one perspective and open up another. The problem of the *Tête-Défense* therefore is not whether to close off or open an existing perspective : it is to place a landmark on the historical axis [...]."

The authorization was given to build above 35 metres (the height at which the construction would become visible under the *Arc de Triomphe*), for the project itself or for "a monumental signal," under the condition that it be of "very high quality" : the project was going to be "a monument." Regarding its volume, the most striking indication was that its "main problem [...] concerns the way of taking into account the historical axis. The monuments on this axis [...] all have an empty space at their center, which all play an essential monumental part [...] in the staging of the successive landscapes on the axis. [...]". They all follow "the tradition of the *grandes compositions* of the French" which one can assimilate with symmetry. Finally, on a technical level, and though the square allowed for a great liberty of shape, the contestants were reminded to verify where

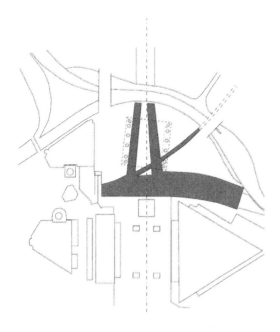

**Fig. 4**
The foundations of the Grande Arche
superimposed on the underground
roads along the axis. Document: LL.
*Data : EPAD/Defacto*

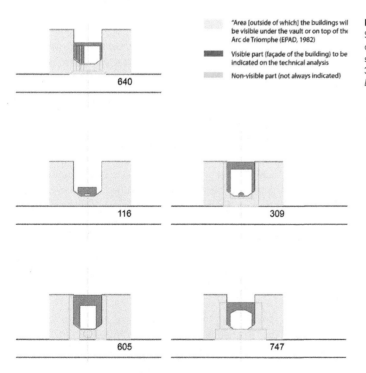

"Area [outside of which] the buildings will be visible under the vault or on top of the Arc de Triomphe (EPAD, 1982)

Visible part (façade of the building) to be indicated on the technical analysis

Non-visible part (not always indicated)

**Fig. 5**
Schemes of analysis by the technical
commission. Profile of the winning
scheme (640) and the projects 116,
309, 605 and 747, as examples.
*Document: LL. Data : EPAD/Defacto*

the existing infrastructures were, so as not to have all the bearing points on them. But the underground roads were themselves along the axis **[Fig.4]**.

It is difficult today not to see in these key points a description of the *Grande Arche*. But that would be forgetting the 400 or so other projects, of which many were also arches. The technical commission noted this in its report: the usual shapes were categorized as "porticos, towers, spheres, pyramids, amphitheaters," often visible under the *Arc de Triomphe*, and "a great majority of these have in mind the creation of a new arch with a central part open west, or the creation of a simple geometric shape [...] on the historical axis".[29] These other arches were present even among the honorable mentions and the laureates.[30] Other projects that were not selected were even very close to the shape of the winning project or were simply enlarged *Arcs* **[Fig.5]**.[31] We could then say that the main idea for the shape of the *Grande Arche* was in the spirit of the era, and had been for some time in several architects' heads.

The classification — portico, towers... — established by the technical commission was followed during the ruling, even though Richard Rogers stated at that time that it was "only a mental approach".[32] With it, the jury intellectualized the projects. All these points allow us to confirm the influence of the jury and the specificity of what happens in a jury room, where, in Jean-Pierre Chupin's words, the jury "conceives" the project.[33]

But the system goes both ways. In fact, Spreckelsen understood and synthesized the demands of the program and showed it with his text on "An open cube. A window to the world [...] THE TRIUMPHAL ARCH OF MAN,"[34] an expression that the jury would use in its report, just as all the poetic arguments put forth by the architect. The jury even added some in its report.[35] For example, the fact that the project was 100X100m and pivoted according to the same angle as the *Cour Carrée* of the Louvre was apparently not mentioned in Spreckelsen's initial report.

The project also had the virtue, in the eyes of the jury, of not being overly costly. Here again, Spreckelsen read the program intelligently and understood the points that were important as well as those where they "did not really know what [they] wanted".[36] With the pivoting of the cube, he avoided having foundations in the wrong place.

On the other hand, even though the amount of details in the program gave life to it, its major component, the International Center of Communication, remained quite vague. Indeed, what does communication mean? Despite a number of analyses, the theme was the least defined of all the *Grands Travaux*, and somewhat an opportunistic choice, imagined by the high-ranking official Serge Antoine.[37] Because of the new companies that were to move into the building, it would be placed at the forefront of the development of communication, and, because of the museum, of its showcasing. But also, the visitors would be at the centre of the world, because it was going to be possible to follow all world "events" by simply going to La Défense.[38] The architect Gérard Thurnauer, a member of the jury for the competition and future advisor for the EPAD, would end up considering the idea too ambitious.[39]

In order to understand the choice of this program, it is necessary to remember a time when computers were becoming ubiquitous. No one yet knew the repercussions that these new technologies would have, but their rapid development was becoming obvious and a Center of Communication was an attempt to be at the *avant-garde*: "The idea was to have all televisions from around the world available at the same time... No one could have imagined that today, we would all have them on our cell phones".[40] This context made it difficult to make choices in terms of programs, so the definition stayed very vague: Jean-Louis Subileau,[41] then director of the mission for the coordination of the great architectural and urban operations of the State (the *Grands Travaux*), recalls that "Serge Antoine was full of imagination, and his program was generous [...] but when I had to defend it in front of the Parliament, I had trouble explaining it... For me, however, the important thing was to create the landmark of La Défense. What was inside didn't matter much".[42] Spreckelsen understood that, so he took the liberty of not respecting the surface area at all. Somehow, he may have felt that it would not be an eliminatory decision.

Lastly, what apparently made the jury lean towards the Dane's project on the last day was its simplicity. In fact, Antoine Grumbach told the other members of the jury that, according to him, "the public would not understand an edifice whose qualities would be too intellectual. [...] The symbol must be 'obvious'".[43] The *Arche* was later qualified as "sensitive" by Zehrfuss, who was also in favor of the project, whereas the front-running project by Viguier and Jodry was seen as representative of "professionalism".[44] The challenge here was clearly to convince and seduce through a poetic and simple form that could be understood by all, and again, to try and create a "landmark" more than an International Center of Communication.

## ▬ The Prince's Choice

The question of the client is here quite difficult to grasp. The EPAD prepared the competition, but sold the land to the State. The government ministries (through their unions), and the municipalities (in particular, Puteaux, on which the site lies) would be the future users, but were not part of the selection process. However, the final choice was presented to them at the end of jury deliberations. [45] The main decision maker was Robert Lion, president of the jury, CEO of the *Caisse des Dépôts et Consignations*, and future president of the *SEM Tête Défense*, which was to become, after the competition, the official client (*SEM: Société d'économie mixte* / French institution which involves public and private funding).

But, in the end, the real client was President Mitterrand. Represented in the jury by Lion, his aura was clearly palpable: "I'm not saying that we would have gotten killed for Mitterrand but... it was unbelievable!". [46] During the jury's sessions, the only real moment of tension that actually occurred was about the President's role — the idea was that the jury would select four projects and that he would make the final choice. [47] Even though the official report does not mention this, the internal notes clearly show that this way of proceeding was controversial, and the members of the jury, especially British and American, rose up against the suggestion that "after working for five days, we would allow anyone, even the President, to select". [48]

Robert Lion insisted during the whole week on letting Mitterrand make the final choice, and even if today Richard Rogers seems satisfied with the way they proceeded, we should not forget that he did not win out. The compromise reached was that the jury would sort the projects or — it seems that they did not agree from the start — that it would choose two winners and two honorable mentions. In the end, the President invited the jury to the Élysée Palace: "In these situations, everyone had the right to express himself; not at all like what goes on today! Despite what may have been said later on, Mitterrand really listened to each one's opinion". [49]

Still, the president took almost a month before officially deciding, [50] and he asked that scale models be built so he could evaluate all four projects. He asked every person he trusted to come and see the project. [51] Mitterrand's choice turned out to be the same as the jury's, although the last race was close between the two front-runners — seven votes for Spreckelsen's project against five for Viguier-Jodry's. In fact, Subileau recalls that some members of the jury even defended Viguier-Jodry's project, because it was the embodiment of modernity. Finally, Mitterrand said: "You might find that it is a good project, why not... But I am President of the Republic, I am accountable for the perspective to the whole nation: the axis must remain open". [52]

This highlights the fact that the history of a jury is a rewriting of reality. When the story is told, the *Grande Arche* seems to have been the exception in the conflict of La Défense, the "new unit" [53] sought after, the logical and obvious choice coming out of an almost perfect competition. However, the jury deliberations during a competition can never be that perfect — they are a moment when opposing ideas are expressed before an agreement is reached; a moment of necessary debate. As Rogers puts it, "There was all this discussion; in fact, there was a lot of time to discuss," even though he states that there never was a "minority vote". [54]

By looking at documents from the jury, we were able, for example, to notice that Spreckelsen's project did not convince the whole jury from the start. Neither was it eliminated only to be given a second chance, like some of the honorable mentions (Bernard Tschumi, for example). However, it only received four votes out of thirteen the second time the jury voted, when they went from 172 projects to 76. In comparison, the project of Jean-Paul Viguier, Jean-François Jodry and Associates then received ten votes, and eleven, half a day later (against six for the *Grande Arche*). However, both projects ended on the last day with twelve votes out of thirteen.

The point here is not at all to put into question the jury's good faith or the quality of its choice, but, on the contrary, to highlight the fact that all competitions are more or less full of debates, which are erased when the result is given out, so as to give extra value to the winning project, when the actual history could do just that. We could say that a jury is a "pedagogical and investigative" situation, where jury members learn more and more about the projects as they select them. [55]

The votes can partly be explained by the quality of the renderings of the two projects: Viguier and Jodry offered detailed designs, in color, prepared to attract the eye; Spreckelsen's rendering, on the other hand, was composed of quite vague sketches and lacked information. The technical commission even stated in its report that, "considering the low level of definition of space, it seems difficult to check the adherence to the program and the functionality of the project". [56] The jury can therefore be praised for having seen the potential of a project whose presentation was scarce.

In the end, Mitterrand followed the jury's decision. The *Grands Travaux* policy was one of the reasons why "the eighties was one of France's most prolific decades in architecture".[57] And yet, the President was very much criticized for having imposed his tastes and his decisions, and was compared to Tutankhamen, Louis XIV and Napoleon. People even talked about the "Mitterrand style, which was described as angular and cold, in one word, pharaonic",[58] made of "simple, geometric forms with transparent structures".[59] According to Subileau, it cannot be said that Mitterrand made a regal decision, but he does admit that the process of the *Grands Travaux* was "a little iffy".[60] Whether advised or not, in the end, every decision was made by the president. The mission for the coordination of the great architectural and urban operations of the state "evidently came under the State's jurisdiction, which violated the fundamental principle of administrative law" requiring that institutions come under the ministries' jurisdiction.[61] However, the unanimous satisfaction[62] that everyone seemed to be feeling overshadowed all criticism.

## The Competition as a Tool

With such an important client, the pressure was high to end up with the best project. Therefore, the competition was presented as the only solution — the right tool — that seems to have fulfilled the president's ambitions. The organizers were also aware that the project might lead to a new controversy, as Robert Lion reminded the members of the jury,[63] so they were careful to remain beyond reproach, and the competition was a means to prove that.

The competition reveals itself to be a powerful communication tool. It offers a form of justification to the project that is to be built, but also the opportunity to create a certain suspense, an expectation, and somewhat of a hype when the results are announced. For the *Grande Arche*, an exhibit was set up, with debates and publications. The "424 projects for the *Tête Défense*"[64] handed in for the competition were presented. However, according to some documents in the archives, 425 projects were judged. The possible counting mistake made in the beginning and perpetuated made it possible to obtain, if not a "round" number, one with a welcomed symmetry (4-2-4).

Being able to recount the story of what happened during the competition — an always rewritten story that puts the winning project forward — is very important for the reception of the building. It highlights the built result :

Spreckelsen's *Grande Arche* was presented as the evident choice. Even though, of course, some other characteristics could be investigated — the budget devoted to the project, for example — the competition shows qualities that help the projects become important in the history of architecture as well as in the history of their neighborhood.

But this can never be set apart from communication and ways of involving the public and the professionals. After the results, for example, a debate was organized by the French Institute for Architecture (IFA) ; during completion, a person — Youssef Baccouche — was in charge of communication and organized some openings to the public right after the inauguration[65] ; later, the rooftop was opened to the public. We think that all these communication tools that were beyond architecture, was one of the factors which made it possible for the *Grande Arche* to be one of the most well-received *Grands Travaux* by the French public — "the only one that the press and the architects did not criticize"[66] :

The debate organized [by the IFA] was very well attended. Antoine Grumbach, member of the jury, praised the 'sublime and eternal scale of this monumental cathedral, and yet so close to life.' As for Roland Castro, [...] he put forth the fact that the concern about Mitterrand's personal tastes no longer existed. 'We know now what he thinks, what he is looking for : something obvious and simple, formal and political, a form of consensus. Spreckelsen's project gives us some air, it is without tyranny : a fine political statement which pleases everyone.'[67]

These statements show the complexity of a competition. When choosing the project, the jury, just like the architect, must try to serve the general interest, and it is put in a puzzling situation, having to seek the "sublime" as wall as the "consensus," without knowing if both are compatible.

As early as October 1979, Gérard Thurnauer had handed in an analysis about the *Tête Défense,* where it was said, "the search for monumentalism at the *Tête Défense* must go beyond that of a formal and aesthetic action. To begin closing the axis in purely architectural terms would be going against the experience of La Défense as it was built and is experienced today. It becomes necessary to have a landmark there [...]. To create a real urban event, a monument that generates use and life [...]".[68] In a way, the *Grande Arche* filled Thurnauer's prophetic expectations : it was more than a mere consensus and was soon called a monument,[69] which makes us wonder if it also became the "event" he was calling for.

## ▬ Cultural Matters

The use of the competition tool is first and foremost a cultural affair. To prove this point, we can look at another competition that gave birth to the Lloyd's (Richard Rogers partnership, 1977-1986), a building that was on the cover of many magazines during those same years. The similarity of their programs, their location in financial districts, their proximity in time, place, and even height (95 m and 111 m[70]), although not in surface, make the two case studies interesting to compare [Fig.6].

Even though the Lloyd's was "the biggest private commission in London since the end of the war",[71] it somehow had to deal with very public issues and with a very traditional context, in a country where the Royal Family is allowed to take a — very conservative[72] — stand on architecture, something that Richard Rogers has always fought against.[73] In fact, since it took the form of a company in the eighteenth century, the Lloyd's institution has always been very important for London, England, and all the way to the Crown. According to Peter Wynne Rees, the current Chief Planning Officer for the City, the company had even more influence in the seventies than it does today, so it was "as if the Queen was asking for a building permit — no matter what her taste, no one would ever say no".[74]

Lloyd's had built a first building for its headquarters in 1928, then a second in 1958, but the two of them failed to fulfill the constantly growing needs in space. As early as 1975, Lloyd's was confronted with this problem once again. The employees had gotten "tired of moving",[75] since some of them had already moved before, so there had to be a good reason to move again.

In 1977, the situation was critical and the work urgent, but Lloyd's committee did not want to be confronted with the same problem again. Ian Findlay,[76] deputy chairman of Lloyd's, thus contacted the Royal Institute for British Architects (RIBA). Considering the importance of the client, Gordon Graham,[77] its president, decided to personally take charge. After only a few meetings, and faced with a number of uncertainties, Graham suggested a limited competition between invited architects. Moreover, he warned Lloyd's that it had to be ready to commit a certain amount of money for choosing between them.[78] The consulting cost the company some 100,000 pounds, of which the architects who were finally not retained received 10,000 each.[79]

As President of the RIBA, Graham could have recommended organizing a more open competition, but such a traditional strategy seemed impossible because of the uncertainties surrounding the future building, making the writing of a detailed program impossible. So he proposed an organization that was "more... not traditional [such as an open competition like the one for the Pompidou Center], but neither Norman Foster nor [Richard Rogers] had ever built an office building before, so it was moderately open. They looked at about sixty projects [of reference], then they came down to six finalists, which were very diverse".[80] The competition was not open, but showed some open-mindedness.

The program was not a real one in the sense that it was not a detailed description of the needs of the future building, its organization, and the areas needed. This was confirmed during the presentation meetings organized by the Committee: the request that was most clearly expressed was that submissions should not be projects, but strategies. As Courtenay Blackmore,[81] Head of Lloyd's Administration and of the project, admitted: "we didn't really know what we wanted to do"[82] — much like what Lion said about the competition for the *Tête Défense*. The only thing they were asking for was flexibility. This could have given the architects a lot of freedom, but these were obviously confused by it. Serete, for example, handed in very elaborate designs, going into every last detail, which caused the agency to be immediately eliminated.[83]

The way the competition was organized was in itself a strategy. Contrary to an anonymous system, Lloyd's committee personally explained the stakes of the competition to the different contestants, meeting the two finalists at least three times. The difference between this procedure and a more traditional one is a question of philosophy. The idea here was that the more the architect knew the client, including his personality, the better his submission would be. Blackmore even explains that the problem with an anonymous competition is that the client could hire an architect whose personality would end up a poor fit.[84] He was thus very pleased with the system they chose: "the formula proved its worth since at the end the interview panel had a very clear idea of each practice's attitude and beliefs, comprehension of an approach to the problem, and the sort of people they were... It was vital for Lloyd's not to select an architect on the basis of an outline design... the method adopted proved to be very successful".[85] Norman Foster was in fact eliminated because he was considered "too much of a loner who would carry the entire project inside his own head"[86] — a judgment based very much on the person and not his architecture.

**Fig. 6a**
The Lloyd's of London. Outside view from St. Mary Axe (the building site on the right is 122, Leadenhall Street, also by Richard Rogers, RSH+P).

**Fig. 6b**
Inside view of the center of the building, the atrium.
*Photographs: LL, October 2013, September 2010*

Such a strategy also reveals the "specific approach" of the advisor Graham[87] or, in other words, his very contextual approach of competitions. It also reveals the somehow liberal approach that is described by other members of the RIBA,[88] which is attributable to cultural matters. More generally, it reveals the importance of the client. In fact, Richard Rogers greatly insisted on this point during our talk, citing Courtenay Blackmore, Robert Bordaz,[89] Peter Green,[90] and Robert Lion. Already, in a 1986 documentary (*Wall of Light*), he had said that important projects such as the *Maison de Verre* (Pierre Charreau, Paris, 1932) are never possible without a great client, and that he himself had had some wonderful ones. For John Young, his partner, it allowed Rogers to design an even more advanced project than the Pompidou.[91] As early as 1981, the RIBA Journal published a file about patronage relating Blackmore's role.[92]

No files in Lloyd's archives can allow us to analyze precisely the decision process. However, it seems to be commonly acknowledged that Rogers was chosen in part for practical reasons such as his nationality, as Blackmore hoped for a UK practice,[93] and the fact that they worked with engineers from Arup, which might have been confused with Arup Associates, the architectural firm. But Rogers' victory can moreover be explained by his good understanding of Lloyd's demands — he was in fact the only architect to understand them. His answer was constituted of multiple-choice propositions for each step of the project, even though the atrium, for example, was present — in a different form — from the very first stage **[Fig.7]**.

It is hard to say in this case that the jury was able to "conceive" the project,[94] because, in fact, it did not ask for one. We could even say that there was no jury as such. On the one hand, the jury was constituted of Lloyd's committee (only), advised by Graham. On the other, all the careful steps proposed by Rogers and his team put the committee — the client, but also the future user — in a situation comparable

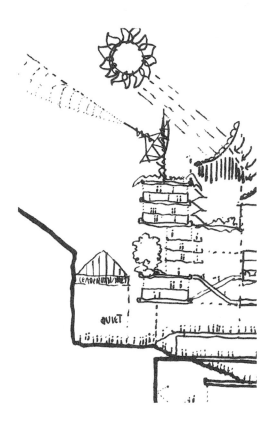

**Fig. 7a**
Rogers and Partners' first studies for the Lloyd's, showing the two sites owned by the firm, and the different possibilities, from the rehabilitation of the existing buildings to a total demolition.

*Source: James S. Russell, John McKean, Gabriele Bramante et Kenneth Powell, Pioneering British 'High-tech', Phaidon, 1999*

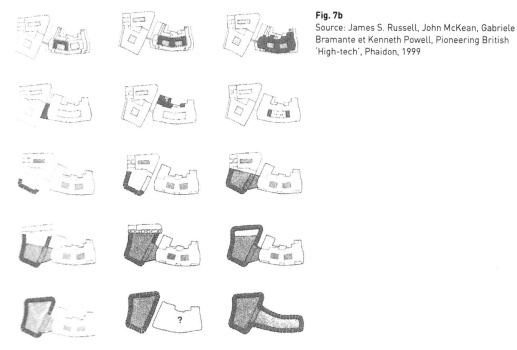

**Fig. 7b**
Source: James S. Russell, John McKean, Gabriele Bramante et Kenneth Powell, Pioneering British 'High-tech', Phaidon, 1999

to a usual commission, where it could discuss the result; or even almost comparable to a participative process, where the architect is chosen more to guide than to design.

But as unusual as this competition was, it still highlights an important phenomenon in a competition process — when an architect understands and identifies with a program. In his previous key projects, Rogers had faced the issue of flexibility — for the PA Technology Laboratory (Cambridge, 1975-1983) and, with Renzo Piano, for the Pompidou Center (Paris, 1971-1977). The flexibility theme had then become a key element of Rogers' architecture. He answered it with the extensive use of materials like metal, allowing prefabrication and assemblage, but, moreover, with a radical application of the separation between "servant" and "served," which Louis Kahn had theorized. Just like for the Pompidou Centre; but in an even more expressive manner, the servant parts were placed on the outside of the building. The resulting space is an empty rectangle, to be furnished according to the changing needs of the client. The program for Lloyd's seems almost to have been tailor-made for an architect like Rogers, allowing him to put his principles into application. Such a radical attitude made the architect Claude Parent write that Lloyd's was "the most perfect kid in the family".[95] The two sides of the decision — the proceedings in this competition and the architect's identification with the program — both led to the same built result. Their combination helped the birth of what is considered an important achievement. The Royal Fine Arts Commission, though conservative, even said that "it should be one of the most remarkable buildings of the decade",[96] an opinion shared by some critics in the architectural press,[97] who even called the project an "event".[98]

This example confirms the important role played by the architect's reading of the program. It especially highlights, in comparison, the specific character of each method used to face the uncertainties, and even each person — be it Graham and Blackmore, or Lion and Mitterrand — who takes charge of the organization of a competition. In the case of Lloyd's, the process was a way of achieving a goal, but the quality of the result was what counted. In the case of the *Grande Arche*, the process was a way of justifying a choice. Richard Rogers, who also took part in the *Tête Défense* process as a jury member, summarizes one consequence of these attitudes when saying that "the Lloyd's was not like the Pompidou or the *Grande Arche* in the sense that it was not as specified nor as open as those competitions. 'Open' may be the wrong word... The big difference was that, if my memory is correct, the Pompidou competition program was probably 3 cm thick of paper, whereas the brief for the Lloyd's was only six pages".[99] These differences in terms of cultures and persons have great consequences on the built result, which, in both cases, was considered an event. But this qualification as event raises questions. Though used by architectural critics, this word is badly defined, and never well separated from its vague relatives, such as "monument" or "icon." Moreover, if both projects are seen as events, but do not spring out of the same methods, are they the same kind of event?

## ▬ Historical Versus Spatial Event

The notion of event is first a historical one, which has been the subject of numerous studies. This has been demonstrated by writers such as François Dosse, who, in his recent major book, took the event only in its original appearance, as a brutal and unexplainable break in time, or as the same break, inseparable from its causes and consequences.[100] It is also a notion used in sociology to define the changes in someone's life — what sociology normally does not define, being more interested in patterns.[101] Trying somehow to combine the two, events are also studied in historical sociology: "Whereas a historian may conceptualize temporality 'as fateful, contingent, complex, eventful, and heterogeneous',[102] the historical sociologist strives to appreciate all this complexity and yet find patterns by looking across cases [...]".[103]

In other words, the challenge that the notion of event poses is the one of explaining something unpredictable. Even though the event has causes, it can never be reduced to them. These causes cannot be reduced to a chain of facts — one leading to another, then another, and finally leading in the end to the event. They are more comparable to a social context, a network of ideas, people, actions from which an event grows. This is clearly explained by Deleuze when he writes "what is possible does not pre-exist, it is created by the event"[104] — the appearance of an event leads the existing facts to be read as causes.

Following the historical tendency, one also has to take into account the consequences of an event. For example, as far as September 11 is concerned, some causes were revealed to us by geopolitical analysts, while the consequences were revealed by the media. Even though the secret services may have been able to detect some sort of danger, no one could have predicted what was to happen.

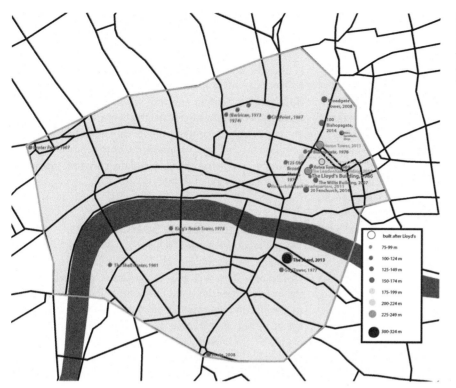

Fig. 8
Map of the tall buildings in the City and its surroundings built before and after the Lloyd's building.
*Documents: LL. Data: Council on Tall Building and Urban Habitat, 2012.*

built after Lloyd's

| | |
|---|---|
| ● | 75-99 m |
| ● | 100-124 m |
| ● | 125-149 m |
| ● | 150-174 m |
| ◉ | 175-199 m |
| ● | 200-224 m |
| ● | 225-249 m |
| ● | 300-324 m |

As for Bin Laden, who made conscious use of the media and was very aware of the symbolic aspect of his act, he still could not have predicted the extent of the repercussions. Even though it was immediately called an event by all television reports around the world, one can consider, going beyond the idea of our "Society of the Spectacle", [105] that they were able to do so because some consequences were already perceptible.

Less cathartic examples can be found: micro-historians, for example, have tried to show the importance of simple situations, and how eventful (in our words) they can be. [106] This introduces the notion of the scale of the event — the framework in which the examples are looked at and must be defined in order to call a fact an event.

When trying to define the event in architecture — a work that, of course, goes far beyond this article [107] — some points need to be investigated. The creation context of the project is thus regarded as part of the background making the appearance of an architectural event possible, not dismissing, however, the suddenness of the event — the moment where things topple over, which can never be entirely planned. Within this background, the competition, through its nature, is supposed to be fairer, through the multiplicity

of ideas that circulate, through its media coverage, but also through the necessity for the client to define more clearly his needs — seems to offer an interesting framework.

More than twenty years later, the *Grande Arche* and the Lloyd's building remain linked to the area they were built in. If we draw in this article from the hypothesis that these buildings are events, we then have to see what type of event they could be, according to the specific context of their competitions, as we have seen the importance of cultural matters for their organization.

The Lloyd's building can be first seen as an event in Richard Rogers' life scale, because of what such a project represents in an architect's career, but not only. [108][109] On another scale, the Lloyd's building contributed to changes in London. Before its construction, few tall buildings had been erected around the axis of Bishopsgate **[Fig.8]**. They were mostly modern office blocks based on square plans with a central core. The major exception was Tower 42 (180m, 1980), which had not been well received. Though not so tall, an atypical building such as the Lloyd's was thus a radical change, "a landmark in the history of City office building". [110]

The very British character of this high-tech building — a British movement, by a British architect, in the

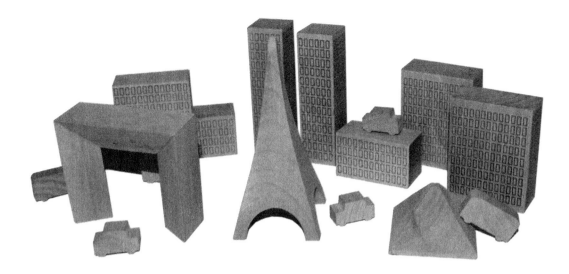

**Fig. 9**
Paris icons as seen by a Japanese design company
(Muji). New York and Tokyo were also edited.

historic center of the capital city — is not to set apart from this judgment. It gave a new example of a high office building that was different and thus forever changed the face of the Square Mile, as it is called, and made it look like a new playing area for architects and developers willing to build high. One might not see it nowadays, hidden behind buildings that are increasingly higher, but at that time, it revealed a dynamic that was contained in the City, but that nobody was really capable of expecting or designing. In that way, we can say that the Lloyd's building is an event in historical terms, at least on London's scale. Some also saw it as an event in the history of architecture: "as the only true building of its time in London, Lloyd's will be as much a milestone in the city's cultural history as the works of Wren and Waterhouse".[111]

The importance of the Lloyd's must also be linked to the process developed here. Such an innovative process, involving the future users — thus making them proud of the result and willing to defend it; engaging lots of time and money — may not entirely explain the result, but might have helped the production of an unusual and ahead of — or maybe very much in-its-time project.

The design was really developed with the client, which avoided many problems and is what makes this competition a unique case. The relation between Spreckelsen and his client was quite different, because he was in the situation of a real anonymous competition and because, besides the explicit and already complex client, there also was an implicit one, the French president.

The decisions were therefore much more difficult to make and, according to us, this is why the project, from the start, and Mitterrand's validation did not change a lot, in order to stay as the president wanted it. As Jean-Louis Subileau put it: "It is the only monument where the form superseded the content. [...] To limit contradiction, we hid behind the masterpiece".[112] A recent report also states that "its functioning is difficult and its defects, which are due to the fact that the project was chosen for its volume, because the program was specified only after, with respect to the winning project, are not easy to correct".[113] The conscious search for a landmark project — and lack of program — put the functional use of the building in the background.

The *Grande Arche* has still become one of the important monuments of Paris and is a landmark of La Défense and of the capital city. A listing of the *Grande Arche* was considered as early as 1994, but the EPAD went against it. However, the State considered selling the ministries' premises and has therefore recently commissioned a new report, so as to protect the building, which "acquired, from its opening, the status of one of the most exceptional monuments of our country, on a symbolic as well as on an architectural level".[114] On a lighter note, a few years ago, a Japanese design company started selling wooden miniatures representing buildings from several world capitals. For Paris, the Louvre Pyramid and the *Grande Arche* were chosen along with the Eiffel Tower **[Fig.9]**.

Here, the history of the site played a great role. In fact, the building was built on a historical axis, of which it has become one of the milestones. Each of the developments, from the *Cour Carrée* of the Louvre to La Défense, is representative of an era, like a constructed timeline. The shape of the building echoes both the axis and the previous arches; its spatial answer to the square and the buildings surrounding it, as well as its formal simplicity, overwrites, in a way, the history — however exciting — of the competition, which is probably not what most will remember. People who work or live at La Défense know the building today as the screen or the stage for entertainment activities, and for its steps, which welcome hundreds of people for lunch on sunny afternoons.

Those facts make us think that we are here in front of a different type of event. While for the Lloyd's, the framework in which to see it is mostly historical — Lloyd's as a mark, a break in the course of time — as it seems here that we are in front of what we could call a spatial event. The *Grande Arche* was no revolution in the history of architecture. But its form and the way it was placed are some of the criteria that make this building important in itself, not even as architecture, but as pure form. In that sense, the research for poetry and simplicity during the jury was reached.

We could then go so far as to say that some events can happen, not in time as the historical ones, but in space, creating a new category of "architectural events." Both of these types of events can exist through the construction of a building; in both cases, competitions offer tools that help and influence the result as architecture as much as event.[115]

### ▬▬▬ **Notes**

[1] Marie Alizard, *François Mitterrand ou le Grand Pari(S)* (les Éd. du Panthéon, 2011), 47.

[2] Jean-Louis Subileau, interview by L. Lenne.

[3] Rémi Rouyer, «Tête Défense,» in *La Défense, dictionnaire et atlas. Architecture/Politique, Histoire/Territoire*, ed. P. Chabard and V. Picon-Lefebvre (Marseille : Parenthèses, 2012).

[4] The area controlled by the EPAD is situated on the grounds of three different cities : Courbevoie, Nanterre, and Puteaux

[5] François Chaslin, *Les Paris de François Mitterrand : Histoire des Grands Projets Architecturaux*, Collection Folio/Actuel (Paris : Gallimard, 1985), 156.

[6] The name *Tête Défense* appeared with Pei's project in 1969. «Un monument en perspective,» in *La Grande Arche de la Défense*, ed. F. Chaslin and V. Picon-Lefebvre (Paris : Le Moniteur, 1989).

[7] Ibid.

[8] *Les Paris de François Mitterrand : Histoire des Grands Projets Architecturaux*, 157.

[9] Rouyer, «Tête Défense.»

[10] EPAD, «Consultation for the Tête Défense,» (Archives EPAD/Defacto, 1980).

[11] Chaslin, *Les Paris de François Mitterrand : Histoire des Grands Projets Architecturaux*, 163.

[12] Jean-Paul Lacaze (born in 1930) was director of the EPAD from 1979 to 1984

[13] Jean-Paul Lacaze, «Interview,» in *Historiographie de la Défense*, ed. J. Beauchard (Archives EPAD/Defacto, 1994), 128.

[14] Richard Rogers, interview by L. Lenne.

[15] Robert Lion, «Interview,» in *Historiographie de la Défense*, ed. J. Beauchard (Archives EPAD/Defacto, 1994), 154.

[16] EPAD, "Program for the Competition for the Tête Défense," (Archives EPAD/Defacto, 1982).
Robert Lion, interview by L. Lenne.

[17] The Ministry of Urbanism and Housing and the Ministry of Environment. See the very positive report by Louis Moissonnier, «Mission d'étude programme, Tête Défense,» (Archives EPAD/Defacto, 1982).

[18] Michèle Champenois, «L'aménagement de la Tête Défense. Le jury international a présenté quatre esquisses à M. Mitterrand,» *Le Monde* (1983).

[19] Currency of the time. EPAD, «Program for the Competition for the Tête Défense.»

[20] Chaslin, *Les Paris De François Mitterrand : Histoire des Grands Projets Architecturaux*, 166.

[21] Lacaze, «Interview,» 129.

[22] EPAD, «Forms for the Analyses of the Projects by the Technical Commission,» (Archives EPAD/Defacto, 1983b).

[23] «Report by the Technical Commission,» (Archives EPAD/Defacto, 1983f).

[24] Oriol Guardiola Bohigas (Spain), Kisho Kurokawa (Japan), Richard Meyer (United States), and Richard Rogers (United Kingdom) ; Antoine Grumbach, Gérard Thurnauer, and Bernard Zehrfuss ; the economist Mahdi Elmandjra (Morocco), the Mayor of Madrid E. Tierno Galvan (Spain), replaced by his deputy, the UIA delegate and professor Jorge Glusberg (Argentina), and the architecture critic Ada Louise Huxtable (United States) ; Robert Lion, Serge Antoine, and Louis Moissonnier. «Program for the Competition for the Tête Défense.»

[25] R. Lion, «Sam'suffit à la Défense,» *Le Monde* (1981).

[26] Thierry Paquot, "Interview De Jean-Paul Lacaze," *Urbanisme*, no. 366 (2009).

[27] EPAD, "Letter to Gerard Thurnauer, 26 January 1983," (Archives Gérard Thurnauer/IFA, 1983d). "Letter to Gerard Thurnauer, 17 February 1983," (Archives Gérard Thurnauer/IFA, 1983c).

[28] All quotes taken from «Program for the Competition for the Tête Défense.»

[29] «Report by the Technical Commission.»

30 Viguier and Jodry proposed a portico closed by a screen ; Gregotti, a window pierced into an office building ; Nouvel and his partners' grid could also be assimilated to a portico ; Autran and Macary designed a dissymmetrical arch ; Jourda and Perraudin, two blocks forming a door, with a glass roof in between ; etc.

31 Projects 112, 116, 209, 401, 407, 431, 530, 605, 647, 742... for the first category. Projects 126, 141, 306, 404, 538, 847... for the second

32 Gérard Thurnauer, «Handwritten Notes, 25-26 April 1983,» (Archives Gérard Thurnauer/IFA, 1983b).

33 Jean-Pierre Chupin, «On the Changing Nature of Architectural Knowledge in a Multipolar World,» in *International Competition and Architectural Quality in the Planetary Age; International symposium*, ed. J.-P. Chupin and G. Adamczyk (University of Montreal : L.E.A.P. / C.R.C., 2012).

34 First lines of the text in Spreckelsen's project (n° 640). Archives of the EPAD/Defacto

35 EPAD, «Jury Report,» (Archives EPAD/Defacto, 1983g).

36 Lion, «Interview.»

37 Serge Antoine (1927-2006) was a high-ranking civil servant in charge of research and innovation in several Ministries from 1962 to 1982, and committed to environmental questions.

38 "Event/Activity — To allow the general public to be in contact with the world and its regions in no time and at any hour." (EPAD, "Program for the Competition for the Tête Défense.") "Event" is of course not to be understood under the exact same definition as the one we will use at the end of the paper.

39 Gérard Thurnauer, «Tête Défense et son environnement,» (Archives Gérard Thurnauer/IFA, 1988).

40 Subileau, «Interview.»

41 Jean-Louis Subileau (born in 1943) is an urban planner. He was the director of the Mission for the coordination of the great architectural and urban operations of the State from 1982 to 1986, and the director of the *SEM Tête Défense* from 1986 to 1991.

42 Subileau, «Interview.»

43 Thurnauer, «Handwritten Notes, 25-26 April 1983.»

44 «Handwritten Notes for the Jury Report. 26 April 1983,» (Archives Gérard Thurnauer/IFA, 1983a).

45 Respectively, 27 and 29 April 1983, from letters sent to Gérard Thurnauer. EPAD, «Letter to Gérard Thurnauer, 5 Avril 1983,» (Archives EPAD/Defacto, 1983e).

46 Subileau, «Interview.»

47 Thurnauer, «Handwritten Notes, 25-26 April 1983.»

48 Rogers, «Interview.»

49 Subileau, «Interview.»

50 The projects were presented to Mitterrand on April 28 but the "Statement from the President", which announced the results, was published on May 25. Archives EPAD/Defacto

51 Lion, "Interview.", Subileau, "Interview."

52 Subileau, «Interview.»

53 EPAD, «Program for the Competition for the Tête Défense.»

54 Rogers, «Interview.»

55 Charlotte Svensson, «Architectural Persuasion : On Quality Assessment in an Architectural Competition,» *Nordic Journal of Architectural Research* 24, no. 1 (2012).

56 EPAD, «Forms for the Analyses of the Projects by the Technical Commission.»

57 Frederic Edelmann and Emmanuel De Roux, «Un Président Bâtisseur,» *Le Monde* (1995).

58 Frederic Edelmann, «M. Mitterrand va inaugurer la Bibliothèque Nationale de France,» ibid.

59 Emmanuel De Roux, «Le Pharaon Et L'architecte,» ibid.

60 Subileau, «Interview.»

61 Alizard, *François Mitterrand ou le Grand Pari(S)*, 143.

62 Chaslin, *Les Paris de François Mitterrand : Histoire des Grands Projets Architecturaux*, 171.

63 Thurnauer, «Handwritten Notes, 25-26 April 1983.»

64 EPAD, «424 projets pour Tête Défense. Concours international d'architecture. Exposition de mai à juillet,» (Archives EPAD/Defacto, 1983a).

65 Lion, «Interview.»

66 Ibid.

67 Chaslin, *Les Paris de François Mitterrand : Histoire des Grands Projets Architecturaux*, 172.

68 Gérard Thurnauer, «Réflexions sur le projet Tête Défense,» (Archives Gérard Thurnauer/IFA, 1979).

69 For example, the jury stated that "The fragile balance between the permanent character of the portico and the transient nature of the low-rise constructions forms a contemporary response to the idea of monumentality" (EPAD, "Jury Report."). The EPAD published a text about "the origins of the monument". The *Canard Enchaîné* ironically wrote that it would now be impossible "to conceive a monument without a hole in it" on the axis C. Bernard, "Le trou du cube," *Le Canard Enchaîné* (1983)..

70 According to the Council on Tall Building and Urban Habitat (CTBUH)

71 Odile Fillon, «Lloyd's Londres,» *Architecture intérieure créée*, no. 211 (1986).

72 Ibid.

73 Richard Rogers, «Order, Harmony and Modernity,» *Architecture and Urbanism, extra edition, Richard Rogers 1978-1988*, no. 12 (1988).

74 Peter W. Rees, interview by L. Lenne.

75 Rogers, «Interview.»

76 Ian Findlay (1918 — 2002) was chairman of Lloyd's.

77 Gordon Graham (1920-1997) was and architect. He was president of the RIBA from 1977 to 1979.

78 Anon, «Richard Rogers and Partners. Architecture and the Program : Lloyd's of London,» *International Architect* 1, no. 3 (1980).

79 Currency of the time. Brian Appleyard, *Richard Rogers : A Biography* (Boston : Faber and Faber, 1986), 236.

80 Rogers, «Interview.»

81 Courtenay Blackmore (1922- 1992) joined Lloyd's in 1971

82 Brian Waters, «The inside Story,» *Building* 249, no. 51 (1985).

83 Appleyard, *Richard Rogers : A Biography*, 238.

84 Courtenay Blackmore, *The Client's Tale : The Role of the Client in Building Buildings* (RIBA Publications, 1990), 38.

85 Anon, «Richard Rogers and Partners. Architecture and the Program : Lloyd's of London.»

86 Appleyard, *Richard Rogers : A Biography*, 238.

87 Rogers, «Interview.»

88 Judith Strong, «The Development on the Competition System,» in *International Conference on Architectural Competitions* (Espoo, Finland 2012).

89 Robert Bordaz (1908-1996) was a high-ranking civil servant appointed by President Pompidou for the completion of the *Centre Pompidou*

90 Peter Green (1924-1996) was chairman of Lloyd's and chairman of Redevelopment Committee

91 Rodney Cooper, «Within These Walls,» *Designers' journal*, no. 20 (1986).

92 Anon, «Patronage,» *RIBA Journal* 88, no. 5 (1981).

93 Blackmore, *The Client's Tale : The Role of the Client in Building Buildings*, 40.

94 Chupin, «On the Changing Nature of Architectural Knowledge in a Multipolar World.»

95 Claude Parent, «Événement. Lloyd's of London : Richard Rogers Partnership,» *L'architecture d'aujourd'hui*, no. 247 (1986).

96 Anon, «Richard Rogers + Partners. Lloyd's New Building,» *Architectural design* 54, no. 3-4 (1984).

97 For example, in Brian Waters, «A Year at Lloyd's,» *Building* 247, no. 38 (1984).

98 Parent, «Événement. Lloyd's of London : Richard Rogers Partnership.»

99 Rogers, «Interview.»

100 François Dosse, *Renaissance de l'événement : Un défi pour l'historien : Entre sphinx et phénix*, 1re éd. ed., Le Noeud Gordien, (Paris : Presses

universitaires de France, 2010).

[101] Marc Bessin, Claire Bidart, and Michel Grossetti, *Bifurcations : Les sciences sociales face aux ruptures et à l'événement*, Collection Recherches (Paris : La Découverte, 2010).

[102] William H. Sewell, *Logics of History : Social Theory and Social Transformation* (University of Chicago Press, 2009), 11.

[103] Elisabeth S. Clemens, «Toward a Historicized Sociology : Theorizing Events, Processes, and Emergence,» *Annual Review of Sociology* 33 (2007).

[104] Gilles Deleuze and Félix Guattari, «Mai 68 n'a pas eu lieu,» *Les Nouvelles Littéraires* (1984).

[105] Guy Debord, *La société du spectacle* (Paris : Buchet/Chastel, 1967). *In.* Dosse, *Renaissance de l'événement : Un défi pour l'historien : Entre sphinx et phénix*, 6.

[106] For example, Carlo Ginzburg, *Il Formaggio E I Vermi* (Einaudi, 1976).

[107] And is in fact the subject of the PhD research I am currently working on, directed by Antoine Picon and Pierre Chabard at OCS (University Paris-Est)

[108] Richard Rogers, «Conference in the Mipim,» (Qatar pavilion, Cannes2012a).

[109] "Richard Rogers RA : Inside Out", 18 July — 13 October 2013, Royal Academy of Arts, London

[110] John Worthington, «Beyond the City Limits,» *Designers' journal* 20 (1986).

[111] Rodney Cooper, «Within These Walls,» ibid., no. 20.

[112] Jean-Louis Subileau, «Pour la noblesse de l'architecture. Discussion avec Jean-Louis Subileau,» in *La Grande Arche. L'événement média* (Archives EPAD/Defacto, 1989).

[113] Michel Brodovitch and Isabelle Vaulont, «Faisabilité d'une procédure de protection de la Grande Arche. Report N° 004798-01,» (La Défense, 2007).

[114] Ibid.

[115] This article was translated from French by Joseph Briaud and Loïse Lenne.

## ▬ References

**Alizard**, Marie. François Mitterrand ou le Grand Pari(S). les Éd. du Panthéon, 2011.

«Patronage.» RIBA Journal 88, no. 5 (1981).

**Anon.** «Richard Rogers + Partners. Lloyd's New Building.» Architectural design 54, no. 3-4 (1984) : 65.

**Anon.** «Richard Rogers and Partners. Architecture and the Program : Lloyd's of London.» International Architect 1, no. 3 (1980) : 25-39.

**Appleyard**, Brian. Richard Rogers : A Biography. Boston : Faber and Faber, 1986.

**Bernard**, C. «Le trou du cube.» Le Canard Enchaîné (1983).

**Bessin**, Marc, Claire **Bidart**, and Michel **Grossetti**. Bifurcations : Les sciences sociales face aux ruptures et à l'événement. Collection Recherches. Paris : La Découverte, 2010.

**Blackmore**, Courtenay. The Client's Tale : The Role of the Client in Building Buildings. RIBA Publications, 1990.

**Brodovitch**, Michel, and Isabelle **Vaulont**. «Faisabilité d'une procédure de protection de la Grande Arche. Report N° 004798-01.» La Défense, 2007.

**Champenois**, Michèle. «L'aménagement de la Tête Défense. Le jury international a présenté quatre esquisses à M. Mitterrand.» Le Monde (1983).

**Chaslin**, François. Les paris de François Mitterrand : Histoire des Grands Projets architecturaux. Collection Folio/Actuel. Paris : Gallimard, 1985.

**Chaslin**, François. «Un monument en perspective.» In La Grande Arche de la Défense, edited by F. Chaslin and V. Picon-Lefebvre, 28-29 : Paris : Le Moniteur, 1989.

**Chupin**, Jean-Pierre. «On the Changing Nature of Architectural Knowledge in a Multipolar World.» In International Competition and Architectural Quality in the Planetary Age ; International symposium, edited by J.-P. Chupin and G. Adamczyk. University of Montreal : L.E.A.P. / C.R.C., 2012.

**Clemens**, Elisabeth S. «Toward a Historicized Sociology : Theorizing Events, Processes, and Emergence.» Annual Review of Sociology 33 (2007) : 527-49.

**Cooper**, Rodney. «Within These Walls.» Designers' journal, no. 20 (1986) : 48-53.

**De Roux**, Emmanuel. «Le pharaon et L'architecte.» Le Monde (1995).

**Debord**, Guy. La société du spectacle. Paris : Buchet/Chastel, 1967.

**Deleuze**, Gilles, and Félix **Guattari**. «Mai 68 n'a pas eu lieu.» Les Nouvelles Littéraires (1984) : 75-76.

**Dosse**, François. Renaissance de l'événement : Un défi pour l'historien : Entre sphinx et phénix. Le Noeud Gordien,. 1re éd. ed. Paris : Presses universitaires de France, 2010.

**Edelmann**, Frederic. «M. Mitterrand va inaugurer la Bibliothèque Nationale de France.» Le Monde (1995).

**Edelmann**, Frederic, and Emmanuel **De Roux**. «Un Président bâtisseur.» Le Monde (1995).

**EPAD**. «424 Projets pour Tête Défense. Concours international d'architecture. Exposition de Mai à Juillet.» Archives EPAD/Defacto, 1983a.

**EPAD**. «Consultation for the Tête Défense.» Archives EPAD/Defacto, 1980.

**EPAD**. «Forms for the Analyses of the Projects by the Technical Commission.» Archives EPAD/Defacto, 1983b.

**EPAD**. «Jury Report.» Archives EPAD/Defacto, 1983g.

**EPAD**. «Letter to Gerard Thurnauer, 17 February 1983.» Archives Gérard Thurnauer/IFA, 1983c.

**EPAD**. «Letter to Gerard Thurnauer, 26 January 1983.» Archives Gérard Thurnauer/IFA, 1983d.

**EPAD**. «Letter to Gérard Thurnauer, 5 Avril 1983.» Archives EPAD/Defacto, 1983e.

**EPAD**. «Program for the Competition for the Tête Défense.» Archives EPAD/Defacto, 1982.

**EPAD**. «Report by the Technical Commission.» Archives EPAD/Defacto, 1983f.

**Fillon**, Odile. «Lloyd's Londres.» Architecture intérieure créée, no. 211 (1986) : 94-97.

**Ginzburg**, Carlo. Il Formaggio E I Vermi. Einaudi, 1976.

**Lacaze**, Jean-Paul. «Interview.» In Historiographie de La Défense, edited by J. Beauchard, 116-33 : Archives EPAD/Defacto, 1994.

**Lion**, Robert. «Sam'suffit à La Défense.» Le Monde (1981).

**Lion**, Robert. «Interview.» In Historiographie De La Défense, edited by J. Beauchard, 149-68 : Archives EPAD/Defacto, 1994.

**Lion**, Robert. «Interview.» By L. Lenne (2012) : 90 min.

**Moissonnier**, Louis. «Mission d'étude programme, Tête Défense.» Archives EPAD/Defacto, 1982.

**Paquot**, Thierry. «Interview de Jean-Paul Lacaze.» Urbanisme, no. 366 (2009).

**Parent**, Claude. «Événement. Lloyd's of London : Richard Rogers Partnership.» L'architecture d'aujourd'hui, no. 247 (1986) : 2-19.

**Rees**, Peter W. «Interview.» By L. Lenne (2012) : 50 min.

**Rogers**, Richard. «Conference in the Mipim.» Qatar pavilion, Cannes, 2012a.

**Rogers**, Richard. «Interview.» By L. Lenne (2012b) : 40 min.

**Rogers**, Richard. «Order, Harmony and Modernity.» Architecture and Urbanism, extra edition, Richard Rogers 1978-1988, no. 12 (1988) : 13-32.

**Rouyer**, Rémi. «Tête Défense.» In La Défense, dictionnaire et atlas. Architecture/Politique, Histoire/Territoire, edited by P. Chabard and V. Picon-Lefebvre, 388-93. Marseille : Parenthèses, 2012.

**Sewell**, William H. Logics of History : Social Theory and Social Transformation. University of Chicago Press, 2009.

**Strong**, Judith. «The Development on the Competition System.» In International Conference on Architectural Competitions. Espoo, Finland 2012.

**Subileau**, Jean-Louis. «Interview.» By L. Lenne (2012) : 90 min.

**Subileau**, Jean-Louis. «Pour la noblesse de l'architecture. Discussion avec Jean-Louis Subileau.» In La Grande Arche. L'événement média, 16-17 : Archives EPAD/Defacto, 1989.

**Svensson**, Charlotte. «Architectural Persuasion : On Quality Assessment in an Architectural Competition.» Nordic Journal of Architectural Research 24, no. 1 (2012) : 97-118.

**Thurnauer**, Gérard. «Handwritten Notes for the Jury Report. 26 April 1983.» Archives Gérard Thurnauer/IFA, 1983a.

**Thurnauer**, Gérard. «Handwritten Notes, 25-26 April 1983.» Archives Gérard Thurnauer/IFA, 1983b.

**Thurnauer**, Gérard. «Réflexions sur le Projet Tête Défense.» Archives Gérard Thurnauer/IFA, 1979.

**Thurnauer**, Gérard. «Tête Défense et son environnement.» Archives Gérard Thurnauer/IFA, 1988.

**Waters**, Brian. «The inside Story.» Building 249, no. 51 (1985) : 38-41.

**Waters**, Brian. «A Year at Lloyd's.» Building 247, no. 38 (1984) : 30-37.

**Worthington**, John. «Beyond the City Limits.» Designers' journal 20 (1986) : 40-47.

# 1.4. A Universal Space for Ageing

**Demographic Changes, Eldercare, and Competitions in Denmark, Norway and Sweden**

**Jonas E Andersson**, Ph.D.
School of Architecture, ABE, Royal Institute of Technology, KTH, Stockholm
Sweden

In the context of an ageing world, theories on welfare regimes as well as their influence on architecture for ageing come of relevance. The key mechanism in these theories is the perceived level of decommodification in society, i.e. various financial measures that the individual subject initiates personally in order to prepare for different stages in his/ her life: bringing up children, education, health and sickness, professional career or retiring from professional life. One concrete social measure is special accommodations for dependent and frail older people, here termed residential care homes (RCH). Decommodification is supposedly most developed in welfare regimes originating from social democratic values, similar to Nordic countries, like Denmark, Norway and Sweden. During the 20th century, these countries have used architectural competitions in order to harmonize socio-political ideals with the architectural realization of RCHs. The present study explores the organizational forms of 77 architectural competitions that were organized in these countries during the period 2000-2012. A sub-sample of 9 competition programmes, three from each country, were analyzed concerning the presence of welfare goals and other prerequisites for the design task in the programming brief. The sample was assembled through key word searches in open and restricted databases. Based on the full sample, restricted competitions appeared as the most used form for RCH competitions. The sub-sample suggested that language and ideological capital, originating from the realization of the Nordic welfare state, adds an additional restriction. Hence, the overall conclusion suggests that that existing socio-political ideals for architecture for the dependent and frail aging process tends to block the integration of international findings on universal space for ageing well.

**Cover**
Wheel of fortune? Or, the glazed ceiling of the interior courtyard at the Galeries Lafayettes in Berlin, designed by architect Jean Nouvel in 1996.
*Photograph by Jonas E Andersson*

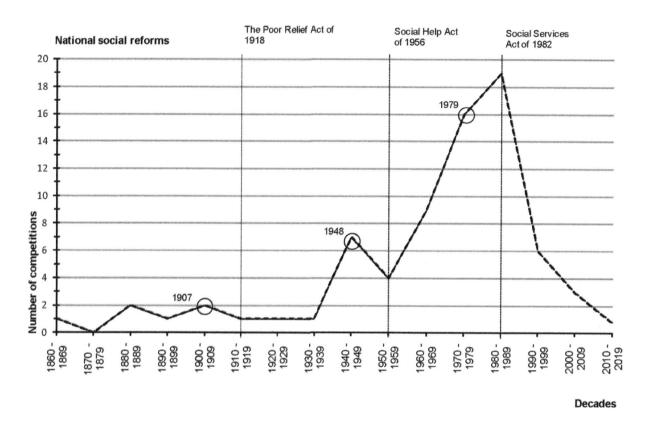

**National social reforms**

The Poor Relief Act of 1918

Social Help Act of 1956

Social Services Act of 1982

**Fig. 1**
During the period 1864 to 2012, some 80 architectural competitions can be identified with
a focus on architecture for older people in both Denmark and Sweden. These competitions
were all acknowledged by the national associations of architects, which suggest the possibility
that other competition-like arrangements may exist. In both Denmark and Sweden, the
majority of competitions were organized as local project competitions that were intended to be
realized. In Sweden, but not in Denmark, stakeholders, involved in civil administration or lobby
organization for improved social welfare, organized three national open ideas competitions,
which preceded three consecutive reforms of the Swedish Social Act in 1918, in 1956, and
the current Social Act of 1982[4] These reforms promoted a change from a lenient approach in
social services to allow only bare necessities in life to an all-inclusive approach that concerned
all citizens, regardless of cognitive or functional capacities, or financial situation.
*Image by author*

In 2011, some 19.9 million people lived in the Nordic countries of Denmark (5.6 million), Norway (4.9 million) and Sweden (9.4 million).[1] Like most western democracies, these countries have a declining nativity rate, a decrease in the working population and an increasing proportion of older people.[2] Among the Nordic countries, Sweden has the largest proportion of people aged 65 years and older, a total of 18.0% (2011). In addition, the proportion of older people aged 80 years and above is the largest, 4.8%. Denmark has the second largest group of people aged 65 years and older, 16.8%, followed by Norway with 15.1%. In these countries, the proportion of older people in higher age bracket is smaller, between 3.4 to 4.5%. By the end of the 20th century, the ageing process changed appearance, and dementia became the most frequently occurring age-related problem, surpassing cancer, heart diseases and mobility impairments.[3]

Denmark, Norway and Sweden have used architectural competitions as socio-political instruments in order to define spatial parameters of ageing with dependency since the end of the 19th century **[Fig. 1]**.[5] Denmark was the first Nordic country to introduce age pensions and special housing for older people.[6] In Sweden, three idea competitions on space for ageing, organized in 1907, 1948, and 1979, prepared for consecutive reforms of the social legislation.[7] In Norway, a competition on homes for dependent and frail elderly was held in 1947 in order to formulate national guidelines for the municipalities to respect, when expanding this type of housing for the dawning welfare society.[8] This continuous definition of the appropriate space for ageing have relied mostly on experience-based findings, and findings on the matter established by research in architecture, caregiving, gerontology or nursing sciences are scarce.

## Architectural competitions on space for ageing

In the European Union, architectural, constructional and engineering services are subjected to the Services Directive.[9] This implies that the tendering process can be organized as open ideas or project competitions, or as competitions with a pre-qualification procurement procedure. In the Nordic context, an architectural competition supposes anonymous competition proposals that are submitted by an individual architect or a multi-professional team of designers in either an idea or project (design) competition. The competition form may be of three organizational types: open ones, restricted ones or competitions with a two-stage procedure. The latter type of competitions implies that the first stage is open, while the second stage is restricted to a selection of awarded or purchased proposals.[10]

The national frameworks for architectural competitions have been harmonized with the EU directive 2004/18/EC through the Danish and Swedish memberships of the European Union. Although not a member of the EU, Norway has adopted the same policies as its neighbouring countries. In the specific context of public stakeholders, both eldercare services and architectural, constructional and/or engineering services are to be published as open notices in daily and professional press in order to promote a fair and transparent competition procedure in view of public commissions or time-limited contracts.[11] About 5-11% of this total is focused on architecture for healthcare (hospital, primary healthcare centres, residential care homes, and other buildings.[12]

## Aims and working hypothesis

The present study is a comparative study of architectural competitions, focusing on space for dependent and frail people, which were realized in Denmark, Norway and Sweden. The study focuses on the period of 2000-2012, during which 77 competitions were organized for renewing RCH architecture: 18 Danish competitions, 34 Norwegian competitions, and 25 Swedish competitions. This paper uses the term residential care homes, RCH, in order to describe this Nordic type of sheltered housing for dependent and frail older people.[13] The objective of the study was to explore competition forms, and how social welfare goals were integrated in programming briefs for new RCH facilities.

The study was guided by a working hypothesis that stated that RCH architecture is an outcome of the existing welfare regime. In the course of time, socio-political ambitions have been transformed into parameters that architects have to address spatially. Consequently, architecture that is intended for social purposes will reflect cultural, ethical and political values that have become integral parts of the welfare regime.[14] This type of architectural space has a slower pace of change, since a change in architectural design depends upon socio-political paradigms that are part of the development of the welfare regime. It constitutes a special field of competence for architects.

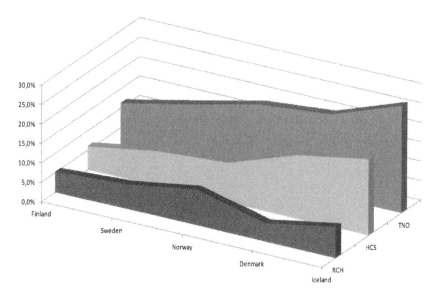

**Fig. 2**
Based on statistics from the Nordic Council, the above three-dimensional graph of eldercare services in the five Nordic countries can be assembled.[26] This demonstrates that home care services and RCH are more frequent in Denmark, Norway and Iceland than in Finland and Sweden. The abbreviation HCS stands for Home Care Services and RCH for Residential Care Homes. TNO is short for Total Number of Older people who benefit from these two types of municipal eldercare. *Image by author*

## ▬ Background

By considering, "*the circumstance that short term policies, reforms, and decision-making take place within frameworks of historical institutionalization that differ qualitatively*"[15], different countries can be analyzed in terms of their, "*institutional arrangements (...) that guide and shape concurrent social policy decisions, expenditure developments, problem definitions.*"[16] In theories on welfare regimes, the term decommodification is essential for defining the type of welfare regime. This concept refers to various services, such as pensions, health or un-employment insurances, eldercare and other societal assistance provided by the state. Their ultimate aim is to reduce the citizens' dependency on the market economy in order to uphold individual well-being.[17] In Western society, three types of welfare regimes can be identified: regimes honouring Christian democratic values, regimes based on a liberalistic thinking or welfare regimes that originate from social democratic values.[18] Christian democratic regimes are based on a subsidiary principle, which often creates social stratification. France, Germany and Italy represent this model. A medium level of decommodification is found in these countries.[19] Liberal welfare regimes affirm the market principle that generates private provisions and social stratification. Canada, Switzerland and the US illustrate this welfare principle. In these countries, a low level of decommodification can be found.

The highest level of decommodification is often said to be found in social democratic welfare regimes, which embrace an egalitarian principle. Societal services are financed by taxation and provided by the state in order to limit the citizens' dependency on variations in market economy. Denmark, Norway and Sweden demonstrate this category of welfare regimes.[20] The Nordic civil administrational model implies three levels: Firstly, the national level that produces general welfare goals with guidelines that are to be implemented nationally. The national level monitors the regional counties, the second and controlling level, which supervises the third level, the municipalities. The municipalities implement and interpret the national welfare goals. In both Denmark and Sweden, eldercare can be provided by the municipalities themselves or by private care entrepreneurs, often active in all Nordic countries. This type of care is accountable for about 20 % of the full stock of eldercare that is realized in these countries.[21] About 80 %

of the Swedish municipalities respect the commissioner-supplier model when commissioning eldercare, whereas it is universally implemented in Denmark. [22] In Norway, some 10%, mainly the larger municipalities implement the principle. [23] Promoting a higher degree of older people's opinions about this care, the individual choice model of eldercare provider was first introduced in Denmark in 2002 and six years later in Sweden. [24] At a slower pace, this model of eldercare has started to be used also in Norway. [25]

## Eldercare and housing for older people in Denmark, Norway and Sweden

Municipal eldercare, provided as home cares services in the older person's individual home or as 24-hour assistance and care for dependent and frail older persons in RCHs, reaches a larger proportion of beneficiaries in Denmark, 27.6%, than in Sweden, 15.3% **[Fig.2]**. Norway assumes an intermediary position with 19.5%. Finland and Iceland are the opposing endpoints on this continuum, but these countries are not part of the study. Eldercare provided by the family is difficult to assess. According to calculations based on Swedish conditions, it is likely that it accounts for about two thirds of all eldercare services provided. [27] In all of the Nordic countries, housing targeting older people aged 55 years or above with few or some age-related problems, can be found in any type of ordinary housing or in special facilities called senior co-housing. This high-quality architecture, often situated in centrally located areas in the cities, can be associated with a dual incentive: to entice older people to leave their familiar home in the green suburbs, and allow young families with children to move out of the city centres to the lush suburbia. As a consequence of the deliberations of the Swedish parliament committee, 2008-2011, so-called safe-haven residences for able and fit elderly have emerged in this country. Such facilities offer services stretching from eldercare to everyday assistance. In Sweden, the official statistics omits detailing this segment of the housing market, while similar housing arrangements accounts for about 2-3% of the housing market in Denmark and Norway. In contrast to Sweden, these arrangements are smaller in scale and forward mutual personal interests among the residents as the fundament for the co-housing principle.

In Denmark, Norway and Sweden, some 204.487 frail older persons live in RCHs, i.e. 1.02% of the full Danish-Norwegian-Swedish population. In the Nordic countries, the main reason for moving to RCHs is either dementia diagnoses or complex long-term medical conditions, which in both cases lead to a dependency on 24 hour assistance and caregiving. [28] However, the same legal framework applies to RCH flats as flats in ordinary housing. [29] The lease of a RCH flat is offered to the older person after an assessment by the municipal eldercare administration of personal needs of assistance and caregiving. Besides a monthly rent, the tenant will pay a fee that is proportional to the assessed need of eldercare services. In a Swedish context, a RCH flat implies a small individual flat of approximately 20-40 m$^2$ (hallway, bedroom and bathroom) with additional space for dining and socializing in communal areas that are adjacent to the flats. In Denmark, the floor plan of the flat is larger, above 35 m$^2$ (hallway, bedroom, living room with kitchenette and bathroom). In addition, the adjacent communal space for dining and socializing is also larger. The Norwegian situation is somewhat different: flats in existing RCHs are similar to the Swedish number, while modern RCHs tend embrace the contemporary Danish guidelines. However, the assessment procedure may also lead to an extended level of home care services, which, currently, is the most likely outcome, since the number of available flats in RCHs has dropped considerably since the beginning of the new millennium. This could also be related to the organization of new architectural competitions on the matter.

## Competition programmes and primary generators

As a field of practice, architecture can be situated to the intersection of four dimensions: The ideological vision of built space versus the concrete realization (vertical axis), and the individual adjustment of the built space versus collective habits of adjusting and using space (horizontal axis). [30] Architecture becomes a tangible form of physical space, shaped by various considerations of an aesthetic, functional, and contextual nature. [31] The axes describe twelve aspects that influence architecture and built environments. The creative phase of conceiving architectural space can be seen as the designer's or group of designers' individual reflections on the design task based upon previous knowledge, the commissioner's wishes and specific requirements for the design task, not to mention discussions with the commissioner. [32] In an iterative process of approving or rejecting random spatial ideas, existing cultural and social beliefs are tested. [33] In this work, architects use generator images that help the architectural idea to evolve into a spatial gestalt. [34]

In the case of an architectural competition, the

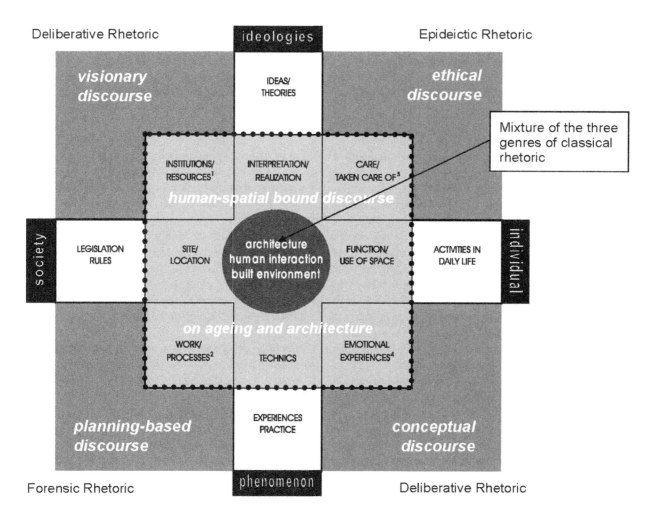

Deliberative Rhetoric

Epideictic Rhetoric

ideologies

visionary discourse

ethical discourse

IDEAS/ THEORIES

Mixture of the three genres of classical rhetoric

INSTITUTIONS/ RESOURCES[1]

INTERPRETATION/ REALIZATION

CARE/ TAKEN CARE OF[3]

human-spatial bound discourse

society

LEGISLATION RULES

SITE/ LOCATION

architecture human interaction built environment

FUNCTION/ USE OF SPACE

ACTIVITIES IN DAILY LIFE

individual

on ageing and architecture

WORK/ PROCESSES[2]

TECHNICS

EMOTIONAL EXPERIENCES[4]

planning-based discourse

conceptual discourse

EXPERIENCES PRACTICE

phenomenon

Forensic Rhetoric

Deliberative Rhetoric

**Fig. 3**
The discursive model of an architectural competition
in a Swedish municipality.
*Image by author*[38]

competition programme will replace the increasingly higher degree of consensus between the architect and the commissioner on the appropriate type of architectural design for the design task in question. The participating architects have to scrutinize the programme for concepts, explicative sentences or hidden meanings in order to find a *bon mot*, which in a their understanding encapsulate the organizer's view on the matter, and, thereby, promote a structuring idea for the competition proposal. [35] This paper acknowledges the parallel between architecture and rhetoric. [36] However, it expands the understanding of the competition programme beyond being merely a text with a primarily utilitarian character into being a multi-faceted document with aesthetical, ethical and existential concerns for the architectural space to address. The competition programme produces primary generators, [37] which guide the creation of a competition proposal.

Based on a previous study on the realization of an architectural competition in a Swedish municipality in 2006-2007, the model for architectural practice can be combined with a discursive model that summarizes the organizer's reasoning about motivating forces for a competition on appropriate space for ageing. [39] Depending on the quadrants between the above-mentioned dimensions, five discourses on an architectural competition and RCH architecture emerge **[Fig.3]**. In the centre, there is a Human-Spatial bound Discourse (HSD) on architecture and ageing that consists of a mixture of the other discourses found in the model. Outside this central think tank, there are four discourses that correspond to one of the classical genres. The Ethical Discourse (ED), similar to the epideictic rhetoric, uses an emotional stance in order to define the appropriate set of constituents for RCH architecture. The Conceptual Discourse (CD) and the Visionary Discourse (VD) are similar to the deliberative rhetoric, which uses logic reasoning in terms of right and wrong in order to conceptualize visions for the future built environment. The Planning-Based Discourse (PBD) is the equivalent of forensic rhetoric, since this discourse defines the set of credible measures that have to be taken in order to realize a certain type of built space within a defined time period.

## ▬▬ Methodology

The present study focuses on the 77 architectural competitions on space for the frail ageing that were organized during the period of 2000-2012. It was realized as a case study with triangulating research methods (document analysis, interviews, questionnaires, and searches in open and restricted databases) in order to retrieve research data. [40] Key word searches (architecture + competition + residential homes in Danish, Norwegian and Swedish) on the Internet were used to circumscribe the competitions. This was followed by searches on the individual web sites of the national associations of architects, which listed architectural competitions. Parallel to this inquiry, a search for complete competition programmes that belonged to any of the targeted competitions was pursued in order to collect detailed research data, which would allow for a semantic analysis (close reading). [41] The full sample was analyzed according to design task; organizational form; presence of welfare goals and profile of organizer. A sub-sample of 9 competition programmes was established. This document analysis adopted a dual perspective, either the organizers' perspective of communicating necessary requirements about the design task to the participating architects, or the participants' perspective of receiving essential information that would allow for composing a competition proposal.

### Principles for analyzing research data

The analysis of the full sample aimed at defining the dominant organizational forms for competitions that focus on RCH architecture. The sub-sample was analyzed according to the previously mentioned discursive model. [42] This implied a structuring of empirical findings similar to Applied Discourse Analysis, ADA, since this analysis does not focus on language itself, but on what is expressed through language. [43] The analyses targeted the programme's capacity to convey the organizer's spatial visions for the intended building to the participating architects. The analyses pertained to the wording of the competition documentation similar to rhetorical criticism. [44] In classical rhetoric, there are three rhetorical genres: Firstly, *Deliberative Rhetoric* that uses dissuasive or persuasive elements in speech or writing to argue a case. Secondly, *Epideictic Rhetoric* analyses negative or positive models in order to define what is to avoid and what is to be desired. Thirdly, *Forensic Rhetoric* is concerned with factual evidence in terms of what is right or wrong.

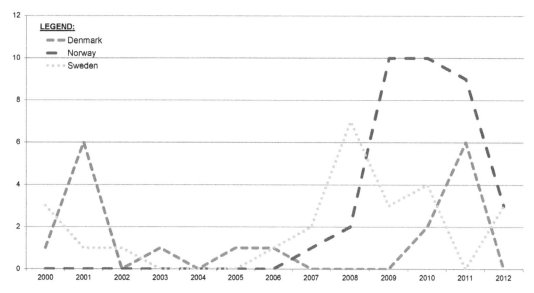

**Fig. 4**

The chronological distribution of the 77 architectural competitions on space for the dependent and frail ageing in Denmark, Norway and Sweden during the period of 2000 to 2012.
*Image by author*

## ▬ Results

This section is divided into two parts. The first part presents findings from the full sample. The full sample supplied an overview of how architectural competitions in the three Nordic countries were used as socio-political instruments in order to generate innovative architecture for the dependent and frail ageing process. The second part investigates a sub-sample of competition documentation. This was a comparative analysis of the programmes that used numeric values in order to describe the perceived presence of welfare goals in the material.

### Architectural competitions listed by professional organizations

Most of the competitions were listed on the websites of the national associations of architects, and the few that were not were awaiting publication. There was a significant difference : On the Danish and Norwegian sites, all architectural competitions were listed, although some of the competitions were organized in a way that the national association did not acknowledge. On the other hand, the Swedish website listed merely competitions that were acknowledged by the association. Unlike its sister associations, the Swedish

professional association enjoys the same position as any other public Swedish stakeholder that have ratified the European Union agreement on how to organize architectural competitions.[45] In that position, the Swedish association represents not only individual architect members and architectural firms, but also construction companies and levels in civil administration. This supremacy may explain the omission of competitions outside the acknowledged framework. This means that the number of competitions in the Swedish case may be higher, although key word searches on the Internet did not indicate this possibility.

### Competitions in a cyclic use

A common denominator for all of the architectural competitions in the sample was that the organizers were local authorities. The chronological organization of the 77 architectural competitions into a graph suggested that architectural competitions were used differently in the three countries **[Fig.4]**. The Danish use of publically organized competitions implied a recurring use with peaks in the number of competitions every 10 year and a normal ratio of 1-2 competitions per year with sudden booms of 6 competitions a certain year. The Norwegian and Swedish graphs looked

**Frequency of use in per cent**

| Nations | IC | ICP | OC | PC | PTC |
|---------|-----|------|-----|-----|------|
| Denmark | 6 | 78 | 0 | 17 | 0 |
| Norway | 29 | 15 | 0 | 0 | 59 |
| Sweden | 0 | 16 | 4 | 80 | 0 |
| **Total %** | **14** | **30** | **1** | **30** | **26** |

Notes: IC = invited competitions; ICP = invited competitions with pre-qualification procedure; OC = open competitions; PC = project competitions; PTC = commission competitions.

**Fig. 5**
Overview of the five re-occurring organizational forms
that were found in the sample.

almost the same, but they were chronologically offset. In these countries, the graphs demonstrated a less frequent use, and intervals between drops and peaks suggested a recurrence interval of above 10 years.

**Three main types of organizational forms**
Concerning the organizational form, the sample with the 77 architectural competitions contained five different forms **[Fig. 5]**. Two organizational forms for architectural competitions, ICP and PC, had the same frequency of use, about 30 %, however, used differently in the individual country. The invited competition with pre-qualification procedure (ICP) was the most used type of competition form in Denmark, but scarcely used in Norway and Sweden. In this case, renowned architectural firms were targeted and invited to participate, often in close collaboration with a construction firm. The Danish competition system requires the listing of consulting fees, constructions costs and financial investments. This can be the case in Norway, but it is seldom the case in Sweden. The second most used competition form was the project competition (PC). Despite the fact that this competition type was not acknowledged by the Swedish association of architects, SA (Sveriges Arkitekter), it was the most used competition form in this country. This

competition form involved a designated plot, often owned by the municipality, and open for a particular use for a limited time. The local authorities searched for new ideas for the use of the plot by open invitations to construction companies and architectural firms, who were supposed to form consortiums. The consortium should submit a full biding proposal for a building proposal with consulting fees, construction costs, investment costs and financial terms for a municipal lease of the building. This type of competition did not exist in Norway, but it was scarcely used in Denmark. In contrast to the SA, this organizational form is acknowledged by the Danish association of architects, AA (Akademisk Arkitektforening).

The third most used type of architectural competition was project and tendering competitions (PTC). This organizational form was only used in Norway, although the Norwegian Association of Architects, NAL (Norske Arkitekters Landsforbund), does not acknowledge this organizational form. Similar to the PC type, participation supposed the collaboration between an architectural firm and a construction company. They should conceive a building proposal with consulting fees, constructions costs and investment costs. The ultimate criterion for winning such competitions was the lowest bid.

**Content in competition documentation**

| Name of competition | Year | Competition documentation | Pages | Separate appendix | Pages | Organizational form | Organizing actor | Nationality | Competition language | building requirements | holistic approach towards space for ageing | competition criteria | project criteria | presence of older persons | discursive character | competition language | nationality of participating architects |
|---|---|---|---|---|---|---|---|---|---|---|---|---|---|---|---|---|---|
| Competition A | 2012 | not possible to retrieve | 5 | Internet-based material from an interactive dialogue with older citizens | 5 | Invited competition with pre-qualification procedure | Gentofte kommune | Denmark | Danish | 0 | 0 | 0 | 0 | 2 | ED | D | 4 Danish architects firms, 1 Swedish architect's firm |
| | | Separate building | 55 | no | | | | | | | | | | | | | |
| Competition B | 2010 | not possible to retrieve | 0 | not possible to retrieve | | Invited competition | Frederiksbergs kommune | Denmark | Danish | 2 | 2 | 0 | 0 | 2 | PB | D | 5 Danish architects firms |
| | | Separate building | 63 | nc | | | | | | | | | | | | | |
| Competition C | 2000 | competition program | 22 | nc | | Invited competition | Aakirkeby kommune | Denmark | Danish | 1 | 1 | 2 | 0 | 0 | HSD | D | 4 Danish consortiums with architects and constructors, 1 Swedish-Danish consortium |
| **Danish cases, mean** | | | 47 | | 5 | | | | | **3** | **5** | **2** | **0** | **4** | | | |
| Competition D | 2009 | competition program | 12 | nc | | Invited competition | Skedsmo kommune | Norway | Norwegian | 0 | 0 | 2 | 0 | 0 | PB | N | 1 Swedish-Norwegian winner, other participants have not been possible to establish. |
| | | Building program | 53 | | | | | | Norwegian | 2 | 1 | 0 | 0 | 0 | PB | N | |
| | | Definition of assignment | 6 | | | | | | Norwegian | 0 | 0 | 0 | 1 | 0 | PB | N | |
| Competition E | 2011 | Combined competition and building program | 22 | nc | | Invited competition with pre-qualification procedure | Time kommune | Norway | Norwegian | 1 | 0 | 1 | 0 | 0 | PB | N | 1 Danish-Norwegian winner, and three other participants, but the nationality has not been possible to establish. |
| Competition F | 2012 | competition program | 13 | nc | | Invited competition with pre-qualification procedure | Vinje kommune | Norway | Norwegian | 0 | 0 | 1 | 1 | 0 | PB | N | 4 Norwegian Architect's firms |
| | | pre-qualification program | 7 | nc | | | | | | 0 | 0 | 0 | 0 | 0 | PB | N | |
| **Norwegian cases, mean** | | | 18 | | 20 | | | | | **3** | **1** | **4** | **2** | **0** | | | |
| Competition G | 2006 | competition program | 32 | nc | | Open competition | Järfälla kommun | Sweden | Swedish | 0 | 1 | 1 | 0 | 0 | HSD | S | 33 participants of which one Danish architects firm. |
| | | no | 5 | nc | | | | | Swedish | 0 | 0 | 1 | 0 | 0 | HSD | S | |
| Competition H | 2012 | competition program | 8 | Building program | | Invited competition with pre-qualification procedure | Linköpings kommun | Sweden | Swedish | 1 | 0 | 1 | 1 | 0 | HSD | S | 4 Swedish consortiums consisting of 6 individual Swedish architects firms and 2 affiliated Danish firms |
| | | pre-qualification program | 5 | no | | | | | Swedish | 0 | 0 | 1 | 0 | 0 | HSD | S | |
| Competition J | 2006 | competition program | 12 | Summary of dialogue with the users of the existing residential space | | Invited competition with pre-qualification procedure | Tingsryd kommun | Sweden | Swedish | 0 | 0 | 2 | 0 | 0 | HSD | S | 3 Swedish architects firms |
| | | pre-qualification program | 1 | | | | | | Swedish | 0 | 0 | 1 | 0 | 0 | HSD | S | |
| **Swedish cases, mean** | | | 19 | | 14 | | | | | **1** | **1** | **7** | **0** | **0** | | | |

Note 1: 0=slightly present, but not elaborated; 1=present and occasionally detailed; 2=present and highly detailed.
Note 2: Type of discourse: CD - conceptual discourse; ED - ethical discourse; HSD - human-spatial bound discourse; PB - planning-based discourse; VD - visionary discourse.

**Fig. 6**
Rhetorical tendencies in competition programmes found in a sample of nine architectural competitions. *Copyright: Author*

The fourth most used competition form was invited competitions (IC). This type of competition also went under the name of parallel commissions for a limited number of pre-selected architectural firms. This type of competition form is not approved by any of the national associations, i.e. the AA, the NAL or the SA. The fifth most used competition form was the open competition form. In the sample, a single Swedish competition of 2006-2007 accounted for this number. This was a competition in a suburban municipality in the vicinity of Stockholm. Seen as an entity, the full sample suggested that invited competitions, with or without pre-qualification procedure, were the main organizational form for competitions on space for the dependent and frail ageing process in Denmark, Norway and Sweden. These types of competitions are acknowledged by the national associations of architects. However, the sample suggested that municipal organizers in Norway and Sweden searched for alternative solutions.

**Rhetoric in competition documentation**

This section presents the sub-sample of nine competition programmes, three from Denmark, three from Norway and three from Sweden. Some elements of the Danish competition documentation could not be established other than items found in tables of contents. Despite this shortage, a significant difference between the competition documentation in the three countries could be established **[Fig. 6]**. The Danish competition programmes along with appendices had a more complex nature. On average, these documents counted 55 pages (47 page programmes plus 5 page appendices). The Norwegian and Swedish equivalents were of fewer pages : In the first case, the average was 18 page programmes with 20 page appendices, while the average in the latter case consisted of 15 page programmes with 14 page appendices. All of the programmes with appendices were written in the national language, and the competition proposals were expected to be submitted in this language.

**Different complexity in documentation**

The Danish competition documentation adopted a holistic approach on the relationship between the dependent and frail ageing process and the design of architectural space. This approach was further developed by use of photographs from exemplary models. The discursive character was rich, and it supposed at least three of the discourses that could be found in the analytical model. The competition documentation forwarded the needs of the older person

and his or her possible demands on the architectural space. Environmental aspects that could be related to older people's satisfaction with the built space, its design and location, were presented and associated with building requirements. In addition, the documentation included technical requirements concerning constructive methods, installation of wireless network systems, sanitation and ventilation. Moreover, the documentation included detailed financial key indicators to respect, since the Danish state subsidizes RCHs facilities with about 3-7 % of the full investment cost. Hence, the competition documents forced the competing architects to include constructional engineers, financial advisors and other experts, who seemed to be essential for the design task. The Danish competition programmes were assembled by a special consultant, whose main speciality was either in architecture, real estate financing or constructive problems.

The Norwegian competition documentation had mostly a technical approach to architecture, without any illustrations or photographs. The programming documentation was mainly written a technical language that used a planning-based discourse. The programmes were oriented towards listing envisioned building qualities and requirements. The documents did not contain financial key indicators with regard to the estimated building costs, but the financial conditions for the future building commission were outlined in the documentation. The competition programmes were centred on the performative nature of the future building, but the relationship between the older person, the ageing process, eldercare and the architectural space was mainly left aside, or present in short descriptive sections in the appendix. The programming documentation was assembled by the organizer of the competition in close collaboration with a consultant, whose main speciality was either in architecture, real estate financing or constructive problems.

The Swedish competition documentation had a rhetorical character that pondered about the appropriate space for ageing without any special concerns for particular environmental aspects to respect. It contained some photographs that described envisioned qualities and requirements that could be associated with the future building. However, these were more an ephemeral character than tangible facts. The older person and his/ her demands on the architectural space were mostly distant, or summarized in short sections in the appendix. In two cases, the appendices highlighted the relationship between the older person, the ageing process and the architectural design ; otherwise, the documentation relied on the participating architects' abilities to foresee the interaction between ageing, eldercare and architecture. The Swedish competition documents were assembled by two key municipal administrations: Often, the municipal real estate office supplied information on the limitations of the competitions, while it also headed the competition. The administration for social welfare and health supplemented this documentation with local policy documents for eldercare and buildings intended as housing for dependent and frail older people in need of 24 hour assistance and caregiving.

## ▬ Discussion

As a direct outcome of the welfare state, socio-political ambitions have been transformed into spatial parameters that architects have to address spatially in Denmark, Norway and Sweden.[46] Consequently, architecture that is intended for this purpose reflects local policies for eldercare and RCH facilities. The architectural design is influenced by cultural, ethical and political values that are integral parts of the local implementation of the welfare regime.[47] The dominance of public organizers when it comes to architectural competitions on space for dependent and frail ageing is consistent with the civil administrational principle of the Nordic countries, since the local level assumes the full responsibility for implementing national welfare goals, predicting needs for appropriate housing within the ordinary housing stock for older people in general or RCHs for dependent and frail senior citizens.[48] In addition, the municipalities will also organize and effectuate eldercare services in either of these residential environments.

However, the recurring use of competition forms, which are not approved by the Norwegian and Swedish associations of architects, suggests that municipalities often chose to deviate from the national framework when it comes to RCH facilities. This could be due to the complexity of the task, which the elaborated lists of building requirements in the Danish and Norwegian programming documents suggest. It could also be linked with the use of approximate national guidelines that promote a generalist approach by the architect, like the Swedish competitions demonstrate. The local implementation of socio-political welfare goals may induce public organizers to engage in a dialogue-based approach in order to share the interpretation task with the participants in the competitions.[49] Such innovative architectural competitions have been realized in Denmark.[50] However, the anonymity principle of the Norwegian and Swedish competition frameworks does not allow for such an exchange of ideas between architects and organizers, which could explain non-conformed organizational forms for competitions.

### National contexts shape architecture for ageing

The varying frequency in using architectural competitions in the full sample can be linked with different approaches in Denmark, Norway and Sweden to prepare for the ageing welfare state. The probable reason for the sudden recession in the Danish use of architectural competitions during the period of 2002-2009 can be linked with the national initiative to rethink this type of architectural design with a holistic approach. In 2003, the Danish Health Department decided to initiate a national research project on environmental aspects that are essential to respect when designing for dependent and frail older people. The project was headed by the Universities of Aalborg and Southern Denmark. It resulted in five research reports on how to design appropriate RCHs. In 2010, new national guidelines were launched that promoted the so-called model programme.[51] This programme adopts the ageing user's perspective, and supplies detailed requirements for the new type of RCH architecture, both architecturally and financially.

The lower Norwegian proportion of older people is the probable cause for the slower preparation for an ageing welfare society in comparison with Denmark and Sweden. The Norwegian graph demonstrates a considerable decline in the number of competitions between 2003 and 2005. It is likely that this recession can be tied to the work of the Norwegian ministry for planning and built environment. In Norway, it is customary to use guiding design principles rather than imperative financial and functional demands to respect. New guidelines concerning appropriate housing for older people in general and RCHs in particular were published in 2009.[52] These guidelines introduce a holistic approach towards architecture for later stages in life by forwarding environmental aspects in the architectural design that are essential for able and fit senior people as well as dependent and frail older persons. These variables are linked with the concept of Universal Design, UD, which have been introduced broadly in Norway since 2007 (also, in Denmark the same year). The UD thinking equips the tandem concept of accessibility and usability in the building code with new leverage to adjust the built environment in order to promote social inclusion for all, regardless of the individual's cognitive or physical capacities.

The Swedish graph demonstrates how the matter of appropriate housing for older people has materialized as an item for the interior political agenda on a regular basis, often in conjunction with the definition of more refined socio-political goals. Since 1982, and with some input from Denmark, which also embraces the idea, the notion of "ageing in place" has influenced the Swedish manner of promoting high architectural quality in housing for senior Swedes, both able and fit elderly and dependent and frail older persons. The Swedish drop in the use of architectural competitions can be linked to a report from the Swedish Board of Health and Social Welfare (NBSW), published in 2006, which highlighted a considerable drop of 22% in the number of available apartments in RCHs, occurring during the first 5 years of the new millennium. [53] This drop was attributed to a municipal reluctance to supply this type of housing, and, instead, promote extended home care services in the ordinary housing. Causing a public dismay with eldercare, the Swedish government appointed a parliamentary committee, the Delegation on Elderly Living, which investigated the matter of appropriate housing for older people over the period 2006-2008. This resulted in two reports : In 2007, a report on ordinary housing for older people in general, [54] followed by a second one in 2008, which targeted RCHs for dependent and frail older persons. [55] In 2010 the Swedish government allocated 50 million Swedish Crowns in order to organize new architectural competitions on space for the fit and the frail ageing. [56] These events fit the edgy look of the Swedish graph for the period of 2008 and 2012. [57]

The present study is a comparative study on architectural competitions in Denmark, Norway and Sweden concerning competition forms and programmes that are used for producing RCH architecture intended for dependent and frail older people and to be used by the local eldercare organization. Several research methods were used to triangulate parallel sources of knowledge about the processes ; close reading, document analyses, interviews, questionnaires, and pattern matching. [58] The study assumed an abductive analysis that aimed at understanding the use of architectural competitions in these Nordic countries in order to realize socio-political ambitions concerning space for the dependent and frail ageing process. [59] This analytic approach was used on a comprehensive level that encompassed the full sample of 77 competitions, and on a sub-level that focused on the wording of programming documentation of 9 separate competitions.

Given the on-going ageing process of the world, the study demonstrated that architectural competitions intended for the dependent and frail ageing process were more of a national than international nature. This type of architecture depended upon the socio-political visions that had assembled during the development of the existing type of a welfare regime. Ipso facto, architectural competitions concerning space for the dependent and frail ageing were part of local and public procurement processes. To some extent, this circumstance challenged the acknowledged plethora of organizational forms for competitions. An overall conclusion from this study is that architecture competitions on new RCH facilities in the three Nordic countries in focus for this study constitute a closed arena for architects who are not familiar with the Nordic contexts and languages. This circumstance tends to block the integration of international findings on universal space for ageing well.

# ▬ Notes

[1] EUROSTAT. Population at 1 January between 2000 and 2011. European Commission. (Strasbourg : European Commission).

[2] Council of Europe. *Recent Demographic Developments in Europe, 2004.*" Council of Europe Publishing. (Strasbourg : Council of Europe, 2005).

[3] NBHW, *Öppna jämförelser inom vården och omsorgen om äldre. Verksamhetens kvalitet. [Open comparative data on caregivning for older persons. On quality of care]*. Socialstyrelsen [National Board of Health and Welfare, NBHW]. (Stockholm : Socialstyrelsen, 2007).

M. G. Parker, K. Ahacic, and M. Thorslund, "Health Changes among Swedish Oldest Old : Prevalences Rates from 1992 to 2002 Show Increasing Health Problems." *Journal of Gerontology : Medical Sciences* 60A (2005).

[4] J. E. Andersson, *Architecture and Ageing. On the Interaction between Frail Older People and the Built Environment.* "Architecture and social ideals for dependent and frail older people."

[5] J. E. Andersson, "Architecture and the Swedish welfare state : three architectural competitions that innovated space for the dependent and frail ageing." *Journal of Ageing & Society.* February, no. 2014. (2014) :1-28.

J. E. Andersson, "Architecture and social ideals for dependent and frail older people." *Anthology about housing for Danish older people (in press)*. Aalborg Universitet. Ed. T. Rostgaard & P. H. Jensen. (Aalborg : Aalborg Universitet [Aalborg University], in press).

M. Dobloug, *Bak verket. Kunnskapsfelt og formgenerende faktorer i nyttearkitektur 1935-1985*. Arkitektur- og designhøgskolen i Oslo, AHO. (Oslo : AHO, 2006).

[6] J. E. Andersson, "Architecture and social ideals for dependent and frail older people."

[7] J. E. Andersson, *Architecture and Ageing. On the Interaction between Frail Older People and the Built Environment.* Kungl. Tekniska Högskolan, KTH [Royal Institute of Technology]. (Stockholm : Kungl. Tekniska Högskolan, 2011).

[8] M. Dobloug, *Bak verket. Kunnskapsfelt og formgenerende faktorer i nyttearkitektur 1935-1985.*

[9] FRI, *FRI-Survey of Architectural and Consulting Engineering Services.* Foreningen af rådgivende ingenjører, FRI [Danish Association of Consulting Engineers]. (Copenhagen : FRI, 1998).

[10] SA, *Tävlingsregler För Svenska Tävlingar Inom Arkitekternas, Ingenjörernas Och Konstnärernas Verksamhetsfält*. Sveriges Arkitekter, SA [Swedish Association of Architects] http ://www.arkitekt.se/s12794.

[11] FRI., FRI-Survey of Architectural and Consulting Engineering Services." SOU2008 :15, *Lov att välja — Lag om valfrihetssystem.*

[12] R. Kazemian, M. Rönn, and C. Svensson, *Arkitekturtävlingar : Erfarenheter Från Finland* (Stockholm : AXL Books, 2007).

[13] The different regulatory statuses, which are found in the European countries and in the US, make it difficult to use a universal term for architecture intended for the dependant and frail ageing process. The American equivalent would be assisted living, and the equivalent term in French would be the EHPAD, (l'établissement d'hébergement pour des personnes dépendantes et âgées). Sources : G. J. Andrews & D. R. Philips, *Ageing and Place. Perspectives, policy, practice.* (London and New York : Routledge, Taylor & Francis Group. 2005). P. Dehan, *L'habitat des personnes âgées, du logement adapté aux EHPAD, USLD, et Unités Alzheimer.* Ed. Le Moniteur. (Paris : Le Moniteur, 2007).

[14] G. Bloxham Zettersten, *Political Behaviour and Architectonic Vision : Two Swedish/ Danish Processes in Comtemporary Public Architecture* . Chalmers Tekniska Högskola, Chalmers [Chalmers University of Technology] (Gothenburg : Chalmers, 2007).

P. Bourdieu, *Esquisse d'une théorie de la pratique. Précédé de trois études d'ethnologie Kabyle.* Edition 2000 (Paris : Éditions Seuil, 1972).

[15] G. Esping-Andersen, *The Three Worlds of Welfare Capitalism.* (Cambridge : Polity Press, 1990), 80.

[16] H.J.M. Fenger, "Welfare Regimes in Central and Eastern Europe : Incorporating Post-Communist Countries in a Welfare Regime Typology." *Contemporary Issues and Ideas in Social Sciences.* August, no. 2007 (2007) : 5.

Esping-Andersen, *The Three Worlds of Welfare Capitalism.*, 80.

[17] *The Three Worlds of Welfare Capitalism.*

[18] Fenger, "Welfare Regimes in Central and Eastern Europe : Incorporating Post-Communist Countries in a Welfare Regime Typology." 6.

Esping-Andersen, *The Three Worlds of Welfare Capitalism.* 26-33.

[19] Fenger, "Welfare Regimes in Central and Eastern Europe : Incorporating Post-Communist Countries in a Welfare Regime Typology." 6.

Esping-Andersen, *The Three Worlds of Welfare Capitalism.* 26-33.

[20] Fenger, "Welfare Regimes in Central and Eastern Europe : Incorporating Post-Communist Countries in a Welfare Regime Typology." 6.

Esping-Andersen, *The Three Worlds of Welfare Capitalism.* 26-33.

[21] NBHW, *Uppföljning av äldreomsorg i Danmark, Norge, England och Kanada.* Szebehely, "Äldreomsorgsforskning i Norden. En kunskapsöversikt."

[22] NBHW, *Uppföljning av äldreomsorg i Danmark, Norge, England och Kanada.* Szebehely, "Äldreomsorgsforskning i Norden. En kunskapsöversikt. "

[23] "Äldreomsorgsforskning i Norden. En kunskapsöversikt."

[24] NBHW, *Uppföljning av äldreomsorg i Danmark, Norge, England och Kanada.* SOU2008 :15, *Lov att välja. Lag om valfrihetssystem [Free to choice. Law concerning the principle of free choice]*. SOU2008 :15. (Stockholm : Statens Offentliga Utredningar [Swedish Government Official Report], 2008).

Szebehely, "Äldreomsorgsforskning i Norden. En kunskapsöversikt."

[25] "Äldreomsorgsforskning i Norden. En kunskapsöversikt.."

[26] NOSOSKO, *Social tryghed i de nordiske lande 2008/09. Omfang, udgifter og finansiering. [Social security in the Nordic countries 2008 and 2009. Expenses, financing and volume]*. Nordisk Socialstatistisk Komité. Ed. J. Nielsen. (Copenhagen : Nordisk Socialstatistisk Komité, NOSOSKO 2011).

[27] M. Jegermalm, *Carers in the Welfare State. On Informal Care and Support for Carers in Sweden*. Stockholms Universitet. (Stockholm : Stockholms Universitet [Stockholm University], 2005).

[28] L. Fratiglioni et al., *Multipla hälsoproblem bland personer över 60 år. En systematisk litteraturöversikt om förekomst, konsekvenser och vård [Multiple Health Issues among People over 60 Years. A Systematic Overview of Prevalence, Consequences and Care]*. SOU2010 :48. (Stockholm : Statens Offentliga Utredningar [Swedish Government Official Report], 2010).

[29] SFS1970 :994, *Hyreslagen [Lease and Tenancy Agreement Act]*. SFS1970 :994 (Stockholm : Sveriges Riksdag [Swedish Parliament], 1970).

[30] B. Cold, H. Dunin-Woyseth, and B. Sauge, "Om arkitekturforskning og arkitekturforskningslandskapet i Norge. [On Architectural Research and the Topography of Architectural Research in Norway]. *Nordisk Arkitekturforskning*, no. 2 (1992) :8-19.

[31] Vitruvius, *Ten Books on Architecture.* Cambridge University. I. D. Rowland (translation and T. Noble Howe (illustrations), Eds. (Cambridge : Cambridge University Press, 1999).

[32] J. Lundequist, *Design och produktutveckling. Metoder och begrepp [Design and Product Development. Methods and Notions]* (Lund : Studentlitteratur, 1995).

D. Schön, *The Reflective Practitionner. How Professionals Think in Action.* Paperback edition. (Aldershot, UK. : Ashgate Publishing Limited, 1983 ; repr., 2003).

[33] G. Bachelard, *La poétique de l'espace.* 8th ed. (Paris : Quadrige/ PUF, 1957).

Bourdieu, *Esquisse d'une théorie de la pratique. Précédé de trois études d'ethnologie Kabyle.*

H. Lefebvre, *La Production de l'espace*, 4th Edition ed. (Paris : Anthropos, 1985).

[34] J. Darke, "The Primary Generator and the Design Process." *Design Studies* 1, no. 1, July 1979 (1979).

U. Jansson, *Vägen Till Verket. Studier I Jan Gezelius Arbetsprocess.* Chalmers Tekniska Högskola, Chalmers. (Gothenburg : Chalmers, 1998).

[35] Dobloug, *Bak verket. Kunnskapsfelt og formgenerende faktorer i nyttearkitektur 1935-1985.*

E Tostrup, *Architecture and Rhetoric. Text and Design in Architectural Competitions, Oslo 1939-1997.* (London : Andreas Papadakis Publisher Ltd, 1999).

[36] Tostrup, *Architecture and Rhetoric. Text and Design in Architectural Competitions, Oslo 1939-1997.*

[37] J. Darke, "The Primary Generator and the Design Process," *Developments in Design Methodology.* Ed. N. Cross. (New York : John Wiley & Sons, 1984) : 36-44.

[38] J. E. Andersson, "Creating Empathetic Architecture for the Frail Elderly. Socio-Political Goals as Criteria in an Architectural Competition." *The Architectural Competition. Research Inquiries and Experiences.,*

[39] J. E. Andersson, "Creating Empathetic Architecture for the Frail Elderly. Socio-Political Goals as Criteria in an Architectural Competition." *The Architectural Competition. Research Inquiries and Experiences.,* M. Rönn, R. Kazemian, and J. E. Andersson, eds. (Stockholm : Axl Books, 2011) :261-301.

[40] R. Johansson, "Ett bra fall är ett steg framåt. Om fallstudier, historiska studier och historiska Studier." *Nordisk Arkitekturforskning* 2000, no. 1-2 (2000) : 65-71.

R. E. Stake, *The Art of Case Study Research* (Thousand Oaks : CA : Sage, 1995).

R. K. Yin, *Case Study Research, Design and Methods,* Third edition. (Thousands Oaks : Sage Publications, Inc, 2003).

[41] B. Brummett, *Techniques of Close Reading.* SAGE (Los Angeles : SAGE Publications, 2010).

[42] Andersson, "Creating Empathetic Architecture for the Frail Elderly. Socio-Political Goals as Criteria in an Architectural Competition."

[43] BL. Gunnarsson, "Applied Discourse Analysis." *Discourse as Social Interaction.* Ed. Teun A Van Dijk, (London Thousands Oaks New Dehli : SAGE Publications, 1998) : 285-312.

[44] S Foss, *Rhetorical Criticism, Exploration and Practice* (Prospect Heights Illinois : Waveland Press, 1989).

M Karlberg and B Mral, *Heder och påverkan, att analysera modern retorik* (Stockholm : Natur och Kultur, 2006).

[45] European Commission, *Council Directive of 18 June 1992 Relating to the Coordination of Procedures for the Award of Public Service Contracts.* 1992L0050-EN-0105.2004-005.001-1 (European Union : 1992).

[46] J. E. Andersson, "Architecture and the Swedish welfare state : three architectural competitions that innovated space for the dependent and frail ageing."

J. E. Andersson, "Architecture and social ideals for dependent and frail older people." *Anthology about housing for Danish older people (in press).*

M. Dobloug, *Bak verket. Kunnskapsfelt og formgenerende faktorer i nyttearkitektur 1935-1985.*

[47] G. Bloxham Zettersten, "The Building of Visions and the Municipal Client's Role ? Findings from an Investigation into Architectural Competitions 1900-1955 for Nordic Civic Projects, as Reconsidered in the Present." *The Architectural Competition. Research Inquiries and Experiences.* M. Rönn, R. Kazemian, and J. E. Andersson, eds. (Stockholm : Axl Books 2010).

[48] SFS1991 :900, *Kommunallagen (Local Government Act).*

[49] J. E. Andersson, "Competition Programs as Socio-Political Instruments for Municipal Architecture Competitions : The Organizer's Articulation of Welfare Goals Concerning Dependent Seniors." *Nordic Journal of Architectural Research.* no. 1 (2012) : 65-96.

[50] Akademisk Arkitektforning, *Hvilken form ?* [*What type of competition ?*] Akademisk Arkitektforening, AA [Danish Association of Architects] (Copenhagen : Akademisk Arkitektforening, 2012).

[51] Erhvervs&Byggestyrelsen, *Modelprogram for plejeboliger.* Erhvervs-og Byggestyrelsen [Danish Authority for Business and Building]. (Copenhagen : Erhvervs- og Byggestyrelsen, 2010). See also *www.modelprogram.dk.*

[52] Husbanken, *Rom for trygghet og omsorg. Veileder for udforming av omsorgsboliger og sykehjem* [Space for Care and Security. Guidelines for the Design of Assisted Living and Nursing Homes]. Den norske stats husbank [Norwegian State Housing Bank]. (Oslo : Husbanken, 2009).

[53] NBHBP and NBHW, *Varför kan inte behovet av särskilda boendeformer tillgodoses ?* Boverket & Socialstyrelsen [ Board of Housing, Building and Planning & Board of Health and Welfare] (Stockholm : Boverket & Socialstyrelsen, 2004).

[54] SOU2007 :103, *Bo för att leva. Seniorbostäder och trygghetsbostäder."* Äldreboendedelegationen [Delegation on Elderly Living] (Stockholm : Statens Offentliga Utredningar [Swedish Government Official Report], 2007).

[55] SOU2008 :113, *Bo Bra Hela Livet. Slutbetänkande.* Äldreboendedelegationen [Delegation on Elderly Living]. (Stockholm : Statens Offentliga Utredningar [Swedish Government Office Report], 2008).

[56] SIAT, *Bo Bra På Äldre Da'r.* Hjälpmedelsinstitutet [Swedish Institute on Assistive Technology, SIAT], *http ://www.hi.se/sv-se/Arbetsomraden/ Projekt/bobrapaaldredar/.*

[57] J. E. Andersson and M. Rönn, Searching for innovative design : architectural competitions in the silvering Swedish welfare state. *Journal of Housing for the elderly.* (In press). (2014).

[58] Brummett, *Techniques of Close Reading.*

Johansson, "Ett bra fall är ett steg framåt. Om fallstudier, historiska studier och Historiska fallstudier."

Stake, *The Art of Case Study Research.*

Yin, *Case Study Research, Design and Methods.*

[59] R. Johansson, "Om abduktion, intuition och syntes." *Nordisk Arkitekturforskning* 2000, no. 3 (2000) : 13-19.

R. Johansson, "Ett explikativt angreppssätt. Fallstudiemetodikens utveckling, logiska grund och betydelse i arkitekturforskningen." *Nordisk Arkitekturforskning* 2002, no. 2 (2002) :19-29.

G. Pearce and L. Geoffrey, "Viva Voce (Oral Examination) as an Assessment Method. Insights from Marketing Students," *Journal of Marketing Education* 31, no. 2 (2009) :120-130.

# ■■■ References

**Akademisk Arkitektforening,** *Hvilken form ?* [*What type of competition ?*] Akademisk Arkitektforening, AA [Danish Association of Architects] (Copenhagen : Akademisk Arkitektforening, 2012).

**Andersson,** J. E. *Architecture and Ageing. On the Interaction between Frail Older People and the Built Environment.* Kungl. Tekniska Högskolan, KTH [Royal Institute of Technology]. (Stockholm : Kungl. Tekniska Högskolan, 2011).

"Creating Empathetic Architecture for the Frail Elderly. Socio-Political Goals as Criteria in an Architectural Competition." *The Architectural Competition. Research Inquiries and Experiences,* M. **Rönn,** R. **Kazemian,** and J. E. **Andersson,** eds. (Stockholm : Axl Books, 2011) :261-301.

"Competition Programs as Socio-Political Instruments for Municipal Architecture Competitions : The Organizer's Articulation of Welfare Goals Concerning Dependent Seniors." *Nordic Journal of Architectural Research.* no. 1 (2012) : 65-96.

"Architecture and the Swedish welfare state : three architectural competitions that innovated space for the dependent and frail ageing." *Journal of Ageing & Society.* February, no. 2014. (2014) :1-28.

"Architecture and social ideals for dependent and frail older people." *Anthology about housing for Danish older people (in press).* Aalborg Universitet. Ed. T. **Rostgaard** & P. H. **Jensen.** (Aalborg : Aalborg Universitet [Aalborg University], in press).

**Andersson**, J. E. & **Rönn**, R. Searching for innovative design : architectural competitions in the silvering Swedish welfare state. *Journal of Housing for the elderly.* (In press). (2014).

**Andrews**, G. J., & **Philips**, D. R. *Ageing and Place. Perspectives, policy, practice.* (London and New York : Routledge, Taylor & Francis Group. 2005).

**Bachelard**, G., *La poétique de l'espace.* 8th ed. (Paris : Quadrige/ PUF, 1957). Bloxham

**Bloxham Zettersten**, G., *Political Behaviour and Architectonic Vision : Two Swedish/ Danish Processes in Contemporary Public Architecture.* Chalmers Tekniska Högskola, Chalmers [Chalmers University of Technology] (Gothenburg : Chalmers, 2007).

"The Building of Visions and the Municipal Client's Role ? Findings from an Investigation into Architectural Competitions 1900-1955 for Nordic Civic Projects, as Reconsidered in the Present." *The Architectural Competition. Research Inquiries and Experiences.* M. **Rönn**, R. **Kazemian**, and J. E. **Andersson**, eds. (Stockholm : Axl Books 2010).

**Bourdieu**, P. *Esquisse d'une théorie de la pratique. Précédé de trois études d'ethnologie Kabyle.* Edition 2000 (Paris : Éditions Seuil, 1972).

**Brummett**, B., *Techniques of Close Reading.* SAGE (Los Angeles : SAGE Publications, 2010).

**Cold**, B., **Dunin-Woyseth**, H., and **Sauge**, B., «Om arkitekturforskning og arkitekturforsknings-landskapet i Norge. [On Architectural Research and the Topography of Architectural Research in Norway]. *Nordisk Arkitekturforskning*, no. 2 (1992) :8-19.

**Council of Europe**. *Recent Demographic Developments in Europe, 2004.* Council of Europe Publishing. (Strasbourg : Council of Europe, 2005).

**Darke**, J., "The Primary Generator and the Design Process." *Design Studies*, no. 1, July 1979 (1979).

**Darke**, J., "The Primary Generator and the Design Process," *Developments in Design Methodology*. N. **Cross**, ed. (New York : John Wiley & Sons, 1984) : 36-44.

**Dehan**, P. *L'habitat des personnes âgées, du logement adapté aux EHPAD, USLD, et unités Alzheimer.* Ed. Le Moniteur. (Paris : Le Moniteur, 2007).

**Dobloug**, M. Bak verket. *Kunnskapsfelt og formgenerende faktorer i nyttearkitektur 1935-1985.* Arkitektur- og designhoegskolen i Oslo, AHO. (Oslo : AHO, 2006).

**European Commission**, *Council Directive of 18 June 1992 Relating to the Coordination of Procedures for the Award of Public Service Contracts.* 1992L0050-EN-0105.2004-005.001-1 (European Union : 1992).

**Erhvervs- & Byggestyrelsen**, *Modelprogram for plejeboliger.* Erhvervs- og Byggestyrelsen [Danish Authority for Business and Building]. (Copenhagen : Erhvervs- og Byggestyrelsen, 2010).

**EUROSTAT**. *Population at 1 January between 2000 and 2011.* European Commission. (Strasbourg : European Commission, 2011).

**Esping-Andersen**, G. *The Three Worlds of Welfare Capitalism.* (Cambridge : Polity Press, 1990).

**Fenger**, H.J.M. "Welfare Regimes in Central and Eastern Europe : Incorporating Post-Communist Countries in a Welfare Regime Typology." *Contemporary Issues and Ideas in Social Sciences.* August, no. 2007 (2007) : 5.

**Foss**, S., *Rhetorical Criticism, Exploration and Practice* (Prospect Heights Illinois : Waveland Press, 1989).

**Fratiglioni L. et al.**, *Multipla hälsoproblem bland personer över 60 år. En systematisk litteraturöversikt om förekomst, konsekvenser och vård* [Multiple Health Issues among People over 60 Years. A Systematic Overview of Prevalence, Consequences and Care]. SOU2010 :48. (Stockholm : Statens Offentliga Utredningar [Swedish Government Official Report], 2010).

**FRI**, *FRI-Survey of Architectural and Consulting Engineering Services.* Foreningen af rådgivende ingenioerer, FRI [Danish Association of Consulting Engineers]. (Copenhagen : FRI, 1998).

**Gunnarsson**, B-L. "Applied Discourse Analysis." *Discourse as Social Interaction.* Teun A Van Dijk, ed. (London Thousand Oaks New Delhi : SAGE Publications, 1998) : 285-312.

**Husbanken**, *Rom for trygghet og omsorg. Veileder for udforming av omsorgsboliger og sykehjem* [Space for Care and Security. Guidelines for the Design of Assisted Living and Nursing Homes]. Den norske stats husbank [Norwegian State Housing Bank]. (Oslo : Husbanken, 2009).

**Jansson**, U., *Vägen till verket. Studier i Jan Gezelius arbetsprocess.* Chalmers Tekniska Högskola, Chalmers. (Gothenburg : Chalmers, 1998).

**Jegermalm**, M., *Carers in the Welfare State. On Informal Care and Support for Carers in Sweden.* Stockholms Universitet, [Stockholm University]. (Stockholm : Stockholms Universitet, 2005).

**Johansson**, R., "Ett bra fall är ett steg framåt. Om fallstudier, historiska studier och historiska Studier." *Nordisk Arkitekturforskning.*, no. 1-2 (2000) : 65-71.

"Om abduktion, intuition och syntes." *Nordisk Arkitekturforskning.*, no. 3 (2000) : 13-19.

"Ett explikativt angreppssätt. Fallstudiemetodikens utveckling, logiska grund och betydelse i arkitekturforskningen." *Nordisk Arkitekturforskning.*, no. 2 (2002) :19-29.

**Karlberg**, M. and **Mral**, B., *Heder och påverkan, att analysera modern retorik* (Stockholm : Natur och Kultur, 2006).

**Kazemian**, R., **Rönn**, R. and **Svensson**, C., *Arkitekturtävlingar : erfarenheter från Finland* (Stockholm : AXL Books, 2007).

**Lundequist**, J. *Design och produktutveckling. Metoder och begrepp* [Design and Product Development. Methods and Notions] (Lund : Studentlitteratur, 1995).

**Lefebvre**, H., *La Production de l'espace*, 4th Edition ed. (Paris : Anthropos, 1985).

**NBHW**, *Öppna jämförelser inom vården och omsorgen om äldre. Verksamhetens kvalitet.* [Open comparative data on caregivning for older persons. On quality of care]. Socialstyrelsen [National Board of Health and Welfare, NBHW]. (Stockholm : Socialstyrelsen, 2007).

*Uppföljning av äldreomsorg i Danmark, Norge, England Och Kanada.* [Follow-up of eldercare in Canada, Denmark, Norway and the UK]. Socialstyrelsen [National Board of Health and Welfare, NBHW]. (Stockholm : Socialstyrelsen, 2009).

**NBHBP and NBHW**, *Varför kan inte behovet av särskilda boendeformer tillgodoses ?* Boverket & Socialstyrelsen [National Board of Housing, Building and Planning & National Board of Health and Welfare] (Stockholm : Boverket & Socialstyrelsen, 2004).

**NOSOSKO**, *Social tryghed i de nordiske lande 2008/09.* Omfang, udgifter og finansiering. [Social security in the Nordic countries 2008 and 2009. Expenses, financing and volume]. Nordisk Socialstatistisk Komité. Ed. J. Nielsen. (Copenhagen : Nordisk Socialstatistisk Komité, NOSOSKO 2011).

**Parker**, M. G., **Ahacic**, K. and **Thorslund**, M. "Health Changes among Swedish Oldest Old : Prevalences Rates from 1992 to 2002 Show Increasing Health Problems." *Journal of Gerontology : Medical Sciences* 60A (2005).

**Pearce**, G., and **Geoffrey**, L., "Viva Voce (Oral Examination) as an Assessment Method. Insights from Marketing Students", *Journal of Marketing Education 31*, no. 2 (2009) :120-130.

**SA**, *Tävlingsregler För Svenska Tävlingar Inom Arkitekternas, Ingenjörernas Och Konstnärernas Verksamhetsfält.* Sveriges Arkitekter, SA [Swedish Association of Architects] http ://www.arkitekt.se/s12794.

**SIAT**, *Bo Bra På Äldre Da'r.* Hjälpmedelsinstitutet [Swedish Institute on Assistive Technology, SIAT], http ://www.hi.se/sv-se/Arbetsomraden/ Projekt/bobrapaaldredar/.

**Schön**, D. *The Reflective Practitionner. How Professionals Think in Action.* Paperback edition. (Aldershot, UK. : Ashgate Publishing Limited, 1983 ; repr., 2003).

**SFS1970 :994**, *Hyreslagen* [Lease and Tenancy Agreement Act]. SFS1970 :994 (Stockholm : Sveriges Riksdag [Swedish Parliament], 1970).

**SFS1980 :620**, *Socialtjänstlagen, SoL.* [Social Services Act]. SFS1980 :620 (Stockholm : Sveriges Riksdag [Swedish Parliament], 1980).

**SFS1991 :900**, *Kommunallagen* [Local Government Act]." SFS1991 :900

(Stockholm : Sveriges Riksdag [Swedish Parliament], 1991).

**SOU2008:15**, *Lov att välja. Lag om valfrihetssystem* [*Free to choice. Law concerning the principle of free choice*]. SOU2008:15. (Stockholm : Statens Offentliga Utredningar [Swedish Government Official Report], 2008).

**SOU2007:103**, *Bo för att leva. Seniorbostäder och trygghetsbostäder.* [*Dwellings for living. Senior housing and safe haven residences*]. Äldreboendedelegationen [Delegation on Elderly Living] (Stockholm : Statens Offentliga Utredningar [Swedish Government Official Report], 2007).

**SOU2008:113**, *Bo Bra Hela Livet. Slutbetänkande.* [*Appropriate dwellings for all stages in life. Final report*]. Äldreboendedelegationen [Delegation on Elderly Living]. (Stockholm : Statens Offentliga Utredningar [Swedish Government Office Report], 2008).Stake, R. E., The Art of Case Study Research (Thousand Oaks : CA : Sage, 1995).

**Stake**, R. E. *The Art of Case Study Research*. Thousand Oaks : CA : Sage, 1995.

**Szebehely,** M., "Äldreomsorgsforskning i Norden. En kunskapsöversikt." [Research on Nordic eldercare, an overview]. *TemaNord 2005:508*, Ed. M. Szebehely (Copenhagen : Nordic Council, 2005).

**Tostrup**, E., *Architecture and Rhetoric. Text and Design in Architectural Competitions*. Oslo 1939-1997. (London : Andreas Papadakis Publisher Ltd, 1999).

**Vitruvius**, *Ten Books on Architecture*. Cambridge University. I. D. Rowland (translation and T. Noble Howe (illustrations), Eds. (Cambridge : Cambridge University Press, 1999).

**Yin R. K.**, *Case Study Research, Design and Methods*, Third edition. (Thousand Oaks : Sage Publications, Inc, 2003).

# 1.5. Greek Concerns and Global Regulations

**Four Competitions for the New Acropolis Museum (1976 - 2000)**

**Sofia Paisiou**, Ph.D.
Institute of Architecture, University of Applied Sciences and Arts Northwestern Switzerland FHNW
Switzerland

Architectural competitions, despite their international appeal and reputation, emerge from the local conditions of *diverse construction scenes*. The definition and rules of competitions are usually connected to the architect's chambers and/or architectural societies. However, the architectural competition may be thought of as an organizational platform derived from local issues and constraints, which framed the urban projects conforming to international regulations and economic rules. International rules and agreements influence the local and global construction scene and provide new regulations for the diverse types of procedures such as tendering, design contest, and parallel studies.

We examine the competitions for the *New Acropolis Museum* in, illustrating how the international and European regulations "landed" on the Greek construction scene, and transformed the competition institutions by altering their procedural structure, thus affecting the competitions' trajectory towards realization. We conclude that the internationalization of design, construction services, and construction markets has multiple affects on the appropriateness of competitions. These affects can be thought of as a network of interrelated reactions and work in multiple levels. These transformations may actually strengthen the competition as an institution and make it flexible to respond to an evolving international landscape.

**Cover**
The arrival of the first sculpture with protests (red panel) at the door of the site.
*Courtesy of Nikos Daniilidis, photographer.*

When private bodies or public authorities spend money in the building sector they are bound to national and international agreements and regulations. International organizations, such as the World Trade Organization, support multilateral trade systems, free trade areas and common market initiatives like the European Union with its common market, the Mercosur in Latin America, the NAFTA for North America and Mexico, or the ASEAN in Asia. A growing volume of building projects have become subject to these international rules and agreements. In other words, these international regulations "connect" the building "problem" to one specific project, or the "job offer" of a client to a specific service. Since 1980 there has been a rapid evolution and growing importance of the procurement systems that are currently being used for architectural and design services[1]. According to Strong[2], the typical procurement system used for the aforementioned services typically distinguishes between three systems of selection: the tendering for the work or call for offers, the selective search to identify a suitable designer, and the architectural competition. In the case of European Union, procurement regulations are captured in special EU Directives 2004/18/EG (European Parliament, Council, 2004a) and 2004/17/EG (European Parliament, Council, 2004b).[3] In this article we argue, and illustrate with the case study for the New Acropolis Museum (NAM), that the internationalization of design, construction services, and markets affects architectural competitions by influencing the structure or modus operandi of the diverse procurement types and thus their results.

To investigate the ways in which the internationalization of design, construction services and construction markets affects the appropriateness of competitions our study will follow two interrelated perspectives:

We first study the appropriateness of competitions in terms of procedure, illustrating how different procurements can be thought as more appropriate to answer current needs. Secondly, we focus on the outcomes of these procurements and study the appropriateness of competitions in terms of results. In other words, how do the local and the global, the economic and the cultural, the ecological and the aesthetic intertwine in the outcome of jury decision-making?

In the first part of this article we briefly introduce the history of competitions, using assemblage theory[4] as a sound basis to conceptualize the "folding in" and also the enduring heterogeneity of the component parts of a competition process.[5]

In the second part of the article we present the case study of the NAM. Here, we study the affect of the internationalization of design, construction services and construction markets on the appropriateness of competitions for the NAM by focusing on two aforementioned perspectives: the procedural organizations and the outcomes. As such, we illustrate how different procurement "platforms" bring together different organizations for the main concerns of the NAM and we study the result that lead to the temporal actualizations and realization.

We conclude that the internationalization of design, construction services and construction markets has multiple affects on the appropriateness of competitions. We argue that these affects may actually strengthen the competition as an institution and make it flexible to evolve in evolving landscape.

## ▬ A Brief Review of the (International) Tradition of Competitions
### Historical and Conceptual Trajectories of Competitions
Architectural competitions, despite their international appeal and reputation, emerged "genealogically" from the local conditions of diverse construction scenes. The definition and rules of these procedures were usually connected with the architects' chambers and/or the architectural societies.[6] More specifically, although the architectural competition is a widely used instrument with a long history, competitions present variations on the procedural types in different countries. Competitions are very flexible procedures, and have evolved to meet the local traditions of the built sector.[7]

Beginning ancient Greece, the competition procedure travelled in space and in time to Italy, and in the sixteenth century, the Italian academic competition system (Concorsi Clementi) emerged with the main goal of architectural pedagogy.[8] In the seventeenth century, the French academic competition system refined the Italian model by introducing the two-stage format–competitions were introduced every month and were considered the heart of academic education. Following the economic and political transformation of the eighteenth century in France, the Revolutionary competition system emerged, deriving from the academic tradition, with the aim of a pluralistic expression and judgment in order to define the building types appropriate to the nation.

Similarly, the Victorian system in the nineteenth century brought forth economic and social changes in England: the expansion of open market principles and decrease in power of the elite and the aristocracy, as well as aspects from the French academic tradition. This system was widespread in England and directly influenced the architectural profession. An example of this influence was the emergence of "competition architects"; meaning architects that participate mainly in public competitions.[9] The particularity of the Victorian system is that it balanced the controversies between markets, styles and professions in England of the nineteenth century. Victorian competitions were transformed by introducing elements from the market competition and by echoing aspects of the French academic tradition, such as the use of two-stage procedures, or the "mistrust" towards perspective drawings.[10] Despite widespread use, the conditions and outcomes of Victorian competitions created strong discrepancies and contradictions in terms of procedural and architectural quality. In 1880, the Royal Institute of British Architects (RIBA) established a permanent committee to review the condition of all competitions and authorize members to participate, with the aim of strengthening architectural practice in terms of expertise and competence by means of competitions.[11] Similar measures were introduced in various other countries, like France (the regulations of 1893 of the French Union Syndicate) or Switzerland (SIA regulations of 1877).

The trajectory of contemporary Greek competitions began in 1830; their initial character was to cause wonder, as the majority of competitions dealt with public buildings of symbolic character. For example, the first competition of the free Greek state concerned the National Monument of the Revolution.[12] Competitions such as these attracted the public's attention, yet they rarely led to realized projects and were thus easily forgotten. Until 1964, competitions without any institutional consolidation were considered unimportant because they were ineffective or related with failures and scandals.[13] According to Filippides, the role of competitions changed due to the increase of international interest towards the unbuilt architecture or the architecture of Utopia. Competitions began to be taken seriously and the participation within competitions was considered important for an architect even if he did not win a prize. In Greece, the first national law for competition was created in 1970 and revisited in 1973. This law formulated a detailed framework for the overall process (selection of the jury, awards, creation of program, obligation of jurors, competitors, etc.) that begins with the following declaration: "An architectural competition [...] is realized only for important projects and if these projects are not an emergency or they are not in the need of very specific work and study" (F.E.K. 1970).

In the twenty-first century in Europe, new procurement regulations now formulate new competition variations, bringing together the "bid"-the economic procurement system and the competition system (Directives 92/50/EEC (European Economic Community,1992) "relating to the coordination of procedures for the award of public service contracts" and 2004/18/EC (European Parliament, Council, 2004) "on the coordination of procedures for the award of public works contracts, public supply contracts and public service contracts"). The Greek law changed to be in accordance with the aforementioned directive (F.E.K. 1998).

This brief look at the genealogy of competitions illustrates that the competition format can be read as a mode of initiating economic and professional change in the building sector. More precisely, the evolution of competitions illustrate that the emergence and transformation of the competition procedures is an international tradition emerging from different countries, but also strongly influenced by the local social and economic context.

With this perspective we argue and illustrate with the NAM case study that the institution of architectural competitions can be thought of as an organizational platform derived from local issues and constraints which framed the urban projects, conforming with international regulations and economic rules. In other words, to find the appropriate solution to an urban problem, architectural competitions need to fit in this twofold frame of international means and regulations and their "landing" to the local realities. In this sense, the appropriate procedure types are "created"–or hybridized–to fit the transforming urban environment and its problems. The architectural competition should therefore not be viewed in opposition to tendering, but rather as a more traditional form of organizing public construction markets. A client asks for a variety of propositions with regard to a given problem and then evaluates the entries to pick the best. Yet, architectural competitions display some key characteristics that are "incompatible" with tendering procedures today. For instance, it is not solely the client assessing the submitted architectural projects, but a jury that comprises of representatives of the client but also of external ("independent") experts. As we illustrate with the case of the NAM, the manner in which architectural competitions

**Fig. 1**
The third prize of the first
competition 1977 : architects
Kandreviotou, Avgoustinos.
*Kontaratos*

**Fig. 2**
The second prize of the second
competition 1979 : architects
Liakatas, Pechlivanidou.
*Architecture in Greece 1981, 224*

and new rules are brought together and deal with the "in-compatibilities" influence the organization of the process and result, thus the appropriateness of competitions.

### Assemblage Theory and the Singularities of the NAM

To investigate the ways in which the internationalization of design, construction services and construction markets affects the appropriateness of competitions we use an "adapted" Deleuzian Assemblage Theory. We argue that assemblage theory [14] provides a theoretical foundation for planning theory [15] and a sound basis to conceptualize the "folding in" and the enduring heterogeneity of the component parts of a public procurement process. More precisely, assemblage theory is based on non-linearity and replaces so-called interior relations with relations of exteriority. This exteriority of relations enables the reconceptualisation of the "political" in competitions as a messy intertwining of regulations and procedures, briefs, representations (both architectural plans and models as well as verbal presentations), personal networks as well as design and planning discourses. [16]

According to DeLanda [17], an assemblage can be viewed as a mostly unintended and not completely determined, emergent product. Its properties are not "given"; when not exercised, they are merely possible. An assemblage is therefore not only an actual formation but also, and in an explicit sense, a virtual one. In other words, assemblages comprise a field of actualities, the exercised properties of components, but also a field of virtuality, the potential properties of the components. Furthermore they comprise a generative field : the intensive, individuating level, which can be thought of as the morphogenetic process from a virtual state towards actualization. [18]

The concept of the virtual organization or "diagram" of singularities [19] is very useful for studying the NAM case. [20] We can consider the NAM problem staged by "singularities"–a set of "main concerns" around which a variety of actualizations of one problem emerge. [21] These virtual organizations are modulated during the trajectory of changing a place from imagination into reality. [22]

From the aforementioned perspective, assemblage theory can help us conceptualize and study the diverse and complex context of the NAM. The trajectory towards realization of the NAM project began after the Greek dictatorship (1967-1974) within a climate focused on the restoration of democracy, and the prospect of Greece becoming a member of the European Union–the prime minister considered the creation of the NAM as top priority.[23] Additional main concerns for the NAM were pollution and the need for a bigger museum to house new archaeological findings, which were being held in open air or old storehouses.[24] Furthermore, the problem of insufficient space was worsened by increased demands due to the large number of tourists who visited the Acropolis and its museum every year.[25]

Under these circumstances the first two competitions were launched in 1976 and 1979: these were one-stage national competitions governed by national laws. The initiator of the two national competitions was the Ministry of Culture. In 1977 Kandreviotou, Avgoustinos won third prize [Fig.1] and Katzourakis, Krokos and Papagianopoulos the fourth, and in 1981 Liakatas, Pechlivanidou won second prize [Fig.2] and Mpiris team the third and Asimomitis, Gerakis and Komninos the fourth.[26] Both competitions did not lead towards a contract or realization due to the restrictive nature of the site chosen for the new Museum in relation to the building program.[27] The site was the Makrigianni site, located on the southeast side of the Acropolis–a difficult building block, with several preservable buildings. The selection of the site created strong opposition from the Chamber of Architects (SADAS).[28]

The competitions of 1976 and 1979 revealed many other problems and concerns. The NAM was the first building project near the "sacred" hill of the Acropolis; its relationship between the Acropolis monument and the capacity of the Greek architecture to respond in a dignified way was also a point of focus. Additionally, the future NAM building had to address the relation between the contemporary city and the Greek society.[29]

1981 saw Greece's entrance into the European Union, and in 1987 the European Union began its trajectory towards a common market with the formulation of the Single European Act. These events signified the entrance of Greek architecture to the European or even global market. As Filippides[30] states, the fusion of Greek architecture with the European and international scene brought new elements to the urban environment such as the urban regeneration of historical sites and restoration of monuments and older buildings.

In the same period, the Minister of Culture aimed to promote Greek culture at home and abroad and prioritized support for the NAM project, as well as the conservation of the Acropolis monuments and the reunification of the Parthenon sculptures displayed in the British Museum. The new museum not only protects and houses the endangered international cultural heritage, its qualities work as a proof of the restoration of Greece and a restitution of its prestige.[31] Thus the initial main concerns for the NAM gain importance and relevance by entering "assemblages" like the "national identity" and "international cultural heritage of the Parthenon sculptures".[32]

The third competition for the NAM was announced in May 1989. It was an international two-stage ideas competition (the first phase ended in April 1990 and the second in November 1990) and followed the framework of the International Union of Architects (UIA). The intent of this competition was to reorganize in order to "fit" the political decision to link the return of the sculptures with the creation of the NAM.

Regarding the issue of the site, the third competition transferred the responsibility of choosing a site to the participants: they could choose between the Makrigianni site, the Dionissos site (with an exceptional view towards Acropolis hill but quite smaller plot), and the Koile site (without direct visual relation with the Acropolis).[33] First prize was awarded to Nicoletti and Passarelli for their "underground" project[34] located in the Makrigianni site. The second prize was awarded to the Mpiris group for their project in the Koile site, and third was awarded to Abraham for his project located in Makrigianni. In 1992 the Ministry of Culture signed the contract with Nicoletti and Passarelli.[35]

The possibility of locating the NAM at the Makrigianni site was the reason that SADAS opposed the international competition from the start, and suggested its members to abstain.[36] In February 1992, SADAS attacked the result of the third competition and instigated a lawsuit at the Supreme Administrative Court (SAC), arguing that the competition was illegal and should be considered invalid.[37] In 1993 the SAC cancelled the third competition on the grounds of formality.[38]

Under these changes and transformations new singularities appear to frame the NAM. ATTIKO METRO S.A. (AM) was created in 1991 (Law N 955/1991 in F.E.K. 1991) and it is financed 50% with European funds, 39% with European bank loans and 11% by the Greek state. AM implements the development of the Athens Metro network. In the first phase of the project, which started in 1992, important archaeological excavations were realized, in collaboration with the Ministry of culture, in the centre of Athens. The decision to locate the metro station in the area near Makrigianni site provided the opportunity to excavate further.[39] The excavation is 2500m$^2$ and unearthed houses, streets, workshops,

**Fig. 3**
Singularities that govern the NAM.
*Source : Sofia Paisiou*

2008 Oppening of the NAM

2004 Olympic games in Athens

EU (2004):
Council Directive
for the coordination of
procedures for the award
of public service contracts.

F.E.K (2000): N2819/2000
Creation of
Olimpiako xorio
(Olympic village)
and other legislation

2000 International closed tender for the NAM
1st prize to Tschumi & Fotiades

1999 second KAS report for the archelogical ruins
in Makrigianni site

F.E.K (1998):
P.D.346. Greek legislation for
the Council
Directive92/50/EEC

1999 definitively cancellation of the contract
by the minister of Minister of Culture E. Papazoi

F.E.K (1997): 909/15 1997
Creation of EAXA

1997 creation EAXA

1996 excavations at Makrigianni site

F.E.K (1994): N2260/94.
Organisation for the
creation of the new
Acropolis Museum

1994 creation OANMA

1993 SAC cancelled the 3rd competition
on the basis of opening the competitors' material
by the technical committee

contract in 1992 between Minister of Culture E. Papazoi
and M.Nicoletti & L.Passarelli

EEC (1992):
Council Directive 92/50/EEC
for the coordination of
procedures for the award
of public service contracts.

1992 lawsuit to Supreme Administrative Court (SAC)
from SADAS (the National Association of Architects)
against the 3rd competition

1992 excavations from Attiko Metro in Acropolis

F.E.K (1991): N955/1991
Attiko Metro S.A.

1991 Attiko Metro S.A.

1989 International two stage ideas comeptition for the NAM
1st prize to Nicoletti & Passarelli

first KAS report 1989 for the archelogical ruins
in Makrigianni site

1987 Single European Act

1984 official request for their return of Parthenon
sculptures submitted to UNESCO

1981 Greece in the E.U.

1979 National one stage Competition for the NAM
in Makrigianni site

1976 National one stage Competition for the NAM
in Makrigianni site

1967-1974 dictatorship

**LEGISLATION** | **EVENTS RELATED WITH NAM**

and other findings covering a period from 3000 B.C. until the Byzantine era. However, these excavations "shrank down" the Makrigianni site from 45000m$^2$ to 30000m$^2$. In 1999, three years after the ruins had been found, the competition and the contract were definitively cancelled by the minister of Minister of Culture. [40]

Furthermore, the initiator of the fourth competition in 2000 was the Organization for the Construction of the New Acropolis Museum (OANMA), created in 1994 according to a legislation related to a "new" singularity, the Olympic Games in 2004 (Laws N2260/94 and N2819/2000 in F.E.K. 2000). The OANMA is private, financed by the state and managed by a nine-member administrative committee, overseen by the Greek Ministry of Culture.

Another private institution strongly influencing in the NAM was the Unification of the Archaeological Sites of Athens S.A. (EAXA). EAXA was created in 1997 (F.E.K. 1997) and implemented a program for unification of the archaeological sites of Athens. The remodelling of Areopagitou Street, which is in front of Makrigianni site was one of the biggest projects of EAXA, began in 1999. [41]

The fourth competition was a part of a hybrid procurement process. The framework of the 2000 competition was given by the European Directive 92/50/EU (European Economic Community, 1992) and the relevant Greek laws. The process lasted from July 2000 to December 2001. The site proposed for the location was again the Makrigianni location, despite the fact of the huge archaeological excavations, the strict urban planning regulations and the long-term plan for expropriations. Tschumi and his Greek colleague Fotiades won the first prize. [42] OANMA and the winning teams moved rigorously towards its realization, and in 2008 the official opening of the NAM. The second prize went to the Libeskind and Potiropoulos proposal, which was a radical solution disregarding the basic of the tender for the reunification of the Parthenon marbles. [43] The third prize was awarded to Tombazis.

To conclude, with the help of assemblage theory we can conceptualize competitions as platforms, which allow the connection of the many **[Fig.3]**. As we illustrate in what follows, the changes in one set of relations of the NAM problem affect the capacities of competition component parts in other sets of relations. [44] Assemblage theory allows us to explore the changes related with aforementioned financial issues, issues of culture and global symbolism, local issues such as urban surroundings, architectural and archaeological concerns, as well as politics, in terms of what these changes "produce" and avoid endless descriptions and weak conceptualizations. [45]

## ▬ The Four Competitions for the NAM

In the previous section we describe the evolving urban landscape of the NAM problem with the help of assemblage theory. In what follows we study the competitions of the NAM and illustrate the appropriateness of the NAM competitions from the following perspectives:

Firstly, in terms procedural organization. We illustrate that each competition case for the NAM acted as a vehicle that brought negotiation to the diverse singularities that structure the NAM problem: the local and the global, the economic and the cultural. Secondly we focus on the outcome of these four cases procurements, and we study appropriateness of competitions in terms of results. In other words, how the local and the global, the economic and the cultural, intertwine in the jury outcome and decision-making.

The initial national competitions of 1976 and 1979 prioritized the democratic political vision of the prime minister and the start of a new European era for Greece. [46] These competitions were governed by the national law and attempted to solve the local problem, which focused one hand on the specific needs of the Parthenon sculptures in terms of space and light, versus the fact that this solution should be found in the small and awkward in shape Makrigianni site. [47] The awarded solutions were not satisfactory and did not lead to a contract, they were however more sensitive towards the existing historical Makrigianni site buildings. [48]

### 1989: An International Ideas Competition for the NAM.

Approximately ten years later, the third competition initiated in 1989. In the meantime the European "dream" was realized with the entrance of Greece into the European Union in 1981. These events enabled the ministry of culture to widely promote Greek culture at home and abroad, and prioritized support for the NAM project, as well as the conservation of the Acropolis monuments and the reunification of the Parthenon sculptures displayed in the British Museum (the first official request for their return was submitted via UNESCO in 1984). [49] Thus, the choice of the UIA-UNESCO framework in 1989 for the international two-stage ideas competition for the NAM was related to the political decision to link the return of the sculptures with the creation of the NAM, a Greek claim supported by UNESCO. This decision shifted the claim for the repatriation of the sculptures to a museological[50] and an architectural one, manifesting the same political claim on those two planes.[51]

The complex organization of singularities was noticeable in the definition of the goal of the third competition, "…an architectural solution for a Museum, which will host the masterpieces of Acropolis"[52]. In terms of the procedure, the UIA framework entailed the following characteristics: first the competition in 1989 was a global open call to all architects approved by the UIA, meaning architects with the right to be active in their country of origin or the country of their residence. Thus it organized a network and an international solution space of architects from twenty-six countries.[53] The competition was considered one of the few occasions where the Greek and international architectural scene overlapped.[54] In the first stage, 25 out of 498 projects were nominated, from which ten projects entered the second competition stage. The second stage dealt with the draft plans for the architectural solution of the building(s) from the ten selected teams.

Secondly, the competition of 1989 was open to experimentation concerning the possible site of the NAM. The participants could choose one of the three sites: the Makrigianni, the Koile and the Dionissos. The competition of 1989 gave importance and detailed information in order to establish relations between the NAM and its physical surroundings: the historical, archaeological and local urban context. The participants become aware of the overall area around the Akropolis hill, of the needs and local character. However the difficult choice of where the museum should be located was "transferred" to participants.

Together with the call for global architecture and the concern about the local urban context, the third competition aimed to express architecturally certain political and symbolic goals. More precisely, the exhibition space where the Parthenon sculptures were going to be placed, expressed the problem of their repatriation in architectural term: their absence and representation by models in a temporary exhibition space is a constant recall of the "demand" to return the Parthenon sculptures to their original context that was to be created in this museum. Thus the Parthenon sculptures play a double role in the virtual organization of the third competition: first, they have an architectural role, since they define the character (as original context) and organize the exhibition spaces of the museum. Second, they have a political role as they recall the demand to return the sculptures located in the British Museum.[55]

In studying the results of the third competition, we began with the winning project of Nicoletti and Passarelli. The project introduced a geological form located in Makrigianni site, bringing together the rocky profile of the Acropolis hill and the urban texture.[56] The minutes from the jury sessions illustrate from the first phase, the jury voted the project of Nicoletti and Passarelli amongst the most appropriate solutions, but underlined a weaknesses in terms of local needs.

*"1022: The big open space on Aeropagitou street connects the museum with the archaeological park. The spaces of the expositions are very satisfactory. The relations with the streets are unclear"*[57].

The Nicoletti-Passarelli project addressed the singularity of local urban surroundings by the exterior figure of the museum, which was dictated by the mixture of diverse landscapes, both urban and natural in the architectural concept of the podium **[Fig.4]**. Additionally, the project of Nicoletti and Passarelli proposed an interior space organized by the dimensions and visual relation with the Parthenon. This dynamic is symbolized by a big window: "the open eye onto the Acropolis," which connects the exhibition room of Parthenon sculptures with the monument of the Acropolis **[Fig.5]**. The eye achieved a continuous relationship with the presence of the Acropolis, and brought this special spatial feeling inside the Museum. Furthermore, the exhibition room of Parthenon sculptures was the museum "core," and was expressed by an abstract invention of a void reproducing the temple dimensions **[Fig.6]**: "around this void the temple sculpture can be exhibited and viewed in the same spatial relations they had on the original building"[58].

The important archaeological content hosted by the NAM functioned as the main idea around which the architectural concepts for the NAM were developed. In this way, the exhibition space and the whole museum expressed the problem of repatriation of the sculptures.[59]

As expected, Nicoletti and Passarelli's project contained weak points, such us the inflexibility of exposition spaces[60] and its relation with the local urban landscape.[61] However, may critics addressed not the winning project but the procedure of the third competition. Specifically, the work of the jury during the first phase when they assessed 426 projects in eight hours, and the inability of the jury in the second phase to generate further development/refinement of the ideas of the first phase.[62] Transparency and anonymity, crucial characteristics of every competition process, were not very well kept. [63] Finally, the Makrigianni site was a point of constant debate, especially by SADAS. The opposition of SADAS and the hesitant stance of the Ministry of Culture produced a feeling of uncertainty about the project's future, which was illustrated by the jurors' comments in 1990:

> A competition can produce an exciting and original concept but it cannot produce the building which should be finally built. Considerations of capital cost and maintenance costs, running costs and environmental performance could not be balanced against the merits of attractive design as shown in the drawings. The reassuring fact is that all the prize winners [...] were by mature architectural firms with great experience. [64]

It is important to state that although Nicoletti and Passarelli's project did not have a strong impact on the evolution of the global architectural scene, it did allow for a broad exchange of opinions and experiences in the local architectural scene. The plans of the third competition, the texts, books and documents fostered a critical dialogue for architecture, which in turn strongly influence the Greek architecture. [65] Or as Loukaki [66] states, the opposition against the third competition reveals a profound need of the Greek architecture to respond to the interpretation of the Acropolis in a creative and coherent manner, with historical appreciation of all periods of Greek civilization.

Recapitulating the third competition procedure answered the need of a "global" political call for returning the Parthenon sculptures and brought Greek architecture to a new international process. Nicoletti and Passarelli's project successfully answered the needs of the "global" call by creating a building based on the relations with the Parthenon. However the NAM was not only a political symbol, it was also a project to be built in a very complex locality. The complexity was derived from other social, political and financial issues, from the close distance to the Parthenon and from the urban fabric. Neither the third competition procedure nor the winning project were able to give clear answers to these issues. The third competition was the appropriate procedure to produce a strong winning concept, which in turn influenced the 2000 competition, and encouraged a strong debate concerning the local architecture. It did not however succeed in answering questions around local problems and opposition, and led to uncertainty concerning the funding of the NAM. [67]

## 2000 : A Hybrid Procedure for the NAM.

Extensive projects like the Makrigianni site metro station/ line and the EAXA regeneration projects changed the area around the Acropolis hill. The organizational experience from the Olympic games influenced the fourth competition with the creation of the "private legal entity" OANMA. OANMA was created in 1994 according to a legislation related with a "new" singularity—the Olympic Games in 2004 (Laws N2260/94 and N2819/2000 in F.E.K. 2000). Thus the fourth procedure formulated a different relationship with the ministry of Culture, using OANMA as an intermediary for the organization of the procedure and the realization of the project. OANMA signified an interval between the organizational structure of the fourth procedure and the political issues, which resulted in a more flexible and continuous trajectory from the initiation of the fourth procedure in 2000 until the completion of the project in 2009.

The aforementioned changes in the political and administrative settings influenced the structure of the procedure. The fourth competition was as equally international as the third, however it was a closed procedure with very detailed and specific criteria in accordance with international and European standards for the participating teams. The criteria comprised official diplomas, "professional level," official statements of non-bankruptcy (art. 29 in European Directive 92/50/EEC (European Economic Community, 1992) and art.30 in the relevant Greek laws), and official statements about the organization of the offices and of the details and contracts of the cooperation between teams. Furthermore, participants were asked to submit biographical information, examples of works from the previous fifteen years, the structure of the team in terms of expertise and organization of the offices, and official statements of office quality (art.32 2.f in European Directive 92/50/EEC (European Economic Community,1992) and art.27.f. in the relevant Greek laws). The call of the fourth competition brought together complex teams and cooperation, with star architects (Tschumi, Isozaki, Libeskind, etc.), local architects (Fotiades, Tombazis, Potiropoulos etc.), providing heterogeneity of expertise and extensive experience gained through relevant types of projects (DENCO, EL.TE.ME., etc.).

The selection of the procurement regulations EU 1992 also allowed for financial certainty for the overall project as stated by the Minister of Culture and the financial support from the third Community Support Framework. [68]

**Fig. 4**
The podium from the project of
Nicoletti and Passarelli.
*Ministry of Culture and
D.O.M.S.1991, 36*

**Fig. 5**
The open eye onto the Acropolis.
*Ministry of Culture and D.O.M.S.
1991, 37*

**Fig. 6**
The open eye onto the Acropolis and the exposition room of Parthenon sculptures from the
project of Nicoletti and Passarelli. *Ministry of Culture and D.O.M.S. 1991, 40*

The financial concerns are also illustrated in the competition brief, as the presence of elements like the budget or the specification of the legislation define the new trajectory for the NAM project:

*OANMA, in order to assign the elaboration of the architectural, engineering and electromechanical study of the NAM, of an overall pre-estimated budget 1 500 000 000 drachmas (plus taxes of added value), initiates the [procedure for the] expression of interest, according to the close procedure as defined by the paragraph 6 of article 2 and article 14 of presidential order (P.D.) 18/2000 (F.E.K. 2000) "transformation of the regulations of the Greek legislation for public service contracts according to the regulations of the directive 92/50/EEC (European Economic Community, 1992) [...]".* [69]

The competition explicitly defined the singularities around which the architectural study should be developed:

- the incorporation of the archaeological excavation to the solution;
- the unity of archaeological spaces of the museum, which should be organized around the sculptures of the Parthenon;
- a high quality exhibition space for the Parthenon sculptures, which stemmed from the dimensions of the Parthenon monument, and the visual relation with the Acropolis monument and the use of the natural light.[70] Both architectural priorities resulted from the 1989 winning project of the third competition by Nicoletti and Passarelli.[71]

Additionally, the fourth competition allowed for the direct involvement of archaeological constraints into the design of the NAM. Since the Makrigianni site contains important archaeological ruins covering 4000m² of the museum site, the location of each of the foundation pillars should be in line with archaeological constraints, such as the archaeological ruins covering half the site should be preserved and exhibited in situ. The rating tables proposed by the brief evaluated the aesthetics and the architecture of the museum, as well as the optimal coverage of its functional needs, according to their compatibility with the engineering studies (*Architecture in Greece* (2002): 158). According to jurors, during the deliberation sessions the archaeologists' opinions were an important aspect to consider. In other words, the load-bearing structure of the museum and the

placement of the foundations in relation to the archaeological excavations in the Makrigianni site structured the search for architectural and functional organization and the realization of the project.

Concerning the surrounding locality, the competition suggested considering the overall site in terms of a radical redevelopment to achieve an appropriate "high quality" urban environment for the NAM.[72] Thus, the fourth competition refers only to the following local surroundings: the new built metro station, the particularities of the site in terms of existing buildings and archaeological ruins and its relation with the Acropolis hill.

All the aforementioned singularities (participants experience, budget, archaeological constrains, museological needs and architectural issues) are hierarchised and rated in tables: for example, the relation with the Parthenon monument and the location of the foundation was given a high rate, and thus are given priority in design.

As we have illustrated, new European regulations and new types of institutions structured the modus operandi of the fourth procedure, as they determine the goal, the participating teams, and the realization of the project according to international market tendering procedures. In terms of the local, the fourth competition recognized the importance of archaeological ruins, the new pedestrian 'look' of Areapogitou street, where the entrance of the NAM should be located, and the metro station 'Acropolis'. The degraded urban surroundings of Makrigianni site were not included in the wishful local environment. On the contrary, the surroundings were the object of regeneration. Or, as Loukaki[73] argues, the NAM was a museum that responded to the needs of three cities: the natural city, comprised of the Acropolis hill and archaeological excavations, the ancient city, deriving from the dimension and orientation of Parthenon monument and to the ideal city, which was defined by the expectation of the NAM to upgrade this part of city of Athens.

The focus of the fourth competition was on the accepted locality, the global symbolism of the Parthenon sculptures and an ideal contemporary Athens. Based on this, OANMA aimed in establishing a long cooperation for the NAM project, a contracting trajectory that began in 2000. The starting point included the OANMA as a constant supervisor of the overall procedure, the Makrigianni site as the location of the NAM, and the complex and multidisciplinary teams as the designers. The trajectory extended to the seven month

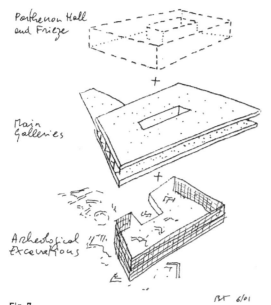

**Fig. 7**
The three layers form the project of Tschumi: the archaeological layer of the ruins, the museum space, the exhibition space of the Parthenon gallery with the same dimensions and orientation as the Parthenon.
*Tschumi Architects, 2010:117*

**Fig. 8**
The arrival of the first sculpture with protests (red panel) at the door of the site.
*Courtesy of Nikos Daniilidis, photographer*

period that the winning team has in order to prepare the pre-study, the final and the realization study of the NAM, as well as the tender financial details which initiated the built phase of the project.

The fourth procurement process gave first prize to a project that proposed a clear hierarchy and organization within the design of the museum, most notably giving priority to the archaeological and political priorities, illustrated in the in **[Fig.7]**:

The Tschumi project divides the problem of the NAM into three specific parts: one for the archaeological ruins, the second for the main museum space, and the third for the Parthenon itself, while taking into account the various particularities of works they each contain.[74] It is the dialogue between these three parts, through layers of movement, which creates a connection between the actual time of visit and the historical time.[75] The dialogue between the aforementioned layers was shaped by the prioritization of the archaeological findings and excavations at the Makrigianni site, as the brief proposed. The winning team negotiated the location of each and every column with archaeologists during the realization phase.[76]

The winning project of the fourth procurement not only acknowledged the singularities, but also clearly expressed how they should be organized in order to realize the project. The project brought together "present" realities, like the archaeological ruins that were found in the Makrigianni site, with "absent" issues such the repatriation of the Parthenon sculptures, which were not present but "presented" by the fourth competition.[77] Furthermore the box-like shape of the NAM was flexible and enabled the archaeological concerns to organize the project in the design but also during realization.[78]

Concerning the degraded locality, its appearance was random in the model and the plans, and it was not given great importance. This indifference or even hostility towards the urban surroundings (Dragonas 2010), which was always "present" in the plans created many problems and protests against the realization of the building.[79] Due to the 2004 Olympics, the Greek government became increasingly heavy-handed in its efforts to move the project forward: a new law was issued, and residents were paid handsomely and sometimes forced to move.[80] According to Tschumi[81], this project was involved in 104 court-cases. It encouraged the organization of the group Citizens' Movement to Prevent Building a ĐĐĐ; caused civil protests, constant obstacles, lawsuits, inquiries and appeals, memorandums and police interventions and a hail of malevolent publications **[Fig.8]**.[82]

Many criticized the architecture of the building and its box-like shape. The building protrudes more than the sloping roof of the Nicoletti and Passarelli project, and refers to a more generic modernism, seemingly more suitable for an embassy. Many suggest that the large building was approved partly because it would not be visible from the Areopagitou pedestrian zone.[83]

Despite these problems, OANMA ensured the realization of the project at the Makrigianni site, as well as the financing by European Union and the technical and legal guidance of the selected partners, Tschumi and Fotiades multidisciplinary teams. The NAM opened in 2008, thirty-one years after the initiation of the first national competition.

———

The internationalization of design, construction services and construction markets has multiple affects on the appropriateness of competitions. In order to map these affects, in this article we examine the appropriateness of the case of the NAM competitions moving from one competition to the other: from the two stages of international ideas competition of the NAM in 1989 to the tender for the architectural, engineering and electromechanical studies for the NAM in 2000.

This study provides a rigorous framework for using assemblage theory as a base to conceptualize architectural competitions as platforms that bring forth negotiations around diverse issues.[84] Assemblage theory enables us to trace the trajectories between the virtual organization of the problem of the creation of the NAM and the different actual settings during the thirty years trajectory of the NAM project. In other words, it enables us to see how the same virtual concerns and singularities are expressed differently by forming different assemblages with contemporary contextual structures of the NAM project.

Furthermore, this article illustrates that the appropriateness of competitions can be examined in terms of procedural organizations and in terms of results. As we argue with our case study, each competition case for the NAM acted as a vehicle that brought negotiation in a specific place and time diverse singularities that structure the NAM problem. In other words, each competition type answers new issues and the problems/failures of the previous one. Comparing the procedures of the national competitions of 1976 and 1979 to the international competition of 1989, the third competition was more appropriate to highlight the issue of the NAM to an international "global" audience,

than to answer the needs of Greece entering a global market and European Union. A comparison between the third competition in 1989 and the hybrid procedure of 2000 shows that the last procedure answers specific local problems of archaeological findings, economic problems of project funding and issues of political commitment that were absent in the latter. In terms of the procedure, we can argue that internationalization of design, construction services and construction markets influence and transform the NAM procedure and allow the formulation of new frameworks more specific to the problems and needs of the project.

In discussing the outcomes of these competitions, we see the effort required to elevate cultural character to a global concern and the challenges of aligning an audience with local architectural sensitivity and aesthetics. The national competition results were more conscious of the local needs and existing buildings, however they could not give a coherent answer to the NAM character as the original context of the Parthenon sculptures.

The third prize in the 1989 competition illustrates that the results can be divided into two "schools" of solutions: one dream-like and poetic–an unarticulated architecture based on feelings deriving from the relationship between old and new.[85] This architecture refers to a critical regionalism, however, it lacked potential as a coherent project. Counter to this, there is also the "rational school" providing solutions oriented towards the global character of the NAM project, answering the musicological needs, and designing a mass tourist destination. From this perspective the third competition's winning project of Nicoletti and Passarelli can be thought as the Greek reply to "big" foreign architecture. The rational school of solutions is more apparent within the fourth competition in 2000. We can argue that as the NAM moves towards a more appropriate "rational" solution for an international mediator and international symbol for Athens and Greece that hosts the Parthenon sculptures, it moves away from the dream-like solutions highlighting local and cultural issues, such as the issues of urban surroundings, the aesthetic and cultural problem of the relation of the NAM with the Parthenon monument and the Acropolis hill. However in the case of the NAM's initial goal, the international character of the building accrues directly as a vehicle for a political request. It can be said the building acts as an international mediator.[86] As Mpouras (2010) noted, it is the request to get back the Parthenon sculptures that motivated the quest for the NAM and not the regeneration or improvement of Greek architecture. Thus in the case of the NAM, we can argue

**Fig. 9**
The visual relation of the Parthenon
sculptures with the Acropolis.
*Courtesy of Tschumi Architects,
2010:118-119*

that the global character of the building was thought of as intertwining with the local, cultural or aesthetic as much as these could support the (local) political request for returning the Parthenon sculptures.

Concluding, we argue that the new regulations in the construction and design sectors have multiple affects on the appropriateness of competitions. As we illustrate with the NAM case, new constraints such as financial issues can transform the project's budget, as well as the type of procurement; they influence both the number and experience of participating teams and thus the architectural result of the competition. The difference in the organization of these singularities derived from the fact that Greek architecture and Greece was entering different assemblages, governed by singularities such as the Olympic Games in 2004, the European Union, the archaeological excavations in 1996. These singularities produced new constraints (like the type of the procurement, the new project budget, the archeological findings in the competition site) which were "folded" in the brief and thus influence the structure and regulations of the final competition. And again, these singularities were unfolded during the procedure by the architects and the judges and thus influence the architectural design and competition outcomes. Furthermore, the production of new architectural innovation influences not only architectural but also procedural knowledge, specifically the way a problem is framed and dealt with by a procedural point of view. This can be seen with the winning project of Nicoletti and Passarelli in the third competition, as it produced new architectural knowledge and innovation and defined the architectural priorities in the competition in 2000; for example, the visual relation with the Acropolis and the exhibition room for the Parthenon sculptures in the dimensions and orientation of the Parthenon **[Fig.9]**. The winning project of Tschumi was able to (re)organize these singularities to achieve the path towards realization of the NAM.

These transformations, used in an unconscious way, may strengthen the competition as an institution and make it increasingly flexible in adapting to an evolving landscape.[87] In the case of the NAM, this is not done on the basis of a strategic blueprint but rather as a result of a trial and error process that lasted several decades.[88] It can be thought of as a school[89] or a dynamic learning process between the international and the local ways of designing and realizing architecture.

# Notes

[1] D. Filippides, "Architectural Competitions and Contemporary Greek Architecture (in Greek)," ed. K. Demiri, Spiridonides, D., Tournikiotis, P. (members of the research committee, Ganotis, S., Sofikitis, M., External collaborators, Athens : GSRT / TCG., 2000).

[2] Judith Strong, *Winning by Design : Architectural Competitions* (Boston : Butterworth-Heinemann, 1996).

[3] Leentje Volker, *Deciding About Design Quality : Value Judgements and Decision Making in the Selection of Architects by Public Clients under European Tendering Regulations* (Leiden : Sidestone Press, 2010).

[4] M. DeLanda, *A New Philosophy of Society : Assemblage Theory and Social Complexity* (Bloomsbury Publishing, 2006).

[5] J. E. Van Wezemael, "Modulation of Singularities — a Complexity Approach to Planning Competitions," in *The Ashgate Research Companion to Planning Theory : Conceptual Challenges for Spatial Planning*, ed. J. Hillier and P. Healey (Ashgate Pub., 2010).

[6] J. Basin, *Architectural Competitions in Nineteenth Century England* (UMI Research Press : Ann Arbor Michigan, 1984).
B. Bergdoll, «Competing in the Academy and the Marketplace : European Architecture Competitions, 1401-1927,» in *The Experimental Tradition : Essays on Competitions in Architecture*, ed. Hélène Lipstadt, Barry Bergdoll, and Architectural League of New York. (New York, N.Y. : Architectural League of New York : Princeton Architectural Press, 1989).
H. Lipstadt, «The Experimental Tradition,» ibid.
J. Dubey, *Le Concours En Droit Des Marchés Publics : La Passation Des Marchés De Conception, En Particulier D'architecture Et D'ingénierie* (Schulthess, 2005).
Filippides, «Architectural Competitions and Contemporary Greek Architecture (in Greek).»

[7] F. Sobreira, "Competitions — Public Strategies for Architectural Quality," *Conditions ; The Politics of Quality Management*, no. 5/6 (2010).
Tridib Banerjee and Anastasia Loukaitou-Sideris, «Competitions as a Design Method : An Inquiry,» *Journal of Architectural and Planning Research* 7, no. 2 (1990).

[8] Bergdoll, "Competing in the Academy and the Marketplace : European Architecture Competitions, 1401-1927."

[9] Basin, *Architectural Competitions in Nineteenth Century England*.
Bergdoll, "Competing in the Academy and the Marketplace : European Architecture Competitions, 1401-1927."

[10] "Competing in the Academy and the Marketplace : European Architecture Competitions, 1401-1927."

[11] Basin, *Architectural Competitions in Nineteenth Century England*.
Bergdoll, "Competing in the Academy and the Marketplace : European Architecture Competitions, 1401-1927."

[12] Filippides, "Architectural Competitions and Contemporary Greek Architecture (in Greek)."

[13] Ibid.

[14] DeLanda, *A New Philosophy of Society : Assemblage Theory and Social Complexity*.

[15] J. Hillier, "Introduction to Part Two," in *The Ashgate Research Companion to Planning Theory : Conceptual Challenges for Spatial Planning*, ed. J. Hillier and P. Healey (Ashgate Pub., 2010).
DeLanda, *A New Philosophy of Society : Assemblage Theory and Social Complexity*.

[16] Van Wezemael, "Modulation of Singularities — a Complexity Approach to Planning Competitions."

[17] DeLanda, *A New Philosophy of Society : Assemblage Theory and Social Complexity*.

[18] Ibid.

[19] Manuel De Landa, "Deleuze, Diagrams, and the Genesis of Form," *Amerikastudien/American Studies* 45, no. 1 (2000).
G. Deleuze and S. Hand, *Foucault* (University of Minnesota Press, 1988).
Gilles Deleuze and Félix Guattari, *A Thousand Plateaus : Capitalism and Schizophrenia*, trans. B. Massumi (Minneapolis : University of Minnesota Press, 1987).

[20] S Paisiou, "Four Performances for the New Acropolis Museum — When the Politics of Space Enter the Becoming of Place," *Geographica Helvetica* 66, no. 1 (2011).

[21] J. E. Van Wezemael and M. Loepfe, "Veränderte Prozesse Der Entscheidungsfindung in Der Raumentwicklung," ibid.64, no. 2 (2009).

[22] Van Wezemael, "Modulation of Singularities — a Complexity Approach to Planning Competitions."

[23] K. Fouseki, "Conflicting Discourses on the Construction of the New Acropolis Museum : Past and Present," *European Review of History — Revue européenne d'Histoire* 13, no. 4 (2006).

[24] S. Kontaratos, "To Adoxo Terma Enos Dromou Met' Empodion," *Architectonika themata. Architecture in Greece*, no. 44 (2010).
A. Loukaki, *Living Ruins, Value Conflicts*, Heritage, Culture, and Identity (Aldershot, England ; Burlington, VT : Ashgate, 2008).
Eleana Yalouri, *The Acropolis : Global Fame, Local Claim*, Materializing Culture (Oxford ; New York : Berg, 2001).

[25] Loukaki, *Living Ruins, Value Conflicts*.
Fouseki, «Conflicting Discourses on the Construction of the New Acropolis Museum : Past and Present.»

[26] S. Kontaratos, "The Acropolis Museum," *Architectonika themata. Architecture in Greece*, no. 12 (1978).

[27] Fouseki, "Conflicting Discourses on the Construction of the New Acropolis Museum : Past and Present."

[28] Loukaki, *Living Ruins, Value Conflicts*.
Fouseki, «Conflicting Discourses on the Construction of the New Acropolis Museum : Past and Present.»

[29] Loukaki, *Living Ruins, Value Conflicts*.

[30] Filippides, "Architectural Competitions and Contemporary Greek Architecture (in Greek)."

[31] Yalouri, *The Acropolis : Global Fame, Local Claim*, 85.

[32] Paisiou, "Four Performances for the New Acropolis Museum — When the Politics of Space Enter the Becoming of Place."

[33] Loukaki, *Living Ruins, Value Conflicts*.

[34] Filippides, "Architectural Competitions and Contemporary Greek Architecture (in Greek)."

[35] Hellenic Parliament, "Minutes of the Session 15.11.1999.," (1999).

[36] Loukaki, *Living Ruins, Value Conflicts*.
Filippides, «Architectural Competitions and Contemporary Greek Architecture (in Greek).»

[37] Loukaki, *Living Ruins, Value Conflicts*.
T. Pangalos and L. Mendoni, «To Chroniko Tou Neou Mouseiou Tis Akropolis,» in *Kathimerini*, 27228 (2009).

[38] Loukaki, *Living Ruins, Value Conflicts*.

[39] Loukaki, *Living Ruins, Value Conflicts*.

[40] Hellenic Parliament, "Minutes of the Session 15.11.1999.."

[41] Filippides, "Architectural Competitions and Contemporary Greek Architecture (in Greek)."

[42] OANMA, "The Competition of the New Acropolis Museum," (Athens : OANMA, 2001).
Loukaki, *Living Ruins, Value Conflicts*.

[43] OANMA, "The Competition of the New Acropolis Museum."
Loukaki, *Living Ruins, Value Conflicts*.

[44] Van Wezemael, "Modulation of Singularities — a Complexity Approach to Planning Competitions."

[45] John Allen, "Powerful Assemblages ?," *Area* 43, no. 2 (2011).

46 Kontaratos, "The Acropolis Museum."
    Fouseki, «Conflicting Discourses on the Construction of the New Acropolis Museum : Past and Present.»
47 Kontaratos, "The Acropolis Museum."
48 D. Filippides, "The Urban Planning Issues," *Design+Art in Greece*, no. 23 (1992).
49 Fouseki, "Conflicting Discourses on the Construction of the New Acropolis Museum : Past and Present."
50 Ibid.
51 Paisiou, "Four Performances for the New Acropolis Museum — When the Politics of Space Enter the Becoming of Place."
52 Ministry of Culture, "Jury Report of the International Competition for Nam, Minutes Phase A," (1990), 12. (free translation)
53 Ministry of Culture and D.O.M.S., "The New Acropolis Museum," (Athens : Ministry of Culture, Directorate of Museum Studies, 1991).
54 Filippides, "Architectural Competitions and Contemporary Greek Architecture (in Greek)."
55 Sofia Paisiou and Joris Ernest Van Wezemael, "The Quest for a New Museum — a Cartography of the Shifting Organizations of Collaboration in the Case of the New Acropolis Museum," *Engineering Project Organization Journal* 2, no. 3 (2012).
56 Ministry of Culture and D.O.M.S., "The New Acropolis Museum," 37.
57 Culture, "Jury Report of the International Competition for Nam, Minutes Phase A," 16.
58 Ministry of Culture and D.O.M.S., "The New Acropolis Museum," 35.
59 Paisiou and Van Wezemael, "The Quest for a New Museum — a Cartography of the Shifting Organizations of Collaboration in the Case of the New Acropolis Museum."
60 Ministry of Culture, "Jury Report of the International Competition for Nam, Minutes Phase B," (1990b), 6.
61 Filippides, "The Urban Planning Issues," 82. (free translation)
62 Paisiou and Van Wezemael, "The Quest for a New Museum — a Cartography of the Shifting Organizations of Collaboration in the Case of the New Acropolis Museum."
63 S. Kontaratos, "The Unfortunate Outcome of the Competition and the Responsibilities of Both the Ministry and Jury," *Design+Art in Greece*, no. 23 (1992).
64 Ministry of Culture and D.O.M.S., "The New Acropolis Museum," 24.
65 Filippides, "Architectural Competitions and Contemporary Greek Architecture (in Greek)."
66 Loukaki, *Living Ruins, Value Conflicts*, 288.
67 Hellenic Parliament, "Minutes of the Session 15.11.1999.."
68 Paisiou and Van Wezemael, "The Quest for a New Museum — a Cartography of the Shifting Organizations of Collaboration in the Case of the New Acropolis Museum."
69 OANMA, "Detail Call for the Preselection of Contributors for the Architectural, Engineering and Electromechanical Study of the New Acropolis Museum," (2000).(free translation)
70 "Detail Call for Contributors for the Architectural, Engineering and Electromechanical Study of the New Acropolis Museum," (2000b).
71 Kouzelis A., Psilopoulou I., and Psilopoulos A., "Innovative Vs. Qualified.The Experience of Competitions in Contemporary Greece," *Nordic Journal of Architectural Research* 21, no. 2/3 (2009).
    Paisiou and Van Wezemael, «The Quest for a New Museum — a Cartography of the Shifting Organizations of Collaboration in the Case of the New Acropolis Museum.»
72 "The Quest for a New Museum — a Cartography of the Shifting Organizations of Collaboration in the Case of the New Acropolis Museum."
73 Loukaki, *Living Ruins, Value Conflicts*.
74 B. Tschumi, "L'architecture : Concepts Et Contexts Aujourd'hui," in *PRIX LATSIS UNIVERSITAIRES 2009* (2009).
75 Loukaki, *Living Ruins, Value Conflicts*.
76 Loukaki, *Living Ruins, Value Conflicts*.
77 Paisiou, "Four Performances for the New Acropolis Museum — When the Politics of Space Enter the Becoming of Place."
78 Tschumi, "L'architecture : Concepts Et Contexts Aujourd'hui."
    Loukaki, *Living Ruins, Value Conflicts*.
79 Paisiou and Van Wezemael, "The Quest for a New Museum — a Cartography of the Shifting Organizations of Collaboration in the Case of the New Acropolis Museum."
80 Loukaki, *Living Ruins, Value Conflicts*.
81 B. Tschumi, "Contested Territories : Bernard Tschumi and Beatriz Colomina," (2005).
82 Loukaki, *Living Ruins, Value Conflicts*.
83 Ibid.
84 Van Wezemael, "Modulation of Singularities — a Complexity Approach to Planning Competitions."
    Paisiou, «Four Performances for the New Acropolis Museum — When the Politics of Space Enter the Becoming of Place.»
85 Loukaki, *Living Ruins, Value Conflicts*.
86 Ibid.
87 Paisiou and Van Wezemael, "The Quest for a New Museum — a Cartography of the Shifting Organizations of Collaboration in the Case of the New Acropolis Museum."
88 J. E. Van Wezemael et al., ""Mattering" the Res Publica : The Architectural Competitions for the Swiss Federal Post Offices in the Late 19th Century as a Foucauldian Dispositif," *disP-The Planning Review* 47, no. 184 (2011). Landau S., «Coming to Terms : Architecture Competitions in America and the Emerging Profession, 1789-1922,» in *The Experimental Tradition : Essays on Competitions in Architecture*, ed. Hélène Lipstadt, Barry Bergdoll, and Architectural League of New York. (New York, N.Y. : Architectural League of New York : Princeton Architectural Press, 1989).
89 Filippides, "Architectural Competitions and Contemporary Greek Architecture (in Greek)."

## ▄▄▄ References

**Allen**, J. "Powerful Assemblages ?". *Area* 43, no. 2 (2011) : 154-57.
**Burton**, Landau S. "Coming to Terms : Architecture Competitions in America and the Emerging Profession, 1789-1922." In *The Experimental Tradition*, edited by H. Lipstadt, 53-78. New York : Princeton Architectural Press, 1989.
**Banerjee**, T, and A. **Loukaitou-Sideris**. "Competitions as a Design Method : An Inquiry." *Journal of Architectural and Planning Research* 7, no. 2 (1990) : 114-31.
**Basin**, J. *Architectural Competitions in Nineteenth Century England*. UMI Research Press : Ann Arbor Michigan, 1984.
**Bergdoll**, B. "Competing in the Academy and the Marketplace : European Architecture Competitions, 1401-1927." In *The Experimental Tradition : Essays on Competitions in Architecture*, edited by Hélène Lipstadt, Barry Bergdoll and Architectural League of New York., 21-51. New York, N.Y. : Architectural League of New York : Princeton Architectural Press, 1989.
**De Landa**, M. "Deleuze, Diagrams, and the Genesis of Form." *Amerikastudien/ American Studies* 45, no. 1 (2000) : 33-41.
**De Landa**, M. *A New Philosophy of Society : Assemblage Theory and Social Complexity*. Bloomsbury Publishing, 2006.
**Deleuze**, G., and S. **Hand**. *Foucault*. University of Minnesota Press, 1988.
**Deleuze**, G, and F. **Guattari**. *A Thousand Plateaus : Capitalism and Schizophrenia*. Translated by B. Massumi. Minneapolis : University of Minnesota Press, 1987.
**Dragonas**, P. "After (the) Acropolis." *Architecture in Greece*, no. 44 (2010) : 128.
**Dubey**, J. *Le concours en droit des marchés publics : la passation des marchés de conception, en particulier d'architecture et d'ingénierie*. Schulthess, 2005.
**European Economic Community**. "Council Directive 92/50/Eec." 1992.

**European Parliament, Council**. "Directive 2004/18/Ec." 2004.
F.E.K. "E27960/1665/70.", 1970.
**European Parliament, Council**. "N2819/2000.", 2000.
**European Parliament, Council**. "P.D.346.", 1998.
**Filippides**, D. "Architectural Competitions and Contemporary Greek Architecture (in Greek)." edited by K. Demiri, Spiridonides, D., Tournikiotis, P.: members of the research committee, Ganotis, S., Sofikitis, M., External collaborators, Athens: GSRT / TCG, 2000.
**Filippides**, D. "The Urban Planning Issues." *Design+Art in Greece*, no. 23 (1992): 80-81.
**Fouseki**, K. "Conflicting Discourses on the Construction of the New Acropolis Museum: Past and Present." *European Review of History — Revue euro-péenne d'Histoire* 13, no. 4 (2006): 533-48.
**Hellenic Parliament**. "Minutes of the Session 15.11.1999.", 1999.
**Hillier**, J. "Introduction to Part Two." In *The Ashgate Research Companion to Planning Theory: Conceptual Challenges for Spatial Planning*, edited by J. Hillier and P. Healey, 111-18: Ashgate Pub., 2010.
**Hillier**, J. *Stretching Beyond the Horizon: A Multiplanar Theory of Spatial Planning and Governance*. Ashgate, 2007.
**Kontaratos**, S. "The Acropolis Museum." *Architectonika themata. Architecture in Greece*, no. 12 (1978): 215-40.
**Kontaratos**, S. "To Adoxo Terma Enos Dromou Met' Empodion." *Architectonika themata. Architecture in Greece*, no. 44 (2010): 130-32.
**Kontaratos**, S. "The Unfortunate Outcome of the Competition and the Responsibilities of Both the Ministry and Jury." *Design+Art in Greece*, no. 23 (1992): 78-79.
**Kouzelis** A., **Psilopoulou** I., and **Psilopoulos** A. "Innovative Vs. Qualified.The Experience of Competitions in Contemporary Greece." *Nordic Journal of Architectural Research* 21, no. 2/3 (2009): 123-41.
**Lipstadt**, H. "The Competition in the Region's Past, the Region in the Competition's Future." In *The Politics of Design: Competitions for Public Projects*, edited by C. Malmberg, 7-27: Policy Research Institute for the Region, 2006.
**Lipstadt**, H. "The Experimental Tradition." In *The Experimental Tradition : Essays on Competitions in Architecture*, edited by Hélène Lipstadt, Barry Bergdoll and Architectural League of New York., 9-20. New York, N.Y.: Architectural League of New York : Princeton Architectural Press, 1989.
**Loukaki**, A. *Living Ruins, Value Conflicts*. Heritage, Culture, and Identity. Aldershot, England ; Burlington, VT: Ashgate, 2008.
**Ministry of Culture**. "Jury Report of the International Competition for Nam, Minutes Phase A." 1990.
**Ministry of Culture**. "Jury Report of the International Competition for Nam, Minutes Phase B." 1990b.
**Ministry of Culture**, and **D.O.M.S.** "The New Acropolis Museum." Athens: Ministry of Culture, Directorate of Museum Studies, 1991.
**Mpouras**, C. "A Spacious and Transparent Museum." *Architecture in Greece*, no. 44 (2010): 136.
**OANMA**. "The Competition of the New Acropolis Museum." Athens: OANMA, 2001.
**OANMA**. "Detail Call for Contributors for the Architectural, Engineering and Electromechanical Study of the New Acropolis Museum." 2000b.
**OANMA**. "Detail Call for the Preselection of Contributors for the Architectural, Engineering and Electromechanical Study of the New Acropolis Museum." 2000.
**Paisiou**, S. "Four Performances for the New Acropolis Museum — When the Politics of Space Enter the Becoming of Place." *Geographica Helvetica* 66, no. 1 (2011): 33-41.
**Paisiou**, S., and J. **Ernest Van Wezemael**. "The Quest for a New Museum — a Cartography of the Shifting Organizations of Collaboration in the Case of the New Acropolis Museum." *Engineering Project Organization Journal* 2, no. 3 (2012): 127-44.
**Pangalos**, T., and L. **Mendoni**. "To Chroniko Tou Neou Mouseiou Tis Akropolis." In *Kathimerini, 27228*, 2009.

**Sobreira**, F. "Competitions — Public Strategies for Architectural Quality." *Conditions; The Politics of Quality Management*, no. 5/6 (2010): 9-16.
**Strong**, J. *Winning by Design : Architectural Competitions*. Boston: Butterworth-Heinemann, 1996.
**Tschumi Architects**. *The New Acropolis Museum*. New York: Skira Rizzoli, 2010.
**Tschumi**, B. "Contested Territories: Bernard Tschumi and Beatriz Colomina." 2005.
**Tschumi**, B. "L'architecture: Concepts Et Contexts Aujourd'hui." In *PRIX LATSIS UNIVERSITAIRES 2009*, 2009.
**Van Wezemael**, J. E. "Knowledge Creation in Urban Development Praxis." In *Knowledge-Based Urban Development: Planning and Applications in the Information Era*, edited by T. Yigitcanlar, K. Velibeyoglu and S. Baum, 1-20. Hershley: Information Science Reference, 2008.
**Van Wezemael**, J. E. "Modulation of Singularities — a Complexity Approach to Planning Competitions." In *The Ashgate Research Companion to Planning Theory: Conceptual Challenges for Spatial Planning*, edited by J. Hillier and P. Healey: Ashgate Pub., 2010.
**Van Wezemael**, J. E., and M. **Loepfe**. "Veränderte Prozesse Der Entscheidungsfindung in Der Raumentwicklung." *Geographica Helvetica* 64, no. 2 (2009): 106-18.
**Van Wezemael**, J. E., J. M. **Silberberger**, S. **Paisiou**, and P. **Frey**. ""Mattering" the Res Publica : The Architectural Competitions for the Swiss Federal Post Offices in the Late 19th Century as a Foucauldian Dispositif." *disP-The Planning Review* 47, no. 184 (2011): 52-59.
**Volker**, L. *Deciding About Design Quality : Value Judgements and Decision Making in the Selection of Architects by Public Clients under European Tendering Regulations*. Leiden: Sidestone Press, 2010.
**Yalouri**, E. *The Acropolis : Global Fame, Local Claim*. Materializing Culture. Oxford ; New York: Berg, 2001.

# 1.6. Should Competitions Always Be International?

**Political Reasons in a Multipolar World (1988-2012)**

**Jean-Pierre Chupin**, Ph.D.
Director of the Research Chair on Competitions and Contemporary Practices in Architecture
Université de Montréal
Canada

Through a research program conducted in 2012 and 2013 at the University of Montreal Research Chair on Competitions and Contemporary Practices in Architecture, we have attempted to deconstruct some contradictory perceptions related to international competitions. Logically seen as signs of "opening to the world," we drew the hypothesis that international competitions could also be seen as potential instruments of multicultural politics. Indeed, in the Canadian context, as can be verified by consulting our on-going database project (the Canadian Competitions Catalogue, *http://www.ccc.umontreal.ca*), there has been a significant increase in the number of international competitions since the end of the 1980s. Historically, this seems to correspond to the adoption of the Canadian Multiculturalism Act in 1988. How are we to interpret this apparent correlation between national and international politics in the organisation of competitions?

Considering competitions as indicators of a genuine "opening of mentalities" and not primarily as instruments of political orientation, we have analysed thirty-nine international competitions organised in Canada since 1988. Combining comparative and hermeneutical analysis of official and media discourses we have identified four categories of international competitions distinguishing figures and intentions related to ideas competitions and project competitions, cultural building and their relationship to national and provincial politics. We also distinguished between landscape architecture and urban design programs as they point to the role of touristic policies and/or municipal marketing and we ended up by locating a series of recent "green" housing competitions displaying a tension between traditional globalisation and environmental globalisation. Amongst these various polarities, remains the search for architectural identity in the complexity of our postmodern cultures.

**Cover**
"Absolute Design Ideas" Competition (Mississauga, Canada. 2005). Project by MAD office (Yansong Ma, Shen Huihui, Yosuke Hayano, Dang Qun, Shen Jun).

## Epistemological Orientation

In architecture, urban design or landscape architecture, when it comes to choosing a competition format (anonymous, restricted, or on invitation) or even more so when it comes to choosing a degree of openness (regional, national, international), various issues are at stake that often go beyond matters of quality, excellence or even collective judgement to reach the fluctuating sphere of political reasons.[1]

Indeed, in our currently multipolar world, where centres of power are somehow fluctuating — be it on an economical, cultural or even political level — it should come as no surprise that the role of international competitions would differ from its traditional recourse in the former bipolar situation of post World War II. As exemplified by the history of what appears to be a praise for international competitions conducted by the *Union Internationale des Architectes*, from the 1950s to the 1970s, international competitions have traditionally been seen as opportunities to conquer new markets, sometimes imposing solutions from one context to another, but also acting as one of various political devices in colonial and even postcolonial frameworks. What would be the reasons for organizing international competitions be in our present world? Should we consider that in a globalized planet every competition should, in practice, be opened internationally and therefore should we interpret "non international competitions" as signs of protectionist politics? After all, and since we enjoy an increasing mobility in many realms of our everyday life, what would be the "good reasons" to organize international competitions and, by symmetry, what would be the reasons not to open a competition at the international level?

Our epistemological orientation considers competitions as research objects and potentially as research methods, in order to produce knowledge. We do not seek to evaluate the efficiency of the competition process per say, as much as we consider competitions as comparative situations offering clearly defined ensemble of documents, design projects, judgements operations and media reactions.1 We therefore follow a scientific path, which takes respectful distance regarding two common and current attitudes concerning competitions studies. The first one adopts an axiological standpoint by discussing the appropriateness of the competition process (be it in favour or against). The second attitude adopts a more sociological posture, generally all embracing, like a meta-discipline: a posture which itself can be subdivided into two trends: (1) to "demystify" designers' intentions or beliefs, as most sociologists still

pretend to do when considering architectural issues; or (2) to endorse and hereby approve "competition studies" by recognizing competitions as "sociological fields" (Lipstadt in Rönn et al. 2010).[2] In these axiological or sociological epistemologies, it is clear however that architecture is subsumed to an all-encompassing discipline (here sociology, in some other cases management, geography, philosophy or history). In other words, in most studies on competitions today, architecture is not considered as a research object nor is it considered as a legitimate and reliable research discipline, with its own questions and methods.

At the *Laboratoire d'étude de l'architecture potentielle* (L.E.A.P)[3] and since 2012 at the *Research Chair on Competitions* (CRC)[4], we consider architectural competitions as disciplinary issues per say, i.e. as architectural phenomena, and in such a theoretical framework competitions are understood as epistemological filters, or prisms, through which the revealing of phenomenological situations allows for the study of disciplinary issues related to contemporary architectural and urban design projects. It is through the inherent comparative nature of a competition process, and even more so through a comparison of competitions during a historical period of time, that we expect to produce new knowledge on architectural practices and theories. Since 2002, through a series of research projects, we have already studied the nature of a (generic) competition situation as being potentially a threefold process of:

1. Reflexivity (as it enhances disciplinary and extra disciplinary debate)[5];
2. Experimentation (since a competition is always supposed to stimulate innovative responses, whether successfully or not); and
3. Multiple judgments (since a competition is the site for at least three other phases of judgement around the jury process itself: a) before, when organisers anticipate the criteria of quality; b) during the process (but before the jury), when competitors have to anticipate the way their proposals will be judged in the competition specific context; c) after the release of the judgement, when media and the public at large are convened to react or comment on the chosen scheme).[6]

In this enquiry on the reasons for international competitions, we chose to focus on a series of comparative and hermeneutical analysis on briefs, regulations and media coverage of international competitions organised in Canada between 1988 and 2012. Was the competition opened to all designers internationally or, on the contrary, was it restricted to national and even local designers? In between these two poles we found a full spectrum of competition types revealing that the choice is not as dualistic as it seems at first glance. For example, there are ways to restrict apparently open international competitions to some "first class starchitects" as there are ways to restrict apparently nationally open competitions to big well-established national firms only. In both cases, younger firms of designers can, for example, be left aside by the selection process in the name of expertise or proven excellence. These phenomena, well known to common competition research, remain nevertheless poorly theorised. In this epistemological gap, what can already be observed is a split between those who favour a restricted access to ensure national and cultural coherence and those who favour internationally open procedures to underline the "world class" level of the architectural and urban issues at stake. In both cases the construction market and industries certainly have a major impact on the level of openness, but in this study we chose to focus on the relationship between the official and explicit reasons given by organisers to choose a competition format (as written in the official documents and as displayed in the immediate media coverage related to a competition) and cultural policies (as evidenced in the same documents, in the type of briefs or program, and at various political scales) be it at the regional, municipal, provincial or national levels. Our main problematic would read as follows: whether regional, national or international:

How are we to consider that a competition becomes an indicator of the openness to the world of a specific cultural or multicultural politics?

- Are international competitions possible instruments of multicultural policies or rather indicators of increasing international multipolar pressures on public actors?

Hence the related research questions:

- For a specific international competition and ultimately for a coherent series of competitions, can we trace both in the official documents and in the media coverage explicit fragments of political rhetoric, and at best clear signs and indicators of an explicit political will (or intention) to open the architectural debate outside the cultural borders of a specific nation?
- What are the various reasons used by a public entity to choose an international competition (in order to realize its most symbolic buildings), which could indicates its level of openness to the world?

As most competitors do, when engaging in a competition, by postponing the answer concerning the efficiency of a competition process and by suspending the question on whether or not, as Shohei Shigematsu, head of OMA New York puts it, "is a competition a form of transparency or a form of abuse?"[7]. We, as researchers, must have the humility to recognize that we cannot yet decide whether a competition is an operative device (an instrument) or simply a revealing device (an indicator). In this prudent theoretical and methodological framework we will follow the Canadian architecture scholar and critic Georges Adamczyk in saying that a competition is a "mise en scène" and should be considered as a "revealing situation."[8]

In the Canadian-specific geopolitical context the question of the correlation between international competitions and politics becomes:

In order to understand the specific nature of the Canadian context, it may be helpful to make some comparisons within a general mapping of national versus international competitions in other western countries (as the figures concerning eastern countries appear rather difficult to gather with enough scientific care). This general mapping can be done in two ways: First, by considering the figures and statistics offered by the UIA archives since the Second World War; second, by gathering data from various official organisations concerned with competitions (be they professional associations, public administrations or semi-public institutions, or in some cases private on-going endeavours such as the *wettbewerbe aktuell* team in Germany). We will come back to the problem of statistical comparisons at the international level in our conclusion **[Fig.21]**.

### ▬ The International Union of Architects (UIA) as International Regulator

Until the end of the twentieth century, when a private organisation or a public institution was to launch an international competition, a general consensus invited this private or public organiser to consult with the *Union Internationale* des Architectes and ideally to get an approval stamp; if only to reassure competitors about the fairness of the general competition process. A comprehensive study by Aymone Nicholas published in 2007, has shown the great impact of this organisation on major competitions through the 1950s to the 1970s giving birth to some of the most prominent buildings of the twentieth century.[9]

About 226 international competitions were approved by the UIA from 1949 to 2010, which is a relatively small number when compared to the few thousands of competitions organised in the meantime. Amongst these 226 international competitions, 28% specifically looked for ideas (63) and 72% for projects (163), since the UIA regulation still distinguishes between ideas and projects.[10] We can already underline the general confidence related to an international opening since three-quarters of the competitions were intended for realizing major buildings through selecting a "project." If we draw a simplified histogram of international competitions approved by the UIA and superimpose a timeline of important financial crisis, we can observe a probable correlation between the lowest numbers of competitions and for example: the student protest of 1967-1968, the 1973-1979 oil crisis and even the major third world crisis of the mid 1980s [Fig.1].

That the dynamics of international competitions can logically be related to the major vectors of global dynamics should come as no surprise, although it would be risky to conclude that they would be more revealing that the number of national or restricted competitions during the same period of time, since there exists no systematic inventory that is reliable enough to the competitions research community. There were nonetheless major competitions won by architects whose names were already in the history book of architecture and some who became big names since: Alvar Aalto for the Seinäjoki Town Hall in 1950, Lucio Costa for the plan of Brasilia in 1956, Aldo Rossi for the San Cataldo Cemetary in 1971, Daniel Libeskind for the Jewish Museum in Berlin in 1988 or Snøhetta for the Bibliotheca Alexandrina in 1988, etc. This is certainly a first indication that there might be a correlation between international competitions and architectural quality. We already attempted to study the new meaning of international competitions during the first CRC/LEAP Montreal conference on the subject in March 2012 at the University of Montreal and we will indeed use some of its results to put the findings related to this research program in our conclusive discussion. In the mean time, another figure to keep in mind, when building a comparative scale, is the impressive number of 278 competitors per international competitions, as a general average for the 60 years span of the UIA accessible data. When compared to the 3 to 12 competitors of common restricted competitions, there is no need to further demonstrate the widespread capacity of attraction and exposure of an international competition — a characteristic powerful enough to attract and to convince administrators, elected ministers and politicians to consider choosing an international opening for political, economic and communicational reasons. But what about the actual will to use an international competition to build and transform a society? What does it say of a cultural or multicultural "opening to the world"?

## ▬ Canadian Statistics Compared to UIA General Figures

Indeed, if we consider the Canadian context, we will find 302 competitions organised since 1945, out of which 63 were opened internationally. In this 21% of international competitions, 46% looked for ideas and 54% for projects. When compared to the UIA picture, there seems to be a more balanced spread, which in fact should be interpreted as an increased recourse of international competitions when looking for ideas than in many other countries. In other words, the "Canadian opening to the world," if confirmed, would encourage ideas as much as buildable projects. Still, the amount of competitions dedicated to realization is slightly more important and this, at least, counts in the general comparative apparatus.

In order to refine the global portrait, we have constructed two comparative diagrams with these general figures. The first diagram superimposes the progression of international competitions in Canada parallel to the UIA ones and it clearly shows a long systematic avoidance of the international procedure between 1958 and 1988, a period during which Canada was not following other countries, and while regularly organising restricted competitions, would never open them to the rest of the world [Fig.2].

Using, in particular, the prominent theoretical essay by Peter Collins, Architectural Judgement (1971), which makes extensive reference to this historical event, we have attempted elsewhere to explain this long refusal by the shock of the 1958 Toronto City Hall competition, which attracted more that 500 competitors, a success which literally provoked a split in the jury and a literal crisis in the profession

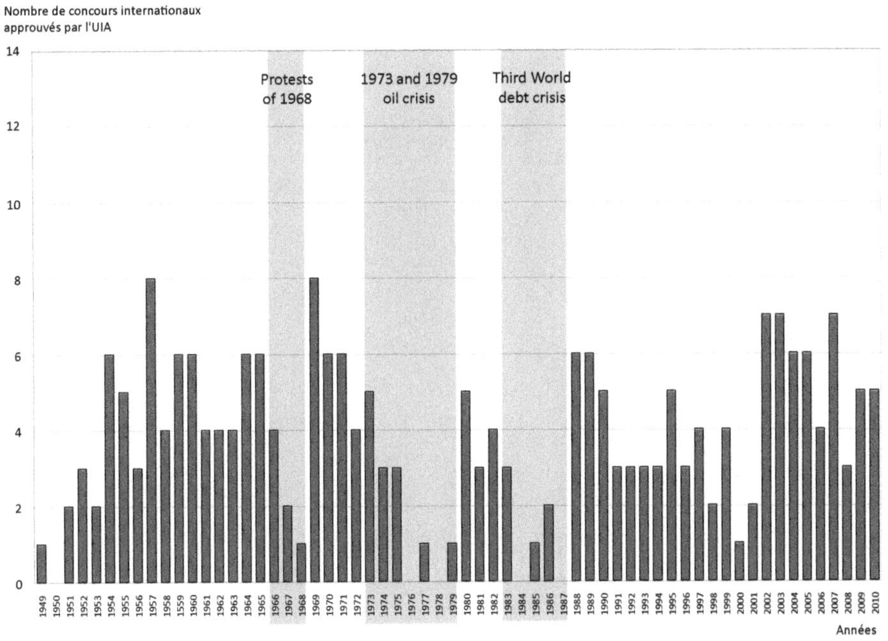

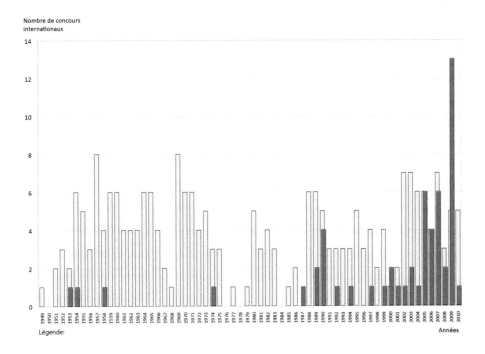

**Nombre de concours internationaux approuvés par l'UIA**

Protests of 1968

1973 and 1979 oil crisis

Third World debt crisis

Années

**Fig. 1**
Histogram of international competitions (in red) (approved UIA) related to three major crises since 1945.

**Nombre de concours internationaux**

Légende:

Années

**Fig. 2**
Number of international competitions (in red) organised in Canada compared to the UIA histogram.

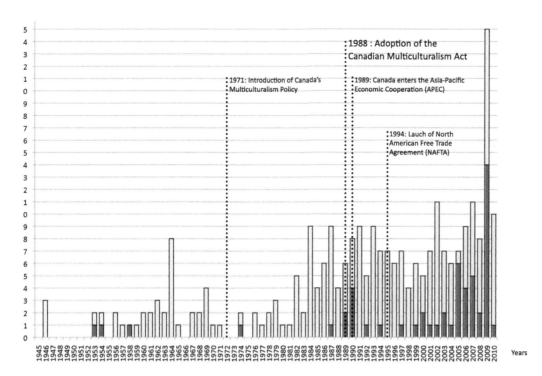

**Fig. 3**
Ratio of international to national competitions (in red), from 1945 to 2010 with
main stages of cultural and economical opening of Canada to the international.

Within the chart:

1971: Introduction of Canada's Multiculturalism Policy

1988 : Adoption of the Canadian Multiculturalism Act

1989: Canada enters the Asia-Pacific Economic Cooperation (APEC)

1994: Lauch of North American Free Trade Agreement (NAFTA)

Years

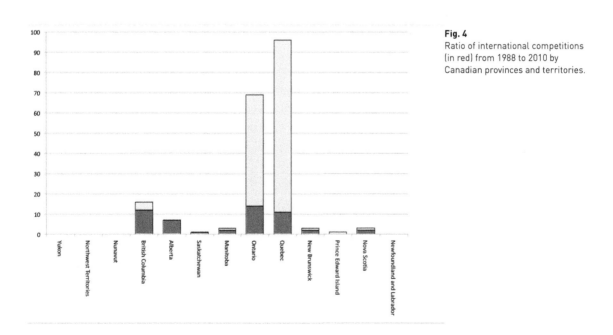

**Fig. 4**
Ratio of international competitions
(in red) from 1988 to 2010 by
Canadian provinces and territories.

as a whole.[11] But how are we to interpret the paradigm shift of the 1980s, and the renewed interest for international openings? It is tempting to look for explanations about this clear rise of international competitions towards the end of the 1980s in correlation to the 1988 *Adoption of the Multiculturalism Act* **[Fig.3]**.

Although the first agreements regarding a multicultural policy go back to 1971, the diagram only shows a possible correlation after the 1988 adoption of the act. There are probably many socio cultural factors to take into account before drawing safe conclusions, but it is also true that since 1988 there has been a clear increase of more than 7% in the percentage of foreign-born population in Canada after more than 30 years of a stable percentage of 15%, the figure quickly rose to 22%. Was the 1988 *Multiculturalism Act* a cause or a consequence, and how did it affect the recourse of international competitions?

## ▬ National Disparities in Some Canadian Statistics

As is well known, Canada's population is rather small (35 millions) but distributed across an extensive slice of land running from the Atlantic to the Pacific Ocean. The second-largest country by total area, Canada is a federal state resulting from an accretion of provinces and territories. As already mentioned, the cultural disparities have been acknowledged as a main constituent of Canada's specificity to the point of protecting this variety of cultures by a federal law in 1988. Beyond the complexity of political reasons, it should be stressed here that this law is still ambiguously perceived by many Canadians as it is not clear whether it is meant to open or close the cultural borders of this all too fragile federation. If we study more closely some statistics regarding national versus international competitions, we find major discrepancies and differences between western provinces like British Columbia and Alberta, both of which barely organised any competitions between 1945 and 2010 and which recently launched competitions almost exclusively at the international level, and eastern provinces like Ontario or Quebec in which more than 83% of all competitions have been organised since 1945, but mostly and clearly at a national (i.e. provincial) level. Regarding the 1988 — 2012 period, we find 33% of international competitions took place in Canada, a meaningless figure when analysed through an interprovincial comparison since it

goes down to 20% in Ontario and to 11% in Quebec: a region of Canada in which almost 50% of all competitions have been organised — a figure equal to the percentage of ideas versus projects competitions in international competitions **[Fig.4]**.

In other words, we would find indications of reluctance to "open to the world" competitions in the Canadian province of Quebec, which devoted the greatest energy to develop and promote the recourse to competitions since the end of the 1980s. If true this would mean facing a clear contradiction or another logic, such as the building of a regional landscape, as demonstrated by Denis Bilodeau's comparative study in his thesis on territorial imagination.[12]

Digging into specific socio cultural differences would certainly be enlightening, although it would go much beyond the scope of this paper, but it is not yet clear that for example a socio economic study would offer clear answers. Alberta, a province in which the gross domestic product per capita has risen to CAD$71 803 between 2005 and 2009, has barely organised ten competitions since 1988, all of which were international; when Quebec, with a gross domestic product per capita of half the amount of Alberta (CAD$37 850) has organised more than a hundred competitions, eleven of which were at the international level: i.e. the same number of international competitions but ten times the overall number of competitions!

There is obviously a scientific limit to these kinds of statistical interpretations, particularly when we try to bring them to the level of an international comparison, but they nonetheless indicate socio political distinctions that need to be made in order to appreciate the differences and the contradictions regarding the validity of any correlation between international competitions and multicultural politics. Facing such a complexity regarding the use of statistics, we have decided to complement the study by engaging in a systematic discourse analysis of competitions organised in Canada since the adoption of the *Multiculturalism Act* in 1988.

**Fig. 5**
"Lower Don Lands" competition.
(Toronto, Canada. 2007). Project
by Michael Van Valkenburgh
Associates, Inc.

**Fig. 6**
"ReCONNECT : The Wildcard"
competition (Vancouver, Canada.
2011). Project by AECOM.

**Fig. 7**
"Jardins Éphémères du 400e " competition (Québec, Canada. 2006). Project by NIP Paysage.

**Fig. 8**
"YUL — MTL Parcours d'entrée de la ville de Montréal" competition. (Montréal, Canada. 2011). Project by Brown and Stoney Architects.

## Comparative and Hermeneutical Analysis of Thirty-Nine Canadian International Competitions (1988 - 2012)

Since 1988, seven of the ten Canadian provinces organised competitions at the international level. The following list shows a significant discrepancy amongst provinces :

- Ontario :14
- Quebec :10
- British Columbia :8
- Alberta :3
- Manitoba :2
- Nova Scotia :1
- Saskatchewan :1

The balance between competitions for ideas (19) and competitions for projects (20) is surprisingly even, but coherent with what we have already observed in the long run since 1945. This can also be analysed by taking into consideration private and public promoters for one-third of the international competitions was launched by private organisations and only three times for actual projects. It should perhaps come as no surprise that the two other thirds were launched by public administrations or semi-public entities.

The typological spread is also quite surprising when one considers that in the general public's opinion, international competitions are often meant for big and symbolic cultural buildings and / or symbolic landmarks. On the contrary, in the selected Canadian corpus we find :

- Urbanism : 11
- Landscape design, parks and public squares : 11
- Cultural buildings : 6
- Housing : 5
- Others : 5 (2 for architecture schools, 2 bridges, 1 administration complex, 1 sport complex)

These overall statistics clearly show that the preconception about cultural buildings does not follow the reality and that, on the contrary, international competitions are considered credible, if not unavoidable tools, foremost at the urban and landscape architecture scales. The interesting sub-distinction to be noted here is the fact that when organising a competition for a more manageable scale of a public square or a park, the organisers were looking for real projects, yet only for ideas when it concerned very complex urban scales, indeed hard to define in a project timeline. This is however coherent with one of the UIA guides that recognises that : (Article 20) : "Town-planning competitions are, by their nature, ideas competitions, since the work is generally carried out by official bodies, frequently on a long-term basis..." [13] **[Fig.5 to 8]**.

## In Search of Direct Effects of the *Canadian Multiculturalism Act* (1988) on Discourses Produced by and Related to International Competitions

Before summarizing the findings of our hermeneutical analysis of official documents, briefs, official declarations and media or public reactions directly related to a corpus of thirty-nine competitions, it may be helpful, especially for non-Canadian readers, to consider the following extracts of a Canadian law at the origin of our hypothesis. The general commentary introducing the law provides a rather technological explanation of its origins by stressing that, "Recent advances in technology have made international communications more important than ever. Canadians who speak many languages and understand many cultures make it easier for Canada to participate globally in areas of education, trade and diplomacy." [14] But the law itself displays a more proactive tone as shown by the following extracts:

> *Article 3 (1) a) "recognize and promote the understanding that multiculturalism reflects the cultural and racial diversity of Canadian society;"*
>
> *Article 3 (1) c) "encourage and assist the social, cultural, economic and political institutions of Canada to be both respectful and inclusive of Canada's multicultural character;"*
>
> *Article 3 (1) f) "promote the understanding and creativity that arise from the interaction between individuals and communities of different origins."*

The nationally oriented nature of these vectors appears clearly in these passages. They are meant to recognise and protect the multicultural character and diversity of Canadian society and are not primarily directed toward developing international relationships in spite of the technological explanation given in the foreword. There are no a priori clear indications or invitations or even injunctions to develop and increase opportunities to "open to the world," through international competitions, for example. Through reading these articles only, it would be hard to anticipate any statistical correlation that constitutes the hypothesis at the origin of this study.

## Synthesis of the Hermeneutical Analysis: Four Reasons to Organize International Competitions

We focussed the analysis on the four most significant program scales (urbanism, landscape, cultural, housing) and looked for traces of discourses in four categories of documents (Calls for competitors (C), Rules and Briefs (R), Official declarations (O), Media reactions (M)). Returning to our main hypothesis and searching in all of these documents, we looked for explicit fragments of political rhetoric and, at best, clear signs and indicators of an explicit political will (or intention) to open the architectural debate outside the cultural borders of a specific nation.

In the following four sections we give some of the most explicit quotations for the purpose of this paper, considering that the full report delivers twenty-five pages of revealing fragments of discourse (n.b. underlining ours). The major common figures, which can be identified throughout these quotations, revolve around four poles of intentions, sometimes conflicting in the same competition related discourses:

a. International competitions as world-class contests
b. International competitions as transfers between local and global models
c. International competitions as global issues (cultural, environmental, etc.) in local contexts
d. International competitions as intercultural openings to the world

Since it appears afterward that these four categories point toward four reasons for organisers to choose in favour of international competitions, it is important to carefully document these "political reasons."

## A. International Competitions as World-Class Contests

### Urbanism (M)

These are **world-leading design teams** *that have come to Edmonton to work with us to plan a new community in the heart of Edmonton." (Mayor Stephen Mandel, "Three European Firms Compete to Redevelop Canadian Airport Lands" in PR Newswire, February 15, 2011).*
[Edmonton Airport Land competition / AL / 2010].

### Cultural (C)

*Cantos envisions a **world-class destination** for public programs, civic engagement, music education, creativity and learning that incorporates, expands and honours the existing historic King Edward Hotel (King Eddy)." ("Cantos Takes Next Step to Create National Music Centre," Cantos Music Fondation, March 9, 2009).*
[Calgary National Music Centre competition / AL / 2009] **[Fig.9]**.

### Cultural (M)

*Royal Ontario Museum president and CEO William Thorsell said that "the outstanding calibre of these architects speaks to... **Toronto's eminent place among international cities. Toronto needs a star turn** — more than one — and the selection of a great architect for the ROM's revival is an essential component in making that happens. (Michael Posner, The Globe and Mail, September 8, 2001).*
[Royal Ontario Museum competition / ON / 2001].

### Housing (R)

*We are interested in spurring creative thinking, among international architects, with the intent of short-listing four to six architectural firms...**The Fernbrook world is a world of difference and originality. A world of bold visions, of challenges met and exceeded.***
[Absolute Design competition / ON / 2005] **[Fig.10]**.

The first pole of key words gathers expressions such as: "world-leading communities," "world-leading design teams," "world-class destination." All of these expressions point towards the existence (real or mythical), of a world ranking and imply that organising an international competition is a way to compete at the "world level," as can be the case for sport activities, for example. In this case, the notion of competition is clearly defined at the primary level of fighting for first place. There is no consideration here of a multicultural intention, but an almost Darwinian understanding of excellence and "natural selection" for survival. In fact, in this category, be it for designing at the urban, cultural or housing scales, we find organisers' intentions that seek to locate their project in the realm of "internationality" almost to the point of negating any value to the local or national levels. In the case of the Royal Ontario Museum (Toronto, 2001), the organisers expect a "great architect for the ROM's revival," or claim that "Toronto needs a star turn," and this can only be found in some international stratosphere more than within the national borders. It may be useful to underline here that Daniel Libeskind won this competition.

**Fig. 9**
"National Music Center of Canada" competition,
(Calgary, Canada. 2009). Project by Allied Works
Architecture/BKDI

**Fig. 10**
"Absolute Design Ideas" Competition (Mississauga,
Canada. 2005). Project by MAD office (Yansong Ma,
Shen Huihui, Yosuke Hayano, Dang Qun, Shen Jun)

**Fig. 11**
"Jarvis Slip" competition (Toronto, Canada. 2007).
Project by Claude Cormier Architectes Paysagistes Inc.

**Fig. 12**
"Orchestre Symphonique de Montréal" competition.
(Montréal, Canada. 2002). Project by De Architekten
Cie./Aedifica inc./Les architectes Tétreault Parent
Languedoc et associés

## B. International Competitions as Transfers Between Local and Global Models

### Landscape (C)

*Waterfront Toronto's mission is* **to put Toronto at the forefront of global cities** *in the 21st century by transforming the waterfront into beautiful and sustainable communities, fostering economic growth in knowledge-based, creative industries, and ultimately redefining how Toronto, Ontario, and Canada are perceived by the world. […] Through the coordination of several international design competitions and the engagement of many of the world's best landscape architects and urban designers Waterfront Toronto have demonstrated its commitment to design excellence. Jarvis Slip will be* **a key component in Toronto's network of world renowned waterfront public spaces.**" *(Competition Brief: Goals of the design competition).*

[Jarvis Slip Public Space competition/ON/2008] **[Fig.11]**.

### Landscape (R)

**An international design competition informed by local technical experts** *and public consultation was chosen as the way to find the best ideas for the park." "The Canadian Tourism Commission states:* "**Canada's tourism industry will deliver world-class cultural and leisure experiences** *year-round while preserving and sharing Canada's clean, safe and natural environments."* *(Introductory remarks: Program, Opportunities, Culture Heritage & Tourism).*

[Point Pleasant Park competition/NS/2005].

### Housing (O)

*"The Absolute partners hope is that* **the competition will also introduce to Canada, design and construction techniques and materials new to the market[...]** *Developers tend to have blinkered vision, a situation forced on them by circumstances," says Mr. Salvatore. "We believe approaching this project in this fashion will prove a breath of fresh air, a new window onto the latest trends and techniques in other cities, other nations."* *(Official declaration, January 30, 2006).*

[Absolute Design competition /ON/2005].

### Cultural (C)

*La formule retenue pour ce concours d'envergure internationale constitue une véritable première au Québec et comporte plusieurs avantages. Ainsi, en plus de favoriser une forte émulation, elle concourt à la notoriété du projet, permet aux firmes d'ici d'enrichir leurs relations avec leurs consœurs d'autres pays, offre aux jeunes architectes la chance d'être de la compétition et, enfin,* **elle contribue au rayonnement mondial de la grande métropole culturelle qu'est Montréal.** *(Ministère de la Culture et des Communications, [Press Release] June 27, 2002).*

[OSM/QC/2002] **[Fig.12]**.

### Cultural (M)

*"This is going* **to put Toronto on the international cultural tourism map,**" *said provincial minister for tourism, Tim Hudak, at a press conference. (Agence France-Presse, 26 février 2002).*

[Royal Ontario Museum competition /ON/2001] **[Fig.13]**.

In the second pole of key words we find expressions such as: "a model for local and global design excellence" or "an architectural statement of international excellence," or even "to put (our city, our region, our nation) at the forefront of global cities, etc." If the first category of intentions was mainly oriented toward a "world level," in this second category there is bipolarity. In this group it is sometimes expected that an international competition will put the organising entity "on the map." This is clearly the case for cultural programs for which a certain level of notoriety is supposed to help the image or the world recognition of the organising entity. This image would function at two levels, sometimes simultaneously: one locally, the other globally. Most of these international competitions can be found at the turn of the century, however, when the debate around the unavoidable globalisation of economies and cultures was at stake. This has slightly shifted towards the idea of "global models" and "international examples" and some cities even insist on the existence of new networks of global cities. In this category, organising an international competition seems to be necessary in order to access the so-called "network of world renowned public spaces" and this is clearly the case when touristic issues are at stake. In this category of expectations, competitions are launched onto the background of an international market — a global market in fact — certainly activated by new communications technologies, in which "branding" is seen as a way for the local to be identified on a global international map. The famous "Bilbao effect" is clearly the underlying paradigm here.

## C. International Competitions as Global Issues (Cultural, Environmental, Etc.) in Local Contexts
### Urbanism (R)

*"This community must be seen as* **a model for local and global design excellence.***" "A very high threshold of sustainability has already been achieved by a limited number of sustainable developments in other parts of the world.* **Edmonton's vision is to expand on the successes of these leading edge communities.***"*
[Edmonton Airport Land competition / AL / 2010] **[Fig.14]**.

### Urbanism (O)

*"The City of Surrey is* **'inviting the world'** *to help provide future vision and design ideas for its five emerging town centres." "***The issues involved in managing the growth we're seeing in our five town centres are shared by other suburbs shifting into complex cities around the globe,***" said Watts. "***By opening ourselves to a world of new ideas***, we'll be able to access and consider the widest possible range of options as we plan the future of our town centres." (Official Press Release, Surrey Contest Issues Global Invitation for Town Centre Design Idea, November 2, 2009).*
[TownShift competition / BC / 2010].

### Housing (R)

*"This is an open worldwide competition and we seek submissions* **from as far a geographic reach as possible***...Vancouver as the epicentre of the 100 Mile radius it is hoped that the* **design principles promoted will be applicable to many locations on our shared planet.***" (Eligibility).*
[100 Mile House competition / BC / 2012].

### Housing (R)

*"The ideas proposed need to consider that the City has adopted a goal to become the* **greenest city in the world...***There might be new forms of housing that work in other cities but have not been tried in Vancouver." (The Challenge).*
[re:THINK Housing competition / BC / 2012] **[Fig.15] [Fig.16]**.

A special category has emerged toward the end of the first decade of 2000s in the Canadian context and seems to shift the drive for globalisation to the cultural and / or the environmental realms. A series of ideas competitions in western provinces, mainly British Columbia, almost entirely relied on reforming the image of cities through the use of international competitions in order to compete for the "greenest city in the world." From economic globalisation to environmental globalisation the gap is not as big as it may seem, since in most cases the competing images are still meant to enhance touristic activities (before or after Olympic games for example). The surprising element would concern the idea of a possible generalisation at the international scale of some design principle supposed to be "applicable in many other locations." There is an almost colonial tone in these declarations thinly disguised by the good intentions of environmental issues that are supposed to belong to an international level of decision and action. In that case, an international competition would become a tool for developing international relationships and the main Canadian cities seem to be very aware of this challenge at the risk of being in competition against each other in order to become a world reference. Projects, but more often ideas, for parks and urban squares seem to be the ideal programs for this kind of international world fair of ideas.

**Fig. 13**
"Royal Ontario Museum" competition. Project by Studio
Daniel Libeskind). *Copyright-Steven Evans Photography /
Source : Studio Daniel Libeskind.*

**Fig. 14**
"Edmonton Airport Land » competition (Edmonton,
Canada. 2010). Project by Perkins + Will.
*Source : Perkins + Will.*

**Fig. 15**
"re :THINK Housing" competition (Vancouver, Canada.
2012). Project by Ian McDonald.

**Fig. 16**
"re :THINK Housing" competition (Vancouver, Canada.
2012). Project by Andrew Neuman.

**Fig. 17**
"Toronto Waterfront" competition, (Toronto, Canada.
2006). Project by DuToit Allsopp Hillier, Schollen &
Company, Diamond + Schmitt Architects, Arup, Halsall
Associates, David Dennis Design

**Fig. 18**
"Canadian Museum for Human Rights" competition.
(Winnipeg, Canada. 2003). Project by Antoine Predock
Architect.
*Source-Antoine Predock Architect*

## D. International Competitions as Intercultural Openings to the World
### Landscape (O)

*"The Jury recognized the wonderful opportunity that an international waterfront competition provides for the City of Toronto and the greater region **to learn about best practices from other parts of the world** and the creative approaches proposed for a more efficient and effective use of urban space for all of our citizens." (Jury Report, Overview, May 30, 2006).*
[Toronto Waterfront competition / ON / 2006] **[Fig.17]**.

### Cultural (R)

*"The issue of human rights is such a worldwide concern that the decision was made to conduct an international architectural competition to select an architect and design for this important project." "The Museum will be a permanent statement to the world about our essential values and beliefs — and **our desire to work with people of every nation** to promote the cause of human rights." "The creative challenge will be to express these critically important issues and transform them into an **architectural statement of international excellence and significance.**" (Brief)*
[Canadian Museum Human Rights competition / MB / 2003] **[Fig.18]**.

### Cultural (O)

*Par ce concours d'envergure internationale, la Grande bibliothèque du Québec souhaite réaliser un triple objectif : établir un haut niveau d'excellence et d'efficacité pour ses futures installations ; **stimuler la créativité des architectes d'ici et d'ailleurs** et **contribuer au rayonnement international du Québec** au plan architectural. (21 janvier 2000).*
[Grande Bibliothèque du Québec competition / QC / 2000] **[Fig.19]**.

### Housing (M)

*"'We're not just doing this for a lark,' insists Lorne Cappe, the competition's coordinator. He says **an international ideas competition was deemed to be the best approach because it would offer the city a wide range of possibilities for developing new types of housing and would not cost a lot of money to run. (...) 'This***

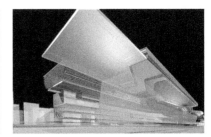

**Fig. 19**
"Grande Bibliothèque du Québec" competition, (Montréal, Canada. 2000). (From left to right)
Projects by Patkau architects/Croft Pelletier, architectes/Gilles Guité, architecte; Saucier et
Perrotte, architectes (Saucier+Perrotte)/Menkès Shooner Dagenais, architectes/Desvigne et
Dalnoky, paysagiste/Go Multimédia intégration technologique; Zaha Hadid architects/Boutin
Ramoisy Tremblay, architectes

*competition won't result in actual buildings, but it will result in legislation,' says [Donald] Schmitt [professional advisor to the competition]." (Victoria Gall, Canadian Architect, Vol.35 No.2, February, 1990)*

[Housing Toronto competition / ON / 1989].

Along with the more traditional understanding of the role of international competition, generally highly oriented by economic issues, even at the cultural level, it is possible to find examples or fragments of discourses that seem to be grounded on a more benevolent call for world expertise and world debate. Expressions such as "inviting the world," "opening ourselves to a world of ideas," "learn about best practices from other parts of the world." Interestingly, we find these generous openings in cases coming from private organisers who sometimes seek to "introduce to Canada design and construction techniques coming from elsewhere" in a kind of knowledge transfer operation. But it is important to underline that there is also a belief that there is an international learning system for these cities, in which the "best practices" contribute to the renewal and diffusion of the city image. This "opening to a world of ideas" does not remain at the technological level; it also reaches the ultimate level of human rights, as is the case for at least one extraordinary competition. In this specific case, hard to generalise, the opening to the world of the international competition is presented as an obvious necessity due to the "world wide issues of tolerance and respect for human rights." In a United Nations-, or rather UNESCO-like system of multicultural values, this kind of international competition would be one of the very few to fall into the expected result of a multicultural policy. But it is also in this category that we find extracts that are literally loaded with multicultural contradictory meanings to the point of seeming meaningless, as is the case for this last quotation:

*"The winning proposal will, in the opinion of an outside Selection Advisory Committee, be one that **puts another piece of Calgary on the international map.**" [...] Characteristics: The architectural style will be memorable and expressive of Canada's diversity of music styles and the variety of cultures that contribute to the breadth of 'Canadian' music, as well as the international spirit of music in general." (Calgary National Music Centre/AL /2009)* **[Fig.20]**.

It is well known that architects who enter a competition process look for challenges, but we can imagine how challenged competitors from the only three countries that sent projects must have been in this openly multicultural case.

**Fig. 20**
"National Music Center of Canada" competition
(Calgary, Canada. 2009). Project by Allied Works
Architecture / BKDI.

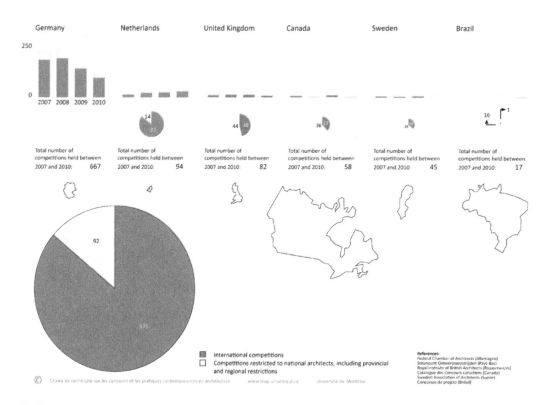

**Fig. 21**
International comparison of the
proportion of international and
national competitions from 2007
and 2010.

**Fig. 22**
"2008 Beijing Olympic Stadium" competition (Beijing, China. 2002).
Nicknamed the "NEST" by the Chinese people, this project was designed
by Swiss architects Herzog and De Meuron architects.
*Courtesy of Carmela Cucuzzella.*

## ▬ Conclusion : Four Reasons for Organizing an International Competition in the Planetary Age

a. International competitions as world-class contests
b. International competitions as transfers between local and global models
c. International competitions as global issues (cultural, environmental, etc.) in local contexts
d. International competitions as intercultural openings to the world

As should be stressed, before concluding this survey, the four categories identified through this corpus of thirty-nine competitions are not mutually exclusive, and it would be erroneous to use the same categories to classify the competitions in proof boxes. In fact, we found traces of intentions jumping from one category to another. Some competitions were clearly meant to look in one direction, but some actually looked in various, almost contradictory, definitions of internationality.

Therefore, how are we to interpret these findings in relation to our original hypothesis since there are almost no clear signs of a direct influence of the *Multiculturalism Act* on these international competitions ? Various classical overall explanations can be given like the ones related to the obvious impact of the new communications systems on a new globalised perception of the world, and of course of widespread use of the Internet, as it has been generalised in our western societies since the mid 1990s. This would be a "feel good" theory, which would perhaps explain why thirty-four of these competitions were organised after 2000 and only five in the 1990s. However, studying the relationship between international competitions and the rise of a digital culture would require another scientific apparatus, for it does not explain the huge disparities encountered when comparing the openness to the world of the various Canadian provinces, theoretically all equally opened to the digital world, but certainly diverging on the need for international competitions **[Fig.4]**.

It is also possible to think of a reverse process of influence coming from the various communities towards the need for some multicultural regulations. In that sense, and there are some indications of this phenomenon, the *Multicultural Act* would be a consequence of multicultural dynamics, of internal pressures for international openings, rather than a cause. In this case, the observed multiplicity of intentions regarding the need for an international opening would give a mirrored image of the search for an identity in the diversity of cultures. In other words it would signify a need for a redefinition of both the notions of internationality and culture in what is now being designated as our multipolar world.

During the Montreal *Conference on International Competitions and Architectural Quality in the Planetary Age*, held at the University of Montreal in March 2012, we were given multiple opportunities to challenge the traditional understanding of the role of international competitions by providing some preliminary statistics gathered from Germany, The Netherlands, Brazil, Sweden and the United Kingdom **[Fig.21]**.[15]

But these remain very fragmentary statistics since there does not yet exist an international network of scholars devoted to the gathering of national data on competitions in spite of repeated calls we have made since the second symposium on competitions research held in Copenhagen in 2010. The information is still dispersed in various administrations, professional associations and sometimes in private enterprises. We will only be able to reach a clear picture when a series of competition databases will be interconnected allowing for comparative studies at a more global level. For now, it appears however that the notion of internationality cannot be dealt within the same understanding of the world as was understood by the *Union Internationale des Architectes* competition organisers of the 1950s and 1960s. And although the UIA revised its guide for international competitions in 1978, it seems that fewer countries still feel the need to require the UIA label nowadays.

We hope to have shown that it does not suffice to label a competition "international" to circumscribe precisely what this means in terms of opening to the world. If indeed it is not proven by our analysis that international competitions were instruments of multicultural policies in the Canadian context since 1988, we hope to have made it clear that the hermeneutical study of discourses shows that they are good indicators of increasing international multipolar pressures on public actors and competition organisers. In fact, some international competitions might be ways to cover otherwise controversial issues — smoke screens — like in the case of some competitions revolving only around environmental issues. It could also be said of international competitions that they are Trojan horses, clever war devices, as was the case for the main buildings of the Beijing Olympics in 2008 ; the stadium won by a "foreign team of Swiss architects,"

as Chinese political leaders put it. In such instances, international opening does not so much mean to be open to the world, as it means to open the world to your own market **[Fig.22]**.

## ▬▬ Notes

[1] Chupin, J.-P. 2008. Documenting Competitions, Contributing to Research, Archiving Events. *In :* Peyceré D. & Wierre, F. (eds.) *Architecture and Digital Archives (Architecture in the digital age : a question of memory).* Gollion : Éditions Infolio.

[2] Lipstadt, H. 2010. Experimenting with the Experimental Tradition, 1989-2009 : On Competitions and Architecture Research. *In :* Rönn, M., Kazemian, R. & Andersson, J. E. (eds.) *The Architectural Competition (Research Inquiries and Experience).* Stockholm : Axl Books.

[3] Since 2002, in a series of research projects focussing on competition cases undertaken at the *Laboratoire d'étude de l'architecture potentielle* (L.E.A.P) and since 2011 in the new *Research Chair on Competitions and Contemporary Practices in Architecture*, both research entities hosted at the University of Montreal, we have been studying issues of architectural quality, architectural experimentation, architectural judgement, heritage conservation, cultural landscapes as well as the impact of environmental norms on the design process (see www.leap.umontreal.ca). These various research programs supported by public funding are both updating and using a systematic documentary database of competitions organised in Canada since 1945 : the *Canadian Competition Catalogue.* This scientific resource, partly open for consultation to the general public, delivers information on 300 competitions, a third of which being well documented, displaying 50 % of the 30 000 documents related to more than 2500 architectural, urban and landscape design projects on the Internet.

[4] Chupin, J.-P. (Ed.) 2012. *Canadian Competitions Catalogue /* www.ccc.umontreal.ca / *Catalogue des Concours Canadiens.* Laboratoire d'étude de l'architecture potentielle (Université de Montréal).

[5] Adamczyk, G., Chupin, J.-P., Bilodeau, D. & Cormier, A. 2004. Architectural competitions and new reflexive practices. *In :* ARCC, E. (ed.) *EAAE ARCC Conference (Between Research and Practice).* Dublin.

[6] Chupin, J.-P. 2011. Judgement by design : Towards a model for studying and improving the competition process in architecture and urban design. *The Scandinavian Journal of Management (Elsevier),* 27 173-184. Chupin, J.-P. & Cucuzella, C. 2011. Environmental standards and judgment processes in competitions for public buildings. *Geographica Helvetica,* 66 13-23. Chupin, J.-P., Gomes, L. J. & Goorts, J. 2007. Le ciel des idées, l'horizon des connaissances. *In :* France, E. & Gravelaine, F. D. (eds.) *Europan France 1998 - 2007 (innover, dialoguer, réaliser).* Paris : Jean-Michel Place.

[7] This is how the architect Shohei Shigematsu, partner and director of OMA New York, summarised the dilemma in his keynote lecture during the Montreal *CRC/LEAP Conference on International Competitions and Architectural Quality in the Planetary Age,* on March 16, 2012. The full video of the conference can be watched at : *http ://vimeo.com/41789025.*

[8] Adamczyk, G. 2008. Le concours d'architecture comme mise en scène in Plante J. *Architecture et spectacle au Québec,* Québec, les publications du Québec.

[9] Nicholas, A. 2007. *L'apogée des concours d'architecture : L'action de L'UIA de 1948 — 1975,* Paris, Picard.

[10] Arrando, J. & Tochtermann, W. 2008. *UIA Guide for International Competitions in Architecture and Town Planning* (Unesco regulations / Terms of application). International Competitions Commission. Article 2 : International competitions may be classified into "Project" or "Ideas" competitions).

[11] Collins, P. 1971. *Architectural Judgement*, Montreal, McGill-Queen's University Press. See also Chupin, J.-P. 2011. Judgement by design : Towards a model for studying and improving the competition process in architecture and urban design. *The Scandinavian Journal of Management (Elsevier)*, 27 173-184.

[12] Bilodeau, D. (Ed.) 2006. *Architectural Competitions and Territorial Imagination : Cultural Projects in Quebec, 1991-2005*, Montreal, Uqam / LEAP.

[13] Farrando, J. & Tochtermann, W. 2008. *UIA Guide for International Competitions in Architecture and Town Planning* (Unesco regulations / Terms of application). International Competitions Commission.

[14] The complete text of the *Multiculturalism Act* can be found on the website of *Citizenship and Immigration Canada : http://www.cic.gc.ca/english/multiculturalism/citizenship.asp*

[15] For more information on this international symposium jointly organised by LEAP lab and the University of Montreal Research Chair on Competitions and Contemporary Practices in Architecture (CRC), please note that the program, list of invited speakers and summaries of presentations can be found at : *http://www.crc.umontreal.ca/index.php ?id = 141&lang = en*.

**Lipstadt**, Helen, and Barry **Bergdoll**. The Experimental Tradition : Essays on Competitions in Architecture. New York, N.Y. : Princeton Architectural Press, 1989.

**Nicolas**, Aymone. L'Apogée des concours internationaux d'architecture : l'action de l'uia, 1948-1975. Collection architectures contemporaines Serie Etudes. Paris : Picard, 2007.

**Rönn**, Magnus, Reza **Kazemian**, and Jonas E. **Andersson**. The Architectural Competition : Research Inquiries and Experiences Stockholm : Axl Books, 2010.

**Tostrup**, Elisabeth, and **Arkitekthøgskolen i Oslo**. Architecture and Rhetoric : Text and Design in Architectural Competitions, Oslo, 1939-90. Oslo : Oslo School of Architecture, 1996.

**Union Internationale des Architectes (UIA).** "Uia Guide for International Competitions in Architecture and Town Planning (Unesco Regulations / Terms of Application)." Paris : Union Internationale des Architectes, 2008.

# ▬▬ References

**Adamczyk**, Georges. "Le concours d'architecture comme mise en scène." In Architecture et spectacle au Québec, edited by Jacques Plante. Québec : Les publications du Québec, 2008.

**Adamczyk**, Georges, Jean-Pierre Chupin, Denis Bilodeau, and Anne Cormier. "Architectural Competitions and New Reflective Practices." In EAAE ARCC Conference (between Research and Practice), edited by EAAE ARCC. Dublin, 2004.

**Bilodeau**, Denis, dir. Architectural Competitions and Territorial Imagination : Cultural Projects in Quebec 1991-2005. Montreal : Uqam / LEAP, 2006.

**Chupin**, Jean-Pierre. Analogie et théorie en architecture (De la vie, de la ville et de la conception, même). Collection Projet et Théorie. Genève : Infolio, 2010.

**Chupin**, Jean-Pierre. "Documenting Competitions, Contribution to Research, Archiving Events." Chap. 29 In Architecture and Digital Archives (Architecture in the Digital Age : A Question of Memory), edited by David Peyceré and Françoise Wierre, 523-34. Gollion : Éditions Infolio, 2008.

**Chupin**, Jean-Pierre. "Judgement by Design : Towards a Model for Studying and Improving the Competition Process in Architecture and Urban Design." The Scandinavian Journal of Management (Elsevier) 27, no. 1 (Special topic forum on Architectural Competitions) (2011) : 173-84.

**Chupin**, Jean-Pierre, and Carmela **Cucuzzella**. "Environmental Standards and Judgment Processes in Competitions for Public Buildings." Geographica Helvetica 66, no. 1 (special issue on competitions research directed by Joris Van Wezemael) (2011) : 13-23.

**Chupin**, Jean-Pierre, dir. "Canadian Competitions Catalogue / Catalogue Des Concours Canadiens (http://www.ccc.Umontreal.ca)." LEAP / CRC, 2002-(2014).

**Chupin**, Jean-Pierre, Lino José **Gomes**, and Jason **Goorts**. "Le ciel des idées, l'horizon des connaissances." In Europan France 1998 - 2007 (Innover, Dialoguer, Réaliser), edited by Europan France and Frédérique de Gravelaine, 39-52. Paris : Jean-Michel Place, 2007.

**Collins**, Peter. Architectural Judgement. Montreal : McGill-Queen's University Press, 1971.

**Europan** (Organisation). Session (8e : 2006), Jean-Pierre **Chupin**, Danièle **Valabrègue**, and Université de Montréal. Laboratoire d'étude de l'architecture potentielle. Europan 8 (Fr) Vu Du Canada : Analyses Interdisciplinaires des projets présélectionnés de la session française : Rapport final, août 2006. Montréal : Laboratoire d'étude de l'architecture potentielle, 2006.

## Section 2
# Competing by Architectural Design

Index of Cited Competitions

*The following index lists all 202 competitions cited in this publication. It is organized by geographical location — first, by continent (Americas / Europe / Africa / Asia), and then by country — and by competition date. Numbers refer to chapters.*

━━ **1866** ━━━━━━━━━━━━━━  ━━ **1908** ━━━━━━━━━━

**England**
London Courthouse, London **3.2.**

**Switzerland**
International Reformation Monument,
Geneva **1.1.**

# Americas
━━ **Brazil**

**1956**
 **Urban Plan for Brasilia**, Brasilla 1.6., 4.4.
**2010**
 **Municipalities National Confederation Headquarters**,
 Brasilla  4.4.
 **Renova São Paulo Competition**, São Paulo 4.4.

━━ **Canada**

**1958**
 **Toronto City Hall competition**, Toronto, ON 1.6.
 **Housing on Toronto's main street**, Toronto, ON 1.6.
**1990**
 **Aménagement du Vieux-Port de Montréal**,
 Montréal, QC 1.6.
 **Place Jacques-Cartier**, Montréal, QC 1.6.
**1997**
 **Bridging — A place for architecture**,
 Montréal, QC 1.6.
**1999**
 **Downsview park**, Toronto, ON 1.6.
**2000**
 **Grande Bibliothèque du Québec**, Montréal, QC 1.6.
 **Ottawa's parliamentary hill competition**,
 Ottawa, ON 1.6.
**2001**
 **Royal Ontario Museum**, Toronto, ON 1.6.
**2002**
 **Ottawa's Bank Street**, Ottawa, ON 5.4.
 **Orchestre Symphonique de Montréal**,
 Winnipeg, MB 1.6.

**2003**
 **City crossing International Design**, Winnipeg, MB 1.6.
 **Musée Canadien des Droits de la personne**,
 Winnipeg, MB 1.6.
 **Canadian Museum of Human Rights**, Winnipeg, MB 5.4.
**2004**
 **Perspective littoral**, Québec, QC 1.6.
 **Art Gallery of Alberta**, Edmonton, AB 5.4.
**2005**
 **Frontierspace**, Vancouver, BC 1.6.
 **Absolute design competition**, Mississauga, ON 1.6.
 **Point Pleasant park international competition**,
 Halifax, NS 1.6.
 **University Boulevard architectural competition**,
 Vancouver, BC 1.6.
**2006**
 **Toronto Waterfront**, Toronto, ON 1.6.
 **Stratford Ontario Market Square competition**,
 Stratford, ON 1.6.
 **Saskatoon Century Plaza Landmark competition**,
 Saskatoon, SK 1.6.
 **Jardins Éphémères**, Québec, QC 1.6.
**2007**
 **Gould street student international competition**,
 Toronto, ON 1.6.
 **POTO : Type**, Vancouver, BC 1.6.
 **Lower Don Lands,** Toronto, ON 1.6.
 **Jarvis Slip,** Toronto, ON 1.6.
**2008**
 **The New Montreal Planetarium,** Montréal, QC 3.1.

**1922** ▬▬▬ **1927** ▬▬▬▬▬▬▬▬▬ **1950** ▬▬▬▬▬ **1956** ▬▬

**Switzerland**
Palais de la Société des Nations,
Geneva

**Brazil**
Urban Plan for Brasilia,
Brasilla **1.6., 4.4.**

**United States**
Chicago Tribune Tower, Chicago, IL **5.2.**

**Finland**
Seinäjoki Town Hall, Seinäjoki **1.6.**

**2009**
>**Townshift,** Vancouver, BC 1.6.
>**Formshift,** Vancouver, BC 1.6.
>**Calgary National Music Centre,** Calgary, AB 1.6.
>**St-Patrick's Bridge design competition,** Calgary, AB 1.6.
>**Gardiner Expressway design competition,**
>Toronto, ON 1.6.
>**Musée National des Beaux Arts du Québec,**
>Québec, QC 1.6.
>**Ryerson post-secondary international competition,**
>Toronto, ON 1.6.
>**Saint-Laurent Library competition,** Montréal, QC 3.1.
>TownShift: Suburb into City, Surrey, BC 5.4.

**2010**
>**Edmonton City Centre Airport lands,** Edmonton, AB 1.6.
>**Pan American Games award pavillion,** Toronto, ON 1.6.
>**Ajout Manifeste,** Québec, QC 1.6.

**2011**
>**Parcours d'Entrée de la ville de Montréal,**
>Montréal, QC 1.6.
>**resTOre,** Toronto, ON 1.6.
>**re : CONNECT,** Vancouver, BC 1.6.
>**Saul Bellow Library Extension competition,**
>Montréal, QC 3.1.
>**Five Park Pavilions,** Edmonton, AB 5.4.

**2012**
>**100 Mile House,** Vancouver, BC 1.6.
>**re :THINK Housing,** Vancouver, BC 1.6.

▬▬▬ **United States**
**1922**
>**Chicago Tribune Tower**, Chicago, IL 5.2.

**1939**
>**Smithsonian Museum of Art**, Washington, DC 5.2.

**1947**
>**Jefferson National Expansion Memorial,**
>Saint-Louis, MO 5.2.

**1962**
>**Boston City Hall,** Boston, MA 5.2.

**1974**
>**Roosevelt Island Housing,** New York, NY 5.2.

**1981**
>**Vietnam Veterans Memorial,** Washington, DC 5.2.

**1985**
>**Humana Building,** Louisville, KY 5.2.
>**Phoenix Municipal Government Center,**
>Phoenix, AZ 5.2.

**1991**
>**San Antonio Central Library**, San Antonio, TX 5.2.

**1997**
>**Illinois Institute of Technology's Student Center,**
>Chicago, IL 5.2.

**1999**
>**Tkts at Times Square,** New York, NY 5.2.

**2001**
>**New England Biolabs (NEB),** Ipswich, MA 5.2.

**2003**
>**Memphis Riverfront,** Memphis, TN 5.2.
>**World Trade Center Design Competition,**
>New York,NY 1.1.

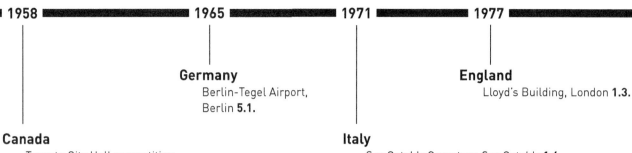

**1958** **1965** **1971** **1977**

**Germany**
Berlin-Tegel Airport,
Berlin **5.1.**

**England**
Lloyd's Building, London **1.3.**

**Canada**
Toronto City Hall competition,
Toronto, ON **1.6.**

**Italy**
San Cataldo Cemetary, San Cataldo **1.6.**
**France**
Centre Beaubourg Inte, Paris

2007
**Broad Art Museum at Michigan State University,**
East Lansing, MI 5.2.
2008
**Baltimore School of Law,** Baltimore, MD 5.2.

# Europe
## ▬ Belgium
2004
**Theaterplein**, Antwerp 1.2.
2009
**International Centre for Art and Culture**, Liège 1.2.
**Rue de la Loi**, Brussels 1.2.

## ▬ Czech Republic
2006
**Czech National Museum,** Prague 5.2.

## ▬ Denmark
2000
**Aakirkeby assisted living facility** (Project competition),
Aakirkeby 1.4.
2001
**Toftehaven residential care home**
(Invited project competition), Ballerup 1.4.
**Hadsten assisted living facility**
(Invited project competition), Hadsten 1.4.
**Vestervang residential care home**
(Invited project competition with pre-qualification), Aarhus 1.4.

**Horsens residential care home**
(Invited competition with pre-qualification), Horsens 1.4.
**Groennehave assisted living facility**
(Invited competition with pre-qualification), Elsinore 1.4.
**Glostrup assisted living facility**
(Invited competition with pre-qualification), Glostrup 1.4.
2003
**Vesterled residential care home**
(Invited competition with pre-qualification), Herning 1.4.
2005
**Soeglimt residential care home**
(Invited competition with pre-qualification), Herning 1.4.
2006
**Rosenhavn residential care home** (Invited competition),
Ballerup 1.4.
2010
**Borgmester Fischers Vej residential care home**
(Invited competition), Frederiksberg 1.4.
2011
**Aabenraa residential care home** (Project competition),
Aabenraa 1.4.
**Frederiksberg residential care home** (Project competition),
Frederiksberg 1.4.
**Vordingborg residential care home** (Project competition),
Vordingborg 1.4.
**Kredsens residential care home** (Project competition),
Frederiksberg 1.4.
**Gentofte : future-oriented residential care home**
(Invited competition), Gentofte 1.4.

**1981** **1982** **1988** **1996**

**France**
Parc de la Villette competition,
Paris **3.5., 4.1.**

**Germany**
Hafen City urban development,
Hambourg

**United States**
Vietnam Veterans Memorial,
Washington, DC **5.2.**

**Egypt**
Bibliotheca, Alexandria **1.6.**

**2001**

**Sweden**

Norra Station residential care home,
Uppsala **1.4.**

**2003**

**Denmark**

Vesterled residential care home,
Herning **1.4.**

**2010**

**Galileum Solingen,** Solingen 5.1.

**2011**

**Landmarke Duhamel,** Ensdorf 5.1.

**▬▬ Greece**

**1976**

**New Acropolis Museum,** Athens 1.5.

**1978**

**New Acropolis Museum,** Athens 1.5.

**1989**

**New Acropolis Museum,** Athens 1.5.

**2000**

**New Acropolis Museum,** Athens 1.5.

**▬▬ Italy**

**1971**

**San Cataldo Cemetary,** San Cataldo 1.6.

**▬▬ Norway**

**2007**

**Rana residential care home**

(Open commission competition), Rana 1.4.

**2008**

**Haugesund residential care home**

(International commission competition), Haugesund 1.4.

**Capralhaugen residential care home**

(International commission competition), Baerum 1.4.

**2009**

**Husebyjordet residential care home**

(Invited competition), Skedsmo 1.4.

**Stagnes, residential care home**

(Commission competition), Harstad 1.4.

**Skjaak residential care home**

(Invited competition with pre-qualification), Skjaak 1.4.

**Helgeland assisted living facility**

(Commission competition), Helgeland 1.4.

**Gjoevik assisted living facility**

(Invited competition), Gjoevik 1.4.

**Bjugn assisted living facility**

(Commission competition), Bjugn 1.4.

**Kristiansand residential care home**

(Commission competition), Kristiansand 1.4.

**Orkanger residential care home**

(Commission competition), Orkanger 1.4.

**Olderdalen residential care home**

(Commission competition), Kaafjord 1.4.

**Foerde residential care home**

(Invited competition), Foerde 1.4.

**2010**

**Geilo residential care home**

(Commission competition), Hol 1.4.

**Stryn residential care home** (Invited competition), Stryn 1.4.

**Residential care home with adjacent hospital centre**

(Invited competition), Sarpsborg 1.4.

**Sortland residential care home**

(Commission competition), Sortland 1.4.

**2004** **2005** **2006**

**Belgium**
    Theaterplein, Antwerp **1.2.**
**France**
    Forum des Halles, Paris **3.2.**

**Germany**
    Porsche automobile museum,
    Stuttgar **5.1.**

**Czech Republic**
    Czech National Museum, Prague **5.2.**
**Korea**
    Gyeonggi-do Jeongok Prehistory Museum,
    Jeongok **5.2.**

**Laerdal residential care home**
(Commission competition), Laerdal 1.4.
**Tynset residential care home**
(Commission competition), Tynset 1.4.
**Mosvik residential care home**
(Commission competition), Mosvik 1.4.
**Sola residential care home**
(Commission competition), Sola 1.4.
**Drammen assisted living facility**
(Commission competition), Drammen 1.4.
**Lynaes assisted living facility**
(Project competition), Lynaes 1.4.
**2011**
    **Vinje residential care home** (Invited competition), Vinje 1.4.
    **Kvernaland residential care home**
    (Invited competition), Time 1.4.
    **Oppdal residential care home**
    (Commission competition), Oppdal 1.4.
    **Tjoerne residential care home**
    (Invited competition), Tjoerne 1.4.
    **Residential care home with adjacent eldercare centre**
    (Commission competition),Hammerfest 1.4.
    **Naeroey residential care home**
    (Commission competition), Naeroy 1.4.
    **Raade residential care home**
    (Commission competition), Raade 1.4.
    **Boe residential care home** (Commission competition), Boe 1.4.

**Extension of residential care in Ski**
(Commission competition), Ski 1.4.
**Ansager residential care home and care centre**
(Project competition), Ansager 1.4.
**2012**
    **Hadsel residential care home**
    (Invited competition with pre-qualification), Hadsel 1.4.
    **Averoey residential care home**
    (Commission competition), Averoey 1.4.
    **Aamot residential care home**
    (Invited competition with pre-qualification), Aamot 1.4.

**Russia**
**2007**
    **Permafrost Museum,** Yakustk 5.2.
**2008**
    **Perm Contemporary Art Museum,** Perm 5.2.

**Sweden**
**2000**
    **Balder residential care home**
    (Project competition), Uppsala 1.4.
    **Myrbergska residential care home**
    (Project competition), Uppsala 1.4.
    **Hoeganaes residential care home**
    (Project competition), Uppsala 1.4.
**2001**
    **Norra Station residential care home**
    (Project competition), Uppsala 1.4.

Index of Cited Competitions   139

**2007**

**Sweden**
> Flottiljen, future-oriented residential car home, Jaerfaella **1.4.**

**Russia**
> Permafrost Museum, Yakustk **5.2.**

**2009**

**Belgium**
> Rue de la Loi, Brussels **1.2.**

**2010**

**Guinea-Bissau**
> Architectural derign for a school, Bissau **4.4.**

**Norway**
> Sola residential care home, Sola

**Canada**
> Pan American Games award pavillion, Toronto (ON) **1.6.**

**2002**
> **Slottshoejdens assisted living facility**
> (Invited competition with pre-qualification), Helsingborg 1.4.

**2006**
> **Hasselparken residential care home**
> (Project competition), Uppsala 1.4.

**2007**
> **Oernen residential care home**
> (Invited competition with pre-qualification), Tingsryd 1.4.
> **Flottiljen, future-oriented residential care home**
> (Open competition), Jaerfaella 1.4.

**2008**
> **Granparkens residential care home**
> (Commission competition), Norrtaelje 1.4.
> **Solbacka residential care home** (Commission competition), Norrtaelje 1.4.
> **Ferlin, residential care home** (Project competition), Uppsala 1.4.
> **Stenhagen residential care home** (Project competition), Uppsala 1.4.
> **Bernadotte residential care home**
> (Project competition), Uppsala 1.4.
> **Saevja residential care home** (Project competition), Uppsala 1.4.
> **Afzeliiskolan safe haven residence for older people**
> (Project competition), Alingsaas 1.4.

**2009**
> **Ljungby residential care home** (Invited competition with pre-qualification), Ljungby 1.4.

> **Nykoeping assisted living facility** (Project competition), Nykoeping 1.4.
> **Hoenekulla By, residential care home**
> (Project competition), Moelnlycke 1.4.

**2010**
> **Rudboda residential care home** (Project competition), Lindingoe 1.4.
> **Ekhaga residential care home** (Project competition), Lindingoe 1.4.
> **Lokomotivvaegen assisted living facility**
> (Project competition), Nacka 1.4.

**2012**
> **Kronetorp residential care home** (Invited competition), Burloev 1.4.
> **Majelden : future-oriented residential care home**
> (Invited competition), Linkoeping 1.4.
> **Fridhem, senior housing** (Invited competition), Gaevle 1.4.

**Switzerland**

**1908**
> **International Reformation Monument,** Geneva 1.1.

**1999**
> **Hegianwand competition,** Zurich 3.3.

**2005**
> **Residential complex Guggach,** Zurich 3.3.

**2008**
> **Avenue de Morges competition,** Lausanne 3.3.

**2011** **2012** **2014**

**Finland**
Serlachius Museum Gösta,
Mänttä **5.2.**

**China**
Port of Kinmen Passenger
Service Center, Kinmen **5.2.**

**Switzerland**
Métamorphose Prés-de-Vidy,
Lausanne **1.1.**
**Canada**
re : THINK Housing, Vancouver (BC) **1.6.**

2009
**Basel Kunstmuseum Burghof Extension,** Basel 1.1.
**Wohnen am Schaffhauserrheinweg,** Basel 3.3.
**Parcelle du Foyer de Sécheron competition,** Geneva 3.3.
2010
**Ersatzneubau Wohnsiedlung Tièchestrasse,** Zurich 1.1.
2011
**Erneuerung Kunstmuseum St.Gallen,** St Gallen 1.1.
2012
**Métamorphose Prés-de-Vidy**, Lausanne 1.1.

# Africa
**▬▬ Egypt**
1988
**Bibliotheca Alexandrina**, Alexandria 1.6.

**▬▬ Guinea-Bissau**
2010
**Architectural design for a school**, Bissau 4.4.

# Asia
**▬▬ China**
1989
**Sino Tower,** Hong Kong 5.2.
2005
**National Palace Museum** (Southern Branch), Taipei 5.2.
2009
**Taipei Pop Music Center,** Taipei 5.2.
2010
**Taiwan Disease Control Complex,** Taipei 5.2.
**Taichung Gateway Park Competition,** Taichun 5.2.
**Taipei City Museum of Art,** Taipei 5.2.
**Kaohsiung Maritime Cultural and Music Center**,
Kaohsiung 5.2.
2011
**Kaohsiung Port and Cruise Service Center,**
Kaohsiung 5.2.
2014
**Port of Kinmen Passenger Service Center,** Kinmen 5.2.

**Section 3**
# Judging Architectural Quality

# 3.1. Judging in a World of Expertise

**When the Sum of the Parts is Less than the Whole**

**Carmela Cucuzzella,** Ph.D.
Design and Computation Arts, Concordia University
Canada

If globally, architects have always felt concerned about the repercussions of their projects on the environment, society, and culture ; paradoxically they now face a plethora of quantitative assessment tools, methods or norms (requiring expertise) that play a significant and decisive role regarding their projects. This paper seeks to identify opportunities, contradictions, and/or the counter-productive effects of environmental certifications on design and judgment in the competition context. Today we are witnessing a particularity in the competition process, where a series of unexpected practices and/or effects related to the use of these certifications are emerging (i.e., unexpected shortcomings of actual environmental performance improvements post-occupancy, shifts in the discourses and debates related to quality, etc.). In the Canadian context, with the introduction of a nation-wide environmental certification system in 2003 (Leadership in Energy and Environmental Design — LEED), there is still far too little research on how such certifications are impacting the practices related to the competition situation, and even less so on the quality of the built environment. By asking how environmental certifications are being used in the competition context, we examine how these may exacerbate tensions in the competition. We seek to identify opportunities, contradictions, and/or counter-productive effects of environmental certifications on design conception and judgment

## The Demand for Environmental Certifications in the Competition Context

Research on tools, certifications, and methods for assessing concerns related to sustainability, particularly the environmental pillar has been conducted since the early 1970s. This reflective, and at times critical activity is growing exponentially as these instruments are continually being improved and new ones introduced to address emerging concerns. Whether this increasing precision is facilitating an approach to a more sustainable development is unclear and is the subject of another research. What is evident is that there is a significant disciplinary gap between an enormous body of research on evaluation tools for environmental, economic or social sustainability, many of which are oriented towards performance optimization, and a very shallow body of research on how these are used in design projects and even less on architectural and urban design competitions.

The competition is an interesting format to study the various operations and practices of sustainable design, as it encompasses many phases of the design process. In addition, the competition functions not only as a cultural mediator and a catalyst of symbolic expression, but also as a device to pass from a brief (a set of requirements and constraints) to forms and figures.[1] As such, the competition process appears, in fact, as a nodal place for considerations and actions related to sustainability along the four pillars of society, culture, economy, and environment together.

For this paper, we focus on the impact that environmental norms have on design and judgment processes, as observed in the architectural competition. Our previous research on evaluation practices and qualitative judgment suggest that the sudden introduction of environmental certifications in the architectural competition may be at the expense of a more qualitative assessment of the design project.[2] This work falls within a larger research that seeks to understand how the definition of quality for public spaces is shifting as a result of the imperatives of a more sustainable development (www.leap.umontreal.ca). The objective here is to understand if environmental certifications are being used indiscriminately in the competition, and if a blind use is exacerbating tensions in the design process and jury debates, along with the legitimate demand for environmental performance. In seeking competitions where the design briefs cannot be easily solved through a lens of environmental performance improvements alone, we selected recent Canadian competitions with culturally oriented programs (2008-2011).

Our epistemological and methodological orientation is grounded on findings related to the general model of precaution versus prevention.[3] This theoretical model will provide the lens through which we articulate the tensions (either limitations or opportunities) of adopting performance measures early on in projects. Although this model is meant to operate at a meta-disciplinary level for design,[4] it is here shown, through a series of cases studies, how it can also be used in the analysis of tensions encountered in the competition process.

We present this model in the first part. This is followed by an analysis of four Canadian competitions. We conclude by presenting a series of questions for future research based on the findings in this paper.

## The Problematic of Design for Sustainability: Precaution vs. Prevention

From the many principles related to sustainability, the precautionary principle is now considered one of the most elaborate in analysing the complexity of design projects in the context of sustainability.[5] This principle originated in the 1970s within the environmental movement in Germany.[6] The precautionary principle is meant to address the failures or limitations of traditional scientific methods — failures that arise from the changing temporality and magnitude of risks or the inaccessibility of data, whether methodologically or epistemologically.[7] Today, most methods for assessing sustainability are oriented towards environmental performance improvements, based on these same traditional scientific methods of assessment: i.e. Life Cycle Analysis (LCA), Leadership in Energy and Environmental Design (LEED), High Environmental Quality (HQE), BREEAM, Minergie, Green Globe, Energy Star, etc.

### Difference Between Precaution and Prevention

Precaution is often confused with the notion of prevention [**Fig.1**]. According to Harremoës, the precautionary principle is a way to formulate an approach to situations where uncertainty beyond statistics, ignorance and indeterminacy dominate the cause-effect relationship. Most of the work conducted in environmental policy focuses on the investigations of the problems and their optimization (preventive problem solving) at the expense of investigations of new or alternative solutions. Yet preventive problem solving may be problematic in cases where the variables of a situation and their values are unknown in advance (methodological

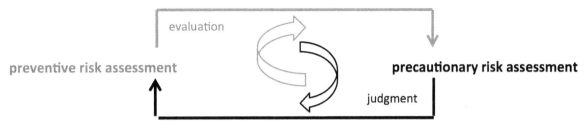

preventive risk assessment

precautionary risk assessment

evaluation

judgment

identification and optimization
fragmented vision of criteria
methodological uncertainty
predictability, repeatability
universality
mechanist worldview

exploratory and anticipative
global perspective of whole and its parts
epistemological uncertainty
prospectivity, projection
contextual significance
complex worldview

**Fig. 1**
The duality between preventive and precautionary risk
assessment and thinking.
*Source: Cucuzzella, 2011.*

uncertainty). In this context, the principle of precaution is essential, as it calls for the exploration of alternatives and the anticipation of their potentialities. This approach redirects environmental science and policy debates from the "what is" (describing and problem solving) to the "what can be" exploring and assessing alternatives.[8] In their book entitled *Le principe de précaution : Rapport au Premier ministre*,[9] Kourilsky and Viney distinguish between prevention and precaution and places each of these terms into context :

*The invocation of the precautionary principle is explained today not only because of the failures of traditional preventive approaches but also because of the emergence of new potential risks. Several recent crises have revealed a posteriori, the gaps in preventive policies and that the precautionary principle was mistakenly invoked several times, for reasons which actually revealed prevention. Failing to consider that the risks are well mastered in the normal process of prevention [...] opinion therefore states that these risks should be avoided much farther upstream of the decision.*[10]

Prevention valorizes universal knowledge and repeatability — the aim is the avoidance of measurable, predictable risks (Werner 2005 ; Ewald 1996). Tools that are based on this approach are often fragmented in terms of the issues that they address, time consuming for collecting data, and are burdensome for designers because they are too data driven. Precaution, on the other hand, relies on context specific projection of intentions and prospective conception which represents a worldview that is more strategic rather than measurable and predictable. Prevention and precaution are highly complementary as **[Fig.1]** shows. The main difference is that prevention is a posteriori, whereas precaution is an a priori based judgment or decision.

### The Precautionary Principle and the Modelling of Tensions in Design for Sustainability

How does this duality between prevention and precaution help contextualize tools such as environmental norms within design thinking ? This temporal relationship can be illustrated in a design situation where preventive problem solving (such as in an environmental impact assessment) are best applied after the detailed design phase or better yet, after the construction phase, since it is only at

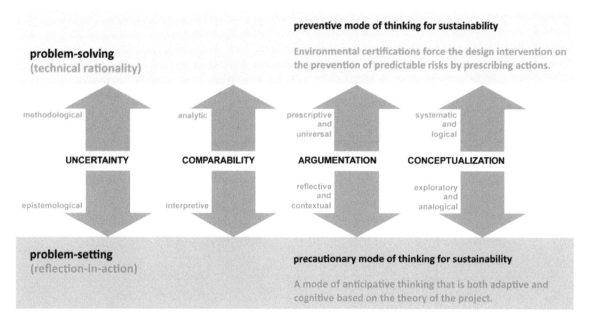

**preventive mode of thinking for sustainability**

**problem-solving**
(technical rationality)

Environmental certifications force the design intervention on
the prevention of predictable risks by prescribing actions.

methodological | analytic | prescriptive and universal | systematic and logical

**UNCERTAINTY** | **COMPARABILITY** | **ARGUMENTATION** | **CONCEPTUALIZATION**

epistemological | interpretive | reflective and contextual | exploratory and analogical

**problem-setting**
(reflection-in-action)

**precautionary mode of thinking for sustainability**

A mode of anticipative thinking that is both adaptive and
cognitive based on the theory of the project.

**Fig. 2**
Design thinking and the precautionary principle:
schematic theoretical model.
*Source: Cucuzzella, 2011.*

that time that enough information is known to make a proper evaluation. Precautionary thinking would therefore be more appropriately located in the early stages of the design process, when no detailed data is available. At these stages, strategies or scenarios are playing a great role in the thinking process. This duality is analogous to the duality between technical rationality and a reflective worldview in design thinking as defined by Schön,[11] in his now commonly accepted thesis on practical knowledge. Preventive and precautionary approaches to design for sustainability, as defined here, are then also analogous to normative design and explorative design.

The underlying theory of the precautionary principle is adopted as a way to articulate the observed tensions in design thinking in order to highlight the dichotomy between a more analytical/universal thinking approach and one more interpretive and prospective for sustainable design **[Fig.2]**. This model is constructed from:

- An understanding of the limits of preventive tools for design for sustainability
- Reflective design practices as defined by Schön
- The underlying theory of the precautionary principle

This model is intended to articulate both the usefulness of and the nature of the difficulty related to assessment tools such as LEED for design thinking.

The four categories of tensions in this model, based on the main activities in design for sustainability are: (1) the way in which uncertainty is understood; (2) the basis of comparability; (3) the logic adopted during the argumentation or communication of proposals; and (4) the approach adopted conceptualizing proposals and describing them. This model helps unveil the value systems embedded within design discourses by identifying where the design discourse resides with respect to the polarities of these tensions — which may also be indicative of the ideal of quality adopted, be it through an explicit or implicit definition of architectural quality.

## The Hypothesis of the Indiscriminate Use of Environmental Certifications and their Exacerbation of Tensions in the Common Competition Format

### Environmental Certifications: The Case of Preventive (Performance Based) Systems

As mentioned, the Leadership in Energy and Environmental Design (LEED) rating system is a green building rating system, and an example of a preventive (or performance based) approach to environmental assessment. Although such methods can greatly contribute to a normative reduction of energy consumption and, in some cases, construction improvements, they represent a fragmented set of indicators, far removed from the complexity of the real world design situation. LEED guides architects through the series of credits that are prescribed for any building type in any region in Canada via a universal prescriptive checklist. Additionally, systems like LEED allow for the break-down and therefore the classification of knowledge. This is intended to help simplify the complexity of the problem, however, this fragmentation may lead to a difficulty in a holistic integration of these concerns, often resulting in a "patch-work" approach.[12]

These approaches, referred to as objective because they use quantitative assessment methods, can only at best promise a partial perspective of the quality of design projects. Furthermore, methods such as LEED allow technocrats to become the experts in urban or architectural projects, thereby reinforcing the local technocracy against the encompassing sustainable and traditional architectural concerns, even if this is not the intent of these norms. Projects adopting such norms may therefore be reduced to expert exercises of checking credits on a grid, rather than complex projects enriched through the reflection, discourse, and unavoidable debates and controversies of the added dimension of these universal norms.

### Environmental Certifications and the Competition Process in Canada

In the majority of today's national and international architectural competitions in Canada, a new series of criteria is being introduced related to sustainable development, or more specifically, to environmental sustainability. This often implies the need to adhere to environmental rating systems in order that potential improvements can be measured and evaluated. In Canada LEED is the nation-wide accepted certification method for Canadian competitions.

### Research Questions

There is an increasing use of environmental certifications in the competitions process today. However, these certifications are also increasingly the subject of controversy as they are exacerbating tensions in the design process, as well as amongst jurors in the selection process. We will be looking for evidence of:

- Is the sustainable development imperative solely defined by the LEED certification in the brief, in the competitor proposals, or in the jury reports? If not, then how? If yes, does this introduce confusion in terms of how to address sustainability, for both the conception of proposals and jury debates?
- What is the basis of the arguments by the competitors and the jurors for highlighting the main characteristics of the projects? Do they resort to universal or standardized knowledge, or are the arguments contextually grounded?
- What is the basis of comparability by the jurors? Do they resort to a strict analysis of best performance? Are they trying to interpret the design intentions of each project, or somewhere in between?
- Is the conception and judgment process in these competitions pointing towards an implicit aesthetic related to environmental certifications?

Each of these above sets of sub-questions is intended to address one of the "arrows" of tensions depicted in the model of **[Fig.2]**.

### Methodology and Corpus

The competitions selected for preliminary analysis all have culturally oriented programs, with a specific requirement related to sustainable development. The public space of cultural projects demands much more than a functional and environmentally efficient solution, since other qualitative architectural elements such as identity, symbolism, form, and quality of space cannot be compromised. These types of competitions are selected as they place a high importance on architectural qualities rather than environmental performance. We conducted a hermeneutic discourse analysis on the major texts related to each of the competitions selected: the brief, the competitor descriptive texts, and the jury reports. The relevant research data may be found in the Canadian Competitions Catalogue public database (see *www.ccc.umontreal.ca*). It should be stressed that this short corpus is mainly to illustrate the cognitive potential of the precaution versus prevention model for addressing the complexity of sustainability in design.

**Fig. 3a**
Winning proposal by Cardin-Ramirez + Aedifica
for the Montreal Planetarium competition, main
entrance — Competition rendering.
*Source: Cardin + Ramirez, 2009.*

**Fig. 3b**
Constructed project 2013.
*Photo: CC.*

**Fig. 4**
Runner-up proposal by Croft-Pelletier + JLP
for the Montreal Planetarium
competition — main entrance.
*Source: Croft-Pelletier, 2009.*

## The Observation and Study of Tensions in Canadian Cultural Competitions requiring Environmental Certifications

The analysis of four Canadian architectural competitions is presented. Two of these four competitions were chosen to illustrate the emerging difficulty in competitions arising from the importance of the sustainability criteria: the 2008 competition for the New Montreal Planetarium and the 2009 Saint-Laurent Library competition. The other two competitions were selected as exemplary in the way that they addressed questions related to sustainability: the 2009 international competition for the Musée national des beaux-arts du Québec (MNBAQ) and the 2011 Saul Bellow Library Extension competition. In all four competitions selected the sustainability criteria are almost entirely defined using LEED.

### The New Montreal Planetarium (2008)

The New Montreal Planetarium competition, launched in 2008 had a LEED Platinum certification requirement — the highest rating of LEED — and the only explicit criterion for sustainable development. The most redeeming quality for the winning project was not the symbolism related to the telescopic canon shaped theatres, representing astronomical instruments since one of the five recommendations the jury made regarding the winning team was: "Further exploration of the symbolism of the cones in terms of iconography and the materiality". [13]

These two canons are the only visible components from street level since the rest of the project is immersed underground **[Fig. 3a] [ Fig. 3b]**. From a media perspective, the most conventional of the projects submitted won, yet it met the strictest LEED standards mainly from "tried and true" technical solutions that were easily understandable by the jury and visible to the public — for example, an extensive green roof. The multitude of press releases and documents connected to the project emphasized the importance of the competition for strengthening Montreal's position as a leader in sustainable development.

The fact that LEED certification was the only criteria for the imperative of sustainable development leads us to the question: Is sustainable development now reduced to LEED? Also, with the heavy importance placed on the LEED certification throughout the competition process, is the implicit purpose of this competition to find the best solution for a public building or to communicate the status of a region's environmental policies?

Consequently, almost 50% of the total descriptive text of the winning project was devoted to LEED — they included an entire section describing how they addressed LEED's six major categories of concern. As such, LEED dominated the design discourse for the winning team. It is important to highlight that this was an international competition that became an important device of communication for the city. The winning project in this instance is a clear case of normative design, yet was considered as the best overall project.

What was interesting about this competition is that the jury, after having selected the winner, highly recommended that the winning team fundamentally rework the fluidity of space, the integration to site, the envelope and the symbolism. One wonders what is left of the architectural project if they were asked to rework these four main design components. These recommendations for improvement led us to question whether the jury appreciated any part of the winning project's architectural qualities? In fact, the heavy emphasis on LEED placed a burden on the jury since it was the runner-up project that was considered "spectacular" in symbolism and spatial aesthetic **[Fig.4]**. This is in direct contrast to how they judged the winning project's architectural qualities. The quote regarding the runner-up project in the jury report stated that, "The jury underlines the exceptional spatial and sculptural qualities and the spectacular response to the site". [14]

So the jury agreed that the runner-up project was remarkable from a spatial and formal perspective, as well as for their response to the site. The runner-up project proposed an experimental solution for addressing the sustainability issues of their project. This solution did convince the jury since they did not consider it feasible. This team was penalized in terms of LEED points for this proposal. Here, it was not the most innovative architectural project that won from an aesthetic, spatial, experiential, technical or environmental perspective, but rather, the most conventional project that had the most green visible elements, and that was perceived most apt to achieve the environmental certification.

Referring back to the theoretical model presented earlier in **[Fig. 2]**, the fact that the winner adopted a technical (tried and true) discourse regarding sustainability to some extent showed a preventive way of design thinking for sustainability — restrictive rather than exploratory using a universal language of technology, rather than a site specific sensitivity to the site and place. Whereas, for the runner-up, based on both the exploratory nature of their proposal with

**Fig. 5a**
Winning proposal by Cardinal Hardy / Labonté Marcil / Éric Pelletier Architecte for the Saint-Laurent Library competition — main entrance — competition rendering. *Source: Cardinal Hardy, 2009.*

regards to sustainability and their site sensitive approach to the form and site, they adopted what is referred to in this paper as a precautionary approach to design thinking for sustainability — context specific and exploratory and prospective (Figure 1 specifies the main differences between prevention and precaution).

**The Saint-Laurent Library (2009)**

The Saint-Laurent Library competition, launched in 2009 for the borough of Saint-Laurent in Montreal is another example of a competition that heavily emphasized the LEED Gold certification. The general requirements for this competition in the brief were stated in the first few pages. This quote summarizes these main requirements: "The preoccupations of universal access, ergonomics, safety, integration of the wooded area, and sustainable development are omnipresent." [15] The question of sustainability would be central, both in the competitor proposals and during jury deliberation. But how exactly did the competition organizers present the requirements of sustainable development? The following quote is extracted from the sustainable development section of the brief:

*[...] the [Montreal] district wants to obtain a LEED Gold certification for the new construction. This action rises from the significant orientation of the responsible management of resources. [...] The objective of a LEED Gold certification for this building will have a strong influence on the decisions that designers make, but they must keep in mind that this certification is a means, with the real objective being an exemplary project in terms of sustainable development from the viewpoint of the environment, health, and work safety."* [16]

This description caused confusion for both the competitors and jurors, since it was not clear what would or could be the most important component in assessing sustainability, or even how to select the best project.

The winning team addressed the sustainability criterion with only LEED credits — all technical solutions that were clearly added to the project rather than integrated with the architecture. These technical environmental solutions were well known to many jurors. For some members of the jury their approach to sustainability was comforting since it provided the assurance that LEED was attainable. For other members of the jury, the winner's design was uninspiring, regardless if the LEED approach was promising.

In fact, the winner's project was self-contradictory — it had a monumental form, with an immense door to the wooded area, which hid much of the forest from the street. This imposing structure implied an overpowering of nature, with little attempt to incorporate the essence of the natural surroundings in the architecture. This depicted little sensitivity to the wooded area rather than being a clear example of valorising the wooded area **[Fig. 5a] [Fig. 5b]**. As Guy and Farmer state:

> [...] our ethical responsibility is in creating a new architectural iconography that has transformative value in altering our consciousness of Nature [...] the role of green buildings is [...] not simply to reduce the energy consumption or the ecological footprint of buildings, but to inspire and convey an increasing identification with Nature and the non-human world. [17]

The tension between the constraints of LEED and the potential challenge of adopting LEED as a means for exploration rather than an end in itself was not resolved in the winning project. For this project, it appeared more important to accumulate LEED points than to explore innovative ways for addressing the given architectural and urban challenges within a context of sustainability.

In fact, the only project that provided an innovative solution for addressing a "new architectural iconography," through its aesthetic details inspired by the nature surrounding the site and connecting these to other architectural elements of comfort and performance efficiency, was also considered by the jury in their report as the riskiest in terms of attaining LEED Gold and therefore rejected. This runner-up team proposed a second skin consisting of a grid that was shaped in the form of leaves, providing both shade and natural light, addressing both comfort and energy efficiency while also being symbolically rich **[Fig. 6a] [Fig. 6b]**.

Was the evaluation related to LEED premature for this project? Ironically, the runner-up project **[Fig. 6a] [Fig. 6b]** offered the most encompassing perspective of sustainability among the four finalists by addressing an integration of concerns rather than a collection of solutions, yet it received the lowest LEED rating.

For some members of the jury, the risk associated with the runner-up's low LEED rating was problematic, while for others the low LEED rating did not signify anything at this stage of the design process. This deadlock in

**Fig. 6a**
Runner-up proposal by Chevalier Morales
Architectes / Les Architectes FABG for the Saint-Laurent
Competition — front view
*Source : Chevalier-Morales, 2009.*

**Fig. 6b**
Detail of double skin light effect on the
interior space.
*Source : Chevalier Morales
Architectes / Les Architectes FABG, 2009.*

the juror process highlighted the fact that the comparison between competitor proposals was done very differently among the different members of the jury. For some, the conceptual interpretation of the ideas presented was the most important. For others, the technical environmental solutions were clearly the most important for selecting the winner, accentuating the very different value systems among the jury members. This conflict experienced in the jury deliberation is an exemplary case of the dichotomy that is depicted in the theoretical model outlined above in **[Fig.2]**. Those jurors that are more comfortable deliberating within a technical rationality take on a more preventive approach to design thinking therefore remaining more analytical than interpretive in their thinking. There are other jury members that are more comfortable with the fluidity and uncertainty inherent in the projects' intentions and prefer to take on a more precautionary approach to design thinking in a context of sustainability implying a more prospective and reflective way of thinking **[Fig.2]**.

The preliminary analysis of these two competitions already indicates that there is an emerging difficulty in the use of environmental certifications for competitions, which has to date been a neglected area of design research. The

dominance of such environmental certifications used in design and decision processes could lead to a compromise of cultural or social sustainability concerns and therefore, in a shifting of repercussions from the environmental to the cultural or social. Yet the use of environmental certifications is no longer negotiable for many public architectural and urban competitions in Canada as it is imposed on most Canadian public space competitions today.

In the next two sub-sections, we describe two competitions examples that although included a LEED requirement did not experience the difficulties and deadlocks described in the above two competitions.

**Musée national des beaux-arts du Québec (2009)**
The international competition for the Musée national des beaux-arts du Québec (MNBAQ), launched in 2009 by the City of Quebec, showed that it is possible to adopt environmental certifications while maintaining a global perspective of architectural quality. In this competition, the LEED requirement was the most basic level of certification. It was not as difficult to attain as the higher levels of LEED expected in the above two competitions. The overarching goal for this competition was stated in the brief as :

**Fig. 7**
Winning proposal by OMA for the MNBAQ competition
*Source : Office for Metropolitan Architecture, 2010.*

*The promoters are seeking the birth of a flagship project, a powerful architectural presence in the urban environment that is modern and innovative, original and distinctive, in short, a new symbol of identity for Quebec at the international scale.* [18]

This was an important international competition for the province of Quebec. When you consider the variety of reasons given by the clients to choose an international competition format, you encounter an impressive list, including : heritage conservation of a natural park ; heritage conservation of a historical museological ensemble ; a religious building with coherent heritage value ; complex urban regulations [19] — in other words, all the ingredients of a complex urban project that seriously consider cultural sustainability.

So even if the environmental sustainability component was included as an important criterion, it did not dominate the competition narrative. In fact, the role of the international dimension of this competition enlarged the design and jurors concerns to beyond those of environmental performance, since symbolism and identity were extremely crucial. The jury described the winning project as evocative,

flexible, and included spectacular dynamic spaces. [20] The local social context of the wood industry representing 'a symbol of identity for Quebec' was deemed very important for the client. This is where the winning project was distinctive in its use of local wood by including an impressive wood structure for the ceiling of the entrance area **[Fig.7]**. The jury chose the OMA project unanimously because of the neutrality of form, the flexibility of space, and the way in which they reinvented the museological experience.

The MNBAQ competition's main objective was about placing this project, and the city, on the international cultural map, especially as the project was a major cultural center for the Quebec City, the capital of the province of Quebec — made clear in the brief. During the jury deliberation, rather than debating the details of the environmental certification as in the above two competitions, once it was established that all the finalists could attain the basic LEED certification, this criteria was taken off the table, and the jurors focused on the qualitative architectural dimensions of the projects of form, composition, materiality, space, etc. The use of an environmental certification for addressing the sustainability criteria in this competition did not force a technocratic analysis of the projects.

**Fig. 8**
Winning proposal by Chevalier-Morales for the
Saul Bellow library extension competition
*Source: Chevalier-Morales, 2011.*

Studying this competition from the perspective of the theoretical model depicted in Figure 2, the jurors seemingly reached an interesting balance between the technical rationality necessary for assessing the mechanical and environmental solutions, and the reflective practices of judging the designers' intentions along with the uncertainties that go hand-in-hand in this way of thinking.

### Saul Bellow Library Extension (2011)

The Saul Bellow Library Extension competition launched in 2011 by the City of Montreal also had a LEED Gold requirement. The competition organizer had already experienced difficulties with LEED in past competition processes. How could the organizer include LEED Gold this time and not have it overwhelm the jury deliberation as it had in previous competitions with high levels of environmental certification requirements? This time, the organizer decided to put into action an innovation for the competition process that may compensate for some of the previous difficulties encountered. The competition organizer required that the winning team establish an Integrated Design Process (IDP),[21] which would take place after the competition. The following quote from the competition brief states that:

*A process organized such as the Integrated Design Process (IDP) is imposed to ensure the maintenance of equilibrium [among stakeholders], to valorise a global perspective, and allow stakeholders to make enlightened and coherent choices from the planning phase until operations. The challenge in such a process is the simultaneous integration of all the actors and all the disciplines of the project in an efficient and orchestrated process in function of the specific requirements.*[22]

This IDP would ensure that the design and construction process would be conducted with the collaboration of the stakeholders of the project. Because of this intense co-design process that would follow the competition, many of the details of the project *could* not be accurately assessed at this early phase (i.e. LEED credits, budget) because of the many changes that the IDP would engender. These considerations could therefore be pushed to after the selection of the winning project. But not all members of the jury were comfortable with this proposal. For some members of the jury, because the data regarding LEED and budget was available, it should be heavily weighted during deliberation. Yet, other members of the jury felt that questions of budget and LEED, even if both the finalist teams and the external competition experts provided estimates for these, they were to some extent meaningless estimates, since the forthcoming IDP would change the projects in major ways.

For this competition, the major decision taken by the jury to exclude specific questions related to LEED (and to some extent the budget) until after the competition, when the IDP would start, was pivotal in selecting the best overall winner. With this, LEED was not used as a focus for deliberation as it was in the previous competitions launched in Montreal. The main driving principle for the jury was the flexibility and adaptability for accommodating future changes. And since adaptability is a fundamental sustainability principle — it is the underlying notion necessary for assigning a second life to artefacts or spaces — the jury adopted a more global perspective of sustainability rather than one reduced to LEED. The 7 criteria used by the jurors were:

1. The potential evolution of the concept through the IDP;
2. Flexibility;
3. Integration to existing building and functionality;
4. Quality of space (light and comfort);
5. Strategies for sustainable development;
6. Budget;
7. Identity and potential for urban renewal.

The winning project was selected for its visual symbolic character, the strong lighting proposals, the functionality, the fact that their proposal presented much future potential, and the perception of flexibility of the project for change, an important characteristic in light of the upcoming IDP. The winning project also did much in this initial phase to address questions of sustainability from an *intrinsic* architectural design perspective, rather than by adopting an ad hoc *additive* approach. It is important to highlight that a tool like LEED does not offer many credits for these important reorientations of design thinking. An example of this intrinsic architectural design for sustainability approach is the way they reduced the impact on the topology of the site since they decided not to dig and destroy the slopes on the site, but rather they decided that these would be part of their project. This resulted in surprising experiences in terms of how users would move across levels of the library. There was also an added economic benefit since this helped reduce the budget **[Fig.8]**. So this initial decision reduced environmental impacts, improved the library experience, and reduced the budget.

The runner-up projects were eliminated because the jury felt that the projects lacked visual character, lacked elements of surprise in terms of lighting, or were predictable in terms of spatial or functional experience. The winning project was selected based on the "excellence of the architectural attitude and intention," [23] These qualitative architectural components could not have been evaluated using a technical rationality alone, as is possible when evaluating LEED credits. Here, because these qualitative characteristics are immeasurable, yet can be judged, a reflective and prospective mode of thinking was adopted. The jury did not consider the environmental performance conducted by external expert evaluators; rather they deliberated the projects' potential for change instead. The following quote from the competition brief suggested this approach to selecting the winning project:

> *This competition is only a first step of the preliminary design of the Project. It is only intended to help choose the architectural part of the Project. The final design will be essentially done following the competition, when the Integrated Design Process will involve the winner, with the engineers, who will be selected by a conventional tender.* [24]

Let us highlight that the IDP is a fairly new approach for architectural design and even more so for architectural design competitions. It is not yet fully understood with regards to its feasibility, its effectiveness, and its ability for respecting the designers' original project intentions. Further research is necessary to understand how the IDP will affect the winning project's core intentions during final design phases and construction.

For this competition however, the fact that the deliberation of the environmental certification credits was moved to after the winning project was selected meant that LEED did not polarize the deliberation process of the jury. Could the shift in temporality (moving LEED debates to after the selection of the winner) be a key to resolve some of the tensions related to the inclusion of LEED in the competition?

**Discussion of Findings**

It is well known that in every design project there are tensions between requirements and proposals, between prescriptive constraints and opportunities for exploration. Architects are used to these types of dichotomies to the point where they are asking for constraints as a stimulant for their design thinking. However, today, with the imperatives of sustainable development, the tensions are directly contradictory, since architects are asked at once to be innovative in their exploration of potentials, yet are required to follow a strict set of environmental guidelines (the certification) with implicit constraints that are taken as universal knowledge and where the goal for the architects/designers is to accumulate as many credits as possible. These choices are only reliably evaluable after the construction phase — yet all this has to be known when the project is submitted to the competition, which is far before the construction phase.

These tensions — between precaution and prevention, between reflexivity and technical rationality, between exploration and prescription, between interpretation of intentions and analysis of results, helped reveal the varying value systems by the many actors involved in the competition. These tensions manifest themselves in some of the following observations:

1. There is varying importance placed on LEED results. Performance results from LEED seem difficult to dispute even though they are laden with uncertainties, given that the constructed project will differ from the winning proposal. In fact, in some competitions LEED arguments "confiscate" the jury debate through a tension arising from the valorisation of the "certainty" of LEED, the need to be analytical (comparison of credits) and technical in the comparison.

2. There are opposing visions of quality — one based on the prescriptive LEED guidelines, the other based on a historical Vitruvian perspective. This tension is related to the fact that there are also conflicting visions of an aesthetic of sustainability since arbitrary references are used to indicate a sustainable aesthetic (for example: avoidance of glass as an envelope).

3. LEED presents itself as a main sustainability principle but is actually just a set of guidelines (an instrument), and there is an inconsistent use of LEED by the varying actors, based on their own perception of what LEED represents. Consequently, since LEED is on the most part presented as the only sustainability criterion, this also reduces the definition of sustainability, causing added confusion as to how sustainability can actually be judged. Sustainable development is defined by four pillars at the international scale, yet is reduced to LEED in many competitions.

4. *Sustainability* branding potential for municipalities places pressure on the judgment process to select a project with communicable *green* elements, where LEED has demonstrated substantial branding power.

It is evident that norms and certifications have an impact on the nature of the competition for decision-makers, whether they are political or institutional, and have led in some cases to competitions being used as the implicit privileged vehicle of communication of environmental policies instead of as a means of finding the best solution, in its entirety, to a given question. This phenomenon is particularly evident in the jury debate where these same environmental norms tend to overpower the more traditional criteria of quality evaluation, presenting themselves as "meta-criteria." Environmental performance thus seems to have become more important than quality of space or constructive choices in the case of some competitions.

——

Our hypothesis regarding the exacerbation of tensions by the indiscriminate use of environmental certifications in the competition directs us towards some new questions:

First, architects, designers, and academics realize that LEED presents limitations with respect to dealing with the complex spectrum of concerns for environmental sustainability, let alone for the four pillars of sustainability (Cucuzzella 2009). Although design practitioners are aware of many of these misconceptions, difficulties, and limits of environmental certifications, they do not seem to have reached politicians or the general public, as far as we have observed in the Canadian context. We do notice however that competition organizers in Canada are relying heavily on environmental certifications for sustainable development.

Second, there is a temporal discrepancy between the best point at which LEED is evaluated in a design project and the point at which LEED must be evaluated in a competition. Can LEED be effectively and accurately evaluated so early in the design process? Why are certifications introduced in a competition knowing that so many changes will take place between the time that the projects are submitted and the time that the projects are realized? Is there a temporal contradiction with the use of certifications in the common competition?

Given the questions related to the temporal gap regarding environmental certifications in the competition format, what alternatives are more compatible with the competition? In other words, are there other ways to formulate the demand for a more sustainable development without resorting to certifications? This question is specifically addressed to environmental experts and policy makers.

On the other hand, we can now wonder if the competition format as understood by most competition organizers is indeed compatible with the legitimate demand for environmental performance, and if it should not be reformulated by taking into account the space for exploration and innovation and the search for quality - both are objectives that competitions are meant to have. Although LEED remains a highly significant environmental rating system helping designers to address a series of ecological concerns, its dominant position in architectural competitions is questioned here, as the design for proposals and the jury debate cannot be aptly accomplished through the "efficient" use of quantitative tools that rely on abstract and fragmented models of a world.

### ▬▬ Notes

[1] Georges Adamczyk, "Concours et qualité architecturale," *ARQ/Architecture Québec* 126(2004); ibid; Georges Adamczyk et al., "Architectural competitions and new reflexive practices," in *ARCC, E. (ed.) EAAE ARCC Conference (Between Research and Practice)* (Dublin2004); ibid.

[2] The counterproductive effects of the use of environmental certifications in the competition process have been studied with regards to the limits they impose on judgment in Carmela Cucuzzella, "Des limites de la norme LEED," *ARQ Architecture-Québec / Le concours : une affaire du jugement* February 2011, no.154(2011).

They have also be studied from the perspective of the narrative of the projects in Carmela Cucuzzella, "When The Narrative Of Environmental Certifications Replaces The Debate On Quality," in *Faire des histoires? Du récit d'urbanisme a l'urbanisme fonctionnel : Faire la ville a l'heure de la société su spectacle*, ed. Christophe Mager Laurent Matthey, David Gaillard, Hélène Gallezot (Geneva : Fondation Braillard Architectes, 2013).

[3] Even if precaution and prevention are terms that are often confounded, since they both represent approaches for addressing consequences, their philosophies differ from an epistemological perspective — prevention is based on statistical analyses, a universal method, whereas precaution is a context specific approach, often where decisions are made with the stakeholders of the situation. There are several authors who have compared the models of prevention and precaution. Of note, Jérôme Bindé, "Toward an Ethics of the Future," *Public Culture* 12, no. 1 (2000); François Ewald, "Philosophie de la précaution," *L'année sociologique*, 46, no. 2 (1996); Christian Gollier, Bruno Jullien, and Nicolas Treich, "Scientific progress and irreversibility: an economic interpretation of the `Precautionary Principle'," *Journal of Public Economics* 75, no. 2 (2000); Daniel Haag and Martin Kaupenjohann, "Parameters, prediction, post-normal science and the precautionary principle--a roadmap for modelling for decision-making," *Ecological Modelling* 144, no. 1 (2001); Phillipe Kourilsky, *Du bon usage du principe de précaution ; Réflections et modes d'action* (Paris : Éditions Odile Jacob, 2002); Marie-Thérése Neuilly, "Prévention et précaution, de préférence à prévision et prospective," *Education Permanente* 176(2008); Andrew Stirling, "On Science and Precaution In the Management of Technological Risk," (Seville: European Commission - JRC Institute Prospective Technological Stidies, 1999).

(Neuilly 2008; Gollier, Jullien, and Treich 2000; Bindé 2000; Stirling 1999; Haag and Kaupenjohann 2001; Kourilsky 2002; Ewald 1996).

[4] In Cucuzzella's doctorate thesis, prevention and precaution are understood as analogs to technical rationality and reflective thinking - Carmela Cucuzzella, "Design Thinking and the Precautionary Principle: Development of a Theoretical Model Complementing Preventive Judgment for Design for Sustainability enriched through a Study of Architectural Competitions adopting LEED" (Université de Montréal, 2011).

[5] The precautionary principle is a controversial principle because it is activated when science fails, in cases of contradiction, doubt, and uncertainty of knowledge. This has been reflected on by several authors, among them: Stephen Byers, "Applying the Precautionary Principle," in *Science and Public Affairs* (2001); Carmela Cucuzzella, "The Limits of Current Evaluation Methods in a Context of Sustainable Design: Prudence as a New Framework," *International Journal of Design Engineering* 2, no. 3 (2009); Carmela Cucuzzella, "Collaborative Design in a Context of Sustainability: The Epistemological and Practical Implications of the Precautionary Principle for Design," in *proceedings for The 14th European Roundtable on Sustainable Production and Consumption (ERSCP)* (Delft, the Netherlands, October 25-29 : Delft University of Technology; The Hague University of Applied Sciences, TNO, ISBN: 9789051550658, 2010); Pierre De Coninck and Carmela Cucuzzella, "Towards Sustainable Lifestyles: A Participatory Approach in a Context of Uncertainty," in *Production et consommation durables : de la gouvernance au consommateur-citoyen*, ed. Sophie Lavallée Geneviève Parent, Georges Azzaria (Quebec : Éditions Yvon Blais, 2008); P. L. DeFur and M. Kaszuba, "Implementing the Precautionary Principle," *The Science of the Total Environment* 288(2002); B. Latour, "Du principe de précaution au principe du bon gouvernement : vers de nouvelles règles de la méthode expérimentale," *Les Etudes* 3394(2000).

[6] P. Harremoës et al., *Late Lessons from Early Warnings: the precautionary principle 1896-2000* (European Environment Agency, Environmental issue report, no 22, 2001); D. Kriebel et al., "The Precautionary Principle in Environmental Science," *Environmental Health Perspectives* 109, no. 9 (2001).

[7] Ewald, "Philosophie de la précaution."; Timothy O'Riordan and Andrew Jordan, "The Precautionary Principle, Science, Politics and Ethics," (The Centre for Social and Economic Research on the Global Environment (CSERGE), 1995); Jan-Peter Voss, Dierk Bauknecht, and René Kemp, eds., *Reflexive Governance for Sustainable Development* (Cheltenham, UK : Edward Elgar Publishing, 2006); K.H. Whiteside, *Precautionary Politics: Principle and Practice in Confronting Environmental Risk* (Cambridge : The MIT Press, 2006).

[8] Carmela Cucuzzella and Pierre De Coninck, "The Contribution of the Precautionary Principle for Decision Making in Situations of Uncertainty for Product and Service Development," in *1st International seminar on Society & Materials, SAM1* (Sevilla, Spain2007).

[9] Kourilsky, *Du bon usage du principe de précaution ; Réflections et modes d'action*.

[10] Kourilsky, *Du bon usage du principe de précaution ; Réflections et modes d'action*, 23.

[11] Donald Schön, A., *The Reflective Practitioner: How Professionals Think in Action* (printed in the USA : Basic Books, 1983).

[12] Graham Farmer and Simon Guy, "Hybrid Environments: The Spaces of Sustainable Design," in *Sustainable architectures cultures and natures in Europe and North America*, ed. Simon Guy and Steven A. Moore (New York : Spon Press, 2005).

[13] Refer to p.7, Ville de Montréal, "Le Planétarium/Concours d'architecture: Rapport du Jury: Étape 2," (2009).

[14] Refer to p.5, Ville de Montréal, "Le Planétarium/Concours d'architecture: Rapport du Jury: Étape 2," (2009)

[15] Refer to p. 4, translation by author, Ville de Montréal, "Programme du concours : Concours d'architecture/Nouvelle bibliothèque Saint-Laurent, centre d'exposition et réserve muséale, arrondissement de Saint-Laurent," (2009).

[16] Refer to p.29, translation by author, "Programme du concours : Concours d'architecture/Nouvelle bibliothèque Saint-Laurent, centre d'exposition et réserve muséale, arrondissement de Saint-Laurent," (2009).

[17] Refer to pages 79-80, Simon Guy and Graham Farmer, "Contested Constructions : The Competing Logics of Green Buildings and Ethics," in Ethics and the Built Environment, ed. W. Fox (London : Routledge : 2000).

[18] Please refer to p. 32, quote translated by author, Ville de Québec, "Concours internationnal d'architecture : Musée national des beaux-arts du Quebec (MNBAQ) : Programme," (2009).

[19] Refer to Chapter 1.6 by Jean-Pierre Chupin of this book.

[20] Refer to p.4, Ville de Québec, "Concours international d'architecture : Musée national des beaux-arts du Québec (MNBAQ) : Jury - étape 2," (2010).

[21] The IDP is ideally based on the facilitation of dialogue among stakeholders who bring different insights to bear on complex issues in a design project : Alex Zimmerman, "Integrated Design Process Guide," (Canada Mortgage and Housing Corporation, 2006) ; ibid ; John Boecker et al., The Integrative Design Guide to Green Building - Redefining the Practice of Sustainability (Hoboken, New Jersey : John Wiley & Sons, Inc., 2009) ; ibid.. It allows the issues to be exposed, and provides a space for dialogue among stakeholders so as to avoid irreversible decisions with incomplete information (Ibid.). Whether or not these promises are realized is unclear, as implementation is sometimes compromised as a result of budget or time constraints ; in many projects, the scope is defined narrowly ; and other projects depart from IDP as described in "theory" due to differing understanding of what an IDP process might/should be. For a reflection on the implications of collaborative design, please refer to Cucuzzella, "Collaborative Design in a Context of Sustainability : The Epistemological and Practical Implications of the Precautionary Principle for Design."

[22] Refer to p.15, translation by author, Ville de Montréal, "Concours d'architecture - agrandissement et réaménagement bibliothèque Saul-Bellow- Lachine - programme & annexes," (2010).

[23] As agreed upon during the jury deliberation for the Saul-Bellow Library Extension competition held on June 8-9, 2011.

[24] Refer to p.5, translation by author, Ville de Montréal, "Concours d'architecture - agrandissement et réaménagement bibliothèque Saul-Bellow- Lachine - Règlement du concours," (2011).

## ▬ References

**Adamczyk**, Georges. "Concours et qualité architecturale." ARQ/Architecture Québec 126 (2004) : 4-24.

**Adamczyk**, Georges, Jean-Pierre **Chupin**, Denis **Bilodeau**, and Anne **Cormier**. "Architectural Competitions and New Reflexive Practices." In ARCC, E. (ed.) EAAE ARCC Conference (Between Research and Practice). Dublin, 2004.

**Bindé**, Jérôme. "Toward an Ethics of the Future." Public Culture 12, no. 1 (2000) : 51-72.

**Boecker**, John, Scot **Horst**, Tom **Keiter**, Andrew **Lau**, Marcus **Sheffer**, Brian **Toevs**, and Bill **Reed**. The Integrative Design Guide to Green Building - Redefining the Practice of Sustainability. Hoboken, New Jersey : John Wiley & Sons, Inc., 2009.

**Byers**, Stephen "Applying the Precautionary Principle." In Science and Public Affairs, 2001.

**Cardin + Ramirez, Ædifica, SNC Lavalin, Dupras Ledoux, and Fauteux et associés**. "Montreal Rio Tinto Alcan Planetarium : Premier Rendez-Vous Avec Le Ciel." In Montreal Rio Tinto Alcan Planetarium Architectural 2008 Competition, Étape 2. Montreal : Ville de Montréal, 2009.

**Cardinal Hardy, Labonté Marcil, Eric Pelletier architectes en consortium, LBHA, SDK, and TEKNIKA·HBA**. "Saint-Laurent Library Competition : Un trait de paysage dans la ville." In Saint Laurent Library 2009 Architectural Competition, Phase 2. Montreal : City of Montreal, 2009.

**Chevalier Morales Architectes**. "Saul Bellow Library Extension Ompetition : Submission." In Saul-Bellow 2011 Architectural Competition, Phase 2, 2011.

**Chevalier Morales Architectes, FABG, AECOM Tecsult, VLAN paysages, LEM experts·conseils, and TEKNIKA·HBA**. "Saint-Laurent Library Competition : Submission." In Saint Laurent Library 2009 Architectural Competition, Phase 2. Montreal : City of Montreal, 2009.

**Croft Pelletier, Jodoin Lamarre Pratte, Dessau, and SDK**. "Montreal Rio Tinto Alcan Planetarium : Le trou noire... L'inconnu." In Montreal Rio Tinto Alcan Planetarium Architectural 2008 Competition, Étape 2. Montreal : Ville de Montréal, 2009.

**Cucuzzella**, Carmela. "Collaborative Design in a Context of Sustainability : The Epistemological and Practical Implications of the Precautionary Principle for Design." In proceedings for The 14th European Roundtable on Sustainable Production and Consumption (ERSCP). Delft, the Netherlands, October 25-29 : Delft University of Technology ; The Hague University of Applied Sciences, TNO, ISBN : 9789051550658, 2010.

**Cucuzzella**, Carmela. "Des limites de la norme LEED." ARQ Architecture-Québec / Le concours : une affaire du jugement February 2011, no.154 (2011) : 22-25.

**Cucuzzella**, Carmela."Design Thinking and the Precautionary Principle : Development of a Theoretical Model Complementing Preventive Judgment for Design for Sustainability Enriched through a Study of Architectural Competitions Adopting Leed." Université de Montréal, 2011.

**Cucuzzella**, Carmela. "The Limits of Current Evaluation Methods in a Context of Sustainable Design : Prudence as a New Framework." International Journal of Design Engineering 2, no. 3 (2009) : 243-61.

**Cucuzzella**, Carmela. "When the Narrative of Environmental Certifications Replaces the Debate on Quality." In Faire des histoires ? Du récit d'urbanisme à l'urbanisme fonctionnel : Faire la ville à l'heure de la société du spectacle, edited by Christophe Mager Laurent Matthey, David Gaillard, Hélène Gallezot. pp. 43-47. Geneva : Fondation Braillard Architectes, 2013.

**Cucuzzella**, Carmela, and Pierre **De Coninck**. "The Contribution of the Precautionary Principle for Decision Making in Situations of Uncertainty for Product and Service Development." In 1st International seminar on Society & Materials, SAM1. Sevilla, Spain, 2007.

**De Coninck**, Pierre, and Carmela **Cucuzzella**. "Towards Sustainable Lifestyles : A Participatory Approach in a Context of Uncertainty." In Production et consommation durables : De la gouvernance au consommateur-citoyen, edited by Sophie Lavallée Geneviève Parent, Georges Azzaria. 662. Quebec : Éditions Yvon Blais, 2008.

**DeFur**, P. L., and M. **Kaszuba**. "Implementing the Precautionary Principle." The Science of the Total Environment 288 (2002) : 155-65.

**Ewald**, François. "Philosophie de la précaution." L'année sociologique, 46, no. 2 (1996) : 383-412.

**Farmer**, Graham, and Simon **Guy**. "Hybrid Environments : The Spaces of Sustainable Design." In Sustainable Architectures Cultures and Natures in Europe and North America, edited by Simon Guy and Steven A. Moore. 15-30. New York : Spon Press, 2005.

**Gollier**, Christian, Bruno **Jullien**, and Nicolas **Treich**. "Scientific Progress and Irreversibility : An Economic Interpretation of the `Precautionary Principle'." Journal of Public Economics 75, no. 2 (2000) : 229-53.

**Guy**, Simon, and Graham **Farmer**. "Contested Constructions : The Competing Logics of Green Buildings and Ethics." In Ethics and the Built Environment, edited by W. Fox. 73-87. London : Routledge, 2000.

**Haag**, Daniel, and Martin **Kaupenjohann**. "Parameters, Prediction, Post-Normal Science and the Precautionary Principle--a Roadmap for Modelling for Decision-Making." Ecological Modelling 144, no. 1 (2001) : 45-60.

**Harremoës**, P. "Ethical Aspects of Scientific Incertitude in Environmental Analysis and Decision Making." *Journal of Cleaner Production* 11, no. 7 (2003) : 705-12.

**Harremoës**, P., D. **Gee**, M. **MacGarvin**, A. **Stirling**, J. **Keys**, B. **Wynne**, and S. **Guedes Vaz**, (eds.). *Late Lessons from Early Warnings : The Precautionary Principle 1896-2000*. European Environment Agency, Environmental issue report, no 22, 2001.

**ISO**. "Environmental Management — Life Cycle Assessment — Principles and Framework." Switzerland : International Standards Organization, 2006.

**Kourilsky**, Phillipe. *Du bon usage du principe de précaution ; Réflections et modes d'action*. Paris : Éditions Odile Jacob, 2002.

**Kriebel**, D., J. **Tickner**, P. **Epstein**, J. **Lemmons**, R. **Levins**, E.L. **Loechler**, M. **Quinn**, *et al*. "The Precautionary Principle in Environmental Science." *Environmental Health Perspectives* 109, no. 9 (2001) : 871-76.

**Lascoumes**, P. "La précaution comme anticipation des risques résiduels et hybridation de la responsabilité." *L'année sociologique*, 46, no. 2 (1996) : 359 — 82.

**Latour**, B. "Du principe de précaution au principe du bon gouvernement : Vers de nouvelles règles de la méthode expérimentale." *Les Etudes* 3394 (2000) : 339-46.

**Neuilly**, Marie-Thérése. "Prévention et précaution, de préférence à prévision et prospective." *Education Permanente* 176 (2008) : 119-26.

**O'Riordan**, Timothy, and Andrew **Jordan**. "The Precautionary Principle, Science, Politics and Ethics." The Centre for Social and Economic Research on the Global Environment (CSERGE), 1995.

**Office for Metropolitan Architecture**. "Mnbaq - Texte Conceptuel - Étape 2 Prestations." (2010).

**Schön**, Donald, A. *The Reflective Practitioner : How Professionals Think in Action*. printed in the USA : Basic Books, 1983.

**Stirling**, Andrew. "Deliberate Futures : Precaution and Progress in Social Choice of Sustainable Technology." *Sustainable Development* 15, no. 5 (2007) : 286-95.

**Stirling**, Andrew. "On Science and Precaution in the Management of Technological Risk." Seville : European Commission - JRC Institute Prospective Technological Stidies, 1999.

**Tickner**, J., and K. **Geiser**. "The Precautionary Principle Stimulus for Solutions and Alternative Based Environmental Policy." *Environmental Impact Assessment Review* 24 (2004) : 801-24.

**Ville de Montréal**. "Concours d'architecture - Agrandissement et réaménagement bibliothèque Saul-Bellow- Lachine - Programme & annexes." 2010.

**Ville de Montréal**. "Concours d'architecture - Agrandissement et réaménagement bibliothèque Saul-Bellow- Lachine - Rapport du jury, étape 2." Montreal, 2011.

**Ville de Montréal**. "Concours d'architecture - Agrandissement et réaménagement bibliothèque Saul-Bellow- Lachine - Règlement du concours." 2011.

**Ville de Montréal**. "Le Planétarium/Concours d'architecture : Rapport du jury, étape 2." 2009.

**Ville de Montréal**. "Programme du concours : Concours d'architecture/ nouvelle bibliothèque Saint-Laurent, centre d'exposition et réserve muséale, arrondissement de Saint-Laurent." 2009.

**Ville de Québec**. "Concours international d'architecture : Musée National des Beaux-Arts du Québec (MNBAQ) : Jury - Étape 2." 7, 2010.

**Ville de Québec**. "Concours internationnal d'architecture : Musée National des Beaux-Arts du Quebec (Mnbaq) : Programme." 2009.

**Voss**, Jan-Peter, Dierk **Bauknecht**, and René **Kemp**, eds. *Reflexive Governance for Sustainable Development*. Cheltenham, UK : Edward Elgar Publishing, 2006.

**Werner**, Wouter, G. "Responding to the Undesired. State Responsibility, Risk Management and Precaution." *Netherlands Yearbook of International Law* XXXVI (2005) : 57-82.

**Whiteside**, K.H. *Precautionary Politics : Principle and Practice in Confronting Environmental Risk*. Cambridge : The MIT Press, 2006.

**Williamson**, Terry, Antony **Radford**, and Helen **Bennette**. *Understanding Sustainable Architecture*. London and New York : Spon Press, Taylor & Francis Group, 2003.

**Zimmerman**, Alex. "Integrated Design Process Guide." Canada Mortgage and Housing Corporation, 2006.

# 3.2. Judging Architectural Quality

## Judgment Criteria and Competition Juries

**Camille Crossman**, Ph.D. candidate
School of Architecture, Université de Montréal
Canada

This chapter is based on a doctoral thesis research, which aims to contribute to the problematic or qualitative judgment in architecture: *How is architectural quality judged?* More specifically, the research analyzes how *architectural judgment* is conducted within the specific context of contemporary architectural competitions.

Considering the complexity of the problematic of architectural judgment within the architectural competition context, this article will focus on one specific aspect of my broader research, namely the role of judgment criteria during the jury process in selecting a winning project. I chose to focus on judgment criteria since it represents some of the most tangible data available in the study of architectural judgment. What is the operative role of judgment criteria within the jury of an architectural competition? How are they used? Do they contribute to the judgment of quality of the projects? Are general criteria more effective than specific criteria in the construction of a collective judgment?

This article proposes to analyze the judgment criteria as well as the jury process of two fictional contemporary architectural competitions created from a larger corpus of architectural and urban design competitions juries, were I was admitted as scientific observer. Using Peter Collins' (1971) theories on the role of architectural "precedents" in the architectural conception as a basis, the hypothesis I propose is that the judgment criteria plays an analogous role in the way the winning project is selected through a collective judgment. More specifically, the reflexive process through which any collective architectural judgment is built is at least partially informed by the judgment criteria as formulated in the brief.

In summary, this essay raises the following question: *What is the effective role of the judgment criteria in the judgment process and in the construction of the architectural judgment?*

**Cover**
Proposed scheme by E.M. Barry
for the 1866 London Courthouse
competition, from Collins (1971).

## ━━ Introduction of the General Problematic of Architectural Judgment[1] in the Context of Competition Juries

*(...) pour reprendre le mot de Kant : il n'y a pas de règle prescrivant comment apprendre à appliquer correctement les règles[2]* — H.-G. Gadamer

### London Courthouse

The competition for the London Courthouse, dating back to 1866, is probably one of the most singular cases of architectural competitions in history. The jury of this historical competition was entirely composed of judges from the legal community. The demanding task of judging the architectural quality of the submissions had been entrusted to law magistrates. Given their knowledge and experiences in *judging*, and because of their great understanding of the courthouse architectural typology as users, the competence of these "professionals of judgment" in dealing with the evaluation of architectural projects to decide a fair, equitable and rational winner were most laborious. After several months of deliberation, the jury, unable to decide which of the propositions was the best project, announced two winners : the first for its plans **[Fig.1]** and the second for its facades and overall architectural style **[Fig.2]**. Following their legal wisdom and using a scoring board, the jury recommended that the two architects merge their designs in order to create the "ideal" courthouse.[3] As noted by historian Peter Collins in *Architectural Judgement*, a rare opus on architectural judgment, the judges had underestimated the fundamental importance of considering the *cohesion* of the concept in the architectural project, as their attempt to formulate a *fair* judgment was most likely of principal concern. Therefore, it appears that the judges' approach to judgment was conducted with an ideal of equity or justice instead of an ideal of architectural excellence.[4]

Despite its exceptional character, this competition illustrates the complexity and the specificity of architectural judgment by raising the question of the judgment criteria : Based on *which criteria* and regarding what issues was the architectural quality judged ? What is the role of these criteria and issues in the construction of judgment by the jurors ? What is the importance of the tacit and complex problematic of the context in which the judgment takes place ?

### Architectural Judgment, Competitions and Criteria

Architectural judgment is a rather complex topic to discuss and study from a scientific perspective.[5] As G. Vickers puts it in his book *The Art of Judgment*, *"the value judgments of men and societies cannot be proved correct or incorrect ; they can only be approved as right or condemned as wrong by the exercise of another value judgment."*[6] In architecture, a multitude of factors or criteria inform judgments that vary regarding the cultural or the historical context. Also, the processes through which architectural judgments are assessed are multiple, sometimes produced individually and other times the result of a collective procedure.[7] In that sense, architectural judgment is a the same time historical, sociological, economical, political, esthetical, technical, etc.[8] In a competition, some of those factors and criteria are *formal*, which mean they leave traces as the urbanism legislation of a city. But some of them remain *informal*, as in the personal taste, ideology, or interest of the actors judging, and are fastidious to analyze.[9] In any case, for the analysis of architectural judgment, architectural competitions present certain advantages, since they leave notable traces. Being a legal procedure, the competition produces written documents, and the juries that take place during the competition produce observable discourses. In fact, during a competition there are several steps and various official documents produced.[10] Throughout each of the steps, various actors must deliver different types of judgments that vary depending on the situation and issues at hand.[11]

In general, the competition process includes five main steps. These steps are :

- The preparation of the brief, including the definition of the judgment criteria ;
- The conception of the projects by the teams (drawings and texts) ;
- The evaluation of the proposals by a jury ;
- The redaction of the jury report at the end of the jury's process ;
- And the reception of the decision, where the winning project is announced, as well as critiqued and commented by the journalistic community (architects and non-architects).

More explicitly, the professional advisors and the clients, and occasionally the members of the jury, firstly develop the judgment criteria, architectural program and competition rules. These actors are already using their values, their experience and their *judgment* to define a preliminary vision of the architectural project at hand.[12]

Then, based on these early guidelines, competitors are asked to design a project that both responds and interprets the program and the judgment criteria requirements. The interpretation of these parameters is formalized through the design of an architectural project–an entity as critical as it is fluctuating, according to the nature of the competition (ideas or project).

Architectural *projects* — as formal interpretations of the program and of the judgment criteria–are then returned to the members of the jury who judge them in order to select the «best» project. At this crucial stage, jurors are required to redefine (or corroborate) their initial vision of the project. These successive reinterpretations enable discussions and debate, through which the jury *builds* a collective judgment thus *designing* the winning project. [13] An account of this deliberation, which takes place behind closed doors, is made public through the jury report. Although never a complete transcription of the discussions, it summarizes the main reasons that led to the selection of the winner, and justifies the selection or elimination of each of the other competitors.

Finally, the results of the competition are received by the public and criticized by the journalistic community; broadcasted in the form of articles. Although these participants mainly intervene after the competition has ended, they represent the public judgment, which is important insofar as it can influence the course of future competitions and the public reception of the projects. Through their comments, the judgment criteria used since the beginning of the competition can serve as a reference to criticism, but the public obviously do not have the obligation to limit their critiques to these criteria to give their own opinions on the project.

As we can observe, judgment criteria crosses the whole competition process. They represent a sizable research object that summarizes a synthesis of the values and concerns that shape the judgment of participants, while incorporating the qualitative judgment resulting in a temporality. Therefore, the traces left by the criteria from their original formulation to their multiple interpretations represents pertinent tool analyze architectural judgment, beyond a sociological study of the juries processes.

### Judgment Criteria

A criterion is defined as *"a character, a principle or an element that is used as a reference to judge, appreciate or define something."* [14] As proposed by A. Nicolas, in a book analyzing twenty-five years of competitions organized by the International Union of Architects (UIA) entitled *L'apogée*

**Fig.1**
Proposed scheme by E.M. Barry for the 1866 London Courthouse competition, from Collins (1971).

**Fig.2**
Proposed scheme by G.E. Street for the 1866 London Courthouse competition, from Collins (1971)

*des concours internationaux d'architecture : l'action de l'UIA 1948-1975,* architectural qualitative criteria are generally divided into six main categories: aesthetic, functional, technical, social, economic and environmental.[15]

However, beyond their function of official or referential documents for the design and the quality assessment, Peter Collins proposes — in his book *Architectural Judgment* that proposes to build a theorization of architectural judgment based on judicial judgment — that *criteria* in architecture are analogous to *principles* in the judicial system.[16] As he puts it, in the judicial system, *principle* refers to a "fundamental reason for deciding *a case one way rather than another, and that this reason is the principle, or fundamental criterion, on which the case has been adjudged."*[17] In that sense, criteria, or principles, are essential in order to judged or *award.* The "external object" that the criteria represent for the juror is fundamental to building an architectural judgment. Why? Because an architectural criteria, or a judicial principle, opens the judgment and links the object judged to a broader *context.*[18] In other words, without external criteria or external principles, judgment would be limited to the internal conception or the personal opinion of the juror judging. This is to say that the criteria or the principle becomes a tool that describes a very specific potential or hypothetical context and supports the way decisions are made or the way judgments are built in order to reach, in Collins' words, a "general agreement"; a "rational judgment."[19], for the potential project at stake in the competition.

In order to formulate a hypothesis regarding the role of criteria in architectural judgment, the second part of this article focuses on the analysis of two fictional competitions based on recent observations of the juries of Canadian competitions. The summary of these competitions' juries highlight how the judgment criteria and the objectives stated in the brief are used throughout the judgment sessions to fulfill the purpose of the competition, which is to identify the *best* architectural solution considering the site, and the architectural problematic as defined by the brief.[20]

## ■ Exemple 1 — Competition A

The next part of this article is dedicated to the summaries of two fictional competition juries, referred to as *Competition A* and *Competition B.* The narrative of these two fictional cases includes the judgment criteria and a summary of the judgment process that specifically focuses on the moments where the jury referred to the judgment criteria. In order to illustrate a greater range of parameters, two very different judgment processes are depicted–as in our *in situ* observations. The first fictional competition concerns an architectural project, while the other concerns an urban design project. The judgment criteria and procedures of judgment adopted by both competitions vary greatly.[21]

## ■ General Description of Competition A

The architectural program of *Competition A* called for a new high school and a public amphitheater. For this one-stage competition, four regional architectural firms were selected upon the submission of their portfolio to propose an architectural design of the project to be built. The judgment process was not anonymous, as the jurors knew the name of the firm that submitted each project. The jury was composed of eight members, including four architects.

The general objectives of the competition were summarized in the program as follows:

- *Provide the community with new a educational facility.*
- *Promote Canadian excellence in institutional architecture.*
- *Affirm Canadian desire to build sustainable architecture.*

The judgment criteria of the competition is described as follows:

- *Quality of the project regarding environmental issues;*
- *Quality and flexibility of the materiality;*
- *Functional and programmatic efficiency;*
- *Quality of the response regarding the social and cultural context;*
- *Overall beauty;*
- *Credibility of the team;*
- *Respect of the budget.*

The selection of the winner, that is to say, the judgment of the projects by the jury, was held behind closed doors. One day prior to the deliberations, the four finalists presented their projects in a public presentation: the time allotted to decide the winning project was limited, the schedule extremely strict. The jury began at 9 a.m. and ended at 3 p.m. at the latest. A coffee break was scheduled at 11 a.m. and a lunch break at 1 p.m.

## Opening of the Jury

At the beginning of jury deliberations, the professional advisor reminded jurors of the judgment criteria. Following this speech, the president of the jury immediately took the floor to remind the jury members that they should not dwell on the "small [architectural] details that are not yet fully resolved by the projects." According to the president, at this stage the jury had to "make an assessment of the entirety of the propositions : that is to say, of the project, presentation and personality of the architect and his team," so that clients will be able to work hand in hand with the winning firm. Finally, he opened the debate by forming a first round table in which everyone was "to mention their first impressions and opinions"–suggesting by that that the jurors set aside the judgment criteria and each express their own preferences, impressions and opinions on the projects, presentations and teams. Finally, along with the professional advisor, the president of the jury suggested that the goal of the first discussion was to eliminate two projects ; a suggestion that was immediately accepted.

## Round Table

During this first round table, initiated by the president of the jury, each juror spoke once, commenting and expressing his opinions on the four projects and indicating which project he would eliminate first. In this phase, no group discussion took place since the round table consisted of successive interventions. However, it should be noted that as the round table advanced, the expressions or opinions articulated by the first speakers were, on several occasions, repeated or reused by the jurors who spoke last, especially when it came to comments that took the form of *negative analogy*.[22] For example, to express the dullness of a particular project, one of the jurors proclaimed, "this project is like white [commercial and tasteless] bread."[23]

## Elimination Votes

After the coffee break that followed this round table — during which informal discussions on the projects took place, but that we were not able to take into account in our observation considering the complexity of the situation[24] — the professional advisor immediately called for an elimination vote by show of hands. One of the projects was eliminated by seven out of eight votes. For two of the projects, three out of eight members were in favor of their elimination. Finally, for one of the projects, none of the members voted in favor its elimination. Following this vote, the professional advisor and the president of the jury decided that their next objective would be to eliminate one of two projects that received three out of eight votes in favor of their elimination.

In contrast to the previous round table that lasted almost two hours, this discussion took the form of a relatively short debate (eighteen interventions in thirty minutes) where everyone was free to speak and respond in his or her own way. In order to respect the tight schedule, the professional advisor ended the discussion. Since the debate did not yield a consensus within the jury, the professional advisor called for another vote, in which a second project was eliminated unanimously.

Without further interventions or discussions, the professional advisor proceeded to call a third vote. He specified that this preliminary vote was intended to give an idea of the opinion of the jury on the two projects remaining in contention. They obtained the same number of votes : four members preferred one ; the other four members preferred the other. The professional advisor then reread the objectives of the competition as described in the program and issued a reminder of the judgment criteria.

## Final Debate

A second discussion followed the series of votes. Without following a predetermined order, the jurors stated their preferences, exchanged opinions and discussed their respective judgments. Some of the earlier analogies used to describe the projects were reused to develop arguments for and against each project. Interestingly enough, no intervention referenced the judgment criteria, whether to build an argument, to compare the two projects, to form opinion, etc. Although members of the jury had used the words "flexibility" and "efficiency" on a few occasions, they did not seem to refer directly to the definitions they were given in the competition's program. This exchange was also relatively short : twenty-seven interventions in one hour, including the last seven that were spent deciding whether the nomination of the winner should be determined through a majority vote, or through unanimous decision. Finally, no clear conclusion could be reached.

## Lunch

Similarly to the coffee break, most of the jurors spent their lunch break discussing the projects in small groups. The interventions of the jurors during this period could not be transcribed. At the request of the professional advisor, the observers were not allowed to discuss with the jury members to avoid influencing their judgment.

## Final Vote

After the lunch break, the professional advisor immediately called for a vote. Nine of the ten members of the jury voted for one of the two projects that remained in contention. The professional advisor then consulted the only member that had voted against the majority to see if he would agree to change his vote–thus rendering the decision unanimous–or if he would prefer to hold his ground–thus making the decision to award the winner a majority. The juror in question decided to rally with the others, thus ending the debate. The judgment criteria were not mentioned again. A short discussion (fourteen interventions in twenty minutes) on the announcement of the winner, the responsibility of the post-trial jury, etc. followed the vote, after which the meeting was adjourned.

## ▬ Example 2 — Competition B

While the narrative of *Competition A*'s judgment process was rather detailed and systematic (chronological), as one-stage competitions tend to be, the narrative of *Competition B*'s judgment process is more synthetic. Competitions held in two stages generally use a similar protocol for both jury meetings; as such, a particular emphasis is placed on the description of the protocol of a fictional two-stage competition. Based on several *in situ* observations, for *Competition B* there is a focus on the description of the moment when the judgment criteria seemed to play a key role in the development of the judgment, for example when judges explicitly referred to the judgment criteria in order to build their evaluation.

### General Description of the Competition

*Competition B* is an urban design competition for the transformation of a large undeveloped area of a city into a new residential area. The designers were asked to propose a master plan including the development of roads and footpaths, parks, public squares and a building plan.

This two-stage competition was held at a national level. The first stage was anonymous. In the anonymous first stage, twenty-six projects were submitted and the jury selected four finalists behind closed doors to participate in the second stage. Similarly to *Competition A*, the finalists were invited to present their projects to the jury in front of a public audience. The day after the presentations, the jury composed of nine members, five of them being architects, met behind closed doors to deliberate and select the winning project.

In the competition program, the main objectives of the project were summarized as follows:

*The purpose of this project is to appropriate and urbanize an important and undeveloped portion of the city. The complexity of the implementation resides in the multicultural and sociological context of the surrounding neighborhood. The project must create links with those neighborhoods as well as create a specific and strong identity for the future residents of the district. The projects must therefore consider all scales of the project, from the major roadsides to the public, private, semi-public and semi-private spaces, as well as the junctions between the circulations and the livable areas.*

The judgment criteria of the competition were defined and divided into several *issues*:

*"The following criteria are proposed to help with the evaluation although the judgment of the jurors is not limited to the criteria"*:

### Social and cultural issues:
*Potential of appropriation of the proposition; opportunities of interaction created for the residents of the sector, the citizens of the whole city and the passing visitors; convenience of the planning for the particular needs of the multicultural residents of the sector.*

### Functional and programmatic issues:
*Facility of accommodation for the daily activities according to the vocations of the buildings surrounding the public space; management of the potential conflicts between the different circulation networks in order to preserve the tranquility of the residents.*

### Aesthetical issues:
*Order and readability of the collective public space; consistency of the links between the public, the semi-public and the private spaces, security of the places at all season and at all time; flexibility of the facilities in order to generate and host diversified activities; participation of the project to the visual identity of the sector.*

*Environmental Issues :*

*Beneficial effects of the interventions on the ecosystems' quality ; comfort of the places in different climatic conditions, quality and sustainability of the plantations, reduction of the environmental footprint of the operations during the realization of the project and at long term.*

## ▬ The judgment process

In *Competition B*, the professional advisor structured the protocol of the judgment process very specifically. At the beginning of both deliberations, the professional advisor began by reminding the jurors of their role, emphasizing the importance of the complementary experiences of each juror as an asset that should allow to building a collective judgment. He then proposed that the judgment period be neither as a selection nor an elimination process, but rather a *debate* on the quality of the projects submitted. The judgment criteria were recalled, the protocol explained, and the judgment period organized. For this competition, the judgment began at 8 :30 a.m. and ended around 6 :30 p.m. for each stage, even if the initial schedule stated that the judgment should be finished at 5 :00 p.m.

Both periods of judgment followed a similar pattern : firstly, the jury held a round table so that each member could state their personal opinion as to what composes the winning project, without referring to any of the proposals. If they should so wish, the jury could clarify or add new judgment criteria. A period of forty-five minutes was then devoted to individual and silent observation of the project boards.

In the first selection period, the jurors were asked to discuss and select the "projects that stood out." After examining the project boards individually, jurors affixed on each project either a red card (to remove the project), a yellow card (to underline certain qualities of a project however not strong enough to be a finalist or winner), or a green card (indicating a project with enough potential to be a finalist or winner and which the juror was ready to defend).

The first selection round began after this step. In the first stage of the competition, the projects that received a majority of red cards were first examined, and then removed. The jury then discussed the remaining projects without following a specific order, to avoid falling into a dynamic evaluation preset (from best to worst or vice versa). During this process, instead of asking those who wished to eliminate the project to explain their choice, those who supported the project exposed the strengths and qualities

they had identified. This selective approach was fruitful– highlighting innovative ideas and strong gestures for each project. Some of the ideas and issues identified within the eliminated projects were deemed so relevant that, on occasion, the judges decided to add them to the list of the judgment criteria. Moreover, this way of operating prevented the division of the jury into those "for" and those "against" a project. It enabled a third possibility : the "maybe"–a category more relevant in initiating discussions and debates on the quality of projects, rather than reverting to a dynamic whose objective is to convince the "opposing party."

Unlike in *Competition A*, the lunch break that followed these proceedings took place around a table, effectively continuing the discussions in a collective and transparent way. After lunch, a second round table took place. The same method–selection by red, yellow and green cards was used. Finally, after a short coffee break, the jury held a period of discussion and debate. In the first stage, this debate led to the selection of four finalists, and in the second stage, it led to the nomination of a winning project. Both periods of judgment were finished one and a half hours later than scheduled with the agreement of all the members of the jury.

### The Judgment Criteria

During *Competition B*, the judgment criteria were systematically referred to by the professional advisor when opening discussions, when returning from breaks and before the final votes of each stage. Generally, the jurors consciously oriented their comments and critiques, basing their arguments on the issues identified by judgment criteria. Moreover, according to their views and their personal expertise, each juror instinctively appropriated certain aspects of the project. Therefore, when a question concerned, for example, the treatment of rainwater, the opinion of the landscape architect was systematically consulted. This way of operationalizing the judgment criteria helped to guide discussions and the evaluation of the quality of the propositions and avoided jurors deviating and formulating their critiques based on personal opinion. Furthermore, in this context, the jury members were more naturally inclined to build an architectural judgment that was collective, that is to say moving towards a consensual decision rather than simply a "majority vote" (whether for the elimination or for the selection of a project). Also, the deliberations were not organized as round tables but rather as group discussions, which seemed to produce more of a debate between the jurors.

| Competition A | | Architectural judgment parameters | Competition B | |
|---|---|---|---|---|
| Variables | | Architectural judgment parameters | Variables | |
| Eliminatory | | General strategy adopted for the selection of the finalist or the laureate | Selective | |
| Vote *Majority. Unanimity if possible* | | Selection strategy adopted for the acchievement of the judgment | Consensus *Unanimity. Majority as a last resort* | |
| "De-constructive" approach *The least worst project should win* | | Overall approach for the construction of the collective judgmen | "Constructive" approach *Collective construction of the winning project* | |
| Controled | | Time management | Regulated | |

**Fig. 3**
Comparison of the procedural protocols as observed in Competitions A and B.

Finally, after the judgment of the first and the second stages, the jurors expressed their surprise in the discovery that the finalists and winning projects, amongst some of the projects, were able to transcend the issues listed by the criteria judgment. Indeed, the strongest projects had all developed the "ideas" constituent of the competition to their full potential, in order to provide innovative and compelling solutions. In terms of design strategy, each of these projects also developed the idea of creating a central community center – a programmatic element that *was not* in the original competition program. This fell into the category of the judgment criteria specifying that the project needed to "punctuate [the site] with publicly or semi-publicly appropriated spaces and can support various forms of socialization." The comments of jury members are quite eloquent with regards to this addition; the juror representing the direction of the urban development of the district even said that he was "surprised to see that the city had completely misunderstood that the site lacked such a symbolic space." Other members of the jury agreed that: "a competition should allow to innovate and consider new ideas to 'educate' the city on new design opportunities." They added that the selected project(s) must therefore "meet and exceed the initial expectations." And that in this regard, "we cannot rule out ideas [or simply eliminate a project] when it shows potential."

## ▬▬ Comparison and Analysis

In addition to summarizing the two fictional examples of competition juries, the main characteristics of the judgment process described in the fictional *Competition A* and *Competition B* were compared. The comparison was made

on three different levels of analysis, based on the definitions generally attributed to Judgment[25] which distinguish what falls under:

1. The *procedures* of judging (the conditions of the judgment);
2. The *processes* of judging and (the results of the judgment);
3. The *act* of judging (how is the judgment mentally built by the subject).[26]

Therefore, to return to the principal question of *"What is the role of the judgment criteria on the judgment process and on the construction of the architectural judgment in the context of competitions' juries?"*, the three levels of analysis for the comparison of the two fictional cases are subdivided as follows:

1. The comparison of the *procedural protocol* followed by the jury;
2. The comparison of the *structure of discussions* between the jurors;
3. The comparison of the *type of arguments* used by the jurors to justify their opinion.

### The Procedural Protocol of Competitions Juries

The procedural protocol concerns the general strategy adopted in order to select the finalist or the winner, and the selection strategy adopted for the achievement of the judgment. In *Competition A*, the professional advisor proceeded by elimination and by majority votes: the jurors were asked if they were for or against the elimination of a project. If a majority (50 % + 1) of jurors were in favour the elimination, the project was eliminated without further discussion. In *Competition B*, the professional advisor proceeded by selection and consensus: few votes were held, and the decision to select a project was consensual. All members agreed on the selection or the elimination of a project after discussing or debating on the quality of said project.

Time management is also an important factor to consider when analysing the protocol followed by a jury. The purpose of observing and comparing how time is managed from one competition to another is not to conclude that *the more time allotted to the judgment the better it is*, but rather to reveal that the way it is divided, regulated, etc., regardless the time allotted, has an effect on the way architectural judgment is built during a constrained or limited period of time. In *Competition A,* the professional advisor *controls* time. After a precise period of time, the professional advisor ends an ongoing discussion without allowing further intervention, in order to respect the schedule. The period allowed for the judgment was from 9 a.m. to 3 p.m., including the lunch break, and the jury finished on time. In *Competition B,* time is *regulated* by the professional advisor who suggests the members of the jury conclude their debate, but always respecting the on going judgment process. The period allotted for the judgment for both stages was from 8:30 a.m. to 5 p.m., but finished at 6:30 p.m. with the agreement of all jurors **[Fig.3]**.

## The Structure of Discussions between Jurors
Regarding the structure of the discussions, the first point of analysis concerns the character or the nature of the discussions and the debates. In the first competition, most of the discussions take place during round tables where jurors emit comments and opinions. The last members to speak often repeated the earlier comments. As observed *in situ,* [27] round tables seem to limit opportunities of group discussions and debates. Instead, jurors formulate opinions or *critical* comments. In the second competition, group discussions are open and free. Exchanges are more focused on the analysis of the projects quality. As observed *in situ,* open discussions regularly led to debates on the definition of a common conception of the architectural quality sought for the project, or to recommendations and precisions to add to the competition's brief. Discussions and debates evolve from one critic to another and argumentative processes and rhetorical arguments are emitted.

The second point of analysis concerns the frequency of the references to the judgment criteria by the jurors. During the jury of *Competition A,* the members of the jury do not refer to the judgment criteria when building their judgment or justifying their opinion, whereas in *Competition B,* the members of the jury would regularly refer to the judgment criteria. Each juror appropriates certain aspects of the project that fall under their field of expertise. In this narrative, the judgment criteria were used as a reference for the evaluation of the projects. New judgment criteria, concerning positive aspects identified in non-winning projects, were added during the judgment processes to evaluate the remaining projects, as if the jurors were acting as designers.

Another point of analysis concerns the general cohesion of the jury. In *Competition A,* collective decisions were made regarding the individual judgment emitted before the vote. During the few debates, comments were oriented to sway disagreeing members by issuing divergent, strong and sharp opinions. In *Competition B,* collective judgments were built through a collective reflexive process. Decisions were made on the basis of consensual agreement as well as comments and questions regarding the pertinence and the potential of the project discussed **[Fig.4]**.

## Type of Argumentative Strategies used by Jurors
The first strategy identified concerns the nature of the interventions of the jurors and the principal justification used in support of the judgment enunciated. In *Competition A,* comments were mainly *opinions.* As observed *in situ,* in this type of competition, jurors made recurring references to the quality of the project's representation (plans, sections, elevations, perspectives) as presented on the boards. The comments were regularly based on the *image* ("too elitist," "too popular," "overly colourful," "too realistic," "not realistic enough," etc.) that could potentially eliminate the project; the design, spatial and functional qualities, etc. were less considered. In *Competition B,* comments primarily took the form of *criticism.* In this situation, the jurors tried to understand the intentions of the designers. Discussions and exchanges between jury members repeatedly questioned the intentions underlying the representations, instead of limiting their appreciation of a project at the superficial level of the quality of the representation (drawings and/or the models submitted by the competitors).

The second strategy concerns the general openness of the jury regarding the judgment criteria. In *Competition A,* the members of the jury did not use or refer to the judgment criteria. In this situation, or with *in situ* observation, it is impossible to evaluate the jury's level of openness regarding the judgment criteria. In *Competition B,* the members of the jury collectively identified new judgment criteria to be incorporated into the evaluation of the architectural quality of the projects remaining. Therefore, the jury was able to identify a deficiency in the competition brief (program),

| Competition A | Architectural judgment parameters | Competition B |
|---|---|---|
| Variables | Architectural judgment parameters | Variables |
| Round table *mainly* | Character / trend of the discussions and the debates | Group discussions *mainly* |
| Maybe once | Reference to the judgment criteria by the jurors | Several time |
| Individual judgement | General cohesion of the jury | Collective judgement |
| Controled | Time management | Regulated |

**Fig. 4**
Comparison of the structure of discussions between
jurors as observed in Competitions A and B.

| Competition A | Architectural judgment parameters | Competition B |
|---|---|---|
| Variables | Architectural judgment parameters | Variables |
| Opinions | Nature of the interventions of the jurors | Criticism |
| appreciation of the "image" *container* | Principal foundation and criteria of the judgment enunciated | Interpretation of the intention *content* |
| Recurrent *mostly negative* | Use of analogical reasoning | Almost absent |
| Not mentionned | General openness of jury regarding the judgment criteria | discussed + emergence of new judgment criteria |

**Fig.5**
Comparison of the types of argumentative strategies
used by jurors as observed in Competitions A and B.

| Competition A | Judgment criteria characteristics | Competition B |
|---|---|---|
| **Variables** | **Judgment criteria characteristics** | **Variables** |
| Rulebook | Part of... | Rulebook |
| List of principles | Organization | 4 issues and objectives |
| Generic / Non-descriptive | Expectations *interpretation of the criteria* | Specific / Descriptive |
| Absence | Adjectives | Presence |
| Absence | Values | Presence |
| None | Weighting | None |
| "Tools of evaluation" | Use / Limitation | "Unlimiting reference for the evaluation" |

**Fig. 6**
Comparison of the judgment criteria used in
Competitions A and B.

thus rectifying it with the addition of a new programmatic element drawn from a particular project (e.g. a new central community center [28]). Following an iterative process and being reflective about the brief, the criteria and the projects at hand, it is pertinent to relate the task of the jurors to the task of the designers.

The last strategy concerns the use of analogical reasoning. In *Competition A*, the jurors would often use analogical reasoning. More specifically, the jurors used negative analogies to describe the aspects they disliked in a project. When a strong negative analogy was linked to a particular project, it became the principal way to refer to it (e.g. "in *the white bread*, we can see that the circulation is problematic" or "*the white bread* would exceed the budget" [29]). In *Competition B*, very few arguments relying on analogy were observed. In this type of competition, the arguments made by the jury members generally demonstrate whether or not the competitor was able to meet the objectives and issues identified by the judgment criteria **[Fig.5]**.

### Overall Approach for the Construction of the Collective Judgment

With regards to the procedural aspect of these two competition juries, there were several major differences that needed to be evident in the fictional cases presented. Although the impact of judgment criteria is part of a broader set of factors that need to be considered when studying architectural judgment, the affirmation that judgment criteria directly contributes to the way architectural judgment is built by the jury allows us to distinguish and define some tendencies.

If we summarize and compare the overall approach of the two competitions, we find that in *Competition A*, the jurors do not refer to the judgment criteria; the reason being, possibly, the way the criteria are formulated in the brief. A quick analysis reveals that they are in fact vague and do not transcend qualitative values or innovative visions for the project. In comparison, *Competition B*'s judgment criteria convey a more precise definition of how the issues identified should be tackled. They become a reference tool for the construction of a collective judgment, and the jurors use them as a means for framing their evaluation **[Fig.6]**. Moreover, the comparison of the two competitions reveals another important difference concerning the procedural protocol followed to determine the winning project.

In *Competition A*, the professional advisor proposes an *eliminatory* process where jurors are asked to discuss the *problematic* aspects of a project in order to decide if it should be eliminated or not. Combined with a less interactive organisation of the discussions (i.e. round tables), the result is a polarization of votes between those who are "for" and those "against." Moreover, it seems that, in this situation, collective judgment is built from a collection of divergent opinions ("I don't like it because..." or "I like it because..."), and a decision reached through a majority vote. In contrast, *Competition B*'s professional advisor proposes a *selective* process where jurors are asked to discuss the *qualities* of each project in order to decide if the project should be selected for the next round. The result was that even though jurors agreed on the elimination of a project, they also identified the strengths of the project in order to refine their judgment criteria for the subsequent projects. Combined with the interactive organisation of the discussions (open group discussions and debates), the method of agreement was that of a consensual decision generally unanimous.

### Comparing *Competition A* and *Competition B*

Considering these different parameters, a preliminary hypothesis about the role of the judgment criteria in the construction of architectural judgment can be summarized as follows: although flexibility in the program seemingly affords more freedom to designers and judges, more defined criteria allows designers to innovate while providing a clear framework for evaluation and critique by jury members. The judgment criteria defined by clear, precise and timely issues represents a more effective framework for architectural judgment and for the selection of a winner. Indeed, *Competition A*'s jury did not seem to have a clear idea of what they were looking for. Jurors were therefore more likely to evaluate the projects according to their respective expertise and to judge whether or not the project met their own personal definitions of architectural quality. In contrast, *Competition B*'s jurors had been given a clear set of ideas of the issues and objectives that the winning project was to meet, and consequently seemed to be more collaborative, critical and rigorous in their evaluation.

Evidently, the criteria are not solely responsible for the way in which a jury evaluates an architectural competition (procedural aspect of judgment) or how the judgment is built (reflexive aspect of the judgment). Other factors, such as the way the professional advisor organizes and animates the judgment period, the expertise and the personal character of each member of the jury, the nature of the competition, etc. are just as fundamental in the construction of architectural judgment. However, these two very different examples of competition juries, when compared, allow a hypothesis on the potential role of judgment criteria in the construction of architectural judgment and the identification of certain parameters of the architectural judgment.

## ▬ Preliminary Hypothesis

In closing, this comparative analysis highlights the fact that while criteria often remain unused, they also represent an important tool for the construction of architectural judgment in the context of competition juries. More defined criteria, transcending values to use adjectives, have the capacity to make more sense to the judges that use them than general and vague criteria. To revisit Collins' theories, the following analogy emerges: judgment criteria would be to architectural judgment what architectural precedents are to the design process. Criteria and precedents allow the project to be linked, either at the conception phase or the judgment phase, to not only the physical context, but also the social, cultural, historical, economic and political contexts—just as fundamental to the development and judgment of the quality of an architectural project.

Naturally, architectural judgment is not solely based on the criteria defined. However, the judgment criteria, when compared to the entirety of the parameters constituent of the architectural design competition, reveal the more critical issues that concern architectural judgment. For example, the way architectural judgment is built could also be analyzed through the type of competition (idea or project), the aspect of anonymity versus non-anonymity in competitions, the procedure adopted for the management of the discussions or the decision making, the recurrence of negative analogies (as made evident in *Competition A*), etc. Likewise, this analysis reveals the importance of the judgment's protocol. In fact, an elimination-style judgment procedure resulted in the judges commenting on the problematic aspects of a project, whereas a selective judgment procedure led judges to comment on the ideas as well as the efficient and innovative solutions of a project. On a larger scale, these different ways of structuring the jury seem to impact the very cohesion of the whole that the competition jury represents.

Launched in 2004, the competition for Paris' *Forum des Halles* is another prime example of the complexity of architectural judgment in the contemporary era. As reported by Françoise Fromonot in a book published in 2005,[30] the jury, under political pressure, ended up nominating a project that was highly contested. Although professional and public opinion was in favour of Rem Koolhaas' innovative project, ultimately David Mangin's project won the competition, despite its conventional and heavily critiqued approach. As explained by Fromonot, the quality of the project's ecological approach, which resulted in–quite literally–a "green aesthetic," was the reason of its nomination. However, it would appear that the emphasis on environmental issues came from political pressure; the architect being preoccupied by the way this iconic Parisian project would be received both nationally and internationally. In regards to commenting on the role of politics in the judgment of architectural quality, this competition raises the issue of the place that sustainability holds within the judgment of architectural quality. More specifically, how do the issues of a society infiltrate and inform the judgment of architectural quality? How do the criteria represent and transcend these issues, and what are their effects on the architectural judgment?

## ▬ Notes

[1] As defined by: (among others) Collins, P. (1971), Saunders, W. S. (2007), Younés, S. (2012), Moore, Steven A., and Wilson, Barbara B. (2013).

[2] Hans Georg Gadamer and Carsten Dutt, *Herméneutique, esthétique, philosophie pratique : dialogue avec Hans-Georg Gadamer* (Saint-Laurent, Québec: Fides, 1998).

[3] MH Port, "The New Law Courts Competition, 1866-67," *Architectural History* (1968).

[4] Peter Collins, *Architectural judgement* (Montreal: McGill-Queen's University Press, 1971).

[5] Jean-Pierre Chupin, "Judgement by design: Towards a model for studying and improving the competition process in architecture and urban design," *Scandinavian Journal of Management* 27, no. 1 (2011).

[6] Geoffrey Vickers, *The art of judgment : a study of policy making*, Centenary ed., Advances in public administration (Thousand Oaks: Sage Publications, 1995).

[7] William S. Saunders, *Judging architectural value*, Harvard design magazine readers (Minneapolis, MN: University of Minnesota Press, 2007).

S.A. Moore and B.B. Wilson, *Questioning Architectural Judgment: The Problem of Codes in the United States* (Taylor & Francis, 2013).

[8] Samir Younés, *The imperfect city : on architectural judgment* (Burlington, VT: Ashgate Publishing Company, 2012).

[9] Michèle Lamont, *How professors think : inside the curious world of academic judgment* (Cambridge, Mass.: Harvard University Press, 2009).

[10] Silberberger, J. distinguishes 3 phases in the process of architectural competition judgment: design, judgment and public reception.

[11] Silberberger, "Organizing the space of possibilities of an architectural competition."

[12] G. Adamczyk, C. Crossman, and J.-P. Chupin, "Qu'est-ce qu'un bon critère qualitatif?," *ARQ, La revue d'architecture, Spécial sur le jugement en architecture*, no. 154 (2011): 33.

[13] Chupin, "Judgement by design: Towards a model for studying and improving the competition process in architecture and urban design."

[14] http://www.cnrtl.fr/lexicographie/critère

[15] Aymone Nicolas, *L'apogée des concours internationaux d'architecture : l'action de l'UIA 1948-1975*, Collection Architectures contemporaines Série études (Paris: Picard, 2007).

[16] Collins, *Architectural judgement*.

[17] Collins, *Architectural judgement*.

[18] The legislative system and in the conception or the judgment of an architectural project are always taking place regarding a specific context, which includes, still following Collins' thought, *the context of history, the context of society, the context of physical and economical environment and the political context.*

[19] Collins, *Architectural judgement*.

[20] Linda N. Groat and David Wang, *Architectural research methods* (New York : J. Wiley, 2002).

Jean Louis Le Moigne, *Le constructivisme*, 2 vols., Collection Communication et complexité (Paris : ESF, 1994).

Pierre Paillé and Alex Mucchielli, *L'analyse qualitative en sciences humaines et sociales*, 2e éd. ed., Collection U Sciences humaines et sociales (Paris : Armand Colin, 2008).

[21] For this paper, we based our analysis on the programs, the rulebooks, the judgment criteria and jury reports, as well as *in situ* observation of the deliberations conducted by the jury behind closed doors of four recent architectural and urban design competitions held in Canada. For these observations, no AV equipment being permitted, every intervention of each member of the jury was carefully noted by hand. These notes were subsequently digitally transcribed. Although there are occasions when words or exact phrasing were not recorded in their entirety (given the rapid discussions), intentions and keywords used by the speakers were always respected. The *in situ* observation of the judgment process as observer has allowed us to note a few trends, especially when we started to compare these observations. In other works, we can refer to this data as "field notes" collected as ethnographers. Concerning our methodological approach, it follows the line of the tradition of the "constructivist" research methods, since we did hermeneutical analysis as well as qualitative analysis. The main methodological references were used were Paillé, P. & Mucchielli, A., Le Moigne, J. L., and Groat, L. N. & Wang, D.

[22] Jean-Pierre Chupin, *Analogie et théorie en architecture : de la vie, de la ville et de la conception, même*, Collection Projet & Théorie (Gollion : Infolio, 2010).

[23] Although the purpose of this article is not to theorize the role of analogical reasoning in the architectural design process as defined by Chupin, J.-P., (2010), it is important to note that it might represent a fundamental object for the theorization of architectural judgment in the jury's competition context. Some juries produce a wide variety of negative analogies ; comments that compare an architectural project, or one of its components, to another object (whatever its nature is) in order to identify weaknesses or eloquently illustrate the element criticized. However, why is analogical reasoning often used for negative comments ? What are the effects of these strong expressions repeated throughout the remainder of the deliberations on the debates and the architectural judgment ?

[24] These kinds of "moments" are inevitable and the exchanges that take place during those periods may at times be fundamental in the development of the judgment. For now, we labelled them the "black boxes" of architectural judgment. They will be integrated in our theoretical modeling as a topic that could constitute furtherer research on the architectural judgment.

[25] The grand philosophers of judgment such as Immanuel Kant generally attribute three definitions to the concept of judgment. Those three definitions distinguish what belongs to the judgment : 1) as a protocol – to build a judgment regarding a value system or an accepted procedure (as in the scientific or the practical judgment as identified by Kant in his first two critiques) ; 2) as a result – which refers to a judgment in his enunciated form (a subject + a predicate) and 3) as an act or a faculty – to judge (as conceptualized by Kant in his third critique). See Blay, M., Castel, P.-H., (2003).

[26] Michel Blay, *Grand dictionnaire de la philosophie* (Paris : Larousse : CNRS, 2003).

Immanuel Kant et al., *Critique de la faculté de juger. Suivi de Idée d'une histoire universelle au point de vue cosmopolitique, et de Réponse à la question : Qu'est-ce que les Lumières ?* , Collection Folio/essais (Paris : Gallimard, 1985).

[27] As mentioned, this part of the analysis also includes general observations made through our observation *in situ*. Four competitions were observed for a total of seven periods of judgment.

[28] Example given in the description of the fictional *Competition B*.

[29] Example given in the description of the fictional *Competition A*.

[30] Françoise Fromonot, *La campagne des Halles : les nouveaux malheurs de Paris* (Paris : La Fabrique, 2005).

# References

**Adamczyk**, G., C. **Crossman**, and J.-P. **Chupin**. «Qu'est-ce qu'un bon critère qualitatif ?» *ARQ, La revue d'architecture, Spécial sur le jugement en architecture*, no. 154 (2011) : 33.

**Blay**, Michel. *Grand dictionnaire de la philosophie*. Paris : Larousse : CNRS, 2003.

**Chupin**, Jean-Pierre. *Analogie et théorie en architecture : De la vie, de la ville et de la conception, même*, Collection Projet & Théorie. Gollion : Infolio, 2010.

**Chupin**, Jean-Pierre. «Judgement by Design : Towards a Model for Studying and Improving the Competition Process in Architecture and Urban Design.» *Scandinavian Journal of Management* 27, no. 1 (2011) : 173-84.

**Collins**, Peter. *Architectural Judgement*. Montreal : McGill-Queen's University Press, 1971.

**Fromonot**, Françoise. *La campagne des Halles : Les nouveaux malheurs de Paris*. Paris : La Fabrique, 2005.

**Gadamer**, Hans Georg, and Carsten Dutt. *Herméneutique, esthétique, philosophie pratique : Dialogue avec Hans-Georg Gadamer*. Saint-Laurent, Québec : Fides, 1998.

**Groat**, Linda N., and David Wang. *Architectural Research Methods*. New York : J. Wiley, 2002.

**Kant**, Immanuel and Ferdinand **Alquié**. *Critique de la faculté de juger. Suivi de l'idée d'une histoire universelle au point de vue cosmopolitique, et de Réponse à la question : Qu'est-ce que les Lumières ?*, Collection Folio/Essais. Paris : Gallimard, 1985.

**Lamont**, Michèle. *How Professors Think : Inside the Curious World of Academic Judgment*. Cambridge, Mass. : Harvard University Press, 2009.

**Le Moigne**, Jean Louis. *Le constructivisme*. 2 vols, Collection Communication Et Complexité. Paris : ESF, 1994.

**Moore**, S.A., and B.B. **Wilson**. *Questioning Architectural Judgment : The Problem of Codes in the United States* : Taylor & Francis, 2013.

**Nicolas**, Aymone. *L'apogée des concours internationaux d'architecture : l'action de l'UIA 1948-1975*, Collection Architectures Contemporaines Série Études. Paris : Picard, 2007.

**Paillé**, Pierre, and Alex **Mucchielli**. *L'analyse qualitative en sciences humaines et sociales*. 2e éd. ed, Collection U sciences humaines et sociales. Paris : Armand Colin, 2008.

**Port**, MH. «The New Law Courts Competition, 1866-67.» *Architectural History* (1968) : 75-120.

**Saunders**, William S. *Judging Architectural Value*, Harvard Design Magazine Readers. Minneapolis, MN : University of Minnesota Press, 2007.

**Silberberger**, Jan. «Organizing the Space of Possibilities of an Architectural Competition.» *Geographica Helvetica* 66, no. 1 (2011) : 5-12.

**Vickers**, Geoffrey. *The Art of Judgment : A Study of Policy Making*. Centenary ed, Advances in Public Administration. Thousand Oaks : Sage Publications, 1995.

**Younés**, Samir. *The Imperfect City : On Architectural Judgment*. Burlington, VT : Ashgate Publishing Company, 2012.

# 3.3. Quality and Iconicity

**A Study on Swiss Housing Competitions (1997-2010)**

**Antigoni Katsakou**, Ph.D.
Associate Lecturer, The Leeds School of Architecture,
London College of Contemporary Arts
United Kingdom

This essay argues that the procedural framework of architectural competitions can strengthen the demand for iconic architectural projects, even in sectors of the construction activity like the residential, where similar concepts were, until recently, less frequent. The author discusses the case of collective housing competitions organized in Switzerland during the last fifteen years; on the one hand, terms such as innovation and innovative design solutions are regularly mentioned in the standard competition brief as one of the principal requisites, while on the other hand, such procedures make up part of broader urban planning policies focusing on the rapid production of new units. In many cases, one of the program's basic requirements is also the unique identity of the future housing estate that needs to function as a regeneration pole for a large urban sector, as well as a "trademark" for its developer.

Thus, although housing competitions have produced in Switzerland, especially since the mid-1990s, quite impressive results in terms of urban forms and apartment types, the public dialogue in their context may be questioned in relation to the definition of "quality" architecture. Besides, the architect's imagination seems of a less daring spirit when it comes to three-dimensional representations of the proposed spatial sequences, frequently using a limited range of themes and rather literal naturalistic representation styles that seem pointed to embellished realities instead of evoking the dynamics of the conceptual process.

**Cover**

Top: Housing competition in Zollikerstrasse (Zurich, 2005), Gigon & Guyer architects, perspective image of the competition project. *Copyright: Gigon & Guyer*

Bottom: Housing competition in Zollikerstrasse, Gigon & Guyer architects, photo of the built project. *Copyright: Thies Wachter*

Competitions dealing with housing projects can be quite different from tendering procedures concerning the construction of a community's public buildings. Traditionally, these last have often made for the object of international competitions, as public buildings function essentially like poles for the majority of urban tissues, and as landmarks representing a certain concentration of activities — drawing "*together the world around them*"[1]; thus they are important to a large number of people, even (and maybe especially) to those that do not live permanently in the specific context (tourists, visitors, etc.). Housing in general can be a rather 'banal' architectural theme, as in many cases it is produced without the involvment of a specialized professional. The larger part of the residential stock is due to developers not necessarily associated with a specific architectural vision, and not forcibly preoccupied with the project's impact on a wider scale. Besides, it is also the link housing constructions bear with the intimate sphere of a person's life that makes it more difficult to associate them with widely accepted aesthetic tastes or architectural tendencies.

The change in the pursuits of the architectural conception with regard to public buildings, and with respect to changing social conditions and the loss or decadence of traditional iconographies, as well as the search for new types of meaning or for the "*enigmatic signifier*," as Jencks puts it,[2] has been largely discussed,[3] as has the idea of the iconic building in relation to public constructions replacing the traditional monuments of the urban tissue and often resulting from international competitions that receive large publicity. It is the goal of this article to argue that through their procedural framework, architectural competitions can strengthen the demand for iconic architectural projects, even in sectors of the construction activity, like the residential, where similar concepts were up to now less frequent. For that purpose Switzerland, where for the last fifteen years an extraordinary activity in the housing sector has been set in place, will serve as case study. In the Swiss context, the promoted quest for architectural quality seems to be working in parallel as a means for promoting other (at first sight extrinsic) attributes. Conveying, for example, the character of a non-profit housing association which is acting as a developer for a specific housing scheme may be to the interest of this construction society and perhaps, to a certain extent, to the interest of the cooperative movement in general, but it is rather unconnected with the quality of an architectural work in itself. Through such a prism, even a fruitful system of competition organizing, as the Swiss background of housing competitions, risks producing less authentically 'qualitative' answers to the posed problems in relation to the users' living conditions.

## ▬ Principal Characteristics of Iconic Projects

Jencks resumes the characteristics of what he calls the "self-important" building[4] in its ability to draw attention, to provoke "public and journalistic excitement" or even a kind of "media saturation" and its association with a "sculptural gesture" that is shaped in most of the cases by the building's "weird form" or "unusual, sometimes awkward geometry". He writes more specifically: "If the building is not new or unusual enough, it will not have sufficient charge to become iconic".[5] An iconic building is for Jencks one that offers "a new and provocative image"[6]; what is more, this image stems often from animate or inanimate objects not particularly charged with meaning; in most cases, the building may 'hint' at qualities of more than one such objects: "if you scratch an iconic building hard enough, it bleeds such meanings: [...]; fish and animals; crystals and our body parts, rhythmical growth forms of plants and galaxies".[7] Mateo, in the publication *Iconoclastia: news from a post-iconic world*[8] describes the icon as "a project that aspires to be exceptionally expressive".[9] He points out that "in the contemporary city, everything is potentially Iconic," while his approach is, to the opposite of Jencks, rather critical, stating as one of the characteristics of the icon its expressive autonomy and disconnectedness with its context:

*Icons do not guide, they do not create hierarchies. [...] The Icon has no thickness, it is pure skin. It knows itself to be pure appearance and does not blend in.*[10]

In the same work, Ivanišin concludes:

*Inevitably, a work of architecture that sets claim to an instant iconic status must rely on immediate perception, and even if some understanding is required, it should not imply too much effort. Consequently, either the differences a work of architecture usually contains have to be blurred in order to create an appealing and unitary image, or a simplified story must be told, joining the parts to excite an observer usually ignorant of architectural matters. In either case, the complex logic of an architectural project must be reduced.*[11]

How many of these features seem to be present in the "successful" application of the competition system in the housing sector of the Swiss construction market? For a start, in competitions' juries the presence of laymen is obligatory. But before actually analyzing the system's parameters, it would be useful to provide some concrete indication of this 'success,' and explain shortly (in the spirit of this scientific meeting that refers to the internationality of the competition phenomenon), how the competition system seems to have evolved during the last fifteen years in the country.

## ▬ Results of the Housing Competition System in Switzerland during the Examined Period

Almost 50% of a total of more than a hundred tendering procedures listed in a database that comprises housing competitions organized during the period of 1997-2010 in various parts of Switzerland [12] have already produced concrete results in the form of completed buildings. This is a relatively high ratio, and even more so considering that almost a third of these procedures are more recent than 2007 and therefore likely to lead to completed projects in the near future. More than half of these construction projects are situated in the canton of Zurich. In Zurich's region, an average of four to five housing competitions are held every year since roughly 1997 (1996 being a year of restructuring for the appropriate State services); these numbers increase especially during the period 2003-2010, reaching sometimes seven housing competitions per year. More than 60% of the procedures listed in this database were conducted with a direct involvement of State administration services on a communal level. In the case of the city of Zurich, the appropriate planning department (Amt für Hochbauten) has been so efficient in bringing about tendering procedures of different kinds that it is also serving as an independent planning office, external to the municipality stakeholders.

Another interesting element is of course the diversity and the wide range of solutions — in terms of urban forms and apartment types — that have been proposed in this framework since the mid-nineties. Housing competitions seem to have worked as a real workshop for new ideas and diversified conceptual approaches, providing at the same time considerable chances for success to a whole new generation of architects. What allows for more optimistic interpretations regarding the operational mode

of competition procedures in the country is the fact that a primary overview of a majority of case studies reveals few significant changes between competition layouts and built projects. [13] This could point to a 'shared' learning process among investors and professionals — a kind of consensus established through the process framework of competitions between the housing market (at least an indicative share of it) and the architectural conception.

### Evolution of the Competition System in Switzerland

Although not evident historically, it seems nevertheless nowadays a bit obsolete to perpetuate terms as 'international' competitions, since participation in tendering procedures, at least for the grand majority of European countries, is not any more limited by country borders. Certainly, it is possible that participation to open procedures be reduced, for example with the obligatory use of a national language. But in general, the situation has changed significantly and seems to be cancelling the need for referring to 'international' tendering procedures, unless of course intercontinental participations are specifically implied.

A clear evolution of the system, regarding the scope of the professionals to which architectural competitions are nowadays addressed, despite the geographical area in which these competitions are launched, may undoubtedly be reported in Switzerland. Strong noted in 1976 while discussing Swiss competitions: "Apart from volume, competitions differ most from those organized in the UK on the question of eligibility. Competitions can be open, but are often restricted to canton or parish or even by religious belief. This has the effect that in normal time and in normal conditions, entries would be no more than about fifty". [14] Restrictions of this type were often decided depending on the importance of the commission. [15] In present days, competitions in Switzerland, in the spirit also of European agreements concerning tendering procedures, normally address architects from all geographic parts of the country without taking into consideration restraining factors, long-time applied in the past. Such a change positively affects the range of proposed solutions and equally promotes the transparency of assessment procedures easily questioned in the case of exclusivist, introverted systems addressing continually the same groups of professionals.

The canton of Valais is one characteristic example of this change of course, regarding the scope of participating architects to competitions organized by State services. Valais is a mountainous canton in the southern part of

Switzerland, rather isolated from the rest of the country because of the land's contour, but in which competitions hold a long tradition ; however, their results have often been contested because of professional clans that often prevailed in the distribution of the available commissions. [16] In support of this point is the interview of the cantonal architect, Bernard Attinger in 1991 (assigned to this post since 1978 ; to the moment of the interview it is commented that he has been already organizing competitions for ten years [17] with a lot of success and an "opening" to other parts of Switzerland) :

> La première répercussion [de l'ouverture de la « scène » architecturale valaisanne, n.d.l.r.] est certainement l'ouverture vers des modèles extérieurs de qualité mais aussi l'ouverture du Valais aux architectes de l'extérieur et inversement celle des architectes valaisans vers la Suisse. On peut comparer cette évolution au phénomène économique de l'ouverture des marchés. Il est très facile de vivre en autarcie en restant entre soi et en vivant son petit train-train quotidien. Dès que les frontières s'ouvrent, les problèmes affluent : concurrence, échanges. Grâce à cette concurrence venue de l'extérieur, le canton y a gagné en dynamisme. [...] Bref, si la concurrence a d'abord été vue d'un mauvais œil, on s'aperçoit maintenant qu'elle a été bénéfique tant pour l'architecture que pour les architectes valaisans. [18]

Despite definite progress, pre-selections concerning the shortlist of participants seem always in practice. Luigi Snozzi points out, in relation to this subject : "While today it is possible to identify some improvements with the opening, for example, above a certain limit, to professionals of other cantons and countries, I think, unfortunately, that with or without the European regulations, the situation is getting worse day by day. I think, for example, of competitions with preselection." [19] In fact Snozzi categorically condemns competition procedures conducted on the basis of preselection, for the sake of young professionals : "Now, in the process above mentioned of preselecting, the architect is left aside, he becomes the last of the group. [...] This is very serious because it entails, in practice, the elimination of the young, that is, of the very figures that need the competition for to be able to emerge". [20]

## Other Significant Features of the Contemporary Competitions System in the Collective Housing Sector of the Country

Apart from a relative evolution regarding the range of participating offices that most possibly affects the quality of the submitted proposals (due to increasing concurrence and the input coming from strongly varied backgrounds), in Switzerland there are still at least two more inherent characteristics depicting a special framework in tendering procedures regarding the construction of collective housing units. On the one hand, it is the fact that terms such as innovation and innovative design solutions are regularly mentioned in the standard competition brief as one of the principal requisites ; they seem to challenge the architects' creativity and bring about a large variety of proposals, with respect to urban forms and apartment layouts. An extensive discourse around the issue of quality housing is equally developed. In the report from the Wohnen am Schaffhauserrheinweg (altes Kinderspital-Areal) competition, for example, it is noted :

> Der Kanton beabsichtigt ein qualitativ hochstehendes, quartierverträgliches und investorentaugliches Wohnbauprojekt zu entwickeln. [...] Um qualitativ hochwertige städtebauliche Vorschläge zu erhalten, wurde das Verfahren eines anonymen Ideenwettbewerbs mit einer Referenzqualifikation gewählt. [21]

"Optimal, innovative apartments" are usually one of the basic competition objectives as expressed in a majority of briefs, where the term figures side by side with the need for "quality and up-to-date urban, architectural and exterior space solutions within new constructions," referring to the planned interventions / housing complexes as wholes. As an example, we quote here an excerpt from the Guggach competition brief :

> Die Wettbewerbsziele lassen sich wie folgt benennen : Städtebaulich, architektonisch und aussenräumlich qualitätsvolle und zeitgemässe Neubauten. [...]; Optimale und innovative Familienwohnungen, die den spezifischen Wohnbedürfnissen von Familien oder anderen Haushaltsformen mit Kindern gerecht werden und einen hohen Gebrauchswert besitzen [...]. [22]

Such indications seem a phenomenon of the last ten years; as in the past, quality did not seem necessarily associated to innovation or up-to-date attitudes, although it was probably equally sought. An excerpt from the Hegianwand competition (1999) that has produced one of the most well-known housing complexes designed by EM2N architects may serve as evidence: "Gefragt waren qualitätsvolle Wohnungen und Aussenbereiche mit hohem Gebrauchswert".[23] Although the exact meaning of innovation in terms of specific expectations in architectural devices or functional solutions that should be integrated in the newly-built housing complexes, is not always quite clear, the term seems related to the idea of a rapidly changing social scenery that demands corresponding solutions, as well as to the idea of densification that seems the appropriate strategy for a country with limited constructible areas and most of all, with especially expensive ones.

On the other hand, housing competitions comprise part of broader urban planning policies with fixed objectives and deadlines, and focus on the rapid execution of the concerned schemes. In the jury report of the Parcelle du Foyer de Sécheron competition it is noted under the title *"Objectifs et critères du concours"*:

*Les futures constructions, qui font l'objet du présent concours, occuperont le cœur d'un quartier qui subira ces prochaines années l'un des plus grands processus de transformation du territoire genevois de ces dernières décennies. À terme, cette portion du territoire ne représentera plus une friche industrielle. Elle est vouée à devenir un véritable centre d'activités, polarisé autour d'édifices importants et de nouveaux espaces publics. [...] Le développement de la parcelle dite du « Foyer de Sécheron », est un enjeu urbanistique et architectural d'envergure pou le site en particulier et pur la Ville en général.*[24]

Future housing estates seem to be expected to function as concentration poles for the regeneration of entire urban or suburban zones, when in most cases, there is little in the context to establish a dialogue with. Housing schemes are called to draw attention in these areas and hopefully serve to their 'relooking.' In the absence of a solidly operating

**Fig. 1**
Wolfswinkel housing complex, Egli & Rohr architects,
parallel study commissions, Zurich, 2004.
*Source: ABZ*

**Fig. 2**
Avenue de Morges housing complex, Fruehauf,
Henry & Viladoms architects, project competition, open
procedure, Lausanne, 2008. The project was described
in the local press as a large green garden.
*Source: FHV architects*

**Fig.3 and Fig. 4**
Tram- / Funkwiesenstrasse housing colony, project competition, restricted procedure, Zurich, 2009; perspective images of the competition proposals of (from top to bottom) Meier & Hug (*source: Meier & Hug*), and Gigon & Guyer architects (*source: Gigon & Guyer*).

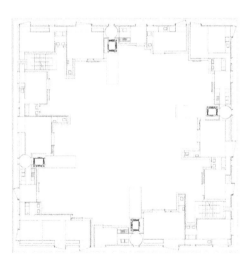

**Fig.5**
Avenue de Morges housing complex, Made-In architects, project competition, open procedure, Lausanne, 2008.
*Source : Made-In architects*

context, they seem to be expected to exist in a fairly autonomous manner until a moment in the future, when they will probably make part of a newly-created network (of housing complexes or drawn-in the neighborhood activities).

Another important factor for the competitions' operational framework is that for the most part, it concerns housing schemes aiming to the replacement of existing complexes. This accentuates the demand for diversification and distinction between the old and the new in order for the project to be considered successful, or really representative of its times. Besides, the public dialogue that is systematically promoted in relation with the competition procedures exposes the projects equally to the appreciation of both laymen and experts, and needs, in order to be effective and arouse subsequent interest, easily 'legible' representation styles.

## ▬ Features of Iconic Architecture Discerned in the Architectural Production Resulting from Swiss Housing Competitions

As already mentioned, one of the principal characteristics of iconic projects is the 'simplification' of their compositional logic that may be supposed to lead to the reduction of their synthetic approach and qualitative aspect. It has also been established that demands associated to the image of the housing complexes to be, seem quite frequent in the respective competition briefs. One can therefore suppose that if simplifications of the projects' compositional logic may be found in the outcome of the competitions procedures, i.e. in the architects' competition proposals, he can safely argue on the system's overall efficiency regarding architectural quality.

In general, it may be said that two principal observations lead to questioning the real efficiency of the system regarding innovation and quality. First, it is quite easy to find in this background residential schemes that seem to seek an excessive expressiveness through their form, either in relation to its extraordinariness, or with respect to their 'detached' symbolism. The formalism of certain submissions (or even already built projects) seems difficult to justify on well-grounded reasons. References to animate or inanimate forms are also quite common **[Fig.1]**.

Second, and this time despite the variety in urban forms and proposed apartment types, the architect's imagination appears less daring, when it comes to three-dimensional representations of the proposed spatial sequences. On the one hand, there exist frequently recurring themes which limit the range of featured spaces. Zones of collective use, such as the common open spaces of the complexes as well as the common spaces of the units — living room and kitchen — seem to be the ones that normally constitute the projects' emblematic pictures; the architects seem to opt mainly for impressive 'snapshots' that may attract attention **[Fig.2]**.

Recurrent spatial themes and compositions in three-dimensional representations seem accentuated by the fact that these last are also the images primarily displayed in the publications concerning these procedures. For example, in the competition reports normally prepared by the city of Zurich, all projects are presented by more or less the same data: principal floor plans and sections, as well as exterior perspectives, often from the same angles; facts that enable a relatively simple comparative reading of the submissions, but at the same time 'flatten' their differences. Additionally, it is not unusual that the architects are asked to submit a perspective image of their project from a specific point of view, a demand surely reducing every submission's particularities to a simple question of 'looking good' from a specific angle **[Fig.3] [Fig.4]**.

On the other hand, in many projects proposing particularly innovative devices no three-dimensional interpretation of these parts of the layout is proposed. This could be interpreted either by limited time frames (that do not allow for an innovative proposal to develop in full) or of course, explained on the basis of unrealistic concepts that cannot lead to real-life architectural solutions. In either case, it is a question of simplifying or rather not completing the project's compositional logic. An example could be offered by the proposal from the office based in Geneva: architectural office Made-In to the Avenue de Morges competition (Lausanne, 2008). The layout of the proposed apartment type is based on a reinterpretation of the bourgeois pattern 'pièces en enfilade,' with absence of connecting spaces between the various rooms. To reach a private room of the unit, the user has to cross other spaces, not solely of collective character. This arrangement introduces a particular hierarchy in the unit's layout and makes necessary the existence of two alternative entries to the apartment. Unfortunately, a more complete idea of the proposal cannot be formed as, among the six presentation boards submitted to assessment, no figuration providing specific information on the space's formation and the apartment's third dimension is available on a larger scale **[Fig.5]**.

Finally, the architect's limited imagination in relation to the innovative aspect of their proposals is also evident in the representation styles predominant among pictorial figurations resulting from housing competitions. Perspective images especially of exterior views, adopt often a rather *literal*, *naturalistic* aesthetic that points to embellished realities and convincing representations of the briefs' requirements, rather than to three-dimensional figurations evoking the dynamics of the conceptual process. An evocative example may be provided by the winning project in the first competition (2009) organized by the Mehr als Wohnen cooperative, a society regrouping more than fifty cooperative associations and foundations in Zurich and having launched its activities with the organization of a significant idea competition in 2007 under the characteristic title "Wie wohnen wir morgen? Zukunft des gemeinnützigen Wohnungsbaus." Although the project, according to the construction program, introduces some breakthrough ideas in matters of social organization and mixing of users of various social backgrounds in the specific housing scheme, its exterior perspective does not reveal the special living conditions reigning in the inside. Besides, few are the cases of projects, where the architects dare to present a *non-finito* illustration of their projects. It is as if the concept would indeed be less convincing otherwise, giving the impression of a less studied solution and probably one that could not be rapidly built **[Fig.6] [Fig.7]**.

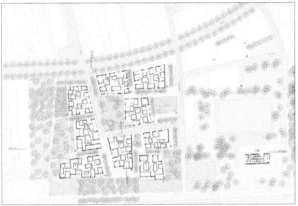

**Fig.6 and Fig. 7**
Housing complex Projekt 1 Baugenossenschaft
Mehr als wohnen, Futurafrosch & Duplex, project
competition, restricted procedure, Zurich, 2009
*Source : Futurafrosch (perspective image: Adrian Koenig)*

Swiss housing competitions lend themselves well to an analysis regarding the relation of the competition system with architectural quality. After several years of their intensive organization in the housing sector, their outcome can help draw conclusions for the 'appropriateness' of the procedure for promoting quality. Although several factors seem to be pointing to a lively architectural research that finds direct applications and improves the housing stock of the country, the system seems to equally present its limits, sometimes disconnecting and voiding this research from its main objectives. In the short length of this essay we cannot provide definite answers. It seems nevertheless important to comment on both sides of the coin, and to question the advantages of competitions, if not for any other reason, just to be sure that these resist doubt.

*The author would like to thank for their help providing original material all the architects mentioned in the text's captions; equally, for its financial support while gathering information the Foundation Research Design Competitions in Zurich.*

## Notes

[1] J. L. Mateo, «Iconoclastia,» in *Iconoclastia : News from a Post-Iconic World*, ed. F. Sauter (Zurich : Actar ETH Zürich, 2009), 4.

[2] Charles Jencks, «The New Paradigm in Architecture,» *Hunch : The Berlage Institute Report*, no. July (2003).

[3] Jencks himself (Jencks, 2006 : 48-61) provides a resuming account of this discussion (Sudjic 2003, 2005 ; Morrison, 2004 ; Jencks 2004, *The Iconic Building-the Power of Enigma* (London : Frances Lincoln Ltd, 2005).).

[4] «The Iconic Building Is Here to Stay,» *Hunch : The Berlage Institute Report*, no. January (2006) : 48.

[5] «The Iconic Building Is Here to Stay,» *Hunch : The Berlage Institute Report*, no. January (2006) : 56-57.

[6] «The Iconic Building Is Here to Stay,» 60.

[7] «The Iconic Building Is Here to Stay,» 60.

[8] Mateo, «Iconoclastia.»

[9] «Iconoclastia,» 4.

[10] «Iconoclastia,» 5.

[11] K. Ivanišin, «Controversy around Images,» ibid., 13.

[12] Antigoni Katsakou, «Recent Architectural Competitions of Collective Housing in Switzerland : Impact of This Framework on Architectural Conception and Innovation» (Swiss Federal Institute of Technology Lausanne (EPFL), 2011), 415.

[13] Considered as significant, are modifications affecting the principal compositional logic of the original layout and/or having an impact on an inherent design parameter that introduces some type of architectural innovation. (see Katsakou, 2012)

[14] Judith Strong, *Participating in Architectural Competitions : A Guide for Competitors, Promoters, and Assessors* (London : The Architectural Press, 1976), 87.

[15] "En règle générale, la participation à ces joutes était ouverte aux architectes établis sur un territoire géographique donnée — commune, canton, région, pays voire au-delà, selon l'importance de l'ouvrage." (Ducret et al., 2003 : 20)

[16] "Thus, after many years characterized by "pseudo-competitions" [...] it has been possible to resume the tradition with the organization of a true competition [...]" ("Così, dopo molti anni caratterizzati da «pseudoconcorsi» [...] è stato possibile ricollegarsi alla tradizione con l'organizzazione di un vero concorso [...]", Attinger, 2000 : 6).

[17] "The '70s were characterized by a definite slowdown and by an unfavorable to competitions political attitude, as the State Council of that time did not want to let a jury impose the allocation of commissions." ("Gli anni '70 sono tuttavia stati caratterizzati da un netto rallentamento e da un atteggiamento politico sfavorevole ai concorsi, in quanto l'allora Consiglio di Stato non volle più lasciarsi imporre da una giuria l'attribuzione dei mandati." Attinger, 2000 : 6].

[18] C. Allenspach, «Le Concours : Une façon d'aborder le débat sur l'architecture (Interview de Bernard Attinger, architecte cantonal du Valais par Christoph Allenspach),» Archithese no. 3 (1991) : 14-17.

[19] "Se da una parte, oggi, è possibile individuare alcuni miglioramenti con l'apertura, ad esempio, sopra una certa soglia, ai professionisti di altri cantoni e paesi, credo, purtroppo, che con o senza le normative europee, la situazione stia peggiorando di giorno in giorno. Penso, ad esempio, ai concorsi su preselezione."
J. Chimchila Chevilli, "La cultura del concorso : Intervista a Luigi Snozzi," Archi, no. 4 (2000) : 12.

[20] "Ora nel processo sopra decrito della preselezione, l'architetto è messo da parte, diventa l'ultima pendina del gruppo. [...] Questo è molto grave, perché comporta, in practica, l'eliminazione dei giovani, cioè proprio di quelle figure che necessitano del concorso per potere emergere."
„La cultura del concorso : Intervista a Luigi Snozzi," Archi, no. 4 (2000).

[21] Immobilien Basel-Stadt, «Wohnen Am Schaffhauserrheinweg (Altes Kinderspital-Areal). Anonymer Ideenwettbewerb Im Selektiven Verfahren. Bericht Des Preisgerichtes,» (Basel : Bau- und Verkehrsdepartement des Kantons Basel-Stadt / Immobilien Basel-Stadt, 2009), 3.

[22] D. Stoffner and R. Wigger, Wohnüberbauung Guggach, Zürich-Unterstrass. Projektwettbewerb Im Selektiven Verfahren. Bericht Des Preisgerichts (Hochbaudepartement der Stadt Zürich, Amt für Hochbauten, 2005), 4.

[23] D. Stoffner and R. Wigger, «Wohnen Am Schaffhauserrheinweg (Altes Kinderspital-Areal). Anonymer Ideenwettbewerb Im Selektiven Verfahren. Bericht Des Preisgerichtes,» 2.

[24] «Parcelle du foyer de Sécheron. Quartier de Sécheron — Concours d'architecture en vue de la réalisation de logements, d'un établissement médico-Social, d'équipements de quartier et d'un parc public,» (Geneva : Ville de Genève, Département de l'aménagement, des constructions et de la voirie, 2004), 3.

# References

**Allenspach**, C. «Le concours : Une façon d'aborder le débat sur l'architecture (Interview de Bernard Attinger, architecte cantonal du Valais par Christoph Allenspach).» Archithese no. 3 (1991) : 14-17.

**Attinger**, B. «Lo sviluppo dei concorsi di architettura in Vallese.» Archi, no. 4 (2000) : 6.

**Chimchila Chevilli**, J. «La cultura del concorso : Intervista a Luigi Snozzi.» Archi, no. 4 (2000) : 12.

**Ducret**, A., C. **Grin**, P. **Marti**, and O. **Söderström**. Architecte en Suisse : Enquête sur une profession en chantier. Lausanne : Presses polytechniques et universitaires romandes, 2003.

**Familienheimgenossenschaft Zürich**. «Überbauung Hegianwand, Zürich. Projektwettbewerb Auf Einladung. Bericht Des Preisgerichts.» Zurich : Familienheimgenossenschaft Zürich, 1999.

**Immobilien Basel-Stadt**. «Wohnen Am Schaffhauserrheinweg (Altes Kinderspital-Areal). Anonymer Ideenwettbewerb Im Selektiven Verfahren. Bericht Des Preisgerichtes.» Basel : Bau- und Verkehrsdepartement des Kantons Basel-Stadt / Immobilien Basel-Stadt, 2009.

**Ivanišin**, K. «Controversy around Images.» In Iconoclastia : News from a Post-Iconic World, edited by F. Sauter, 6-13. Zurich : Actar ETH Zürich, 2009.

**Jencks**, Charles. «The Iconic Building Is Here to Stay.» Hunch : The Berlage Institute Report, no. January (2006) : 48-61.

**Jencks**, Charles. The Iconic Building-the Power of Enigma. London : Frances Lincoln Ltd, 2005.

**Jencks**, Charles. «The New Paradigm in Architecture.» Hunch : The Berlage Institute Report, no. July (2003) : 251-68.

**Katsakou**, Antigoni. «Housing Competitions-Elaborating Projects in Their Specific Process Framework.» Nordic Journal of Architectural Research 24, no. 1 (2012) : 174-200.

**Katsakou**, Antigoni. «Recent Architectural Competitions of Collective Housing in Switzerland : Impact of This Framework on Architectural Conception and Innovation.» Swiss Federal Institute of Technology Lausanne (EPFL), 2011.

**Kiss**, Virág, and Ursula **Tschirren**. Neubau Project 1 Der Baugenossenschaft Mehr Als Wohnen, Zürich-Leutschennbach. Projektwettbewerb Im Selektiven Verfahren, Bericht Des Preigerichts. Hochbaudepartement der Stadt Zürich, Amt für Hochbauten, 2009.

**Kiss**, Virág, and Ursula **Tschirren**. Wie Wohnen Wir Morgen ? : Zukunft Des Gemeinnützigen Wohnungsbaus : Stadtraum Zürich : Ideenwettbewerb Für Alle : Bericht Des Preisgerichts. Hochbaudepartement der Stadt Zürich, Amt für Hochbauten, 2007.

**Mateo**, J. L. «Iconoclastia.» In Iconoclastia : News from a Post-Iconic World, edited by F. Sauter, 4-5. Zurich : Actar ETH Zürich, 2009.

**Stoffner**, D., and R. **Wigger**. Wohnüberbauung Guggach, Zürich-Unterstrass. Projektwettbewerb Im Selektiven Verfahren. Bericht Des Preisgerichts. Hochbaudepartement der Stadt Zürich, Amt für Hochbauten, 2005.

**Strong**, Judith. Participating in Architectural Competitions : A Guide for Competitors, Promoters, and Assessors. London : The Architectural Press, 1976.

**Sudjic**, Deyan. The Edifice Complex : How the Rich and Powerful--and Their Architects--Shape the World. New York : Penguin Press, 2005.

**Ville de Genève**. «Parcelle du foyer de Sécheron. Quartier de Sécheron — Concours d'architecture en vue de la réalisation de logements, d'un établissement médico-social, d'équipements de quartier et d'un parc public.» Geneva : Ville de Genève, Département de l'aménagement, des constructions et de la voirie, 2004.

have

the

to be

ARCH — ... Spare me.

ART — All of a sudden th

mistake becomes an

wolves

d this

horizon of knowledge

amati-

sburger

something you had

versions

PH — Wait a second. I

frames of referenc

int "cre-

creativity

ART — I would say a s

quite dif-

electrical installa

n the whole

ARCH — But answer

do with architec

es".

mention?

mes of refer-

ll of this as it

ART — I came up v

capability to

that a mistake

extremely pro

# 3.4. The Honourable Mention

## A Fictitious Discussion

**Jan M. Silberberger**, Ph.D.
ETH Wohnforum — ETH CASE, Department of
Architecture, ETH Zurich
Switzerland

In effect since 1998, SIA regulation 142 defines the formal procedure of an architectural competition in Switzerland. Among others, SIA regulation 142 defines a specific instrument, the so-called "honourable mention". This instrument provides the jury board with the opportunity to award outstanding projects that critically violate terms specified in the competition brief. Competition entries that are awarded an honourable mention can even be ranked on the first place and recommended for further development and completion.

The paper at hand argues that the honourable mention is to be considered an integral part of the architectural competition. Yet, it obviously creates a conflict with basic principles of public procurement (transparency, non-discrimination and equal information), the latter being paralleled by a total bindingness of the information given in the brief.

Referring to an ethnographic study on the work of jury boards of four Swiss architectural competitions, several interviews with competition organisers and to a specific case, the paper orients towards a philosophical discussion of the honourable mention focussing on its relation to the quality of the outcome a competition generates.

The paper at hand revolves around the so-called honourable mention. In its regulation 142 (Art. 22.2), the Swiss Society of Engineers and Architects (SIA) defines that "outstanding entries, that were initially excluded from the awarding of prizes because of critical violations of terms specified in the competition brief, can be awarded an honourable mention". Moreover (Art. 22.3), "Competition entries that are awarded an honourable mention can be ranked by the jury on the first place and can be recommended for further development and completion. This option has to be explicitly mentioned in the brief. Furthermore are required a decision of the jury with a 3/4 majority and the explicit agreement of all representatives of the contracting authorities."

The paper draws on findings of an ethnographic study on the work of jury boards of four Swiss architectural competitions, several interviews with competition organisers and on the "Workshop Honourable mention" (3rd of November 2011, Zurich) held by the Committee SIA 142. In preparation for this workshop the Committee SIA 142 provided every attendant with a hand-out comprising of short descriptions of three recent cases where an honourable mention had been awarded. Additionally to the above cited definition of the honourable mention, the Committee SIA 142 states in this hand-out, that "(t)he honourable mention has a long tradition and is deeply rooted in the essence of competitions and the procedural regulations. Also the regulations on public procurement provide for the honourable mention. And nevertheless it is a disputed issue".

The paper at hand explicitly draws on one of the three examples featured in the hand-out, namely the competition regarding new training facilities for the fire brigade squads of four Swiss cantons (that is, the competition "Ostschweizerisches Feuerwehr-Ausbildungszentrum Bernhardzell"). Section 2 provides the segment of the hand-out that deals with this example.

In section 3 the paper gathers various perspectives on the honourable mention. The format used is borrowed from Plato's dialogues. In this way the reasoning becomes an argumentative action. Furthermore, rhetorical devices like irony or allegories can be applied and the clash of different positions as well as hypothesis and assumptions can be presented in an elegant way. Finally, unsolved separate questions — like in this case the juridical evaluation of the honourable mention — can be neglected. Although the discussion presented in section 3 is fiction, that is, it did not take place as such, the different parts and perspectives described stem from various field notes. In this sense the fictitious discussion can be considered a vignette as the

author used it in his paper "Jury sessions as non-trivial Machines" (2012) and especially in Van Wezemael et al. (2011).

Section 4 provides the reader with references and comments considering certain lines of thought featured in the discussion. The paper is concluded in section 5.

## ▬▬ The hand-out

Example Honourable Mention: O0stschweizerisches Feuerwehr-Ausbildungszentrum Bernhardzell (New training facilities for the fire brigade squads of four Swiss cantons)

### Problem

In order to be able to train close to reality the fire brigade squads of the cantons Appenzell Innerrhoden, Appenzell Ausserrhoden, Thurgau and Sankt Gallen must be provided with adequate practice venues and objects. The contracting authority decided to use the military training ground Bernhardzell as the location for the future building.

### Type of Procedure

Open project competition with a potential further development. 51 projects have been submitted and allowed.

### Result

An honourable mention was ranked on the first place and recommended for further development and completion (*locus foci*, Streiff Architekten, Zurich).

### Violation

Accessing the site from the north thereby trespassing the safety zone. This safety zone was confirmed in the competition's Q&A-catalogue.

### Condition for realisability

Redefinition of the safety zone according to insights gained from clarification with military authorities during jury sessions.

### Jury's explanatory statement regarding the recommendation for further development

...The project captivates with its clear and simple construction, with its horizontal separation of the different types of utilizations and with its clever placement in the existing topography. This is, however, also due to the accessing via the safety zone.

## ▬ The fictitious debate

As mentioned in the introduction we will now enter a fictitious discussion on the honourable mention. From time to time debaters will refer to the example presented in section 2. The fictitious debaters are: a moderator (MOD), the head of a research and development department (RD), an artist (ART), a professional athlete (PA), a philosopher (PH), an architect (ARCH) and a spin doctor (SPIN). A building law expert has been invited, however, did not show up.

**MOD** — One could come up with the following confrontation: Imagine a football game. Now think of a linesman being interviewed after the final whistle. Imagine him saying in the camera: "The ball was clearly out. Yet, the whole play was so brilliant, so beautiful, that I decided to let play continue". One could argue that in the same way as this linesman's action conflicts the laws of football awarding the honourable mention conflicts the basic principles of public procurement — transparency, non-discrimination and equal information. [1]

**PA** — I am so sick of those sports metaphors. All those guys doing the 100 metres in 15 seconds talking about Champions League or world-class. But let's drop that subject. Your comparison is flawed.

**MOD** — In what way?

**PA** — Sports is based on clear, universally valid rules. That's the charm of it. Nobody wants to have that kind of linesman. If at all, sports are about finding scope within the existing rules. It is definitely not about abrogating rules at times.

**PH** — In a late essay, the French philosopher Gilles Deleuze [2] mentions the relation between innovation and style in sports. Referring for instance to the development in high jump — from the scissor jump to the belly roll to the Fosbury flop — he points out that the history of sports runs through these inventions, which, according to him, in each case amount to the unexpected. Do you mean such inventions when you speak of the search for scope within an existing structure of guidelines?

**PA** — The point is, the three styles you mentioned are all according to the rules. For instance, there is no rule that forbids jumping backwards over a high jump bar.

**PH** — I consider the existence of the honourable mention to be founded in the demand to provoke unforeseen, unexpected problem-solving approaches. The honourable mention extends the search for unforeseen, unexpected solutions beyond the solution space defined in the competition programme. You, in contrast, advocate to limit this search to the space of possibilities as defined in the competition brief.

**PA** — I do not advocate anything. I just say that in sports it is completely uninteresting to search beyond the solution space as defined by the rules and standards. This obviously seems to be different in architecture.

**ARCH** — It is absolutely possible to find unexpected, unforeseen problem-solving approaches within the solution space defined by the competition brief. [3]

**ART** — Creativity is essentially about breaking rules. Even by definition. You can look that up in the Encyclopaedia Britannica.

**PH, pulls out her iPhone and checks on Wikipedia** — Here it says: "In a summary of scientific research into creativity Michael Mumford (2003) suggested: 'Over the course of the last decade, however, we seem to have reached a general agreement that creativity involves the production of novel, useful products'. Beyond this general commonality, authors have diverged dramatically in their precise definitions, with Peter Meusburger (2009) claiming that over a hundred different versions can be found in the literature". Under the point "creative process" it says, for example, that "creativity arises as a result of the intersection of two quite different frames of reference". But nowhere in the whole entry you find the term "breaking the rules".

**ART** — Well, combining two quite different frames of reference is sort of a taboo, isn't it? But be all of this as it may. I consider the opportunity - or the capability to be more precise - to conceive an infringement of the established horizon of knowledge against the background of aspects of quality to be essential. Do you know what I mean?

**RD** — I think I do.

**PH** — Well I think I don't. Would you please explain to us what you exactly have in mind when you mark combining two quite different frames of reference as a taboo?

**ART** — Imagine it is 1968. We are on a construction site. A residential building comprising of 120 apartments. Now imagine the typical parents' bedroom of that time: A king-size bed in the middle and to the left and to the right those bedside tables with the reading lamp ...

**RD** — What is the difference to our present situation? (laughs)

**ART** — Good question. But the point I am trying to make is: This set-up meant that you had to install two sockets at a distance of let us say 2.5 metres in the wall on the head side of every parents' bedroom. Now let us imagine that the electrician on our construction site installed these sockets in a wrong way. That is, in a way so that the typical king-size bed slash bedside table combination cannot be set up properly. The architect in charge appears on the construction site. He notices the electrician's mistake. He calls the electrician down and wrathfully leaves the site. However, on the way to his car he suddenly comes to a standstill. He reflects and abruptly asks himself: What kind of perception with regard to living, with regard to family, with regard to work does such an arrangement of sockets transport? If we want to organise society differently, our flats have to be different. Which means that our bedrooms have to be different, which means that these sockets have to be arranged differently …

**ARCH** — … Spare me!

**ART** — All of a sudden there is a new perspective: The mistake becomes an infringement of the established horizon of knowledge, that is, it provokes you to realize something you had not been able to see.

**PH** — Wait a second. I still don't get which two different frames of reference are combined in your example.

**ART** — I would say a serious reading of Guy Debord[4] and electrical installation.

**ARCH** — But answer me this: What does all this have to do with architectural competitions and the honourable mention?

**ART** — I came up with that example in order to illustrate that a mistake, which is a breach of the rules, can be extremely productive — in case one reflects on it. And I think that the architectural competition could be one of the rare sites where such mistakes can be reflected and interpreted.

**RD** — You must not forget that such an infringement of the established horizon of knowledge to use your words again…

**ART** — … I guess I stole this term from Henry Miller …

**RD** — … that the assertion of such an infringement needs a certain virulence.[5] A virulence that makes society adopt the infringement. This is the case with every invention, every new paradigm.[6]

**ART** — That's the jury's job. That's what these jurors have to do when ranking an honourable mention on the first place — to see to it that the required virulence to get the project realised is generated.

**ARCH** — Let me tell you this: An architectural competition is not the place for such profound, radical inventions as you have them in mind.

**ART** — Architectural competitions are always described as struggles for excellence. People constantly argue that architectural competitions produce excellent, exceptional solutions.

**ARCH** — People argue that architectural competitions produce high quality solutions.

**MOD** — Just to clarify this: What do you mean by exceptional? There is a researcher on architectural competitions, who employs the term exceptional practice for competitions, which should provoke the submission of unconventional design proposals…[7]

**ART** — What does unconventional mean?

**MOD** — Outside the norm, outside the routine. For him — I am very rough here - exceptional practice applies to prestige projects, signature buildings, one-off spectacles.

**ART** — I guess I meant the exact opposite. I meant by exceptional — just a good idea.

**SPIN** — Come on, if you take that example described in that hand-out you gave us — a training centre for a fire brigade squad some place you never heard of — I mean, look who won — Streiff Architekten — with all due respect that's not the major leagues. This whole competition is definitely no spectacle and yet it produced an exceptional, unexpected project.

**RD** — Maybe exceptional ideas or inventions are the opposite of spectacles. Take the Walkman, probably the most successful invention of the enterprise I represent. You had the transistor radio, you had the portable cassette player, you had headphones. But then you had to do the unexpected: you had to remove the loudspeakers to replace them with headphones. It's as simple as that.

**MOD** — I would like to go back to that aspect of connecting two different frames of reference. There is a researcher from Canada,[8] whose studies on architectural competitions can be related to that practice. In short, this researcher considers the evaluation of competition entries as a design process. Drawing on design methodology literature he describes the winning project as the product of two design processes: the first taking place in the architect's studio, the second taking place in the jury's meeting room. This reminds me of your socket example. It needed someone who construed the electrician's installation. Without that act of interpretation the electrician's work would have stayed an annoying mistake, which had to be eradicated as soon as possible. So when this researcher describes the evaluation — the construal - of competition entries as a design process he stresses the explorative nature of that inquiry and points out that the jury's work has to be regarded a major factor in the creation of a winning project. In the sense that the jury performs a general, profound scheme transformation of the field of competition entries into a winning design project.

**RD** — I think this is an important point. A jury board of an architectural competition is no tender panel. Let's see what this means for the honourable mention. We can start from the premise that we have a highly complex interplay of deliverables - we have maybe hundreds of different dimensions. Therefore, it is virtually impossible for a jury to make a ranking with a rational choice process, that is, in a predictable, calculable manner. Such a form of transparency is impossible. By necessity the jury has to come up with a different mode of assessment. The outcome of its decision-making is not the outcome of a rational choice process but the result of its commitment to the winning project...[9]

**MOD** — ... Which is completely comparable to the decision-making in the course of designing.

**RD** — Juries in architectural competitions as well as designers rationalize this commitment in retrospect. Yet, one cannot analyze it prospectively, that is, we cannot rationally explain its creation.

**SPIN** — "Although we read with our minds, the seat of artistic delight is between the shoulder blades. That little shiver behind is quite certainly the highest form of emotion that humanity has attained when evolving pure art and pure science. Let us worship the spine and its tingle." That's Nabokov.

**RD** — Furthermore, one could also regard the set-up of a competition programme as a design process. That process involves "reflective practice" as well. During the course of writing a competition brief its authors constantly experiment with the competition's space of possibilities : they widen it, narrow it down, re-widen it, narrow it down again. Writing a good competition programme in the same way as designing a good competition entry requires a certain critical distance, that is, the ability and willingness to challenge assumptions time and again.[10]

**ARCH** — You're addressing the competition programme now. Yet, this does not get us any further. At first sight,

an honourable mention obviously reveals a mistake, a flaw in the competition brief. However, when taking a closer look you will notice that there are cases where serious thought and money has been put in the preparation of the brief — for instance, several development studies have been carried out — so that the published brief was so to speak almost perfect — and nevertheless an honourable mention has been recommended for further development and completion ...

**RD** — ... Which is just consequent ...

**ARCH** — ... Which means that the honourable mention does not correlate with the quality of the competition programme.

**SPIN** — Did you at all listen to that guy with his sockets ?

**ARCH** — Excuse me ?

**SPIN** — I claim that there is a correlation. The better the brief, the higher the chances that there is an honourable mention.

**ARCH** — What ?

**SPIN** — I think we all agree that awarding an honourable mention needs some courage. It's easy to say that those sockets are installed incorrectly. But to recognize their installation as absolutely right, which in turn means that you declare that your assumptions regarding the design of bedrooms or whole apartments respectively had been wrong — for this you have to be anxiety-free. Hence, we can say the better the jury the more likely the awarding of an honourable mention.

**ARCH** — So what ?

**SPIN** — As I understand, the guys that are involved in setting up the competition programme usually act as jurors later on. Is that correct ?

**ARCH** — Many of them do, that is correct.

**SPIN** — So tell me this : Why should someone who put little effort in setting up a brief all of a sudden start to work when it comes to assessing the entries ? Why should someone who never really cared suddenly challenge things ?

**ARCH** — That's purely hypothetical. Besides, why didn't the jury in that fire brigade squad training centre competition start challenging the assumptions on which the brief bases during questions and answers ?

**RD** — That is consequent as well. It needs an outstanding entry to provoke you to challenge your assumptions. During Q+A there is nothing to provoke you. There is just a question, which you have dealt with and which you have decided during the preparation of the brief.

In the same way mediocre projects do not provoke you to challenge your assumptions. A mediocre project accessing the site through the safety zone would have simply been excluded from the competition.

**MOD** — This is exactly to what the administrative court objected to in its decision. I quote: "The boundary conditions have been changed a posteriori on the grounds of further clarifications with representatives of the army. These clarifications and changes, however, have been solely oriented towards the project of the appellee."

**SPIN** — These judges do not have the slightest idea how designers work.

**RD** — What if we regard the whole course of the competition, the whole procedure, as a design process? If we do so, the honourable mention becomes an integral part: it is the chance to profoundly reflect and rework the perception of the design problem through the examination of concrete problem-solving approaches. [11]

**SPIN** — That SIA probably hired one of the lamest PR agencies ever!

**MOD** — What's that supposed to mean?

**SPIN** — Do you know that famous campaign by Dane, Doyle and Bernbach for Avis? No? Well, here is the situation: We're at the beginning of the 60ies. Hertz is the number one car rental firm. Then there is a rather huge gap and then we have Avis, Budget and National, I think, more or less sharing second place. So Avis asks DDB to do a campaign for them and what does DDB come up with? No one? "We try harder"! Avis uses this slogan for almost 50 years now! We're number two, but we do everything to get to the top. That's why we provide you with the best service.

**ARCH** — The SIA is not a business company.

**SPIN** — That is totally beside the point. In that hand-out the SIA itself writes, I quote, "The honourable mention has a long tradition and is deeply rooted in the essence of competitions and the procedural regulations. Also the regulations on public procurement provide for the honourable mention. And nevertheless it is a disputed issue." Sounds like a PR-problem to me.

**ARCH** — So how would you solve this problem?

**SPIN** — "We people at the SIA comprehend the architectural competition as a dynamic procedure. That is, as an instrument by means of which we can appropriately approach the complex nature of architectural problems. We let the competition entries speak. Even to the extent that we allow them to provoke us to see the problem in a different, a new light". Something like that. You have to sell the honourable mention as an essential possibility to adapt the competition's solution space according to findings gained - no, to treasures captured - on the jury's courageous exploration of the space of possibilities opened up by the submitted architectural projects. They've got my number. Why don't they use it?

———

Roughly speaking we can regard an architectural competition as three processes of translation or transformation. At first, the client's intention is translated into a competition programme. Then, the competing architecture offices translate the competition brief into various competition entries. Finally, the board of jurors "transforms" the bundle of competition entries into a project, which it recommends for further development and completion. While the second transformation is obviously a design process, there is, as we have seen, research that describes the third and also the first transformation as a design process as well.

Against the background of this body of literature, which analyses each of these three sub-processes as a design process, that is, as a non-linear, iterative process, the paper at hand proposes to regard the whole competition procedure as a full-blown design process and puts forward the hypothesis that it is the instrument of the honourable mention that allows for full-blown iteration leaps throughout the whole sequence of an architectural competition. Put differently, without the honourable mention, the paper argues, an iterative course of action would possibly be threatened - as for instance a profound rethinking or reworking respectively of the client's intention as (temporarily) fixed in the competition brief when engaging with the competition entries would possibly be impossible.

## ■■ Endnotes

[1] For a detailed discussion of EU-law requirements for public procurement (which also apply to Switzerland) see Volker (2010).

[2] In his essay "Mediators" (1992), Deleuze discusses qualitative transformations within various fields of society.

[3] Van Wezemael, Silberberger and Paisiou (2011) describe how a competition entry (which does not violate any of the terms specified in the brief) provokes a new, unexpected perspective on the design problem.

[4] For a detailed description of the Situationist movement and Guy Debord's work, readers are referred to McDonough (2004) and Wark (2008).

[5] The term "virulence" as well as its concept are borrowed from Gladwell (2002).

[6] Kuhn (1957) provides a detailed account of the resistance a new paradigm in physics has to get over in order to substitute the established one.

[7] The researcher mentioned here is Schmiedeknecht (2010).

[8] The researcher mentioned here is Chupin (2010; 2011).

[9] The researcher mentioned here is Kreiner (2006; 2007a; 2007b; 2010; 2011).

[10] Silberberger (2011) referring to Chupin (2010; 2011) describes the action of setting up a competition brief as a design process.

[11] For a detailed discussion regarding the instrument of the honourable mention and its integral role within the competition procedure readers are referred to Silberberger (2012).

## ■■ References

**Chupin**, Jean-Pierre. *Analogie et théorie en architecture : de la vie, de la ville et de la conception, même*. Collection Projet & Théorie. Gollion : Infolio, 2010.

**Chupin**, Jean-Pierre. "Judgement by Design : Towards a Model for Studying and Improving the Competition Process in Architecture and Urban Design." *Scandinavian Journal of Management* 27, no. 1 (3/ 2011) : 173-84.

**Deleuze**, Gilles. "Mediators." In *Zone 6 : Incorporations*, edited by J. Crary and S. Kwinter, 281-94. New York : Zone Books, 1992.

**Gladwell**, Malcolm. *The Tipping Point : How Little Things Can Make a Big Difference*. Boston : Little, Brown, 2000.

**Kreiner**, Kristian. "Architectural Competitions — a Case Study [2006]." *http://www.clibyg.org/en/knowledge_bank/index.php ?item_id=21*.

**Kreiner**, Kristian. "Architectural Competitions : Empirical Observations and Strategic Implications for Architectural Firms." In *The Architectural Competition : Research Inquiries and Experiences*, edited by Magnus Rönn, Reza Kazemian and Jonas E. Andersson, 101-26. Stockholm : Axl Books, 2010.

**Kreiner**, Kristian. "Constructing the Client in Architectural Competition [2007a]." *http://www.clibyg.org/en/knowledge_bank/index. php ?item_id=11*.

**Kreiner**, Kristian. "Strategic Choices in Unknowable Worlds [2007b]." *http://www.clibyg.org/en/knowledge_bank/index.php ?item_id=33*.

**Kreiner**, Kristian, Peter **Holm** Jacobsen, and Daniel **Toft Jensen**. "Dialogues and the Problems of Knowing : Reinventing the Architectural Competition." *Scandinavian Journal of Management* 27, no. 1 (3/ 2011) : 160-66.

**Kuhn**, Thomas S. *The Copernican Revolution ; Planetary Astronomy in the Development of Western Thought*. Cambridge, : Harvard University Press, 1957.

**McDonough**, Tom, ed. *Guy Debord and the Situationist International : Texts and Documents*. Cambridge, Mass. : MIT Press, 2004.

**Meusburger**, Peter. "Milieus of Creativity : The Role of Places, Environments and Spatial Contexts." In *Milieus of Creativity : An Interdisciplinary Approach to Spatiality of Creativity*, edited by Peter Meusburger, Joachim Funke and Edgar Wunder. Knowledge and Space V 2, 97-153. Dordrecht : Springer, 2009.

**Mumford**, M. "Where Have We Been, Where Are We Going ? Taking Stock in Creativity Research." *Creativity Research Journal* 15, no. 2 (2003) : 107-20.

**Schmiedeknecht**, Torsten. "Routine and Exceptional Competition Practice in Germany as Published in wettbewerbe aktuell." In *The Architectural Competition : Research Inquiries and Experiences*, edited by Magnus Rönn, Reza Kazemian and Jonas E. Andersson, 152-77. Stockholm : Axl Books, 2010.

**SIA**. "Regulation Sia 142, Schweizerischer Ingenieur- Und Architektenverein / Swiss Society of Engineers and Architects (Sia)." Zürich (unpublished draft version), 2009.

**Silberberger**, Jan M. "Jury Sessions as Non-Trivial Machines : A Procedural Analysis." *Journal of Design Research* 10, no. 4 (2012) : 258-68.

**Silberberger**, Jan M. "Organizing the Space of Possibilities of an Architectural Competition." *Geographica Helvetica* 66, no. 1 (2011) : 5-12.

**Van Wezemael**, **Joris** E., Jan M. **Silberberger,** and Sofia **Paisiou**. "Assessing 'Quality' : The Unfolding of the 'Good' - Collective Decision Making in Juries of Urban Design Competitions." *Scandinavian Journal of Management* 27, no. 1 (2011) : 167-72.

**Volker**, Leentje. *Deciding About Design Quality : Value Judgements and Decision Making in the Selection of Architects by Public Clients under European Tendering Regulations*. Sidestone Press, 2010.

**Wark**, McKenzie. *50 Years of Recuperation of the Situationist International*. Forum Project. New York : Buell Center / FORuM Project : Princeton Architectural Press, 2008.

# 3.5. Competitions as Generators

**From the Redevelopment of Les Halles to a Theoretical Critique of "Compositional" Urbanism**

**Françoise Fromonot**, Professor
École Nationale Supérieure d'Architecture
de Paris-Belleville
France

Contemporary urban planning is in crisis. We shall not dwell here on the challenges it faces from a broad range of new phenomena as they have been frequently and adequately identified, quantified and discussed in numerous works published over the last twenty years — global urban demographic growth, the exponential development of world cities in so-called emerging economies, shifts in the idea of public space in its historic sense and the increasing privatization of the latter — along with their primary consequence, the extension of heritage concerns to our environment at large, with the increasing demand for "sustainable design". But what models is this massive urbanization drawing on today, explicitly or implicitly? Conversely, what references are guiding the contemporary practice of urban planning, the discipline supposed to embody higher knowledge when it comes to organizing the changes being produced in the urban environment?[1]

**Cover**
Aerial view of the old
"Marché des Halles"
in the 1960's

A study of proposals submitted to various recent urban design competitions in France — a fundamental scrutiny for any critic interested in theoretical positions in the field — provides rich material for hypotheses. The articulation of the programs, the types of practitioners most often invited and the nature of the winning projects show that, in many respects, the dominant ways of thinking today's cities are a fading reflection of a set of doctrines rooted in the 1970s. However this was a period when modernization as an ideal was in retreat, whereas today it has been revived at the planetary scale with exponential effects. In light of this paradoxical situation, what paths lay open to renewed criticism of contemporary urbanism at this juncture? On what basis and by what means should it operate in order to influence both theory and practice?

These themes have been fuelling a work in progress I began several years ago[2] in an attempt to more precisely formulate these queries and to suggest responses, whose genesis and provisional conclusions I will outline in this text. One particular event was the catalyst for this reflection and the generator of its framework: the 2002 to 2004 competition for the renovation of the Les Halles district in Paris, a central sector of the French capital for at least two reasons: it occupies its geographic and historic centre, and for more than fifty years it has concentrated the many difficulties, scandals, dilemmas, and even deadlocks of Parisian urbanism. I propose to retrace the process that led my research from an analysis and an extrapolation of this particular case study, to a tentative theoretical interpretation of the situation of contemporary urbanism, yielding prospective propositions that I hope will generate discussion and action.

## ▬ Prologue

In spring of 2001, the socialist Bertrand Delanoë was elected head of the city of Paris, putting an end to twenty-three years of neo-Gaullist domination of municipal management. In his campaign program, the new mayor had promised to rehabilitate the Les Halles district, decried since its brutal renovation in the early 70s, and in a premature state of disrepair due to the intensity of its use. While this district clearly required improvements to its public spaces as well as its image [Fig.1], the operation was initially motivated by the need to update security standards in the underground RER station, a colossal hub that absorbs and dispatches 800,000 commuters from the entire Parisian periphery daily. The program also called for a resurfacing of what was originally the largest pedestrian zone in Europe, more specifically the redesign of the gardens.

The procedure of a "marché d'étude de définition" (literally a "definition study tender") was preferred to the usual design competition. This was a significant methodological innovation with the purpose of bringing together the municipality, the designers of the projected urban transformation and the local stakeholders, such as neighbourhood associations. It prescribed a threefold process. After the public was informed and consulted, all the protagonists, including the architects, brainstormed together on the problems and issues at stake on the site. This collective phase resulted in the drafting of a program that each team interpreted in their proposal during the final, individual phase. Four multidisciplinary teams had been selected following an international call for tenders by the competition organizer, the "Société d'Economie Mixte (SEM) Paris-Centre": two French (David Mangin, Jean Nouvel) and two Dutch (OMA-Rem Koolhaas, MVRDV-Winy Maas).[3] Their proposals were examined by an assembly of municipal politicians and also presented to Parisians through an exhibition, which triggered public and media controversies that raged for months in the capital. This reaction was by no means surprising. The polemics had barely ever let up since Les Halles (the site of the wholesale market since the Middle Ages) were first emptied in the late 60s for the sake of De Gaulle's modernization of Paris and its pavilions destroyed in 1971. Bertrand Delanoë's decision for the umpteenth renovation of the district couldn't fail to spark a new wave of criticism [Fig.2] [Fig.3].

The mayor announced that he would entrust the urban and landscape redesign of the site to David Mangin, with what he considered the most neutral and realistic, solution, and that another, architectural, competition would be held for the only building featured in this scheme: a huge flat, green roof over the former "Forum".[4] This second competition, which was delayed for a further three years, was finally awarded to Patrick Berger and Jacques Anziutti [Fig.4], whose enormous, curved, green "Canopy" won out against nine other international offices. After many financial, political and technical tribulations, the two projects are currently under construction (as of the end of 2013), with anticipated completion dates of 2014 for the building and 2016 for the landscaping.

**Fig. 1**
Aerial view of garden and Forum des Halles in the middle of the 1980's

**Fig. 2**
Photomontage of the winning project by team SEURA-David Mangin in December 2004.

**Fig. 3**
Front-page of French newspaper *Libération* (December 16th 2004, the day after the press conference held by Bertrand Delanoë, socialist mayor of Paris, to announce the winning scheme).

**Fig. 4**
Nocturnal perspective of winning project by team Berger-Anziutti for the roof concept imagined by David Mangin, June 2007

**Fig. 5**
Aerial view of the old "Marché des
Halles" in the 1960's with the future site
of Pompidou Centre in the foreground.

**Fig. 6**
The demolition (destruction) of the "Pavillons de
Baltard" starting August 1971.
*Photo by C. Caroly, APUR, Paris-Projet n°25-26, 1985*

**Fig. 7**
One of many manifestoes reacting
to the demolition of the pavilions
in 1972.

**Fig. 8**
The "hole" of the Halles during the
building of the underground train station
which will be opened in 1977.
APUR, Archives de Paris

The 2002 urban design consultation and its peculiar terms, its specific site, and the arguments of the subsequent public debate made this new Les Halles affair an exemplary case study. Firstly it presented an historical interest. Delanoë's project was one of a long line of transformations, each being marked by significant proposals and controversies. Looking back over this past illuminates the explicit or latent challenges faced by this new attempt to resolve a recurrent problem: an opportunity to sharpen our understanding of the urban questions that were once again brought to the surface, and to resituate the solutions proposed by the four teams within the long history of ideas that have shaped the city.

Secondly, this event was of critical interest. Between them, the four proposals addressed most major themes of current urbanism: the understanding of history, modernity and context, the place of infrastructure, the role of program, the problem of urban vs. architectural scales, the methods of representation, and, ultimately, how the contemporary city projects in the imagination. Deciphering the approach of each team, analyzing their projects in detail, reading them in the context of the declared doctrinal positions of their authors, and comparing their respective responses to the question asked, were all ways of revealing oppositions or unexpected convergences.

Thirdly this competition presented a theoretical interest, for the findings of its historical and critical investigation were to lend themselves almost naturally, as we shall see, to a broader speculation. Hence the tentative typology of the strategies at work in contemporary urbanism in which this study has resulted. I will outline this theoretical attempt and address some of the questions it poses in turn: its position vis-à-vis an anterior baseline survey, its confrontation with more recent ones, and suggested investigations to be pursued in the fields of history, criticism and theory.

## ▬ History: Modern Projects, Postmodern Inversions

In the 1950s, Les Halles Centrales, the wholesale market that supplied the capital of a country in full economic expansion at the time, was still located in its historic site in the centre of Paris. It was housed in the majestic iron and glass pavilions designed in 1854 by Victor Baltard at the request of Napoleon III as part of Haussmann's urban renovation. However, one century later, under the pretext of mounting logistical problems (difficulty transporting goods to the

centre, functional congestion, hygiene and health issues), the Gaullist government decided to implement the shift that had been debated intermittently for nearly three centuries, now made inevitable due to the drastic infrastructural reform undertaken by the regime. At the beginning of the 1960s, it was decided that the Les Halles Centrales market be exiled in part to Rungis — an area in the southern suburbs well connected by new infrastructure (highways, airport) — and in part to the modernized slaughterhouses of La Villette. Les Halles continued to operate as a wholesale market until 1969, at which point the wholesalers migrated one by one to these new locations **[Fig.5]**.

While this transfer stripped the pavilions of their initial function, their architecture of large volumes and open plans connected by covered streets clearly had potential for reconversion. Their fate was sealed, however, by another decision made right before the evacuation: the connection of the principal RER suburban train lines (Réseau Express Régional de transports ferrés) to form the future Châtelet-Les Halles station by open-air excavation. The excavated site would then be filled with commercial equipment, a project inspired by the "subterranean urbanism" theorized by Edouard Utudjian and his GECUS research group. This "three-dimensional urbanism" had its supporters in the upper echelons of the State. Utudjian advocated the subterranean construction of public facilities accessible by vehicles, thus freeing public space for the use of pedestrians. In addition to these functional and land-use arguments, the destruction of Les Halles was meant to etch in the fabric of the capital a shift towards the future, doing away with 19th century buildings as well as the associated social and urban fabric.

In 1971 the demolition of the metallic pavilions began **[Fig.6] [Fig.7]**, in an atmosphere of controversy and drama, despite the public's calls for their conservation. Parisians were attached to the phantom-like buildings, which had become a popular place for cultural activities pending their demolition. To the outrage of the population and observers alike, they were demolished and sent to the scrap yard and the site was gutted over several hectares to build the underground RER interconnection station, inaugurated in 1977. The site remained an enormous, gaping pit for years (the infamous "Halles hole" **[Fig.8]**), waiting to be filled by the colossal subterranean mall that was to be activated by the flows from the station. The first phase of construction was for the Forum on the eastern half of the site, a shopping mall with a public space atrium on the lowest of three levels,

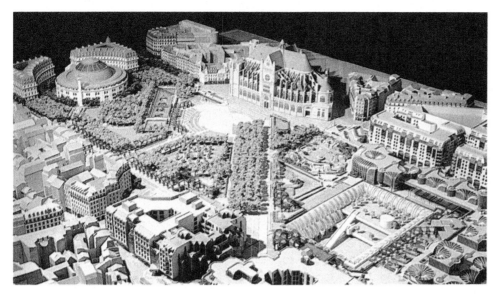

**Fig. 9**
Model of project by Louis Arretche and APUR (Atelier Parisien
d'Urbanisme) for Jacques Chirac mayor of Paris in 1979.
(APUR, Paris-Projet n°25-26, 1985)

open to the sky and surrounded by glass-walled galleries. The second phase of construction, called the "New Forum", completed the west side of the site, its underground cultural and sports facilities distributed around a square and a large gallery emerging near the Bourse du Commerce.[5]

Finally, again in line with subterranean urbanism, the Les Halles megastructure is presented as a "composite construction, sometimes more of a building, other times more a work of civil engineering"[6] of an unprecedented structural complexity anchored in limestone some thirty meters below the surface. Criss-crossed by RER lines, perforated by rapid automobile traffic, composed of giant, reinforced concrete caissons divided into hermetic fireproof areas capable of dilating in every direction, this gigantic volume forms a "substratum" that ensures the "complete integration, on a technical level, of the urban infrastructure, private and public buildings, that lose their structural independence and their exclusive link to an outline on a land parcel plan".[7] These structural barriers have built a sort of immutable three-dimensional plot in the subterranean levels, which summarizes the impressive mutation, as radical as it is imperceptible on the surface, sustained by the historic city centre.

While the infrastructure work was underway, a series of competitions was held to redesign the space "freed up" on the surface following the destruction of the pavilions. After much hesitation, changes of heart, and following a change in the capital's administrative status,[8] it was decided in 1977 to insert a garden into the vast pedestrian space. Post-modernism was in full swing, influencing urban policies and the aesthetic of official architecture. The contextualist return to the regulatory traditions of Parisian urbanism, already operational in practice for a few years at this point, was integrated into the new land-use plans. In 1979, mayor Jacques Chirac decided to entrust the planning of a public and consensual garden to the Atelier parisien d'urbanisme (APUR), headed by Louis Arretche. At the base of Saint Eustache church, a small plaza was inspired by the Campo in Siena, while elsewhere, paths, rows of trees and fountains were surrounded by buildings mimicking the traditional tripartition of Parisian buildings. On both sides of the Forum, metallic pavilions designed by Jean Willerval in collaboration with Jean Prouvé, an allusion to Baltard's architecture, would house public facilities. Ostensibly, the project was intended to close the still raw wound by applying soothing references drawn from stylistic conventions supposedly shared by ordinary Parisians **[Fig.9]**.

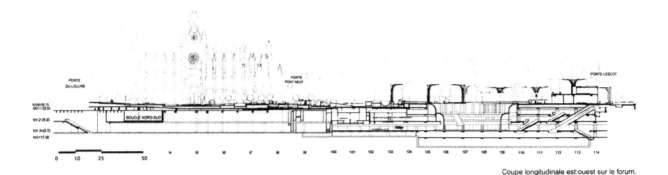

**Fig. 10**
Longitudinal section of the entire site with its underground megastructure, in 2002. (SEM Paris-Centre)

This coup, coupled with Arretche's mediocre project, triggered an international counter-competition of ideas, organized by the Syndicat de l'architecture in which a young Jean Nouvel was actively involved. A jury comprised of eminent architects and intellectuals of the time examined more than 600 projects, however the authorities gave it no consideration and it remained a last stand.[9] Thus, the centre of Paris inherited the master plan designed by Arretche and Chirac in lieu of Baltard's pavilions and the associated atmosphere: municipal post-modernism of the late 1970s superimposed on the State modernism of the late 1960s.

In 2002, when the competition we are concerned with here was launched, all that remained of the former Les Halles was their secular commercial vocation along with the high volume flows characterizing this activity. Thus, the site's only real permanence is programmatic, as opposed to morphological, for in all other respects this district was profoundly transformed. Its modernization has resulted in multiple inversions of its nature and role. The first of these inversions is *topographic*: what had always been an urban ground had become a roof, the upper deck of an enormous invisible building anchored in the Parisian limestone. Raised above street level by the landscaping of its garden surfaces and thickened by massive waterproofing systems devised to protect the underlying commercial spaces, this slab has replaced the paved ground partially sheltered by the pavilions and their covered galleries that used to stage the activities of Les Halles. Unlike the former market, the garden covering this concrete terrace, where rows of trees struggle to grow between meagre bushes, generates no secondary activities in the neighborhood. In 2002, it was merely a green space cut up by service components (stairs, access and exit elevators from the underground levels, ventilation grids, skylights, etc.), as new as it was foreign in relation to the Parisian tradition of parks and gardens.

The second inversion is *typological*. The modular assembly of Baltard's light, glazed pavilions was replaced by a blind, subterranean building, a massive feat of civil engineering made out of reinforced concrete entirely lacking the flexibility of the former market. Had the pavilions not been demolished, their generic spaces could have easily been converted into a shopping centre, or cultural facilities. On the contrary, being buried deep underground the Châtelet-Les Halles megastructure is deprived of the sole quality afforded to this type of programmatic concatenation, its potential for growth. Its static mass acts as an artificial

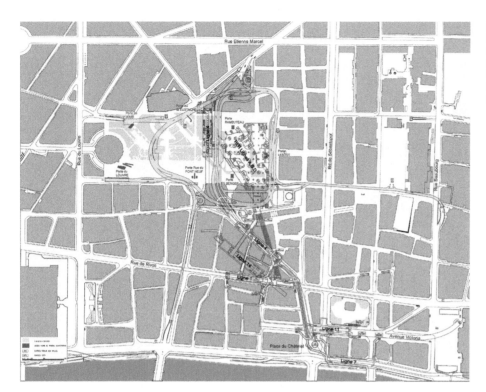

**Fig. 11**
Superimposed plans of the public spaces showing the various levels: above ground gardens (in green), below ground car lanes (in yellow), and public transportation, metro and train (in red)

geology, an unmoving three-dimensional plot that imposes its internal logic on everything else, constraining the evolution of the whole site over time **[Fig.9] [Fig.10]**.

The third inversion, with the most serious consequences at the scale of Grand Paris is *geographic*. Whereas the Parisian train stations of the industrial era unloaded their passengers on the threshold of the former Wall of the Farmers-General, and at street level, the main entrance to the public transport system is now situated underground in the middle of the historic city. While Les Halles market was located in the heart of Paris, the underground labyrinth that is the Châtelet-Les Halles station, an extension of the periphery plugged into the centre, has become de facto the centre of Greater Paris. The lack of a suburb-to-suburb public transport system has accentuated the station's function as an interchange hub, in contrast with the district's former role of centralizing and distributing foodstuffs. In the time of the market, the extra-muros zone supplied Les Halles with material goods, whereas now it dispatches commuters. The sprawling network of the RER map converges in this colossal station, crossed daily by hundreds of thousands of suburbanites, whether commuting to work or attracted by the entertainment,

leisure and shopping facilities. It is primarily business from these visitors, children of the working class that was gradually banished to the outskirts of Paris after the war, that sustains the shops and cinema theatres of this "leased city", as it is called since it has been outsourced to a major property management group. This massive buried hive remains invisible from the "inherited city" on the surface, which has progressively become more gentrified and less dense. The transformation of Les Halles signified the arrival in the historic centre of a commercial scheme that is quintessentially suburban: the shopping mall.

However, the cruellest inversion was *symbolic*. The "belly of Paris", a romanticized and fascinating neighbourhood where all kinds of urban activities ebbed and flowed with the day's trade, full of shops of all kinds, restaurants and cafés, had been elevated into an urban and social myth by writers and artists.[10] And now, this exemplary metropolitan setting has been mocked for a quarter of a century for its gaudy architecture and the shoddiness of its overall design.[11] Its mediocrity stands out all the more for its immediate proximity to the Georges Pompidou Centre, which represents a certain panache in the political and decision-making process, with Piano and Rogers winning the design competition three weeks before demolition began on Baltard's pavilions. Conversely, even though highly frequented, the modernized then post-modernized Les Halles are perceived as having precipitated the decline of the 19th century ex-capital within the new Gotha of world cities **[Fig.11]**.

## ▬ Critique: Four Projects, Two Types of Projects?

The redevelopment program set in motion in 2002 by the new mayor of Paris clearly had a larger and more complex technical and urban repercussions than the cosmetic intervention originally envisioned within a limited sector. It required the competition entrants to take a critical stance in relation to the impacts of the modern and postmodern periods on the whole area, and in fact to tackle most of the dilemmas that globalization causes for large Western cities. In addition to the necessary destruction of certain obsolete structures such as Willerval's pavilions, the reduction in the number of underground automobile lanes feeding the complex, and the redistribution or addition of programmes, some of which would be left up to the architects, the idea was that, the design teams would come up with solutions to the problems generated by the drastic mutations to the site. To facilitate exit flows from the station, there was a need for new passageways, but how was this possible in a closed, solid megastructure? To recreate the garden, the architects had to find a way to circumvent its physical constraints and invent a new landscape, but what would this landscape be? The challenge was to work with the functional status of the site within the economy of flows on the scale of Greater Paris while articulating it with the local scale, and to reinvent a place capable of restoring the image of the centre of the capital while allowing it to vie with emerging megalopolises.

If we sum up the stance taken by each of the four teams in one emblematic document, the board of site photographs presented by David Mangin — twelve black and white pictures of everyday life in the perimeter, with only one depicting the underground levels — is certainly the most telling. This calculated reference to historic views of working-class Paris announced a proposal centred on life at street level, therefore at a local scale, and an intention to strengthen existing uses on the site. Mangin proposed to restructure the garden around a longitudinal axis following the existing rows of lime trees, in reference to Barcelona's

*ramblas*, a large "path" connecting the drum of the Bourse de commerce to the pit of the former Forum. He intended to cover the latter with a large roof laid on top of it like a lid, a copper-clad square plane measuring 145 x 145 metres (the width of the site **[Fig.12] [Fig.13]**).

Referred to as the "Carreau", this roof hovered 9 m above the garden level and housed retail areas and public facilities. Inside, the Carreau took on spectacular dimensions, its height amplified by the pit of the Forum, its space crossed by the extension of the axis as an "arcade", with rays of light streaming through the perforated roof. The resulting "department store" atmosphere was depicted in a large perspective drawing. Sections of the underground arteries were sealed off to restore continuity in the streets adjacent to the garden (currently crisscrossed by access ramps) and one of the freed up tunnels was converted into a shopping area in order to boost the profitability of the underground levels. The vocabulary used by Mangin borrowed from that of the historic city and, correspondingly, the style of the drawings conformed to traditional modes of architectural representation: detailed elevations, watercolour tones, etc. Mangin put particular emphasis on his desire to reinsert Les Halles into the "natural" urban succession of prestigious public spaces on the Right Bank, from the Palais Royal to the Place des Vosges, thus stressing the coincidence between the dimensions of the latter and those of the "Carreau", using an aerial photograph where these urban spaces were highlighted in green.

Nouvel, on the other hand, claimed to operate on a more explicitly doctrinal level, that of a contextualism attuned to "strong specificities anchored in history and geography": "to be modern means modifying the conditions by which we read a territory all the while respecting it", "making the desires of the people who live in the neighbourhood the essence of the proposed architecture", "working with" and "here and now". [12] In order to effectively deal with every problem in the neighbourhood, Nouvel proposed multiple "micro-projects" federated around a completely redesigned garden **[Fig.14]**.

These architectural interventions, totalling an extra surface of some 60,000m², were highlighted red on a large site plan and simulated by elaborate digital perspectives. These perspectives were sometimes akin to large tableaus and sometimes to a series of vignettes (or "contact boards"). His proposal revolved around three planted areas (where "the tradition of parks and gardens would meet the contemporary sensibility for nature in the city") located at three

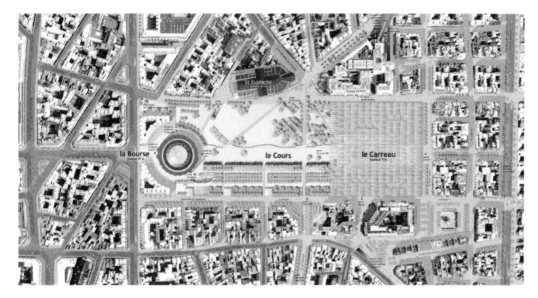

**Fig. 12**
Project by team David Mangin (SEURA) : block plan
(SEM Paris-Centre)

**Fig. 13**
Project by team David Mangin (SEURA) : model.
*Photo Benoît Grimbert - SEM Paris-Centre*

**Fig. 14**
Project by team Jean Nouvel (AJN, with Michel
Desvignes landscape architect) : block plan
(SEM Paris-Centre)

different heights that, when added up, totalled a surface of 7 hectares. At street level the largest of these gardens, the size of the nearby Palais Royal, was to be planted with tree varieties native to forests in the Île-de-France. The two other gardens were designed as terraces: the first, on top of a narrow linear building proposed on the southern edge of the quadrangle to close it, and the other, on top of a canopy-roof raised by metal pillars 27 meters above ground, over the old Forum (which incidentally Nouvel also called the "Carreau"). Underneath, the passenger hall was to receive natural light from windows in the lower part of the Forum, mirrors and images projected on the walls, as well as planted areas around the access escalators compensating for "the poor quality of the underground spaces".

The Dutch had a completely different approach. Winy Maas explained that he saw in the current Les Halles a schizophrenic overlay of two sectors unaware of one another: underground, a dark, dense but extremely busy "catacomb" and on the surface, a vast deserted space whose architectural treatment was unworthy of a metropolis. MVRDV proposed to do away with this division and restore the splendour of Les Halles by tapping into the underground energy of the site to revitalize the lifeless gardens.

The team's "urban strategy" took its cue from the buried part of the site. By emptying the Forum all the way to the passenger hall, and by clearing all other recoverable underground spaces — the Grande Galerie, some of the underground roads, parking space, etc. — the station was opened upwards and turned into a "cathedral of circulations" receiving natural light from a glass roof [Fig.15].

To relocate the activities that were removed from the underground and to complete the programming in the neighbourhood, MVRDV added an aerial layer at street level: a 5-meter high podium containing public services, retail and recreational spaces along its perimeter, as well as a new garden at its centre, accessible by large ramps. The central, glazed part of the podium, set between the thematic beds designed by landscape architect Adriaan Geuze, commanded a view down to the bottom of the "valley", glimpses of whose intense activity rose to the surface. Garden and public space, place of passage and event, revelation and spectacle, the elevated garden became the "horizontal rose window of the three-dimensional underground city", the city's "new dance floor".

As for Koolhaas, he re-assessed the site within the chronology of its recent history, declaring his ambition to reinvent an architectural and urban modernity capable of

coexisting with the historic city, on the very spot that had marked the end of this modernity in Paris. His proposal, symbolized as the elevation view of an iceberg, took the form of a strategy in three acts. Act one: Renovating the site by acting upon its quantitatively most important section — its underground infrastructure. Circulation in the shopping mall was restructured, the north-south highway exit was blocked off and partially opened upwards to create a rift known as the "canyon" connecting the fourth basement level (the Salle des Échanges) and the garden, and thus establishing a direct link between the station and the surface. Through a meticulous work of spatial connectivity, he improved the comfort in underground transit spaces, organizing them into a great "interchange gallery" open to the world above through the canyon, and increasing porosity between the transit system and the neighbourhood.

Act two: Integrating the underground commercial city with the residential city of the surface, and vice-versa. The levels of the megastructure were represented in diagrammatic section by a superimposition of colour-coded lines relating to the programs, swelling up periodically to emerge in the garden, while, conversely, the garden spilled into the canyon. These "eruptions" of thin pyramidal volumes of varying dimension and height endowed the buried program with aerial extensions and a new visibility, thereby reintegrating this hidden part of Parisian history in the urban landscape [Fig.16].

Act Three: Creating a new type of garden on the entire perimeter of the surface, as an actor and witness to the "green modernity" which Koolhaas wished to instate there for Paris. Strewn with circular parterres, associated or not with the protruding volumes, this garden covered the entirety of the site. Diagrams depicted a field of dots in many shades of green depending on their program, traversed by rows of the existing and conserved trees and perforated here and there by the volumes emerging from below [Fig.17].

In both intention and form, the opposition between the two categories of projects was obvious. The French had approached the problem from the top down, seeking to repair the area *on the surface* through an urban composition associating historic Parisian buildings and public spaces (gardens, terraces, and axes). However, their proposals neglected to deal with the underground spaces — those with the most traffic — such as the station and the shopping mall, and in fact disregarded their regional dimension. Maas and Koolhaas, on the other hand, had envisaged the site from bottom to top, approaching it in its depth (the

**Fig. 15**
Project by team MVRDV: perspective on the "vallée de la gare"
(SEM Paris-Centre).

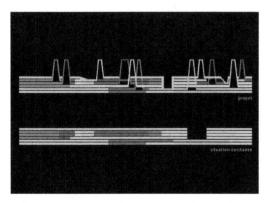

**Fig. 16**
Project by team Rem Koolhaas (OMA with
XDGA and One Architects): conceptual
diagram of section
(SEM Paris-Centre).

**Fig. 17**
Project by team Rem Koolhaas (OMA with XDGA and One Architects) : model.
*Photo Benoît Grimbert - SEM Paris-Centre*

underground infrastructure and its associated commercial program) and insisting on the metropolitan scale of this unprecedented space in Parisian history. Consequently, forms on the surface resulted largely from the underground transformations. While the two French offices sought to revive intangible models of traditional public space, the Dutch took the historic inversions as a given, and sought rather to profit from them, tapping into the symbolic power of infrastructure, a synonym of functionality, animation, and the spectacle of consumption. While Nouvel sought to elevate gardens on his superstructures, Koolhaas wanted to bring greenery, air and light to the underground levels. The French had thought in plan, the Dutch, in section.

This divide was apparent in the respective conceptions of the urban planning work put forward in the proposals. Mangin and Nouvel had designed *formalized projects*, substantiating their urban compositions through detailed drawings of their buildings ; OMA and MVRDV proposed *strategies of principle*, deliberately stopped short of their transposition to architecture. Means of analysis and representation therefore differed to the point of caricature. The French had preferred conventional methods : detailed plans, sections and elevations displaying the degree to which their proposal was resolved, digital perspectives simulating the future reality, as well as carefully drawn cadastral divisions and poché in the sections. The Dutch teams had, for their part, produced far more schematic documents : diagrams in bright colours, collages that insisted on types of activities, quantities and potential combinations, completed by perspectives that were more suggestive than realistic, in any case certainly marginal with regards to analytical representations.

These two distinct approaches also attested to diametrically opposed understandings of the hierarchy that links architecture and urbanism. Having identified the multiple and specific stumbling blocks of the immediate context, Nouvel sought to respond through an addition of architectural tactics meant to endow inner Paris with a new urban ensemble. Koolhaas, on the other hand, proposed a three-dimensional global strategy in order to establish coherency between the domains and scales that were linked in spite of themselves by the situation — infrastructure, urbanism, architecture and landscape — leaving for later, or rather for others, the strictly architectural design of his small buildings.

**Fig. 18**
Covers of the original edition of Françoise Choay's
book, *L'urbanisme, utopies et réalités — Une anthologie*,
Paris (Éditions du Seuil), 1965

**Fig. 19**
"Program-based" urbanism: OMA,
plan of Euralille, 1988-1995

The clear opposition between two forms of urbanism was consequently brought into stark relief: on one hand, the "urban project", the large-scale extension of the urban architecture that came to the fore in France from the end of the 1970s; on the other, an urbanism based on the primacy of program and flows, which flourished in the Netherlands during the same period, referred to by some as a "second modernism".

## ▬ Theory? From Utopia in Reality to Reality as Utopia

Could this bipartition be considered to sum up the scope of current positions on urban design? No, insofar as it seemed to primarily reflect the bipartition in the nationalities of the selected competitors. How then might these partial conclusions serve as a basis to further elucidate contemporary tendencies in urban design? Let us return to key texts in which theories on urban planning have already been studied typologically, and in particular to the work that still acts as a leading reference: *L'urbanisme, utopies et réalités: Une anthologie*, published in 1965 by Françoise Choay **[Fig.18]**.

In her now classic introduction, [13] the historian identified three major ideological directions that the discipline had rallied itself around to reflect on the "planning of the machinist city":

- The progressist model (the futurist tendencies born out of the social utopias of the 19th Century, then promoted in the 20th Century by the main figures of hygienist and rationalist modernism, Le Corbusier and Hilberseimer);
- The culturalist model (the anti-industrial nostalgic school advocating the spatial coherence of hamlets and medieval towns, developed in England by Ebenezer Howard and Raymond Unwin, though initiated before them in Austria by Camillo Sitte),
- The naturalist model (the later, organicist, individualistic and essentially American trend represented by Frank Lloyd Wright).

She associated each of these historical models with typical urban forms and with the bastardized derivatives they lapsed into in the post-war era: For the first, large slab housing estates and the brutal renovation of historic quarters; for the second, new towns; for the third, suburbia.

However this text coincided with a crisis in the discipline marked by the sentiment of the failure of progressist urbanism, still dominant at the time, and by a sense of change being imminent, all circumstances by which Françoise Choay justified the necessity of her clarification. 1965 was marked by the death of Le Corbusier. While architectural and urban modernism everywhere still appeared to be triumphant, its decline was already underway. Movements contesting all its outcomes were beginning to take hold, within the profession as in society at large. Associated by dint of its 'ism' to the State-run planning of the post war economic boom, and to its authoritarian, top-down implementation, urbanism came to be contested for its name, and its scientific vocation, for its claim to control urban phenomena as much as for its inability to harness them, that is, in all the terms by which Choay defined it to elaborate her history of ideas.

Unlike the Modern Movement, which had hoped to substitute reality for its own ideal models, the emerging post-modernism sought to reconstruct the doctrines of thought and action by drawing on reality, or better yet, by extrapolating them from the real : a shift in priorities that would be transposed as the inversion of the respective precedence of *utopia* and *reality.* The whole spectrum of current positions in urban design has inherited and endorsed that shift. Coming back to Les Halles, we have seen how the four architects' discourse, beyond their differences and even their oppositions, insisted and drew from features of the existing situation, be it through uses (Mangin), context (Nouvel), flows (MVRDV), program (Koolhaas), and history (all architects, albeit each in their own way).

### ▬ Three Post-Modern Urbanisms

An attempt to update contemporary urban planning categories can therefore not use pre-existing theories as its sole discriminating criterion, but rather — in light of that shift — should examine the ways urban design deals with the two basic, concrete *realities* of any project — the designated site for the implementation on the one hand, and on the other the program meant to be to implemented upon it. One then observes that the massive increase in construction, which has gone hand in hand with the global economic growth since the 1990s has made program the main, near exclusive reason for most operations, reducing sites to mere holding zones. From Houston to Shanghai, from Mumbai to Dubai, mainstream real estate developers seek to make maximum profit out of the pragmatic arrangement of massive quantities of useable space on abstracted landscapes. Two opposing but complementary templates are favoured :

vertical stacking and horizontal sprawl, downtown and suburbia. One is synonymous with concentration, the other with dispersion, or rather, to paraphrase Bernardo Secchi, with the two models of the standing city and the diffuse city. [14]

But what considered alternatives to this essentially quantitative, efficiency-oriented production exist ? How then can we rethink a typology of the modi operandi of current urbanism that might have a theoretical impact based on these two terms of the project ? A critical examination of recent operations, carried out on the basis of the relations they create between site and program identifies three major methods of conception and action. To provide different solutions to the same challenges — those of a modernization on a worldwide scale — some architects have been looking for ways to exploit the potential of "metropolitan congestion", invented by the modern metropolis. To do so, they are advocating the condensing of all sorts of activities into large-scale urban artefacts, true autonomous and artificial sites activated by transport infrastructure. By "retroactively" making sense of the pre-existing context, these cities within buildings are meant to regenerate its "condition". The protagonists of the Dutch Second Modernist movement represent the most radical proponents of this first position, which we could also call *program-based urbanism* **[Fig.19]**.

A second, opposing attitude consists in granting priority to the site, in order to draw from its geographic, historic and symbolic substrate the very principles of its transformation. Through the decryption of their nature, the anamnesis of their past, and the patient extrapolation of their intrinsic qualities, sites thus bring about the program of their own evolution locally, through a perpetually unfinished process that constitutes the project itself. Both determinist and critical, this *revelation-based urbanism* was initially the prerogative of certain landscape architects, and, more recently has become that of a generation of architect planners who promote as paramount the notions of use, sustainable environment and event-based urban action. [15]

The third approach, in principle, merges some aspects the two others, while being fundamentally distinct from them both. It articulates the site to the program through the intercession of a third element — the preliminary outline of public spaces and a set of regulations — which guarantee typical urban forms. Since it takes into account — in principle — the given site *and* the programs to come, thus dealing with two fundamental terms of the project, and since it also evokes the extension to city plans of the architectural composition that was practiced with worldwide success

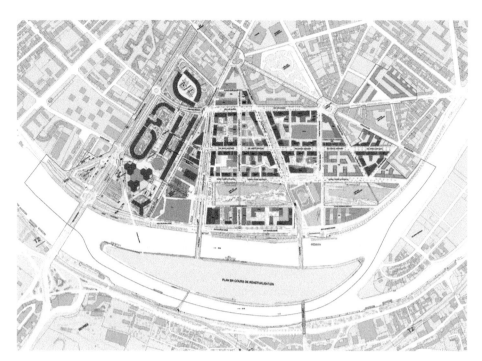

**Fig. 20**
"Composition-based" urbanism:
ground plan of the ZAC Boulogne
Rives de Seine (SAEM Boulogne
Rives de Seine)

at the École des Beaux Arts in early 20th Century Paris, let us call it *composition-based urbanism.* This tendency coincides with the "urban project *à la française*", which was gradually substituted in France by modernist-inspired planning in France at the end of the *Trente Glorieuses,* or with New Urbanism as it is practiced in the United States and elsewhere. [16]

Despite the fact that they relate to quantitatively asymmetric practices and that neither is totally isolated from the other two, these families of strategies in a way define three poles, forming a dynamic field in which current projects and ideas can be identified. Moreover, this typological outline opens the door to many new questions in the interrelated fields of history, criticism, and theory **[Fig.20]**.

## ▬ A story to be written

These three tendencies stem from parallel evolutions, marked by simultaneous phases within the same period: emergence in the late 1960s, materialization in different projects and realizations starting in the early 1980s, and explicit doctrinal formulation or reformulation in the mid 1990s. The first tendency is inseparable from the emergence

of one figure, Rem Koolhaas, and following him, of a neo-modernist "school" that has generated in turn its own avatars. After *Delirious New York,* [17] the product of a reflection rooted in the culture and the debates of his years as a student at London's Architectural Association School of architecture, a manifesto with which he forged his doctrine and launched his career, Koolhaas embarked on a second wave of theorization inspired by his projects and realizations, as he was delivering Euralille. In two important texts, *Whatever Happened to Urbanism,* and *Bigness,* both written in 1994 and later published in his "auto-monograph" *S, M, L, XL,* he advocates an anti-functionalist regeneration of progressist urbanism, as initiated by his reading of the Manhattan skyscraper, by focusing on the question of program according to three watchwords: congestion, contamination, instability. [18]

The second tendency corresponds to the *invention of a profession,* landscape architect and its subsequent admittance to expertise in matters of urban planning. In the Anglo-American world, this profession arose in the wake of ecological planning, as theorized and put into practice in the 1960s by Ian MacHarg, founder of the University of Pennsylvania landscaping department. His former students

Anne Whiston Spirn and James Corner, amongst others, are prominent contemporary proponents of "landscape urbanism", based on the concrete transfer of landscaping knowledge to urban planning. [19] In France, the *École d'Horticulture de Versailles* was founded anew as a landscaping school in the mid 1970s. Its principal figures — Michel Courajoud and Alexandre Chemetoff, among others — have contributed to the rise of lateral thinking regarding territorial planning, for which the Parc de la Villette competition (1983) was an essential stepping stone. [20] A decade or so later, philosopher Sébastien Marot, a long-time companion of these practitioners and keen observer of their work, took on the role of exegete, discovering in the ancient culture specific to gardeners, which binds them to the earth in a special way, the conditions for a "landscape alternative" to the historic modes of urbanism. [21] The affinities of this "revelation-based urbanism" with Geddes' evolutionist thought and survey methods, as with the theories of his disciple Lewis Mumford, designate it as an heir to the humanistic, "anthropological" urbanism that Françoise Choay saw as a critique of the progressist urbanism born outside of the specialized milieu of urban planners and architects. [22]

The third tendency is first and foremost concerned with the *recapitalization of a heritage*, that of the neo-classic city, whose urban know-how it wishes to update, in order to renew with a history thrown into disarray by the modernist rupture. In France, it is mainly the doing of architects of generation 68, for whom the rejection of the Beaux-Arts approach prompted the discovery and importing of research conducted outside French borders, particularly those of the Italian typo-morphological school, which was very popular at the time. [23] As is the case with the other two tendencies, the initiatives aimed to legitimize this tendency by theorizing it appeared when the practice was well established. There again, significant attempts to codify it were made in the mid-1990s: an institutional manual in two volumes from architect and historian Pierre Pinon, entitled precisely *Composition Urbaine*, which exposed its motivations, actuality and results [24] to erect them as models; the text from a lecture given by Christian Devillers at the Pavillon de l'Arsenal, in Paris, in which the architect and urban planner set the expectations and methods of the "projet urbain" ("urban project"). [25]

This French version of composition-based urbanism would deserve a thorough analysis, and particularly, an in-depth investigation of its ideological and professional construction. While the designation "urban project" refers to a practice and a doctrine whose domination on intellectual, professional, and institutional levels verges on hegemony in France (as exemplified once again by the result of the Les Halles competition), the period in which this tendency earned its place has, for the moment, been the subject of very few historical studies, other than those of its followers. [26] The underlying hypothesis of the suggested investigation may seem paradoxical. In contrast with the practical and theoretical break with progressist urbanism, to which the partisans of the urban project claim to adhere — and which also fitted with the classification outlined above — it postulates that a strong cultural, professional, and institutional continuity of a specific earlier tradition, that of the Beaux-Arts, spans both modernism and post-modernism in France. This uniquely French trait is attested to by the adding of "à la française" the expression "urban project".

The Les Halles episode provides interesting proof of this continuity. Beyond their differences, oppositions, even, in their architectural persuasions, the two French architects indeed proposed surface compositions for the site that were elaborated in plan. David Mangin, a student in the post-68 period, was taught by the theoreticians and practitioners of urban architecture and typo-morphology from Arretche's studio at the École des Beaux-Arts. He had titled his watercoloured ground-floor plan "tripartite composition" and drawn out its real or simulated symmetries to substantiate the impression of the appeasement of the site through a mere embellishment. As for Jean Nouvel, who had so energetically disputed the Chirac-Arretche plan and its poor historicist references, [27] he proposed to replace it, in 2004, by an assemblage of architecture formally derived from his own buildings — the Nantes Courthouse, the Cartier Foundation — arranged around a geometric garden explicitly inspired, as we have seen, by the Palais-Royal. [28]

## ▬ A critique to construct

Secondly, although the classification of contemporary urbanisms outlined above contributes to clarifying the panorama of current tendencies, it also raises questions regarding the limitations of and contradictions within the types of thinking which it attempts to define. Program-based urbanism claims to take into account all phenomena of the "contemporary condition" and their related data, for which reason it is qualified as "a-critical" by its detractors. This type of urbanism, however, neglects one important phenomenon: the rise of environmental preoccupations and the increasingly pressing demand for the integration of "sustainable" development into urban planning. Founded on a futuristic rhetoric of the instantaneous, on the cult of quantity, artificiality and the dissipation of energy this involves, this thermodynamic urbanism seems, by its very nature, rather incompatible with this new imperative, which tends by definition to its opposite. Certain explorations by the generation following Koolhaas' remain to be examined in this perspective : for example, MVRDV's attempt to include the ecological agenda in their interest in density, or also that of FOA in theorizing a new organicism based on the potential of digital technology.

As for the revelation-based urbanism, it naturally presents the opposite drawback. Founded on a delicate archaeology of territorial specificities, on the exaltation of memory in all its dimensions, on a conception of time in which what is to come is an extrapolation of what already exists, this urbanism struggles to accommodate the massive injections of new programs necessary in large-scale urban transformations, notably in the conversion of peripheral or industrial sites, which have become its elective hunting ground. However, its favourite field of practice remains urban public spaces in all forms, though more particularly gardens, whose planted components and minimal programmatic planning fit into the advocated process, without surpassing it. When confronted with the integration of a great many exogenous activities, it risks veering into the other two types of urbanism, particularly when it must take responsibility for the social consequences of an increase in property value caused to the public domain by its interventions, or to accept large programs imposed from above.[29]

In the case of composition-based urbanism, its complications arise from the discrepancy between the idealized historic references it invokes, and the reality of the problem it wishes them to solve. At Les Halles, Mangin's project merely succeeded in producing an updated version of Arretche's plan, implemented twenty-five years earlier on the same site. He even used practically the same terms to justify his proposal. This stuttering comes across as an admission of theoretical impotence ; it essentially stems from the denial of the effective consequences of the modernist rupture and testifies to of a constitutive inability to accept them at their most blatant : a surprising contradiction in an urban planning theory elaborated on the basis of making historic knowledge a prerequisite for the lucid urban transformation. The disinterest, disdain even, for operations undertaken during the *Trente Glorieuses* expressed by this mode of intervention based on the "reflexive" recourse to earlier models, extracted from the circumstances and culture that produced them, seems to condemn it to a form of autism. The "return to the city" then takes place at the cost of an ossification of the notion of history on which it is supposedly founded, leaving it disconnected from the lived-in thickness of cities. It ends up generating the same a criticism that was also levelled at progressist urbanism.

In this regard, there remains to produce a documented critique of thirty years of Parisian ZACs (mixed-use zones). Their imposed procedures and their recurring architectural ingredients have ended up creating a peculiar genre in itself, a paradoxical mix of cadastral erasure, formal historicism, and real-estate cynicism.[30] The idea of "urban architecture" upon which the revisions of the 1970s were founded, and the Rossiesque conception of dialectic relations between architecture and the city from which they stemmed[31] has mutated into a division of labour serving public relations and urban planning services. The "urban project" is meant to determine a master plan whose layout guarantees the continuity of the future urban fabric with its historic precedents. It then assigns to the architecture of the forthcoming buildings the task of redeeming this conventional morphology with their formal creativity. At Les Halles, the result of the first, urban planning, tender concluded in the need for a second, architectural, competition. Having chosen an "urban project" that was academic to the point of blandness in order to quell the polemic, the mayor of Paris was hoping for a formally spectacular building that would serve him as an icon.

### ▬ A Theory Worth Pursuing

In the light of this triple critique of the three types of approach to urbanism in the neo-liberal era, and in an attempt to surpass them, would it be possible to identify, define and theorize a fourth category capable of reconciling attentiveness to the reality of the site and the necessity of its programmatic transformation without resorting to the mediation of formally preconceived public spaces ? Might we imagine an open, fluctuating project process combining the symmetric concerns of program and revelation free of the anachronistic prosthesis of composition ? And develop an approach capable of pursuing the dynamics of a history from which no heritage would be excluded *a priori* ? In other words, is it possible to imagine an unclassifiable, opportunistic and specific urbanism, impossible to define as a model that would create the site from the program and vice-versa ?

For some time now, architect-planners have been developing stimulating ideas by adopting an approach in which they recognize today's city in its totality, give consideration to all of its landscapes without exception, attempt to define the identities of these landscapes and take strong and risky stances on their needs through original methods and modes of representation. The necessary next step in furthering this investigation will be to identify and build a critical anthology of projects that do not fit the actual production systems of the city, and thus fall into this fourth category. In order to define this newfound and elusive urbanism without confining it, one would need to search for occurrences that do not fit within the three aforementioned categories, and that stand out as singular. The Les Halles public consultation brought about one of those singularities, paradoxically due to the major protagonist of the category previously defined as program-based urbanism. Koolhaas and his team's strategy consisted in turning the site's weaknesses into strengths, tapping into the existing program, its only historic continuity. It indulged in a *programmatic revelation* by fusing the two opposing ways to approach a project, drawing from their common tendency to extrapolate reality. Present reality, the legacy of a past utopia, became the basis of its own transformation by subversion of its own identity: the atavistic fascination for program and organization, responsible for the thick artificial soil that is the underground part of Les Halles today. In order to reverse this in turn, Koolhaas drew on the situation created by the inversions in the neighbourhood, materializing with a range of emerging volumes the possibility of a proactive development of the program that would double as a retroactive manifesto of the site.[32]

This original proposal was made possible thanks to two factors. On the one hand, it was favoured by the nature of Paris' new centre, a hub of commercial activities buried there by a particular, "subterranean", brand of progressist urban planning; on the other hand, by the measure of freedom afforded to teams due to the flexibility of the program, which imposed neither method nor result and guaranteed an original proposal. The public consultation for Les Halles offered teams the rare opportunity to think outside the box.

Were a third term to be brought into play between site and program through such *negotiation-based urbanism*, it could be the commission in itself, which determines both site and program and whose formulation generally escapes the prerogatives of designers. Finally, if this demonstration were to be of use to urban planners and to those who commission them in identifying or re-asserting priorities, it would point towards actions to transform the leftover urban territories bequeathed by modern utopias, in accordance with their singularities. These two suggestions conclude by closing the loop, albeit temporarily, since, in a way that is doubtless optimistic and perhaps paradoxical, they place their faith in the ability of theories to influence reality.

## ▬▬ Notes

[1] This text is based on a paper presented at the University of Montreal on 23 September 2008 as part of the L.E.A.P. lecture series entitled "À quoi sert la théorie?" ("What use is theory"?)

[2] This project began in 2004 as part of the writing of a topical book on the consultation of Les Halles - Françoise Fromonot, *La campagne des Halles: Les nouveaux malheurs de Paris* (Paris: La Fabrique, 2005).

[3] Out of convenience, the teams will be designated here as they were in the press during the consultation, by the names of their respective proxy architects. In reality, their composition was much more complex, each team being comprised of a group of associated architects, a landscape architect and consultants from various fields — structural, commercial, transport, etc. The complete list of team members can be found on the last page of each team's pamphlet in *Paris-Les Halles: Concours 2004*, (Paris: Moniteur, 2004).

[4] For details on this public consultation, the objectives, its nature and reasons for the process, progression, media firestorm, and the motives for the result, see *La campagne des Halles: Les nouveaux malheurs de Paris*. The main documents of the consultation are published in *Paris-Les Halles*, op. cit.

[5] Claude Vasconi and Georges Pencreac'h designed the Forum (1972-1979) whereas Paul Chemetov is the designer of the Grande Galerie, and the New Forum's pool (1979-1985).

[6] Société d'économie mixte pour l'aménagement des halles (SEMAH). Paris, «Dix ans d'activité aux Halles,» (1980), 25.

[7] See Benoît Carrié and Thierry Roze, «Le quartier des Halles à Paris — diagnostic patrimonial des années 1975-2000,» (SEM Paris Centre, 2004). Société d'économie mixte pour l'aménagement des halles (SEMAH). Paris, «Dix Ans D'activité Aux Halles.»

[8] Until 1977, the management of the city depended directly on the State though a prefect and a council. In 1977, the capital was brought to common law and instated a mayor. Jacques Chirac, first to be elected to the post, took over the planning of Les Halles from the State.

[9] This jury was comprised of "personalities from the arts and culture" (Roland Barthes, Henri Lefebvre, Bruno Zevi) and "foreign architects" (Diana Agrest, Philip Johnson, Carlo Aymonino). See Association pour la consultation internationale pour l'aménagement du quartier des Halles., *600 contreprojets pour les Halles: Consultation internationale pour l'aménagement du quartier des Halles, Paris* (Paris: Éditions du Moniteur, 1981).

[10] In *Le Ventre de Paris* (Paris: G. Charpentier, 1873), Emile Zola makes the neighbourhood the metaphor of a whole city and era, while the Situationists chose it as the setting for one of their psycho-geographical *derives*. Abdelhafid Khatib, "Essai De Description Psychogéographique Des Halles," *Internationale situationniste* 2(1958).

[11] A place that would "shame a provincial Bulgarian town", "the biggest planning failure of all European capitals" summarized a prominent British journalist at the time of the last consultation. John Lichfield, «Les Halles, ce crime contre l'urbanisme,» *The Independent (2004)* (2004), http://www.courrierinternational.com/article/2004/05/27/les-halles-ce-crime-contre-l-urbanisme.

[12] These quotes are transcribed from Nouvel's oral presentation in front of the pilot consultation committee on April 7, 2004 (document on film, SEM Paris Centre). The source text of the presentation is transcribed in *Paris-Les Halles : Concours 2004, 50*. He has since developed his arguments in other texts, for example the Louisiana Manifesto.

[13] Françoise Choay, *L'urbanisme, utopies et réalités : Une anthologie* (Paris : Editions du Seuil, 1965).

[14] See Bernardo Secchi, «Villes sans objet, la forme de la ville contemporaine,» (Montreal : conference given at the Canadian Centre for Architecture (CCA), Montreal, September 4th, 2008, 2008). According to Secchi, the third urban form is the 'compact city', as embodied by the city centre of 19th Century Paris.

[15] For the latter, ephemeral aspect, let us cite as an example the actions of the Roman collective Stalker, or the nocturnal discovery of European capitals organized by Parisian group AWP in the context of its "Protocole Troll".

[16] Let us refer here to the classification of urbanisms in the United States put forth in 2005 by Douglas Kelbaugh, the former dean of Taubmann College of Architecture, at the University of Michigan, in which New Urbanism holds the same position as Urbanism of Classification does in ours. Its classification revolves around three major tendencies. New urbanism comes first, promoting nuclear urbanism inspired by historic European cities, a sustainable alternative to sprawl. Secondly, Post Urbanism presents itself as a producer of great metropolitan objects conceived as datascapes, in phase with information technology. The third is Everyday Urbanism, dedicated to the concrete enhancement of daily life, and opposed to any globalizing or utopian aims, in line with Venturian grassroots and populism. See also the three volumes of the 'Michigan debates on Urbanism' : Kelbaugh, Douglas. *Michigan Debates on Urbanism (Vol. I-III)*. Ann Arbor : University of Michigan, Taubman College of Architecture and Urban Planning, 2005, which includes *Everyday Urbanism — Margaret Crawford vs. Michael Speaks* (vol. I), *New Urbanism — Peter Calthorpe vs. Lars Lerup* (vol. II), and *Post Urbanism & ReUrbanism — Peter Eisenman vs. Barbara Littenberg and Steven Peterson* (vol. III). Kelbaugh takes on the role of advocate of New Urbanism. See also Kelbaugh, Douglas. 'Further thoughts on the three urbanisms', *in* D. Kelbaugh and K. McCullough, *Writing Urbanism : A Design Reader* (Taylor & Francis, 2008).

[17] Rem Koolhaas, *Delirious New York : A Retroactive Manifesto for Manhattan* (New York : Oxford University Press, 1978). / Koolhaas, Rem. *New York Délire - Un manifeste rétroactif pour Manhattan*, French translation by Catherine Collet. (Paris : Éditions du Chêne), 1978.

[18] See «Whatever Happened to Urbanism ?,» in *Small, Medium, Large, Extra-Large : Office for Metropolitan Architecture, Rem Koolhaas and Bruce Mau*, ed. Rem Koolhaas, Mau, Bruce, Sigler, Jennifer, Werlemann, Hans, Office for Metropolitan Architecture. (New York, N.Y. : Monacelli Press, 1995), 969.
"Bigness or the Problem of Large," in *Small, Medium, Large, Extra-Large : Office for Metropolitan Architecture, Rem Koolhaas and Bruce Mau*, ed. Rem Koolhaas, Mau, Bruce, Sigler, Jennifer, Werlemann, Hans, Office for Metropolitan Architecture. (New York, N.Y. : Monacelli Press, 1995), 494-518.

[19] See J. Corner, *Recovering Landscape : Essays in Contemporary Landscape Theory* (Princeton Architectural Press, 1999), 13. We have seen the extended notion of landscape urbanism grow considerably in the academic field since the eponymous publication of James Corner, Detlef Mertins and Ciro Najle's "Landscape Urbanism" in *Landscape Urbanism : A Manual for the Machinic Landscape*, edited by Mohsen Mostafavi and Ciro Najle, London : Architectural Association Publications, 2003.

[20] It was also the case for future spokespeople of all three tendencies. For a detailed account of this consultation, see François Chaslin, *Les Paris de François Mitterrand : Histoire des Grands Projets Architecturaux*, Collection Folio/Actuel (Paris : Gallimard, 1985), 214-28.

[21] See in particular Sébastien Marot, «L'alternative du paysage,» *Le visiteur* 1(1995) : 54-81. Marot calls "sub-urbanism" this subdued, landscape approach to urban design and opposes it to the flamboyant, program-based Koolhaasian "super-urbanism".

[22] "Anthropopolis : pour un aménagement humaniste", *op. cit.,* pp. 58-64.

[23] On this question, see J.L. Cohen, «La coupure entre architectes et intellectuels, ou les enseignements de l'italophilie,» *In extenso*, no. 1 (1984).

[24] P. Pinon, «Composition urbaine,» in *I - Repères, II - Projets* (Paris : Éditions Villes et Territoires - DAU-STU-Ministère de l'Equipement, 1994).

[25] Christian Devillers, Pierre Riboulet, and Pavillon de l'Arsenal (Paris France), *Le projet urbain Le 4 Mai 1994 / Christian Devillers. La ville comme oeuvre Le 12 Janvier 1994 / Pierre Riboulet*, 2e éd. ed., Les Mini Pa (Paris : Pavillon de l'Arsenal, 1996). Myriads institutional publications, meant to celebrate rather than theorize, have dealt subsequently with the many facets of this subject.

[26] Jacques Lucan, *Architecture En France, 1940-2000 : Histoire et théories*, Architextes (Paris : Le Moniteur, 2001).

[27] Ironically, one of the winners of the counter-competition for which he had been one of the instigators in 1979 was the team of Steven Peterson and Barbara Littenberg, a duo chosen by Douglas Kelbaugh a quarter century later, to defend the category of 'Re-Urbanism' against Peter Eisenman. See Eisenman, *Post Urbanism & Reurbanism : Peter Eisenman Vs. Barbara Littenberg and Steven Peterson*.

[28] Nouvel, regardless, often explained how he had obtained his diploma, in 1967, with a text, as opposed to the typical plans, sections, and other expected drawings, in order to make a provocative statement. On this persistence and even on the restitution of the Beaux-Arts system in France by those who had dismantled it in May 1968, see Françoise Fromonot and Julie Rose, «The Beaux-Arts : Model, Monster... Phoenix ?,» *Log*, no. 13-14 (2008) : 41-52. and Françoise Fromonot, "De l'identité nationale considérée comme un des Beaux-Arts," *Criticat*, no. 6 (2010) : 40-53.

[29] The finalization of a decade's work by Alexandre Chemetoff on the island of Nantes, which in France became one of the most stimulating laboratories of this project philosophy on a significant scale, may yet refine or prove wrong the critique of this type of approach.

[30] They remained until now rather rare and fragmentary. See for example Philippe Genestier, «Reflexion : Que vaut la notion de projet urbain ?,» *L'Architecture d'Aujourd'hui*, no. 288 (1993) : 40-46. ; Fromonot, *La campagne des Halles : Les nouveaux malheurs de Paris*, 112-17. ; Raphaël Labrunye, "L'urbanisme Tupperware," *Criticat*, no. 3 (2009) : 114-23.

[31] Partially reformulated by Bernard Huet, in France, and two decades after the original publication of *L'architettura della Città*, in his famous article "L'architecture contre la ville", Bernard Huet, «L'architecture contre la ville,» *AMC* 14(1986) : 10-14.

[32] OMA continued this type of approach on another site, in 2008, with a strategy for the future of La Défense by "waking the slab's unconsciousness".

# ▬ References

**Association pour la consultation internationale pour l'aménagement du quartier des Halles**. *600 contreprojets pour les Halles : consultation internationale pour l'aménagement du quartier des Halles, Paris*. Paris : Éditions du Moniteur, 1981.

**Calthorpe**, Peter, Robert **Fishman**, and Lars **Lerup**. *New Urbanism : Peter Calthorpe vs. Lars Lerup. Michigan Debates on Urbanism* Vol. 2. Ann Arbor : University of Michigan, Taubman College of Architecture and Urban Planning, 2005.

**Carrié**, Benoît, and Thierry **Roze**. «Le quartier des Halles à Paris — Diagnostic patrimonial des années 1975-2000.» SEM Paris Centre, 2004.

**Chaslin**, François. *Les Paris de François Mitterrand : Histoire des grands projets architecturaux*. Collection Folio/Actuel. Paris : Gallimard, 1985.

**Choay**, Françoise. *L'urbanisme, utopies et réalités : Une anthologie*. Paris : Editions du Seuil, 1965.

**Cohen**, Jean-Louis. «La coupure entre architectes et intellectuels, ou les enseignements de l'italophilie.» *In extenso 1*. Paris, rapport de recherche S.R.A., École d'Architecture Paris-Villemin, 1984.

**Corner**, James. *Recovering Landscape : Essays in Contemporary Landscape Theory*. Princeton Architectural Press, 1999.

**Corner**, James, Detlef **Mertins**, and Ciro **Najle**. «Landscape Urbanism» in *Landscape Urbanism : A Manual for the Machinic Landscape*, edited by Mohsen Mostafavi and Ciro Najle. London: Architectural Association Publications, 2003.

**Crawford**, Margaret, and Michael **Speaks**. *Everyday Urbanism : Margaret Crawford vs. Michael Speaks. Michigan Debates on Urbanism* Vol. 1. Ann Arbor : University of Michigan, Taubman College of Architecture and Urban Planning, 2005.

**Devillers**, Christian, Pierre **Riboulet**, and **Pavillon de l'Arsenal** (Paris France). *Le Projet urbain Le 4 Mai 1994 / Christian Devillers. La ville comme oeuvre Le 12 Janvier 1994 / Pierre Riboulet*. Les Mini Pa. 2e éd. ed. Paris : Pavillon de l'Arsenal, 1996.

**Eisenman**, Peter, Barbara **Littenberg**, Steven **Peterson**, Roy **Strickland**. *Post Urbanism & ReUrbanism : Peter Eisenman vs. Barbara Littenberg and Steven Peterson. Michigan Debates on Urbanism* Vol. 3. Ann Arbor : University of Michigan, Taubman College of Architecture and Urban Planning, 2005.

**Fromonot**, Françoise. «De l'identité nationale considérée comme un des Beaux-Arts.» *Criticat*, no. 6 (2010).

**Fromonot**, Françoise. *La campagne des Halles : Les nouveaux malheurs de Paris*. Paris : La Fabrique, 2005.

**Fromonot**, Françoise, and Julie Rose. «The Beaux-Arts : Model, Monster... Phoenix ?». *Log*, no. 13-14 (2008) : 40-53.

**Genestier**, Philippe. «Reflexion : Que vaut la notion de projet urbain ?». *L'Architecture d'Aujourd'hui*, no. 288 (1993) : 40-46.

**Huet**, Bernard «L'architecture contre la ville.» *AMC* 14 (1986) : 10-14.

**Kelbaugh**, D., and K. **McCullough**. *Writing Urbanism : A Design Reader*. Taylor & Francis, 2008.

**Kelbaugh**, Douglas. *Michigan Debates on Urbanism (Vol. I-III)*. Ann Arbor : University of Michigan, Taubman College of Architecture and Urban Planning, 2005.

**Khatib**, Abdelhafid. «Essai de description psychogéographique des Halles.» *Internationale situationniste* 2 (1958) : 13-18.

**Koolhaas**, Rem. «Bigness or the Problem of Large.» In *Small, Medium, Large, Extra-Large : Office for Metropolitan Architecture, Rem Koolhaas and Bruce Mau*, edited by Rem Koolhaas, Mau, Bruce, Sigler, Jennifer, Werlemann, Hans, Office for Metropolitan Architecture., New York, N.Y. : Monacelli Press, 1995 : 494-518.

**Koolhaas**, Rem. *Delirious New York : A Retroactive Manifesto for Manhattan*. New York : Oxford University Press, 1978.

**Koolhaas**, Rem. «Whatever Happened to Urbanism ?». In *Small, Medium, Large, Extra-Large : Office for Metropolitan Architecture, Rem Koolhaas and Bruce Mau*, edited by Rem Koolhaas, Mau, Bruce, Sigler, Jennifer, Werlemann, Hans, Office for Metropolitan Architecture., New York, N.Y. : Monacelli Press, 1995 : 969.

**Labrunye**, Raphaël. «L'urbanisme Tupperware.» *Criticat*, no. 3 (mars 2009) : 112-17.

**Lichfield**, John. «Les Halles, ce crime contre l'urbanisme.» *The Independent* (2004). Published electronically 27 mai 2004. *http://www.courrierinternational.com/article/2004/05/27/les-halles-ce-crime-contre-l-urbanisme*.

**Lucan**, Jacques. *Architecture en France, 1940-2000 : Histoire et théories*. Architextes. Paris : Le Moniteur, 2001.

**Marot**, Sébastien. «L'alternative du paysage.» *Le visiteur* 1 (1995) : 54-81.

*Paris-Les Halles : Concours 2004*. Paris : Moniteur, 2004.

**Pinon**, Pierre. «Composition urbaine.» In *I - Repères, II - Projets*. Paris : Éditions Villes et Territoires - DAU-STU-Ministère de l'Equipement, 1994.

**Secchi**, Bernardo. «Villes sans objet, la forme de la ville contemporaine.» Montreal : conference given at the Canadian Centre for Architecture (CCA), Montreal, September 4th, 2008.

**Société d'économie mixte pour l'aménagement des halles** (SEMAH). Paris. «Dix ans d'activité aux Halles.» p.25, 1980.

**Zola**, Émile. *Le Ventre de Paris*. Paris : G. Charpentier, 1873.

# 3.6. Design Combat

**American Competitions and Decision-Making**

**Susanna Sirefman**
President, Dovetail Design Strategists
United States

It can be argued that one of the reasons that architecture competitions are held less frequently in the United States than elsewhere is that there are so many choices in which to go about identifying and hiring a design team. The all too common misunderstanding that architecture is an add-on rather than the rubric under which all else occurs and the lack of any regulatory schemes add to this phenomenon. The wide range of architect selection process choices in America is excellent from the point of view of possibility, yet it is this very freedom that has contributed to the architecture competition construct not being the "go-to" process for design selections.

**Cover**
The BIG U — Rebuild by Design
Competition, 2013-2014

Credit : BIG — Bjarke Ingels Group

## The Architecture Competition Construct

Architecture competitions do not exist in cultural or societal vacuums. The country within which an architecture competition takes place, be it a public or private venture, informs the rules, regulations, procedures, protocols, process, input and outcome of that competition. The American architecture competition offers a mirror of contemporary American cultural, socioeconomic, political, and behavioral mores.

In fact, making a decision, almost any decision, large or small, important or irrelevant is influenced by the cultural background and the cultural context of the decision-maker.[1]

The construct of the architecture competition, understood as a complex, multi-layered process, is directly influenced by the way in which individuals make choices. The deeply complex competition process requires an interdependent, multivalent series of linear and lateral decisions that culminate in one final decision. Most often, a final choice is reached by consensus amongst an appointed committee.[2]

The competition process has very different goals than the goals of making a building. In the broadest possible terms, the elements of making a building can be boiled down to four major components: site, program, resources (budget), and design. Site and program are usually established givens in an American architecture competition, but not always. Competition sponsors may sometimes be looking for fresh program ideas; other sponsors might have a notion of the building program but have not determined the site yet. Budget may also be provided in a competition brief, but again, not always. Consistently, the main element that is always absent, intentionally left out, is the building's design – the architect's act of invention **[Fig.1]**.

In addition, there are usually a myriad number of layered, sometimes conflicting goals, objectives, and agendas for running an architecture competition. This is true wherever an architecture competition is taking place, in either America or abroad.

*The selection of an architect is merely one of the several purposes of design competitions. Competitions can have educational purposes (e.g. educating students, challenging 'conventional wisdom'), political reasons (e.g. enlarging support, marketing a project, running architecture politics, coordinating different fields of interests), cultural aims (e.g. creating a dialogue on design, contributing to the cultural dimension of the built environment, expanding the boundaries of design), and economical reasons (e.g. increasing competition, gaining insight in competences or assuring quality through jury assessment).*[3]

The very nature of a design competition, especially one for something as important as a building, provokes a difference of opinions. Add to that the aforementioned mix of agendas and politics and the diverse individual and collective cultural attitudes towards choice, and the construct of the design competition grows exponentially in complexity.

## American Individualism

Place is central to the way in which choice and decision-making can be understood. Academic studies crossing multiple disciplines — mathematics, social science, behavioral science, economics, and psychology — have examined how and why people make the decisions that they do at all scales: from choosing which type of chocolate to eat, to which medical treatment to undergo and which individual life insurance plan to purchase.[4]

For Americans, individual freedom of choice is considered a basic right that is written into the Declaration of Independence, our Constitution, and the Bill of Rights. Independence is a core American value and freedom of choice is a part of our daily lives.

In her book *The Art of Choosing,* Sheena Iyengar, Professor of Business at Columbia Business School, explores how different cultures perceive the act of decision-making and the areas in which different cultures desire choice.[5] Iyengar cites the work of social psychologist Geert Hofstede to support the belief that Americans are fiercely individualistic. In the late 1970's, Hofstede collected data from IBM employees in over 70 countries, establishing an expansive system for ranking a country's level of individualism. According to this 1980 study, which has been periodically updated, the United States is indeed the most individualistic country in the world.[6]

Americans, as individualists[7], will privilege themselves over a group when faced with making decisions. Decision-making is not predicated on what might be best for the family, community, or nation but what is perceived as the best choice for the individual.

Americans fully expect to make choices about every area of their lives: what they eat, where they work, whom they marry, and how they spend their leisure time.

Americans are also obsessed with personal (individual) achievement, competitive sports, and contests, as evidenced by the proliferation of popular television reality shows such as *Project Runway*, *Cupcake Wars*, and *Survivor* where contestants compete to design the best frock, bake the most delicious cupcake, or to endure the most hardship on an isolated tropical island. Yet there are no popular reality shows in the U.S. titled *America's Next Top Architect* or *Trial by Charrette*, pitting one design team against the other in a timed challenge to produce a sexy, innovative public space.

This carries over into the professional arena of the built environment, as sadly, unlike in Europe or increasingly in Asia, where architecture competitions are either governmentally required or de rigueur for all significant public and private buildings, design competitions are not standard practice here in the States.

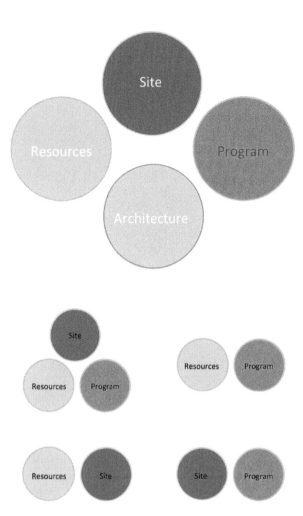

**Fig. 1**
Four Components to Making a Building and Competition Variations. Credit : Dovetail Design Strategists. *Copyright : Dovetail Design Strategists*

### ▬ Choice Study

A seminal breakthrough in the analysis of choice, an experiment popularly known as the "Jam Study" also conducted by Sheena Iyengar along with her colleague Mark Lepper [8], compared two sets of shoppers in a high-end supermarket who were invited to receive a $1-off coupon for one gourmet jam if they took a taste of jam samples that were laid out on display. The first set of shoppers were given a choice of twenty-four different jams to sample, while the second set of shoppers were given a choice of only six jam varieties to taste-test. While the larger display of jam attracted more testers, the researchers were surprised to learn that those who had been offered twenty-four choices were statistically substantially less likely to purchase any jam at all in relation to the purchases made by those who had been offered only six sample choices.

The ramifications of this study and subsequent work have established that more options do not always guarantee a better outcome. The understanding that offering fewer, clearer choices will result in more chances of a purchase has led to dramatic changes to the way many industries now do business.

The notion that "less is more" is an important one, but what is equally elucidating about the "Jam Study" is how it establishes the clear power of the experiment's curators to influence the buyer.

In their influential bestseller, *Nudge: Improving Decisions about Health, Wealth, and Happiness*, authors Richard Thaler and Cass Sunstein describe experiential curators as "choice architects." In other words, this duo defines choice architects as the persons with "the responsibility for organizing the context in which people make decisions." Choice architects create choice architecture — the space within which outcomes can be influenced by the way that possibilities and choices are presented.[9]

For instance, the order in which we encounter options has the power to affect how and what we choose. "We tend to better remember the first and last options in a group, so rather than focus on the merits of each alternative, we may be influenced primarily by the position in which it appeared."[10]

Frequently choice architects are not visible or even tangible to those for whom they have structured a decision-making process. The design of voting ballots may bias which candidates get the most votes, map design has the power to steer us towards a particular direction or travel route, and menu design can manipulate us into choosing the more expensive items on offer at a restaurant.

The food industry and its stakeholders in particular spend enormous resources on studying how environments can be designed to influence people's choices. In America's fight against obesity, much research has been done on how to get children in a lunchroom to choose healthier options like salads and fruit over potato chips and cake. Some interior design solutions that have been remarkably successful seem quite obvious, such as relocating vending machines with unhealthy snacks away from the cafeteria or manipulating cafeteria traffic patterns in order to force students to move past a salad bar or fruit stand to get to the cash wrap.[11]

People have their own inherent, internal systems for making decisions. These decision-making capabilities are aligned with individual biases, habits, experiences, and the complexity of the choice. "People adopt different strategies for making choices depending on the size and complexity of the available options."[12]

The frequency that one is faced with making particular decisions affects the decision-making process, as does the reaction or response once the decision has been made. These two tenets go hand in hand, as the more often a particular type of decision has to be made, the more opportunity there is to gather feedback. Our understanding of the features or elements of complex options directly affects the quantity of choices that we can handle. People have the ability to hone in on specific elements of an option, thereby creating a grouping of options that exhibit that particular element. This allows for the elimination of the options lacking that characteristic.

Social scientists have confirmed that complex choices require expertise, whether acquired personally or sought from outside counsel. Deep knowledge of a particular topic allows options to be simplified, prioritized, and categorized.[13]

Think of the different ways in which a house can be perceived depending on a person's level of knowledge — in general terms as a house, with slightly more detail as a single-family residence, or in specific detail as a 2,500 square foot, two-story house designed by architect X.

*Developing expertise in a given domain is one remedy for coping with a multitude of choice. Expertise enables people to understand options on a more granular level, as the sum of their characteristics rather than as distinct and indivisible items.*[14]

Expertise allows for interpretation of options according to their attributes, which then translates into the capability to recognize patterns, classify categories and therefore grapple intelligently with a wider set of options. If expertise can be applied to a set of choices, the number of options can be reduced to a manageable size.[15]

The obvious question that follows this line of investigation is: how do people make the best possible choice in an area in which they have no expertise? The obvious answer would be to turn to others who have that particular expertise. Thaler and Sunstein take this a step further and advocate for the creation of "choice architecture" that promotes those with expertise to provide a framework to assist people in making better choices about their lives — the thesis of their previously mentioned book *Nudge*.[16]

## ▬ Architecture Choices and Choice Architecture

The framework and process of the architecture competition is a choice architecture. There is, of course, the added caveat that the choice architecture must be equitable, objective, and transparent. The architecture competition has been described as a social technology.[17]

Reflecting Absence

Dual Memory
Garden of Lights
Passages of Light: Memorial Cloud
Lower Waters
Inversion of Lights
Suspending Memory
Votives in Suspension

**Fig. 2**
Winning and Finalist Proposal Titles/World Trade Center Site Memorial Competition. Credit: Dovetail Design Strategists. *Copyright: Dovetail Design Strategists.*

> *It is a technology for picking a winner in a competition for primacy. The fact that we need a carefully designed 'technology' for accomplishing this task is an indication of its complexity. Not only must the technology ensure that there is something attractive to choose between; it must also ensure that the choice of the winner is legitimate and that the 'transaction costs' in terms of time and effort are not prohibitively high.* [18]

Architecture competitions are decipherable as a social technology. They are a social technology that utilizes a choice architecture. The more complex the competition, the more the choice architecture must be explicit.

Just as the goals of designing and constructing a building differ from the goals of an architecture competition, the choice architecture of an architecture competition is different from the choice architecture required to design that building. This is a critical distinction.

The framework for the choice architecture driving a building's design must be embedded in a competition brief as part of the architecture competition process, but the decisions to be made throughout an architecture competition do not mirror those to be confronted in a typical client/architect design process.

Adding to the amalgamated aspirations of an architecture competition is the conceptual nature of the materials from which decisions must be made. Two dimensional drawings, three-dimensional renderings, physical models, and digital animations, while rich illustrations of future physicality, are, in fact, only notations, visual narratives of an imaginary final product. Choices must be made without experiencing the actual physical environment.

This raises many issues about potential realities. What role do promise and possibility play in such instances, when the future product is not experiential? Multiple narratives of who we are, who we think we might be and who we will become are buried in the choices made during an architecture competition.

Therefore, each step of a design competition is loaded with differing meaning for those involved in the decision-making process.

## Instagram

It is a long-standing tradition that entries in American architecture competitions, particularly those involving public space, include project titles. Purely anecdotally, if you look at the finalist and winning project titles from the World Trade Center Site Memorial Competition held in 2003 in New York City it is quite revealing **[Fig. 2]**.

This epic competition for a "single memorial that remembers and honors all loss of life on September 11, 2001 and February 26, 1993," received the largest response to an open architecture call ever, with 5 201 submissions from 63 countries and 49 states received.

While it is impossible and inadvisable to draw any conclusions after the fact, the argument can certainly be made that the cogency of a winning project title, such as *Reflecting Absence,* is in keeping with the eloquence of the winning architectural design.

**Fig. 3**
The West Front of the U.S. Capitol, Architects Dr. William Thornton and
Benjamin Henry Latrobe. Credit : Architect of the Capitol.
*Copyright : Architect of the Capitol.*

How important are words, titles and names to decision-making ? Choice theorists have been looking at this question for some time now and it seems that names are quite potent. A 2010 study, "A Rose by Any Other Name : Would it Smell as Sweet" [19] looked at "whether presenting an odor with a positive, neutral, or negative name would influence how people perceive it," disproving Shakespeare. Fifteen different odors ranging from unpleasant to neutral to pleasant were presented to subjects with positive, negative or neutral names such as "carrot juice," a numeral, or "moldy vegetables." No matter what the smell really was, if it was presented to the study subjects with a positive name it automatically was rated as more pleasant than when it was sniffed under the guise of a negative name. Heart rates went up when smelling a positively-titled smell and people took notably more sniffs. [20]

Obviously using olfactory skills as part of design analysis is not something jurors are typically asked to do when judging an architecture competition. The Rose Name study is referenced here to illustrate the hidden context of choice as demonstrated by the latent power of titles and semantics. Social scientists, advertisers, and marketers have been studying names for decades, and apparently names really do matter.

In the long laundry list of choices that a design competition traverses, this one snapshot (or Instagram image) dissecting an incrementally important element of a competition entry represents how charged every aspect of a submission is.

Jurors are asked to make layer upon layer upon layer of decisions, all ripe with both blatant and subliminal complexities of time, place, personality, politics, personal experiences, and culture.

#### ▬ The History of the American Architecture Competition

A speedy zip through the history of the American architecture competition reveals how Americans have collectively waxed and waned in their enthusiasm for architecture.

The first known American design competition, challenging amateur and trained architects alike, was for a design for a new public library in Philadelphia in 1789. This was followed three years later by the first federally-sponsored contest, for the design of a new US Capitol building. [21]

It is striking to note that the winner of these two first-recorded architecture competitions was the same designer :

a medical doctor and amateur architect originally from the West Indies, Dr. William Thornton. In 1789, Thornton was awarded five pounds as the winner of a competition by the Philadelphia Library Company for his neo-Palladian design for a new brick library. [22]

Three years later Thornton was awarded the commission for the U.S. Capitol as the winner of the first federal architecture competition in America. [23] Launched in 1792 at the request of Secretary of State Thomas Jefferson, the broad terms of this national competition open to anyone in the country promised to: "award $500 and a city lot to whoever produced the 'most approved plan' for the U.S. Capitol Building." [24] Seventeen plans were submitted but none were awarded the commission.

Long after the competition deadline had passed, the competition organizers, three government Commissioners appointed by President George Washington, reviewed plans authored and submitted late by Thornton **[Fig. 3]**.

Although construction began in 1793, in 1803, Benjamin Henry Latrobe, considered the first professional architect and engineer to work in America took over, tweaking the design and overseeing the buildings' construction. [25]

Architectural historian Sarah Bradford Landau credits these first two architecture competitions as promoting an appreciation of design and architecture in the U.S. and believes that American ideology and the notion of freedom of speech attributed to the development of our competition practices.

*Lacking firm evidence, we can only surmise that Jefferson associated the competition procedure with the democratic ideals of the new Republic...By the same token, the constitutionally guaranteed right of free speech surely encouraged criticism of the process from its outset.* [26]

Before and during America's Civil War, architecture competitions proliferated despite dissolute rules and regulations. Often the buildings that resulted were of unsanctioned mixed authorship. All too frequently a winner would be selected for their conceptual design, given the commission, and then be asked to blend elements from the less fortunate entries into the final edifice. [27]

Following the Civil War, "standards of fair practice" were instituted when, in 1867, the American Institute of Architects — the professional organization for licensed architects in the United States, which was founded in 1857 and is now known as the AIA — issued guidelines for architecture competitions that included recommendations on what sort of program and site information should be provided to participants and what should be considered a sufficient timeframe for submission preparation. The AIA also advocated for compensation for design work done in the course of the competition. A version of these recommendations was ratified by the AIA as Competition Code in 1900. [28] Not surprisingly, not much variation in competition process or competition administration occurred throughout the 20th century in the U.S. [29]

Architecture in the U.S. has historically been perceived as an elitist affair. Rarely does a building capture the American public's attention. Several prominent regional architecture competitions have received local celebrity over the last hundred years, yet very few competitions have infiltrated our national consciousness, entering into typical household conversations across the nation and across socioeconomic divides.

One of the best-known American architecture competitions was held in 1922, when the publishers of The Chicago Tribune, Robert R. McCormick and Joseph Patterson held an open and invited contest challenging architects to address the aesthetics and function of a new commercial tower **[Fig. 4]**.

The Tribune, the windy city's most popular newspaper since the 1850's up through to today, staged an enormous marketing effort around the competition in order to demonstrate its dedication to the betterment of the public realm. The publicity resulted in global attention and the winning scheme, designed by Raymond Hood and John Mead Howells, is now considered iconic. [30]

America has always been and remains a conservative country where it can take decades for new, innovative design ideas to be accepted. Historically, architecture competitions have served to educate the public to possibilities, even if the winning avant-garde designs were not ultimately built.

Modernism was brought to the attention of the general public through architecture competitions in the late 1930's and 40's. Much has been written about four important contests, which were launched as America (and the architecture profession) was recovering from the Great Depression. In 1938, the College of William and Mary in Virginia solicited designs for an Art Center, as did Wheaton College in Illinois. In the same year, Maryland's Goucher College challenged the profession to design a new campus plan. The Smithsonian Institution in Washington

D.C. held a competition a year later for a museum building. The contest was won by Eliel and Eero Saarinen, whose design was then rejected by the Commission of Fine Arts and, remarkably, never built. While only Goucher implemented a design garnered through the competition process, these contests were early testing grounds for the likes of architectural stars such as Walter Gropius, Richard Neutra, Eero & Eliel Saarinen, and Pietro Belluschi, and were closely followed by students and professionals. [31]

Zooming ahead to the early 1980's, it is fascinating to note that the two most recent American architecture competitions to capture the nation's — and the world's — full attention were not for buildings but for memorials : the Vietnam Veterans Memorial, recognizing those that lost their lives serving in the U.S. military during the Vietnam War, and the World Trade Center Site Memorial, discussed earlier. [32]

It stands to reason that these competitions received so much attention because they were for memorials, created specifically to honor the dead, and addressed multiple emotionally-charged issues such as patriotism, nationalism, bravery, grief, and mourning. Both of these competitions were surrounded by highly-publicized controversies about the "appropriateness" of the winning designs.

The 1981 competition for the Vietnam Veterans Memorial was a national contest open to any U.S. citizen, 18 years of age or older. A one-stage competition, the winning scheme, designed by Maya Lin, a 21-year old architecture student at the time, was chosen over 1,400 entries. At the time of the competition, Lin's winning design, a monolithic black granite wall inscribed with the names of over 58,200 fallen soldiers, was divisive — people around the country took sides over the meaning and suitability of the design.

Sited between the Lincoln and Washington monuments on the National Mall in Washington D.C., Lin's abstract design for the memorial has been credited as the impetus for America's culture wars of the 1980's. This is difficult to imagine today, as the Memorial is now thought of as a national treasure **[Fig. 5]**.

Twenty-one years later, Maya Lin, now a design star, served as a juror for what was probably the most closely-followed architecture competition of all time, the World Trade Center Site Memorial Competition. In 2003, following closely upon the remarkably complex, politically loaded, and emotionally charged architecture competition administered by The Lower Manhattan Development Corporation (LMDC) for a master plan for Ground Zero, the international two-stage competition for the WTC Memorial was held. The large-scale, abstract, symbolic nature of Arad's winning design, embraced quite readily by the public is most surely a direct legacy of Lin's Vietnam Veterans Memorial.

## ▬ Spoilt for Choice

America today, in 2014, does not have enforceable regulations for architecture competitions. This is due in part to the Federal Trade Commission's concern that regulation of design competitions would cause a "restraint of trade." [33] There are professional guidelines for competition organization and execution. These guidelines have no legal standing and are framed as recommendations in *AIA The Handbook of Architectural Design Competitions,* which was first published in 1988 and then comprehensively revised in 2010. This overhaul was deemed necessary due to the various different "models and structural systems" for architecture competitions that have cropped up in the last ten years. [34]

The *Handbook* identifies nine different competition formats : [35]

- One And Two Stage Competitions
- Developer/Architect Competitions
- Design/Build Competitions
- RFQ Competition
- Interviews With Design Concepts
- International Union Of Architects (UIA) Competition
- Hypothetical [36]
- Competition Limited To Students

These formats are to be further combined with three categories of entry eligibility :

- Open
- Limited
- Invited [37]

Alternative formats exist such as "hybrid" competitions that hark back to competitions of the early 20th century, combining an invited shortlist with an open call. A relatively recent example was held in upstate New York in 2009, titled From the Ground Up : Innovative Green Homes. Run by the Syracuse University School of Architecture, the two-stage competition sought designs for inexpensive, sustainable, and small single-family homes through an open call for three teams to compete with four pre-selected firms. [38]

Multiple-site competitions are increasing in popularity, such as the National Mall Design Competition held in Washington D.C., September 2011 through May 2012. Sponsored by the Trust for the National Mall, this was a three-stage competition to select a design team(s) to redesign three different sites included within the National Mall Plan. The competition format as described on the Trust for the National Mall website states :

*The process includes (1) portfolio evaluations to select up to eight potential lead designers for each site, (2) team interviews to select up to five potential design teams for each site, and (3) a design competition to select a design for each site* **[Fig. 6]**. [39]

Rebuild by Design : Hurricane Sandy Regional Planning and Design Competition, launched in June 2013 by the Hurricane Sandy Rebuilding Task Force, was a multiple-stage, multiple-site, multi-aspirational competition.

*Design Solutions are expected to range in scope and scale — from large-scale urban and multi-functional green infrastructure, to small-scale distributed flood protection measures and resilient residential structures, for example. The competition process will also strengthen our understanding of regional interdependencies, fostering coordination and resilience both at the local level and across the United States.* [40]

The competition was eligible to teams that included a minimum of professionals in at least three of the following disciplines : infrastructure engineering, landscape design, urban design, architecture, land-use planning, industrial design, community engagement, and communications design. This was a competition in four stages that included a comprehensive, commissioned planning phase, community/partner engagement aspects, and led the Federal Government through the U.S. Department of Housing and Urban Development to distribute $930 million dollars in implementation funding to six winning teams.

In addition to the independent competitions described above, the General Services Administration (GSA), a federal agency and America's biggest landlord and developer runs its own architect selection/procurement program. Known as the Design Excellence Program, the format follows a Request For Qualifications followed by a design concept competition.[41]

Recently, the U.S. Bureau of Overseas Buildings and Operations (OBO) instituted a similar Design Excellence Program under the auspices of Secretary of State Hilary Clinton. These programs have influenced other civic procurement methodologies.

Most notably, the City of New York Design + Construction Excellence instituted in 2006 under the leadership of Mayor Michael Bloomberg's administration centered on "Quality-Based Selection" of architects through an RFQ process that selects a pool of firms to be considered for a diverse array of projects. While by no means a design competition, these significant changes in civic procurement do signal a growing interest in design excellence.

## ▬ More Is Less

In *The Paradox of Choice : Why More is Less*, author Barry Schwartz[42], a professor of social theory and social action at Swarthmore College, posits that our American culture of abundance and choice overload is restricting rather than empowering.

Schwartz has concluded through both anecdotal evidence ; (i.e.: the overwhelming plethora of choices faced when buying jeans at the Gap) and the careful examination of academic research into contemporary choice and decision-making, that culturally we are all collectively suffering from having to make too many choices and having too much to choose from.

Schwartz observes that, "A way of easing the burden that freedom of choice imposes is to make decisions about when to make decisions."[43]

This is, once again, a different way of stating the results of Iyengar's "Jam Study." It is simpler to make a choice when faced with fewer options, no matter the magnitude of that choice and, indeed, the default position when encountering a complex decision is to not make a choice at all.

It can be argued that one of the reasons that architecture competitions are held less frequently in the United States than elsewhere is that there are so many choices in which to go about identifying and hiring a design team. The all too common misunderstanding that architecture is an add-on rather than the rubric under which all else occurs and the lack of any regulatory schemes add to this

phenomenon. The wide range of architect selection process choices in America is excellent from the point of view of possibility, yet it is this very freedom that has contributed to the architecture competition construct not being the "go-to" process for design selections.

For sure, an architecture competition is not always appropriate for every project. But for public projects, public/private partnership projects and particularly important, complex projects, an increase in architecture competitions would raise the bar for architecture here in much the same way competitions have raised the bar in Europe.

The well-managed architecture competition would bring architecture and design into the public eye, raise the status of the architecture profession here in the States and create excitement and interest in the specific projects under exploration.

It is apparent that whether looking at the big picture of the frequency with which architecture competitions are held through the lens of decision-making theory or exploring one moment of the process that informs an incremental decision, every step of an architecture competition represents an abundantly loaded moment of choice, ripe with complexities of time, place, personality, politics and culture.

## ▬ Notes

[1] For a fascinating discussion of how culture and decision-making are intertwined see Iyengar, S. 2010. *The Art of Choosing*. Chapter 2, 57-60. New York: Twelve.

[2] Architecture competition is defined here as a formal contest that requires competitors to provide the representation of their independent design concept in a specific format in order to compete with a group of other independently authored submissions which are then judged by a collective body typically known as a Jury.

[3] Volker, L. 2010. *Deciding About Design Quality: Value Judgments and Decision Making in the Selection of Architects by Public Clients Under European Tendering Regulations*, 79. Leiden: Sidestone Press.

[4] For a concise overview of the history of decision-making theory, see Volker, L. 2010. 41-68.

[5] Iyengar, S. 2010. *The Art of Choosing*.

[6] Iyengar, S. 2010. *The Art of Choosing*, 34-35. Iyengar cites Geert Hofstede's book *Culture's Consequences: International Differences in Work-Related Values* (Sage Publications, 1980). Hofstede's findings put the United States as the most individualistic country, this system rated Ecuador as the most collectivist country.

[7] Individualist is defined as "one that pursues a markedly independent cause in thought or action." Individualist. *In Merriam-Webster.com*. Merriam-Webster, n.d. Web. 20 Nov. 2014. http://www.merriam-webster.com/dictionary/individualist.

[8] Iyengar, S. 2010. *The Art of Choosing*, 183-7.

[9] Thaler, R. H. and Sunstein, C. R. 2009. *Nudge: Improving Decisions about Health, Wealth, and Happiness*, 3. New York: Penguin Books.

[10] Iyengar, S. 2010. *The Art of Choosing,* 121. Iyengar points out some of the real ramifications of this observation: "This is why items displayed at either end of a store shelf sell more than those in the middle, and it's also the reason an interviewer might unwittingly pay more attention to the first and last candidates in a job interview."

[11] Thaler, R. H. and Sunstein, Cass R. 2009. *Nudge.*

[12] Ibid, 96.

[13] Iyengar, S. 2010. *The Art of Choosing,* 192. "When we learn, through study and practice, to simplify, prioritize, and categorize elements and to recognize patterns, we are able to create order in seeming chaos."

[14] Ibid, 191-192.

[15] Ibid, 193. "As we can see from the nature of expertise, when talking about choice it's important to make a distinction between the number of options available in the environment and the number actually faced by the chooser."

[16] Thaler, R. H. and Sunstein, Cass R. 2009. *Nudge.*

[17] Kreiner, K. 2010. "Designing Architectural Competitions: Balancing Multiple Matters of Concern." *CONDITIONS: Independent Scandinavian Magazine on Architecture and Urbanism.*

[18] Ibid.

[19] Djordjevic , J. 2008. A Rose by Any Other Name: Would it Smell as Sweet. *Journal of Neurophysiology 99* 386-93. The Shakespeare reference is from *Romeo and Juliet* (II, ii, 43-44): "What's in a name? That which we call a rose / By any other name would smell as sweet"

[20] Further discussion about this phenomenon can be found in Rosokvsky, I. "Was Shakespeare Wrong? – Would a Rose by Any Other Name Smell as Sweet?", *Pyschology Today,* 2010

[21] The birth of the American architecture competition is discussed in depth in Sarah Bradford Landau's essay, Coming to Terms: Architecture Competitions in America and the Emerging Profession, 1789 – 1922. *In* Lipstadt, H. [ed.], *The Experimental Tradition: Essays on Competitions in Architecture.* New York: Princeton Architectural Press.

[22] Landau, S. B. 1989. Coming to Terms, 55. *In* Lipstadt, H. [ed.], *The Experimental Tradition: Essays on Competitions in Architecture.* New York: Princeton Architectural Press.

[23] History of the U.S. Capitol. In *Architect of the Capital.* Web. 20 Nov. 2014. www.aoc.gov/history-us-capitol-building

[24] Ibid.

[25] *Architect of the Capitol.* Web. 20 Nov. 2014. www.aoc.gov/architect-of-the-capitol/benjamin-henry-latrobe

[26] Landau, S.B. 1989. Coming to Terms, 53.

[27] Ibid, 57-59.

[28] Ibid, 53.

[29] There are two wonderful essays, appearing back-to-back, that outline the history of the American architecture competition in great detail by Lipstadt, H. 1989. They are: In the Shadow of the Tribune Tower· American Architecture Competitions, 1922 – 1960; and Transforming the Tradition: American Architectural Competitions, 1960 to the Present. *In* Lipstadt, H. [ed.], *The Experimental Tradition: Essays on Competitions in Architecture,* 79-114. New York: Princeton Architectural Press.

[30] Landau, S.B. 1989. Coming to Terms, 71.

[31] Bentel, P. 1986. The Re-examination of Modern Architecture: A Review of Modernism in America: 1937 – 1943, Places/Volume 3, Number 1.

[32] About the World Trade Center Site Memorial Competition. In *World Trade Center Cite Memorial Competition.* Web. 20 Nov. 2014. www.wtcsitememorial.org/about

[33] Collyer, G.S. 2004. Competitions by Country. In Collyer, G.S. [ed] *Competing Globally in Architecture Competitions,* 244. UK: Wiley Academy.

[34] American Institute of Architects, 2010. *Handbook of Architectural Design Competitions,* 4. Washington D.C.: American Institute of Architects. The Handbook Preface states: "While not wholly outdated, that document [previous edition] needed to be revised in view of the proliferation of the new varieties of competition types and because competitions have become more visible and common."

[35] These nine different competition types are characterized as follows. One-stage and the two-stage competition are counted as two separate formats. **One and Two Stage Competitions:** One-stage juried competitions select a winning design following upon one sequential design phase and one required submission. Two-stage juried competitions select a winning design after two culling phases: an initial submission leads to the selection of finalists who are requested and typically compensated to do further work. A winner is selected based upon their second submission.**Developer/Architect Competitions:** An architect is required to team up with a developer in order to participate in the competition. These types of competitions are usually formatted as one or two stage competitions as outlined above. Submissions typically include a financial component addressing proposed land values and speculative development costs that are not included in design only competitions. **Design/Build Competitions:** An architect is required to team up with a contractor in order to participate in the competition. These types of competitions are usually formatted as one or two stage competitions as outlined above. Submissions include a financial component addressing the streamlining of construction costs in greater detail than are typically included in pure design competitions. **RFQ Competition:** This is a qualifications-based process to select an architect not a design. An architect is chosen on the basis of prior work and frequently an interview rather than the solicitation of a project specific design. **Interviews with Design Concepts:** This format is a combination of a qualifications-based selection process that then leads to a one or two stage design competition. **International Union of Architects (UIA) competition:** Follows the UIA guidelines as listed on www.uia-architectes.org/en. **Hypothetical:** This is a competitive process that solicits design concepts for a speculative project.**Competition Limited to Students**

[36] Hypothetical competitions are design ideas competitions defined as organized, targeted challenges that request professional solutions to complex problems that are not intended to be built. Design Ideas competitions are a way to call public or political attention to an issue, unearth a wide range of potential solutions and gage interest in a project.

[37] The following are definitions of the three major competition eligibility categories: **Open:** This is a competition that casts as broad a net as possible, may or may not include students, interns or other design professionals. Prerequisites and required accreditations are up to the competition sponsor. **Limited:** Restrictions on who can enter such a competition vary but typically revolve around geographical location, level of experience, office size or familiarity with a particular building typology. **Invited:** For an architect to be an included in such a competition they need to be formally asked to participate by the competition sponsor.

[38] soa.syr.edu/events/2008/greenhomes/index.php

[39] The Competition. In *National Mall Design Competition.* Web. 20 Nov. 2014. design.nationalmall.org/design-competition

[40] Rebuild by Design, 2013. REBUILD BY DESIGN: Hurricane Sandy Regional Planning and Design CompetitionDesign Brief. Web: http://portal.hud.gov/hudportal/documents/huddoc?id=REBUILDBYDESIGNBrief.pdf

[41] Collyer, G. Stanley. 2004. Competitions by Country, 244. More information can also be found at www.gsa.gov

[42] Schwartz, B. 2004. *The Paradox of Choice: Why More Is Less: How the Culture of Abundance Robs Us of Satisfaction.* New York: Harper Perennial.

[43] Ibid, 113.

## ▬ References

**Architect of the Capitol.** Web 20 Nov. 2014.
www. aoc.gov/architect-of-the-capitol/benjamin-henry-latrobe

**Bentel**, Paul. The Re-examination of Modern Architecture: A Review of Modernism in America: 1937 – 1943. *Places*/Volume 3, Number 1. 1986.

**Collyer**, G. Stanley. Competitions by Country. In Collyer, G.S. [ed] *Competing Globally in Architecture Competitions*, 244. UK: Wiley Academy, 2004.

**The Competition.** In *National Mall Design Competition*. Web. 20 Nov. 2014. design.nationalmall.org/design-competition

**Djordjevic**, Jelena. A Rose by Any Other Name: Would it Smell as Sweet. *Journal of Neurophysiology 99* [2008]: 386-93.

*Handbook of Architectural Design Competitions*, 4. Washington D.C.: American Institute of Architects, 2010.

**History of the U.S. Capitol.** In *Architect of the Capital*. Web. 20 Nov. 2014.

**Iyengar**, Sheena. *The Art of Choosing*. New York: Twelve, 2010.

**Kreiner**, Kristian. "Designing Architectural Competitions: Balancing Multiple Matters of Concern." *CONDITIONS: Independent Scandinavian Magazine on Architecture and Urbanism*. 2010. Web. Dec. 28, 2010. http://www.conditionsmagazine.com/archives/1767

**Landau**, Sarah Bradford. Coming to Terms: Architecture Competitions in America and the Emerging Profession, 1789 – 1922. In *The Experimental Tradition: Essays on Competitions in Architecture*, edited by Hélène Lipstadt. New York: Princeton Architectural Press, 1989.

**Lipstadt**, Hélène. In the Shadow of the Tribune Tower: American Architecture Competitions, 1922 – 1960. In *The Experimental Tradition: Essays on Competitions in Architecture*, edited by Hélène Lipstadt. New York: Princeton Architectural Press, 1989.

**Lipstadt**, Hélène. Transforming the Tradition: American Architectural Competitions, 1960 to the Present. In *The Experimental Tradition: Essays on Competitions in Architecture*, edited by Hélène Lipstadt. New York: Princeton Architectural Press, 1989.

**REBUILD BY DESIGN: Hurricane Sandy Regional Planning and Design Competition Design Brief.** 2013. Web: http://portal.hud.gov/hudportal/documents/huddoc?id=REBUILDBYDESIGNBrief.pdf

**Schwartz**, B. *The Paradox of Choice : Why More is Less*. New York: Harper Perennial, 2004.

**Thaler**, Richard H. and Cass R. **Sunstein**. *Nudge: Improving Decisions about Health, Wealth, and Happiness*. New York: Penguin Books, 2009.

**Volker**, Leentje. *Deciding About Design Quality: Value Judgments and Decision Making in the Selection of Architects by Public Clients Under European Tendering Regulations*, Chapter 4, 79. Leiden: Sidestone Press, 2010.

**World Trade Center Memorial Competition.** About the World Trade Center Site Memorial Competition. In *World Trade Center Cite Memorial Competition*. Web. 20 Nov. 2014. www.wtcsitememorial.org/about

## Section 4
# Archiving Architectural Knowledge

100
MARIA GRAZIA DALLERBA-RICCI
*Italy*

104
ALISON & PETER SMITHSON
*Great Britan*

148
BAKKER & BLEEKER
*Netherlands*

248
ARRIOLA / FIOL / GALI / QUINTANA
*Spain*

312
HARUYOSHI ONO
*Brazil*

323
ROLAND CASTRO
*France*

327
OFFICE FOR METROPOLITAN ARCHITECTURE
*Great Britan*

335
HIROSHI HARA
*Japan*

409
ÉQUIPE TRAC
*France*

620
ALAIN SARFATI
*France*

726
ÉQUIPE ZAHA HADID
*Great Britain*

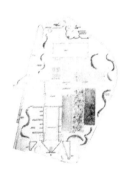

736
CEDRIC PRICE
*Great Britan*

749
ÉQUIPE BERNARD TSCHUMI
*United States*

802
KISHO KUROKAWA
*Japan*

803
TEAM ZOO
*Japan*

949
MARIO GALVAGNI
*Italy*

# 4.1. Competitions as Laboratories
## On the So-Called 'Experimental' Nature of Architecture Competitions

**Bechara Helal**, Ph.D. candidate
School of Architecture, Université de Montréal
Canada

There seems to be a general belief that there exists a close link between competitions and experimentation in architecture : architectural competitions would be these special events where new and audacious ideas are offered, dramatically changing the course of the field. One can read such an idea into the naming of the renowned 1989 exhibition on competitions curated by Hélène Lipstadt, "The Experimental Tradition : Twenty-five Years of American Architecture Competitions, 1960-1985." However, if this link is generally assumed, it needs to be nuanced and refined. What exactly is "experimental" about architectural competitions ? Are there specific conditions that make a competition "experimental" ? Are there types of competitions that are more "experimental" than others ?

Looking at competitions through the lens of a theory of experimentation, this presentation proposes a clarification of the multiples forms of experimentation (artistic, scientific... architectural ?). Through a reading of the famous 1982 La Villette Park competition along two axes (the competition as a space of architectural experimentation and the architectural competition as an experimental process), this essay discusses how these multiple definitions of the notion of experimentation can be used to describe in a new way the operations underlying the competition process.

**Cover**

'La Villette as Laboratory', a collage of a limited number of entries in the large database incorporating all the projects submitted to the 1982 La Villette Park International Competition. From the top down and from left to right, the proposals are those submitted by Maria Grazia Dallerba-Ricci ; Alison and Peter Smithson ; Bakker & Bleeker ; Arriola / Fiol / Gali / Quintana ; Haruyoshi Ono ; Roland Castro ; Office for Metropolitan Architecture ; Hiroshi Hara ; Équipe Trac ; Alain Sarfati ; Équipe Zaha Hadid ; Cedric Price ; Équipe Bernard Tschumi ; Kisho Kurokawa ; Team Zoo ; and Mario Galvani. The numbers assigned to the proposals are those that were attributed at the time by the *Établissement Public du Parc de La Villette* to the competing teams in order to identify them during the anonymous judging process.

In 1988, the Architectural League of New York presented "The Experimental Tradition : Twenty-Five Years of American Architecture Competitions, 1960-1985",[1] a retrospective exhibition covering twenty-five years of American architecture competitions — an era curator Hélène Lipstadt describes as one of a "so-called 'competition revival'".[2] Widely considered by many as a seminal event in the study of architecture competitions, the exhibition was paired with a catalogue that included, in addition to the exhibited documents, a number of essays proposing a historical study of American architecture competitions from the fifteenth century to the present time **[Fig.1]**.[3] The naming of the exhibition draws a clear link between architecture competitions and the notion of experimentation. One would think that the essays presented in the exhibition catalogue would largely focus on this link, but the reference to experimentation in the context of architectural competitions remains largely unexplained. In fact, a survey of the words used in the writings of the catalogue shows that the notion of experimentation is hardly ever referred to.[4] The only explicit yet brief explanation of the naming of the exhibition can be found in Lipstadt's own introductory essay to the book :

> 'Experimental Tradition' should not be taken as an affirmation of a historical association of competitions with great style-forming moments of innovation in architecture. Rather, it reflects the nature of architecture competitions, for these ephemeral events with permanent results are endlessly repeated and always changing.[5]

This statement opposes two approaches of the notion of experimentation. The first describes a certain quality of competition results ("innovation in architecture"), whereas the second is related to the competition process itself ("the nature of architecture competitions"). Even though Lipstadt clearly favours the second approach, the link hinted by the exhibition between experimentation and architecture competitions remains to be studied in depth.

What is experimental about architecture competitions ? From this very general interrogation stem three more precise questions. What exactly does "experimentation" mean in the field of architecture ? Are there specific competition conditions that ensure the production of "experimental architecture" ? Can architecture competitions be considered experimental processes ? This essay will tackle these questions by considering one main case study, the La Villette Park architecture competition in Paris, France.

## The Multiple Definitions of Experimentation

What exactly does "experimentation" mean? The notion of experimentation in architecture may appear familiar because of the numerous mentions of "experimental architecture", a term widely used — one (could even say overused) — yet hardly ever thoroughly defined.[6] This lack of a proper definition can be linked to the ambiguities identified by architectural historian and theorist Aaron Betsky that lie at the very heart of the notion of experimentation itself. As Betsky writes in his entry on "experimental architecture" in the *Metapolis Dictionary of Architecture*, "the notion of experimentation was given contradictory impulses by 19th century scientific revolutions and by art making practices of the 20th century."[7] As architecture is often described as a discipline at the crossroads of the fields of art and science, it is only natural that, in order to better inform the multiple definitions of experimentation in architecture, one must take a step back and analyze the "contradictory [historical] impulses" identified by Betsky.

### The Science of Experimentation

The Scientific Revolution of the nineteenth century marked a major change in how the sciences were built. Up to this point, according to the Aristotelian tradition, sciences were built through deductive reasoning. As the Scientific Revolution transformed the field of science, this approach was replaced by an inductive and empirical process based on observation[8]; experimentation became the preferred method through which sciences were built **[Fig.2]**. According to this method, a scientific fact is built on a rigorous and structured iterative process that starts with a research question. The scientist formulates a hypothesis to this research question and proceeds to test it through an experiment that will need to be previously devised (design of the experiment apparatus and identification of the variables). The results of this experiment will then be measured through measuring protocols, which the scientist will also need to establish (these measuring protocols can take into account quantitative as well as qualitative information). The measured results are then recorded and categorized, which implies, in turn, a previous effort of description and analysis of the collected information. In a final step of the process, the categorized and analyzed information is evaluated according to a number of pre-identified quantitative and/or qualitative judgment criteria. If the evaluation is positive, the initial hypothesis is validated and a scientific fact is constructed. However, in the case of a negative or inconclusive evaluation, the process goes through a new iteration with a new corrected hypothesis (or, if necessary, a new corrected experiment).

In the field of science, experimentation takes the form of the experimental method, which can be best described as a research process that builds new knowledge. As we will see, this is very different from experimentation in the arts.

### Experimental Art

The first references to the notion of experimentation in the arts can be traced back to the work of Russian avant-garde artist Aleksandr Rodchenko. In 1920, when Rodchenko presented his work in the context of the 19th State Exhibition in Moscow, he chose to pair it with a strong typewritten manifesto entitled "Everything is Experiment" (*Vse-opyty*) **[Fig.3]**, in which he redefines all his work from the point of view of experimentation:

*We are experiments for the future. I created today in order to seek the new tomorrow. [...] The old painters put everything that was done before them into their works... But in each work, I make a new experiment without the addition of everything old — belonging to others — and in each work I set different tasks. If you look at all my work over time, it is, in fact, one huge work, and completely new, and if you want to add on the old, then you can go to a museum and think about it.*[9]

Rodchenko's manifesto strongly advocates a clear and total break from the past and an adventurous and constructive stance towards the future. This approach to the arts is in line with the general attitude of the Russian society, which seeks to redefine itself entirely and collectively after the major historical break that was the 1917 Russian Revolution. In his Moscow diary in 1927, Walter Benjamin writes:

*Each thought, each day, each life lies here as on a laboratory table. And as if it were a metal from which an unknown substance is by every means to be extracted, it must endure experimentation to the point of exhaustion. No organism, no organization, can escape this process... This astonishing experimentation — it is here called remonte — affects not only Moscow; it is Russian.*[10]

**Fig. 2**
Schematic iterative diagram of the experimental method in science.
*Diagram : Bechara Helal after Steven G. Darian (2003).*

The "new" Russian artist must produce art that goes beyond personal expression and tackle issues common to the whole society of which he is part. In that sense, the notion of experimentation referred to by Rodchenko in the context of art is a direct reference to the field of sciences : experiments require rigor, method, and subjectivity. However, the term "experimental art" has become synonymous today with the kind of art produced by these early avant-garde movements : heroic, utopic, and highly adventurous. It is these to qualities that the notion of "experimental architecture usually refers, and, in that sense, the term usually describes the formal characteristics of the resulting objects rather than the process that produced them. Going back to Rodchenko's manifesto, the experimental work of art can be described as the result of a research for new models for the future.

## Experimentation and Research in Architecture

"A research process that builds new knowledge" or "a research for new models for the future" : be it in the sciences or the arts, the notion of experimentation is always related to the activity of research. But, as stated by Aaron Betsky, it follows "contradictory impulses" depending on the studied field. Scientific experimentation is a process for thinking (i.e. building new knowledge) whereas artistic experimentation is a stance for making (i.e. building new objects). The former is related to the process and can therefore be best described as methodological and epistemological, while the latter is concerned with the results and can be described as reflexive and operative. Experimentation in architecture can follow either of these impulses : indeed, a distinction can be made between "experimentation in architecture" as a constructive process and "experimental architecture" as a result with specific qualities. It is interesting to note that this is in line with the distinction made by Hélène Lipstadt between two different readings of experimentation (the competition process itself vs. the quality of its results). We will now see how these two somewhat contradictory understandings of experimentation in the field of architecture can be applied to the study of architecture competitions.

## The Competition as a Space of Production of Experimental Architecture

Let us consider, in a first step, experimentation in architecture as seen from the point of view of the project. As previously discussed, "experimental architecture" can be described as the result of a research for new models for the future. Can architectural competitions be considered as a space of production of "experimental architecture"? And, if so, are there specific conditions that ensure this kind of result? In order to provide answers to these questions, we will study the remarkable case that was the La Villette Park international architecture competition. Because of the particular qualities of the architectural results, the competition process itself, and the available information, this case proves ideal in regard to the notion of experimentation this essay tackles.

The La Villette Park architecture competition is particular in that there was not *one* but *two* separate international competitions.[11] The first competition was an idea competition that took place in 1976 under the presidency of Valéry Giscard d'Estaing. The competitors were asked to rethink the fifty-five-hectare site that was once used by the La Villette slaughterhouses by integrating a large array of programmatic components including offices, housing (a maximum of 4500 residences), an industrial zone and a fifteen-hectare park, while reconditioning a number of existing architectural structures and a neoclassical fountain. 167 competitors presented schemes for this first competition but no unique winner was ever officially announced and the competition did not have any built materialization. A few years later, having taken office in 1981, socialist president François Mitterrand initiated Les Grandes Opérations d'Architecture et d'Urbanisme, a construction program that included a large number of important urban and architectural public projects.[12] In the context of this program, a new international competition was set up for the La Villette Park in 1982. This new competition excluded some of the original programmatic elements of the first competition (such as housing and office space) and took into account a number of the conclusions that followed the 1976 ideas competition such as the need of a larger park (over thirty hectares instead of fifteen hectares) and the integration within this park of an auditorium and of a Musée des Sciences, des Techniques et de l'Industrie. This time however, the competition was a project competition and 471 competitors from 41 countries presented schemes. While the competition was supposed to be limited to a single round, nine joint first

**Fig. 3**
"Everything is Experiment": Aleksandr Rodchenko's work displayed with typewritten text at the 19th State Exhibition, Moscow, 1920.
*Copyright: Aleksandr Rodchenko and Varvara Stepanova Archive, Moscow.*

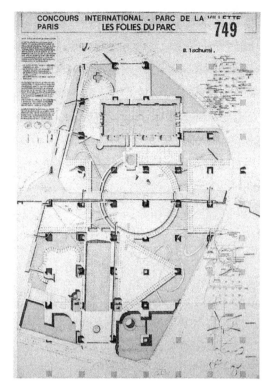

**Fig. 4**
Bernard Tschumi Architects (USA) entry for the La Villette
Park International Competition, 1982 — Winning Scheme.

**Fig. 5**
Office for metropolitan Architecture/Rem Koolhaas,
architect (UK) entry for the La Villette Park International
Competition, 1982 — Runner-up scheme.

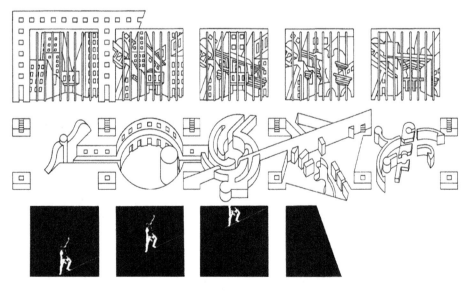

**Fig. 6**
*The Manhattan Transcripts*,
Bernard Tschumi, 1967-1981.
*Copyright: Bernard Tschumi (1981).*

**Fig. 7**
*The City of the Captive Globe*, a project by Rem Koolhaas produced with the collaboration of Zoe Zenghelis at the *Institute for Architecture and Urban Studies* in New York. *Copyright: Rem Koolhaas (1972).*

prizes were awarded, and these nine "finalists" were asked to refine their schemes in a second round. [13] The competition ended with Bernard Tschumi, (USA) being awarded the winning prize **[Fig.4]**, while OMA/Rem Koolhaas, (GB) was nominated as the runner-up **[Fig.5]**. These two very particular projects will be the focus of our study.

Can the projects presented by Bernard Tschumi and OMA/Rem Koolhaas be considered "experimental architecture"? In order to answer this question, it is necessary to go back in time to the beginning of the 1980s, as the La Villette Park competition was taking place. Back in 1982, Tschumi and Koolhaas were still relatively unknown. The most important work both architects had produced at this point was not located within the boundaries of the professional field of architecture but rather in the realm of theoretical thinking. Tschumi had produced his now classic *Manhattan Transcripts* project (1976-1981) and published *Architectural Manifestoes* (1979), a collection of theoretical writings on architecture **[Fig.6]**. [14] Koolhaas had followed a similar path and his production of theoretical projects such as *The City of the Captive Globe* (1972) had become part of a major theoretical publication, *Delirious New York* (1978) **[Fig.7]**. [15] Both the entries of Tschumi and OMA/Koolhaas for the 1982 La Villette Park competition are the embodiment in the professional field architecture of an important theoretical rethinking of the discipline itself. In that sense, both competition propositions can be considered as theoretical projects testing the possibility of radical new and future architectures. The approach at the heart of the work of both Tschumi and Koolhaas is very similar to the stance adopted by Rodchenko and the Russian avant-garde artists who explored the possibilities of a new type of art.

But, while Rodchenko advocated a complete break with the art of the past, the projects presented by Tschumi and Koolhaas can be linked to past architectures, albeit not the architectures of the classical, modern or even postmodern movements. In fact, one can find in the entries of both Tschumi and OMA/Koolhaas direct references to the architectures produced by the avant-garde movements of the 1920s and 1960s; in other words, "experimental architectures" boasting an open approach to research. Bernard Tschumi's project can be explained by referring to the plastic work of Iakov Chernikov's *Architectural Fantasies* (1933) and to the urban approach of Archizoom in projects such as *No-Stop City* (1970). In the same way, OMA's scheme can be directly linked to the programmatic considerations at the heart of Ivan Leonidov's *Lenin Institute* project (1927) and

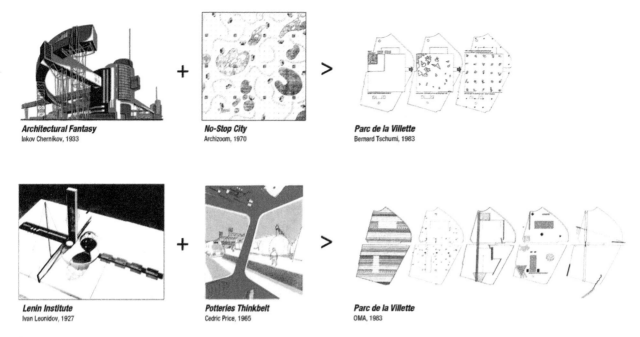

**Architectural Fantasy**
Iakov Chernikov, 1933

**No-Stop City**
Archizoom, 1970

**Parc de la Villette**
Bernard Tschumi, 1983

**Lenin Institute**
Ivan Leonidov, 1927

**Potteries Thinkbelt**
Cedric Price, 1965

**Parc de la Villette**
OMA, 1983

**Fig. 8**
1920 / 1960 / 1980: Linking the projects of Bernard Tschumi and OMA for the La Villette Park
competition in 1982 to the 'experimental architecture' of the 1920s and 1960s avant-gardes.
*Copyrights : Museum of Modern Art, New York (Iakov Chernikov); Deganello Archives, Milan
(Archizoom); Bernard Tschumi Architects (Bernard Tschumi); The Standard Catalogue Company
Ltd., London (Cedric Price); Office for Metropolitan Architecture (OMA)*

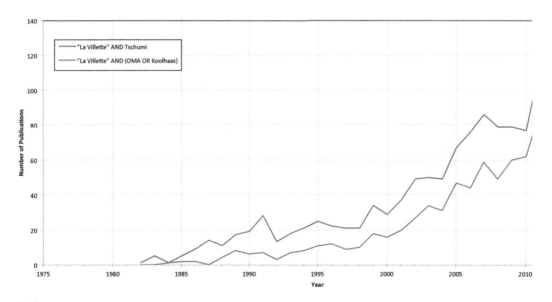

**Fig. 9**
Number of publications referring directly to the work of Tschumi and OMA/Koolhaas on the
La Villette Park as referenced on Google Scholar.

the vector dynamics structuring Cedric Price's *Potteries Thinkbelt* project (1965) **[Fig.8]**. Tschumi's and OMA's proposals can therefore be seen as new materializations of theoretical models generated by previous "experimental architects". However, the language used by the Tschumi and Koolhaas to explain their projects leaves no doubt : these new materializations must not be considered as simple architectural objects.

An analysis of the discourse of the architects show that both Tschumi and Koolhaas have always refused to describe their propositions in terms of professional projects. In a 1984 interview, Bernard Tschumi states :

*The first stage presented at the competition expressed a principle ; the second stage developed this principle ; neither project nor park... We are interested in conceiving a set of principles, which can then be developed and inserted among the constraints presented* [16]

Clearly, for Tschumi, his proposition is not to be considered as a final and completed project but rather "a set of principles" of what a park should be in 1982. Rem Koolhaas uses the same kind of language in the presentation text of OMA's proposition to the second phase of the competition :

*We insist that at no time have we presumed to have produced a designed landscape. We have confined ourselves to devising a framework capable of absorbing an endless series of further meanings, extensions, or intentions without entailing compromises, redundancies, or contradictions.* [17]

Here too, the architect refuses to consider that his entry is a completed and closed project ("a designed landscape") : he insists that it must be seen as a "framework" that can be adjusted and tweaked. What both architects clearly state is that their proposals must be understood as u-topian architectures in the literal sense of the term, i.e. "without topos," — not rooted in any physical site.

It is a well-known fact that the projects of Tschumi and OMA/Koolhaas on the La Villette Park are important contemporary milestones in the history of architecture. This can be corroborated by a survey of all academic publications referring to them from their inception in the 1980s, all the way to today **[Fig.9]**. [18] We believe that the number of direct references to a given project in the architectural literature is a good indicator of its importance and impact

on the history, theory and practice of the discipline. Even thirty years after the competition, both projects are referred to regularly (more than a hundred times each in 2012), and it is most telling that the project by OMA/Koolhaas remains an object of study even though it was not the winning scheme. Clearly, the importance of both these projects goes beyond the simple formal answer to a given professional problem. [19] In that sense, both Tschumi's and OMA's projects must be seen as models rather than objects ; and these models are clearly geared towards an architecture of the future.

New models for the future devised through theoretical research and built in the continuity of experimental work by previous members of the avant-garde : clearly, Tschumi's and Koolhaas' schemes for the La Villette Park competition must be considered true and major works of "experimental architecture." One could wonder if a direct link can be found between the production of this kind of projects and the particular design context that is the architecture competition. Why did the La Villette Park competition produce two of the more important examples of "experimental architecture" in recent history ? Four hypotheses can be investigated to explain this remarkable case : a) the intentions and contradictions of the competition program ; b) the complexity and heterogeneity of the competition jury ; c) the format of the competition itself ; and, finally, d) the stability of the architectural discipline.

## Intentions and Contradictions of the Competition Program

The architecture and urban program of the La Villette Park competition may appear very simple and straightforward — the construction of a new thirty-hectare urban park in Paris — but, a study of the documents released by the French Presidency of the Republic announcing the competition show a clear intention to go beyond the physical and formal project. This is probably made most clear in the one-page official presidential communiqué which sums up the objectives of the competition :

*The future La Villette Park [...] will be an urban Park, alive and busy and, owing to its cultural nature will become, if possible, a model for all XXI$^{st}$ (sic) century urban parks.* [20]

What is asked of the competitors by the highest authority goes beyond the simple answer to a set of architectural and urban problems : it is, spelled out very clearly, what

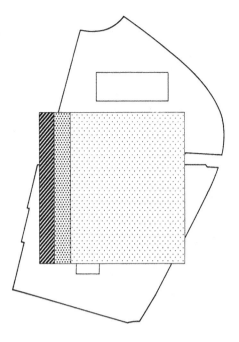

**Fig. 10**
Diagram of the La Villette
Park competition program
superimposed over the physical
site plan, as included in the
text presentation of OMA/Rem
Koolhaas' competition entry.

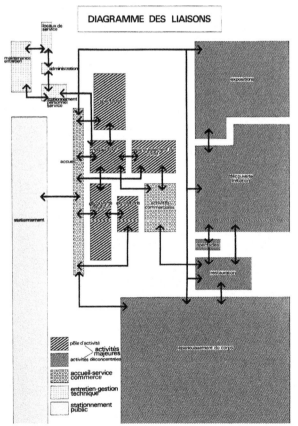

**Fig. 11**
Diagram of programmatic relationships
in the brief of the 1982 La Villette Park
International Competition.
*Source: Établissement Public du Parc de
La Villette (1982).*

we previously called a "model" for all future parks set in urban environments. It is little wonder that such an explicit request for a complete rethinking of the traditional urban object that is the park yielded projects like the ones presented by Tschumi and OMA/Koolhaas. In addition, the usual competition program presented a number of issues. In a violen article she wrote a few years after the competition, renowned architectural theorist and historian Françoise Choay — a member of the competition jury — had very harsh words regarding the program, which she described as:

  a. *over-inflated;*
  b. *over-constraining;*
  c. *contradictory: a collage of contradictory logics, this program... asked for a park at once: rural and urban, vegetal and mineral, closed and open; still a park yet something entirely new and innovative.* [21]

Koolhaas had already also noted that the program of the competition went beyond the physical limitations of the site and had built his design approach on that fact using the operative theory of congestion he had previously developed in *Delirious New York*. As OMA's competition presentation text makes very explicit from the onset, the size of the program is not, in fact, a problem, but rather an opportunity to propose something entirely different:

  *As the diagram reveals* **[Fig.10]**, *the site of La Villette is too small, and the program too large, to create a park in the recognizable sense of the word... At this stage, it would be nonsense to design a detailed park. We have read the program as a suggestion, a provisional enumeration of desirable ingredients. It is not definitive.* [22]

The fact that the program could be seen as "over-constraining" as suggested by Choay is evidenced by the complexity of the network of programmatic relationships that was part of the brief of the competition **[Fig.11]** [23] But what is most interesting in Choay's criticism is the "collage of contradictory logics" she identifies: "rural and urban, vegetal and mineral, closed and open; still a park yet something entirely new and innovative." One could say that such contradictions in a competition program make it impossible to propose a coherent project, but we argue that these contradictions are precisely what allowed participants such as Tschumi and Koolhaas to propose the kind of schemes they did. The complexity of the program and the contradictions

within it enable architects to project over the canvas of the competition their own intentions and understanding of the issues at play and, by doing so, to go beyond the limits that would be fixed by a traditional and coherent program. In other words, a complex and contradictory program can become an opportunity for an "experimental architect" to ask new questions that go beyond what is explicitly asked of him. [24]

**Complexity and Heterogeneity of the Competition Jury**

The competition jury was chosen by François Barré, once editor-in-chief of the prestigious magazine *Architecture d'Aujourd'hui*, and director of the Établissement public du Parc de La Villette, a body founded in order to manage both the competition and construction of the new La Villette Park. The international jury included twenty-one members from nine different countries and was presided by Brazilian landscape architect Roberto Burle Marx **[Fig.12]**. A study of the professional occupations of the jury members shows that a total of nine of the members — more than 40 % of the jury — are directly related to the field of architecture, which is almost double that of members related to the field of landscape architecture (a total of five). This is a somewhat surprising fact given that the program of the competition — a park — should, in theory, be considered more a problem of landscape architecture than one of architecture. One could wonder what role the architects played in the selection of the winning and the runner-up schemes, two projects clearly originating in the field of architecture. The fact that the decision of the jury was not unanimous, but the result of a majority vote makes this question even more relevant. In her article, Françoise Choay, a clear supporter of the scheme presented by OMA/Koolhaas, [25] criticizes the decision of the jury:

  *The verdict was inspired by fear:*
  • *Fear of innovation and of the unpredictable, from the programmers who had been asking for it and refusing it at the same time.*
  • *Fear by lack of understanding, from the non-professional members on the jury.*
  • *Fear by too much understanding, from the same architects on the jury.* [26]

Choay criticizes the position — and decision — of the jury faced with the "experimental model" the program called for, with all its complexity and contradictions. It is

| | country | occupation | affiliation | related to the field of | |
|---|---|---|---|---|---|
| | | | | architecture | landscape architecture |
| François Barré | F | Architect | Établissement public du Parc de La Villette | x | |
| Bernard Bourgade | F | Architect-sociologist | Collectif La Villette | x | |
| Lucius Burckhardt | CH | Sociologist | | | |
| Roberto Burle Marx | BR | Landscape architect | (Jury president) | | x |
| Françoise Choay | F | Architecture and urban studies theorist | | x | |
| Pierre Dauvergne | F | Landscape architect | Société Française des Paysagistes | | x |
| Christian Dupavillon | F | Architect | Ministry of Culture | x | |
| Paul Friedberg | USA | Landscape architect | | | x |
| Mathias Goeritz | MEX | Sculptor | | | |
| Vittorio Gregotti | IT | Architect | | x | |
| Gottfried Honegger | CH | Painter | (Jury vice-president) | | |
| Arata Isozaki | JP | Architect | | x | |
| Henri Laborit | F | Biologist | | | |
| Luigi Nono | IT | Composer | | | |
| Renzo Piano | IT | Architect | | x | |
| Simone Robert | F | Councillor | Seine-Saint-Denis department | | |
| Bernard Rocher | F | Deputy Mayor | | | |
| Joseph Rykwert | UK | Architecture historian and theorist | | x | |
| Jacques Simon | F | Landscape architect | | | x |
| Jean Tribel | F | Architect | Direction de l'Architecture | x | |
| Hans Friedrich Werkmeister | CH | Landscape architect | | | x |
| | | | TOTAL | 9 | 5 |

**Fig. 12**
List of the jury members of the 1982 *La Villette Park* architecture competition.

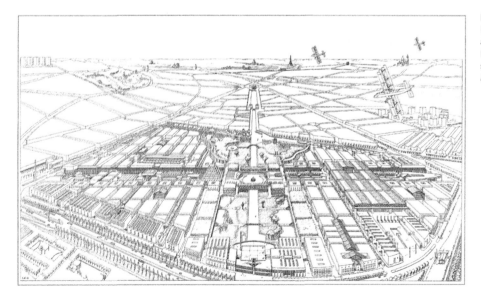

**Fig. 13**
Panorama of the New Quartier at an Altitude of Three-Hundred Metres": Leon Krier's proposed scheme for the 1976 *La Villette Park* architecture competition.

interesting that she blames as much the non-architects as the architects for what she considers a bad decision, and that which she blames the architect-jurors for is precisely the fact that they understood all too well what the daring architectural schemes by Tschumi and OMA/Koolhaas implied for their discipline. Would the decision have been any different if the jury included more (or less) members from the field of architecture? Would a jury less geared towards architecture still have chosen a clearly "experimental" architectural scheme? Given the limited information on the confidential La Villette Park jury available to us, it is hard to answer these questions. It is however safe to assume the jury debates would have been much different had architects been more or less represented. The subject of the ratio of architects in an architectural competition jury is sure to play an important and direct role in the selection of the winning proposal and should therefore be closely considered in the context of architecture competition studies.

**Types of Architecture Competition**

In the context of architectural competition studies, a distinction is commonly made between two major types: the project competition and the idea competition. Because they do not necessarily take into account the constructability of a project, a usually important hindrance to radical and creative design, idea competitions might appear as more prone to the production of experimental architecture. But is this really the case? In order to test this potential link between the type of architecture competition and the production of experimental architecture, let us compare the two La Villette Park competitions: the 1976 idea competition and the 1982 project competition. The case study of the La Villette Park competitions is ideal in the sense that it enables the direct comparison of two types of architecture competitions on a single site with different yet similar programs within a very limited timeframe.

As previously mentioned, the 1976 idea competition did not end with a single official winner. Instead, the jury chose to congratulate a number of competitors for their design "in close continuity with the existing urban fabric" while deploring "the expression of an excessively rural type that did not match a city such as Paris."[27] Such comments from the jury may be understood as a sign that the entries of this first competition were judged as being, in general, not innovative or experimental enough. This is corroborated by the analysis carried out by architecture and urban studies historian Giovanni Cerami, according to

which all the competition proposals could be categorized in three major groups:

The first group can be considered as the "heir to the Athens Charter," worthy of respect, but the least innovative.

*The second group aims for a reassertion of a link with a historically consolidated — yet, in practice, out-dated — tradition, and is geared towards the investigation of a possible reordering through morphology and typology. It includes the projects having the strongest links with values stratified within "history" (such as the projects of Krier, Huet, and Ciriani) — in other words, the projects more linked to a "rational construction" of the city.*

*Finally, the third group seems to put forward an approach less dubious, less linked to the "new found tradition," and therefore more innovative in regards to the acceptance of a certain amount of "disorder." Such is the case, for example, of the project of Porro or that of Grumbach and Nicolas; projects that tend to invent a new urban landscape made of memorization and transgression.*[28]

Cerami's categorization shows that only a few of the competitors — the third group — chose to turn their back on the traditional schemes of landscape architecture and urbanism in order to tackle more contemporary questions through innovative projects. It is ironic that the project that is best remembered from the first La Villette Park competition — the entry by the young British architect Leon Krier — is not one of these. Krier's proposal is not a vision that projected into the future but rather a project that advocated an idealized return to the historical tradition of the city [Fig. 13]. Entitled "For a New Quartier (A City within a City)," Krier calls his entry a "project of re-urbanization... which attempts to restore the city to itself."[29] Although not avant-gardist in the true sense of the word — an approach in advance of those generally accepted in the field — it would be absolutely wrong to consider Krier's project a pragmatic one. Architecture historian Vincent Scully calls it "an excellent example" of Neorationalism:

*The Neorationalists regard themselves as ideologically directed, but like all art their own is effective because of its form. Neorationalism is in fact peculiarly formalistic, wedded to pure form. But it is also ideological and authoritarian, much as the International Style before it was."*[30]

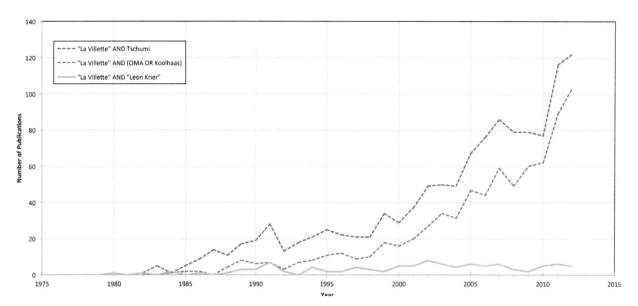

**Fig. 14**
Number of publications referring directly to the work of Leon Krier, Bernard Tschumi and
OMA/Koolhaas on the La Villette Park as referenced on Google Scholar.

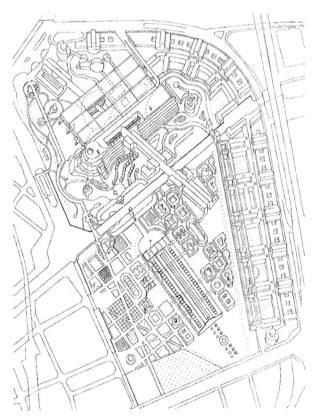

**Fig. 15**
Bernard Tschumi's proposed
scheme for the 1976 *La Villette
Park* architecture competition.

Krier certainly considered his competition rooted in ideology. It is however not an ideology that projected towards the future, but rather towards an idealized past considered lost. This aspect of Krier's project is made evident by its inclusion in *New Babylon : The Value of Dreaming the City of Tomorrow*, a congress where architects, historians, and critics discussed the "course that 'radical', 'neo-avant-garde' architecture took through the 1960s and on into the 1970s" that followed Constant's New Babylon project. [31] As made evident by the book's structure, for the conference organizers, Krier's proposal for the La Villette Park marks the end of the visionary projects of the 1960s and 1970s :

> *Starting with the playful but practically inspired futurological scheme of Yona Friedman's Paris Spatial [1959-61], we move through the early Archigram revolution — Plug-in City [1963-66] ... — towards the seminal works of Italian Architettura Radicale. We look closely at No-Stop City [Archizoom Associates, 1969-72] and the Continuous Monument [Superstudio, 1969], discovering that... Archizoom and Superstudio were in many ways polar phenomena. [...] After the great clean-up act, the overcoming of Architecture in the Fundamental Acts (lyrical autobiography as architecture) [Superstudio, 1972-73], we truly enter the age of post-modernism : the final of utopian speculation in the metaphorical Exodus [Rem Koolhaas and Elia Zenghelis with Madelon Vriesendorp and Zoe Zenghelis, 1972] and the return to the 'traditional city' in Krier's [Project for the New Quartier of] La Villette [1976].* [32]

For many, Leon Krier's project is the first clear expression of what will become the New Urbanism movement in the United States a decade later. [33] Although repeatedly criticized by contemporary architects, the fact that this movement is still active two decades later is a testimony to the relevance of Krier's ideology. However, a survey of all academic publications referring to Krier's work for the 1976 La Villette Park competition shows that while still recurrently referred to, it has never gained the same recognition as the entries of Bernard Tschumi and OMA/Rem Koolhaas for the 1982 competition **[Fig.14]**. [34] Leon Krier's 1976 entry might not be labeled "experimental architecture" but it nonetheless contained ideas that had an impact on the architecture that followed.

The comparison between the 1976 and the 1982 La Villette Park competitions shows that the type of the competition (idea vs. project) does not have a direct impact on the type of architecture produced. Both competitions have produced ideology-rooted projects, although, contrary to what could have been thought, the one that generated the most forward-thinking entries was the project competition.

## Stability of the Architectural Discipline

The fourth hypothesis that could explain the remarkable production of "experimental architecture" in the context of the La Villette Park competition is totally independent of the competition process. In his introduction to the book on the 1983 Tête Défense competition, Joseph Belmont, president of the Administrative Board of the Etablissement public pour l'aménagement de La Défense, links the need for architecture competitions with the status of the architecture discipline :

> *Ten years ago, it was easy to choose an architect, one only had to nominate the best at a time when there was one international form of architecture. Nowadays it is much more difficult, because architecture is bubbling with ideas and expanding in all directions, so the choice of a creator goes hand in hand with that of a school of architecture. For this reason, it seemed advisable to organize a competition for the Tête Défense operation, as being the best way to provoke the spontaneous emergence of an architecture for our epoch, and to avoid any arbitrary selection.* [35]

At the beginning of the 1980s, the field of architecture is going through a period of major crisis and instability, as postmodernism is increasingly criticized and abandoned. As previously noted, the La Villette Park competition was the subject of two distinct competitions : the first in 1976 and the second in 1982. Bernard Tschumi presented schemes for both competitions **[Fig.4] [Fig.15]**. As he states himself in a 2001 interview, the projects are very different :

> *It is at this time that I became conscious of the limits of composition. Strategically, methodologically and formally, I did not like at all the project of 1976... But after that, I worked a lot, mainly at a theoretical level, and this was the right choice given that I could win the 1982 competition... Between the two competitions, a generation leap took place... A new generation emerged.* [36]

This "generation leap" mentioned by Tschumi required new tools, new theories : in other words, a new architectural language. Theoretical research carried out by architects

**Fig. 16**
Schematic diagram of the
architecture competition process.
*Diagram : Bechara Helal.*

such as Tschumi and Koolhaas was precisely aimed at defining this new language. In a monograph dedicated to Tschumi's completed La Villette Park project, architecture journalist Alain Orlandini devotes a whole chapter — one sixth of the book — to what he calls a "body of doctrine" developed by Bernard Tschumi in relation with the design of the competition proposal. [37] The characteristics of this "body of doctrine" as listed by Orlandini clearly situate it in reaction to the instabilities of the postmodern world and in the continuity of the work of the preceding avant-gardes :

- *The incertitude of the postmodern world — which calls for the design of "neutral" spaces permitting modes of appropriation not defined a priori ;*
- *The complexity of the postmodern world — which renders obsolete "all-encompassing" composition schemes in favour of spatial structures dealing with density and rupture ;*
- *The artificiality of the postmodern world — which speaks in favour of a design of the park as an artefact ;*
- *The urbanization of the territory — which would imply a "built" approach of the concept of the park ;*
- *The acceleration of the historical time — which would call for the production of "dynamic" spaces ;*

- *The Surrealist Beauty — which, by replacing the concept of harmony with the notions of shock and incompatibility, would enable the staging of an "un-consciousness" of the social ;*
- *The avant-gardes — which, because they acknowledge the loss of meaning, would call for the production of a project "devoid of meaning." [38]*

The architectural discipline was shaken by a number of crises during the twentieth century. The break from classicism in the 1920s and the fall of modernism in the 1960s were some of them. These dates coincide with new efforts in architectural theorization and an important production of "experimental architecture." [39] As architecture lives through a new crisis in the 1980s, the discipline was in need of new theories and the 1982 La Villette Park competition timing was ideal for the experimental proposals of Tschumi and Koolhaas.

According to the fourth hypothesis discussed here, the remarkable production of "experimental architecture" is linked, not to the architecture competition as a process, but rather to the disciplinary dynamics shaping the field of architecture. The 1982 competition for the La Villette

Park simply happened to take place at a key moment in the history of architecture, when, in the wake of postmodernism, the time was ripe for new architectural theories and practices. However, one could argue that, ever since the beginning of the 1980s, the field of architecture has been in a state of constant crisis as it is subjected to an unending influx of new theories and practices. In a way, this would mean that contemporary architecture competitions are more likely to see "experimental architecture" be produced than ever before.

## ▬▬ The Architecture Competition as an Experimental Process

As we have seen, the Park de La Villette competition is remarkable, in part, because it has enabled the production of two of the most important examples of recent "experimental architecture." It would however be wrong to pretend that, building on this study, *all* architecture competitions generate such architecture. Many factors can influence the type of architecture produced in response to a competition. The ones we have discussed here — the competition program, the composition of the jury, the type of competition, and the disciplinary crisis — are only some of them. Operating on these factors might potentially encourage the competitors to submit projects that can be labeled as "experimental architecture," but, in truth, if architectural competitions can sometimes generate experimental architecture, they do not do so consistently. However, a further study of the Park de La Villette case brings to light another, more consistent link between architecture competitions and experimentation. After having considered the notion of experimentation from the point of view of the result, let us now consider it from the point of view of the process: in what way can architecture competitions be considered experimental processes?

The architectural competition is a process through which a project is selected in response to a given architectural problem (usually defined by a context and a program). The selection process goes through a number of phases, the first of which is the formulation of the competition brief, which is submitted to a number of competitors (limited in the case of a closed competition, unlimited in the case of an open competition). Each of these competitors then produces a solution to the given problem. All these solutions are then subjected to an evaluation process, which can be subdivided into three general phases: a phase of analysis where the proposals are studied independently; a phase of

categorization where the proposals are compared to each other; and finally, a phase of evaluation where an optimal solution is identified (the winning project). In the case of a two-phase competition, the evaluation phase will end with the identification of a number of schemes, which will then go through another cycle of development and evaluation ending with the selection of a winning project. However, the evaluation phase could also end with a reassessment of the whole process and the formulation of a new competition problem.

This simplified description of the competition process is clearly analogous to the research process of the experimental method in science previously described **[Fig.2]**, which makes it possible to propose a similar diagram for the competition process **[Fig.16]**. This reading builds a series of analogical links between sets of variables and operations: the competition program and the research question; designing a project and designing a project; evaluating according to judgment criteria in both cases; etc. One could also link the selection of a winning project with the construction of a scientific fact, although it must be stressed that these elements do not hold the same weight: the former is relative (the selected project is judged as being the best of a set), while the latter is absolute (a scientific fact is a reflection of a certain physical truth[40]).

The proposed competition process diagram shows clearly that the results of the competition process are not limited to the selection of a winning project: the process generates, in addition to the chosen final scheme, a number of other non-winning proposals. These could be seen as the results of a large array of individual experiments. With the attention generally focused on the winning scheme of a competition, these projects tend to be discarded and forgotten. But it is possible to incorporate them into a database, just as the results of scientific experiments are annotated, categorized and archived. It is precisely such a database of projects that was compiled in the case of the 1982 Park de La Villette competition by the Etablissement public du Parc de La Villette, in the form of a published book containing all the competition entries **[Fig.17]**.[41] These are organized in three large chapters: the first chapter ("Casting Out the Nine") details the nine projects that were selected for the second phase, while the second chapter ("The Seven Families") presents the general schemes of all the other entries categorized in seven groups, each group characterized by a specific approach to the competition problem. Finally, a third chapter ("God is in the Details") focuses on

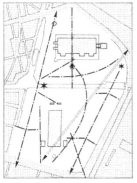

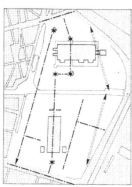

**Fig. 18**
Comparative analyses carried out by Lodewijk Baljon
of the alignments of different entries for the 1982 La
Villette competition : from the top down and from left
to right, the proposals are those of Franco Zagari,
Bakker and Bleeker, Hirochi Hara, and Zaha Hadid.
*Source : Lodewijk Baljon (1995).*

how specific elements of the program (play areas, kiosks, signage, furniture, fences, etc) were tackled by the competitors. A categorized archive of partially analyzed projects, the book summing up the Park de La Villette 1982 competition is clearly a database of raw information.

But raw information is simply an addition of meaningless data and remains at the state of potential knowledge. An operation of theorization is required in order to transform it into actualized knowledge. It is precisely this theorization that landscape architect Lodewijk Baljon carried out through his doctoral studies at the Wageningen University. Baljon had participated to the 1982 La Villette Park competition as a member of Bakker and Bleeker (NL), one of the nine joint winners of the first phase of the competition. His Ph.D. thesis focused on the new principles in landscape design that were showcased in the context of the La Villette Park competition and was the basis of a book entitled *Designing Parks : An Examination of Contemporary Approaches to Design in Landscape Architecture, Based on a Comparative Design Analysis of Entries for the Concours International : Parc de La Villette, Paris, 1982-3.* [42] Baljon's book goes beyond the simple raw data presented in the 1984 book published by the Etablissement public du Parc de La Villette. After a first section that serves as an introduction to the question of urban parks in general and to the specific case of the La Villette Park competition, a second section presents a comparative analysis of a selection of fifty competition entries described as follows :

> Our analysis consists of four successive decompositions : firstly, the decomposition of the park as a (representation of a) graphic composition ; secondly, the decomposition of the layout and the spatial coherence of the park ; thirdly, the decomposition of the design principles ; and fourthly, the analysis of the styling of the design. [43]

The intent behind this comparative analysis is to "reveal the concept behind the design" **[Fig.18]**. [44] The results of the analysis are then studied and reflected upon in a third section, which concludes with a meaningful description of the major characteristics of contemporary approaches to landscape design. Baljon's work is clearly the transformation of raw case-specific information into actualized disciplinary knowledge through an operation of theorization.

While the goal of the competition was to select a project for a very specific architectural problem, the process itself enabled the production of a larger array of data that had the potential of going beyond the limited time and space of the project itself in order to inform the discipline as a whole. The projects by Tschumi and OMA/Koolhaas for the La Villette Park may have been experimental in form, but the competition process is, in itself, experimental, in the sense that it generates not only formal objects but also potential knowledge.

### ▬ The Competition Project as "an Offering to Architecture"

In her introduction to the catalogue of the *Experimental Tradition* exhibition, Lipstadt cites architect Louis I. Kahn, who is reported to have described "the competition project as an offering to architecture." [45] For Lipstadt, this is taken to mean that the architect working on a competition proposal must invest a lot of effort while being financed in a limited way, and, in the end, does not get much in return. There is however another way of understanding Kahn's quote. The competition project can be seen as a true "offering": an object holding new ideas offered with a sense of selflessness as a contribution to the larger discipline of architecture. Only one of the entries in a competition will eventually become a realized project, but every single proposal has the potential to enrich — or even transform — the discipline. In that sense, the competition process is truly an experimental process as it generates, above all, knowledge.

This is precisely what the case study of the La Villette Park competition teaches us: on one hand, it shows us is that there is more to architectural competitions than the qualities of their winning schemes. Given the right conditions, architectural competitions can produce formal solutions that can be labeled as "experimental architecture." These will provide not only answers to the competition problem, but also ask new questions that will, in turn, influence the future theories and practices of the discipline. On the other hand, the La Villette Park competition show us that the competition process can also produce knowledge that is not limited to the sole context of the problem to be solved. The archives compiling all the projects generated through the competition process become databases of raw information that architecture researchers can use to build new theoretical knowledge that become a direct contribution to the discipline as a whole.

In few words, used to their full extent, architecture competitions can be experimental in the sense that they will have an impact on the future of the discipline through the construction of knowledge. Maybe the best way to sum this up is by referring back to the point of view of architecture critic Talbot F. Hamlin on the subject of competitions, as quoted by Lipstadt, who wrote, in 1938:

*Competitions lead inevitably to experimentation in design, and the effect of the experimentation will be seen not only in the building finally erected, but even more in the education they give to juries, to architects, to clients and to the public.* [46]

### ▬ Notes

[1] "The Experimental Tradition: 25 Years of American Architecture Competitions, 1960-1985" exhibition, organized by the Architectural League of New York and curated by architectural researcher Hélène Lipstadt, was presented at the National Academy of Design in New York from May 17th to July 31st, 1988. It featured ten pivotal design competitions held in the United States over the previous twenty-five years.

[2] Hélène Lipstadt, "Experimenting with the Experimental Tradition, 1989-2009: On Competitions and Architecture Research," *Nordic Journal of Architecture Research* 21, no. 2/3 (2009): 12.

[3] *The Experimental Tradition: Essays on Competitions in Architecture* (New York, N.Y.: Architectural League of New York; Princeton Architectural Press, 1989).

[4] The word 'experimentation' (and terms related to it, such as 'experiment' or 'experimental') is used only 11 times in the whole catalogue, which is much lower than the 104 occurrences of the term 'tradition.'

[5] Hélène Lipstadt, «The Experimental Tradition,» in *The Experimental Tradition: Essays on Competitions in Architecture*, ed. Hélène Lipstadt (New York, N.Y.: Architectural League of New York; Princeton Architectural Press, 1989), 9.

[6] One can't even find a clear definition of 'experimental architecture' in the book published by avant-garde architect and Archigram member Peter Cook on the subject; see Peter Cook, *Experimental Architecture* (New York,: Universe Books, 1970).

[7] Aaron Betsky, "Experimental Architecture," in *The Metapolis Dictionary of Advanced Architecture: City, Technology and Society in the Information Age, ed. Manuel Gausa and Instituto Metápolis de Arquitectura Avanzado* (Barcelona: Actar, 2003).

[8] On the transformation of scientific thinking and the advent of experimentation, see chapters 4 to 6 of Chunglin Kwa, *Styles of Knowing: A New History of Science from Ancient Times to the Present* (Pittsburgh: University of Pittsburgh Press, 2011). Philosopher Ian Hacking presents a clear survey of the debates surrounding the relationship between experimentation and theory in Part B ("Intervening") of Ian Hacking, *Representing and Intervening: Introductory Topics in the Philosophy of Natural Science* (Cambridge; New York: Cambridge University Press, 1983).

[9] Aleksandr Rodchenko, "Everything Is Experiment," in *Aleksandr Rodchenko: Experiments for the Future: Diaries, Essays, Letters, and Other Writings*, ed. Aleksandr N. Lavrentiev (New York: Museum of Modern Art, 2005), 109.

[10] Walter Benjamin, "Moscow," in *Selected Writings - Volume 2, Part 1, 1927-1930*, ed. Michael William Jennings, Howard Eiland, and Gary Smith (Cambridge, Mass.: Belknap Press, 1996), 28-29.

11 François Chaslin presents a thorough history of both competitions in François Chaslin, *Les Paris De François Mitterrand : Histoire Des Grands Projets Architecturaux*, Collection Folio/Actuel (Paris : Gallimard, 1985).

12 Mitterrand's *Grandes Opérations d'Architecture et d'Urbanisme program* — also known as the *Grands Travaux* or *Grands Projets Culturels* — included eleven projects in Paris (of which the Grande Arche de La Défense; the Grand Louvre; the Musée d'Orsay; the Institut du Monde Arabe; the new Ministry of Finance; the Opéra Bastille; the Cité de la Musique; the Cité des Sciences et Techniques and the La Villette), five projects in the rest of France and even one project outside of Metropolitan France (the Tjibaou Cultural Centre in Noumea, New Caledonia). All these public projects — excluding the Grand Louvre which was directly entrusted to Chinese American architect I.M.Pei — were completed through national or international architecture competitions.

13 The nine finalists were Bernard Tschumi, architect (USA) ; Office for Metropolitan Architecture (OMA)/Rem Koolhaas, architect (GB), Bernard Lassus, landscape architect (F) ; Gilles Vexlard, landscape architect (F) ; Sven Ingvar Andersson, architect / landscape architect (DK) ; Arriola/Fiol/Gali/Quintana, architects (ES) ; Alexandre Chemetoff, architect / landscape architect (F) ; Bakker & Bleeker, landscape architects (NL) ; Jacques Gouvernec, architect, with Jean-Pierre Raynaud, landscape architect (FR).

14 Bernard Tschumi, *The Manhattan Transcripts* (London : Academy Editions, 1981). and *Architectural Manifestoes*, Revised and expanded [ed.] ed. (London : Architectural Association, 1979).

15 *The City of the Captive Globe* is the work of a 1972 collaboration between Rem Koolhaas, Elia Zenghelis, Madelon Vriesendorp and Zoe Zenghelis (who were to later found OMA in 1975). It was reprinted in a slightly modified form in Rem Koolhaas, *Delirious New York : A Retroactive Manifesto for Manhattan* (New York : Oxford University Press, 1978), 243-45.

16 Bernard Tschumi interviewed in Marianne Barzilay, Catherine Hayward, and Lucette Lombard - Valentino, eds., *L'invention Du Parc : Parc De La Villette, Paris. Concours International, International Competition 1982-1983* (Paris : Graphite Editions; Établissement Public du Parc de la Villette, 1984), 28.

17 Presentation text - presentation text, Phase 2 La Villette Park International Competition, 1983 also in Rem Koolhaas et al., *S, M, L, Xl* (New York, N.Y. : Monacelli Press, 1995), 934.

18 The number of references for a given year was found by using the Google Scholar search tool (www.google.com/scholar/). A search for simultaneous mentions to both "La Villette" and Tschumi was used to establish the number of written references to Tschumi's project, while a more complex search string ("La Villette" AND Koolhaas OR OMA) was used to find references to OMA's competition proposal.

19 Tschumi's project for the La Villette Park was also the subject of a special event in October 2005 of *Supercrit*, a series organized by *EXP*, the *Research Center for Experimental Practice in Architecture* at the University of Westminster, which "revisits some of the most influential projects of the recent past and examines their impact on the way we think and design today." This even was followed by a publication, Samantha Hardingham and Kester Rattenbury, eds., *Bernard Tschumi : Parc De La Villette*, Supercrit (Oxon : Routledge, 2012). Other events of *Supercrit* focused, amongst others, on work by Cedric Price (*Potteries Thinkbelt*, 1966), Robert Venturi and Denise Scott Brown (*Learning from Las Vegas*, 1972), Richard Rogers (*Centre Pompidou*, 1971-77) and Rem Koolhaas (*Delirious New York*, 1978).

20 Présidence de la République Française, "Parc De La Villette : Communique from the Presidency of the Republic," news release, 8th April, 1982, 8th April, 1982.

21 Françoise Choay, "Critique," *Princeton journal : Landscape* 2 (1985) : 211-14.

22 Koolhaas et al., *S, M, L, Xl*, 921.

23 The person in charge of the program was Christian Dupavillon, architect at the Ministry of Culture. Dupavillon has worked on the programs on many of the competitions of Mitterrand's *Grandes Opérations d'Architecture et d'Urbanisme* program. According to sociologist and architecture researcher Jean-Louis Violeau, Dupavillon often repeated that a competition program should never be longer than two sides of a single sheet of paper. The complexity Choay mentions has less to do with the number of programmatic elements than with the relations between them.

24 The ability to ask new questions in order to find new answers is one of the main characteristics of the "experimental architect" as described by American architect Lebbeus Woods, co-founder of the *Research Institute for Experimental Architecture (RIEA)*. See Lebbeus Woods, "Introduction," in *Riea/Research Institute for Experimental Architecture : The First Conference* (New York, N.Y. : Princeton Architectural Press, 1990).

25 From the onset of her article, Choay states upfront, and not without heavy irony, that "according to the established order, Rem Koolhaas' project... could not possibly have won the competition : it was, by far, the best entry." (Choay, "Critique," 211.)

26 Ibid., 214.

27 Chaslin, Les Paris De François Mitterrand : Histoire Des Grands Projets Architecturaux, 61.

28 Giovanni Cerami, *Il Giardino E La Città : Il Progetto Del Parco Urbano in Europa* (Roma : Laterza, 1996), 171.

29 Geert Bekaert, "'Une Mise À Nu De L'architecture Par Ses Adorateurs Mêmes' : Maurice Culot and Leon Krier : A Forgotten Episode," in *Exit Utopia : Architectural Provocations, 1956-76*, ed. Martin van Schaik and Otakar MáĐel (New York, NY : Prestel, 2005), 305.

30 Vincent Scully, "Where Is Modern Architecture Going?," *GA (Global Architecture) Document* 1 (1980).

31 The congress was held at the Faculty of Architecture in Delft University of Technology on January 26-27, 2000 and was followed by the publication of *Exit Utopia : Architectural Provocations, 1956-76* in 2005. Martin van Schaik, "Introduction," in *Exit Utopia : Architectural Provocations, 1956-1976*, ed. Martin van Schaik and Otakar MáĐel (Munich : Prestel, 2005), 9.

32 Ibid.

33 It is only in 1993 that the Congress for the New Urbanism was founded in Chicago, IL.

34 As for the academic references to the projects of Tschumi and Koolhaas, the number of references to Leon Krier's 1976 project was found by using the search string "La Villette" AND "Leon Krier" in the Google Scholar search tool (www.google.com/scholar/).

35 Joseph Belmont, "Pourquoi Un Concours? / Why Hold a Competition?," in *423 Et 1 Projets Pour La Tête Défense : Le Concours International D'architecture De 1983*, ed. Établissement Public pour l'Aménagement de la Région de La Défense (Paris : Electa Moniteur, 1989), 7.

36 Bernard Tschumi interviewed by Alain Orlandini in Alain Orlandini, *Le Parc De La Villette De Bernard Tschumi, Un Architecte, Une Œuvre* (Paris : Somogy, 2001), 96.

37 "Chapter III — Bernard Tschumi : A Body of Doctrine" in ibid., 30-43.

38 Ibid., 9.

39 One could think, for example, of the work of the Russian Constructivists and the new approach to architectural education of the Bauhaus in the 1920s. In the 1960s, experimental work was produced by architectural groups such as Archigram, Superstudio, and Archizoom, while the Architectural Association in London became a radical center of architecture education. Having either studied or taught at the Architectural Association, both Koolhaas and Tschumi were very familiar with these movements as we have previously noted.

40 It is important to note that many philosophers and scientists, such as Bruno Latour, have defended the idea that scientific facts are only true until they are falsified, therefore undermining the notion of absolute truth in science. See Bruno Latour and Steve Woolgar, *Laboratory Life : The Social Construction of Scientific Facts*, Sage Library of Social Research (Beverly Hills : Sage Publications, 1979).

41 Barzilay, Hayward, and Lombard - Valentino, *L'invention Du Parc : Parc De La Villette, Paris. Concours International, International Competition 1982-1983*.

42Lodewijk Baljon, *Designing Parks : An Examination of Contemporary Approaches to Design in Landscape Architecture, Based on a Comparative Design Analysis of Entries for the Concours International, Parc De La Villette, Paris, 1982-3* (Amsterdam ; Woodbridge, Suffolk, U.K. : Architectura & Natura Press ; Garden Art Press distributor, 1995).

43 Ibid., 50.

44 Ibid.

45 Quoted in Lipstadt, "The Experimental Tradition," 10.

46 Talbot Hamlin, "Competitions," *Pencil Points* (1938) : 565. quoted in Lipstadt, "In the Shadow of the Tribune Tower," 79.

# ▬▬ References

Baljon, Lodewijk. *Designing Parks : An Examination of Contemporary Approaches to Design in Landscape Architecture, Based on a Comparative Design Analysis of Entries for the Concours International, Parc De La Villette, Paris, 1982-3*. Amsterdam ; Woodbridge, Suffolk, U.K. : Architectura & Natura Press ; Garden Art Press distributor, 1995.

Barzilay, Marianne, Catherine **Hayward**, and Lucette **Lombard-Valentino**, eds. *L'invention Du Parc : Parc De La Villette, Paris. Concours International, International Competition 1982-1983*. Paris : Graphite Editions ; Établissement Public du Parc de la Villette, 1984.

Bekaert, Geert. "'Une Mise À Nu De L'architecture Par Ses Adorateurs Mêmes' : Maurice Culot and Leon Krier : A Forgotten Episode." In *Exit Utopia : Architectural Provocations, 1956-76*, edited by Martin van Schaik and Otakar Máđel, 299-308. New York, NY : Prestel, 2005.

Belmont, Joseph. "Pourquoi Un Concours ? / Why Hold a Competition ?". In *423 Et 1 Projets Pour La Tête Défense : Le Concours International D'architecture De 1983*, edited by Établissement Public pour l'Aménagement de la Région de La Défense, 7-8. Paris : Electa Moniteur, 1989.

Benjamin, Walter. "Moscow." In *Selected Writings - Volume 2, Part 1, 1927-1930*, edited by Michael William Jennings, Howard Eiland and Gary Smith, 22-46. Cambridge, Mass. : Belknap Press, 1996.

Betsky, Aaron. "Experimental Architecture." In *The Metapolis Dictionary of Advanced Architecture : City, Technology and Society in the Information Age*, edited by Manuel Gausa and Instituto Metápolis de Arquitectura Avanzado, 208. Barcelona : Actar, 2003.

Cerami, Giovanni. *Il Giardino E La Città : Il Progetto Del Parco Urbano in Europa*. Roma : Laterza, 1996.

Chaslin, François. *Les Paris De François Mitterrand : Histoire Des Grands Projets Architecturaux*. Collection Folio/Actuel. Paris : Gallimard, 1985.

Choay, Françoise. "Critique." *Princeton journal : Landscape 2* (1985) : 211-20.

Cook, Peter. *Experimental Architecture*. New York, : Universe Books, 1970.

Darian, Steven G. *Understanding the Language of Science*. Austin : University of Texas Press, 2003.

Hacking, Ian. *Representing and Intervening : Introductory Topics in the Philosophy of Natural Science*. Cambridge ; New York : Cambridge University Press, 1983.

Hamlin, Talbot. "Competitions." *Pencil Points* (September 1938 1938) : 565.

Hardingham, Samantha, and Kester **Rattenbury**, eds. *Bernard Tschumi : Parc De La Villette*, Supercrit, vol. 4. Oxon : Routledge, 2012.

Koolhaas, Rem. *Delirious New York : A Retroactive Manifesto for Manhattan*. New York : Oxford University Press, 1978.

Koolhaas, Rem, Bruce **Mau**, Jennifer **Sigler**, Hans **Werlemann**, and Office for Metropolitan Architecture. *S, M, L, Xl*. New York, N.Y. : Monacelli Press, 1995.

Kwa, Chunglin. *Styles of Knowing : A New History of Science from Ancient Times to the Present*. Pittsburgh : University of Pittsburgh Press, 2011.

Latour, Bruno, and Steve **Woolgar.** *Laboratory Life : The Social Construction of Scientific Facts*. Sage Library of Social Research. Beverly Hills : Sage Publications, 1979.

Lipstadt, Hélène. "The Experimental Tradition." In *The Experimental Tradition : Essays on Competitions in Architecture*, edited by Hélène Lipstadt, 9-19. New York, N.Y. : Architectural League of New York ; Princeton Architectural Press, 1989.

Lipstadt, Hélène, ed. *The Experimental Tradition : Essays on Competitions in Architecture*. New York, N.Y. : Architectural League of New York ; Princeton Architectural Press, 1989.

Lipstadt, Hélène. "Experimenting with the Experimental Tradition, 1989-2009 : On Competitions and Architecture Research." *Nordic Journal of Architecture Research 21*, no. 2/3 (2009) : 9-22.

Lipstadt, Hélène. "In the Shadow of the Tribune Tower." In *The Experimental Tradition : Essays on Competitions in Architecture*, edited by Hélène Lipstadt, 79. New York, N.Y. : Architectural League of New York ; Princeton Architectural Press, 1989.

Orlandini, Alain. *Le Parc De La Villette De Bernard Tschumi* [in fre]. Un Architecte, Une Œuvre. Paris : Somogy, 2001.

Présidence de la République Française. "*Parc De La Villette : Communique from the Presidency of the Republic*." news release, 8th April, 1982, 8th April, 1982.

Rodchenko, Aleksandr. "Everything Is Experiment." In *Aleksandr Rodchenko : Experiments for the Future : Diaries, Essays, Letters, and Other Writings*, edited by Aleksandr N. Lavrentiev, 439. New York : Museum of Modern Art, 2005.

Scully, Vincent. "Where Is Modern Architecture Going ?". *GA (Global Architecture) Document 1* (Summer 1980 1980) : 6-11.

Tschumi, Bernard. *Architectural Manifestoes*. Revised and expanded [ed.] ed. London : Architectural Association, 1979.

Tschumi, Bernard. *The Manhattan Transcripts*. London : Academy Editions, 1981.

Van Schaik, Martin. "Introduction." In *Exit Utopia : Architectural Provocations, 1956-1976*, edited by Martin van Schaik and Otakar Máđel, 8-9. Munich : Prestel, 2005.

Woods, Lebbeus. "Introduction." In *Riea/Research Institute for Experimental Architecture : The First Conference*, unpaginated. New York, N.Y. : Princeton Architectural Press, 1990.

4.1. Competitions as Laboratories — Helal

253

# 4.2. The Canadian Competitions Catalogue

**Digital Libraries of Projects as Collective Legacy**

**Jean-Pierre Chupin**, Ph.D.
Director of the Research Chair on Competitions
and Contemporary Practices in Architecture
Université de Montréal
Canada

After presenting a short history of the *Canadian Competitions Catalogue* (CCC) (www.ccc.umontreal.ca), we propose to reflect on a decade of personal experience in the building and use of digital libraries of competitions projects, here presented as "Electronic Libraries of Projects" (ELP). From a more epistemological perspective, we question the problematic location of the entity "clients" in the ontological structure of any competition database as an invitation to recognize that the logical structure of a specifically designed and long-tested relational database, such as the CCC, already offers itself as a theoretical reconstruction of this complex temporal phenomenon called "design competition." We conclude with an appeal to develop and connect multiple libraries of competition projects, at an international level, as a form of recognition of the inherent value of the numerous unbuilt architectures produced through competitions. Indeed, this world of possibilities, solutions and ideas should be seen as contributing to an extensive reservoir of "potential architecture" partaking of a collective legacy, if not a world heritage, of environmental design projects.

**Cover**
Island of Utopia. Plate from Thomas More, *Libellus vere aureus nec minus salutaris quam festivus de optimo reipublicae statu, deque nova insula Utopia*, Louvain (1516).

## Overview of the Canadian Competitions Catalogue (CCC)

The Canadian Competitions Catalogue (CCC) is the digital and bilingual library (French and English) for architecture, urban design, and landscape architecture projects designed in the context of competitions in Canada.[1]

The Canadian Competitions Catalogue (CCC) was created in 2002 by three researchers at the Laboratoire d'étude de l'architecture potentielle,[2] namely, Jean-Pierre Chupin, Denis Bilodeau and Georges Adamczyk, in order to facilitate comparative research on contemporary architecture. In 2006, the CCC became partially accessible to the public through a web interface, gradually becoming a true collective resource with few equivalents worldwide. Since 2012, the CCC is a publication of the *Research Chair on Competitions and Contemporary Practices in Architecture* at the Université de Montréal **[Fig.1]**.[3]

In July 2014, this vast library of projects already comprised information and documentation on over 126 of the 361 listed competitions, which corresponded to nearly 3,255 projects and 38,060 documents related to projects imagined or realized in Canada since the middle of the twentieth century. This collective resource is regularly updated in accordance with the advancement of research projects, but its updates are more and more frequent thanks to the generosity of professional firms and competition organizers across the country.

The CCC is not an endeavour controlled by professional corporations, it remains directed by scientific goals and above all it remains firm on one sustaining principle: every project, even those that are not laureate and even not realized, should be considered as both a source of knowledge and new ideas. Along with this principle, the CCC earned much recognition from the Canada Foundation for Innovation (CFI) in 2012. Seeking to construct the present, each project anticipates the future, while reflecting on the past. The spotlight projected upon the winner of a competition is perhaps what blinds us from seeing that the non-winning projects are not merely the remains of a selection process, but represent "potential architectures" with an equally important role in the edification of cultures and societies. Submitted to the challenge and rigour of a collective and qualitative judgement, each competition proposal seeks a better way of redefining our living environments, as a manifesto for the quality of our buildings and places.

Within the framework of a major grant obtained from the Canada Foundation for Innovation and the Quebec Ministère de l'Enseignement supérieur, de la Recherche, de la Science et de la Technologie, but also thanks to funding from the Fonds Québécois de Recherche sur la Société et Culture, from the Office of Research and Development at the University of Montreal, and its Faculté de l'aménagement, the Research Chair on Competitions and Contemporary Practices in Architecture has entirely redesigned its relational and documentary database in 2013-2014. The new infrastructure, unveiled to the public on February 2014, optimizes and systematizes the study of competitions understood as privileged experimental situations, allowing for a comparative analysis of projects and design strategies, identifying technical innovation, and contributing to the history of Canada's built environment.

The public website of the CCC offers the maximum information on competitions and projects, and uses the best of contemporary technology in terms of global positioning, visual indexing, search tools and interactive display. A specialized dynamic web-based interface for simple data consultation is now compatible with many mobile platforms available to researchers, professionals and the greater public (with access restricted to public data). For competitions organized prior to 1995, where documents were not in digital format, the new system allows for the production of on-site digital documentation in firms or archives, which include hemispherical photographic animations of physical models (3D photography by Ortery Technologies) **[Fig.2]**.

Considering that in a digital library of projects, each competition is exemplary for conducting scientific comparisons — and in fact constitutes a research project in its own right — and considering, above all, that each architectural, urban planning, design, or landscaping project is a true object of research and of culture, we expect that the new infrastructure of the Canadian Competitions Catalogue will become an unparalleled scientific research resource within a few years. By allowing a cross-comparative analysis of thousands of projects, the CCC resource is expected to grow comparable, relatively speaking, to the great databases that precipitated the dramatic evolution of knowledge in many fields.

## What is a "Client" in a Theoretical Model of the Competition Phenomena?

Of an epistemological nature, and considering the need for ontological definitions in parallel to ongoing case studies on competitions in the world, we propose to address the paradoxical definitions of "client" and "clients" in a general theoretical framework for research on competitions. A simple comparison of two types of electronic resources on competitions, mainly typical websites and online databases, can support a questioning of common representations (if not clichés), and potential controversies about the gap between clients and designers in the process. Competitions are often said to establish a distance between clients and designers. We formulate the hypothesis that this preconceived representation comes in part from the communicational and media potential of competitions rather than the design / judgement process itself and that it comes from a misunderstanding of what a competition represents. In our digital age, the impact of competitions websites on the dissemination of some clichés about competitions cannot be underestimated.

How can we define the notion of client in a theoretical model of the competition process? While it is clear that a competition is a temporal phenomenon involving a great variety of actors, it is more difficult to define, a priori, what a client represents in this process. One might argue that there are various clients all along the process. To the question: "who is the client?", a possible answer may be: "the one who launches and ends the competition." This answer is unsatisfying since a professional organiser can perform these actions without being the client, even more so if we admit that this service, as a professional act, precisely is addressed to a client, either private or institutional. The head librarian may be considered the client of a competition for a new public library when she is in fact only one of the representatives of the public mandate giver, depending on the various levels of hierarchy.

In this intertwining of responsibilities, typical of public spaces and places, the "client" either tends to be seen at one extreme or the other of the chain of decisions. However, can a administrative director or even a minister of culture or of education be considered the client of a school or a library, when everybody in a democracy is eligible to receive the title of client of a public space or building?

A sociological answer will not be more satisfying by replacing the client with the user. Client and user are not synonymous entities; furthermore they tend to belong

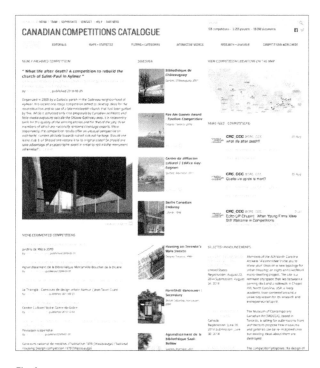

**Fig. 1**
Screen shot of the Canadian Competitions Catalogue web site designed by the Research Chair on Competitions at Université de Montréal.
*http://www.ccc.umontreal.ca*

**Fig. 2**
Still view of an interactive (3D) photography of a competition model as displayed on the Canadian Competitions Catalogue. Project by Chevalier & Morales, architects, Montreal.

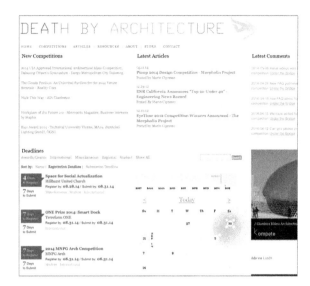

**Fig. 3**
Front page of the Deathbyarchitecture website
*www.deathbyarchitecture.com* pioneer of all websites
displaying announcements and basic
data on competitions.

**Fig. 4**
Front page of the EuropaConcorsi website
*www.europaconcorsi.com*, an example of a user
generated content website on competitions projects.

to opposite sides of the project in architectural terms. Although designers must work with some representation of the user, and while there obviously are users of buildings, there is no user of a "project" per se. In other words, if we stay within the logical structure of a competition, the user is implicit during the process and becomes explicit only when the building is realised. On the contrary, and logically speaking, everybody should be considered a client in a competition process for a public building, including designers themselves. Like the notion of "user," the notion of "client" is not easy to circumscribe at an epistemological level.

But there is an entity, typical of the competition process, which is entitled to behave as a potential client, and that is the "jury." Indeed, we can consider, by definition, that the jury theoretically is the representative of the public in a competition. As such, the jury is the ultimate, albeit temporary, client to which designers submit their projects. In other words the jury is the closest representation of an "ideal model of the clients" formulated by a specific competition framework. To make this even clearer, and to use an extreme case, it is not rare to see private organisers perverting the collective nature of a jury by asking to be the sole members of a jury for a private building and to see public organisers' dream of the same kind of restrictive jury composition. The weight of French president François Mitterand in the questionable judging of some famous competitions in Paris in the 1980s is well known in that respect, as shown by French critic and journalist François Chaslin. [4]

In general, juries are composed to be representatives of public interest and some competition rules consider that neither the elected politicians nor the administrative representative should be a jury member, as they can be tempted to emphasize political or institutional interests above general public needs. In fact, the history of competitions is a testimony of the difficult equilibrium requested to compose a fair, knowledgeable and "representative" jury and I would even add that the history of competitions is a slow and ongoing movement toward the democratic recognition of public interest: the same way that the history of the Internet mirrors the tensions between transparent communication and manipulative propaganda.

In the following two sections we evaluate both explicit and implicit representations of clients, first in a general survey of competitions websites and second in a more scientific database like our own Canadian Competitions Catalogue. This comparison is not meant to act as a methodological apparatus, but mainly as a reflective device.

## Where are the "clients" in the pages of various websites on competitions?

More than 150 websites on competitions, from 45 countries,have already been compiled in a special on-line resource regularly updated by the Research Chair on Competition (C.R.C) and the Laboratoire d'étude de l'architecture potentielle (L.E.A.P) labs at Université de Montréal.[5]

When examined closely, it appears that dozens of competition websites give access to inconsistent levels of data and information. Although they display considerable amounts of images, these websites are rarely grounded on a coherent definition of the competition. Even a reliable resource like "competitions.org," long directed by Stanley Collyer, will often display announcements or results by considering the organisers of a competition as clients but also as "sponsors." If we take for example a case related to the Ullswater Yacht Club Design Competition, it is said that the Royal Institute of British Architect (RIBA) was the mandated sponsor and the notion of client appears only in a sentence like: "The report should also include an elemental cost statement to demonstrate how the scheme can be delivered within the client's identified budget." Although this distinction is accurate, it is clearer that this kind of informative website puts the emphasis on the competition process considered as an event in itself.

For another semi-private/semi-public competition like The spaces between: An urban ideas competition, the client is named as follows: AIA Utah YAF/ Salt Lake City Downtown Alliance in which the American Institute of Architects, Utah section is one of the clients. But it is also explained in the summary of the competition brief — as such a text coming from the organisers themselves that "Two winning projects and fifteen finalists will be eligible for the People's Choice award." In this complex case, there is a mix of collective judgement through a regular jury and public vote, which demonstrates how ambiguous the notion of client appears when we browse competition websites.

We can distinguish three types of websites and attempt to categorise them through their main purpose:
1. Billboard announcements
2. Promotional displays
3. Journals

It is difficult to qualify the first and biggest category—what we call the "billboard announcements" type of websites, but the well-known "Death By Architecture" website perhaps best illustrates this category [Fig.3].[6] This kind of calendar resource of registration deadlines is very useful and surprisingly enough, they do not come from public international organisations supposed to support competitions like the Union International des Architectes, but from personal initiatives. Mario Cipresso, in that specific case, launched his own website as early as 1995! On such online resources, relying on their power of dissemination throughout the architectural community, you will not find competitions listed by clients' names but rather by categories, deadlines, juries and all basic information needed to decide whether you want to register or not. Although "awards" are distinct processes and should not be considered as competition per se, you will find them often mixed with competitions announcements.

The second category is perhaps the most intriguing since it appears to play mostly on the communicational potential of competitions sometimes coming from clients but more often from designers. On the one end, clients' websites like Design Montreal or Montreal Ville Unesco de Design[7] in Canada, display a series of competitions in order to promote their own politics on design strategies for the enhancement and promotion of public projects. On the other end, designers' websites like the Italian "Europa Concorsi" are based on what architects upload of their own projects, sometimes even when they were runner up and not laureate.[8] As it presents itself: "it is a user-generated content architecture website" which means that participants are encouraged to publish their own projects on the platform [Fig.4]. When entering a key word in the research engine, it appears that the emphasis is placed on projects rather than on competitions and it often displays a strong disparity between search results for competitions, with only one project documented, and search results for projects, without basic information on the original competition. Also this site is supposed to document European competitions; if you type "Canada" for example, you will get fifty-three projects, one announcement and eight competitions (when our own Canadian Competitions database lists more than 300 competitions organised since 1945). It is true however, that in the case of Europaconcorsi.com, and when the information is published by the editors, you will find the clients' names, but along with project managers and general contractors and in the category of "Buildings," confirming, if necessary, that this kind of website is about architects' self promotion (about their projects or their buildings), rather than about objective documentation of competitions.

**Fig. 5**
Some results of the "client" queiry on WA
(wettbewerbe aktuell), the German website and
database on competitions complementing the
famous journal founded in the 1970's.
*www.wettbewerbe-aktuell.de/en/home.html*

"Journals," the third type of website, may be the smallest in number of items, but remains the soundest in terms of the amount of information displayed for each documented competition. Journals like the already mentioned *Competitions* in the USA or *wettbewerbe aktuell* in Germany, have a long history of objective displays of both announcements and results. A journal like *wettbewerbe aktuell* distinguishes between the clients of a competition and the clients of a project, but does not differentiate between private and public clients **[Fig.5]**. Needless to say, they started as printed journals and are now offering digital versions. One can suspect that the editorial rigor imposed by the old technologies of printed press is probably what still assures a level of discipline governing the content in these valuable cases (see section 5 of the present book).

Without operating a complete and systematic survey of online resources, we can easily guess that any potential client wishing to understand what a competition is about or how clients are being respected in the process through these websites, might find it discouraging rather than enlightening. This situation is problematic while potential clients may use such websites when trying to figure whether they should follow what appears the riskier path of a competition process. But since in most of these resources, as in mundane discussion about competitions, the emphasis is put on the winner and rarely on debating or even explaining why this project won and how it influenced the client's understanding of his or her own needs and expectations, the risk of a distorted representation of competition is increased.

The study of competitions through these websites may have a sociological pertinence as such, but research on competitions cannot expect to rely on the basic requirements of rigorous documentation as do true relational documentary databases. It seems that most competition websites propagate inappropriate myths about the competition process, first of which is that competitions are for designers and not for clients and users. It should not come as a surprise that competitions are less regarded as research objects than as fluctuating and problematic phenomena and in some cases as "generators of controversies"; but even this last issue appears to be a myth. Indeed, as shown by Bruno Latour and more particularly by Albena Yaneva in the design disciplines, design projects are, by definition, designed and built at the core of a complex network of controversies. It is not so much that design projects suffer from controversies as they are actually made of these paradoxical tensions as clearly shown by Yaneva in *Mapping Controversies in Architecture.*[9] Framed by actor-network theory, her approach allows theorizing what she calls the "architectural" rather than "architecture" that usually concentrates on buildings rather than processes. In that respect, the principles of a competition database as we would like to evaluate now, would fall into the field of architectural processes, regardless of issues of scale. It is the variety and heterogeneity of actors, which is at stake in such a representation of competitions, understood both as a procedural and as a temporal phenomenon **[Fig.6]**.

## ▬ Where are the "clients" in the ontological structure of a database of competitions?

Databases of all kinds are all too often considered as mere archival devices — as digital shelves — and when they offer a public interface on the Internet, they sometimes appear as websites. Two main differences should be underlined here: First, you can design a website page after page with no specific logical structure of the main subject, and second, you can sometimes "search" in a website but the results will rarely be comparable and structured. For example, you can design a website on bread, even to sell a variety of breads, without understanding how bread is made. You can even design a website on bread using the same structure that was used for a website on cheese. To follow this example, you may do some research on this page-by-page website, but you will not be able to compare the various types of bread. Any reliable comparison needs an ontological structure and the theoretical mapping of an entity/relation diagram of the subject. This is precisely why a database of competition projects can be considered a research tool and as such contribute to the theoretical modelling of this complex phenomenon still too often generically called "competition" **[Fig.7]**.

The first database we designed focuses on Canadian competitions and the second on a certain type of competition best known under the name Europan, still considered the largest competition-organising body in Europe. The Canadian Competitions Catalogue (CCC) aims, in the long run, to document all competitions organised in Canada since World War II. Compared to the European context, this challenge seems eventually achievable. Unlike Switzerland, which organises approximately 200 competitions a year, or Germany which organises more than 600 per year, and unlike France, where more than a thousand competitions were organised every year, at least during the 1980s and 1990s, the Canadian catalogue would cover less than 350 competitions identified between 1943 and 2013. In July of 2014, we had only achieved one-third of the task set before us. This represents, however, several thousand projects since, for some competitions, and as is the case everywhere in the world, more than a hundred teams were involved. However, it is important to underline that, across Canada, there are major geographic and cultural disparities and of the ten Canadian provinces and territories, Quebec has organised the most competitions. From this perspective, the archive already gives us an insight into contemporary Canadian history. It should also be noted that, in the majority of cases, the competitions were organised by private organisers (sometimes with a percentage of public funding), despite the fact that in Quebec, the Ministry of Culture tried to drive this process in the 1990s. North American governments have been torn between the principles of free market economics and the unpredictability of competition juries, and the very principle of competition itself. The CCC can also serve as a measuring tool to evaluate these tensions.

What about the European situation? The issue of digital data is raised to an altogether different scale, if we consider that the Europan-France phenomenon involves several thousand projects. If the Europan-Europe Catalogue, for which we have designed a prototype, provided a comprehensive record of all competitions organised since the beginning, the database would give access to more than 15,000 projects! For example, the ninth session of Europan Europe gathered more than twenty-two participating countries and offered seventy-three sites to competitors. For the French session alone, six sites were proposed to competitors, for which approximately 200 teams designed development proposals.

In summary, the Canadian Catalogue offers a relatively limited corpus, covering a very large territory, with no apparent coordination: a collection that is constantly but randomly growing, making comparative research very difficult. The Europan Catalogue likewise covers a very large territory, with a rapidly growing corpus, but there is a certain level of control and coordination from the Europan management team. Theoretically, this should ensure ideal conditions for operation, observation and comparison, both for archivists and for researchers. Nevertheless, each competition session highlights the urban and territorial issues affecting a given period. The Europan phenomenon is a bit like a snapshot of the generation of architects and the urban issues in play.

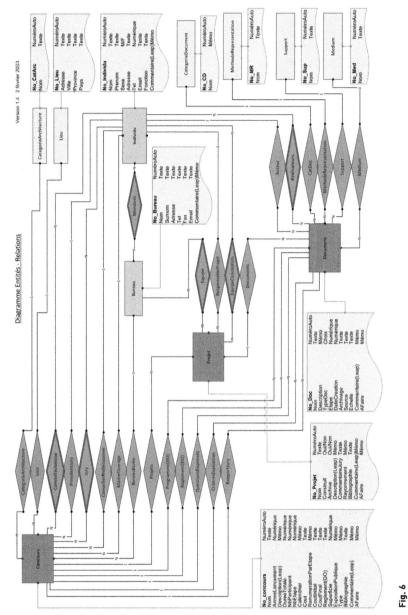

**Fig. 6**
Diagram of the general logical structure of the former 2006 version of the Canad an Competition Catalogue.

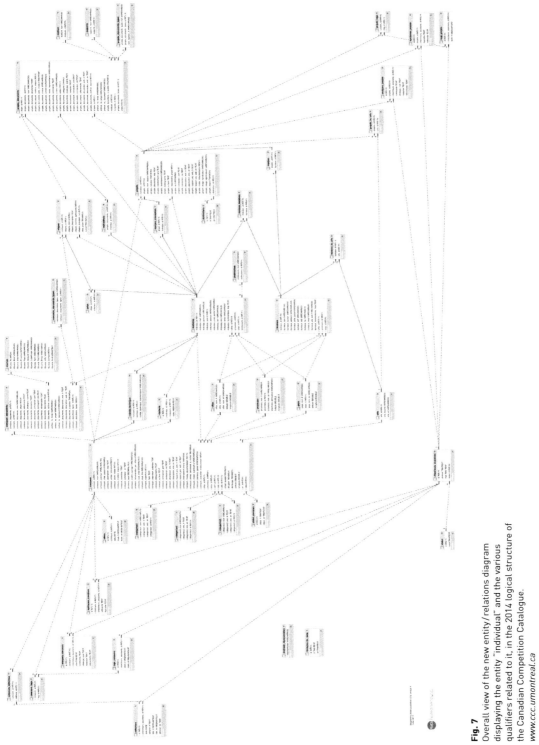

**Fig. 7**
Overall view of the new entity/relations diagram displaying the entity "individual" and the various qualifiers related to it, in the 2014 logical structure of the Canadian Competition Catalogue.
*www.ccc.umontreal.ca*

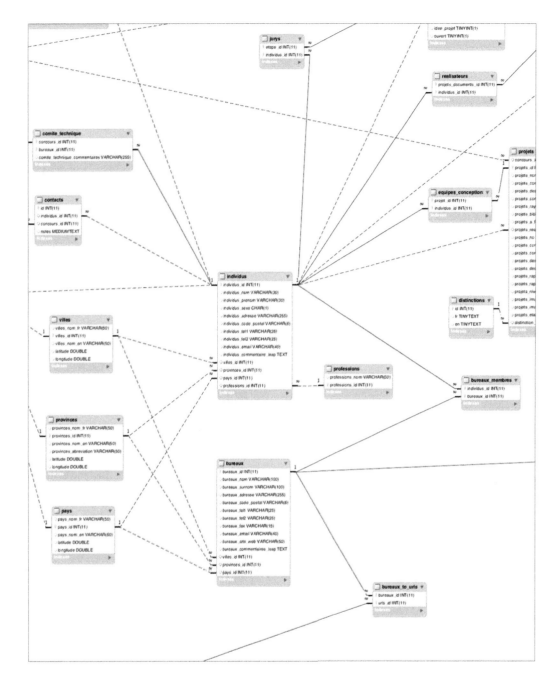

**Fig. 8**
Diagram showing various sub entities to the super-entity
individual ("individus") in the ontological hierarchical
structure of the Canadian Competition Catalogue.

For researchers, designing and compiling a documentary database—even more so a relational database—is an invitation, a challenge even, to start theorising about the phenomena through defining the contours of certain disciplinary concepts. This is, of course, the main advantage of a relational database system—enabling an architectural event, such as a competition, to be reconstituted or at least theoretically modelled to a certain extent. The bottom line is that the projects in themselves are in some ways less important in such a digital archiving system than the complex fabric of relationships that can be represented and, even more importantly, that researchers can uncover using the documentation tool. When an IT technician asks simple questions such as, "What is an architectural competition?" or "What is a design project?", "Is a project a set of procedures, a set of documents, or both?" The researcher needs to clarify some epistemological assumptions. In such an archiving endeavour it becomes necessary to take the risk of defining the relationships between research objects, if only to subsequently think more clearly about the weaknesses of the modelling hypothesis.

As in any scientific model of a phenomenon, there are ontological gaps and practical choices, which make the classificatory paradoxes of these apparently coherent ensembles closest to some difficulties encountered throughout the history of library science or even biology as described by French philosopher Michel Foucault in his seminal book *The Order of Things*[10].

In order to design the CCC, we have developed an ontological structure, which distinguishes between concepts (country, teams of designers, offices, technical committee and individuals, etc) and qualifiers or descriptive terms (categories, types of documents, stages, etc). Behind the concept "individuals," you will find at list six entities : project manager, project superintendent, professional advisor, jury member, author, etc) but the entity "client" as such, and for all the reasons developed in the introduction of this paper, does not exist in the ontological structure of our database! The notion of "project owner," although it is a poor translation of the French *maître-d'oeuvre*, would nevertheless be the closest to what a client may be in our representation of competitions **[Fig.8]**.

## Database of competition projects as scattered archives but potential libraries

However, we can already be sure that these databases will never be completed, for the simple reason that the records are at best scattered and at worst mostly destroyed. Databases and their respective search engines and web interfaces are designed to enable comparison within a single site, across different sites and according to topics suggested by the organisers etc. It goes without saying that the scale of this archiving task represented a real challenge to our organisational capacities and to our ability to convince architect offices to contribute to the undertaking.

In the case of Europan, the plethora of prints and presentation books led to the destruction of archives by the organising countries themselves **[Fig.9]**. On the other hand, for the Canadian competitions, which were more conventional in nature, it is sometimes easier to find drawings from the 1960s than digital files from the late 1990s ; and even more difficult to open and read these files 15 years later.

If we go beyond these technical issues, genuine theoretical questions can also be formulated. To do this, it is important to distinguish between two types of digital archives. Firstly, archives that aim chiefly to store and preserve (and most of such archives feature two layers : the first of which is composed of a set of digital documents and a second layer comprising an elementary contextualisation of such data). We say elementary, because when comparing what these archives offer and what we are aiming to offer, we cannot help but notice a major difference in the area of data contextualisation — our aim being to genuinely "model an architectural competition." In our case, the ordering operations went from formulating research questions to identifying the corpus, then compiling documentation and finally analysing the data. In some ways, the fact that our databases are now being used as historical records is simply one of the many paradoxes that we live with on a daily basis in research.

Although databases can appear as depositories, their first mandate is not to preserve documents, but to preserve ideas and "representations of projects." Indeed a competition database is closer to the notion of a "library of projects," than it is to a digital archive and we propose to call these digital resources ELP (Electronic Libraries of Projects). This naming is a way to underline the idea that each competition is like a book (or research object) of which each stage and even each project is like a chapter or section (and research cases or experiences). The library may not

**Fig. 9**
Front page of the Europan-France database website
designed by Laboratoire d'Étude de l'Architecture
Potentielle at Université de Montréal.
*http://www.arclab.umontreal.ca/EUROPAN-FR/listsessions.php*

**Fig. 10**
When the potential nature of any competition project is
doubled by its own title: Project submitted by Richard
Tabesse architecte et Sylvia Rochonnat entitled "La politique
de nos immenses possibilités" to Europan 6 (2000).

contain every published or printed book, but each book is a
coherent entity in itself. If a library is to be also considered
as an archive, it is therefore an archive of projects, more
than an archive of objects.

## ▬ Are Electronic Libraries of Projects (ELP) threatening communicational devices?

Some books are dangerous; some libraries have a restricted
access, and the history of libraries show how powerful they
have been in the rise of modern civilisations and democracies. How far then can we keep the analogy between
competitions and books? Would Electronic Libraries of
Projects be threatening communicational devices due to
their transparency and projected light on the comparative
phenomenon? A corollary of such questions would be the
issue of innovation: Do competition databases stimulate
innovation or encourage repetition? This complex issue
has important implications in the client's representation
of what a competition actually does.

Contrary to our expectations, some rather surprising reactions have ensued the public launching of these
databases. When we presented the model of our system to
the various organisers in other European countries in the
summer of 2006 at an international Europan-Europe forum
in Dordrecht, the Netherlands, some national managers
were surprised that our system gave as much credence to
the losers as to the winners. Even though the system clearly
announces the results including competition winners and
all shortlisted and mentioned projects, some organisers
were worried that all the projects were being shown, instead
of eliminating projects that the juries had not selected. In
simple terms: why keep the looser? A similar attitude can
be noted within professional architecture offices that lose
too many competitions and end up rejecting some of their
own projects. In this frame of thinking it seems as if a project
can only acquire its proper value in the field when a jury
confers such value. Architectural history, which is made up
of project-to-project transfers and influence, would seem
to categorically contradict this incorrect assumption.

Indeed, these "non-wining" projects do have an architectural value that goes beyond their selection by a competition jury, and the history of architectural competitions
is regularly marked by unsuccessful competition projects,
which influence the practices and the discipline as a whole,
sometimes in a more profound way than the project actually
built or at least in a comparable way. Two well-known
modern paradigms of this phenomenon are for example

Le Corbusier's Palais des Nations project in 1927 or Rem Koolhaas' Parc de la Villette project in 1982. But in our view, all projects designed in a competition setting represent an architectural heritage, indeed poorly known, and as such they constitute a formidable reservoir of neglected "potential architecture" **[Fig.10]**.

This theoretical interpretation does not mean that clients who favour the competition process to a their project easily recognise that they participate in a collective endeavour and the production of architectural knowledge. At best they see competitions as a way to communicate with the public at large, and it is more and more frequent nowadays to encounter situations in which a client's representative under the name of "communication adviser" will control the competition process. These new actors do not consider competitions as scholars would do—as reservoirs of potential architectures, ideas and solutions—but, on the contrary, often threaten their clients about the dangerous transparent power of a process that is supposed to open the gate to controversies and counter-effects within the press and the public. As a result, it becomes sometimes impossible to display a newly-judged competition in a documentary website since it would open the way to a criticism of the jury's judgement. This paradigm shift in the way clients deal with competitions becomes a new problem, which makes the systematic documentation of competitions and its display on the web a rather risky path. As explained by Emmanuel Caille, chief editor of French journal D'A (D'Architectures), in a special issue on competitions in April 2013, competitions are now being seen as instrumental in the communication strategies of cities and big institutions (not to speak about companies and private institutions).[11] Documenting a competition sometimes becomes impossible when communication offices on both sides of clients and designers are willing to control the display of information following a competition. At a time when information is being transmitted in almost real time, it is precisely the transparent, fair and democratic characters of the competition phenomena, which are at stake.

The paradoxical nature of the process, however, is such that its spectacular and media potential threatens the competition phenomenon and the experimental nature, quite often turns into a polemical dead end. Without digging into the sociological aspect of this displacement, we can underline here, that in general, only the winning projects are disseminated and the public exhibitions at the end of the selection process do not do enough to ensure lasting

visibility for the different projects. True comparisons—for example by potential clients—are therefore difficult, if not impossible, and the other projects—the losing projects—are doomed to be forgotten in the depths of professional architectural offices. This paradox only serves to enhance the dispersion of documents and ideas, and further devalues architecture in "project" form. Whether they are run for cultural, heritage or domestic programmes; competitions, by their very nature, offer the basis of an empirical situation well suited to comparing projects. Each competition, by definition, is based on the confrontation between interpretations of a request formulated as a brief. Each competition is in some way a type of analogous experimental process understood as early as 1989, by Helen Lipstadt in her famous work on American competitions, *Experimental Tradition*, even though we should now be more careful to distinguish between experimentation in projects (as designers do) and the experimental nature of the empirical competition process itself.[12]

## ▬ Architectural Knowledge and the Preservation of Projects: A Borgesian paradox?

To what extent do these Electronic Libraries of Projects change our research methods? The consequences for research are diverse and fruitful. As shown above, the comparative nature of each competition is better respected when not only the winner but also all competitors are presented objectively along with original expectations, judgement criteria, jury report and media reception.

A particular disciplinary issue that can be addressed through an ELP concerns the understanding of the design process. From an architect's perspective, asking what aspects of a project architects and clients are willing to show or keep can help reveal how they summarize the process through a selection of documents. This issue is crucial and reinforces the distinction between archives and libraries. While an archive should ultimately be expected to look for exhaustivity; a library, ideally speaking, is always a choice and a cultural construct—even in the case of the American Library of Congress. In general terms, to what extent does an architectural project have to be documented in order to do it justice? Does the whole design process need to be reconstituted? As researchers in the field of design thinking and design processes, we feel that this idea is illusory and pointless, the chief concern being however to ensure that the relationship between the project and the competition is well preserved. The validity of this "slimmed down" approach is supported by the fact that the architects themselves identify some sketches as emblematic of a project, despite our observation that with the advent of digital design tools since the middle of the 1990s, the relationship with drafts has radically changed.

Although in some ways ELP enable contemporary architectural productions to be made available, let us not forget that their primary purpose is to enable research in the field of contemporary architecture. One of the most helpful features of relational documentary databases is their ability to integrate analysis levels at every scale, and these analyses are in themselves layers of interpretation for the data stored within the archive. One example of the new capacity this provides is in distinguishing those winning projects that genuinely bear witness to their historical era from shortlisted projects that sometimes reveal ideas whose full meaning only becomes clear with historical hindsight. In Brest in 1997 (Europan France competition, session 5), the jury selected a project inspired by fractals and a certain 1980s deconstructivism, but did not seriously consider a project which now highlights a widespread fascination for its "hybrid networks," and which has therefore since acquired a new value. By juxtaposing projects and comparing them, with hindsight, one can see, as in the 2003 Nanterre competition (Europan France competition, session 7), that the issue of tower blocks was starting to raise its head again in the Paris scene and that Rem Koolhaas' ideas were a major influence on most competitors. [13]

From this point of view, these collections of projects become historical tools that, in some cases, can assist in political decision-making. If Electronic Libraries of Projects contribute to the production of knowledge through their use by designers and researchers alike, can we consider that in the new "knowledge markets," ELP become efficient knowledge dissemination devices? In the strict sense of the term, a documentary database is no more an archive or a communication tool than pressed flowers or butterfly collections represent archives of living nature for a true biologist. However, these relational and, most of all, contextual documentary databases represent a method for archiving these competitions as events. Documenting a competition is of course about documenting projects and gathering information by which the competition conditions and parameters can be understood. Architects seem to accept more and more the need to preserve a presence of their projects within the global scene or event of the competition. Finally, one unforeseen consequence of our work has been to realise that our databases are now starting to be considered as collective archives in which architects in some way entrust their ideas and proposals to us, to keep their memory. On both sides, there is a form of generosity. Archiving the event has become a way of "re-presenting" it, particularly if we consider that many architects enter competitions to renew their ideas and develop their practice through this confrontation with other architects. It becomes clear that if a project is not merely a collection of drafts, neither is a competition merely a collection of projects. It is a complex encounter between a client's brief, designers' proposals in the form of projects, expert knowledge of all kinds, and jury members' value systems and deliberations—all of which are somehow redefined during each competition process. Competitions are closer to what we would call, after the seminal works of Donald A. Schön, [14] "reflective practices" or, more precisely, as we would like to coin it, "reflective collective situations."

As reservoirs of collective intelligence, competitions and even more so Electronic Libraries of Projects, can be seen as collective reflective devices. As shown by theoretician of artificial intelligence Pierre Lévy, collective intelligence supports the process of democratization, which, for what regards competitions, should be seen as a coherent quality. [15] The ontological search for the "client" takes on a different scale when we consider these ELP at the level of world heritage preservation. But contrary to the world heritage list of the UNESCO, which has become an issue of political and economic interplay between governments and touristic markets, ELP are still protected by the paradox of classification. This paradox, briefly expressed by the expression "classification as disorder," brings archivists, librarian, researchers and architectural designers together around the notion of ordering. Michel Foucault has highlighted the role of order in the development of modern science and has shown that mankind only became a knowledge-bearer after the Renaissance epoch, once a vast range of correspondences and relationships had been exhausted. From this perspective, "knowing" would seem to be a question of creating relationships and classifying [Fig.11] [Fig.12].

A conclusive story can illustrate how ordering should be seen as a way of building knowledge, be it at a figurative or literal level, as paradoxical as any attempt to write a book on the future of knowledge [Fig.13]. Foucault was much amused by "a certain Chinese encyclopaedia" that is cited in a novella by Jorge Luis Borges, and Foucault himself is well known to have cleverly used this image in the preface to his monumental work *The Order of Things* (1966). As he quotes, in this typically Borgesian encyclopaedia, "animals are divided into: a) belonging to the Emperor, b) embalmed, c) tame... f) fabulous... i) frenzied j) innumerable... n) that from a long way off look like flies." Although archivists would probably find this monstrous classification method amusing, the same seems to apply to designers, and this may be why their imagination is wired in such a strange way. To come back to our subject, this may be why designers' archives are organised so strangely too and why architects' libraries are so important in the end as if architectural knowledge was to be found in between archives and libraries. This is even more intriguing since Borges was clearly referring to the ordering of books in a library and there was one Belgian librarian to whom Borges was alluding—a famous one indeed—Paul Otlet. Let us continue Borges's quotation up to the passage that implicitly refers to Otlet: "The Bibliographical Institute of Brussels also resorts to chaos: it has parcelled the universe into 1000 subdivisions: Number 262 corresponds to the Pope; ... Number 263, to the Lord's Day; Number 268, to Sunday Schools... It also tolerates heterogeneous subdivisions, for example, Number 179: "Cruelty to animals. Protection of animals. Moral Implications of duelling and suicide. Various vices and defects. Various virtues and qualities..."

Paul Otlet, at times called the "man who wanted to order the world," was the symbol of a new way of ordering knowledge following the positivistic trend in science at the beginning of the twentieth century.[16] Surprisingly, Foucault did not pick up on this important, even crucial reference, since Borgesian criticism focuses first on decimal classification and its potentially absurd yet potentially brilliant juxtapositions! It is well known that decimal classification was invented by Melvil Dewey (1876), and that it was perfected, but also adapted to a more complex level by Henri La Fontaine and Paul Otlet. Along with Henri Lafontaine and later Le Corbusier, Otlet dreamt up the Mundaneum, an ambitious project to say the least, which aimed to document the whole world's knowledge in one single location. Needless to say, the Mundaneum was never constructed, but the classification made its way as a virtual architecture of knowledge: a pure "utopia" so to speak **[Fig.14]**.

Having said this, however, who has not, in the well-ordered shelves of a university library, found himself or herself selecting a book just next to, two shelves further on, than the

**Fig. 11**
Classifying butterflies is neither a reservoir, nor an archive of the living, but it is already a path to knowledge.

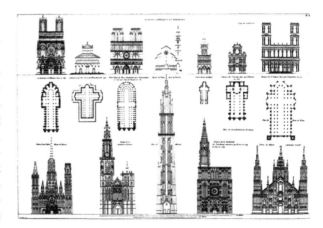

**Fig.12**
Comparison and analysis as a basis of architectural knowledge. Comparative plate of "gothic and modern churches" from Jean-Nicolas-Louis Durand, *Recueil et parallèle des édifices en tout genre, anciens et modernes, remarquables par leur beauté, par leur grandeur ou par leur singularité (1800)*. p 8.

**Fig. 13**
Front cover of: Pierre-François Lacome,
*Le futur sans fiction*, Paris (1958).

**Fig. 14**
Island of Utopia. Plate from Thomas
More, *Libellus vere aureus nec minus
salutaris quam festivus de optimo
reipublicae statu, deque nova insula
Utopia*, Louvain (1516).

one that he actually came in to look for? Browsing in a competition database often present the reader with the same wonderful opportunity: looking for something and finding something even more interesting. Finally, this Chinese encyclopaedia whose incomprehensible classification of the real and imaginary so amused Foucault, had a name in Borges' novel, although this fabulous name was also, and even more strangely, omitted by Foucault. [17] Borges' encyclopaedia was entitled "The Celestial Emporium of Benevolent Knowledge." Is this not the very definition of any database of competitions projects? It seems that this type of "Emporium of Architectural Knowledge" ought to start being compiled over the next few years as Electronic Libraries of Projects come into contact one with another, across cultures and oceans, like a true collective legacy.

## ▬▬ Notes

[1] See: Canadian Competitions Catalogue at *http://www.ccc.umontreal.ca*
[2] See: Laboratoire d'étude de l'architecture potentielle (L.E.A.P) at *http://www.leap.umontreal.ca*
[3] See: Research Chair on Competitions and Contemporary Practices in Architecture at *http://www.crc.umontreal.ca*
[4] Chaslin, François. (1985), Le Paris de François Mitterand, Histoire des grands projets architecturaux. Paris, Gallimard, 1985.
[5] See: *http://www.leap.umontreal.ca/index.php?id=85&lang=en*
[6] See: *http://www.deathbyarchitecture.com/recent.html;jsessionid=016E9F54 B29374ACAFAB22166345AA56?method=Search*
[7] See: *http://mtlunescodesign.com/*
[8] See: *http://europaconcorsi.com/*
[9] Yaneva, Albena, (2012), Mapping Controversies in Architecture, Ashgate Publishing Limited.
[10] Foucault, Michel, (1966), Les mots et les choses (Une archéologie des sciences humaines). Translated in 1970 as: The Order of Things (An Archeology of Human Sciences). London: Tavistock Publications Ltd.
[11] Caille, Emmanuel, (2013), « Peut-on encore critiquer les projets d'un concours » in D'A (D'Architectures), 216, avril 2013, pp 76-77. See also: Caille, Emmanuel, (2013), « Le concours instrumentalisé par les communiquants : bienvenue dans le monde des popstarchitectes », in D'A (D'Architectures), 216, avril 2013, pp 73-75.
[12] Lipstadt, Helen (1989), The Experimental Tradition, Essays on Competitions in Architecture. New York, Princeton Architectural Press.
[13] We already commented these cases in: Chupin, Jean-Pierre, Gomes Lino José and Jason Goorts, "Le ciel des idées, l'horizon des connaissances" in Frédérique de Gravelaine, dir. Europan France, Innover Dialoguer Réaliser: 1998-2007, Jean-Michel Place, Paris, 2007.
[14] Schön, Donald A., (1983), The Reflective Practitioner: How Professionals Think in Action. Basic Books, New York.
[15] Lévy, Pierre. (1994), Collective Intelligence: Mankind's Emerging World in Cyberspace. New York, Basic Books (1999, for the English translation).
[16] Levie Françoise, (2006), L'homme qui voulait classer le monde. Paul Otlet et le Mundaneum. Les impressions nouvelles, Brussels.
[17] Borges, Jose Luis (1967), Otras Inquisiciones (Translated as Other Inquisitions, University of Texas Press, 1964).

# Rerefences

**Architectes**, Union Internationale des. "Uia Guide for International Competitions in Architecture and Town Planning (Unesco Regulations / Terms of Application)." Paris : Union Internationale des Architectes, 2008.

**Borges**, Jose Luis. *Other Inquisitions 1937-1952.* University of Texas Press, 1967.

**Chupin**, Jean-Pierre. *Analogie et théorie en architecture (De la vie, de la ville et de la conception, même).* Collection Projet et Théorie. Genève : Infolio, 2010.

**Chupin**, Jean-Pierre. "Archivage numérique des concours canadiens et re-connaissance de l'architecture." In *Archives : Pour une (re) connaissance de l'architecture (Livre blanc des archives de l'architecture en Fédération Wallonie-Bruxelles) Sous la direction de Chantal Dassonville,* pp. 92-103. Bruxelles : Cellule architecture de la Fédération Wallonie-Bruxelles, 2012.

**Chupin**, Jean-Pierre. "Concourir à la qualité de l'architecture scolaire ". In *Dassonville, Chantal Et Cohen Maurizio, Monographie sur la rénovation de l'athénée Royal Riva Bella.* Collection Visions, pp. 36-43. Bruxelles, 2013.

**Chupin**, Jean-Pierre. "Documenting Competitions, Contribution to Research, Archiving Events." Chap. 29 In *Architecture and Digital Archives (Architecture in the Digital Age : A Question of Memory),* edited by David Peyceré and Françoise Wierre, 523-34. Gollion : Éditions Infolio, 2008.

**Chupin**, Jean-Pierre.. "Judgement by Design : Towards a Model for Studying and Improving the Competition Process in Architecture and Urban Design." *The Scandinavian Journal of Management (Elsevier)* 27, no. 1 (Special topic forum on Architectural Competitions) (2011) : 173-84.

**Chupin**, Jean-Pierre. "Quand juger c'est « concevoir un projet »." *ARQ, La revue d'architecture, Spécial sur le jugement en architecture (sous la direction de Jean-Pierre Chupin),* février 2011 2011, p. 48-51.

**Chupin**, Jean-Pierre. "Some Reflections on the Problematic Location of the Entity Client in the Ontological Structure of Electronic Ressources on Competitions." Paper presented at the The 5th International Conference on Competitions, Delft University of Technology, 2014.

**Chupin**, Jean-Pierre (Rédacteur invité). "Dossier spécial "Que savons-nous des concours ?"." *d'a (D'architecture),* no. no.216 (avril 2013) (2013).

**Chupin**, Jean-Pierre, dir. "Canadian Competitions Catalogue / Catalogue des concours canadiens ( *http ://www.ccc.umontreal.ca* )." LEAP / CRC, 2002-(2014).

**Chupin**, Jean-Pierre, Lino José **Gomes**, and Jason **Goorts**. "Le ciel des idées, l'horizon des connaissances." In *Europan France 1998 — 2007 (Innover, Dialoguer, Réaliser),* edited by Europan France and Frédérique de Gravelaine, 39-52. Paris : Jean-Michel Place, 2007.

**Europan** (Organisation). Session (8e : 2006), Jean-Pierre Chupin, Danièle Valabrègue, and Université de Montréal. Laboratoire d'étude de l'architecture potentielle. *Europan 8 (Fr) vu du Canada : Analyses interdisciplinaires des projets présélectionnés de la session française : Rapport final, août 2006.* Montréal : Laboratoire d'étude de l'architecture potentielle, 2006.

**Foucault**, Michel. *Les mots et les choses (Une archéologie des sciences humaines).* Paris : Gallimard, 1966.

**Foucault**, Michel. *The Order of Things (an Archeology of Human Sciences).* London : Tavistock Publications Ltd., 1970.

**Levie**, Françoise. *L'homme qui voulait classer le monde. Paul Otlet et le Mundaneum.* Brussels : Les Impressions Nouvelles, 2006.

**Lévy**, Pierre. *Collective Intelligence : Mankind's Emerging World in Cyberspace.* New York : Basic Books, 1999.

**Lipstadt**, Helen, and Barry **Bergdoll**. *The Experimental Tradition : Essays on Competitions in Architecture.* New York, N.Y. : Princeton Architectural Press, 1989.

**Schön**, Donald A. *The Reflective Practioner : How Professionals Think in Action.* New York : Basic Books, 1983.

**Yaneva**, Albena. *Mapping Controversies in Architecture.* Ashgate Publishing Limited, 2012.

Welcome to KONKURADO – the information platform about architectural and engineering competitions (present, past and future) within the framework of public and private procurement in Switzerland.

This platform provides a forum for the exchange of information between project owners and contracting authorities, planners, architects and engineers, researchers and research institutions and other potential users, such as building authorities, the press and anyone else with an interest in the subject.

KONKURADO is both a database of knowledge on the built and unbuilt environment and a tool supporting professional competition planning, calls for tenders, publication and implementation.

▶ **Competition notices**

▶ **Offer announcements**

▶ **Previous competitions**

▶ **Implemented projects**

▼ **Competition map**

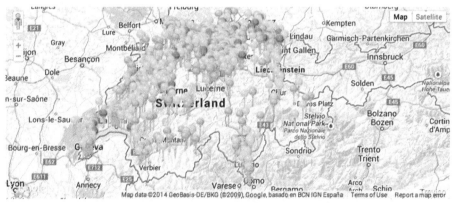

AG  AI  AR  BE  BS  BL  FR  GE  GL  GR  JU  LU  NE  NW  OW  SG  SH  SO  SZ  TG  TI  UR  VD  VS  ZG  ZH

● Wettbewerbe  ● Study contracts

Sign up to Konkurado

**Search**

[            ]    Search

**Partner & Sponsor**

s i a

**Sponsors**

**Konkurado in numbers**

| | |
|---|---|
| 568 | Study contracts |
| 613 | Wettbewerbe |
| 1011 | Documents |
| 1265 | Companies/institutions |
| 4518 | People |

RECHERCHE CONCOURS D'ETUDE

Contact details | Legal notice | About us

**Cover**
Konkurado | Web of Design Competitions.
*www.konkurado.ch*

# 4.3. Capturing Competition Data

**Involving Stakeholders in a Swiss Competition Database**

**Ignaz Strebel**, Ph.D.
ETH Wohnforum — ETH CASE
Department of Architecture, ETH Zürich
Switzerland

**Jan M. Silberberger**, Ph.D.
ETH Wohnforum — ETH CASE
Department of Architecture, ETH Zürich.
Switzerland

**Denis Raschpichler**, eng.
Swiss Society of Engineers and Architects (SIA).
Switzerland

We report on the first phase of a process to build a web-accessible database on architectural competitions in Switzerland. The goal of this database is to provide data for applied research as well as for stakeholders within the competition business. This application aims at supporting existing competition practices, and to eventually optimize competition procedures. According to our estimation, around 400 solution-oriented forms of procurement are publically announced in Switzerland each year ; approximately 80 % of these competitions are advertised by public awarding authorities and 20 % by private clients. This number includes an unratable number of non-advertised, and therefore difficult to trace competition procedures. This database should be able to continuously provide a significant amount of data on all types of procedures, capturing a large diversity of competition procedures in Switzerland. Our work is based on a user-centered approach, which aims at studying and improving work cooperation between people and information technology. Having chosen to take stakeholders and potential users as a starting point to build the conceptual framework for this database, our starting point for this project is the practices of those involved in the competition business, with tasks such as competition advertising, administering prequalification documents, submitting projects, and participating in jury/board meetings. From here, we ask not only how to archive completion data but how the planned internet-platform can support this work.

Two polarizing scenarios of data handling and logging have been put forward : an approach to *ad hoc* data acquisition and document management "during the competition processes" as opposed to an archival approach, which involves data handling "after accomplishment of the competition procedure." In this way, the web interface is more than an entry mask used to enter data and upload documents, as it will be designed as an interactive tool for competition organizers and participants who may accomplish various work tasks over the internet — this may include advertising, submission of prequalification documents, and the publication of competition programs. We expect this tool-based approach to the documentation of information will be of high quality, as data will be uploaded 'live'. However, there are significant risks related to this approach : the interface will only work if its supportive capacity and added value were obvious to its users ; and, after this conceptual work, it was also not clear how the data entered into the system by the user will be used for research on competitions and what its epistemic value is.

This is a report on the first phase of an applied research project that aims at building a web-accessible database on architectural and planning competitions in Switzerland. The goal of this database is to provide data for applied research as well as stakeholders within the competition business. By now, the project is completed and the database named KONKURADO | Web of Design Competitions is available online.[1] This paper provides a retrospective reflection on the process involved in developing a conceptual framework for this archive. In this text, we do not intend to describe the final outcome of the project, but rather want to demonstrate how we have proceeded in the opening and empirical phase to build an appropriate conceptual framework for this application.

The project is linked to its partnership and its financial structure as a science-to-market initiative. On the one hand, five public awarding authorities, including the public works offices of four of the seven largest Swiss cities and of one canton are involved; the third largest Swiss bank; the biggest retailer; the Swiss Society of Engineers and Architects (SIA); and four private planning offices and specialists in competition organization. On the other hand, we have solicited viewpoints from four research groups on architectural competitions and academic institutions. The scientific part of the project is funded through the Swiss government's innovation promotion agency CTI.[2]

In this project we have carried out a detailed requirement analysis to better understand which data and information is needed by which stakeholders within the Swiss competition business, and what kind of technological support the database could potentially provide to optimize workflows within the competition business. From the onset of the project, we assumed that an online research platform can become a strategically significant work tool that could potentially provide the distribution and coordination of work tasks and better data handling, which would possibly shorten awarding procedures and make competitions accessible and manageable for a wider group of clients. To follow this strategic aim we opted for a user-centered approach that allows for the conceptual framing of the architectural competition as cooperative work, which is and can be supported by various information and communication technologies. Beginning with this conceptual choice, the strategic potential of the tool is required to be embedded within the actual competition business in Switzerland. We started focusing on the organizational and procedural aspects of the Swiss competition business by examining an

expressive data sample of eighteen competition procedures in Switzerland. This organizational study was paralleled by an analysis of existing data management practices and inventory of user requirements.

The aim of this analysis was to estimate the potential for improvement that an archive and online database could bring to the Swiss competition business. This strategic and organizational analysis provided the foundation for a basic initial requirement specification of the platform that was presented to the project partners at mid-term of the project. In this paper, we restrict ourselves on the requirements analysis and present the basic requirement specification that emerged from this process.

## Method

The project was originally set up using a user-centered approach, based on the idea of carrying out workshops with stakeholders, in which an appropriate structure and classification of the database would be negotiated. User-centered approaches aim at integrating human factors into the earliest stages of the design project. They base successful design on an understanding of the work context involved and on knowledge of stakeholders' requirements. A web-interface has to be designed for a work practice. The question to be asked therefore is whose work the system should support. It might well be that one system is useful for one person's work practice, while at the same time making another person's work difficult or even impossible. By identifying all potential users' needs and requirements, it is possible to create generic tools and avoid this kind of problem. Ideally, user-centered design involves three steps: (1) Studying the work context and the particular work to be supported by the system; (2) Identifying the requirements of potential users and stakeholders; and (3) Building a prototype of the system, which will then be tested and developed further with real users.

In this paper, we will describe how the research project covered the above-mentioned steps (1) and (2). At the start of the project, our original aim to limit ourselves to stakeholder workshops was reconsidered: instead of carrying out workshops in which people would talk about competitions, we opted for a different methodology in order to better understand what people actually do, when they organize, participate, and are involved in competition procedures. Following this new approach, we studied actual competitions as they happened, and not as 'best practice' or as considered in instructional documents, which describe competitions as how they should ideally be carried out.

The analysis to be carried out will incorporate the following principles. Firstly, it should be work-oriented, meaning that the focus of the analysis is on the workflow of competition organization. Based on this first principle, we have directed our attention towards competition organizers, such as planning and architecture departments within public and private institutions, or planning offices specialized in competition organization that would be contracted by clients. Secondly, the study was group-focused. We assume that organizing a competition is not the affair of a single professional, but rather a cooperative work. For example, a project-leader and a jury moderator interact and communicate with each other, but also with competition participants, experts, and jury/board members. Thirdly, the study focuses on the relationship between human actors and technologies. Competitions cannot unfold without various technologies being used as resources to accomplish certain work tasks. These may be digital technologies such as computers, servers, email and websites, but, more importantly, they may also encompass the buildings and rooms in which jury/board meetings take place, the act of postal sending, and the physical format of competition contributions. Finally, we study the cooperation between users and analysts. In Switzerland, the competition business is surveyed by the regulating body of the Swiss Society of Engineers and Architects and lawyers working in the field of public procurement.

The analysis of the competition business was carried out in the three following steps. Firstly, a study of recent competition databases and archives aimed at understanding local practices in archiving architectural processes and documents. Secondly, eighteen case studies of recent and current competitions were carried out. These case studies aimed at achieving a better understanding of the organization and sequencing of competitions and, more specifically, of the production and use of documents in these procedures. Thirdly, we have carried out eight stakeholder focus groups. This third step aimed at surveying user and stakeholder needs and testing the first ideas of the conceptual framework of the database and web interface.

## Requirements Analysis of the Swiss Competition Business

Aiming at understanding the requirements for the new online tool, our analysis elaborates on the following three themes: document and information management practices; the workflow of competition organization; and requirements for the system expressed by potential users.

### Document and Information Management Practices

In the requirement analysis, the design and data structures of four different internet-archives were carefully considered. In addition, through our case studies of eighteen competitions organized and carried out by our project partners, we have documented the data management and archiving practices of each of the analyzed competition procedures.

We can distinguish between three approaches to competition Internet platforms.

Firstly, the profession-oriented database of the Swiss Society of Engineers and Architects (SIA) presents on its website data manually and centrally fed from a database. All competition advertisements of public awarding authorities are systematically and manually copied in the system from the Swiss Official Gazette of Commerce.[3] Competitions advertised by private awarding authorities are only saved to the database if they are sent to the SIA offices. The structure of this database is elaborated and classified according to the vocabulary used by the SIA Regulation 142 (architectural competitions) and 143 (study commissions). Although the data structure provides for information on results and realization of buildings to be captured, this information is not updated. The database works according to the business model of the SIA, and aims at regulating the building market and delivering information on behalf of their members. Users of the SIA website can either search actual advertisements or buy and configure an email newsletter through which newly advertised competitions are sent to members of this service.

The second documented database, *Tec21*, works in a similar way. This professional journal has recently updated its website and has initiated its online web portal named Espazium.[4] Competitions are reported directly by public and private clients and then advertised on the platform. Information is accessible for the public and for registered members. The SIA database and the Espazium Webportal use their information reciprocally, however data transfer is done manually and not through an interface between the two systems. Both *Tec21* and SIA platforms sufficiently cover the needs of architectural offices as potential competition participants.

Secondly, Internet platforms such as, for example, the Canadian Competitions Catalogue, [5] are built for research purposes. The information housed by this system is collected and added by a centrally located group of researchers. Some selected information about the competition and project documents (plans, images) are available to the public on the web interface. Competitions and projects are documented systematically. This application is increasingly used by researchers and is of more and more interest to competitors who understand the archive as a way of showcasing their built and unbuilt projects.

Finally, the fourth documented Internet platform is similar to a social network. Competition Online [6] is a recent example of a communication platform that aims at bringing clients together and architects. This web tool distinguishes itself from the research and the profession-oriented approach in that it focuses not only on competitions, but provides an internet platform that clients and architectural offices can use to advertise for jobs, showcase their firm beyond just projects, and broadcast other information related to their activity. For the most part, data capturing is left to the users of the system. The disadvantage of this strictly decentralized and uncontrolled data capturing leads to many entries of poor quality and incomplete data. The quality of the data is visibly poor at a first glance.

In addition to the study of a selected number of existing web-based competition platforms, we have surveyed the archival practices of the competition organizers involved in the project. The archival practice follows a general pattern, which is less routed in the specificity of the competition nature than in the administrative system and technology. Competition organizers (public and private) administrate and archive digital documents locally, proceeding according to internal rules. Documents are created and edited on the personal computer of the project leader, who in turn saves them on a central server within the institution. The public administration department or firm provides a local structure of folders to be used for data management. Project leaders interpret this structure and use, extend or shorten it in various ways. General documents can be found when searching file names manually, or by using various sort functions: for example, the date of creation, the file format, the size of the files, or by using search engines provided by the operating systems in use. One competition organizer — a public architecture department — uses a file-naming format (ISO 9000 certification).

None of the investigated firms and departments uses a document management system (DMS). After the completion of the competitions, no protocol of how to archive data and documents is currently in use.

We find also that competitions produce the following documents:

- Documents of process organization
- Competition entries
- Documents addressed to competitors and the public
- Media documents and documents of public discussion
- Pre-competition documents (development studies, clarification documents, decision-making with regard to the type of competition to be chosen)
- Post-competition documents (design, occupancy and maintenance of the building)

**Workflow of Architectural Competitions**
A preliminary report summarizes the findings of the ten interviews we conducted with the project managers of the 18 chosen competition procedures. In addition to these interviews, we examined approximately 150 documents per competition procedure or case study, respectively. As a result, we were able to elaborate how the different administrative bodies and planning bureaus manage their data, as well as the differences and similarities regarding data handling amongst different types of competition procedures. Despite the significant differences regarding the type of procedure as well as the building task amongst the 18 examined case studies, one can identify a distinct pattern of tasks that is oriented around the milestones "publication of the call to tender" or "publication of the competition brief" respectively, and "jury assessment sessions" / "publication of the jury's final report."

The pattern of tasks mirrors the complexity of the building task and the chosen type of procedure. For instance, a two-stage competition produces a different structure of the pattern of tasks than a one-stage. In the case of a restricted procedure, the publication of the call to tender does not necessarily coincide with the publication of the competition brief — an extension to an exhibition hall for fine arts in a historic city center needs more clarifications (which most likely include a so-called "development study") than a reconstruction of a tramway waiting booth. Yet, on a more abstract level of the structure of the pattern of tasks regarding which decisions have to be made at which time, there is a high degree of accordance between the 18 examined cases. For example, in all 18 cases the composition of the jury was determined before the publication of the call to tender or the competition brief, and the preliminary technical examination of the entries were established prior to the jury's evaluation process.

In all 18 examined cases, there is generally one person — the project manager — who oversees the entire process. The project manager organizes the writing of the competition brief, the publication of the call to tender, the undertaking of the technical control of the entries. In a sense, the project manager brings together the various threads of the competition procedure. He makes sure that information, decisions and determinations are present at the required point of time. For that purpose the project manager creates a detailed sequence plan using appropriate project management software.

**User Requirements**

To document the requirements of potential users, we have carried out stakeholder workshops in which forty-four invited stakeholders participated. Workshops were organized for the following groups: competition participants, public awarding authorities, private awarding authorities (including private investors, housing cooperatives and consulting firms in estate management), competition organizers, regulators, jury-board members, researchers and the press (media and specialized journals). Each focus group was invited to lead an open discussion around three main questions: What are potential user needs? What additional value would the system have for individual stakeholders? What documents and data would participants be able to provide and possibly enter themselves into the planned system?

After the workshops, the following ten requirements were edited and grouped:

1. Developing synergies: Participants and competitions organizers agreed that synergies in the competition practice nowadays are not publicly made available. The competition practice should learn not from ideal models of architectural competitions, but rather from existing local experiences.

2. Systematic documentation: Currently in Switzerland there is no systematic documentation of architectural competitions available. For example, regulators and researchers demand information about what kind of competitions are carried out, who is involved, which competitions are aborted and which regulations are applied.

3. Added value: The system should not build on the "good will to archive," but must deliver concrete added value for stakeholders. From the workshops a list of potential added values was generated.

4. User Involvement: The user of the system–the various stakeholders–should be involved in archiving procedures. Users want to control their own data and they are interested in using the platform as a work tool for things such as data management, visualization of data, communication during the competition process, and the use of classification systems.

5. Completeness of data: Data on competitions in Switzerland can be found by means of using search browsers on the internet, specialized journals such as *Tec21* or *wettbewerbe aktuell* (*wa*). Available competitions are selected and published by stakeholders with particular interests. This field should now be extended to all competition procedures currently applied in Switzerland. The challenge here is that not all competitions are publicly advertised. Those that do not leave a trace in public — such as many invited study commissions — are often carried out by private clients. Completeness of data does not only concern the field of competition procedures, as data depth is also required for individual competitions, as end-to-end information. Therefore data for each of the phases of competition procedures must be gathered and include decisions made on the competition procedure, decisions made within the competition, the design phase and construction phase of the selected project.

6. Actuality of data: Workshop participants have clearly stated that most of the documents and data archived would only be of use if they reflect actual events in Switzerland, such as advertised, executed, and realized projects, or decided and realized competitions. Other data, like historical or aborted competitions, would only be of use for researchers and possibly those who study the development of regulations in the Swiss competition business. It is therefore necessary to tag every competition with its status, such as "in-progress," "aborted," "realized."

7. Publicity of the data: Users of the system should decide upon which data is publicly available for which kind of user groups. These requirements would open up a practical dimension of the system. Users would be able to show, share and organize data with smaller groups, such as work colleagues, jury/board members or competition participants. The platform should

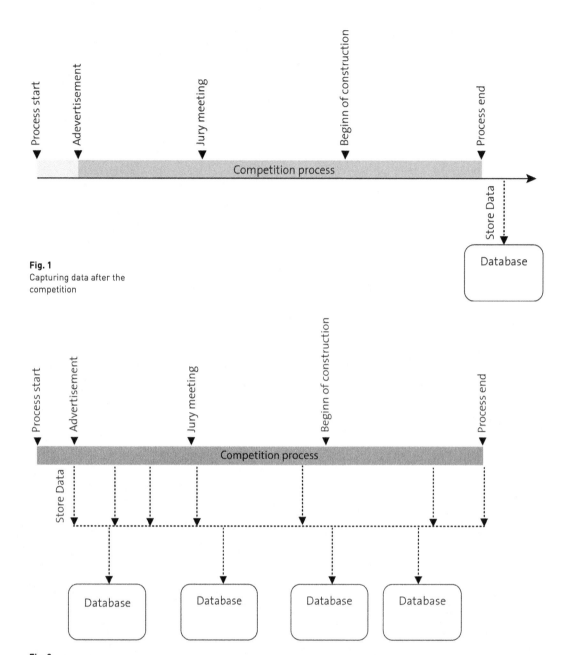

**Fig. 1**
Capturing data after the
competition

**Fig. 2**
Capturing data during the
competition.

therefore not only instruct the user to capture data, but define the visibility and copyright of data entered.

8. Process support: Workshop participants could imagine using the system to accomplish various work tasks, which can be easily standardized: i. Advertise competitions on the Internet; ii. Upload and publish information about competitions; iii. Provide "question and answer" blogs as well as information to research participants; iv. Provide documents and information to jury/board members; v. Use the system to validate and possibly label competitions, which is a specific requirement of the SIA; vi. Use of the system by the competition organizer as a data management system.

9. Searching for specific information: A series of criteria were mentioned in the workshop, all related to various needs and professional aims of the stakeholders. It is important to note that in the specific workshop with competition participants, the system was not seen as providing information about projects and current architectural design practices. The following list of search criteria emerged from the workshops: the names of jury/board members; clients and their expertise; good practice in competition organization; projects (unbuilt, awarded and realized projects); juridical information; competition program; jury reports; particular architectural solutions (for example, deepness of floor plans); and prize-money sums.

10. Analytical information: Various gaps in the information on architectural competitions have been mentioned. For example, statistical information, cross-reference of various competitions, end-to-end visualisations of competitions, best practice, benchmarks (for example, size of flats in housing projects), operating figures, and maps of competition localizations.

## ▬▬ Scenarios of Data Capturing

Strategic potentials of technological applications, such as the planned information platform, are only accomplishable if the organization of workflows is adapted. This is the major challenge of every technological implication. Schwabe suggests building on two kinds of scenarios of implementation.[7] A more conservative scenario aims at understanding the usage of a technology without changes to the workflow. Alternately, a more progressive scenario of implementation aims at building on changes to the workflow to optimize the usage of the technology. Ideally the comparison of the two scenarios leads to the strategic direction of impact of technology implementation. In our project we have distinguished two scenarios: 'capturing data *after* the competition', and 'capturing data *during* the competition process. In the following, these two scenarios will be presented as two ideal practices of data capturing.

### Capturing Competition Data after the Competition Has Taken Place

If we capture data after the competition has taken place the administrator of the database has full control over the quality, the integrity, and the quantity of data and documents introduced. This approach is intensive, probably less in terms of designing the catalogue, but rather because data collection and data entry are laborious. If the financial means are available to finance a team of researchers or research assistants that collect and feed data into the database, this approach is certainly of high value. However there are some disadvantages to this approach. Firstly, data is not easily available as it is difficult to trace and to receive from various individuals, organizations and institutions, mostly because the various data owners lose control over their data. Secondly, training of the data collection and data entry team is time consuming and happens at relatively high costs as information and documents have to be asked for, filtered, entered into the system and continuously updated **[Fig.1]**.

### Capturing Competition Data during the Competition

Data is entered in the system by its producer and at the very moment of its production. Data and documents are entered into the system not for archiving but for working purposes, and the archive or database becomes part of the competition process. The producer has practical reasons to enter data–he or she advertises competitions, subscribes to newsletters, shares information, asks questions, responds, publishes documents, and submits projects over the system. From such an approach, raw data could be added to the system without the intermediary interpretation of a research institution. The system turns into something that is more than an archive, it is considered as a tool that significantly supports the competition process. An example of when this archiving process was altered is an experience from an art school, where students were asked to upload their final dissertations after graduation into the school database system. It was difficult to motivate the students to do that work. Why would they do so now, as they are about to leave the institution? The school then changed their policy and claimed that final dissertations would only be assessed, if

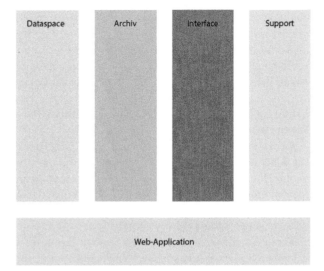

**Fig. 3**
Four function blocks.

examiners can download dissertations from the system. It is this small change — the integration of the archive into the process of studying — that made it a useful tool for the student. In this case the archiving process became a crucial supporting tool to the workflow.

These two scenarios led to a compromise : We tend to capture data during the competition processes : Primarily, we have very carefully listed which stakeholder would get what kind of added value from his involvement and in turn from the system ; and we have carefully thought about how the continuity, the integrity and the completeness of data and database can be warranted. We secondly added a supporting data-team, which enters new and historical data in the system, supplements exiting data sets and surveys data and documents entered into the system by stakeholders **[Fig.2]**.

## Requirements Specification
### The Vision
In total we have fourteen stakeholders groups who will potentially use the system. The design of the web-interface and database cannot respond to all fourteen users. A selection had to be made and a confined list of people who specified their needs :

1. Competition organizers and awarding authorities, who advertise and carry out competitions ;
2. Researchers, who archive, classify, describe, order and analyze data ;
3. Competition participants, who search for advertised competitions ;
4. Regulators, who observe, regulate the competition business and survey single competitions.
5. Furthermore the requirements that were identified in the workshops have been reduced to four user needs :
6. Actuality : The system will be of importance if it mirrors the actuality of the competition business.
7. Publicity : At the heart of each competition are three documents : advertisement, competition program and jury report.
8. End-to-end documentation : The system should be able to follow competitions over longer periods of time, and it should be able to absorb changing responsibilities for one procedure, so access rights can be forwarded and changed from one project leader to the next.
9. Completeness and profoundness : The system should be able to accommodate all kinds of competition procedures currently conducted in Switzerland.

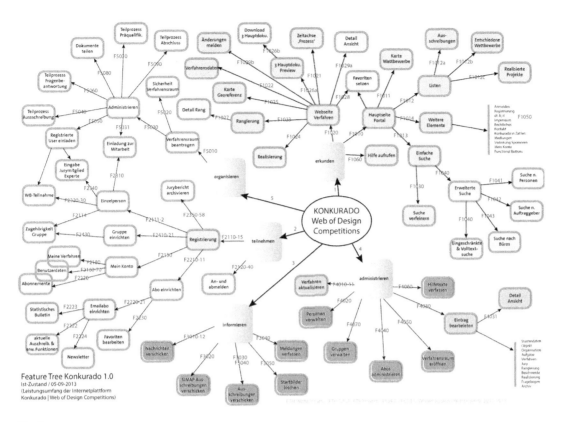

**Fig. 4**
Konkurado | Web of Design Competitions
(Feature Tree, September 2013).

## The system should have the following abilities:

1. Minimal effort for data entry.
2. Flexibility: The system should have a certain degree of elasticity so that changes in the competition business can be reproduced. Datasets must be adaptable for research and regulation, so that they can work on their own (research) questions.
3. Process-support: The system should not simply reproduce the competition process and deliver information about the competition business; it should actively support the process, as the system is of tool character.

## Functional Details

We then derived four function blocks [Fig. 3]. The first block 'dataspace' is the archive, at the heart of the system. Datastructure and metadata are adaptable for scientific purposes and organization; entry masks for each of the three data groups are available.

The second block is what we call the procedural space, where entry structures of data will be modeled. Ideally a competition can be processed from beginning to the end. Transfer of data ownership and data governance will be implemented according to a generic model that can absorb various competition modalities. Data captured in this process is in principle confidential–project owners will be able to decide upon the public character of various parts of the dataspace and of all documents and information.

The third block consists of an interface that allows connection to the systemic context. Other databases and systems should be able to use an interface to download information from the system according to their needs. In conjunction with this, other systems should be able to feed their information into the system. The aim here is to implement automatic uploads and allow manual data transfer.

The fourth block is the support team to be implemented. This is a tripartite instance consisting of a competence

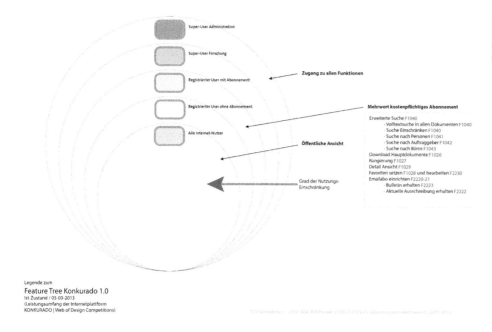

**Fig. 5**
Konkurado | Web of Design
Competitions.
(Caption, September 2013)

Super-User Administration

Super-User Forschung

Registrierter User mit Abonnement — Zugang zu allen Funktionen

Registrierter User ohne Abonnement — Mehrwert kostenpflichtiges Abonnement

Erweiterte Suche F1040
· Volltextsuche in allen Dokumenten F1040
· Suche Einschränken F1040
· Suche nach Personen F1041
· Suche nach Auftraggeber F1042
· Suche nach Büros F1043
Download Hauptdokumente F1026
Rangierung F1027
Detail Ansicht F1029
Favoriten setzen F1028 und bearbeiten F2230
Emailabo einrichten F2220-21
· Bulletin erhalten F2223
· Aktuelle Ausschreibung erhalten F2222

Alle Internet-Nutzer

Öffentliche Ansicht

Grad der Nutzungs-
Einschränkung

Legende zum
Feature Tree Konkurado 1.0
Ist-Zustand / 05-09-2013
(Leistungsumfang der Internetplattform
KONKURADO | Web of Design Competitions)

centre, which collects competences within the context of the Swiss competition business and makes them available online — this competence centre is also responsible for further development of the system.

In this chapter, we have focused on the conceptual development phase of a web-based competition database. The aim was to demonstrate how a conceptual framework emerged from an empirical study of the Swiss competition business and its practices that involved a large group of competition stakeholders. The steps following this conceptual phase, which have not been discussed in this text, included, on the one hand, the specification and development of an appropriate software solution to implement the conceptual aspects of this project, and on the other hand, the functional implementation and introduction of the web-interface into practice.

Figures 4 and 5 show the final design of the platform (in German) as it was handed over in September 2013 after a two-year phase of programming and testing to the SIA, who has been decided upon to be its future operator and developer **[Fig.4] [Fig.5]**.

Inside the project partnership and after the presentation of the conceptual aspects of the project, the idea of capturing data during the competition process has been intensely discussed and received with a healthy amount of scepticism. In the context of the actual amount of available information on competitions, and practical issues of competition organization, data handling within public and private institutions, the idea of a procedural space in which competitions can be planned, administrated and advertised generated at this stage a lot of fascination.

Obviously, the here-described initial phase would have to be evaluated against the outcome of the following phases. How do you translate the established conceptual framework into a prototype? How did stakeholders receive the prototype in the testing phase? Did initial concepts change or were they abandoned? Not at last we would have to critically discuss our approach against the actual needs of stakeholders and the ways the competition business in Switzerland is developing. We have limited ourselves in this paper to describe the conceptual framing of the project.

The actual web-based platform KONKURADO provides features, such as, for example, the possibility for users to create their own competition portfolios and define their roles in individual competitions. In terms of the procedural space, we have limited the design to administrate several basic organizational tasks. In this procedural space, competitions can be advertised, organizers can collect questions and answer online, documents can be shared with various users, a prequalification can be organized over the tool, and, finally, the project space can be used to archive data in a searchable database. Access to project space and user rights can be handled by the space owner — usually the competition organizer — who can invite, according to the needs of a given procedure, jury/board members, competition participants and co-workers of his organizational unit to enter the project space and to view, download and/or edit data.

## ▬▬ Notes

[1] "KONKURADO | Web of Design Competitions, accessed July 2, 2014, http:// www.konkurado.ch

[2] "Towards 'Planning Competitions' as a Knowledge System", 2010-2013, research grant CTI No 11834.1 PFES-ES

[3] "SIMAP", accessed July 2, 2014, http://www.simap.ch

[4] "Wettbewerbe" Espazium, accessed July 2, 2014, http://www.espazium. ch/tec21/wettbewerbe

[5] "Catalogue des Concours Canadiens", accessed July 2, 2014, http://www. ccc.umontreal.ca

[6] "Competition Online", accessed July 2, 2014, http://www.competitionline. com/de

[7] Gerhard Schwabe, "Bedarfsanalyse," in CSCW-Kompendium, ed Gerhard Schwabe, Norbert Streitz, and Rainer Unland, (Berlin : Springer, 2001), 361-372.

## ▬▬ References

**Schwabe**, Gerhard "Bedarfsanalyse," in CSCW-Kompendium, edited by Gerhard Schwabe, Norbert Streitz, and Rainer Unland, 361-372. Berlin : Springer, 2001.

"**KONKURADO | Web of Design Competitions**". Accessed July 2, 2014, *http:// www.konkurado.ch*

"**Wettbewerbe**" Espazium. Accessed July 2, 2014, *http://www.espazium.ch/ tec21/wettbewerbe*

"**Catalogue des Concours Canadiens**". Accessed July 2, 2014, *http://www. ccc.umontreal.ca*

"**Competition Online**". Accessed July 2, 2014, *http://www.competitionline. com/de*

"**SIMAP**". Accessed July 2, 2014, https://www.simap.ch

# 4.4. Design Competitions in Brazil

**Building a [Digital] Culture for Architectural Quality**

**Fabiano Sobreira**, Ph.D.
Professor, Uniceub University — Brasilia
Architect, Brazilian Parliament
Brazil

The ongoing and increasing digital revolution, along with multiple and decentralized possibilities for disseminating, publishing, archiving, debating, networking and sharing ideas have changed the way we think on architectural culture and competitions. Bringing together editorial, academic and professional perspectives, the author reflects on recent experiences related to the "digital revolution" and the promotion, diffusion and judgement on architectural competitions in Brazil. In the first part of the paper, after reviewing the competition culture in the country, the author proposes some reflections on the role of internet-based tools towards the building of an architectural quality culture based on competitions, and presents–in this context–its editorial experience ahead of the website and electronic magazine *concursosdeprojeto.org*. In the second and final part of the paper, the author presents some recent experiences related to the diffusion and promotion of on-line competitions and their role in the democratization and dissemination of architectural competitions in Brazil.

**Cover**
Competition for a school of
Guine-Bissau (competition in
2010 built in 2012),

**Fig. 1**
School for Guine-Bissau — Architecture
Competition — First Prize — Board 02/06 Architects:
Bruno Giugliani, Cintia Gusson Etges, Karen Bammann.
*Source : concursosdeprojeto.org*

## On-line Competitions : A Digital Culture for Architectural Quality

On the west side of the Atlantic Ocean, in the "new nations" of North and Latin Americas, we find a less consolidated tradition of the State as policy maker. Consequently, the politics of architecture is either affected by the strength of market-based and liberal decisions (North America) or by the weakness of democracy, economic fragility and government instability (Latin America). Our premise is that such a political scenario partially explains the fragility, or even the absence of a consolidated competition system or policy in North and Latin American countries, in opposition to European ones. [1]

In Brazil–just as in Canada or the United States–there is no appropriate political space for design competitions as effective instruments in determining architectural quality. Between 1857 and 2007 approximately 690 architectural competitions were organized in Brazil [2] – an average of less than six events per year. In other words, in 150 years, Brazil has promoted fewer competitions than France promotes in one year. Other "less celebrated" Latin-American countries, such as Colombia, seem to have a more established quality-based architecture policy than Brazil. Despite Brazilian federal law, which since 1993 recommends competitions as the main instrument for commissioning architectural design, in practice, competitions are exceptions. [3] Most managers of public administration simply ignore the procedure or have pre-conceived ideas of architectural competitions as bureaucratic, expensive, time-consuming and wasteful. According to Kreiner : "Asking many people to work in parallel to produce alternative solutions to the same task, knowing that only one of them will be implemented, is, in retrospect, a wasteful procedure. But the wastefulness is rationalized as a necessary investment in creativity." [4]

Considering that competitions could sometimes be viewed as necessary but wasteful procedures, how could one make the process less wasteful, while making it more attractive and fair for all the actors involved ? One of the possible answers to the concern of wastefulness, as we argue in this paper, is adapting the competition procedure to the possibilities offered by the so-called digital revolution : electronic storage, diffusion and high-speed transmission of graphic information and data. In other words, promoting on-line competitions ; that is, procedures in which parts or even the whole process is based on digital resources and electronic means, including its diffusion, the submission and exhibition of projects, and sometimes even the judgement. [5]

The diffusion and promotion of on-line competitions is a direct response to three interrelated concerns: (1) diminishing the wastefulness of traditional competitions; (2) contributing to effective transparency, equality, democracy, and sustainability of the process; (3) preventing the memory loss of potential architecture culture. But, how is the digital revolution affecting the architectural culture and, consequently, the promotion of design competitions in Brazil?

## ▬ Architectural Culture, Knowledge Sharing and the Digital Revolution

In 1964, when Tadao Ando (Pritzker Prize Japanese architect, 1941) was twenty-three years old and decided to become an architect, he embarked on a journey around the world: from the Yokohama port by ship to Nakhodka (at the east end of Russia, then, Soviet Union), where he took the Trans-Siberian train to Moscow; from here to Finland, France, Switzerland, Italy, Greece and Spain. On the way back to Japan, he took a cargo ship passing by South Africa, Madagascar, India, Philippines and, finally, Japan. It was a seven-month trip, to learn about architecture.

For an architect, traveling is definitely a rich and constructive experience. But, how many architectural students (or even professionals along their whole career) are capable of making such a fantastic architectural journey? We know that before having the opportunity (if one ever has it) to see and feel in situ the masterpieces from Le Corbusier, Alvar Aalto, Antoni Gaudi or Michelangelo (just to mention the names Tadao Ando highlighted from his pilgrimage), students and professionals usually start their learning experiences "traveling" on books and magazines. For example, architects and students learnt that Brasilia is a built and living icon of modern architecture and urbanism; that it was the result of a competition won by the urbanist Lucio Costa in 1956 and that it gathers the main Oscar Niemeyer architectural masterpieces. They probably have distinct and particular opinions about the city, but how many of them have actually ever visited the Brazilian capital? Probably, most of those impressions and opinions were formed from reading books or magazines. But now an even cheaper and ever spreading source–the Internet–is sharing the role in the architectural learning process with printed books, magazines and travels.

At the beginning of the 1980s, computers were exceptions in architectural firms.[6] Nowadays it is hard to imagine an architectural office working without a digital platform, or even disconnected from the Internet. The digital culture in architecture started with CAD technologies in the 1980s, but it is with the spreading and popularization of the "World Wide Web," and especially, after recent improvements in recording and sharing graphic data (specifically speed transmission and storage capacity), that one could say the digital revolution really started and we are living it.

With the digital revolution constantly evolving, it is not only the everyday work of architectural offices that is changing, but also the whole concept of architectural culture: learning, teaching, researching, cataloguing, and sharing. Using any portable wireless gadget (perhaps mentioning tablets or smartphones could sound outdated to someone who reads this paper in five years time), one can easily travel through the architectural world–from its historical architectural icons to contemporary ideas; drawing from the most recent competitions around the world. Via the Internet, one can also access the projects (and design processes) of the main architectural offices– an experience which offers a level of detail and interactivity not available from printed sources. For example, recent developments in Virtual Reality (VR) by Columbia University allow students to "travel" through three-dimensional interactive images of architectural masterpieces via the Internet. Such advances mean that most architectural students and professionals are no longer limited to borrowing a book at the library or anxiously waiting the delivery of next month's magazine, as they can find and learn about whatever they want, wherever they are, through the "web." After all, as we've said, some of these websites offer a learning experience even deeper and more interactive than the average printed books and magazines.

However, the flipside of the digital revolution is the risk of superficiality, highlighting the difference between sharing information and promoting knowledge. Today, one witnesses an excess of information circulating in a free, diverse, intense and fast manner, but which part of such information has been properly retained as knowledge and is effectively forming a contemporary architectural culture? Would such superficiality be a side effect of a so-called tweeting culture, whose essence is based on texts limited to no more than 140 characters? Not necessarily. After all, the superficiality of quickly browsing a webpage, looking for "fancy" architectural images, is not so different from quickly leafing through the pages of a printed book or magazine. According to Antoine Picon:

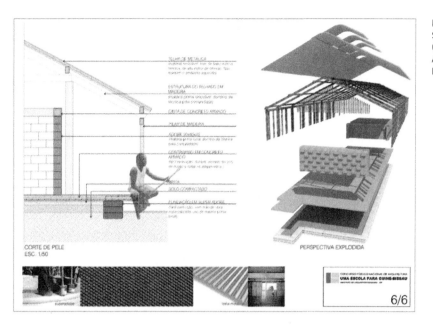

**Fig. 2**
School for Guine-Bissau — Architecture
Competition — First Prize — Board 06/06
Architects: Bruno Giugliani, Cintia Gusson
Etges, Karen Bammann.

*The incredible explosion of digital technologies forces us to rethink the question of time and memory. (...) the Internet has achieved an unheard-of feat in becoming both an incredible archive, the largest archive ever known to man, and at the same time appearing to have almost no memory.[7]*

In such a new world of digital transmission of ideas and concepts and also in a new context of debates on archiving and memory, competitions definitely have a special place and an important role to play on the building of contemporary architectural culture.

We argue that the diffusion of architectural competitions contributes to the collapse of time and space in learning and reflecting experiences. It reduces the distance and the time that used to separate students and professionals all over the world from the freshness of contemporary ideas and debates in architecture. Competition projects can be the shortest and fastest path between the learning/reflecting professional and such cutting edge architectural concepts and debates. After all, considering the amount of time and effort (social, political and economical) needed to convert a concept into construction, new architectural concepts are usually primarily published and disseminated as non-built ideas, and those ideas used to play an important role in the building of the architectural culture. Thus, studying contemporary architecture as a cultural expression through recently conceived and non-built ideas, such as those generated from competitions, could allow for a better understanding of its contemporaneity and its context–aspects which tend to be lost in the lapse of time between the architectural conception and its materialization.

Therefore, considering that a competition project, as "potential architecture [...] belongs to these activities of architectural thinking located exactly at the crossroads of discipline and profession"[8], its purpose and utility go beyond the need of choosing an idea for a specific building or space: it is also a learning tool, a reflective source on possibilities for design and planning strategies and, in such a competitive world, it is also an important instrument of propaganda and promotion of architectural offices. That is why, despite the apparent "wastefulness of the procedure"[9], architects used to acknowledge the importance of competitions as reflective and creative exercises and they used to archive or even display and publish their experiences in competitions, even when they were not the winners. A recent relevant experience is the exhibition and book about the Pritzker Prize winner, Portuguese architect Eduardo Souto de Moura, which displayed projects from fifty competitions, encompassing thirty years of work.[10] According to Alberto Campo Baeza, in his essay for the exhibition book:

*We are not as much concerned here with Souto de Moura's constructed work as with the competitions and the tremendous effort and enviable inner strength required to participate in every one of them. This is an exhibition showing all the competitions that this architect has entered, no matter if he has won or not. It is like a collection of dreams, some of which have come true and others have not. (...) Souto de Moura's designs for these competitions may be considered his most radical ones, something that we should always demand of ourselves in competitions: strong and extreme ideas, capable of generating the best possible architecture.*[11]

But before the digital revolution there used to be a considerable delay between the conception of an architectural idea in a competition and its diffusion to the general audience. At that time, if you were not part of a privileged professional or academic circle, or if you were not living in the same city or country where the competition exhibition would take place, you would probably have access to these new and fresh ideas only after a couple of months or even years later, through books or magazines; or maybe never, if the competition boards were discarded (as usually they were) after the exhibitions. Nowadays, projects are diffused via the web even before the competition ends, and in some competitions the organizers even use the Internet to collect the community impressions on competition proposals, before the final jury decision.

Without the possibilities of digital technologies, competition projects (especially those not qualified as winners by the jury) used to be easily and simply discarded and, as a consequence, lots of potential ideas and concepts were lost. It's not a coincidence that the LEAP (one of the most internationally acknowledged initiatives on research and cataloguing competitions) started in 2001, under the flourishing of the digital revolution. For the LEAP team of researchers, the cataloguing and research efforts go beyond the competition project and focus on the whole event:

*It becomes clear that if a project is not merely a collection of drafts, neither is a competition merely a collection of projects. It is an encounter between a brief, some projects, experts and juries (p. 543).*[12]

But this "new era" also brings new challenges for the dissemination and use of digital archives. According to De Meyer:

*The role of the archivist – traditionally the gatekeeper of the archive – has evolved towards the gate opener, the one who facilitates access. (...) Facilitating access to archives is not only about providing access to more documents, but also about creating better ways of connecting them.*[13]

In this sense, another feature of the digital revolution is the diversity and decentralization of publishers and the multiplicity of information sources. Considering that culture formation depends on sharing information, and information means power, it leads to an era of power decentralization and cultural diversity on the editorial world as well, expressed by the multiplicity of publishing vehicles. According to De Meyer:

*Until 2003-04, content creators accounted for a marginal fringe of web users, but today we tend towards a situation in which the internet user becomes as much a creator of information as he is its consumer. (...) We are leaving the information provider model for another model in which content is generated, reviewed, corrected, criticized permanently in a much more diffuse way among all participants in the community.*[14]

The model described by De Meyer is the one in which we would like to situate the recent editorial experience that will be described in the next section: *concursosdeprojeto.org*, a Brazilian website and electronic magazine specialized on architectural competitions.

**Fig. 3**
School for Guine-Bissau — Architecture
Competition — Second Prize — Board 01/06
Architects: Luciano Rocha de Andrades, Rochelle
Rizzotto Castro, Silvio Lagranha Machado.

**Fig. 4**
School for Guine-Bissau — Architecture
Competition — Second Prize — Board 06/06
Architects: Luciano Rocha de Andrades, Rochelle
Rizzotto Castro, Silvio Lagranha Machado.

**Fig. 5**
School for Guine-Bissau — Architecture
Competition — Third Prize — Board 05/06
Architects: Bernardo Richter, Fernando Caldeira de
Lacerda, Pedro Amin Tavares.

**Fig. 6**
School for Guine-Bissau — Architecture
Competition — Third Prize — Board 06/06
Architects: Bernardo Richter, Fernando Caldeira de
Lacerda, Pedro Amin Tavares.

## www.concursosdeprojeto.org : A Web-based Editorial Experience on Architectural Competitions

In 2008, as one of the products of a post-doctoral research developed at LEAP (Université de Montréal) related to a comparative analysis of competitions in Brazil and Canada, the website *concursosdeprojeto.org* was idealized and created. The idea originated from three motivations : (1) the need for an on-line tool for publishing and sharing data and information related to the on-going post-doctoral research with other lusophone researchers ; (2) the lacking within the Brazilian editorial field, of a publication specializing in competitions ; (3) the aim of contributing to the building of a culture of architectural quality based on competitions in Brazil.

*Concursosdeprojeto.org* is a non-commercial editorial project based on two simultaneous formats : a website (with a continuous flux of publications) and a monthly electronic magazine, with registered ISSN (International Standard Serial Number : 2238-1430). Three main sections, with regular publications, define the editorial project : competitions announcements (anúncios de concursos) ; results and projects (resultados e projetos) and built projects (obras construídas). Besides, there are other special sections, with less regular publications : essays and debates (ensaios e debates), interviews (entrevistas), researches and publications (pesquisas e publicações). It is yet a quite small, modest and experimental editorial project, especially if compared to the main international on-line architectural magazines and websites. Yet, at the beginning of 2015, *concursosdeprojeto.org* was the main lusophone source of information on "concursos de arquitetura" (architectural competitions) on the Internet.

The project was not conceived as a competitions catalogue, but as an on-line interactive platform that could gather all parties interested in the issue of competitions and related themes, such as professionals and students looking for announcements of national and international competitions ; architectural offices aiming to diffuse their winning and built projects (resulting from competitions) ; competition organizers interested in the diffusion of their events ; students and professionals interested in public architecture ; researchers and academics with pedagogical and reflecting purposes.

It is worth mentioning that as an open and interactive platform, the website and electronic magazine *concursosdeprojeto.org* is also an environment of debate on contemporary architecture, urban development and public policy, all from the perspective of competitions, among other related issues. As such, readers are able to publish comments (always moderated by the editors) and are invited to register their impressions about each new publication. Naturally, as one could expect in the democratic and diverse arena of the Internet, comments vary from simple words, to rich and deep analysis, offered by students, academics and professionals.

In discussing the sharing of information on the Internet, it is inevitable to consider copyright laws. In this matter, *concursosdeprojeto.org* follows and shares the principles and the vision of *Creative Commons* (*creativecommons.org*) – a free, public, and standardized infrastructure that creates a balance between the reality of the Internet and the reality of copyright laws. Its mission is to develop, support, and steward legal and technical infrastructure that maximizes digital creativity, sharing, and innovation. Since its launch in 2008, *concursosdeprojeto.org* has been the "stage" for important discussions related to competitions and public architecture in Brazil ; acting at the same time as a platform for the diffusion of contemporary architecture, as well as a permanent forum for debates and the promotion of competitions as instruments for architectural quality. Among these issues, one is particularly worthy of mention in this paper : the promotion and diffusion of on-line competitions. In the following section, we present and discuss two recent experiences on the promotion of on-line competitions in Brazil.

## A School for Guinea-Bissau

In 2010, as the result of diplomatic exchanges between Brazil and Guinea-Bissau, the Brazilian International Cooperation Agency (ABC), a department of the Brazilian Ministry of International Affairs, asked the Brazilian Architects Institute (IAB-DF) to donate an architectural design for a school to be built in Bissau, capital of Guinea-Bissau. As a response to that demand, the IAB-DF suggested the promotion of a national architectural competition. At that time the "wastefulness" and "bureaucracy" of competitions, especially for architects who decided to compete, was a recurrent theme at the IAB, and there were several discussions about formats and possibilities to reduce costs and minimize the exploration of competing professionals. Acknowledging the potential of digital resources and inspired by a previous experience with the promotion of a Students Architectural Competition, the IAB-DF decided to

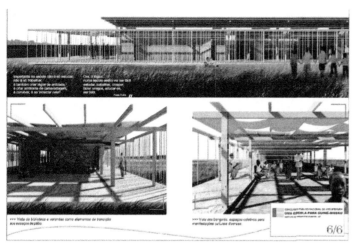

**Fig. 7**
School for Guine-Bissau — Architecture
Competition — Honored Mention 01 — Board 06/06
Architect: Mirelle Papaleo Koelzer.

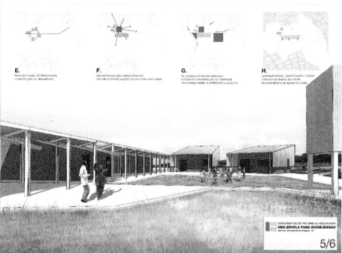

**Fig. 8**
School for Guine-Bissau — Architecture
Competition — Honored Mention 02 — Board 05/06
Architects: Bruno Salvador, Carlos Augusto Ferrata,
Cesar Shundi Iwamizu, Eduardo Pereira Gurian.

**Fig. 9**
School for Guine-Bissau — Architecture
Competition — Honored Mention 03 — Board 06/06
Architects: Cassio de Lucena Carvalho, Edmar
Ferreira Junior, VinÌcius Martins ¡vila.

launch the Guinea-Bissau On-line Architectural Competition as a first professional experience of a completely on-line procedure. Launched in August 2010, the competition was run completely by electronic procedures via the Internet: from the diffusion, registration, design submission, exhibition and inclusively – judgement. In fact, because of budget restrictions, the on-line procedure was the only possible way to ensure competition feasibility, particularly in regards to the high costs of the traditional judgement procedure.

Considering the opportunity and the potentialities of the electronic procedure and the challenge of the proposed on-line judgement, the organizers decided to compose a jury combining locals with nationally and internationally acclaimed architects, most of whom had considerable experience in competitions. The eighty-three projects submitted in .pdf format (each project composed of 04 boards, A3 size) were analyzed and evaluated by the jury in the electronic format during nine days of on-line procedures. The jury did not gather, so the only communication established among the jury members was via the Internet, specifically through e-mail exchanges and an on-line forum moderated by the competition coordinator. Each jury member could visualize, from his or her computer screen, all eighty-three projects, both in small and high resolution, as a virtual exhibition. The on-line judgement procedure followed the same sequence of a traditional (in situ) one: a first set of individual analysis to define shortlists, followed by a final collective evaluation of the selected propositions (the finalists). The final result was consensual, but not unanimous: the winner was decided according to votes, following a collective (on-line) discussion. Despite acknowledging some limitations of this first experience with an on-line collective debate and judgement when compared to the traditional in-situ experience, the jury members and the competition coordinators agreed that it was a valuable and necessary experience requiring immediate improvement so that it could be implemented and disseminated in the near future.

At the beginning of 2012, the school was under construction in Guinea-Bissau. The architectural design authors, competition winners (young architects from Porto Alegre, south of Brazil) spent six months in 2011 in Guinea-Bissau, supervising construction. After the Guinea-Bissau on-line experience, the same year, another National Architectural Competition was promoted through on-line procedures: CNM (Municipalities National Confederation Headquarters in Brasilia). This time the jury gathered in-situ, but the analysis was based on electronic platforms, and

the projects were displayed and analyzed through computer screens and projections. Jury members acknowledged that the electronic format was far more practical, comfortable and productive when compared to the traditional format of printed boards.

## ▬ Renova São Paulo – Urban Infrastructure and Social Housing

In December 2011, Brazil was proclaimed the sixth largest economy in the world, overtaking the UK. And according to IMF (International Monetary Fund), Brazil was expected to climb past France to become the fifth-largest economy by 2016. But at the same time, according to the World Bank (2011), Brazil became the world's eighth worst country in terms of income concentration, and such figures had clear effects on its urban and social development: according to the Brazilian Institute of Geography and Statistics (IBGE), in 2011, 43% of Brazilian homes or 25 million, are not considered adequate for habitation, and 11 million Brazilians live in slums.

In acknowledgement of existing challenging realities (despite the most recent economic developments), such as social exclusion, income concentration and urban poverty, the Brazilian government has invested (in the last ten years) a considerable amount of effort and investment in social inclusion programs. At least, that is the message one can read from a recent government official slogan: "a rich country is a country without poverty." Among these programs, the social housing projects and slums improvement plans seem to be priorities for public administration. A recent and internationally acclaimed example is the social housing program implemented by the city of São Paulo. According to the housing department of São Paulo City Hall their purpose is not to eliminate the informal city, but rather to improve it:

*Since 2005 the city of São Paulo has chosen to take the risk by stating that informal settlements and slums are not a degenerative disease of the contemporary city. (...) the slums are part of what constitutes the urban reality of the state capital."* [15]

In this context, the Social Housing Department of São Paulo City Hall, in partnership with the Brazilian Architects Institute, decided to promote a national competition in 2010 with the purpose of selecting, through architectural design and urban planning ideas, architects and urban planners to

**Fig. 10**
School for Guine-Bissau — Winning Design — Building
Process — Winning Design — 2011.

**Fig. 11**
School for Guine-Bissau — Winning Design — Building
Process — Winning Design — 2011.

**Fig. 12**
School for Guine-Bissau — Winning Design — Building
Process — Winning Design — 2011.

work on a multi-million urbanization project for twenty-two peripheral areas in São Paulo. But how does one organize, on a tight schedule, such a complex competition, managing simultaneous registrations and proposals for twenty-two areas of intervention, each one with its specific briefs (dozens of subsiding documents and graphic data for each area), keeping it anonymous and transparent, and at the same time making it cost-effective for public administration and attractive for the competing architectural offices ? The answer proposed by the IAB was the promotion of an on-line competition.

Following the examples of Guinea-Bissau and CNM Headquarters competitions, the Renova São Paulo Competition was also run by electronic procedures through the Internet (including diffusion, registration, design submission and winning designs exhibition). Following the same principle of design synthesis that marked the previous on-line competitions, competitors were asked to submit their proposals (architectural and urban design preliminary ideas) in electronic format (pdf–04 boards, A3 size). All winning designs were published on the competition's official website as soon as the winners were announced. Besides the agility of the process, the electronic procedure also included, in this case, an interactive registration panel, which allowed potential competitors to know the number of candidates for each one of the twenty-two areas. As such, a potential competitor could consult the panel and the number of candidates for each area, before registration. In 2011 the winners signed contracts to develop their projects, and new competitions are expected to be launched to continue with the social housing program in São Paulo.

After these recent experiences, one can affirm that on-line procedures could help to demystify the idea of competitions as wasteful procedures. On the contrary, on-line competitions can help to make the procedure more economic, agile, transparent and sustainable. But just as democracy, as an institution, is not enough to guarantee social inclusion, transparency and fairness ; competitions alone (on-line or not), are not enough to guarantee the desired quality of the built environment. Both democracy and competitions depend on public commitment and constant management of conflicting interests ; otherwise, it would be "nothing more than a democratic facade on an autocratic decree".[16]

Answering the initial proposed question: Can digital archiving of competitions projects enhance the building of a planetary architectural culture? The answer could be yes, if we think on such a planetary architectural culture from an ethical perspective and not necessarily from its aesthetical expressions. After all, aesthetical values may differ locally, but ethical values can be planetary. In this sense, more than archiving competitions projects, it is essential to disseminate and discuss the competition culture as a basis for quality judgement. And such dissemination, in the "planetary age" depends and must rely on the potential of the digital revolution for worldwide archiving, publishing, sharing, debating and promoting competitions as instruments for architectural quality.

Finally, someone could ask: Thanks to the digital revolution, could Tadao Ando's seven-month journey around the world to learn about architecture, in the "planetary age" be replaced by a seven days on-line navigation through the web? Certainly the intensity of being on site and the essences of experiencing a culture in situ will never be replaced by any virtual experience. But accessing and sharing architectural concepts and ideas (real or potential) through digital resources and the Internet will probably help to make the in situ learning adventure more deep, valuable, profitable and enjoyable.

## ▬ Notes

[1] F. Sobreira, «Competitions: Public Strategies for Architectural Quality,» Conditions Magazine. The Politics of Quality Management, no. 5-6 (2010).

[2] M. H. Flynn, «Concursos De Arquitetura No Brasil: 1850-2000» (Universidade de São Paulo, 2001).

[3] F. Sobreira, «Le concours et la réglementation au Brésil,» Architecture-Québec. Les Concours: une affaire de jugement, no. 154 (2011a).

[4] K. Kreiner, «Designing Architectural Competitions: Balancing Multiple Matters of Concern,» Conditions Magazine. The Future of Competitions, no. 7 (2010): 14.

[5] F. Sobreira, «Concursos Em Meio Eletrônico: Razões E Recomendações,» Concursosdeprojeto.org March 2011, no. 28 (2011b), http://concursosdeprojeto.org/2011/03/20/concursos-em-meio-eletronico-razoes-e-recomendacoes.

[6] A. Picon, «Architecture and Digital Memory,» in Architecture et archives numériques: l'architecture à l'ère numérique: un enjeu de mémoire, ed. D. Peyceré and F. Wierre (Genève: Infolio, 2008).

[7] A. Picon, «Architecture and Digital Memory,» in Architecture et archives numériques: l'architecture à l'ère numérique: un enjeu de mémoire, ed. D. Peyceré and F. Wierre (Genève: Infolio, 2008)., 69-70.

[8] J.-P. Chupin, D. Bilodeau, and G. Adamczyk, «Reflective Knowledge and Potential Architecture,» in Colloque international conjoint de l'American Research Consortium et de l'Association Européenne pour l'Enseignement de l'Architecture, ARCC / AEEA (McGill University, Montreal2002), 2.

[9] Kreiner, «Designing Architectural Competitions: Balancing Multiple Matters of Concern,» 14.

[10] M. Souto, «Eduardo Souto Moura,» in Concursos. Competitions. 1979-2010, ed. Eduardo Souto Moura (Universidade do Porto, Portugal: Faculdade de Arquitectura, 2011).

[11] A. Baeza, «Souto, Souto, Souto,» ibid., 30.

[12] J.-P. Chupin, «Documenter Les concours, concourir à la recherche, archiver l'Évènement / Documenting Competitions, Contributing to Research, Archiving Events,» in Architecture et archives numériques: l'architecture à l'ère numérique: un enjeu de mémoire, ed. D. Peyceré and F. Wierre (Genève: Infolio, 2008).

[13] De Meyer, «New Challenges for the Dissemination and Use of Digital Archives,» ibid., 440.

[14] De Meyer, «New Challenges for the Dissemination and Use of Digital Archives,» ibid., 440.

[15] Elisabeth França and F. Serapião, «São Paulo Social Housing Department,» Revista Monolito: The urban guerrilla fighter, no. 7 (2012): 46.

[16] D. Lawrence, «The Dilemma of Democracy,» Conditions Magazine. The Future of Competitions, no. 7 (2010).

## ▬ References

**Baeza**, A. "Souto, Souto, Souto." In *Concursos. Competitions. 1979-2010*, edited by Eduardo Souto Moura. Universidade do Porto, Portugal: Faculdade de Arquitectura, 2011.

**Chupin**, J.-P. «Documenter les concours, concourir à la recherche, archiver l'évènement / Documenting Competitions, Contributing to Research, Archiving Events.» In *Architecture Et Archives Numériques: L'architecture À L'ère Numérique: Un Enjeu De Mémoire*, edited by D. Peyceré and F. Wierre, 523-44. Genève: Infolio, 2008.

**Chupin**, J.-P., D. Bilodeau, and G. Adamczyk. «Reflective Knowledge and Potential Architecture.» In *Colloque international conjoint de l'American Research Consortium et de l'Association Européenne pour l'Enseignement de l'Architecture, ARCC / AEEA*. McGill University, Montreal, 2002.

**De Meyer**. «New Challenges for the Dissemination and Use of Digital Archives.» In *Architecture et archives numériques: l'architecture à l'ère numérique: un enjeu de mémoire*, edited by D. Peyceré and F. Wierre. Genève: Infolio, 2008.

**Flynn**, M. H. «Concursos De Arquitetura No Brasil: 1850-2000.» Universidade de São Paulo, 2001.

**França**, Elisabeth, and F. Serapião. "São Paulo Social Housing Department." *Revista Monolito: The urban guerrilla fighter*, no. 7 (2012).

**Kreiner**, K. «Designing Architectural Competitions: Balancing Multiple Matters of Concern.» *Conditions Magazine. The Future of Competitions*, no. 7 (2010).

**Lawrence**, D. «The Dilemma of Democracy.» *Conditions Magazine. The Future of Competitions*, no. 7 (2010).

**Picon**, A. «Architecture and Digital Memory.» In *Architecture et archives Numériques: l'architecture à l'ère numérique: un enjeu de mémoire*, edited by D. Peyceré and F. Wierre. Genève: Infolio, 2008.

**Sobreira**, F. «Competitions: Public Strategies for Architectural Quality.» *Conditions Magazine. The Politics of Quality Management*, no. 5-6 (2010).

**Sobreira**, F. "Concursos Em Meio Eletrônico: Razões E Recomendações." *Concursosdeprojeto.org* March 2011, no. 28 (2011b). *http://concursosdeprojeto.org/2011/03/20/concursos-em-meio-eletronico-razoes-e-recomendacoes*.

**Sobreira**, F. «Le concours et la réglementation au Brésil.» *Architecture-Québec. Les concours: une affaire de jugement*, no. 154 (2011a): 41-43.

**Souto**, M. "Eduardo Souto Moura." In *Concursos. Competitions. 1979-2010*, edited by Eduardo Souto Moura. Universidade do Porto, Portugal: Faculdade de Arquitectura, 2011.

**Section 5**
# Publishing Architectural Ideas

297

# 5.1. wettbewerbe aktuell
## Competitions as Impetus for German Building Culture

**Thomas Hoffmann-Kuhnt**, Chief Editor
wa wettbewerbe aktuell
Germany

The journal called, wa — wettbewerbe aktuell was founded in 1971 and has since been dedicated to architectural competitions: award-winning designs are documented impartially with true-to-scale reduction of the design, photos of the model and the comments of the jury. The journal is suitable for archiving to allow the subscriber to create his own private design-archive. This design-archive, developed since 1971, comprises approximately 6,000 competitions and 30,000 designs. It presents an impressive and unique testimony of contemporary architecture. Initially only German competition results have been published, but since the early 1990s interesting international competition results have been increasingly published as well as the presentation of completed competition projects.

The significance of the wa-specific documentation of competitions shall be highlighted by the case studies concerning the HafenCity Hamburg, the Porsche Museum Stuttgart, and several examples for everyday architecture. Due to these examples it was possible to train the perception of certain trends, to notice aesthetic developments in architecture and to provoke critical debates – to allow future generations to understand which specific criteria at what time conclusively determined the criteria for an ambitious architecture.

**Cover**
The intial idea was maintained from the competition design up to the completed building. *Aerial view of Hafen City (Hamburg)*

Competitions in Germany are of extraordinarily high significance, much higher than in most other countries. To illustrate this, one needs to highlight the development after the Second World War in that the reconstruction of destroyed cities led to an immense building boom, which resulted in an increased need for architects.

At that time there was a ministerial decree that demanded architectural competitions for all state-aided buildings, such as schools, town halls, etc. Inevitably all architects who were interested in the planning of public buildings had to participate in competitions. Success in competitions during the '60s was the start for many architects who are now internationally renowned. For example, Meinhard von Gerkan and Volkwin Marg, GMP Architects, got their first contract for the Airport Berlin-Tegel as newcomers; and Günther Benisch, for the 1972 Olympia buildings in Munich.

### ▬▬ Formation of the Publishing Company wettbewerbe aktuell in 1971

With the steadily increasing significance of competitions as important acquisition vehicles, the need for information grew larger. All interested architects wanted to know the names of the prizewinners, the look of the winning designs, the general trend of selection, and how the jury deliberated. However, at that time no communication medium existed that could fulfill this demand. I noticed this lack of information in 1968 when I began studying architecture in Munich. As a result, I developed a concept for a journal which could document the most important competitions—with the intent of being impartial and non-judgemental. I deliberately chose to abandon a critical review. The reader target group would be exclusively architects, as they would like to form their own opinion. Another idea was to create a way to file the documentation divided by subject, so that at the end of the year the reader got a kind of reference work on architectural competitions. Therefore, I founded, while still a student, a publishing company. The first issue appeared in June 1971 with the name wa wettbewerbe aktuel–a rough english translation of this would be something like "competitions up-to-date," and the publication is published on a monthly basis.

This founding principle to provide an extensive non-judgemental space to archive documentation has been kept until today. Over the last forty-one years the journal has been improved in many respects, as one can see from the development of the cover [Fig.1]. The trend in drawing techniques has changed dramatically since the beginning of the digital age of the 1990s–before it was perspective ink drawings, and now it is CAD and architectural renderings.

### ▬▬ The Concept of the Journal wa wettbewerbe aktuell

The concept of wa is divided in 3 parts:

The first part comprises general competition information, starting with a guest commentary, index, calendar with all current competitions, newest tenders, and results of those competitions, which are not documented in the second part. But mostly pictures and plan material are available on the homepage of wa.

The second and most important part of the journal comprises the competition documentation. First the international competitions are documented, and afterwards the German ones. Normally, the first page of the document is comprised of the general information, such as the timetable, jury, and prizewinners with their co-workers, as well as the assignment, in both German and English. At times photographs of the models and competition area are included. The following pages document the awarded projects and feature the most important design material. Each are presented in accordance with the layout of the respective author, and if available, the jury´s assessment [Fig.2].

The third part of the magazine consists of completed projects with photos, design material and the comments of the architect, in both German and English [Fig.3].

Currently, the wa company publishes additional books for competitions of a particular subject. In addition, a publication which deals exclusively with student competitions is published annually [Fig.4].

In the present digital age the online database which is updated daily plays an important role in offering the readers an access to all Europe-wide tenders for architects and engineers [Fig.5].

### ▬▬ Significant Changes in the Field of Architectural Competitions due to the Introduction of EU Regulations in the 1990s

To begin to understand the problems of competitions in Europe, one has to turn back the clock.

The dramatic political and social changes at the end of the 1980s, together with Germany´s reunification and the establishment of the European Union, fundamentally altered the field of competitions.

**Fig. 1**
The development of the cover of
**wa** *wettbewerbe aktuell.*

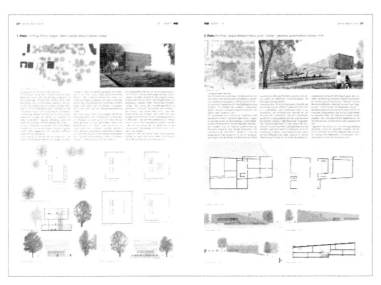

**Fig. 2**
Calendar and newest tenders.

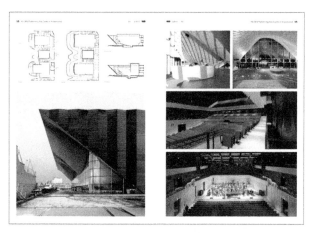

**Fig. 3**
Typical competition documentation
shown by "Grimms World in Kassel"
as an example.

**Fig. 4**
Subject Books "Schools And
Kindergardens","Museums"
and *wa*-vision.

**Fig. 5**
The *wa* homepage, updated daily.

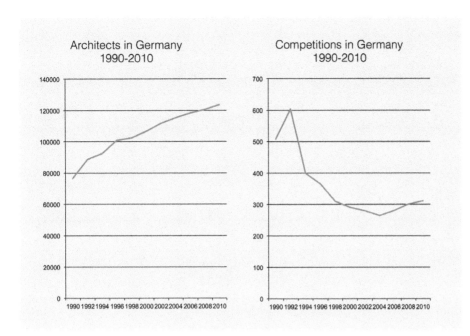

Architects in Germany
1990-2010

Competitions in Germany
1990-2010

**Fig. 6**
The proportionality of German architects and competitions over the last twenty years.

The inner-European principles of non-discrimination required an amendment of the Rules of Competition. From this point on regional competitions were no longer allowed and, apart from invitational ones, only Europe-wide tenders are admitted. These were divided into open and limited open competitions. Open competitions indicate that every architect based in Europe is allowed to participate. Limited open competitions state that everyone may apply, however the client may select the participants according to predetermined criteria.

These regulations regarding Europe-wide competitions are discouraging many clients from the open competitions. Consequently, the most chosen competition form is limited open, with an application procedure. Here every participant must prove his ability and is judged along several criteria, such as success, office size, and office equipment. This inevitably leads to a situation where the same established offices are selected more frequently, and young architects rarely have the opportunity to take part.

The development over the last twenty years since the reunification of Germany demonstrates a problem. The number of German architects increased from 76,000 in 1990 to over 124,000 today, with a declining number of inhabitants of approximately 82 million. There has also been

a a reduction of competitions from approximatley 600 in 1992, to 300 today **[Fig.6]**. These numbers explicitly reveal a dilemma, expecially considering there are currently 6,000 new architects per year who are graduating from universities and entering the labour market. These statistics were retrieved from the *Federal Chamber of German Architects (BAK)* in Berlin.

## ▬ Case Study : Hamburg HafenCity

Hamburg's HafenCity is an excellent example for successful urban development based on competitions. In the mid-1990s, it was decided that a completely new district would be developed between the River Elbe and the listed warehouse district on mainly run-down wasteland **[Fig.7]**.

In 1998, the first master plan for an area of more than 150 hectare was developed, which proposed to extend the city by 40% with an urban mix-use development with areas for housing, services, culture, leisure, tourism and trade. In 1999, an urban ideas competition was carried out ; First prize went to Kees Christiaanse / ASTOC architects in cooperation with Hamburgplan, a planning association of several architects and city planners from Hamburg **[Fig.8]**.

**Fig. 7**
The area for Hamburg's
HafenCity in 1990.

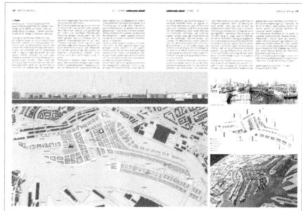

**Fig. 8**
The publication of the first-prize
winning Kees Christiaanse/ASTOC
architects proposal.

**Fig. 9**
Masterplan 2000.

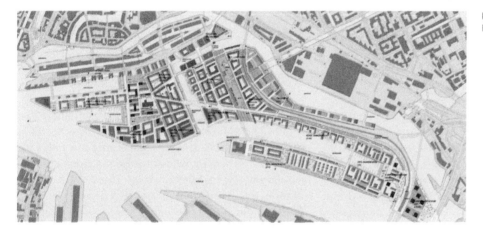

**Fig. 10**
Aerial photo 2011. *Aerial view of
Hafen City (Hamburg).*

The new master plan was based on this design with proposed 5,800 apartments and more than 45,000 work places, over 2 million square metres gross ground floor area, and 26 hectares of public parks **[Fig.9]**.

The first realization of competitions began as early as in 2001. In 2004 an exciting row of residential houses was already completed. The aerial photo from 2011 **[Fig.10]** depicts the further completion of the project — it is remarkable how fast a former wasteland was developed into an attractive city district.

Besides residential housing, office buildings are another integral aspect of the HafenCity. A typical office building is the so-called Spiegelhaus. This is the administrative and editorial building which houses the news magazine *Der Spiegel*.

This competition was launched in 2007 as a limited competition, and was published in *wa* in 11/2007. There were three first prizes awarded and they went to: first Henning Larsen Architects, Copenhagen, whose proposal envisaged two congeneric buildings in different sizes **[Fig.11]**; second KSP Engel and Zimmermann, Braunschweig, who proposed two bent building discs; and third Jan Störmer and Partner, Hamburg, set several angles against each other.

The implementation of the project was carried out based on a revised version of Henning Larsen's design, and was completed in summer 2011 and published in *wa* 12/2011 **[Fig.12]**. Here one can see how the first concept of the design, a tipped over cover of the magazine "Der Spiegel," could be consequently maintained from the competition design up to the final completed building **[Fig.13]**.

Altogether there have been 63 competitions for the HafenCity, with 300 participating architectural offices, and according to the masterplan there will be additional competitions for the eastern section.

## ▬ Case Study: Porsche Museum

Innovative and spectacular designs are found in many German museum competitons. At the beginning of 2005, Porsche launched a competition for its new automobile museum in Stuttgart: First prize went to Delugan Meissl Architects, Vienna, with their design for a seemingly floating exhibition area on top of a polygonal building base **[Fig.14]**.

Second prize went to Staab Architects from Berlin. This team recommended a resting solitaire at its Core—a sculptural structure growing as symbol of the Porsche idea and encased with an innovative translucent stone facade **[Fig.15]**.

The third prize went to Allmann Sattler Wappner architects, from Munich, who designed a cubic

volume covered with an abstract façade, combined with an inviting spiral shaped ramp running through the inside of the building **[Fig.16]**.

The fourth prize went to Lamott + Wittfoht architects, from Stuttgart. They planned a triangular building structure with two exhibition areas and a façade with a large-scale honeycomb structure.

The museum was completed within three years based on the design of the first prizewinners **[Fig.17]**. It was inaugurated in 2009. The floating effect of the exhibition area was increased.

## ▬ Case Study: Everyday Architecture

As significant as these spectacular projects are, especially in the media, we must also draw attention to the importance of smaller buildings, the everyday architecture that characterizes the principal image of our cities.

### Kindergarden Schwetzinger Terrasse Heidelberg

A typical example is the competition for a kindergarden in Heidelberg. The first prize went to the office of Behnisch Architects **[Fig.18]**, demonstrating that renowned offices not only successfully participate in big international competititons, but in small ones as well. The second prize went to K9 Architects **[Fig.19]**, where their proposal embraced the entire kindergarden area with a trellis structure for climbing plants. The third prize went to Harris + Kurrle Architects, while the fourth-prize team of Hermann Architecture detached themselves from an urban framework, and proposed a powerful solitaire building shaped like an elevated tree house.

### Galileum Solingen

The second example of everyday architecture is a small but an extraordinary one. In many cities in Germany there are numerous unused and unsightly gasometers. A competition was launched In the small town of Solingen for the conversion of such a gas-ball into a planetarium and observatory. The first prize went to mvm + starke **[Fig.20]**, who proposed a tower-like extension beside the ball; the second prize went to kister scheithauer gross **[Fig.21]**, who placed a satellite next to the gas-ball. The third prize, töpfer bertuleit, focused on an underground extension. The fourth prize, Bernhardt and Leeser, placed an elevated building alongside the pre-exisitng structure.

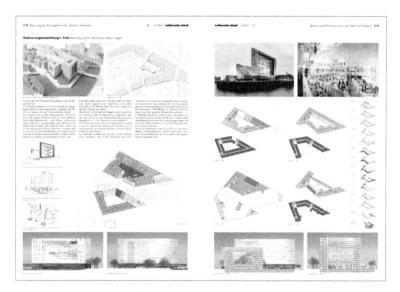

**Fig. 11**
The competition draft of Henning Larsen Architects, Copenhagen in **wa** 11/2007.
*Aerial view of Hafen City (Hamburg).*

**Fig. 12**
This project was completed in summer 2011.
*Aerial view of Hafen City (Hamburg).*

**Fig. 13**
The intial idea was maintained from the competition design up to the completed building.
*Aerial view of Hafen City (Hamburg).*

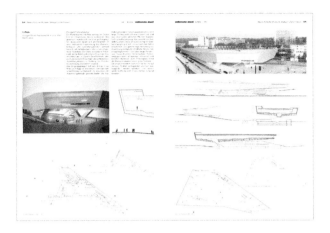

**Fig. 14**
The Project of Delugan Meissl
Architects, Vienna.
*Porsche Museum*

**Fig. 15**
Project proposal by Staab Architects, Berlin.
*Porsche Museum*

**Fig. 16**
The Project of Allmann Sattler
Wappner architects, Munich.
*Porsche Museum*

**Fig. 17**
The museum was completed in three
years based on the design of the first
prizewinners. *Porsche Museum*

**Fig.18 (left)**
First prize Behnisch Architects.

**Fig.19 (right)**
Second prize K9 Architects.

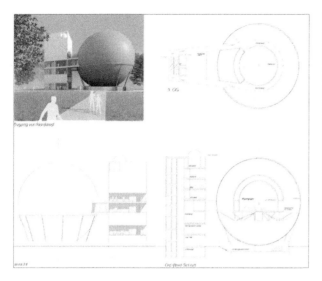

**Fig. 20**
First prize mvm + starke.
*Landmark Halde Duhamel (Ensdorf).*

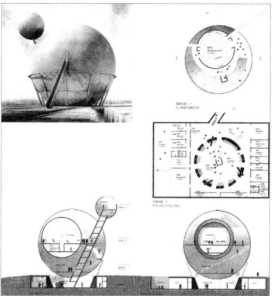

**Fig. 21**
Second prize kister scheithauer gross.
*Landmark Halde Duhamel (Ensdorf).*

**Fig. 22**
First prize Pfeiffer and Sachse.
*Landmark Halde Duhamel (Ensdorf).*

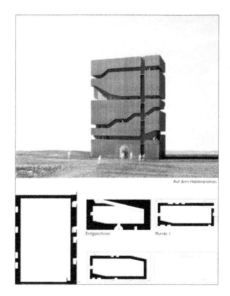

**Fig. 23**
Second prize Florian Kirfel.
*Landmark Halde Duhamel (Ensdorf).*

## Landmark Halde Duhamel in Ensdorf

As a final example I will address the competition for the Landmark at the Waste Rock Pile

Duhamel in Ensdorf whereby the cooperation between architects, landscape architects and artists was required. A suprising first prize was the proposal by Pfeiffer and Sachse **[Fig.22]**. This design focused on the long-distance view, as the project looked different from each direction. The second prize went to Florian Kirfel **[Fig.23]**, whose project can be viewed as a cross-section of the region´s geology with tunnels and shafts lifted up to the surface. The third prize, Hackl + Hoffmann, evoked an open book cover.

These projects are very rarely published in the architectural press. Rather, the local papers on occasion cover the outcome of such a competition.

To conclude, in analyzing the landscape of media it is evident that a large portion of the media is primarily interested in completed projects. The competition phase is especially interesting as one can promptly detect the newest trends of architecture. Here, in direct comparison with the designs which are based on the same site with the same building program, debates emerge, which could indeed contribute to the further development of architecture. Therefore it can be said the publication of competititon projects is of special importance. Competitions are true vehicles for the critical debate on architectural quality.

An important question remains as to what the future holds for architecture in the digital age, and how we can bring architectural quality closer to the public. One possibility is that those of us in the media can stimulate the debate about architectural quality with ongoing suitable online and print publications. On the other hand, one has to show tenders and clients that competitions lead to the best solution for their building projects, and that they may also contribute to positive public relations.

In general, the competition procedure is still regarded as relatively expensive and elaborate, and this should change. For example, *wa* has developed an extremely reasonable online tendering program. Thanks to free online access, all competition material can be sent without postage and expensive printing, and the application phase or first phase of a two-phase competition can be handled in a fast and cost effective manner.

# 5.2. www.competitions.org

**Competing Globally
in the Information Age**

**G. Stanley Collyer**, Ph.D.
Director. The Competition Project, Inc.
United States of America

The advent of the Internet has had a profound effect on the way in which design competitions are organized. First of all, with all the communication advantages provided by the Internet, advertising a competition is now comparatively easy and inexpensive. The downside of the internet era, with its reduction in advertising and processing costs, is a lowering of standards and the proliferation of ideas competitions. Now almost anyone can advertise an ideas competition, and there are enough examples of architects setting themselves up as competition sponsors, without a real client in the background. Without a specific site in mind certain competitions tend to be very theoretical in nature, and often are asking the participants to come up with a program.

The proliferation of competitions administered in two stages marks a significant change. There are two common scenarios:

- A limited competition preceded by a Request for Qualifications (RfQ) to arrive at a shortlist.
- An open stage competition followed by a second stage with shortlisted finalists

The RfQ variety is often looking for teams having previous experience with the subject at hand. The latter variant can give younger designers an opportunity to break through the glass ceiling and gain an important commission.

**Cover**
New England Biolabs, Ipswich (MA),
USA (Weston Williamson, 2002-2005).
*Copyright: Richard Mandelkorn (2005).*

Before the 1980s, most competitions around the world were open and anonymous, with European and Asian nations leading the way. On the other hand, open competitions in the United States were few and far between. However, the 1922 Chicago Tribune Tower competition did much to influence the course of modern skyscraper design. The second place winner of that competition, a stripped-down modernist design by Eliel Saarninen, did much to usher in that new era of modern design in the U.S. Although not the competition winner, the interest this entry generated resulted in Saarinen's move to Michigan as the head of Cranbrook Academy. From there Eliel and his son Eero were successful in several competitions, most notably the 1939 Smithsonian Museum of Art competition — never built because of World War II — and the Jefferson National Expansion Memorial (St. Louis "Gateway Arch"), won by Eero Saarinen in 1947 [Fig.1][1].

In the first three decades after WWII, there were several open competitions of note in the U.S., such as the Boston City Hall Competition, won by Kallmann, McKinnell and Knowles. However none were international in nature. Roosevelt Island Housing (1974/75) was the first major international competition to be held in the U.S. after World War II, but this was an anomaly.[2] Ten years later The International Cities Design Competition (1985) took place, the first and last competition approved by the UIA in North America. In the 1980s several invited competitions with international participation occurred, one being the promising Phoenix Municipal Government Center (1985) won by Barton Myers, but also including foreign participation, including Arata Isozaki of Japan and Ricardo Legorreta of Mexico, the latter also winning an invited competition for the 1991 San Antonio Central Library [Fig.2]. Finalists in an invited competition for the design of the Humana Building in Louisville, Kentucky, won by Michael Graves in 1985, included Foster Partners of the UK.

Why did so few competitions occur in the U.S. during this period? The main reason is that the American Institute of Architects (AIA) remained on the sidelines primarily as the result of a 1970s legal restraint-of-trade ruling by the Federal Trade Commission, which voided the AIA's power to approve competitions for participation by its members. Instead, there was an increased number of invited competitions, which for the most part are devoid of any institutional regulation. One exception to this unregulated format was a program adopted enthusiastically by the U.S. government's General Services Administration (GSA) for many of its federal courthouse projects — coined the "Excellence in Architecture" program. Yet again, none of these were open to foreign architects. During the Bush administration this policy was put on the back burner but there are signs that it is being resurrected under the Obama administration.

An impetus to the invited competition format in the U.S. during the 1980s came from abroad, with Berlin's International Building Exposition (Berliner Internationale Bauaustellung or IBA). The German Director of the IBA, Josef Kleihues formerly of Cooper Union in the U.S., invited numerous American architects to participate in the invited competitions he was coordinating in Berlin.[3] As many of the architects he invited were well known in their countries of origin, this in turn contributed to the "star" system which was to become so prevalent in later invited competitions around the world. As a result, it has become commonplace to see names such as Foster, Libeskind, Perrault, Ando, Zaha Hadid and Snøhetta represented among invitees for major competitions, not only in Europe, the Middle East and Asia, but also in the U.S.

One would have assumed that the successful Vietnam Veterans Memorial competition on the Washington Mall in 1981 would have validated the open, anonymous process. Its validation can also be seen in the numerous memorial designs up to the present day, which have much in common with this memorial. Apparently the bureaucracy only viewed this program as a model for memorial architecture, for the country as a whole has embraced the invited format for large projects almost without exception. This has also been the prevailing attitude in the private sector. Museum competitions are almost all by invitation only, with "star architects" as the usual suspects. There are two reasons for this, as clients are more comfortable with a proven commodity, and many of these projects depend on fundraising, and the perception of unknowns is that they do not generate much enthusiasm with potential donors. Thus the question that will be debated into the future is: do open, anonymous competitions produce higher quality architecture than the invited format?

**Two-stage Competition Formats**
There are various scenarios for competitions organized in more than one stage:
- an anonymous, open competition, whereby finalists are picked for a second stage;
- a Request for Qualifications (RfQ) to determine competition participants.

**Fig. 1**
"Gateway Arch", Jefferson National Expansion
Memorial, St. Louis (MO), USA (Eero Saarinen, 1947).
*Copyright : Debbie Franke Photography, Inc.*

**Fig. 2**
San Antonio Central Library, San Antonio (TX), USA
(Legorreta + Legorreta Architects, 1991-1995).
*Copyright : Legorreta + Legorreta Architects.*

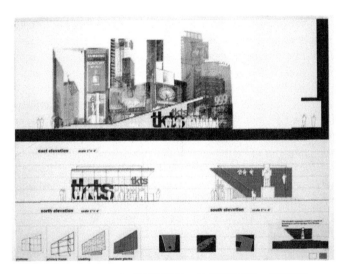

**Fig. 3 to 5**
TKTS Times Square, New York City (NY),
USA (John Choi + Tai Ropiha, 1999-2008).
*Copyright : Van Alen Institute.*

All of the latter competitions may be further limited geographically, either by country or province, and the official language can be a further limitation.

There can be a number of rationales for two-stage competitions:

- To determine the ability of each architectural team to fine-tune their designs to accommodate the needs of the client;
- To convince the client that the team favored by a selection committee is capable of managing a large-scale project;
- Compatibility with the client and community, in case the issue of fund-raising is high on the agenda.

## ▬ International Winners in the U.S.

Opening the first decade of the new millennium, there were several open competitions in the U.S. with international participation, several of which are either already built or under construction. The first was for tkts at New York's Times Square in 1999, won by an Australian team led by John Choi I Tai Ropiha of Sydney. Finally completed in October 2008, this design was the result of 683 entries from around the world [Fig.3] [Fig.4] [Fig.5].[4]

Another open, international competition of note was the Memphis Riverfront Competition (2003). Won by RTM Architects of Buenos Aires, their design prevailed over five shortlisted finalists from 171 first-stage submissions and has been partially realized.[5] The New England Biolabs competition was the result of over 300 entries, almost half of which came from outside the borders of the U.S. Again a two-stage competition with five finalists in the second stage, it was won by Weston Williamson, a team from the U.K and completed in 2008. Of invited competitions during this period making headlines, the Illinois Institute of Technology's 1997 Student Center competition [Fig.6] [Fig.7], won by The Office of Metropolitan Architecture (Rotterdam), featured three of the five finalists from abroad including Zaha Hadid of London, and SANAA of Japan.[6]

Zaha Hadid was to later win an invited competition for the new Broad Art Museum at Michigan State University (2007) in East Lansing, Michigan. The finalists in this competition also included Coop Himmelb(l)au of Vienna. In the 2008 Baltimore School of Law invited competition, Behnisch Architekten of Stuttgart won over five other finalists, including Dominique Perrault of Paris and Foster Partners, London [Fig.8].[7] The building was completed in late 2013.[8]

In concert with the expansion of the global economy, architects are now crossing international boundaries in increasing numbers, not only competing with local professionals for prime projects but raising the bar in terms of new materials and structural innovation [Fig.9].

### The New England Biolabs Competition (2001-2004)

The New England Biolabs (NEB), a leading source of products for molecular biology research in Ipswich, Massachusetts was the location of one of the more successful open and international competitions in the U.S. It is noteworthy that N.E.B turned to this open two-stage competition format, as the prevailing conventional wisdom in the U.S. is that open competitions are not appropriate for specialized buildings, where prior experience with the building type is thought to be crucial. However the suitability of a project as a competition subject actually depends on more specific and subtle distinctions. In this instance, competitors were not asked to reinvent the specialized elements of the laboratories themselves. The client and his architect, Douglas F. Trees, had already fine-tuned a laboratory configuration during four phases of development at the company's present facility in nearby Beverly.

Trees brought this background to the role of competition advisor. With the desired lab configuration as a given, the competitors' tasks were the broader architectural ones: organizing the new construction and required parking most effectively on the sensitive site. The variety of possible layouts presented an excellent opportunity for an open competition.

In order to protect its exceptional open spaces from intensive development and reinforce its non-residential tax base the town of Ipswich has had a policy of encouraging commercial use of its several surviving estates, assuming their principal assets are preserved. Under its Great Estates Preservation zoning, the town can approve projects subject to strict limitations. The mansion and three of its outbuildings constructed between 1894 and 1914 had to be restored to Department of Interior. New construction may be approved for up to 5 times the square footage of the existing, which in this case allowed for 285,000 square feet, of which the company planned to build only 150,000 at the time. An agreement with the town for this project capped the construction at 160,000 square feet for 10 years.

After the conclusion of the competition, the mansion was rehabilitated to house the company's administrative

**Fig. 6**
Illinois Institute of Technology McCormick
Tribune Campus Center, Chicago (IL), USA
(Office for Metropolitan Architecture, 1997-2003).
*Copyright: G. Stanley Collyer.*

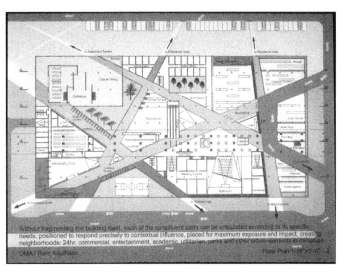

**Fig. 7**
Illinois Institute of Technology McCormick Tribune Campus
Center, Chicago (IL), USA (Office for Metropolitan Architecture,
1997-2003) — Competition panel.
*Copyright: Office for Metropolitan Architecture.*

**Fig. 8**
The John and Frances Angelos Law Center for
the University of Baltimore, Baltimore (MD), USA
(Behnisch Architekten, 2008-2013).
*Copyright: Behnisch Architekten.*

**Fig. 9**
New England Biolabs, Ipswich, MA, USA
(TRO Jung|Brannen, 2002-2005).
*Copyright: Richard Mandelkorn (2005).*

offices, and the outbuildings adapted for such uses as a day-care center and visitors' housing. An area near the mansion large enough to offer many layout options is designated for the new laboratory structure. In deference to the landscape — and the sometimes harsh weather in Ipswich — the owners are committed to locating half of the required parking under the new building, and the town will not count that square footage in the zoning calculation.

## The Competition

After studying other recent design competitions and the fate of winning schemes architect Trees tailored a two-stage process for this project. To attract a wide range of firms, both established as well as fledgling, a total of $222,500 in prize money was allocated. For the first stage five finalists received $7,500 each, and five Honorable Mentions $5,000 each. In the second stage, the finalists vied for first, second, and third awards of $50,000, $40,000, and $30,000, with $20,000 each for those who came in fourth and fifth.

Notice of the competition was mainly disseminated by Internet, and all required materials were posted for free on the competition website. Only 5 of 300 participants requested a printed brochure, which was priced at $100 to cover reproduction and express shipping, while those using the web paid no entry fee. Unregistered participants could find these items on the website. In the end 200 of the eventual 300 participants registered in advance. The use of electronic communication undoubtedly facilitated participation by foreign teams, who submitted about half the entries.

The competition program envisioned the expansion of the Biolabs from its present 230 employees to 400. Of these, 315 were to work in the new structure, 85 in the 57,000 square feet of the renovated estate buildings. A tropical winter garden was required as it was a feature of the company's present home. Operating without air conditioning and relying solely on circulating outside air, this conservatory had to be separated from working spaces, but in a manner that gave views into it from circulation and meeting spaces.

There were a number of other design considerations the competitors had to deal with. An enclosed connection between the mansion and the new lab building; and since the town would allow no wings attached to the historic building, an underground connection was dictated.

The owner wanted to employ "green" strategies, including recycled materials, photovoltaics, energy-efficient HVAC systems, high insulation values, and energy transfer systems for ventilation air. The mechanical plant would also have a solar aquatic greenhouse as a component of sewage treatment. The recycling of wastewater to flush toilets and water the landscape was also envisaged.

The first stage was identified as a "concept" competition with participants limited to specified graphic and verbal material on two 24" x 36" boards. All entries were displayed in the mansion for viewing on-site for a two-week period for local residents, company employees, and any other interested parties. The objective of stage one was to select "the 5 concepts that were deemed most appropriate to the stated design objectives of New England Biolabs, the planning objectives of the Town of Ipswich Planning Board, and that express the highest level of design mastery, consistent with realistic costs of construction." The jury for stage one consisted of:

- Donald G. Comb, founder and president of the company
- Donlyn Lyndon, FAIA, of Lyndon Buchanan, architects, of Berkeley, California
- Jane Weinzapfel, FAIA, of Leers Weinzapfel, architects, of Boston
- Bruce Wood of Kallmann McKinnell & Wood, architects, of Boston

A technical jury advising the voting members included the chair and a second member of the five-member Ipswich Planning Board, Michael Comb, son of Donald G. Comb, biologist and president of Cell Signaling Technology, and Linda Narekian, an artist who has advised Donald G. Comb on his extensive collections.

The first-stage jury chose five award winners, which included two U.S. entrants, three foreign entrants, plus five honorable mentions. The second stage began with visits to the site by the award winners. They were briefed on local regulations and examined the site and the company's present facilities. Each finalist heard recommendations based on first-stage jury deliberations. Their second-stage presentations could cover any number of 24" x 36" boards, but were still limited to that two-dimensional format. They then had almost six months to produce submissions at the "preliminary design" level. In-person presentations of second-stage designs, envisioned in the competition announcement, were in the end considered unnecessary.

The second-stage decisions — among entries already selected for awards by the professional jury — was reserved for the owner himself, with the advice of his staff, employees, and anyone else he wished to consult.

## Costs

The competition program stated an intention to build the new structure for $200 per square foot, or $30 million. In the first stage cost was a factor only if the jury considered a scheme "impossible to construct... at or near the stated budget." After the first-stage jury, the owner discussed cost with the architect jurors who agreed that all five award-winning schemes would be similar in cost and that all would exceed $200 per square foot. As the jurors all had experience in designing buildings with labs, they immediately recognized that the square foot cost would be closer to $300, thus raising the cost by at least 50 %. In the final analysis the budget had to be increased to $71.5M, and the client approved this number.

## Second Stage Choices

The five finalists all had a different approach to the siting of the building. When they were reviewed in the second stage, the entry by C.P.R. Architects of Caracas, Venezuela **[Fig.10] [Fig.11] [Fig.12]** was fairly quickly assigned fourth place. Both C.P.R. and fifth-place entry Kling Lindquist of Philadelphia responded to first-stage criticism in ways that failed to improve on their original concepts.

The C.P.R. scheme was the most plainly utilitarian of the award-winning schemes. With its industrial imagery and New England Biolabs spelled out on it in large letters, its second-stage version still lacked sensitivity to the site compared to other contenders.

The third-place design by the Madrid team UNO-h arquitectura **[Fig.13] [Fig.14] [Fig.15]** snaked wings around existing groves of trees. Although it proposed engaging forms and spaces, it was nevertheless considered by some to look somewhat like a finely designed public school. Narrow wings, single-loaded corridors, and a buried garage not under the building would add to its cost. And while splitting the winter garden in two parts was permitted, it became clear during judging that a single garden was preferable.

New York architect Michael Louis Gallin's design **[Fig.16] [Fig.17]** was admired for the way its series of linked lab structures arced around a central lawn and its specimen beech tree. However, it would also have eliminated many fine trees. Its very visible roofs demanded expensive material and multiple winter gardens were considered less desirable than a single one. In the end the design was a strong second.

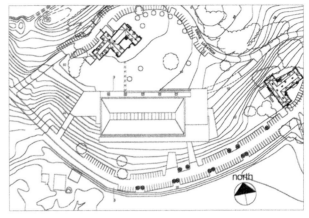

**Fig. 10 to 12**
Proposal by fourth-place finalists C.P.R. Arquitectos (Caracas, Venezuela) for New England Biolabs architecture competition (Ipswich, MA, USA, 2002).
*Copyright : C.P.R. Arquitectos.*

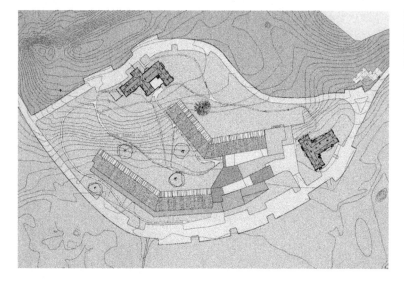

**Fig. 13 to 15**
Proposal by third-place finalists UNO-h arquitectura
(Madrid, Spain) for the New England Biolabs
architecture competition (Ipswich, MA, USA, 2002).
*Copyright : UNO-h arquitectura.*

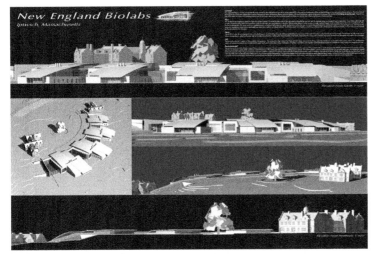

**Fig. 16 and 17**
Proposal by second-place finalist Michael Louis Gallin
(Dobbs Ferry, NY, USA) for the New England Biolabs
architecture competition (Ipswich, MA, USA, 2002).
*Copyright : Michael Louis Gallin Architect.*

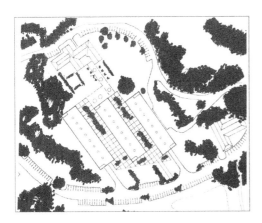

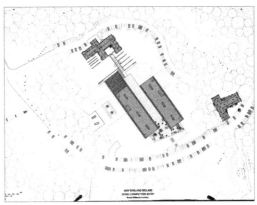

**Fig. 18 and 19**
Winning scheme by Weston Williamson (London, England) for the New England
Biolabs architecture competition (Ipswich, MA, USA, 2002).
*Copyright : Weston Williamson.*

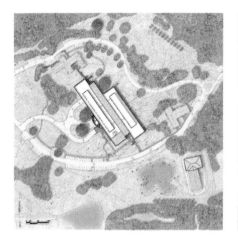 

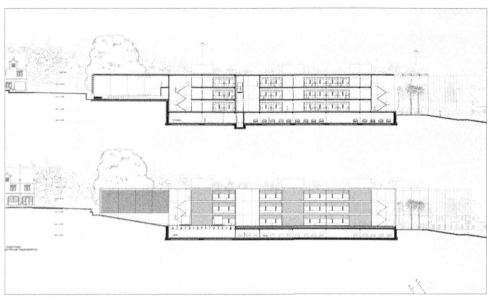

**Fig. 20 to 23**
Winning scheme by Weston Williamson (London,
England) for the New England Biolabs architecture
competition (Ipswich, MA, USA, 2002).
*Copyright : Weston Williamson.*

**Fig. 24**
New England Biolabs, Ipswich (MA),
USA (Weston Williamson, 2002-2005).
*Copyright: Rick Feehery, courtesy TRO
JunglBrannen, Inc.*

**Fig. 25**
New England Biolabs, Ipswich (MA),
USA (Weston Williamson, 2002-2005).
*Copyright: Richard Mandelkorn (2005).*

The winning scheme by Weston Williamson **[Fig.18 to 28]** stacked its labs three stories high flanking a linear "street" that leads to a winter garden at the down-slope end. During the first stage the architects laid out their labs in narrower wings along two "streets," an arrangement that lacked clarity and covered a lot of ground. Switching to a single linear structure unified the design. The three floors of labs, which needed clearance for intensive mechanical services, threatened to break through the site's 45-foot height limit. Though the limit could be waived for sufficient reason, it was not desirable. These conflicting demands were successfully reconciled with a floor-to-floor height of 14'-6".

Having the competition in two stages benefitted Weston Williamson, as the improvements they brought to the second stage led to a marked improvement in their concept. On the other hand, in the eyes of the selection committee Michael Louis Gallin's second stage design did not mark a significant improvement over the first stage entry. Here, a two-stage competition altered the dynamics of the selection process.

Since the winning firm was small and located in England, Weston Williamson was designated design architect and the larger local firm of Jung Brannen was chosen as the architect of record. Construction began in September 2002 and the building was completed in two years. [9]

### ━━ Americans Competing Abroad

Since there have been so few open competitions in the U.S. where lesser-known architects could gain recognition, many U.S.-based architects joined their global colleagues in competing in the international arena. There have been several success stories by American firms in international competitions — Paul Rudolph's winning Sino Tower competition entry **[Fig.29]** in Hong Kong, and Steven Holl's Kiasma Museum in Finland from 1993 are two isolated examples. And until the beginning of this century, the Grands Projets of François Mitterrand in France were the highest profile international competitions in Europe.

Even Russia has seen international participation in recent competitions: The Permafrost Museum competition of 2007 was won by Leeser Architecture with Balmori Associates, New York, with Antoine Predock Architects, Albuquerque, New Mexico, as a finalist in that competition. Acconci Studio + Guy Nordenson and Associates, New York, received a "Purchase" prize in the Perm Contemporary Art Museum Competition (2008) in Perm, Russia as did another New York firm, Asymptote Architecture.

**Fig. 26**
New England Biolabs, Ipswich (MA), USA (Weston
Williamson, 2002-2005).
*Copyright: Richard Mandelkorn (2005).*

**Fig. 27 and 28**
New England Biolabs, Ipswich
(MA), USA (Weston Williamson,
2002-2005).
*Copyright: John Morris Dixon.*

**Fig. 29**
Paul Rudolph's winning proposal
for the Sino Tower architecture
competition (Hong Kong, 1989).
*Copyright: Paul Rudolph Foundation.*

The two young U.S.-based firms included in the final round of the Czech National Museum Competition in 2006 were Tom Wiscombe I Mona Marbach from Los Angeles and John Reed Architect from New York (Tom Wiscombe was also the Second Place Winner in the 2014 Port of Kinmen Passenger Service Center International Competition in Taiwan). Korea has also been the site of a select number open competitions, with one of the more recent being the Gyeonggi-do Jeongok Prehistory Museum (2006) where Second and Third Place winners were from young U.S. firms — Paul Preissner, Chicago and Easton + Combs, Brooklyn, New York, in that order.

But the greatest opportunities for participation in open, international competitions have been in Taiwan, where projects are fully funded, and where U.S. firms have performed remarkably well. Among those competitions where Americans made the final cut are:

- National Palace Museum — Southern Branch (2005)
- Taipei Pop Music Center (2009)
- Taiwan Disease Control Complex (2010)
- Taichung Gateway Park Competition (2010)
- Taipei City Museum of Art (2010)
- Kaohsiung Maritime Cultural and Music Center (2010)
- Kaohsiung Port and Cruise Service Center (2011)

Two of the above competitions were won by Reiser + Umemoto of New York for the Taipei Pop Music Center and Kaohsiung Port and Cruise Service Center.

Other U.S. firms that did well in the above competitions are:

- Antoine Predock Architect — Winner of the National Palace Museum Competition
- Studio Gang of Chicago — Runner-up in the Taipei Pop Music Center Competition and Third Place in the Kaohsiung Maritime Cultural and Music Center Competition.
- Office dA I Daniel Gallagher, Boston — Third Place, Taipei Pop Music Center
- Morphosis, Santa Monica, California — Honorable Mention, Taipei Pop Music Center
- Asymptote Architecture, New York — Second Prize, Kaohsiung Port and Cruise Terminal
- HMC Group I Raymond Pan, Los Angeles — Honorable Mention, Kaohsiung Port and Cruise Terminal
- Mack Scogin Merrill Elam of Atlanta — Honorable Mention, Kaohsiung Maritime Cultural & Music Center

- Stoss, Inc, Boston — Second place, Taichung Gateway Park Competition

All of this does not include the large numbers of invited competitions which have taken place in Singapore, Australia, Vietnam and especially China, whereby the organizational rules and formats vary considerably from place to place.

## Taipei Pop Music Center (2009-)

As an anchor for a new "Innovation Research and Development Corridor" in Taipei, Taiwan, who would have guessed that pop music would have been showcased as the main event for a brand new complex in the center of this mix? The Nangang district in Taipei — the center of this new activity — has long been an industrial area, host to a number of large and small manufacturing enterprises. Most of the businesses are being moved to the city's edge and the area is being retooled to resemble the local equivalent of a Silicon Valley. As an industry that has benefitted and fallen victim to high technology, pop music would seem to be a logical fit for this area. It attracts a younger generation, simultaneously engaged in those new enterprises, which are on the cutting edge of technology.

The site chosen for this project is located near a new metro rail station, part of a mammoth project which foresees the burying of the existing and new rail systems. It was in an area where exhibition space was to be expanded, in addition to commercial, residential and retail. The configuration of the site posed a real challenge for the competitors. Instead of a very symmetrical, high-density site, the north end of the site is spread like two prongs extending along the previous rail corridor. This invitation to incorporate this additional space into the total design scheme was to have implications in the final selection of a winner. The client left much up to the competitor in this area, stating, "The design team may choose to reference directly to the site plan and proportions, or offer a new one."

Besides indicating flexibility in dealing with the site, the client stated that this was about "creating a space which will produce creativity." Professional knowledge was most important in the design of the performance venues — concert halls, Hall of Fame, etc. But these buildings were simply there to provide a "framework, a basic infrastructure that would allow for pop music to have its own creative space to develop."

As has been the case in previous Taiwan competitions, this edition was completely open to licensed architects throughout the world. For the second short-listed, stage of the competition, the finalists were expected to include other members on their teams, which could provide the necessary expertise in areas such as acoustics, engineering and landscape design. The competition attracted 114 entries from 33 countries, including several Pritzker Prize winners. When it came down to a final shortlist none of the latter was in the mix, as the three finalists were all relatively young firms from the United States. They were:

- Reiser + Umemoto RUR Architecture, New York **[Fig.30 to 34]**
- Studio Gang, Chicago **[Fig.35 to 42]**
- Office dA | Daniel Gallagher, Boston **[Fig.43 to 47]**.

## The Final Selection Process

Entering the second stage of the competition, Studio Gang's proposal, the central focus of which was a large building containing most of the necessary program requirements, could have been considered the favorite. Juror Michael Speaks characterized it as a city within a city and thought it reflected much of the aspirations of the client. Although not overpowering, the structure itself was quite impressive in its architectural expression, functionality, and relationship to the site. Studio Gang's idea was that it was the Taiwanese concept of the "big tent", and by containing most of the functions within the structure, Jeanne Gang stated that this allowed the large border-like sliver along the north edge to be freed up as a public park. Also, by providing some shelter for the large outside open performances where as many as 15,000 people might gather, Studio Gang's idea was to shelter the crowd from the frequent rains which pelt the island.

The winning entry by Reiser +Umemoto (RUR) dramatized several features in the second stage that impressed the jury.

Firstly, the model they presented was exceptional and helped to reinforce the team's innovative design concept. In contrast to Studio Gang's proposal, the functions were not all connected under one roof, but interspersed on an elevated platform over the site, with retail and parking located underneath. They conceived of a flexible theater configuration, which could be adjusted to different types of performances, large and small, and to various audience sizes, partially based on a moveable stage on rails. This all resulted on a large, elevated open space which created not only a large space for people viewing outside performances, but also a large plaza. If outside jurors had any concerns about such a large public space above grade, they would find out that such elevated areas are not unusual in Taipei. Thus the RUR scheme differed from Studio Gang in that it utilized the sliver at the north end of the site as part and parcel of its functions.

Office dA took an entirely different approach, using the idea of perforation of the site from the street to attract the public and lend an aura of comfort to the composition. Speaks stated that this scheme looked like it could fit in Madrid or Rotterdam, as well as Taipei. Thus the final decision really boiled down to the other two finalists, Gang Studios and Reiser + Umemoto.

Two important differences in the approaches of the above competitors most likely swung the balance in favor of Reiser + Umemoto:

- The design of the "livehouse" function — areas reserved for music groups presently scattered throughout Taipei — was left to the creative efforts of those groups by RUR, while designed very much in detail by Studio Gang. Speaks remarked that these groups often performed in industrial lofts and may feel more constrained or not at ease in a highly designed environment located at the opposite end of that park.
- In the second stage Gang Studios brought in West 8 to design the open park space. Speaks found this design to be too metaphoric for this setting, and wondered if it hadn't been better for Gang Studios to just let it remain open for further development. In this case, it was the "best of both worlds and the worst of both worlds." Overdesigning turned out in this case to detract from an otherwise well-conceived plan.

Finally, the jury was somewhat concerned that all of the finalists were relatively young firms without many large-scale projects on their resumes. But RUR had brought in a very strong team, including Arup (Beijing), to strengthen its position.

The first-stage participants who received honorable mentions also had impressive resumes. Toyo Ito and Morphosis both had Pritzkers in their pockets. Notably, several high-profile firms failed to make the cut. One might have expected monumentality from one of the better schemes, and Toyo Ito's design certainly fulfilled this formula, concentrating most of the performance functions

**A Gradient of mixed-use spaces, from the fully public realm to the interior of the audi-**
torium, allows the visitor to partake of the event dynamic however they choose to visit this complex. Whether they
plan a night of music or are browsing the myriad shops, markets, cafes, and restaurants, the complex will be a 24-hour attraction independent of the schedule of performances in the theaters. 一個有斜度的混合使用空間，從完全地公共領域到室內的觀眾席，使得訪客參與動態的事件無論他們選擇
基麼方法去參訪這個綜合體(complex)。集論他們想第一個音樂之夜或是瀏覽各式各樣的商店、市場、Cafe'和餐廳，這個綜合體將會是一個24小時的吸引力，有著獨立於劇場表演的時刻表。

**Fig. 30 to 32**
Winning entry by Reiser + Umemoto / RUR Architecture PC (New York, NY, USA) for the Taipei
Pop Music Center Competition (Taipei, 2009). *Copyright: Reiser + Umemoto / RUR Architecture PC.*

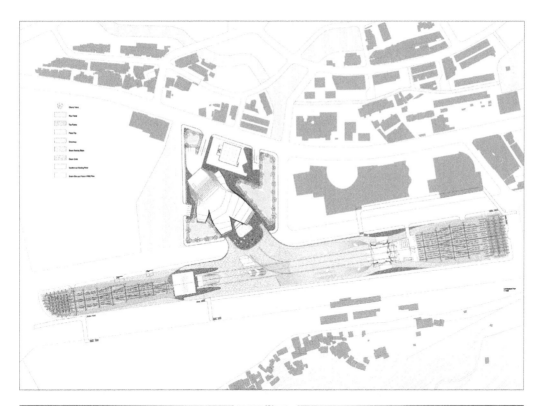

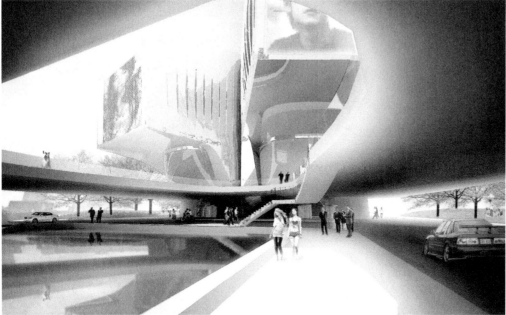

**Fig. 33 and 34**
Winning entry by Reiser + Umemoto / RUR Architecture PC (New York,
NY, USA) for the Taipei Pop Music Center Competition (Taipei, 2009)
*Copyright : Reiser + Umemoto / RUR Architecture PC.*

**Fig. 35 to 39**
Entry by finalist Studio Gang (Chicago, IL, USA) for the
Taipei Pop Music Center Competition (Taipei, 2009)
*Copyright : Studio Gang.*

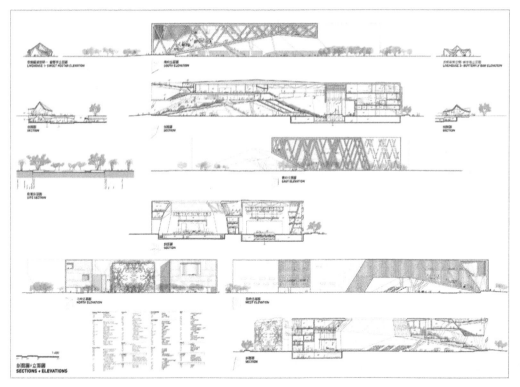

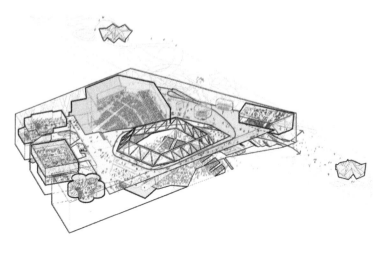

**Fig. 40 to 42**
Entry by finalist Studio Gang (Chicago, IL, USA) for the
Taipei Pop Music Center Competition (Taipei, 2009)
*Copyright : Studio Gang.*

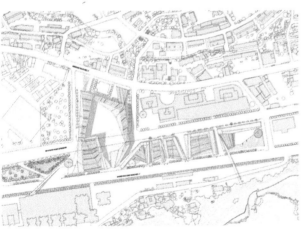

**Fig. 43 to 45**
Entry by finalist Office dA / Daniel Gallagher (Boston MA, USA) for
the Taipei Pop Music Center Competition (Taipei, 2009)
*Copyright : Office dA / Daniel Gallagher*

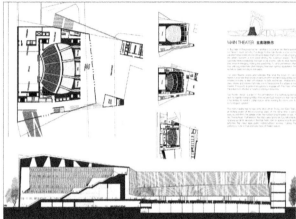

**Fig. 46 and 47**
Entry by finalist Office dA / Daniel Gallagher
(Boston MA, USA) for the Taipei Pop Music
Center Competition (Taipei, 2009)
*Copyright: Office dA / Daniel Gallagher*

right within the confines of a giant container bordering directly on the street. Morphosis also implied a degree of monumentality by creating a large arrival feature surrounded by a huge slanted facade.

This competition presented participants with an interesting set of challenges, as here was a real contemporary design problem with many variables. In the end it was the creative juices of the finalists who researched the site in depth that brought them to the final stage. Adding and subtracting was one of the deciding factors, which tipped the scales in favor of the winner. But the others were not far behind. It was a close call. [10]

To summarize the results of the above two-stage with an anonymous first stage competition, the results might have well been different had the selection process ended at the end of Stage I. The refinement of Weston Williamson's design to win the NEB competition, and the addition by Studio Gang of West 8 to their team in the Taipei Pop Music Center competition — leading to the 'overdesign' of their scheme — illustrate just how such changes in design progression, in a highly competitive competition, can tip the scales to the advantage of one party or the other.

## ▬ E-Competitions and the Internet Revolution

The advent of the internet has had an extraordinary effect on the way in which competitions are administered. Before websites and email, advertising a competition was a substantial item to be considered by any sponsor, as mailings and ads in professional publications were not free. Currently cost of advertising a competition is incidental and may only require the expense of a computer person for several hours a week. In an age where passing items through customs is problematic, sending entry files through email and ftp sites has greatly simplified the process.

In some cases E-competition files are sent separately to jurors where they examine them at their leisure. They are charged to pick their favorites before convening for a final, on-site session. At the November March 2012 symposium on competitions at the Université de Montréal, one participant voiced reservations about this system, maintaining that it is a necessity to be familiar with the site before the adjudication process begins. Actually, familiarity can occur far from the site if the competition brief is thorough. If it were true that local architects have a definite advantage over outsiders who have never seen the site, one might assume that the former would be overwhelming favorites to win anonymous competitions. Actually, this has almost never been the case. As with many international competitions, the Spanish winner of the recent Serlachius Museum Competition in Finland, MX_SI Architectural Studio, had never visited the country beforehand.[11] But professional advisers are united in advocating that competition jurors should have a face-to-face session before selecting a winner for an important project.

The only negative aspect of administering competitions via the internet is that this procedure enables anyone with a website to advertise an ideas competition. This has become a serious problem, as some sponsors — here the website owners are usually the sponsors — require substantial registration fees without offering commensurate awards. Moreover, many of these competitions are often very theoretical and essentially ask the participant to design their own program. In one recent case, a sponsor asked potential participants to select an abandoned military airfield anyplace in the world, and convert it to a new use. How could any juror possibly be familiar with all of the site locations around the world? Since there is no international institutional body to evaluate these competitions, design professionals and students are left up to their own devices to navigate these challenging waters. Websites such as *competitions.org* may attempt to screen out the most egregious offenders, but preventing them from trivializing the nature of this inherently democratic process is an ongoing struggle for those who honor it.

———

Media coverage of competitions is a snapshot of the state of architecture, and society. It may even indicate a consensus — or lack thereof — concerning new approaches to solving urban issues in these changing times. Analyzing the selection process and encouraging those involved to discuss their priorities when ranking the entries is certainly beneficial for the profession and adds to an ongoing dialogue about design. This is where media shoulders its greatest responsibility.

## ▬ Notes

[1] Travis C. Jr. McDonald, «The Smithsonian Institution Competition for a Gallery of Art,» in *Modernism in America 1937-1941*, ed. Ed. James D. Kornwolf (Williamsburg: Joseph and Margaret Muscarelle Museum of Art, 1985).

[2] Paul D. Spreiregen, *Design Competitions* (New York: McGraw-Hill, 1979). pp. 162-178

[3] Josef Kleihues, «Interview with Josef Kleihues,» *Competitions* 2, no. 2 (1992).

[4] Kira L. Gould, «The View's the Thing,» ibid.10, no. 1 (2000).

[5] Stanley G. Collyer, «Making the Mississippi Connection,» ibid.13, no. 4 (2003).

[6] Kevin Pierce, «lit at a Crossroads,» ibid.8, no. 2 (1998); Michael Dulin, «Beyond Mies,» ibid.13, no. 4 (2003).

[7] Stanley G. Collyer, «A Second Midwest Commission for Zaha Hadid,» ibid.18, no. 2 (2008).

[8] Tom Reasoner, «Baltimore Law School Raises the Bar,» ibid.9, no. 1 (2009).

[9] *This article appeared in an expanded version, COMPETITIONS, Vol. 18, #2. John Morris Dixon, «New England Biolabs Competition,» ibid.12, no. 2 (2002). See also: «A Modern Fit for a Traditional Park Setting,» Competitions 18, no. 2 (2008).*

[10] *This article appeared in an expanded version, COMPETITIONS, Vol. 20, #1. Michael Speaks, «Taipei Pop Music Center as Urban Catalyst,» ibid.20, no. 1 (2010).*

[11] William Morgan, «Bucolic Site as Museum Context,» in *Competitions Annual*, ed. Stanley G. Collyer (Louisville: The Competition Project Inc., 2011).

## ▬ References

**Collyer**, Stanley G. «Making the Mississippi Connection.» *Competitions* 13, no. 4 (2003): 24-41.

**Collyer**, Stanley G. «A Second Midwest Commission for Zaha Hadid.» *Competitions* 18, no. 2 (2008): 26-41.

**Dixon**, John Morris. «A Modern Fit for a Traditional Park Setting.» *Competitions* 18, no. 2 (2008): 20-25.

**Dixon**, John Morris. «New England Biolabs Competition.» *Competitions* 12, no. 2 (2002): 16-27.

**Dulin**, Michael. «Beyond Mies.» *Competitions* 13, no. 4 (2003): 16-23.

**Gould**, Kira L. «The View's the Thing.» *Competitions* 10, no. 1 (2000): 52-61.

**Kleihues**, Josef. «Interview with Josef Kleihues.» *Competitions* 2, no. 2 (1992): 50-57.

**McDonald**, Travis C. Jr. «The Smithsonian Institution Competition for a Gallery of Art.» In *Modernism in America 1937-1941*, edited by Ed. James D. Kornwolf. Williamsburg: Joseph and Margaret Muscarelle Museum of Art, 1985.

**Morgan**, William. «Bucolic Site as Museum Context.» In *Competitions Annual*, edited by Stanley G. Collyer, 26-37. Louisville: The Competition Project Inc., 2011.

**Pierce**, Kevin. «lit at a Crossroads.» *Competitions* 8, no. 2 (1998): 4-23.

**Reasoner**, Tom. «Baltimore Law School Raises the Bar.» *Competitions* 9, no. 1 (2009): 4-19.

**Speaks**, Michael. «Taipei Pop Music Center as Urban Catalyst.» *Competitions* 20, no. 1 (2010): 22-43.

**Spreiregen**, Paul D. *Design Competitions*. New York: McGraw-Hill, 1979.

# 5.3. d'architectures

**Regional Identity and Cultural Diversity in the Wonderful World of *Starchitects***

**Emmanuel Caille**, Chief Editor
d'a (d'architecture journal)
France

The practice of architectural competitions, whether open to international teams or not, has permitted the improvement of the quality of public buildings in France for the past three decades. Gradually, and driven by local government, architectural competitions are now gaining interest from the private sector. If it is understood today that the organization of project management consultation has generated a higher production quality, this does not mean that the system is without its flaws. In the practice of architecture, competitions can be seen as the site of crystallized fantasies, paranoia, bitterness and jealousy, all due to a profession confronted with constant competition. If the way competitions operate is still debated, no one in today's France is questioning this selection method. I would add that from a certain size of program and budget — say 10 million — an architectural competition loses much credibility if no foreign teams are invited.

**Cover**
Extract of Winning project by OMA for the exhibition parc of the Toulouse urban area (PEX) in 2011.
*Copyright : OMA*

## Publishing the Results of Competition in an Architecture Magazine

As editor of an architectural magazine with a mandate to provide a critical view of competitions and architectural production, I often end up collecting grievances, false confessions, and all sorts of rumours that feed the drama that takes place around each competition **[Fig.1]**.

There is never a competition in which one of the unsuccessful candidates does not confide in me that they were to be the winner, but the evil forces of lobbying and arbitrariness have stolen their victory. This is often true, but sometimes what these "victims" of the system forget is that they themselves had perhaps submitted their project by using arguments that were not particularly architectural as well.

We obviously try to exercise our critical thinking towards architectural and urban qualities of analyzed projects. I will not deny that it is tempting, when one is aware of somewhat transparent strategies implemented in order to influence the selection of the winner, to act as a vigilante. Unlike juries in courts of criminal justice, architectural juries are largely composed of members with ties to the candidates : professional, financial, involving family, etc. — this type of inbreeding is rampant and the links are somewhat public. However, it is evident that in the case of Freemason connections, quite common in this environment in France, it is impossible to know for sure, or at least with certainty, the totality of the interconnectedness.

Phases of pre-selection are even more prone to risk and submission to the circles of influence, since the choices do not have to be justified. However, it is a balance between lobbying and neutralizing the worst effects, since we must recognize that during major consultations we rarely find teams that clearly do not meet the status of excellence required. If this is indeed the case, then the choice, even if awkward, generally reflects the desire to offer a chance to an unknown young team with the intent of repeating the success of the Sydney Opera House or the Centre Pompidou.

In the case of our publication *d'a* (d'architectures), we choose an architectural consultation every month and publish and analyze all the proposals, whether or not they are successful **[Fig.2] [Fig.3]**. This column on competitions has now been running for seven years under the direction of architect and critic Richard Scoffier. While we try to select different consultations in terms of program, location and size, our requirement in terms of quality leads us naturally to consultations where international teams are present.

A retrospective analysis of these projects submitted by non-French architects provides two ideas that we found compelling. First, the proposals are an expression of identity or local cultural specificity. Second, the teams are chosen due to their international status in a bid to open the field of proposals to the widest cultural diversity possible.

Before focusing on these questions and to help better understand how I address them, I wish to firstly elaborate upon the specificity of the French context. The context in France is obviously related to its location in the heart of the European community. This is a hybrid situation since all European communities can participate in a competition in France. Officially, all members of this community are treated equally. In reality, Spanish or Austrian applicants are still considered international and it is probably for this identity they will be chosen to compete. This discrepancy between the two statutes — as both an international applicant and member of the same community and the fact that these countries are undergoing profound change and therefore should eventually be combined — has made the quest to objectify this analysis quite difficult.

I would like to briefly explain how and when France became a land of competitions and how this is the result of a "system of fine arts." I would like to conclude (hopefully with a little self-mockery) with the issue of internationalization of competitions in terms of French chauvinism.

## France : A Case Study

Until the late sixties, France was not open to international competitions. Major national projects were split between winning architects of the Grand Prix de Rome. This award crowned students at the end of their studies at the École des Beaux-Arts in Paris **[Fig.4]**.

The entire organization of education was focused on this final contest, which means that the competition was already completely integrated within the education system. In 1971, the call for the future Centre Pompidou in Paris was one of the first major open competitions.However since the 1980s, this practice has become increasingly common due to the policy of major projects launched by the President of the Republic Mitterrand, with the exception of the transformation of the Louvre in 1983 entrusted to the Chinese-American architect Ieoh Ming Pei. A series of major international competitions began with the Parc de la Villette won by Bernard Tschumi in 1982, and the Parisian Court of Justice in 2011 won by Renzo Piano **[Fig.5] [Fig.6]**.

**Fig. 1**
Extract from *"La Renommée distribuant les couronnes"* by Paul Delaroche. This painting depicts The famous Hemicycle of the École des Beaux-Arts in Paris. Ictinos, Apelle and Phidias: the architect, the painter, and the sculptor at the center of this emblematic composition. On the front row, "Fame" is about to through a crown of laurel.

**Fig. 2**
Front cover of the French journal d'a (d'architectures).

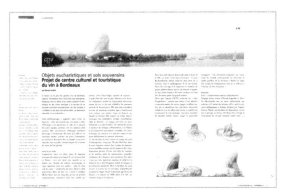

**Fig. 3**
Publication in d'a for the CCTV competition of Bordeaux. All the projects are presented and are the object of a critique.

**Fig. 4**
The "cour des Etudes" of the Ecole des Beaux-Arts (Paris). Félix DUBAN.
*Copyright: Photo RMN-Grand Palais — H. Lewandowski.*

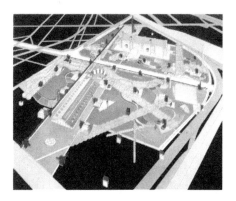

**Fig. 5**
Rendering for the Parc de
la Villette competition, won
by Bernard Tschumi in 1982.
*Copyright : Bernard Tschumi*

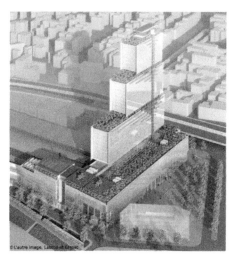

**Fig. 6**
Rendering for the Tribunal de Grande
Instance of Paris competition, won in
2011 by Renzo Piano.
*Copyright : Renzo Piano*

**Fig. 7**
Charles Garnier in the Drafting Room
while designing the competition for
the New Paris Opera, photography
by Louis-Émile Durandelle, 1870.
*Copyright : Metropolitan Museum of Art*

**Fig. 8**
Jury meeting for the Georges Pompidou Centre
in 1970, Oscar Niemeyer at the extreme left, Jean
Prouvé at the center, and Philip Johnson towards
whom all gazes converge.
*Copyright : Centre Georges Pompidou*

**Fig. 9**
Philip Johnson comments on the
project by Renzo Piano and Richard
Rogers during the competition jury for
the Georges Pompidou Centre in 1970.
*Copyright : Centre Georges Pompidou*

## The Legacy of the Fine Arts

The influence of the Parisian École des Beaux-Arts on world architecture until the mid-twentieth century was critical, and placed France in a dominant position — at times even considered one of intellectual arrogance — vis-à-vis the rest of the world. Paradoxically, this dominant position, which drew young architects to Paris from around the world, also immensely influenced academics. This led to infinite interpretations when graduates returned to their countries of origin and developed their own interpretation of the Fine Arts model. The curriculum was very academic, and it is anachronistic to think that once released, the powerful ethnocentrism of the teachers was saturated by values provided by their students. When Louis Sullivan attended the school in 1874, I doubt that his teachers took the opportunity to open themselves up to the challenges of the New World. Until the thirties many French architects were invited to compete abroad, often by former students. They found themselves in the context of international competitions, a situation which would prepare them to better accept this type competition in their own country **[Fig.7]**.

The international competition for the Centre Pompidou was launched in 1969, just one year after the dismantling of the École des Beaux-Arts in 1968. It was Georges Pompidou, President of the French Republic and instigator of the project who raised the question of participation by foreign architects. As reported by Robert Bordas and Bernadette Dufrêne in their book on the Centre Pompidou (2007), Pompidou declared "It seems to me essential that a substantial part of the jury be reserved for foreign architects with a worldwide reputation". The rest is history; as in 1971, the jury led by Jean Prouvé particularly welcomed Oscar Niemeyer and Philip Johnson — the winners were from England and Italy — Richard Rogers and Renzo Piano **[Fig.8] [Fig.9]**.

The question that arises is: Is the legitimacy of international competitions as has been established in the recent decade still relevant at the time of planetary age? I will tackle this by addressing the following sub-questions:

1. What remains today of the national or local identity of an architect and of its architecture in a competition which includes international teams?
2. Is this identity still decisive enough to motivate the invitation of an international architect?

## Local identity?

Working outside of their cultural background, are architects still designing projects that are an expression of their identity or local cultural specificity?

This question obviously arises not only for a competition, as it addresses wider issues of globalization. Once local determinants which confront every architect when eliminated, whether allogenous or not, when building within a defined space — i.e. climatic, regulatory and economic constraints — can we still speak of a regional or national architecture today? In Europe architects are trained according to a common curriculum, then they travel, participate in student exchange programs or do internships outside of their country. For example, while teaching at the Paris-Belleville National School of Architecture I had 14 students. In this pool, one student was from Scotland, one from Hungary, three from Mexico, one from Korea, and one from China. In addition, references broadcast by the architectural press are now international. And regulations in terms of safety, accessibility, and environment are becoming standardized.

This homogenization has two direct consequences on the internationalization of competitions: it is becoming easier to work in a country other than one's own since conditions are becoming increasingly similar, and the specificity of each candidate and their international cultural contributions that enrich the diversity of sensible proposals are slowly disappearing. A recent example shows, however, how the various influences and references are complex and can sometimes lead to opposing meanings. In 2011 the city of Bordeaux organized a competition for the Centre Culturel et Touristique du Vin (CCTV). Four French teams were selected of which two are partners with international designers, including the winner. By observing and analyzing the proposals, it is difficult to guess the origin of national projects, especially the winning project: the Parisian agency X-TU combined with British designers Casson Mann Limited. Their proposal was meant to evoke the movement of the wine when turned in a glass in order to smell its perfume, and was indeed a product of the temptation of the "Bilbao Effect" **[Fig.10] [Fig.11]**.

Strangely, it was Japanese Toyo Ito's project that seemed to want to pay homage to the eighteenth century facade of the Bordeaux riverbanks (one of his drawings seemed to materialize this very clearly). However, for those who know something about the achievements of Toyo Ito, the arcade system reminds us of the library of Talma in Tokyo designed by Ito in 2004 **[Fig.12]**.

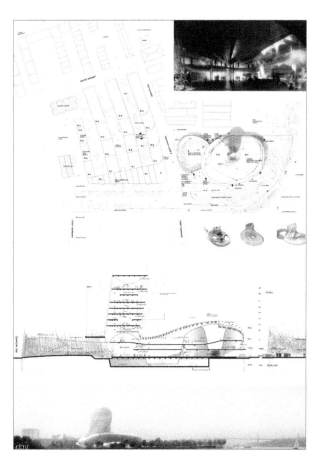 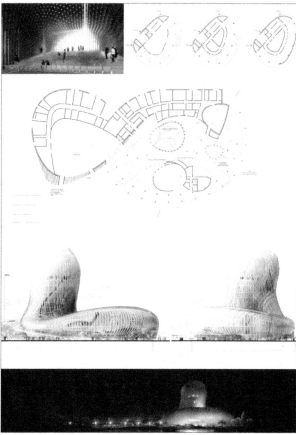

**Fig. 10 and 11**
Two panels of the winning project by the firm X-TU for
the Cultural and Tourist Centre for Wine in Bordeaux
competition in 2011.
*Copyright: X-TU.*

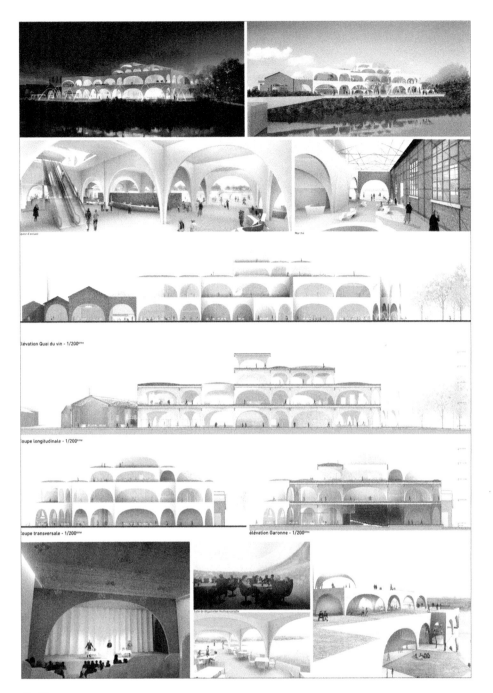

**Fig.12**
Panel for the project by Toyo Ito's firm for the Cultural and
Tourist Centre for Wine in Bordeaux competition in 2011.
*Copyright : Toyo Ito*

**Fig. 13**
(from left to right)  Montage of 6 digital renderings
of proposals by Shigeru Ban; Stéphane Maupin;
Herzog & de Meuron; Foreign Office Architects; Nox
architekten and Dominique Perrault, for the Centre
Pompidou-Metz competition in 2003.

## Cultural Diversity ?

Are international teams then selected for their international status in a desire to promote cultural diversity ?

This is obviously a question that is difficult to confirm without conducting research that traces all discussions in the initial selection, and absolves all personal ties that bind decision makers to applicants. Although I often receive complaints and secrets from various protagonists of these competitions, it is difficult to verify. My view remains broad and I affirm this, not as a scientist but rather as a journalist. Nevertheless, I have attempted to identify some recurrences within a few examples, which may eventually lead to a full research.

## Competition for the Antenna of the Pompidou Metz Center

In 2003, the competition for the antenna of the Centre Pompidou in Metz took place in eastern France. Six teams were selected: Shigeru Ban-Stéphane Maupin, Herzog & de Meuron, Foreign Office Architects, Nox architekten and Dominique Perrault. The jury was seemingly seduced by architect Shigeru Ban's poetic idea of the Chinese straw hat. The volumes of the new museum were covered with a superstructure consisting of a structural weaving that can be found in Asian hats. Shigeru Ban said he had found the hat in a shop in Paris, and also added that when viewed from above, the new building will consist of a hexagon, "just like the map of France." Here I must point out that Shigeru Ban was not alone in this adventure, although it was only he who generally appeared in the media as the winner. He was indeed associated with French architect Jean de Gastines, and Anglo-Armenian Philip Gumuchdjian, longtime employee and partner of Richard Rogers, who was in fact the distinguished guest speaker of the panel [Fig.13].

We see here that the composition of the team is an obvious strategy with each member serving a purpose. The brief explicitly stated that the clients wanted a building, "which does not give the feeling of being lost or insignificant" and "without a monumental gesture," integrating "vegetation," and also one that can "surprise and destabilize the visitor." The idea understandably is to re-edit the major event from the Centre Pompidou by Piano and Rogers that everyone has come to recognize as the reference of twentieth- century architecture.

In 2003, French architects were no longer fascinated by England or Italy as they were in the late sixties. After Tadao Ando, the new idols are from Switzerland or Japan, namely Toyo Ito, Shigeru Ban, Kazuyo Seijima or Kengo Kuma. Swiss architects Herzog & de Meuron are widely recognized for their expertise in museums and contemporary art, however, they embody the world of rich collectors and major foundations; the image of patronage, art or business of large institutions, just like the Tate Modern in London.

Shigeru Ban, with his habitat projects and emergency halls made of a cardboard structure has the perfect profile: new, oriental, offbeat, light and sustainable. The beautiful wood mesh structure of the building he designed proved costly, technically absurd and functionally inadequate. However, the straw hat has done wonders in terms of communication and, contrary to the reception he had reserved in Piano and Rogers' building, the audience applauded [Fig.14] [Fig.15].

## Competition for 130 Social Houses in Paris, 16th District

Did we really expect a Japanese architect to understand and revolutionize Parisian homes ? This is obviously a question that seeks to address the interrogation of internationality in competitions. In 2006, after winning the international competition for the new Louvre in Lens, on a mining wasteland of northern France, Kazuyo Seijima and Ryue Nishizawa (SANAA agency) were invited to a competition for social housing in Paris. The invitation is not without intent. France invited them so that they could win. And this is ultimately what happened, probably less for the actual quality of the project then what was embodied by the two architects.

The project is located in the 16th district on the edge of the Bois de Boulogne in the most chic and expensive district in Paris. Its inhabitants are apprehensively anticipating the arrival of new social housing. This apprehension is based on classism towards the low-income people to be housed in these buildings, and the rejection of modern architecture by bourgeois inhabitants of the district. By ignorance, they associate all modern buildings in defiance of the Parisian heritage, to social housing and therefore to the suburbs and all related racial and class based insecurity [Fig.16]. We understand how SANAA was instrumentalized by the City of Paris — a traditionally bourgeois-bohemian left-wing trend — which organized and controlled the competition against the mayor of the sixteenth district, who was traditionally right-winged. It is obviously not the qualities of the Japanese project that count, but instead the image embodied by Sejima and Nishizawa. We do not imagine them as accomplices of guilty French architects that have built horrible soulless suburbs — they enjoy the clichés about Japan : discretion, lightweight, refined exoticism, etc. They were not yet Pritzker Prize, but they have in their hand, the institution with the most heritage in France, the Louvre.

The examples are numerous where foreign architects are invited, thanks to the visibility that their fame provides for consultation, and their presence also sometimes offers visibility to other candidates. A young architect or agency that has received little recognition is provided access to the big leagues, and this effect obviously reaches its maximum when the underdog wins. The foreigner, if not always a starchitect, is a figure marked by media professionals. It would never occur to anyone to seek out the participation of an unknown architect from Russia, China, or Canada, although the quality of their achievements could legitimize the invitation. The call for international teams is often a desire for quality and visibility. However, the next step — the announcement of the winner — does not always reflect the intentions of the sponsors. In other words, the star does not win every time ; in fact, they are almost always exploited, but not necessarily to their advantage. This could include cases where many starchitects were often invited without winning competitions or who have to wait a long time before obtaining a less prestigious project. For example, Steven Holl, Peter Eisenman, and more notably, Rem Koolhaas and Zaha Hadid have been frequently invited to prestigious French consultations without ever having a project selected.

## ▬ Two Major figures ; Koolhaas and Hadid

Since 1982, Rem Koolhaas has been invited to participate in major competitions at least a dozen times. He won one in 1994 in Lille, north of France, but has won no other major competition until a modest city library in Caen last year, and a more ambitious development project for a large exhibition center in Toulouse, southwest of France [Fig.17] [Fig.18].

Zaha Hadid was also invited to participate in one of the most prestigious competitions : the Museum of Civilization from Europe and Méditerranée, the Paris Philharmonic Concert Hall, the Seguin Island Bridge, the Lens Louvre, and the Louvre Paris for the collections of Islamic Art. She has not won any of the aforementioned competitions, but in 2002 she won a major contract in Montpellier called "Living Stone," which included three departmental equipments : the archives, the central library, and sports facilities. The initial budget was clearly not suited to the fees and the complexity of Zaha Hadid's architecture, and so the project took ten years.

Some projects were not so fortunate. *Toyo Ito* won the competition in February 2004 for the Regional Fund for Contemporary Art of Picardie in Amiens, north of Paris. Five months later the operation was abandoned. There were multiple causes, including political change and opposition by river associations, but the main reason seemed to be the exceeding budget. This was probably underestimated by programming — as is usual in French competitions — but Toyo Ito's draft exceeded 70% of the surface that was originally planned. This did not matter, since the jury saw the project — which recycles the aesthetics of Tod's Omotesando Building in Shibuya-ku Tokyo — as an opportunity to offer the city of Amiens international visibility. Steven Holl, who was also invited and perhaps sensed the trap, chose not to design his project. In this case, the architect is not fooled by this instrumentalization ; he plays the game, but in the end, he ends up being a victim in the situation. The first victims are of course the artists and the inhabitants of Picardy, who never see this center for contemporary art. The search for a win-win situation ends up with both parties losing [Fig.19] [Fig.20].

It is therefore necessary to face the fact that the international quality of architecture has now been almost entirely overshadowed by that of starchitects. Therefore, the issues of open competitions in the international scene can be addressed in another manner. The goal is not entirely to seize the opportunity of cultural diversity, but is at best a means to achieve excellent results, and at worst, a way have to quick and cheap access to greater visibility in the race to the attractiveness of cities.

## ▬ Publish, Display, Discuss, Appeal, Win : The Strategy of Market Occupation by International Teams

The European context, which allows any community member to participate, reporting on the presence of international teams is an almost trivial matter. However, an international team, European or not, still occupies a special place, and this status does not correspond to anything formal. The reasons for choosing such a candidate are never actually formulated, even if implicitly everyone may assume the motivations behind the choice. For an international team, getting invited to a competition in France is often the result of a communication strategy : one must first get invited to conferences and exhibitions in prestigious venues.

**Fig. 14 and 15**
The completed project of the Centre Pompidou-Metz
(architects, Shigeru-Ban, Jean de Gastines,
Philip Gumuchdjian).
*Copyright: photos Emmanuel Caille*

**Fig.16**
Winning project for the competition of 135 social housing
apartments located in the bourgeois neighbourhood of the
16th District of Paris by the Japanese architectural team of
SANAA. The buildings which were to be delivered in 2011
are still not yet in construction.
*Copyright: sanaa*

**Fig. 17**
Winning project by OMA for the
CAEN Library in 2010.
*Copyright: OMA*

**Fig. 18**
Winning project by OMA for the
exhibition parc of the Toulouse
urban area (PEX) in 2011.
*Copyright: OMA*

**Fig. 19 and 20**
Project by Toyo Ito for the "Fonds d'art contemporain"
de Picardie (FRAC) in Amiens. Winning project in 2004
but abandoned because of budget overruns.
*Copyright : Toyo Ito*

**Fig. 21 and 22**
Morphosis Exposition at the Georges Pompidou Centre in 2006.
Thom Mayne was recently awarded the Pritzker prize, was invited to
the competition for the highest tower in France at the Défense and
won a few months later.
*Copyright : Centre Georges Pompidou and Morphosis*

**Fig. 23 and 24**
Digital perspective of the winning project by Kengo Kuma for the FRAC of Marseille in 2007 and view of completed project in 2013.
*Copyright : Kengo Kuma and Xavier Zimmermann*

### Tadao Ando

Tadao Ando, to whom was devoted one of the first major exhibitions at the Centre Georges Pompidou in 1993, waited a few years before being invited to the great competitions of the Musée du Quai Branly in 1999, and in the Pinault Foundation's private consultation on the Seguin Island.

### Thom Mayne

For Thom Mayne of the Morphosis agency, things have been accelerating. The Californian architect was the winner of the Pritzker Prize a few months before the opening of a 2006 solo exhibition dedicated to him at the Centre Pompidou. Frederic Migayrou, chief curator of architecture and design at the National Museum of Modern Art, the Centre Pompidou, invited him. It is important to highlight that regardless of the quality of the work, the architects themselves largely carry out such exposure. Their highly self-promotional nature is undeniable. During this exhibition Thom Mayne presented some lectures. While he has never built in France, he was invited in the prestigious "Lighthouse Tower" in la Défense, in Paris. Ten months after this exhibition he won this competition, despite the fact that the most prestigious starchitects were participating **[Fig.21] [Fig.22]**.

### Kengo Kuma

Kengo Kuma gave several lectures in France : in 2004 at the Cité de l'Architecture et du Patrimoine and in 2006 at the exhibition dedicated to him at the Regional Fund for Contemporary Art in Orléans. Two months later, he was selected to compete in the Cité des Arts de Besançon competition, a contract combining another Regional Fund for Contemporary Art and the Conservatory of the city. A month later, Kengo Kuma was selected again for the assistance of another Regional Fund for Contemporary Art, in Marseille. He won both competitions in July and November. In 2010, he also won the competition for the Conservatoire de Musique d'Aix-en-Provence **[Fig.23] [Fig.24]**.

### Bjarke Ingels

The most recent and most iconic case is that of Bjarke Ingels (BIG). This young Danish architect, formerly with OMA, is probably the most formidable competition creature in architectural history. His lectures are like events, and he is no longer simply a starchitect but rather a pop-starchitect. Table 1 shows the list of projects he has won in the brief span of two years **[Fig.25]**.

**Fig. 25**
Bjarke Ingels in conference.
*Copyright : dr*

**Fig. 26**
Digital perspective of the winning project for the MECA
in Bordeaux by the firm BIG (associated with Freaks
Free architects) 2012.
*Copyright : BIG*

**Fig. 27**
Digital perspective of the winning project for the
"Musée du corps humain" in Montpellier by the firm
BIG (associated with A+architectures) 2013.
*Copyright : BIG*

**Fig. 28**
Glenn Murcutt. The only architect to win the
Pritzker prize that refuses to built outside his
Australian birthplace.

## One Year of Winning Projects by BIG

- January 25, 2011: A new waste-to-energy plant + ski slope in Copenhagen
- February 9, 2011: Greenlands National Gallery
- March 15, 2011: International E2 (Economy + Ecology) timber competition in Finland
- March 22, 2011: The Stockholmsporten Master Plan
- May 4, 2011: The Tirana cultural center in Albania
- October 25, 2011: The transformation of the Transitlager in Switzerland
- November 18, 2011: Extension of the university of Jussieu in Paris
- December 12, 2011: A ski resort in Lapland, Finland
- February 12, 2012: The Kimball Art Center in Utha, USA
- February 15, 2012: Residences in Stockholm

Ingels created his own solo exposition, which he then sold to various institutional organizations related to architecture around the world. The exhibition was accompanied by a manifesto in comic book form published by Taschen. The exhibition is a boon for exhibition centers that do not yet have large budgets, and is an opportunity to conduct a speaking tour. Bjarke Ingels offered his "Yes is more" exhibition and lecture to the Arc en Rêve Centre d'Architecture in Bordeaux from June to October, 2010.

Ingels then gave a lecture at the School of Architecture of Paris-Malaquais at the same time as Rem Koolhaas. He was invited shortly after the competition to the new research center at the University Pierre and Marie Curie on the Jussieu campus in Paris. On November 18th, 2011, he was the only architect invited to the major International Symposium on the Future of Cities — Paris in 2030, held in the gilded salons of the Hôtel de Ville in Paris. He has just now been named winner of the Jussieu competition, and in spring of 2012 he was the winner (in association with the French team Freaks Free Architects) of the MECA, a prestigious cultural center in Bordeaux. He subsequently wins the competitions for the upcoming Europa City leisure and commercial complex in the parisian suburbs and finally the competition for the Museum of the Human Body (Cité du Corps Humain) in Montpellier in 2013. If the last case appears ludicrous, these strategies are not always deliberate on the part of architects. This route, leading from media attention to victory, is mainly the result of local promoters, directors of cultural institutions, critics, or contract authorities, whose motivations lie in sincere admiration for the architects that they wish to invite [Fig.26] [Fig.27].

With a few exceptions, the starchitect status is itself under construction. Participation in international competitions is both a means of accessing the status as well an effect of this status. All starchitects now participate in international competitions, with the exception of course of Australian Glenn Murcutt, the famous Pritzker Prize winner that refuses to build outside his home country. He may seem like the worst person to discuss in the context of this conference, but I would be curious to hear from him [Fig.28].

# 5.4. Competitive Process
## Leveraging Design Competitions for Effective Urban Development

**Ian Chodikoff**, Architect
Director, Architecture Canada
Former Editor, Canadian Architect magazine (2003-2012)
Canada

This paper will discuss the critical significance of carefully structuring a design competition so that the desired outcome can best represent the goals of the client while ensuring the highest caliber of design excellence possible. Managing, brokering and promoting a successful creative process through the mechanism of a design competition demands a level of sophistication on the part of both the organizers and sponsors, from the inception of a critical idea to the management of post-competition results in the media and public sphere. This paper will discuss a number of Canadian competitions over the past decade to illustrate the lessons that can be learned, so that future competition organizers and sponsors can achieve the maximum benefits from the mechanism of a design competition. Factors to consider when evaluating the capacity of competitions to achieve useful debate in the public realm include the ability of the competition organizers, the clients, and the winning design team to remain committed to the project through effective post-competition management. The greatest role the media and publications play in the success of any design competition is the power to translate architectural ideas with the goal of fostering critical debate on realizable, high-quality architectural designs **[Fig.1]**.

**Cover**
A team led by Montreal-based Saucier + Perrotte Architectes was one of the five shortlisted teams that were selected for the doomed Bank Street Competition in Ottawa. Image courtesy Saucier + Perrotte Architectes.

A design competition should ultimately provide the client with a strategic outcome which is usually a building that can be feasibly built and is able to respond to either a distinct set of policy or business objectives, hopefully both. A successful design competition is also able to mitigate risk in both the political and the public spheres. After all, the great unknown in any design competition is the uncertainty of the winning submission. However, if the design competition is viewed as part of a larger process, rather than the savior of the commissioning process, the procedures set in place to professionally manage the timeline of creating such a dynamic building that responds to the sponsor's established objectives will be preserved. As for the scrutiny of the media, if there is a perceived unfair practice built into the process — as what may have been the case of some recent Canadian architecture competitions such as the Art Gallery of Alberta, or the Canadian Museum of Human Rights (Manitoba) — then the credibility of sponsorship and ensuing fundraising potential may be jeopardized. Such accusations are difficult to prove, as no jury is infallible to biases, personal or otherwise. In other cases where a design competition has not been carefully tied to long-term funding objectives, the final schemes may appear as the result of an "ideas competition" and will not be taken seriously. In all likelihood, as is the case for the TownShift competition in Surrey, British Columbia, the results were part of an ideas competition. In situations like these, commission and/or winning design may simply be left to wither and hopefully disappear with no further action (i.e., risk) on the part of the client as what was seen in Ottawa for the Bank Street competition.

Failure to achieve the successful management of a design competition in the media — after a winner has been selected — will more often than not result in raising the anxiety of already nervous clients and/or politicians. In conjunction with this, the general public may express a diminished lack of faith in the value of a winning competition entry over issues such as escalating costs, appropriateness of site, or the ability to fulfill a larger mandate. As is the case of the Canadian Museum for Human Rights in Winnipeg, the slow pace at which competition organizers decided to reveal the winners caused a diminished faith in the media–and profession–as to the viability of the design competition in the first instance (*Canadian Architect* June 2005; Bellamy, 2012).[1]

An important issue to consider in any design competition is risk management. Many competitions fail to effectively communicate risk, while other architectural competitions completely lack the necessary vision or clarity of purpose to attract sufficiently high-quality submissions. This often happens in ideas competitions where the eagerness and boundless energy of the competition organizers is readily apparent but a lack of committed sponsors prevents the competition from achieving any real positive impact on the public realm — as what can be seen in the TownShift competition in Surrey, British Columbia.

Assessing the ways in which media responded to a selection of architectural competitions over the past few years (both single and multiple-stage competitions), the usefulness in studying the efficacy of design competitions across Canada and how results can vary depending upon the region often reveals two important themes: the competition's ability to leverage local political and economic culture; and the ability of competition organizers, clients and winning design teams to remain committed to the project during the crucial stage of effective post-competition management.

Briefly exploring case studies of design competitions in Edmonton, Alberta; Surrey, British Columbia; Ottawa, Ontario; and Winnipeg, Manitoba can explain some of the successful and problematic dynamics associated with competitions.

### ▬ City of Edmonton: From the Art Gallery of Alberta to Park Pavilions

The City of Edmonton has often felt as though it lives in the shadow of Calgary. The provincial capital of Alberta, Edmonton has often been viewed as the cultural capital of the province while Calgary has become, relatively speaking, an active city engaged in a variety of rich city-building exercises. Nonetheless, the City of Edmonton has played host to two types of significant design competitions over the past decade. The first was the selection of an architect for the re-christened Art Gallery of Alberta, and the second design competition (or series of small design competitions) recently occurred when the City of Edmonton held a series of calls for five park pavilions in five different city parks in 2011, where they defined a design competition in the following way:

> *Architectural competitions level the playing field between firms of all experience levels and backgrounds. The focus of an awarded competition is not the profile of an individual firm, but the challenges and objectives of the project at hand. They allow for a less restrained showcasing of skills and a greater variety of outcomes. An architectural competition allows for a broad display of inspiration, innovation and creativity.* [2]

**Fig. 1**
Gh3 was the winning firm for the Castle Downs District Park in the successfully run City of Edmonton-sponsored design competition. Image courtesy gh3 architects.

Under the direction of City Architect Carol Bélanger, a young architect and city-builder hired by the City of Edmonton, Bélanger has been instrumental in helping Edmonton develop a series of thoughtfully prepared architectural competitions to improve the public realm. Edmonton's recent experience with design competitions exists as an invaluable case study whereby the park pavilions competition created excitement for the community, demonstrated a low level of risk, and attracted high-calibre design responses **[Fig.2]**.

In an October 2005 non-city initiated Edmonton design competition, the Art Gallery of Alberta (which changed its name from the Edmonton Art Gallery) announced that Los-Angeles based Randall Stout Architects won the architecture competition for the expansion of its new gallery **[Fig.3]**. From an initial field of 25 submissions, four teams were shortlisted. The three other finalists were as follows: Alsop & Partners (London, UK) with Quadrangle Architects (Toronto); Arthur Erickson/ Nick Milkovich (Vancouver) with Dub Architects (Edmonton); and Zaha Hadid Architects (London, UK) with Kasian Architecture (Edmonton). When Randall Stout won the competition, he described his building as:

**Fig. 2**
The original Edmonton Art Gallery was designed by Don Bittorf and completed in 1968. The image seen here was before its renovation and expansion. Image courtesy Ian Chodikoff.

> *[A]n alluring composition of metal and glass [embodying] regional references, including the stacked rock compositions of 'inukshuks.' The ephemeral, lucid forms of the stainless steel draw inspiration from the 'aurora borealis.' The building design may be seen as the largest object in the Gallery's collection. Its fluidity frees the mind of convention, representing an entire institution that evokes experimentation* **[Fig4]**. [3]

**Fig. 3**
The new Art Gallery of Alberta was designed by
Randall Stout Architects and replaced the Edmonton
Art Gallery. Image courtesy Robert Lemermeyer.

**Fig. 4**
Finalists for the Art Gallery of Alberta. TOP Randall
Stout Architects. BOTTOM, LEFT TO RIGHT Zaha Hadid,
Arthur Erickson/Nick Milkovitch, and Will Alsop.

In addition to their permanent collection, the new art gallery was supposed to comprise 80,000 square feet of new and renovated space dedicated to Western Canadian and First Nations art. The decision for the new gallery was also intended to revitalize Edmonton's core, acting as a catalyst for future development. Funding for the project was split between the federal government's $10 million Alberta Centennial Grant and a last-minute $15 million investment from the province of Alberta.

The original Edmonton Art Gallery was designed by Don Bittorf in 1968. Over time, its Brutalist exposed-concrete design lost favor with the general public. Museum standards had changed and the building experienced increasing challenges to maintain stable temperatures and humidity levels, limiting the gallery's ability to host traveling exhibitions. The purpose for renaming the building as the Art Gallery of Alberta was to simply expand its fundraising potential beyond city limits. As Shafraaz Kaba noted in an article commissioned by *Canadian Architect* magazine[4], former Executive Director Tony Luppino, the sponsor of a design competition for the gallery's expansion had noted that, "One of our main patrons, John Poole was very much in favour of the competition." John and Barbara Poole persuaded the gallery to spend a significant sum of their $5-million donation to pay for the design competition rather than going to a typical RFP process **[Fig.2] [Fig.3]**.[5]

The exhibition of the four finalists, entitled *Building a New Vision : Four Perspectives*, featuring the models was on display at the Art Gallery of Alberta for a month-long exhibition and provided considerable excitement surrounding the renewal of the Edmonton Art Gallery. The media enjoyed covering the competition as it contained much drama surrounding rumors about who the competition organizers wanted to win, versus which scheme was favored by the general public. Fortunately, the media coverage also had the positive effect of raising the profile of the competition in the local community, while also contributing to increased political volatility surrounding the competition.

The Edmonton Art Gallery Board approved an architectural competition in late 2004. Holding a competition by the Architectural Association of Alberta took some time to negotiate, but the requests for Expressions of Interest were released in winter 2005. When the four shortlisted firms presented their work at the Architecture Canada | Royal Architectural Institute of Canada's (RAIC) Festival of Architecture in May 2005, each of their presentations were highly telling of their individual philosophies regarding the future of Edmonton. The four finalists presented were not yet presenting their specific design response for the new art gallery. Will Alsop (partnering with Toronto-based Quadrangle Architects) presented a game-changing approach to culture, offering the gallery as an incubator for art. Using a relatively old-fashioned slide projector to present his credentials, the late Arthur Erickson (who was partnering with Nick Milkovich/Dub Architects) delivered a time-honored speech on the value of a well-crafted civic building as anchor to place-making. The team led by Zaha Hadid (with Edmonton-based Kasian Architecture) was represented by a young Briton who flew in from London for the weekend to deliver a rambunctious presentation based largely on an evocative yet formal approach to architecture. Finally, it was Randall Stout's (of Randall Stout Architects) turn to reveal his architectural roots under the tutelage of Frank Gehry. Stout, the architect who ultimately won the competition, used his formal-to-near-iconic design approach to woo senior gallery officials, and his strategy worked **[Fig.5]**.

Less than five months later, the four finalists exhibited their conceptual designs for the gallery renovation and expansion to the public, who could weigh in on the final schemes. This was a highly unusual process and one that increased the volatility of the public's reaction to the project, since they were given a chance to evaluate the four finalists even before the jury could convene. Inspiring numerous articles and letters to the editor in the *Edmonton Journal*, the competition was viewed as a success, which inevitably helped it garner patrons and interested supporters that would see the $66-million project come to fruition. However, once the gallery opened it failed to receive the critical success that many had hoped. This was largely due to the architectural aesthetic, not to mention its lack of contextualism and inability to engage with its surrounding context. Despite these setbacks, admission has increased considerably, unlike other cultural institutions like the Royal Ontario Museum in Toronto, which after its estimated $275-million renovation completed in 2007, has seen a disappointing decrease in attendance after it reopened.

The competition was very time-consuming for senior museum employees who claimed that the process, "...was beyond what we imagined. We learned a lot about who we are as an organization and our relationship to the community," notes Luppino when asked to comment on the overall process.[6]

Nevertheless, the Alberta Art Gallery competition was certainly advantageous in bringing the staff of the institution closer together while clarifying their own mandate as to what their mandate should be in the eyes of the general public. The new architecture, notes Luppino, would eventually become the biggest 'brand' or identity element for the gallery".[7]

Most importantly, Luppino noted that, "We could have used more direction and input from the Alberta Association of Architects [who] need to think about how they can facilitate the process rather than being regulators of the process." The Gallery used Toronto-based architect Peter Berton as the professional advisor with local architect Rick Arndt assisting throughout the process. "Even if you have an advisor, these things are being initiated by people like me, who are not architects, and the competition process is much more complex than one who isn't an architect may realize," admits Luppino.[8]

Of the 25 responses to the Art Gallery of Alberta's Expressions of Interest–many of which came from international firms, the final four contained ideas that were certainly not without risks associated with their design. What is interesting to note about the Edmonton experience is how Luppino wishes that, "It would be great to have an exchange network to share experiences with other organizations that have gone through the experience or are planning to do a competition".[9] No such forum exists on a strategic level. The lesson learned from the Edmonton Art Gallery is that identifying the goals and expectations of the client is more important than engaging the services of an architect.

Led by City Architect Carol Bélanger, the City of Edmonton launched a design competition in 2011 for five individual park pavilions in five separate parks: Borden Park, Castle Downs Park, John Fry Sports Park, Mill Woods Sports Park, and Victoria Park. The results were exceptional in that not only were the winners' entries quite buildable, but the competition was structured in such a way as to allow local citizens to feel part of the process while creating an opportunity for public-private partnerships after the competition results were declared **[Fig.1] [Fig.6]**.

A five-person jury examined each project independently, and each park pavilion jury had the same four members, of which one was the City of Edmonton architect Carol Bélanger. The fifth jury member included a member of City staff who had more intimate knowledge of each site.[10]

**Fig. 6**
Gh3 was the winning firm for the City of Edmonton-sponsored design
competition for the new Borden Park Pavilion. Image courtesy gh3 architects.

Individuals or teams had to have been eligible for registration with the Alberta Association of Architects. This was part of the requirements for the project to be officially sanctioned by the Alberta Association of Architects. Having a provincial association endorse a design competition is an important aspect to architecture competitions in Canada, as to ensure that a fair process protects the creative efforts of the architecture teams submitting their designs in a competition format.[11]

The City of Edmonton decided to eschew the typical RFQ and RFP process to reinforce the City's "commitment to 'cutting edge' quality design, and ensuring that it is brought to all civic projects regardless of size or budget." Managed through the City of Edmonton Building and Construction Branch, winners of the competition would also have an opportunity to develop a portfolio of work with the City of Edmonton, a bonus when responding to future RFQs and RFPs. This is also a welcome component to design competitions that wish to promote emerging firms who have not had previous opportunities to work with significant clients like municipalities.

This architectural competition is for the design of five pavilions and has a portion of the program for each pavilion to be funded by the City of Edmonton with a portion to be funded by a partner organization. Stipulating a phase for the base building components allowed the opportunity for the City of Edmonton to pay for those elements, with the partner organization completing the project as required.

It remains to be seen how the winning pavilion designs[12] will look once complete. However, the ways in which the City of Edmonton stewarded the process leaves no doubt that the efforts and talent promoted through this competition for park pavilions will only elevate the culture of architecture and design in the City of Edmonton for years to come.

## Making a Case for the Canadian Museum for Human Rights

With a projected budget of $350 million, the Canadian Museum for Human Rights (CMHR) in Winnipeg, Manitoba will be the first national museum to be created in Canada since 1967, and the first to be located outside of the National Capital Region. The idea for the museum first originated from local businessman Israel Asper, who died in 2003. Asper wanted to establish a museum devoted to the idea of human rights. In keeping with the contemporary ways in which large public buildings are realized, the museum was a public-private development that would include the three levels of government as well as the Forks Renewal Corporation and the newly established Friends of the Canadian Museum for Human Rights, a charitable organization that was able to raise 40 percent of the funds through private donations. The construction process for the CMHR began in the summer of 2008, with a projected completion date of 2012 **[Fig.7]**.

Supporting an endeavor of this magnitude demands a high degree of sophistication in which a design competition represents only a fraction of what must transpire for the project to become a reality. Firstly, government and institutional support is required at all levels. Clearly, the support of the federal government for the CMHR required significant political will and commitment. Other stakeholders included Library and Archives Canada, the Canadian Heritage Information Network, McGill University Archives, The National Film Board, CBC/Radio-Canada, Rotary International, the Global College at the University of Winnipeg, the University of Manitoba, as well as additional institutions in Europe and in the United Kingdom.

During the first stage of the competition process in late 2003, 30 architectural firms spanning 12 countries were selected out of an original 500 architectural firms who indicated their initial interest. [13] By March 2004, the Architectural Review Committee selected eight architectural firms for Stage 2 of the competition. The eight were chosen from the 30 architectural firms who submitted their design proposals. Each of the eight winning firms received $12,000 and had their proposals exhibited at The Forks Market in Winnipeg, and for a brief period of time the proposals were featured on the museum's website where the public had the opportunity to submit their feedback. At the beginning of April, the Architectural Review Committee interviewed the eight semi-finalists, of which three were invited to participate in Stage 3 of the competition. Each of the three finalists in Stage 3 was to receive $100,000. The eight firms included the following: Antoine Predock Architect (USA), Charles Correa Associates (India), Dan Hanganu Architects with The Arcop Group (Canada), Mashabane Rose Architects (South Africa), Michael Maltzan Architecture, Inc. (USA), Saucier + Perrotte architectes (Canada), Schmidt Hammer Lassen (Denmark), and Schwartz Architects and EHDD Architecture (USA). The three finalists that were eventually chosen were the following: Saucier + Perrotte architectes, Antoine Predock Architect, and Dan Hanganu Architects & The Arcop Group **[Fig.8]**.

At the time of the competition much information was available to the public, including information on the competition process, along with a list of the Architectural Review Committee and Technical Review Committee members. For the shortlisted firms in Stage 2 of the process, The Asper Foundation published a highly prescriptive and weighty three-volume series of architectural and programmatic guidelines to describe the requirements of the project.

On April 15th, 2005, after months of rumors over the winner of the CMHR design competition, the Asper Foundation officially and finally announced that New Mexico-based Antoine Predock won the competition. Predock's design for the CMHR was described as an architectural path for the visitor that moved from darkness to light. The architectural journey began with the Museum's "roots" that rose up from the ground of The Forks—the concrete base manifests this. Once inside visitors ascend a series of bridges, encountering various human rights-related stories and the people who lived them along the way. The journey through the building culminated with the arrival at the Tower of Hope, a 23-storey glass structure that was a key design feature the Asper Foundation ultimately wanted. According to the Architectural Review Committee, Predock's design was seen as one that "exhibits the substantial presence of an iconic building." The Asper Foundation was explicit in its desire for a tower. Those that deviated from this notion, or who attempted to reinterpret its meaning on a deeper architectural level were ultimately eliminated.

The 11-person jury for the competition was comprised of five architects and one landscape architect. The jury deliberations for the eventual winner were recorded but never released. A decision was finally made to select Antoine Predock from a shortlist of the two other finalists, both of which were Montreal-based architect teams: Saucier + Perrotte architectes and Dan Hanganu with the Arcop Group (*Canadian Architect*, June 2005). [14]

**Fig. 7**
The winning entry for the new Canadian Museum
of Human Rights was won by Albuquerque-based
architect Antoine Predock. Image courtesy Antoine
Predock Architect.

**Fig. 8**
Montreal-based Saucier + Perrotte Architectes were
one of three finalists for the competition for the new
Canadian Museum of Human Rights in Winnipeg.
Image courtesy Saucier + Perrotte Architectes.

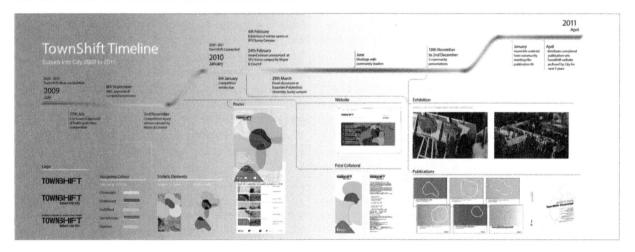

**Fig. 9**
The timeline chart for the TownShift ideas competition in Surrey, British
Columbia. Image courtesy Sean Ruthen.

At the time, it was felt that The Asper Foundation made a significant error in judgment by waiting several months before announcing the winner. "They didn't do the right thing by waiting for so long," notes Hanganu, one of the finalists. "Future international competitors will have to ask themselves if Canada is a worthwhile market to engage in design competitions".[15]

As is the case for many design competitions, firms invest not only a lot of time, but also a lot of money into submitting for the competition. The $100,000 that each of the finalists received to defray their costs to enter the competition certainly did not allow the finalists to recoup the costs incurred on their design proposals. As Gilles Saucier noted at the time "Winning means that you are good enough to win. Not winning means that you have done the research".[16]

Commenting on the jury deliberations, jury member Raymond Moriyama remarked that the non-designers were more easily swayed by metaphors and phraseology throughout the adjudication process than were the designers on the jury. "The visual people read what they need to read. You can easily manipulate people with words. It's much harder to manipulate people through imagery," says Moriyama. Predock's scheme is certainly more metaphorical in its allusions to snow and the Canadian North. It was generally acknowledged that the designers on the jury were not as convinced about Predock's architecture. Nevertheless, as jury member and former Director of the School of Architecture at McGill University noted, "You don't walk out of these arenas. When you accept to participate, you also agree to a set of rules".[17]

To be sure, the Asper Foundation and the incredible machinery working to ensure the success of the future CMHR had many measures of success to balance throughout the process of conducting the design competition. Was the competition process successful in fostering design excellence, or did it merely act as a due diligence process to secure publicity for the building? As one jury member anonymously remarked to *Canadian Architect* at the time, the result of the competition "is an inspiration to non-architectural thinking".[18]

Currently the museum is well-under construction and beyond the post-competition management phase, and the CMHR continues to be challenged with meeting the targets of its operating budget. Completing a building is only the beginning of an ongoing challenge of realizing an architectural commission. Garnering constant support from private and public donors, in addition to creating adequate linkages with individuals is critical to the long-term success of the CMHR. This, along with a clear mandate for the museum, is an important issue to consider, even during the design competition phase.

Undoubtedly, the CMHR design competition and capital campaign is a difficult challenge. However, it remains to be seen how the museum's management will be able to ensure the programmatic and design elements of the museum are maintained while ensuring that operational cost requirements can be met over the long-term.

### ▬▬ Surrey TownShift : The Inertia of Ideas

"TownShift : Suburb into City" was an open international ideas competition intent on rethinking five of Surrey's established "Town Centres" : Guildford, Fleetwood, Cloverdale, Newton and Semiahmoo that was launched in 2009 and continued through 2010. The purpose of the competition was to think of new ways to intensify the future of these rapidly growing centers and alter the public's perception of the public nature and public space of these centers. How can we think of making the suburb more sustainable and productive? The concept of TownShift, developed through the efforts of architects and/or critics Allen Aubert, Trevor Boddy, John Sprung, Scott Kemp and Sean Ruthen who initiated debate and awareness of Surrey's changing urban dynamics amongst architects, urbanists and the general public. The goal of the ideas competition was to "generate visions of how architectural and urban design for new private and public development might 'shift' Surrey from its suburban legacy towards a bolder, more inclusive, and more sustainable urban future" **[Fig.9] [Fig.10]**.[19]

As British Columbia's second most populous city, Surrey is located to the east of Vancouver with a 2011 population of 468,251. This represents an 18.6% population increase from 2006, as compared to the national average growth of 5.9%. Surrey is a municipality that was formed by amalgamating several old farm communities about 50 years ago. Developed as a suburb, sprawl has not been kind to Surrey. Today, it boasts an extremely multicultural population, the largest school system in British Columbia and it counts universities as its fastest-growing employers. It is becoming so big that architects can no longer avoid the need to cultivate a more important identity for itself.

The competition cost over $300,000, and attracted 138 submissions from 20 countries. The five-member jury

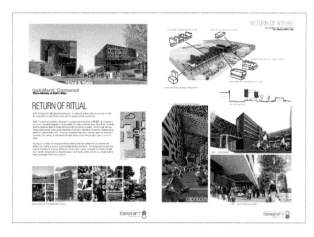

**Fig. 10**
Renante Solivar was the overall winner for the
TownShift ideas competition in Surrey, British
Columbia. Image courtesy Renante Solivar.

**Fig. 11**
A team led by Montreal-based Saucier + Perrotte
Architectes was one of the five shortlisted
teams that were selected for the doomed Bank
Street Competition in Ottawa. Image courtesy
Saucier + Perrotte Architectes.

selected 27 finalists. The $75,000 in prize-money was distributed to winners for each of the five sites. Most tellingly, Surrey did not commit to build any of the winning schemes, but the entries were published as an attractive six-volume box set of booklets that were intended to be used to promote the potential of Surrey's urbanity. Unfortunately, this promotion did not work past the initial media blitz coordinated by the competition's organizers. Although an ideas competition, the strategic relevance of TownShift was severely lacking and had little association with concrete initiatives that the municipality had been undertaking over the past number of years. In essence, the ideas competition amounted to a public relations campaign that set out to merely draw Vancouver's creative class out to Surrey.

Renante Solivar of Vancouver took the overall top prize for his entry "Return of Ritual" which proposed structuring a new bold, brightly colored construction along 152nd Street in front of Guildford Mall. Solivar, an architect at the Vancouver firm Musson Cattell Mackey Partnership, contributed a design that called for vibrant red buildings and outdoor courtyards to draw focus to 152nd Street and create a zone called «Superbia." In addition to winning best overall design and $15,000, Solivar also won $10,000 for placing first in the Guildford-area category.

Needless to say, reactions from the press were very positive, but polite. Media attention largely focused on how this ideas competition was attempting to rebrand Surrey as a challenging and dynamic suburb, rather than a maligned suburb in the Lower Mainland.

As the TownShift competition indicated, there is a fundamental gap in the results of the ideas competition and the subsequent release of Surrey's Economic Action Plan, which occurred a few months after the competition winners were announced. Further to this, Surrey's Economic Investment Action Plan that was designed to foster economic growth through capital investment, strategic partnerships, and a focus on clean technology industries shared little with the results of the TownShift competition. Similarly, the Build Surrey Program that examined key strategic investment considerations such as the promotion of a clean energy hub, business incubator areas, new strategic partnerships, and extending the municipality's economic investments zones shared very little with the results of the competition. As an extension of its $465 million capital investment program that will see the completion of a new City Centre Library and City Hall, as well as swimming pools, recreation centers, pedestrian and cycling trails, and new parkland across

Surrey–all of which will near completion by 2016, it seemed positively naive for esteemed architectural critic and one of the competitions organizers Trevor Boddy to note that TownShift, "is a rare opportunity to have a visually-driven public discussion about urban alternatives," only adding that, "These meetings will provide Surrey residents with a visual gateway into shaping the future of their city". [20]

## ▬ Ottawa : A Political Reality

When Ottawa's Bank Street Competition was cancelled in 2005, it was largely due to political reasons. The government repositioned its priorities, and as a result, plans to build the first new building in 70 years in the parliamentary precinct of the Nation's Capital were cancelled.

As Elsa Lam wrote in *Canadian Architect* magazine, [21] a design competition was announced in 2002 for a building located at Bank and Wellington Streets. With a projected budget of over $275 million, the building would contain about a dozen committee rooms for the House of Commons, 39 offices for senators, underground parking for 300 vehicles and a materials handling facility. It would have been the first new building to grace the parliamentary precinct in almost 70 years.

In June 2005, Public Works Canada announced the results of the celebrated competition and then cancelled the project based on changing government priorities. The West Block was deteriorating and this shifted the capital expenditures elsewhere.

The Bank Street building would have ushered the Parliament Hill precinct into the twenty-first century. The steep topography of the site itself was challenging, but the proposed 200,000-square-foot facility would have achieved a LEED-Gold status, in addition to responding to strict security requirements. The building was also supposed to be both contemporary in nature, while remaining stylistically sympathetic to the precinct's Gothic Revival architecture.

Five teams of architects were shortlisted to submit entries to the competition, and they are as follows : Diamond + Schmitt Architects in collaboration with Katz Webster Clancey Associates was postmodern in its approach, while Kuwabara Payne McKenna Blumberg Architects in joint venture with Gagnon Letellier Cyr architectes and Barry Padolsky Associates presented a 10-storey structure that alluded to the Neo-Gothic (complete with a copper roof), while emphasizing its verticality in its detailing. Montreal-based Dan Hanganu, in collaboration with Lemay Dorval

Fortin Doyle & Associates and Mill & Ross Architects presented a low podium with a sunken courtyard and narrow tower placed on top experimental massing. The Hanganu-led collaboration combined a low podium with a slim, contemporary tower whose cleft form evoked the Gothic spires of Parliament. Finally, the submission by Provencher Roy, in collaboration with the Zeidler Grinnell Partnership and Hotson Bakker Architects, was a particularly dramatic entry. It emphasized the connection to the building site, as it took advantage of the steep topography. However, it was Saucier + Perrotte architectes' entry–developed in joint venture with Stantec and Cohos Evamy–that was seen as the jury's favorite. "It was a refreshing, modern scheme that didn't make any concession to stylistic contextualism," noted jury member and architect Edward Jones. "Instead, it addressed the site guidelines not with condescension or over-deference, but with a good piece of modern architecture". [22]

Bhagwant Sandhu, former Director-General of Public Works, noted at the time of the competition's cancellation the $1.5 million paid to the shortlisted architects remains a valuable investment as the competition helped develop prototypes for committee rooms, innovative risk analysis protocols, and the experience of working with a competition tendering model as lessons that will inform future projects **[Fig.11]**.

Indeed, when the federal government prepared a long-term vision and plan (LTVP) for the Parliamentary Precinct a few years after the cancellation of the failed Bank Street competition, their intention was to review a framework that could provide a direction for renewal of the precinct that would see not only a restoration and preservation of the parliamentary architecture, but a plan to modernize the facilities to be implemented in five phases over a 25-year period. The government accelerated the restoration of the West Block due to advanced deterioration and the presence of asbestos and other health and safety concerns. Other reasons included : a broader review of the LTVP to examine issues such as security, circulation, and the deterioration of the masonry of the precinct's buildings, an increase in overall estimated costs for the Bank Street Building project, and general concerns with regards to soil contamination.

As Lam notes, "architects stand to profit from the considerable creative effort mustered by the competition. Its proposals represent the results of extensive design research into key contemporary issues of sustainability, heritage, and Canadian architectural identity. For these lessons, they deserve to be discussed, appraised, and celebrated". [23]

There are many instances across Canada where design competitions continue to attract young talent, while reassuring anxious clients that hosting a design competition will yield the best results when it comes to attracting new ideas to solve real issues for the client. Quebec is often cited as a jurisdiction in Canada where open design commissions have enjoyed a rich history of and track record of sponsoring successful design competitions. One firm that has benefitted from such a program is Montreal-based firm Atelier TAG, comprised of life partners Manon Asselin and Katsuhiro Yamasaki. The couple operates a small firm in Montreal and has completed nearly six library commissions to date, all of them garnered through design competitions. However, the firm has not completed much else. Content with the slow but intense evolution of their firm's portfolio, the pair represents one of the few strong design firms in Quebec to emerge with a female principal leading the charge. Although the firm is a recipient of several choice design commissions as a result of the competition format, the couple is clear that there needs to be a much stronger competition system in the province with which to award projects. They also believe that architects would be more effective if they were implicated in the development of a project's measure of success at the outset of a client's desire to go out and seek the services of an architect. Even in Quebec, there needs to be much more work done to ensure that sponsors of design competitions are more adequately guided through the process to produce the most successful result possible.

Competitions are effective at raising the profile of particular issues, and ideas competitions are especially effective in this regard. The client, who generally receives free information, or an abundance of creative ideas for little or no financial and/or political risk, also appreciates them. In the case of a community group or non-profit, ideas competitions help coalesce the political or social interest in a given cause.

However, ideas competition lacks the spirit of commitment that one finds in invited or open design competitions intended to produce a building. Ideally, the best design competition has established a clear set of guidelines so that the desired outcome–the winning team with the best designs–will have their project carefully handheld so that the project will be able to be built.

As for managing the inadequacies of media and publishing, ideas online and those in print, there remain considerable obstacles. The purpose of media interested in design competitions is to learn how to translate the key purpose and goals of any design competition, so that either the general public or a professional audience remain engaged and committed to the value of any given design competition, far beyond the announcement of the winner.

Many competitions fail to relate such risks effectively, while others completely lack the necessary critical debate to attract sufficiently high-quality submissions. In such situations, it is only logical that the winning competition entry's design will remain vague or unable to address the real and valuable issues associated with the purpose of the competition. There is a future for design competitions, and we need the full support of sponsors, public officials and the media to make it perfectly clear that the design competition is ultimately a small but essential component of building better communities.

## Notes

1. "Antoine Predock and the Aftermath of the Canadian Museum for Human Rights Competition," *Canadian Architect*, June 2005, 15.
Brent Bellamy, «Inspiration Comes with a Cost,» *Winnipeg Free Press*, January 2, 2012, http://www.winnipegfreepress.com/opinion/columnists/inspiration-comes-with-a-cost-136526313.html
2. "Park Pavilion Design Competition," City of Edmonton, 2012.
3. "Randall Stout Wins Edmonton Art Gallery Design Competition," *Canadian Architect*, Novermber 2005, 13.
4. Shafraaz Kaba, "The Edmonton Art Gallery Competition," *Canadian Architect*, December 2005, 14-15.
5. Id., 15.
6. Ibid., 15.
7. Ibid., 15.
8. Ibid., 16.
9. Ibid., 16.
10. The other three other jury members were: Steve McFarlane (Vancouver), Janet Rosenberg (Toronto), and Pierre Thibault (Quebec City). For each of the five projects, a separate individual was appointed to the jury as the fifth member and these included three City of Edmonton landscape architects: Jim Black (for the Mill Woods Sports Park and the John Fry Sports Park); Martina Gardiner (for Borden Park and Castle Downs Park) and Gilbert Catabay (for Victoria Park)
11. For more information on the Architecture Canada | RAIC guidelines for competitions, please visit http://www.raic.org/architecture_architects/architectural_competitions/index_e.htm
12. The winners were as follows: gh3 won first place for Borden Park and the Castle Downs District Park. Marc Boutin Architectural Collaborative Inc. won the competition for the John Fry Sports Park. Dub Architects Ltd. won the Mill Woods Sports Park and Rayleen Hill Architecture + Design won the Victoria Park competition.
13. A sub-committee jury for this phase of the competition was comprised of Gail Asper, David Covo, Gustavo Da Roza, Robert Fulford, Moe Levy and Raymond Moriyama.
14. The jury included landscape architect Jane Durante and the following five architects: Max Bond, David Covo, Gustavo da Roza, Roisin Heneghan and Raymond Moriyama. The six "word" people included Gail Asper, Michael Bliss, Robert Fulford, Moe Levy and Victor Rabinovitch
15. "Antoine Predock and the Aftermath of the Canadian Museum for Human Rights Competition," *Canadian Architect* June 2005, 15.
16. "Id.
17. "Ibid.
18. "Ibid.
19. Sean Ruthen, "Visions for Surrey: Townshift: Connected," Surrey: City of Surrey, Build Surrey Program, 2010, 5-12.
20. Kent Spencer, "Let's Add Sparkle to Centres: Mayor," *The Province*, November 3, 2009, http://www2.canada.com/theprovince/news/story.html?id=a7650556-58fe-4442-a3e1-1c6c1b28bb94
21. The Cancellation of one of Canada's most important design competitions was a blow to the architectural profession in thins country, but the proposals by the five shortlisted teams represent significant progress on issues of sustainability, heritage, and Canadian architectural identity. Elsa Lam, "Don't Bank on Bank," *Canadian Architect*, November 2005, 20-24.
22. Elsa Lam, "Don't Bank on Bank," *Canadian Architect*, November 2005, 20.
23. Id., 21-22.

## References

"Antoine Predock and the aftermath of the Canadian Museum for Human Rights competition." *Canadian Architect* 50, no. 6 (2005): 15. Accessed May 10, 2012. http://www.canadianarchitect.com/news/antoine-predock-and-the-aftermath-of-the-canadian-museum-for-human-rights-competition/1000196130/.

*A Proposal to establish the Canadian Museum for Human Rights.* Winnipeg: The Asper Foundation Inc., Winnipeg, 2001.

"Randall Stout wins Edmonton Art Gallery design competition." *Canadian Architect* 50, no. 11 (2005): 12.

**Brodbeck**, Tom. "If you build it, they won't come." *Winnipeg Sun*, January 31, 2012. Accessed July 17, 2014, http://www.winnipegsun.com/2012/01/31/brodbeck-if-you-build-it-they-wont-come

**Bellamy**, Brent. "Inspiration comes with a cost." *Winnipeg Free Press*. January 2, 2012. Accessed May 10, 2010. http://www.winnipegfreepress.com/opinion/columnists/inspiration-comes-with-a-cost-136526313.html

**Canadian Museum of Human Rights**. *Summary of Corporate Plan and Operating and Capital Budgets for 2011-2012 to 2015-2016.* Winnipeg: Canadian Museum of Human Rights, 2012.

**CBC News**. (April 14, 2010). Edmonton unveils winning park pavilion designs. Retrieved on May 10, 2012, http://www.cbc.ca/news/canada/edmonton/story/2011/04/15/edmonton-park-pavilions-designs.html

**"Park Pavilion Design Competition**." City of Edmonton, 2012. Accessed May 10, 2012, http://www.edmonton.ca/attractions_recreation/parks_river-valley/park-pavilion-design-competition.aspx

*Build Surrey Program. Investing in our City's Future.* City of Surrey, 2011.

**Kaba**, Shafraaz. "The Edmonton Art Gallery Competition." *Canadian Architect*. 50, No. 12 (2005): 15-16.

**Kaba**, Shafraaz. "Art for Art's Sake." *Canadian Architect*. 56, no. 1 (2011): 24-28.

**Lam**, Elsa. "Don't Bank on Bank." *Canadian Architect*. 50, no. 11 (2005): 20-24.

**Lett**, Dan. "A portrait of the artist." *Winnipeg Free Press*. September 4, 2010. Accessed July 17, 2014 http://www.winnipegfreepress.com/local/a-portrait-of-the-artist-102209924.html

**Public Works and Government Services Canada**. (2008) *Long-Term Vision and Plan for the Parliamentary Precinct*, Ottawa, 2008 Accessed May 10, 2012 http://www.tpsgc-pwgsc.gc.ca/rapports-reports/rpp/2007-2008/section-3b-eng.html

**Ruthen**, Sean, ed.*Visions for Surrey: TownShift: Connected.* Surrey: City of Surrey, 2010.

**Spencer**, Kent. "Let's add sparkle to centres: Mayor." *The Province*, November 3, 2009. Accessed July 17, 2014 http://www2.canada.com/theprovince/news/story.html?id=a7650556-58fe-4442-a3e1-1c6c1b28bb94

**Threndyle**, Steven. "Surrey: where the future lives." *Vancouver Sun*, November 19, 2010. Accessed on July 17, 2014 http://www2.canada.com/vancouversun/news/archives/story html?id=6155c51d-8288-443d-8d73-fc95eecc8f82

# 5.5. NAJA and EUROPAN
## Advantages and Constraints of Two French Trademarks

**Jean-Louis Violeau**, Ph.D. HDR
Professeur, École Nationale Supérieure
d'Architecture (ENSA) , Paris-Malaquais
France

Every new promotion drives back by orders of magnitudes its predecessors in the history of architecture. How do the winners of "marketing formulas" fit into the French competition system ? This paper will discuss the following : First, the origins and the professional trajectories of the winners renewing the Nouveaux Albums des Jeunes Architectes (NAJA, 2002). Second, the winners' paths listed and quoted for the first twenty years of the Europan competition (1988-2008). Third, the detailed analysis of the situation that took place in Nantes from 1995 to 2005, where three winning teams of the Europan competition (Devin-Rannou, Garo-Boixel, DLW) were in turn called to realise their projects under the leadership of George Décréau, first on behalf of Société Anonyme des Marchés de l'Ouest (SAMO), then for Nantes' inhabitants. And finally, I will look back at an innovative procedure, launched by the same client : in this 2003 competition, competitors spent two days reflecting on issues of innovations in housing while "locked away" in basements of homes in Nantes. The winner, François Delhay, then realised his project by constructing a series of fifty-five units named "La sècherie" completed by the end of 2008 by the Boskop cooperative, consisting of François and his daughter, Sophie Delhay. Rather "innovative," quickly publicised and part of a dynamic eco-district located in Nantes (La Bottière-Chénaie), Sophie Delhay obtained… the Albums as early as 2006.

This double-sided coin, played both on a national and local scale, should lead to a better understanding of how issues of decentralization are broken down, and how they have dramatically changed the practice of architecture in France over the last thirty years. François Mitterrand's major projects (1981-83) have coincided with Gaston Defferre's decentralization (1983), and the way it kept alive an "elite" group of architects capable of undertaking public commissions while dissemanating, throughout a competition's entire process, their contribution to the entire country.

**Cover**
Project by Boskop (François Delhay, Sophie Delhay, Franck Ghesquière, David Lecomte, Laurent Zimny) built in la Sècherie, éco-quartier de la Bottière-Chenaie near Nantes, in 2009.
*Photos : Jean-Louis Violeau (2014).*

If we were to choose a series of international competitions that attracted local interest, President Mitterrand's projects in France would be prime candidates. Coupled with a vast decentralization movement, they have influenced even the most modest architectural scenes. How many small town media libraries and town halls have been inspired by these great projects? This phenomenon can be observed over multiple mediations that have led to some surprising results. After this first phase in the mid 1990s just after the housing crisis of 1993, the competition procedure had reached such prominence that France was sometimes appearing as a small paradise of creativity. Technocrat Contenay Florence, who had accompanied the standardization of the competition procedure since its inception at the Department of Architecture on the eve of the events of May of '68, noted in a report (1995) that, "the French public order, by its prestige and quality, has polarized, perhaps to excess, architecture into certain niche markets, such as public facilities or new construction of social housing, and monopolized the research effort on new markets and competition practices that are too nationally exclusive."[1] Is this statement an excess of satisfaction or act of contrition? Certainly, it was also encouraging "the greatest" French architects to come out of their cocoons so they can tune in with the globalization that we were announced at a great expense.

The situation was of course much more complex, as demonstrated by the rest of the report. These great projects themselves have never evoked a uniform and monolithic symbolism. There were several periods as well as several submission types, and there were also multiple types of competitions, some open to public submission, and others upon invitation only. There were also many ways to elaborate an architectural program, and to engage an architectural reflection. We can see how both features of Jack Lang's cultural vitalism and youth are reversed in the program for the Parc de la Villette[2] competition, written by François Barré, when he was appointed to the head of the public construction establishment in May 1981. A very interesting text offering general guidelines was inserted in the preamble to more technical documents, forming one of the richest programmatic documents of the past twenty years, at least for the intention and the general philosophy that it emanated.

The first phase of the international open competition was held in June 1982 with great success, heralding the emergence of landscape architecture in French architectural culture, in opposition with the consultation held in 1976 organized by Giscard, who had specifically revealed a project by Leon Krier. To demonstrate this vitalism and youth, we need only consult François Barré's introductory text, which speaks of a "new spirit" (p.2): "The aim is to create a park design adapted to the reality of today, as well as that of tomorrow; the ambition is to successfully create a park worthy of the twenty-first century," in contrast with traditional Parisian parks, "somewhat disconnected from the new forms of urban life." The park should therefore be "active, popular with many adults and teenagers (…) and not only meeting the needs of children and the elderly."

This view on life is fundamentally hedonistic and individualistic, and seeks "democratic" values and consumerist freedom that was observed throughout the 1980s. In addition, the document reflects a strong philosophical bias that separates a certain view on life from spatial practices, rather than connecting function and space. Unlike the program for "la Cité de la Musique" nearby, its general intentions were rather poor but strictly regulated and highly spatialized. Two hundred and fifty pages of this document dealt with specifying the size of the cello cases in the dressing rooms, while data concerning the park were very informative, but not actually geographically located.[3]

Symbolically, this phase of the major projects was destroyed by the rise of transparency in France. The age of Mitterrand's projects has retained some of its secrets despite the passage of time. Why then has transparency, a physical property, been assimilated as a moral imperative and why has this property revealed a formal translation in architects during the 1980s? We can recall, for example, a number of discussions concerning Dominique Perrault's National Library and its transparency, which were the subject of endless critiques devoid of arguments, aimed towards such an anti-urban project. Intellectual war will rarely find its participants more helpless. Among architects, the concept is certainly inseparable from competitive design, and the assessment of the competition as a means of awarding public projects. Transparency does not suffer the indeterminate: it is inevitable to choose a site.

"The Mitterrand Generation" (coupled with the "moral generation") — is it not true that only seniors could come up with such a nickname to label the younger generation? At the same time, but not by the same measure, the French government developed a series of relays promoting the renewal of generations of architects and ways to allow the younger generation access to contracts. In doing so it introduced a parallel series of new benchmarks, following the decision in 1969 to eliminate the benefits associated with obtaining the Prix de Rome.[4] In fact, it is not because the Prix de Rome and its benefits had disappeared, as the state instead had not felt the need to confirm and certify the "quality" of architects that it was educating and putting to work with public funds. The real "title" is therefore not the diploma, but the validation and legitimization methods that the state, and local authorities, since 1983, had put in place for forty years. The New Architecture Program [NAP] had been launched in 1972 when the former academic benchmarks had collapsed **[Fig.1]**.

## ▬ Are Prizes a Governmental "Technique"?

To inventory and create a hierarchy of various prizes, awards, and distinctions that regulate a part of the life of architects led to questions about ways to govern. A discovery? A feat accomplished? A medal. A building? A medal. Freedom — Equality –Emulation (and Decoration): could it be the new motto of our Republic? In any case it brings us back to a state born in the eighteenth century by enlightened philosophers and rationalized by nineteenth-century administration, and confirmed in the twentieth century by management, recognised as an academic discipline. Utilitarian Jeremy Bentham, author of the Panopticon, a memoir establishing a new principle to build institutions, and namely prisons (1780), was also the author of a theory of rewards (1802).

The United States is accustomed to lists and rewards: its tolerance to inequality is high and the valorisation of success stories is rooted in deep-seated meritocratic individualism. This is certainly one of the foundations of high-profile "celebrity culture" and research devoted to it in the Anglo-Saxon part of the world. Nathalie Heinich drew an overview to better understand their relative invisibility in France, which would dismantle a "very slow normalisation" in the scientific world.[5] This is obvious also since Anglo-Saxon publications are constantly dealing with this issue while we remain relatively silent. Although it could be said that all actors care about prizes, especially in a world governed by a dominant edge in competitions and the competitive standing. In France at least, we are still very far away from these Anglo-Saxon books or special issues of journals devoted in recent years to this question of Fame, or "How to Become a Famous Architect." For us to judge: "Fame

**Fig. 2**
Anonymous. Ironic collage about the Nouveaux Albums des Jeunes
Architectes (NAJA(x)) in the 2002 edition of the epynomous album. The
allusion with Ajax should perhaps be underlined.

and Architecture," special issue of *Architectural Design*
published in November 2001 (Wiley-Academy), *Famous*, by
*Perspecta*, the distinguished Yale Architectural Journal in
its 37th issue published in 2005 (MIT Press), *the Architecture
of Power*, fifth volume published at the end of the winter of
2006 (AMO / C-LAB / Archis), or even *the Architect's Guide
to Fame* led by Paul Daviesand Torsten Schmiedeknecht
and published in 2005 by Oxford's Architectural Press. [6]

But when merit is involved, we must inevitably resort
to evaluation, and faithful to its "Republican" model, France
has maintained the tradition of a mixed model where the
weight of public institutions and public bodies rule in their
own way when evaluation is involved. That said, this governmental technique still relies on emulation : to be the first. [7]
Emulation rather than force as a technique of power : In a
world where contenders are supernumerary, a universe
governed by competitions and the tournament of reputations, the competition is, after all, an insurance like any
other, reducing some of the risks of trading art. It is a way
to distribute individuals on a social scale, assigning each a
rank and function, and encouraging them to fight for these
places. In pursuit of efficiency, it is also by seeking recognition–the magic triangle (reward-motivation-performance),

is at the heart of liberal philosophy, as it forms the basis of
good practice and republican institutions. Hence the ground
of collusion, often criticized, which can be found between
public ministries and private media groups. For example,
*Le Moniteur* journal and its prizes, the Equerre d'argent and
the Goncourt prize for architecture **[Fig.2]**.

### ▬ Nouveaux Albums des Jeunes Architectes

What would be the ideological reasoning prior to the establishment of "promotional formulas" in the world of
architecture ? To simply give younger talent an opportunity
to shine ? It would be too simple. There is talent and work
involved, but also "luck," the notion of first chance. In-depth
analysis of the trajectories and sociological characteristics
presented by 451 architects (of the 3.000 under the age
of 35) candidates for the "Nouveaux Albums des Jeunes
Architectes" (NAJA), a distinctive and promotional formula
relaunched in 2002 by the Department of Architecture at the
Ministry of Culture, has allowed us to test many of these
assumptions about youth, generations, talent and prizes... [8]

These NAJA offered to a younger group, a relative comparative competition model. We could locate in this model: substantial individual differences, the importance of past achievements (although they are often embryonic), and the existence of an effective system, upon submission of a normalised profile. Essentially, the "measurable" and "immeasurable" could be found within. However, and this is perhaps due to its "Republican" specificity: NAJA combined both a principle of classification and at the same time amplified the differences between submissions.

Given the diversity of the group, these 451 candidates allowed us to use their creations as "data," finally revealing the situation of all those who are next to or behind the "inspired" and the "elected"–often one and the same. They offered us not necessarily a "representative" sample, but a high-contrast one or a *geological* section (rather an exceptional one incidentally) revealing almost all segments of the world of architects, which we know as highly composite, sometimes wrong to even consider it a "profession." [9] Both structural and fragile, these labels associated with age are only as good as the support and credit that large institutions provide them. Every new promotion pushes back its predecessor by another notch in the history of architecture (or sometimes even makes it disappear).

The albums are in fact an institutional rite where one utters: you're a "young" architect (but you're also "only a young architect") and you just have to be what you are, that is to say a (good) "young" architect. Since Norbert Elias and especially since the work of Pierre Bourdieu, we know that this game is a question of incorporation (of constraints and rules), and a player is all the more relevant and effective when he forgets he is playing (and it therefore calculates his moves). The problem is therefore to know what is implied when using the adjective "young"–hence our willingness to extend such questioning to "young" architects who, at the time, did not claim their status as "young architects" since they were employees within an agency. [10] As in most artistic and cultural careers, an architect who is less successful in the first phase of his or her career and who is especially slow to seek recognition of his or her work is exposed to a mechanism of cumulative disadvantage. And we already perceived, within early careers, young architects working for the best of the best create vast possible worlds within which they later seek to narrow their field of work over time.

These "Nouveaux Albums des Jeunes Architectes" by the extreme diversity of the 289 submitted applications, illustrate the socially constructed character of youth, between the construction of collective identities, scientifically developing categories and tracking that operates in ordinary life. [11] It was indeed a flanking glance in the sense that these grandchildren of '68 (almost 70 % of them were born between 1967 and 1971), though they have characteristics related to their age and their social trajectories, reproduce some of the less salient features that characterize the traditional "profession." Firstly, as soon as one focuses on the cultural and artistic world, this division between Paris and the provinces is striking–even if this new session trimmed a little excess from the previous few. Then, the persistence of what was called, until the early 1970s, "the place" (for almost 70 % of candidates), consisted of learning the art in an agency and explaining the trajectories. If strategies and figures were already emerging, as with certain types of trajectories, they were indeed much related to the original school or choice of teachers supervising the completion of their studies, than the first wages–all of which are also often more or less related. Finally, it was noted that even relative marginalization of women were still under-represented (123 women compared to 330 male candidates) in relation to feminization of the student body for over twenty years. This is apparent even if the distribution of women within teams, and the high value of mixed gender teams also gave rise to new divisions and new hierarchies. It was also striking that the great traditional divisions, if they were reproduced each time were also each time (slightly) redefined by the fraction of age.

Another striking element, similar to the proportion of women in architecture, is that the proportion of team applications fell in relation to the applicant's grades. Individual applications were predominant even for the last category, with the lowest evaluation, where in about 108 cases there are only 23 teams, which tells us about the conditions under which these young architects, sometimes very lonely, began their exercise. In contrast, some groups, similar to the original "collective" forming less transition between school and professional practice itself, are creating very noticeable submissions. In his thesis, under the direction of anthropologist Alban Bensa, the architect Miguel Mazeri elaborates the idea of recognition, [12] quoting the X'TU duo, accustomed to these promotional competitions in their early days in the 1990s, [13] and who choose the comparison with a "rock band" to characterize these moving and passionate gatherings presiding often over the best careers: "We do things and then we see"!

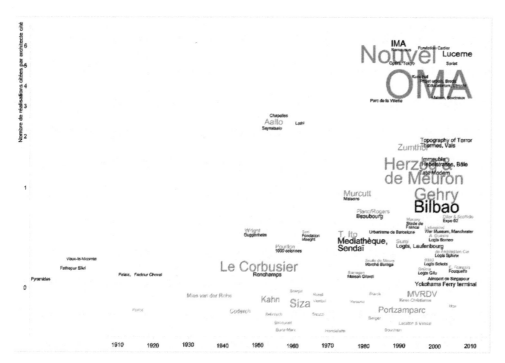

**Fig. 3**
Chronological ordering of architects and projects as designated by Europan laureates as major "references" after being asked : What are your references ? Do you follow any architect in particular ? What is the most important building of the recent years ? In grey, architects, in black, buildings. Abscisse : temps / ordonnée : nombre de réalisations citées par architecte cité.
Diagram published in Pommier Juliette and Violeau Jean-Louis, *Notre histoire à 20 ans*, Archibooks, Paris, 2007.

In this case, with the study on the population of the candidates to the achievement of these new Albums, it was not a matter in the least to denounce, but simply to attempt to unveil certain implicit rules that anyone who is interested (incorporated within this world or "serious" candidates to the incorporation) knows, but never formulates explicitly. Even while trying to unveil the mechanisms of selection of NAJA candidates, we hardly had the impression to have liberated a number of young architects ! On the contrary, if one trusts the stable amount of interested candidates ten years after the revival of the formula... Clearly, there is no recipe for when we deliver–or try to deliver– and it is shared by all — or too many people–it is worthless. A glorious elder, Viollet-le-Duc, had told anyone who would listen that there is a perfectly conceived "uniform system, a rigid education system, calculated to elevate young people at an equal level in institutions like polytechnics or Saint-Cyr," before they "provide an annual quota of professionals for the country," while a number of artists ultimately mattered little : "in painting or sculpture, as in poetry or in music, there is but one level : General or nothing !" **[Fig.3] [Fig.4]**. [14]

## ▬ Europan

A researcher needs to work on topics that are working him. Generational fractures and incorporation in the artistic and cultural worlds have been concerning us for several years. In the same branch of questioning, our attention is indeed very quickly reaching the Europan competition, successor of the PAN [Programme Architecture Nouvelle] on the trajectories of its recipients, its organization and its expectations... First of all, we are analyzing the proposals submitted during the sixth session, [15] and also looking back more generally on two decades of competitions. At the dawn of the ninth session, and twenty years after its

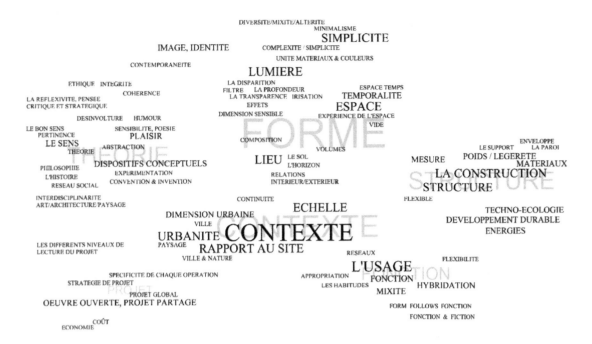

**Fig. 4**

Graphic interpretation of the architectural concepts or principles as mentionned by the laureates and winners of Europan following the question : What are the notions that you generally refer to when explaining your projects ? In black the notions as quoted, in grey the analogous terms on a semantic level. The frequency of quotation of a same notion is mesured by its distance between two concepts. : fréquence d'apparition d'un terme ou d'une catégorie (somme des termes qui la constituent). Six categories have been identified to regroup most quoted notions. Diagram published in Pommier Juliette and Violeau Jean-Louis, Notre histoire à 20 ans, Archibooks, Paris, 2007.

launch (1987, the first session is evaluated in 1989), heads of the Europan competition wanted results. Twenty years of organizing and reflection, collection and recovery of urban and architectural innovations, collaboration between masters and project management, from developing the theme of the competition and research sites, up to performance monitoring. In addition to its openness to all architects under forty years of age and to its "European" character, the competition distinguishes itself by its willingness to allow its recipients to carry out their projects first as an urban study conducted under the guidance of the municipality that has provided a site for the competition, then possibly in the form of a contract, often a housing contract.

The results sought by officials of Europan-France has thus turned into a kind of self-examination : almost a chore, at least one questionnaire stretching over ten pages, sent to 150 winners, listed and quoted for the first seven sessions. Fifty responded in total, one-third

of which received the questionnaire ; this was considered quite satisfactory. In 2006, the ten winners and honourable mentions of the eighth session in France were added and twelve teams comprising at least one French architect, winners, mentioned or quoted elsewhere in Europe. Ten of them responded, which was quite satisfactory again. The questionnaire was organized into five chapters :

- Training and emulation competitions : the foundations of an architectural career ;
- Today's professional practice ;
- Intellectual activities (teaching, research, publications…) ;
- Historical and cultural references, in architecture but also more generally references referring to an entire generation ;
- European sentiment, through the Europan competition, but also in terms of European construction and its recent milestones (from 1989 to 2005).

**Fig. 5 to 7**
Project by Nicole GARO et Marc BOIXEL architects winners of
Europan 2 (1991). Theme: *"Habiter la ville aujourd'hui. Requalification
des sites urbains* ZAC du Moulin du Tillay / Saint-Herblain (NANTES
Nord)". Built in 1995 under the leadership of Georges Décréau
(Société Anonyme des Marches de l'Ouest / SCIC).
*Photos: Jean-Louis Violeau.*

Beyond the influence of a competition on an individual's trajectory, an investigation with Juliette Pommier, architect, has endeavoured to trace the outlines of a generation. She was published in 2006 under the title: *Notre histoire, Europan à 20 ans. Sociologie des architectes lauréats du concours Europan* by Archibooks editions. Exceeding the basic question, that of the results of the competition, we wanted to examine the social and cultural environment in which the recipients were changing, some for nearly over two decades. This variable geometrical circle drawn around the winners of Europan is not defined by its degree of orthodoxy, for example, to a formal school or an urban theory. Indeed it was observed again with the results of this long questionnaire that the expression of generational reports demonstrated a strong ambivalence: it may well occur at both a rupture and continuity, all depending on the issues discussed. One can also declare in favour of affiliation (and its recognition) and the idea of transmission, while also displaying a willingness to break away or at least to restate.

In general, this intermediate generation has been called upon to manage the contradictions of this double heritage: "sixty-eighter" and "eighty-one-er"–revolutionary and reformist. An urban "à-la-French" project crossed by as many interruptions as continuations. Continuities can be found with the contribution of the humanities as a sort of reunion with a first look upon urban planning from the early twentieth century around the founding fathers Henard, Jaussely, Agache, Prost, Poëte, and Bardet. In addition, we can identify sources of renewal and rupture, since the city has gradually emerged as a subject far too complex for it to be reduced to standards used to design space.

These contradictions between revolution and reform, right to the city / rights of the city, etc., relate broadly with the "mystery" of the 1980s. How has the urban landscape, for example, an important element of the seventies, been deeply redefined so suddenly since the eighties, forcing its way into management? This intermediary generation (the "68-ers" and "81-ers") could be said to be supporting the institution while not being afraid to go against it, and their lives directed by this polarity: on one hand a rationalism, and on the other a utopianism which fights for change, and still believes that art and architecture have the power to affect vested interests **[Fig.5] [Fig.6] [Fig.7]**.

## A Local Scene (Nantes) and a Contracting Authority

How have multi-year winners managed to create a path through the mess of contract attainment? In Nantes, the work of a contracting authority, George Décréau, as director of the SAMO[16] and of "la Nantaise d'Habitations," which provided work for three Europan winners, provides a good overview of professional careers. The three contracts seemed to emanate a dominant theme currently concerned about social housing, density, and a common goal: to allow the masses access to the qualities traditionally associated with the individual house and the intimacy associated with the use of exterior extensions.

In St. Herblain, Nicole and Mark Garo Boixel, winners of the second Europan session in 1992, delivered in 1995 on behalf of the SAMO four "city-block villas," each composed of a fifteen-unit building, a house and garden.[17] In line with the boulevard, the foundations of the buildings are extended by walls that surround the city block and define a shared garden in a "ZAC[18] du Moulin du Tillay" nearing completion. Contributing to the "Rezé" site, a former market garden at the foot of the "Cité radieuse" and the immediate vicinity of the sensitive "Château de Rezé," the two young architects were, from the very beginning, faced with the same problems in St.Herblain when they started construction two years later. In Tillay, as in Rezé, nature and the countryside are nearby and neighbourly with parts of the city, like an urban countryside. Quiet, touted for its proximity to the shops of Tillay, but primarily supermarkets Carrefour (Dervallières) and Leclerc (Atlantis) nearby, the surrounding area is undoubtedly an element of value. We can also find a certain architectural questioning, having preoccupied architects for a long time, at least since Le Corbusier and his "immeuble-villas." Not unlike Le Corbusier, in demiurge, seeing his project addressing this harmonious relation between individual life and collective life, this new building is in many ways an alternative to the production of "ordinary" family housing.

On boulevard d'Alby in Nantes, offering once again for the SAMO a diverse mix of housing supply and collective houses, Isabelle Devin and Catherine Ranou (with Quadra Architects) wanted to break the uniformity of bland social housing.[19] Pursuing the idea to exacerbate one by one each of the functions of living (sleeping, eating ...) which had made them the winners of the Europan 1 (1989, Habiter la ville), they proposed a double typology at an apartment building where each house is "individualized," distinguished by a set of additions and extensions of volumes in a cubic facade of terraced houses facing gardens. The additions, four square meters each, are randomized and extend living rooms, bedrooms or even bathrooms. Located in the end of the plot, the six-storey houses are located along a vast public park. They provide a transition to the thirty-four units aligned along the boulevard: five-storey buildings aligned along the circulation axis and two-storey houses, and between the two, a courtyard offering a view of the sky. This connects the façade and neighbouring rooftops and reminds one of the visual sequences that characterize Nantes' suburbs, near the train station. In the district, small workshops and warehouses can still be found, connected by small streets or alleyways connected to the boulevard d'Alby, dotted with small shops, markets and two-storey homes. The colourful facades (bright blue plaster and wood formed concrete with wood stain color, having been redone by the SCIC[20]) fit in well with the profile of the boulevard. Finally, elevating the houses by one meter ensures a separation from the boulevard where traffic is still quite heavy **[Fig.8 to 11]**.

Finally, DLW[21] has delivered in 2001, this time on behalf of La Nantaise d'Habitations, a set of forty-seven units, spread over two wings along the streets of Rieux and Fouré with the addition of a plot to catch the alignment of the Rieux street. The building is wide open, situated on a triangular plot, and hosts, on the windowed ground floor, a nursery comprised of sixty cradles and its adjacent service areas. Initially winners in 1995, on the site of Athis-Mons during Europan 4 (Construire la ville sur la ville), the young architects had to revise much of their designs. They managed to maintain some of their main ideas, but have also admitted to having stretched some. Athis-Mons was primarily an urban project along the N7, consisting of disconnection and design on a large scale, inspired by the strip in Las Vegas. Nantes is however on another scale: the urban landscape is already completed and the project is confined to the scale of the building, even if it must also fit into the suburb where Nantes city hall launched a "ZAC" since the dawn of the 1990s by placing it under the direction of town planner Jean-François Revert. The congress center is the "Lieu Unique" on the site of the old LU factories: large equipment has progressively structured this district that stretches from Canal St. Felix in the east to the base of the Madeleine in the west, the transformation "of an old suburb in new central district."[22] Architects have drawn from this the idea for an open city block, traversed by semi-public circulation, extending existing alleys. The inverted duplexes open their living rooms at the last level. The accommodations feature

**Fig. 8 to 11**
Project by Isabelle DEVIN and Catherine RANNOU architects winners of Europan
1 (1989). Session with no designated sites under the theme *"Evolution des modes
de vie et architectures du logement"*. Project built in 1994 in Nantes under the
leadership of Georges Décréau (Société Anonyme des Marches de l'Ouest / SCIC).
*Photos : Jean-Louis Violeau.*

a living area spanning the entire length of the building. The access to apartments is organised by small alleyways and the volumetric organisation of the nursery show once again the "experimental" character of the proposal: an attempt to subltly change domestic life **[Fig.12] [Fig.13] [Fig.14]**.

These three projects also show in their own way the difficulty of realising either a strictly theoretical reflection (for winners of Europan 1) or on other sites for the other two teams. Therein lies the ambiguity of the ideas competition in general and in particular that of Europan.[23] Central to these three trajectories, we find the contracting authority both paternalistic and demanding with these young teams, in what might be considered a training mission. During the long conversation we had together, he mentioned: assimilate the "young architect" to risk himself acting as an obstretitian:

*The young architect must be able to do. It's like the young artist. But he must also work with "real" contract authorities. I have lived this with every Europan laureate. When they arrive, they have concepts, a ton of ideas in mind. I respect architecture, but it must be sellable or at least leasable. The architect is not there to put himself in my shoes, or in the shoes of inhabitants. However, he can contribute to society's adaptation. From that point of view, there is no reason why one should not work with young architects. A big mistake would be to be too brutal from the start. It is a compromise. I'm always amazed; architects are not trained and have very little experience regarding these discussions. But Europan is, for me, a symbol of quality. I do not have to wonder if they are any good. There is a viable filter. When I have room for manoeuvre on an operation, I am inclined to hire people who were winners of a competition rather than organize one. But in a firm like mine, you also have protectionists, people who tilt towards management, who look only towards sustainability. Therefore, we need to help them accept other points of view. If you persist, you end up with both purpose and durability, all the while having derogated. And everyone wins, young architects as much as us.*

Thereafter, the DLW trio made a remarkable breakthrough in the 2000s, winning competitions regularly, often for social housing operations but also for a police station and small projects, such as for the school board, nurseries or technical centers. Their work now extends throughout Brittany, and their agency is part of structures that "count" on Nantes. It has received the prize for architecture in 2006 from Great-Britain for housing on "port du Légué Plerin-Saint Brieuc." Francois Dussaux teaches at the School of Architecture of Nantes, the ENSAN. For their part, Isabelle Devin and Catherine Rannou are not building anything any longer; Catherine now teaches at the architecture school of Rennes, ENSAB. Finally, the couple formed by Nicole Garo and Mark Boixel maintains a continuous stream of activities and designs small habitat projects (mostly social) in the Nantes region. Mark also teaches at ENSAN.

George Décréau loves architecture. He told us so and we have seen him regularly at events organized by the Regional House of architecture–of which he is a member of the board of trustees. Décréau likes architecture and the risk it represents–he has proven this by launching an innovative competition in spring 2003 on a site bordering a social housing neighbourhood in Nantes, the Breil-Malville. He had invited twenty candidates to reflect on "experimental and innovative projects of dense and individualized housing." The competition, accessible only through invitation, privileged reiteration: before choosing its invitees, the sponsor first looked at the architect for what he has done rather than what he would be able to do. Basically, Décréau went against the tide by offering this "en loges" competition, renewing its bond quite consciously with the Prix de Rome. Supported by the City Council, the Urban Community and the CROA,[24] he "locked up" the candidates in his basement to force them to "walk the plank" **[Fig.15 to 20]**.

These candidates were chosen not by reference (only a College registration was required) but on a letter of intent surrounding the idea of innovation and experimentation in housing. Not working only 8 hours or 24 hours (and not as far as the 72 to 110 days imposed to Prix de Rome finalists) but the intermediate compromise of 12 hours. An anonymous evaluation took place on the next day. Advertisements were officially released in *Le Moniteur* of March 21, 2003. Forty-eight architects responded, thus overcoming the reluctance of some, confused by this "open" (a little too much!), unusual procedure. The letter of intent actually counted and some experienced candidates were not successfully received, having only presented their credentials without taking a few hours of their time to write a two-page ad hoc text.

**Fig. 12 to 14**
Project by DLW architectes (François Dussaux, Aurélien Lepoutre, Vincent Wattier) former winners of Europan 4 (1995) on the site of Athis-Mons, south of Paris. Theme, "Construire la ville sur la ville". Project built in Nantes in 2001 under the leadership of Georges Décréau (Société Anonyme des Marches de l'Ouest / SCIC).
*Photos: Jean-Louis Violeau.*

**Fig. 15 to 20**
Project by Boskop ((François Delhay, Sophie Delhay, Franck Ghesquière, David Lecomte, Laurent Zimny) built in lla Sècherie, éco-quartier de la Bottière-Chenaie near Nantes, in 2009.
*Photos: Jean-Louis Violeau (2014).*

None of the twenty pre-selected teams had previously worked with the "Nantaise d'habitations," even though they worked on around fifteen operations per year.[25] Within each team, only one member was invited, always punctual, arriving at 8:00 a.m. The participants had at their disposal: paper, an A3 photocopier and booklet containing info for the site with images, maps and topographical plans at a scale of 1:500. They were provided food and board, in addition to 800 euros. Fearing being given nothing at all, some participants–but very few finally (about four or five)–still brought their personal laptop and printer for their submission. Only two of them had nothing submitted by the end of the day. Architects who had accepted these conditions were quite young, and again, among them many regular "promotional frames" Albums and Europan, and some were even older, who could recall the "renaudisme" and "l'habitat intermédiaire" throughout the 1970s in their letter of intent.

The competition invited architects to reflect on innovative and experimental dense residential zoning and individualized housing in France, however, many communities were beginning to develop their PLH (Programme Local de l'Habitat) imposed by the law SRU (Solidarité et Renouvellement Urbain) launched in December 2000. Competitors were all focused on qualities of housing: separated entranceways, intimacy, terraces, diversified corridors and semi-private spaces, and especially large homes. As we already explained, Décréau George had just made the trip to Holland, a ritual at the time, the "docks Bornéo et Java d'Amsterdam": "Individual housing in town, we must show that it could also exist in Nantes."[26] In his mind everything was related: from renewing typologies, distributions, but also competitions' procedures, and thus seeking to grasp momentum, in the early 1970s, when an urgency of change was present, by REX (Réalisations Expérimentales), the MI (Modèles Innovation) and PAN.

After a second round held the following fall, François Delhay's proposal, an architect from Lille, topped all three committees (architect, contracting authority, local officials and external members). Turning his reflection onto modularity and scalability, he had worked on articulation and assembly around a central courtyard. Displaying a willingness to confront managing surface area and quantifying space,[27] he had proposed an ingenious system of differentiated access and "extra rooms." The latter is unaffected, accessible by a passageway connected to several adjacent homes, suggesting adaptable housing for the lifespan of a family.

In a France affected by a very complex phenomena of transmission (especially in cultural worlds), the mature and experienced architect (graduating in 1972[28]), has forwarded his winning project to his daughter, Sophie Delhay, born in 1974 and having graduated in 1999. Beginning in 2004, she took the opportunity to build his agency with him: Boskop, a cooperative structure with a viaticum of this first competition. The following year, what happened? With such a fine project, she was declared winner of the "Albums des Jeunes Architectes" in 2006 (NAJA). And in 2011 she was appointed professor at the School of Architecture of Nantes. In the aftermath she built the project on a site other than the one suggested in the competition, but still within the city of Nantes–the Bottière-Chénaie–a sustainable neighbourhood. Considered a very tasteful project in a France preoccupied by "sustainable development," the eco-district became the new password to continue developing "new neighbourhoods." Fifty-five low income homes were developed on "rue de la Sècherie," for an "innovative and experimental operation of dense urban individual homes." The project was given major media coverage. The young agency was therefore on the way to new adventures–father and daughter working together–their steps guided them to the neighbouring community of Rennes. They were invited by the "atelier des nouvelles formes urbaines" led by Jean-Yves Chapuis, an urban planner and politician constantly looking for innovative housing projects. They continued in 2007 on their reflection of housing density coupled this time with "social cohesion," another key word of the "SRU years" in France. The project consists of cleverly arranged round plots, surrounded by a subdivision of 150 homes coordinated by Nexity, a developer largely concerned in the 2000s with the principles of "quality," defended by public projects.

This (short) story (from Nantes and Rennes) tries to tell how the rules in France are held up on two feet: liberalization (and thus a competition between designers) and a decentralization of submissions; therefore, architects followed the general slope that was taken by French society at the same time. Although competition is never quite a hindrance to the process of repetition and circular flow of reputations...[29] Behind all this, the state was deeply transformed, and this "fetish" hasn't held out on architecture (and other cultural worlds) as a monopoly to establish symbolic hierarchies.[30]

# ━━ Notes

[1] Florence Contenay (dir.), *Rapport du groupe de travail architecture et exportation*, Direction de l'architecture et de l'urbanisme, Ministère de l'aménagement du territoire, de l'équipement et des transports, mai 1995, (145 p.) p. 14. *http://www.ladocumentationfrancaise.fr/rapports-publics/954149900/index.shtml*

[2] Archives de l'Etablissement Public de La Villette.

[3] See: Jacques Allégret, Benoît Chalandard, and Jean-Louis Violeau, "La formulation de la commande publique en architecture," ed. mimeographed report (research funded by the Plan construction et architecture, 1998).

[4] At first through a gradual extinction of the "corps des architectes en chef des Bâtiments Civils et Palais Nationaux" and in the end by the automatic registration of the "prix de Rome" winners on approved lists for major ministries requiring construction contracts (Post, Health, Education … ) which had, before the decentralization, both hands on public building contracts.

[5] Nathalie Heinich, "La culture de la célébrité en France et dans les pays anglophones," *Revue française de sociologie* 52, no. 2 (2011): 368. The author argues for «the issue [of fame] to be taken seriously by a sociological practice that is both empirically supported and theoretically ambitious, going beyond case studies without overflowing into general issues concerning "social aspects" or "postmodernism."

[6] The book revolves around a series of case studies each of which scans a national culture, its recent history, its dynamism, its dominant figure, its networks, its mysteries. After a recent reflection on the fate of "theoretical architecture," it contains insights into Switzerland ("Botta: Fame and Scale"), Italy ("Rossi: Fame and Familiarity"), the Netherlands ("Koolhaas and the Profession at Play"), Germany ("(Un) editedArchitecture; wettbewerbe aktuell"), Spain ("The Fame Game") and the United States ("Ground Zero: 1.776 ft Into Thin Air"). Strangely, France is absent. "Fame and Architecture," *special issue of Architectural Design, Wiley-Academy* November 2001 (2001). Brendan M Lee and Mark Jarzombek, «Perspecta 37» Famous»: The Yale Architectural Journal,» (2006). «The Architecture of Power,» *AMO, C-LAB, Archis* fifth volume published at the end of the winter of 2006 (2006).
Paul Davies, Torsten Schmiedeknecht, and Julie Cook, *An Architect's Guide to Fame*, vol. 1 (Routledge, 2005).

[7] See: Olivier Ihl, *Le Mérite et la République. Essai sur la société des émules* (Paris: Gallimard, 2007).

[8] This work was published in condensed form at the opening of the catalog devoted to NAJA under the title W. DIEBOLT and P. JOFFROY, «Les 'premiers collés' volontaires de l'architecture,» *Les Nouveaux Albums des jeunes architectes — Le Moniteur Architecure hors série — IFA / DAPA*, no. 5128 (2002).

[9] We have extended these methodological questions with the article: Jean-Louis Violeau, "Profession : Architectes de moins de 35 ans " *AMC-Le Moniteur architecture*, no. 127 (2002). And with a conference that brought together the 12 architects nominated for the Prix de la première œuvre 2006 décerné par Le Moniteur : Karine Dana and Jean-François Drevon, «Douze Premières Œuvres En Action,» *AMC-Le Moniteur architecture — annuel 2006 — Les 100 bâtiments de l'année*, no. 166 (2007).

[10] Gricha Bourbouze et al., «Le projet partagé « *AMC-Le Moniteur architecture*, no. 134 (2003).

[11] Given this construction of the "young architect," we can identify with the discussion led by Alain Desrosières on the construction of socio-professional categories. See Alain Desrosières and Laurent Thévenot, *Les catégories socio-professionnelles*, Coll. Repères (Paris: La Découverte, 1988) and Alain Desrosières, *La politique des grands nombres. Histoire de la raison statistique* (Paris: La Découverte, 1993).

[12] Miguel Mazeri, «L'étoffe des héros. Pour une histoire des Albums des Jeunes Architectes (1980-2006). De l'arbitrage de la reconnaissance à l'insertion professionnelle de jeunes architectes» (2012).

[13] Winner of the Europan 1 (1990), of Pan Université (1991) and of the Albums in 1992 — without having built anything at the time, opting for photos of scale models (« Since it is more professional ») to build up their portfolio.

[14] L. Vitet and E. E. Viollet Le Duc, «L'enseignement des arts : Il y a quelque chose à faire (1862),» in *A propos de l'enseignement des arts du dessin : Suivi de l'enseignement des arts, Il y a quelque chose à faire* (Paris: ENSBA — Ecole Nationale des Beaux-Arts, 1984), 122.

[15] A short article, Jean-Louis Violeau, «Europan 6 — Dire le réel « *Urbanisme*, no. 322 (2002). And a much longer version on CD-rom (that many people would not read) will accompany the issue.

[16] Société Anonyme des Marchés de l'Ouest.

[17] These architects from Nantes reproduce a similar typology a few years later, erecting three housing blocks facing the landscaped park in Saint-Nazaire (for municipal office, Silène).

[18] The "Zone d'Aménagement Concerté" of France limits a specific perimeter over which are applied many special design procedures while providing all necessary financial instrumentation prior to any operational planning.

[19] This was already, among the "architectures remarquables" in the early 2000s, as identified in Nantes by a team of architects and scholars on behalf of "Nantes aménagement". See Colette David et al., *Nantes, Architectures Remarquables* 1945/2000* (Nantes: Nantes aménagement, 2000), 46. S'agrégeant, à la nébuleuse de jeunes architectes née de l'exposition Concours perdus (Galerie Philippe Uzzan, Paris, hiver 1995-96), the Devin-Rannou duo will gather in Venice in the fall, during the VI Biennale d'Architecture, for the young French architecture organized by devices in partnership with the DAPA and the AFAA. They also participate in the exhibition "A la recherche de la Maison modèle," organised the following year by "Arc-en-Rêve, la DAPA et l'AFAA".

[20] SCIC, « la Société Centrale Immobilière de la Caisse des Dépôts et Consignations » was originally a subsidiary of the Caisse des Dépôts. It consisted of ESH, as well as SAMO, "Entreprises Sociales pour l'Habitat" building with collection agencies including the 1 % housing. It was located in France, next to the Municipal Offices, the second largest hub of social housing. In 2003, opening to shareholders rather than the Caisse des Dépôts, the SCIC has changed his surname and now denominates "Icade. Since then, the Icade financial institution moved away from housing and gradually moved its operations to private development — always mixed in France.

[21] François Dussaux, Aurelien Lepoutre, VincentWattier. This Nantes operation was the first realization of a team born from Europan (and promotional competitions in general, since these three graduates from ENSAIS (1993) were first gathered around a submission for the CIMBETON competition of 1995). They are a young team that has partnered with SARL in 1998, following their victory in the fourth session and at the start of the project for Nantes that came afterwards. In autumn 2001, when they have applied to "Nouveaux Albums des jeunes architects" (team 102) their cover letters also highlighted the fact that this was in fact a sort of initiation, extended by the cycle of training in urban management organized by the Department of Architecture and, bringing forth a dozen winners of the last sessions of Europan.

[22] Patrick Rimbert, First Deputy Mayor of Nantes and vice president of the Urban Community in charge of major urban projects, *in* Ariella Masboungi, Frédérique de Gravelaine, and Bert McClure, *Nantes: La Loire Dessine Le projet* (Paris: Éd. de la Villette / Communauté urbaine de Nantes / Ministère de l'Equipement, 2003), 65.

[23] This is an ambiguity emphasized by Jean-Pierre Chupin in his contribution Jean-Pierre Chupin, Lino José Gomes, and Jason Goorts, «Le ciel des idées, l'horizon des connaissances,» in *Europan France: Innover Dialoguer, Réaliser: 1988-2007*, ed. Danièle Valabrègue and Anne Vigne (Paris: Jean Michel Place, 2007), 38-51.

[24] Conseil Régional de l'Ordre des Architectes.. In France, the profession is divided up into "CROA"s, each represented nationally at the CNOA, Conseil National.

[25] The pre-selected teams were : Martine Arrivet-Jean-Charles Zebo, Atelier de la Maison rouge, Barclay-Crousse, Beau-Seltzer, Delhay architectes, Nicolas Guillot-Radu Molnar-Pascal Piccinato, Jean-Luc Hanier, IGLOO (Aubry et Goulard), Eric Lapierre, LINE A, Evelyne del Moral, Christophe & Guy Murail, Vincent Perraud, PLAN 01, Khmaphet & Khamseuk Sakda, Frédéric Schlachet, Eric Schneller, TEKHNÊ, TOA architecture, Oscar Valenzuela.

[26] Georges Décréau, interview by Jean-Louis Violeau, May 28, 2003.

[27] To read more about this competition, see two articles in the *AMC* : "Concours à Nantes : Une journée pour l'innovation dans le logement social," *AMC-Le Moniteur architecture*, , no. 136 (2003).
"Concours : Un modèle pour des logements individuels," *AMC-Le Moniteur architecture*, no. 138 (2003).

[28] François Delhay's trajectory is, in its own way, quite typical of that of a generation : in the mid 1970s, he split his time between his project and those of the "Atelier Populaire d'Urbanisme de l'Alma-Gare." Then in the late 1980s, he worked with Jean-Paul Baïetto, the first developer of Euralille, and then worked daily with Rem Koolhaas, for which he was partner from 1989 to 1996. He was also an architectural consultant of "CAUE du Nord" and regularly saw his work exhibited or published.

[29] In France in 2010, 80 % of agencies with an annual turnover of more than 500,000 euros participated in competitions against only 39 % of those with a turnover of less than 50,000 euros. In addition, 70 % of architects associated through an agency reported participating in competitions, and they were only 37 % among sole proprietors. Annually, it is usually half the French agencies who regularly participate in competitions. Source : *http://www.architectes.org/outils-et-documents/la-profession-en-chiffres/observatoire-de-la-profession-2011/* See in particular page 22

[30] This article was written at the same time as Pierre Bourdieu gave his enlightening course at the College of France, 1989 à 1992 *Sur l'État*. The sociologist concludes with a text dedicated to the housing market and one of the concise formulas of which he had the secret : the state is much more Superphénix than Phoenix houses ! Pierre Bourdieu et al., *Sur L'état : Cours Au Collège De France, 1989-1992* (Éd. Raisons d'agir, 2012).

## References

**Allégret**, Jacques, Benoît **Chalandard**, and Jean-Louis **Violeau**. "La formulation de la commande publique en architecture." edited by mimeographed report : research funded by the Plan construction et architecture, 1998.

**AMO, C-Lab**. "The Architecture of Power", *Volume* magazine #5, Winter 2006

**Bourbouze**, Gricha, Denis **Eliet**, David **Fagart**, Cécile **Graindorge**, Julien **Monfort**, and Nicolas **Sallavuard**. "Le projet partagé". Round-table exchanges collected by Karine Dana et Jean-Louis Violeau. *AMC-Le Moniteur architecture*, no. 134 (2003) : 14-20.

**Bourdieu**, Pierre. *Sur l'état : Cours au collège de France, 1989-1992*. Éd. Raisons d'agir, 2012.

**Chupin**, Jean-Pierre, Lino José **Gomes**, and Jason **Goorts**. "Le ciel des idées, l'horizon des connaissances." In *Europan France : Innover Dialoguer, Réaliser : 1988-2007*, edited by Danièle Valabrègue and Anne Vigne, 38-51. Paris : Jean Michel Place, 2007.

**Dana**, Karine, Jean-François **Drevon**, and Jean-Louis **Violeau**. "Douze premières oeuvres en action." *AMC-Le Moniteur architecture — annuel 2006 — Les 100 bâtiments de l'année*, no. 166 (2007) : 59-65.

**David**, Colette, Michel **Bazantay**, Frank **Gerno**, Romain **Rousseau**, Philippe **Ruault**, and Mireille **Durand-Garnier**. *Nantes, architectures remarquables* 1945/2000*. Nantes : Nantes aménagement, 2000.

**Davies**, Paul, Torsten **Schmiedeknecht**, and Julie **Cook**. *An Architect's Guide to Fame*. Vol. 1 : Routledge, 2005.

**Décréau**, Georges. "Interview with Georges Décréau." By Jean-Louis Violeau (May 28, 2003).

**Desrosières**, Alain. *La politique des grands nombres. Histoire de la raison statistique*. Paris : La Découverte, 1993.

**Desrosières**, Alain and Laurent **Thévenot**. *Les catégories socio-professionnelles*. Coll. Repères. Paris : La Découverte, 1988.

"Fame and Architecture." *Special Issue of Architectural Design, Wiley-Academy* November 2001 (2001).

**Heinich**, Nathalie. "La culture de la célébrité en France et dans les pays anglophones." *Revue française de sociologie* 52, no. 2 (2011) : 353-72.

**Ihl**, Olivier. *Le Mérite et la République. Essai sur la société des émules*. Paris : Gallimard, 2007.

**Lee**, Brendan M, and Mark **Jarzombek**. "Perspecta 37" Famous" : The Yale Architectural Journal." (2006).

**Masboungi**, Ariella, Frédérique **de Gravelaine**, and Bert **McClure**. *Nantes : La Loire dessine le projet*. Paris : Éd. de la Villette / Communauté urbaine de Nantes / Ministère de l'Equipement, 2003.

**Mazeri**, Miguel. "L'étoffe des héros. Pour une histoire des Albums des Jeunes Architectes (1980-2006). De l'arbitrage de la reconnaissance à l'insertion professionnelle de jeunes architectes." Thèse de doctorat de l'EHESS sous la direction d'Alban Bensa, 2012.

**Violeau**, Jean-Louis. "Concours : Un modèle pour des logements individuels." *AMC-Le Moniteur architecture*, no. 138 (2003) : 18-20.

**Violeau**, Jean-Louis. "Concours à Nantes : Une journée pour l'innovation dans le logement social." *AMC-Le Moniteur architecture*, , no. 136 (2003) : 19-22.

**Violeau**, Jean-Louis. "Europan 6 — Dire le réel ". *Urbanisme*, no. 322 (2002) : 20-21.

**Violeau**, Jean-Louis. "Les 'premiers collés' volontaires de l'architecture." *Les Nouveaux Albums des jeunes architectes — Le Moniteur Architecure hors série — IFA / DAPA*, no. 5128 (Novembre 2002) : 8-15.

**Violeau**, Jean-Louis. "Profession : Architectes de moins de 35 ans ". *AMC-Le Moniteur architecture*, no. 127 (2002) : 24-27.

**Vitet**, L., and E. E. **Viollet Le Duc**. "L'enseignement des arts : Il ya quelque chose à faire (1862)." In *A propos de l'enseignement des Arts du dessin : Suivi de l'enseignement des arts, Il ya quelque chose à faire*. Paris : ENSBA — Ecole Nationale des Beaux-Arts, 1984.

# Final Cut

A Remarkable Cross-Section of
Architectural Tendencies

# Final Cut

## A Remarkable Cross-Section of Architectural Tendencies

**Georges Adamczyk**, MScA
Codirector, Laboratoire d'Étude de l'Architecture
Potentielle, Université de Montréal
Canada

This essay examines the question of representation of architectural projects and more specifically projects submitted in competitions. Among the conventional drawings : plan, elevation, section and perspective view, it is the section that can render visible the formal and spatial qualities of the interiority offered by the design of the building, as well as the relation of the interior with the exterior. Section is always required in competition. Comparing sections designed by the architects permits to take the measure of their particular conceptual positions. Further than just describing the building, its vertical and technical properties, section drawings are also a figurative process of ideas or researches, opening for the observer a potential field of interpretation for the contemporary theory of architecture.

**Cover**
Elevation and longitudinal section of the project for the Lapérouse mausoleum by Henri Labrouste. Corinne Bélier, Barry Bergdoll and Marc Le Cœur, *Labrouste* (1801-1875), architecte : *la structure mise en lumière* (Paris : Nicolas Chaudun : Cité de l'architecture & du patrimoine : Bibliothèque nationale de France ; New York : The Museum of Modern Art, 2012), p.72.

The introduction of the jury report for the Centre Beaubourg International Design Competition (1971) highlights the ways an international competitioniss an opportunity which offers a, "remarkable section view of all the trends and research of a period."[1] Seeing in perspective or in section is literally and figuratively part of an architect's skill set. Even so, what is the utility of the section drawing at the project stage? Historians such as Jacques Guillerme and Hélène Vérin have studied and well demonstrated the specificity of the Section, its poetic value and its technical efficiency.[2] Because the section offers a view through the body of the building, these drawings are generally unavoidable in architectural competitions. What ca we learn on architectural competitions when looking closely at the use of the section?

Architectural drawings are often enigmatic to non specialists. Only perspectives, which are directly readable, stimulate viewers to imagine a portrayal of what might be seen in reality. Viewers may decipher a plan or elevation, taken in isolation, by calling upon their ability to use maps and familiarity with house plans, and by reading catalogues, tourist guides, and books about buildings that illustrate their physical features. The section, however, is always more mysterious. One orients oneself carefully, starting at ground level and going up floor by floor. But this type of drawing is ultimately very abstract and inaccessible. When drawings are taken as a system in which the plan, the elevation, and the section fit together, their comprehension is reserved for architects, builders, and connoisseurs. Numerous research projects study the geometry and space distribution of plans, or compare one to another. One may also study elevations for their composition, ornament, or shadows — in short, everything that can be understood as the expression of a style. The section drawing is considered, rather, an auxiliary figure, without the symbolic status and instrumental value that are accorded to the plan and the elevation.

In architectural competitions, as we said, section drawings are almost always required, while at certain times in the history of competitions, directives have been issued to limit, or even prohibit, the use of perspectives seen as a potential fallacious device. One may thus deduce that the section drawing plays a decisive role in figuration of the design and representation of architecture. In a certain way, it speaks the truth. Refering to the disctinction proposed by Richard Wolheim for the study of drawings, at the jury stage of the competition, the section is clearly at the intersection of a judgement of quality (the beauty of the execution of the drawing of the section) and a judgement of interest (what the drawing reveals about the architecture).[3] This short essay looks at the utility of the section drawings in architecture for the jugdment of interest in competition context. We shall focus on spatial and formal qualities as revealed by the section.

## ▬ The Architectural Drawing

Documenting architectural competitions is one of the new tasks in contemporary architectural research. With origins that go back to antiquity, competitions are a mode of access to private or public commissions, and their popularity has varied depending on the country and the era. Thus, considered for their societal position and intellectual production, competitions are a source of original knowledge for architectural theory and practice and provide insight into changes in the discipline over time. This is the objective pursued in the most recent research. Approached from the institutional, professional, and educational angles, the architectural competition is a sort of barometer and benchmark of doctrines and ideologies; its function is as much regulatory as innovative.[4]

Another approach consists of addressing competition entries as graphic works, since the documents submitted by the architects to communicate their proposals consist essentially of images. Some of these images "objectively" describe the proposed building with drawings that are determined by convention: plans, elevations, sections. These drawings fit within a cognitive protocol that architects have shared since the Renaissance. Many other images, addressed directly to observers outside of the profession, are perspective drawings composed as if they were paintings, so that potential visitors or users may project themselves into the scene. They give a "rendering" of the completed building, and they may exceed the anticipated reality and push the illusion to the point of showing features that will never exist.[5] These different modes of figuration, objective and subjective, constitute a specialized graphic language, useful for description, instruction, and, more generally, communication. Thus, architectural drawings may be read as statements, and their settings as rhetorical strategies. In a competition situation, images aim to convince observers of the value of the architect's proposal.[6]

To better understand the significance of architectural drawings, their instrumental dimension, and their imaginative potential, we must pick up the thread of the history of the drawing within the history of architecture. This area of architectural research has been active since 1968.[7] The link between architectural theory and architectural drawings has now become obvious; in 1989, the Canadian Centre for Architecture inaugurated its new building with an exhibition entitled *Architecture and Its Image*. Drawings do not simply illustrate discourse; they are part of discourse. In addition, we can consider architectural drawings to be not solely the expression of an architect's idea, but also part of a process of development of thought and imagination.[8] Although architectural drawing has advanced thanks to technical and scientific progress, from optical geometry to mechanics, the instruments and media used are also very important; for instance, the introduction of tracing paper in the eighteenth century, and of the computer much more recently, may be seen as having generated new paradigms.[9] In spite of these changes, however, architectural figuration, which has gradually replaced verbal and written communication since the medieval era, maintains its function of emulation of reference models. The advent of computer-assisted design has allowed the ambiguity of these models to be cultivated to the point of proposing virtual replicas.[10] At the design stage, figurative operations and the resulting figures are diverse, and studying them is quite complex.[11]

A "morpho-genetic" approach to architectural drawings may, however, be more fruitful for the historical study of "variants" in a project, for understanding the architect's intentions, for interpreting the transactions between architect and client or between architect and construction-site collaborators, or for "reconstructing" the process of discovery.[12] The notion of *disegno*, as conceptualized during the Renaissance to accurately distinguish design from execution and make the drawing "active information on the space and the edification,"[13] is essential here. But architectural drawings also have their limitations, and an analysis of graphic documents can also reveal this. Robin Evans emphasizes the distinction between composition and projection and discusses the creative and cognitive issues that their necessary relationship poses. We can thus consider this relationship a fundamental architectural question.[14]

Architectural representation also leads theory toward a more philosophical horizon. Perspective, introduced during the Renaissance, is usually interpreted as a great artistic and scientific upheaval that marked, conveyed, and supported a new vision of the world. The advent of the inversion of the heavenly and human worlds is seen as a privileged moment for symbolization. This new world has disappeared, swept away by the technical power of human activity.[15] The fading of humanist culture is often identified with the rise of modernism in architecture. Perspectives were erased from the creative process in favour of axonometric drawings that combine in a single figure an object's plan, elevation, and section. For the avant-gardes, the ideal was for architecture to free itself from gravity and material limitations thanks to new construction techniques. A new conception of scope made space and movement the central themes of architectural creativity.[16] These new architectural theories and practices led, at the same time, to a crisis in architectural representation. Nevertheless, in spite of this program of new ideas, the great architects of the modern movement continued to rely on perspective drawings to elaborate their projects. Dialogue between interior and exterior, architectural promenades, the context of the city as work of art, and the site as landscape are all themes that have reinforced the use of perspective in the design and dissemination of architectural projects.

## ▬▬ The Section Drawing

The section is often compared to a surgical operation. It is, indeed, a drawing of an object that is seen as if it were cut along a vertical plane. This cut into the material is perceived analogically as a cut into the body of the building. There is certainly a relationship between the dissection performed in order to learn more about living beings and the modes of discovery and teaching in architecture. But the section drawing is of interest not only for its role in representing the structure, as was observed in the Middle Ages, when it first made its appearance on construction sites **[Fig.1]**; it also shows what the deployed materials contain — that is, the interiority of the building, its habitability, the void that can be occupied. In his study on representations of interiors during the Italian Renaissance, Wolfgang Lotz retraced the path that led from section drawing with perspective of the interior to section drawing with orthogonal projection of the interior. According to Lotz, the first theory of the section with orthogonal projection was presented by Raphael in a letter that he wrote to Pope Leo X in 1519. In this letter, he distinguished the work of the painter from that of the architect and established the convention that made the plan the representation of a building's footprint; the elevation, the view of its exterior; and the section, the view of its interior. The same system of orthogonal projection applies to these three figures that are drawn at the same scale.[17]

**Fig. 1**
Drawing of the exterior buttressing system of the
Reims choir by Villard de Honnecourt. Roland Recht,
*Le dessin d'Architecture : Origine et fonctions*
(Paris : Société nouvelle Adam Biro, 1995), p. 30.

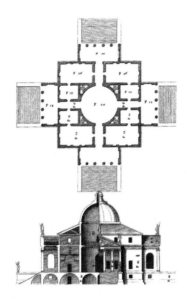

**Fig. 2**
Plan and section of a villa designed by Palladio. Adolf K.
Plackek, *Andrea Palladio : The Four Books of Architecture*
(New York : Dover Publications, 1965), p. 47.

**Fig. 3**
Section of the project for the Opera by
Étienne-Louis Boullée. Jean-Marie
Pérouse de Montclos, *Étienne-Louis Boullée
(1728–1799): de l'architecture classique à
l'architecture révolutionnaire* (Paris: Arts et
métiers graphiques, 1969), p. 295.

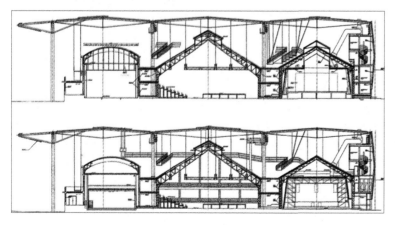

**Fig. 4**
Cross section. Studio des arts
contemporains Le Fresnoy à
Tourcoing, France, by architect
Bernard Tschumi. Gevork Hartoonian,
"Bernard Tschumi : Return of the
Object," *Architecture & Ideas*, Vol. 4,
No. 2 (2004) : 37.

These were the three figures used by Palladio in his *Four Books on Architecture* around 1570 **[Fig.2]**.

For Henri Stierlin, "only elevations and sections provide an understanding of the transition from plan to volume and space."[18] Although the section was not considered isolated from its close connection to the plan, which remains the "generator" of the building's measurements and qualities, it is clear that it provides access to an evaluation of spatiality. One might even venture to propose that the section represents the proposal for a spatial experience of a particular project. An examination of several famous sections, such as those by Boullée and Tschumi, provides ample proof of this **[Fig.3] [Fig.4]**. In teaching the design of collective housing, there is probably no more famous section whose operative character is still current than that of the apartments in Le Corbusier's Unité d'Habitation in Marseille **[Fig.5]**.

A reading of "Précisions sur un état présent de l'architecture et de l'urbanisme" (Precisions on the present state of architecture and city planning), which Le Corbusier published in 1930, is particularly enlightening. Concluding his lecture entitled "Le plan de la Maison moderne," he analyzed the Villa de Poissy project, then under construction. After describing the site, the volume, and the interior, which began to sound like a description of a promenade, he said, "To conclude, look at the section : air circulates throughout, light is in every corner, penetrating throughout. The circulation provides architectural impressions of a diversity disconcerting to any visitor unaware of the architectural liberties brought about by modern techniques. The simple posts of the ground floor, judiciously placed, cut the landscape with a regularity the effect of which is to suppress any notion of 'in front' or 'behind' the house, or 'beside' the house."[19] These statements are illustrated by a large sketch of the section, which shows the "suspended box" : the dwelling's top (the solarium), bottom (the *pilotis*), and underground (the cellar). The stairway and ramp are indicated by two graphic gestures that express the motion of climbing. Does the section summarize the analysis, or is it at the origin of the project ? If the analysis is the conception of the project in reverse, the second possibility might be true, and the figurative operation that is the section drawing would thus show the principal idea of the project. Le Corbusier's description is of movement and spatiality : interior and exterior interpenetrate, and materials no longer impose limits. Thus, a lecture entitled "The Plan" concludes with a section !

To see how important the section was to Le Corbusier, one just has to peruse the *Poème de l'Angle Droit* ("Poem of the Right Angle"). Of three drawings illustrating the *Esprit,* two are schematic sections — one of a house and the other of a collective housing unit.[20] These are, in fact, the only drawings in the "Poem" that refer to architectural drawings. If the "*Esprit*" is associated with the idea of imaginative intelligence, the section is a fundamental figure for the modern architect.

The exploration of figurative operations that enable modern architects to redefine the spatial experience of buildings has been addressed in a number of remarkable studies. For instance, the work by Claude Vié and Henri E. Ciriani helped to clarify notions such as "the horizontal extension of space" and "ascending spatial extension," and they inventoried the mechanisms designed by modern architects — for instance, Ciriani was interested in documenting continuous movement of matter — in order to obtain these spatial qualities in their projects.[21] The analysis of forms of "spatial sequence" in Le Corbusier's early work is very significant. A very strong relationship between the circulation of air and communication among rooms is implemented in the Villa de Carthage project in 1928 **[Fig.6]**. This section drawing led, in a way, to the increasingly frequent use of the section today to represent the ventilation of a building's interior spaces.[22] Comparative studies between the "Raumplan" proposed by Adolf Loos and Le Corbusier's "free plan" do not hesitate to compare the figure of one's section to the figure of the other's plan.[23] Although one might wonder about such graphic correspondences, it is easy to see that use of the section for spatial analysis is indispensable **[Fig.7]**.

To return to section drawings in architectural competitions and to extend my observation that these figurative operations may be considered decisive in the representation of an idea supported by a project, I will take two examples : first, the schematic section submitted by the winning architects, Renzo Piano and Richard Rogers, in their documents accompanying the presentation boards for the Centre Beaubourg competition in Paris in 1972 ; second, section drawings for the Peak project in Hong Kong by Zaha Hadid in 1982–83. In the case of the Centre Beaubourg, the schematic section is striking for its simplicity. The suspended box contains the platforms and frees up the square in the historic Les Halles district of Paris. A second square (the terrace), is accessible at the top, and touches the Parisian sky. The project is literally above the district, and it has

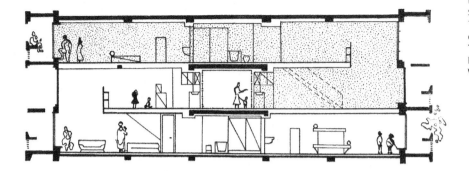

**Fig. 5**
Section showing Le Corbusier's "bottle rack" system for the Unité d'habitation in Marseille. Donald Tomkinson, "The Marseilles Experiment," *Town Planning Review*, Vol. 24, No. 3 (October 1953): 201.

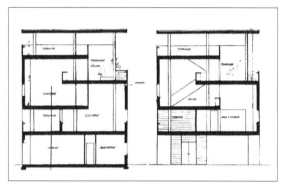

**Fig. 6**
Cross sections of the Villa Baizeau in Carthage by Le Corbusier. Jacques Lucan, *Le Corbusier une encyclopédie* (Paris : Éditions du Centre Pompidou/CCI), p. 373.

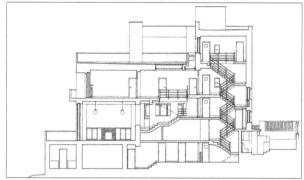

**Fig. 7**
Section of the Villa Müller by Adolf Loos. Leslie van Duzer and Kent Kleinman, *Villa Müller: A Work of Adolf Loos* (New York : Princeton Architectural Press, 1994), p. 85.

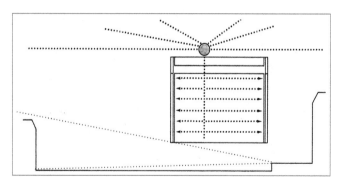

**Fig. 8**
Schematic section of the project by architects Piano, Rogers, and Franchini for the Centre Beaubourg. *Rapport du Jury du Concours international pour la réalisation du Centre Beaubourg*, Établissement public du Centre Beaubourg (Paris, 1971), p. 104.

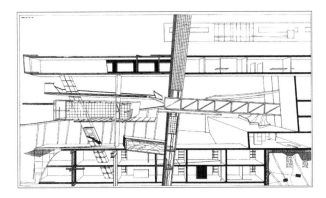

**Fig. 9**
Detail of a section for the project "The Peak, Hong Kong" by Zaha Hadid. Peter Wilson, "The Park and the Peak — Two International Competitions," AA files, No. 4 (1983) : 87.

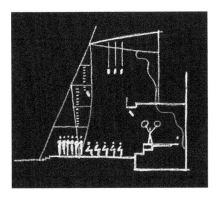

**Fig. 10**
Project by Dan S. Hanganu Architects for the Salle de spectacle de Rimouski, 2001.

the entire capital city as a horizon **[Fig.8]**. The perspective section of the project for luxury residences at the Peak in Hong Kong is but one of the many very beautiful drawings produced by Hadid for this competition. The most striking ones are those that evoke the architecture of the Russian Suprematist movement and give the impression that the project is floating above the city. The section corresponds well to the description of this project, which, according to Hadid, could be seen as a slice cut by a knife through the site. The sports club is suspended in a great open void, built against the mountain and overlooking the city. This void is situated in the clearance created by the distance separating the lower part, anchored to the site, and the upper part, floating over the site. These two parts contain the residences. This deconstruction would have certainly made the builders anxious at the time, but the section concretely shows the project's potential. One might say that the essence of the project is portrayed in it **[Fig.9]**.

## ▬ The Space of the Section Drawing in architectural competitions in Quebec

Architectural competitions in Quebec require participants to submit section drawings. These particular drawings, as I have mentioned, are integrated into a presentation strategy that is also meant to be a rhetorical strategy. It is thus a mistake to attempt to isolate individual drawings from these coherent groups of graphic documents prepared by the architects who enter these competitions. But as I am focusing on the figurative operations that are section drawings, I shall attempt a brief analysis of several of them. I will examine how these drawings convey the architects' spatial concerns, knowing that these concerns overflow into a space other than that contained by the building itself. As Benoît Goetz has written about Le Corbusier, "It is no longer about the space of the work, but about the space opened up by the work : the architect makes tangible a space that is not his." [24]

### The schema and the section

In Dan Hanganu's team's project for the Salle de spectacle de Rimouski (2001) and the project for Habitations Georges Vanier in Montreal by Richard de la Riva (1991), the section shows the architects' intended tripartite composition, progressing from the public space into the depths of its interior. Hanganu's sketch compresses the building, since it is less about measurements than about differential qualities **[Fig.10]**. De la Riva's section drawing shows the

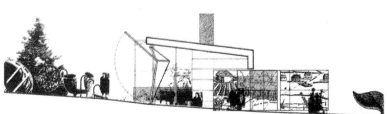

subtraction of a threshold in front and the addition of a raised exterior domestic space at the back. Each of the three floors has its own specific habitability qualities **[Fig.11]**.

### The project constructs the site

The section of the promenade at Pabos by Atelier Big City (1991) and the sections of the Théâtre du Vieux-Terrebonne by Manon Asselin (Atelier T.A.G.) and Jodoin Lamarre Pratte (2002) clearly indicate the project's relationship with the territory and the role played by the existing topography in the former case, and by the invented topography in Terrebonne in the latter case. At both sites, the project constructs the landscape **[Fig.12] [Fig.13]**.

### Addition and intermediary space

Dealing with an existing building may be seen as adding a new building to a previous composition. In three cases — the project for the Faculté de l'Aménagement by Saucier + Perrotte, Menkès Shooner Dagenais (1994), the Centre d'archives de Montréal by Dan Hanganu/ Provencher Roy et Associés (1997), and the Centre d'accueil et d'interprétation de la Place Royale in Quebec City by Atelier Big City (1996) — an intermediary space places the

old and the new in tension. Saucier + Perrotte and MSD proposed an interior courtyard that clearly divides the project: the studios opening onto the garden and the auditorium facing the broad avenue **[Fig.14]**. Hanganu chose instead a large hall separating the archives, in protected areas, from the auditorium, open to the public. The large hall gave the archive floors room to breathe while offering a magnificent area, bathed in natural light, for people to meet **[Fig.15]**. Atelier Big City chose to slide the new building from the top of the hill toward Place Royale. This shift was suspended to open an interstitial space between the façade that was to be preserved on the public square and the new structure. The interpretation is in the project **[Fig.16]**.

### Constructing the Void

Buckminster Fuller's geodesic structure and Cambridge Seven's platforms were valorized in the project by the Consortium Blouin, Faucher, Aubertin, Brodeur, Gauthier/ Desnoyers, Mercure et Associés (1991). The project for the Montreal Symphony Orchestra on the Balmoral block in Montreal is that of the winners, De Architekten Cie and Ædefica (2002). Both section drawings meet the challenge of portraying a large architectural space in which the

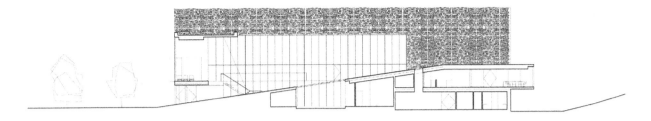

**Fig. 13**
Project by Manon Asselin (Atelier T.A.G.) for the competition for Théâtre du Vieux-Terrebonne, 2002.

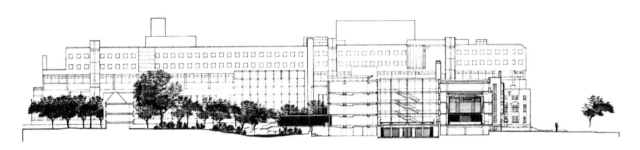

**Fig. 14**
Project by Saucier et Perrotte architectes (Saucier + Perrotte), architect René Menkès, and Deshaies, Raymond, and Blondin, Barone, architectes-paysagistes for the competition for the Faculté de l'aménagement de l'Université de Montréal, 1994.

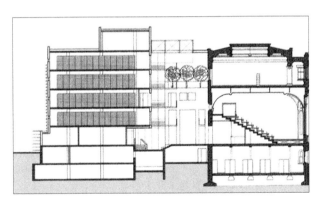

**Fig. 15**
Project by Dan S. Hanganu Architects Provencher Roy + associés architectes for the relocation of the Centre d'archives de Montréal, 1997.

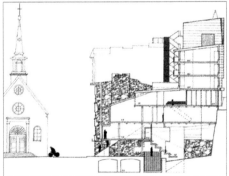

**Fig. 16**
Project by Cormier, Cohen, Davies, architectes (Atelier Big City) for the competition for the Centre d'accueil et d'interprétation de la Place Royale, 1996.

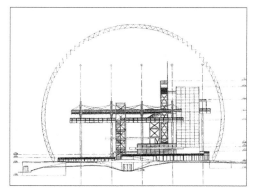

**Fig. 17**
The Biosphère de Montréal, Blouin Faucher
Aubertin Brodeur Gauthier/Desnoyers
Mercure et associés, architectes, 1991.

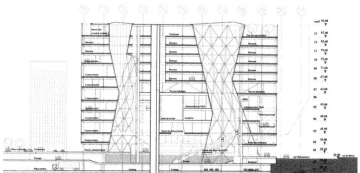

**Fig. 18**
Project by the consortium of De Architekten Cie./Aedifica inc./Les architectes
Tétrault Parent Languedoc et associés for the competition for the Montreal
Symphony Orchestra (MSO), Complexe culturel et administratif, 2002.

emblematic figure of the column disappears. The constructive concept makes the project. Certainly, the architects who restored the Biosphere deliberately chose to favour the platform as an elevated public space in order to place people literally in the centre of the sphere, whose light structure filters the landscape of the river **[Fig.17]**. In the case of the large cube that houses the concert hall, immense conical structures support the building while freeing up interior voids that open to the sky **[Fig.18]**.

### Cross or longitudinal section

Sections are conventions, but are these conventions related to drawing or to composition? A classic longitudinal section divides the building into two parts that are often symmetrical. This geometrical regularity is shown in the longitudinal section for the Outremont library by Brillant/ Mercier Boyer-Mercier (1994). The overhead lighting is right at the centre of the building, along the line where the section is taken **[Fig.19]**. In the case of the proposal by Atelier Big City with Borkür Bergmann and Desnoyers, Mercure, it is the cross section that is the most significant, especially because it clearly breaks with classical symmetry and shows the "overpasses" created by the circulation

ramps. More than an architectural promenade, the project is entirely conceived as a choreography of matter in motion, housed in a perforated envelope that tends to reserve the "surprise" for those who dare to cross the threshold of the library **[Fig.20]**.

### Spatial compression and extension

The winning project proposed by the team of Patkau, Croft Pelletier, and Gilles Guité for the competition for the Bibliothèque Nationale du Québec (2000) stands out for its compactness. By "compact," I do not mean compression of the space. This is revealed perfectly in the cross section, which shows the opening of the project to the surrounding neighbourhood and to the landscape of the city as a whole. In addition, the interpenetration of spaces is obvious. The link between the public space below grade and the metro station counterbalances the large opening of the stepped readers' promenade **[Fig.21]**.

This overview is all too brief, but it certainly indicates that the section drawing conveys the essence of the spatial ideas and proposals formulated by architects in the context of architectural competitions in Quebec.

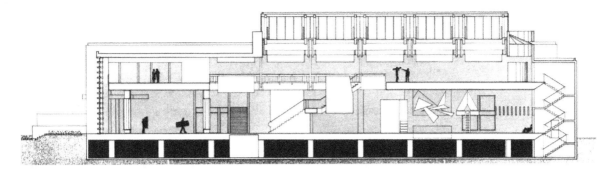

**Fig. 19**
Project by Brillant/Mercier
Boyer-Mercier, architectes for the
Bibliothèque d'Outremont, 1994.

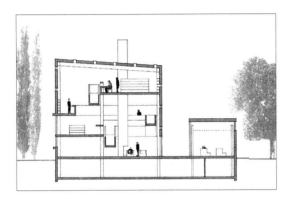

**Fig. 20**
Project by Cormier, Cohen, Davies, architectes (Atelier
Big City), architect Borkür Bergmann, Desnoyers,
Mercure et associés, architectes for the competition
for the Bibliothèque d'Outremont, 1994.

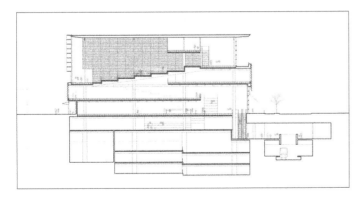

**Fig. 21**
Project by Patkau Architects/Croft Pelletier,
architectes/Gilles Guité architecte for the Grande
Bibliothèque du Québec, 2000.

Returning to the making of architecture and the developpment of this specific skill of the architect, we undertand that when the studio professor talks with a student at his drafting table, where a computer sits beside sketching paper and cardboard for model-making, and he suddenly says, "You should do a section!," it is less to urge the student to conform to a convention than to give him the means to better see and think about how his project will be made. Seeing and designing are intertwined in this figurative operation, as in all others. However, the section drawing, combined with the plan and the elevation, does not overcome the difficulty of designing a complex form. Robin Evans provides a good example of this when he describes Hans Scharoun's process of designing the Berlin Philharmonic concert hall between 1956 and 1963. After making perspective sections of the interior, he had to return, as Raphael would have hoped, to sections with orthogonal projections of the interior, multiplying them like successive slices into the building to master how the unusual space would be constructed. But, at the same time, and this was Evans's main argument, should we not wonder about the persistence of these figurative operations, which come from the classic age and limit the spatial imagination of contemporary architects? In fact, is it not paradoxical to portray a three-dimensional space in two dimensions? And further, is not this figurative system a protection against the unimaginable?[25] In their project for a research centre in Waterloo, Saucier + Perrotte used computers to multiply the number of longitudinal sections in order to precisely define the cross sections, which governed the crossing movements of people, light, and views. Thus, the question of geometry will continue to challenge architectural drawing, and this question is crystallized in the attempt to perceive space through section drawings as much as through the "vanity" of perspective drawings.

The relevance of the section drawing must also be understood in the correspondence that is established between a precedent and a new project. In fact, in certain cases one refers less to the building previously erected than to its section. We might interpret the publication of a recent book by Richard Weston as a figurative parallel with Palladio's treatise and as a collection in which section drawings achieve relative autonomy in terms of grasping the multiple forms of architectural space created by twentieth-century architects.[26] Similarly, documentation of architectural competitions constitutes a source of knowledge for a better understanding of these figurative operations, which will continue, despite their limitations and the strong imperatives of the construction industry to determine their form, to make the architectural act one of imagination and symbolization that is fundamental The study of architectural competition anable us to depict the paradigm shifts of the discipline and pratice of architecture that can be particularly well observed in looking closely at the Section, as an idea and as a drawing of an idea.[27]

## Notes

1 Rapport du Jury du concours international pour la réalisation du Centre Beaubourg, *établissement public du Centre Beaubourg* (Paris, 1971)

2 Jacques Guillerme and Hélène Vérin, The Archeology of Section, Perspecta No 25 (1989) pp. 226-257

3 Richard Wolheim, Why is drawing interesting ? British Journal of Aesthetics, Vol. 45, No 1, January 2005. Pp. 1-10

4 See Hélène Lipstadt (ed.), The experimental Tradition, New York : Princeton Architectural Press, 1989.

5 Jacques Guillerme, "L'ingestion du rendu," *A.M.C.* No. 35 (1974) : 29–32.

6 Elisabeth Tostrup, *Architecture and Rhetoric : Text and Design in Architectural Competitions* (London : Andreas Papadakis, 1999).

7 Roland Recht, *Le dessin d'architecture* (Paris : Adam Biro, 1995) ; see, in particular, chapter 1, "Actualité du dessin d'architecture," pp. 9–19.

8 A brief, general history of architectural drawings is offered in Helen Powel and David Letherbarrow (eds.), *Masterpieces of Architectural Drawing* (New York : Abbeville Press, 1989), pp. 12–60.

9 James S. Ackerman, *Origins, Limitation, Conventions* (Cambridge : MIT, 2002). See the chapter "The Conventions and Rhetoric of Architectural Drawing," pp. 292–317.

10 Mario Carpo, "Topos, stéréotype, cliché, clone," *Architecture d'Aujourd'hui*, No. 343 (2002) : 42–51.

11 See, notably, Philippe Boudon and Frédéric Pousin, *Figures de la conception architecturale* (Paris : Dunod, 1988).

12 Marc Grignon, "Les archives d'architecture, document ou monument," *ARQ* No. 66 (1992) : 18–20.

13 Joselita Ciaravino, *Un art paradoxal, la notion de "Disegno" en Italie (XV–XVIe siècles* (Paris : L'Harmattan, 2004).

14 Robin, Evans, *The Projective Cast, Architecture and its Three Geometries* (Cambridge : MIT Press, 1995).

15 See, on this subject, Alberto Perez-Gomez and Louise Pelletier, *Architecture Representation and the Perspective Hinge* (Cambridge : MIT Press, 1997). See also Alberto Perez-Gomez, "The Revelation of Order : Perspective and Architectural Representation," in Kester Rattenbury (ed.), *This is not Architecture* (London : Routledge, 2002), pp. 3–25.

16 See Yve-Alain Bois and Bruno Reichlin, *De Stijl et l'architecture en France* (Brussels : Mardaga, 1985).

17 Wolfgang Lotz, *Studies in Italian Renaissance Architecture* (Cambridge : MIT Press, 1977), pp. 1–65.

18 Henri Stierlin, *Comprendre l'Architecture universelle* (Fribourg : Office du livre, 1977), pp. 9–18.

19 Le Corbusier, *Précisions sur un état présent de l'architecture et de l'urbanisme*, facsimile of the 1930 book (Paris : Éditions Altamira, 1994), pp. 123–39.

20 Tim Benton and Al Benton, *Le Corbusier and The Architecture of Reinvention* (London : Architectural Association, 2003), pp. 58–97. This book reproduces all the plates of Le Corbusier's "Le Poème de l'Angle Droit."

21 Claude Vié and Henri E. Ciriani, *L'Espace de l'Architecture Moderne*, research report, Paris-Belleville, 1989.

22 Bruno Reichlin, "Solution élégante, L'utile n'est pas beau," in Jacques Lucan (ed.), *Le Corbusier, une encyclopédie* (Paris : Centre Georges Pompidou, 1987), pp. 369–77.

23 Pierre Boudon, "Plan + coupe + élévation, Propos sur la Villa Savoye et autres édifications parallèles," *Silo*, No 4 (1990) : 10–17.

24 Benoît Goetz, "L'espace-surprise' : pensée et sensation," *Les Cahiers philosophiques de Strasbourg*, No. 1 (1994).

25 Evans, *Projective Cast*, pp. 119–21.

26 Richard Weston, *Plans, Sections and Elevations : Key Buildings of the Twentieth Century* (London : W.W. Norton & Company, 2004).

27 This essay is a new version of a previous one that has been published under the title : Notes on Architecture Drawing : The Section, written for the Catalogue : Architecture Competitions and Territorial Imaginations : Cultural Projects in Quebec 1991-2005 (Centre de Design UQAM-Leap, 2006).

## References

**Ackerman**, James S. *Origins, Limitation, Conventions*. Cambridge : MIT (2002) : 292–317.

**Benton**, Tim and Al **Benton**, *Le Corbusier and The Architecture of Reinvention*. London : Architectural Association, (2003) : 58–97.

**Bois**, Yve-Alain and Bruno **Reichlin**, *De Stijl et l'architecture en France*. Brussels : Mardaga, 1985.

**Boudon**, Pierre. "Plan + coupe + élévation, Propos sur la Villa Savoye et autres édifications parallèles," *Silo*, No 4 (1990) : 10–17.

**Boudon**, Philippe and Frédéric **Pousin**. *Figures de la conception architecturale*. Paris : Dunod, 1988.

**Carpo**, Mario. "Topos, stéréotype, cliché, clone," *Architecture d'Aujourd'hui*, No. 343 (2002) : 42–51.

**Ciaravino**, Joselita. Un art paradoxal, la notion de "Disegno" en Italie (XV-XVIe siècles). Paris : L'Harmattan, 2004.

**Chupin**, Jean-Pierre. "Les 40 prochaines années : le doctorat en architecture à la charnière des enjeux disciplinaires et professionnels," *Trames*, no. 15. Montreal : Université de Montréal, (2004) :121–44.

**Egbert**, Donald Drew. *The Beaux-Arts Tradition in French Architecture*, Princeton : Princeton Architecture Press, 1980.

**Evans**, Robin. The Projective Cast, Architecture and its Three Geometries. Cambridge : MIT Press, 1995.

**Goetz**, Benoît. "L'espace-surprise' : pensée et sensation," *Les Cahiers philosophiques de Strasbourg*, No. 1 (1994).

**Grignon**, Marc. "Les archives d'architecture, document ou monument," *ARQ* No. 66 (1992) : 18–20.

**Guillerme**, Jacques. "L'ingestion du rendu," *A.M.C.* No. 35 (1974) : 29–32.

**Guillerme** Jacques and Hélène Vérin, *The Archeology of Section*, Perspecta No 25 (1989) pp. 226-257

**Le Corbusier**. *Précisions sur un état présent de l'architecture et de l'urbanisme*, facsimile of the 1930 book. Paris : Éditions Altamira, (1994) : 123–39.

**Lipstadt**, Hélène. *The Experimental Tradition*. New York : Princeton Architectural Press, 1989.

**Lipstadt**, Hélène. "Le concours, lieu de représentation de l'architecture," *ARQ* No. 59 (1991) : 8–11.

**Lotz**, Wolfgang. *Studies in Italian Renaissance Architecture*. Cambridge : MIT Press, (1977) : 1–65.

**Perez-Gomez**, Alberto. "The Revelation of Order : Perspective and Architectural Representation," in, Kester Rattenbury (ed.). *This is not Architecture*. London : Routledge, (2002) : 3–25.

**Perez-Gomez**, Alberto and Louise **Pelletier**. *Architecture Representation and the Perspective Hinge*. Cambridge : MIT Press, 1997.

**Powel**, Helen and David **Letherbarrow**. *Masterpieces of Architectural Drawing*. New York : Abbeville Press, (1989) : 12–60.

**Recht**, Roland. *Le dessin d'architecture*. Paris : Adam Biro, (1995) ; 9–19.

**Reichlin**, Bruno. "Solution élégante, L'utile n'est pas beau," in Jacques Lucan (ed.), *Le Corbusier, une encyclopédie*. Paris : Centre Georges Pompidou, (1987) : 369–77.

**Stierlin**, Henri. *Comprendre l'Architecture universelle*. Fribourg : Office du livre, (1977) : 9–18.

**Tostrup**, Elisabeth. Architecture and Rhetoric : Text and Design in Architectural Competitions. London : Andreas Papadakis, 1999.

**Vié**, Claude and Henri E. **Ciriani**, *L'Espace de l'Architecture Moderne*, research report, Paris-Belleville, 1989.

**Weston**, Richard. *Plans, Sections and Elevations : Key Buildings of the Twentieth Century*. London : W.W. Norton & Company, 2004.

# Author Biographies

## Georges Adamczyk

Georges Adamczyk is professor at the School of Architecture of Université de Montréal. He was the Head of the School from June 1999 to June 2007. Previously, since 1977, he was professor at the Department of Design of the Université du Québec à Montréal. From 1992 to June 1999, he was the Director of the Design Center at UQAM, a gallery dedicated to exhibitions and discussions on the city, architecture, landscape, design and graphic media. He participates regularly in advisory committees, juries on architecture and design competitions. He has contributed to the book Architectural installations published by the Canadian Center for Architecture (1999). He has directed the exhibition (2000) and written the catalogue (2004) of Maisons-Lieux/Houses-Places for the Biennale de Montréal. He was the curator of the exhibition Objets trouvés installed by Saucier + Perrotte at the Canadian Pavillon of the Venice Biennale (2004). He also contributed to Substance over Spectacle by Andrew Gruft (2005) and to the Guide de l'architecture contemporaine de Montréal by Nancy Dunton and Helen Malkin (2008). As co-director of Laboratoire d'étude de l'architecture potentielle (L.E.A.P), he contributes to the Canadian Competitions Catalogue since the inception of the project in 2002.

## Jonas E Andersson

Jonas E Andersson graduated as architect in 1990, and he is member of the Swedish Association of Architects, SA. As a practicing architect, he works with residential architecture in different shapes, but also with RCs for dependent and frail older people, hotels and offices. In 2003, he commenced his Ph D project, and his licentiate thesis was published in 2005. In October 2011, Andersson defended his doctoral thesis, "Architecture for Ageing, on the interaction between frail older people and the built environment at the School of Architecture, Royal Institute of Technology, KTH, in Stockholm, Sweden. During the period of 2012 to 2013, Andersson was employed as researcher at the Danish Building Research Institute. Here, he focused on accessibility and usability issues in architecture and the built environment. Parallel to research on architecture for ageing and architecture competitions, he is working as an assistant professor in continuing education courses or elective courses at the School of Architecture, Royal Institute of Technology, KTH, in Stockholm.

## Emmanuel Caille

Architect and architectural critic, Emmanuel Caille is chief editor of the French journal *d'architectures* (d'a) (www.darchitectures.com). From 1985 to 2000, he participated as architectural designer in several major international competitions. Invited author for numerous publications on architecture, he regularly direct public debates related to the dissemination of architectural culture. Since 2007, he has been teaching in various French national schools of architecture and has been directing the masters studio "Questionner, formuler, projeter" at the National School of Architecture Paris-Belleville since 2009. He was appointed member of the Advisory Board of the École Polytechnique Fédérale de Lausanne (EPFL) in 2009.

## Ian Chodikoff

Ian Chodikoff is an architect, educator, and journalist, currently Director of Architecture Canada. He directed Fora Strategic Planning Inc., a consultancy focused on urban-related issues such as public health, social inclusion, economic development, multiculturalism and migration. Ian was the Editor of Canadian Architect magazine from 2003-2012 and remains its Editorial Advisor. He holds a Master of Architecture from the University of British Columbia and a Master of Architecture in Urban Design from the Harvard University Graduate School of

Design. Ian has taught and lectured in various universities and cities, has served on numerous design juries, and has volunteered for various causes relating to engaging a greater sense of community. He is a Fellow of the Royal Architectural Institute of Canada. In 2013, he ended his three-year tenure as a member of the City of Ottawa's Urban Design Review Panel which provided him with a privileged overview of Ottawa's development process. As for juries and competitions, Ian is currently the professional advisor for an ideas competition relating to increasing the level of private market rental housing development in York Region. Ian also has considerable experience conducting various policy research and visualization projects relating to the intersection of social issues and the built environment. He curated an installation focusing on the importance of designing for those suffering from dementia at Toronto's Harbourfront Centre in 2014 as part of his ongoing investigations relating to linking various aspects of public health and urban design. In 2008, Ian began studying the effects of ethnicity and multiculturalism on the process of urban development in our cities with a specific focus on the Greater Toronto Area. Further to this, other independent studies have included work on the influence of transnational migration between Italy and Senegal.

## Jean-Pierre Chupin

Jean-Pierre Chupin is professor at the Université de Montréal School of Architecture, where is holds the Research Chair on Competitions and Contemporary Practices in Architecture and co-directs of the Laboratoire d'étude de l'architecture potentielle (L.E.A.P). Jean-Pierre is an architecture graduate from Nantes (France), and Portsmouth (UK). He holds a Masters in History and Theory of Architecture from McGill University and a PhD from the Université de Montréal. He has taught at the Université du Québec à Montréal (Uqam), Toulouse School of Architecture and Lyon School of Architecture before joining the Université de Montréal in 2000. Historian and theoretician of architectural design and architectural ideas, Jean-Pierre Chupin has been working for more than two decades on the role of "analogical thinking" in architecture. The first volume of his research on Analogy and Theory in Architecture (On life, on the city, and on design thinking, even) has been published in French in 2010 by Swiss Infolio Editions (in the series Projet et Théorie). The second edition, revised and augmented, came out in 2013 and is currently under translation for a publication in English. Prof. Chupin conducts research projects on contemporary architecture, competitions processes and practical and theoretical issues such as tectonics, architectural judgment and architectural excellence and experimentation. He coordinates the ongoing updates of two major competition databases (libraries of projects): in Canada (Canadian Competitions Catalogue) and in Europe (EUROPAN-FRANCE competitions (1989-2009)).

## G. Stanley Collyer

In 1986 G. Stanley Collyer became the director of The Competition Project, Inc., a Louisville, Kentucky-based non-profit organization charged with the sole mission of editing and disseminating information on design competitions. As such, he has been the editor of the U.S.-based quarterly publication, competitions, for 20 years and now oversees the internet E-zine and year-end publication of the competitions Annual. Besides the quarterly, competitions, now being published in China, he has authored a number of articles and publications, including Competing Globally in Architecture Competitions (Wiley-Academy, John Wiley and Sons, 2004). He has also been a featured speaker at AIA conventions as well as at universities. Before taking over his duties with competitions, G. Stanley Collyer lived for 20 years in Europe, initially in the U.S. military, then as a student and lecturer in Berlin, Germany, and finally in Vienna, Austria as a journalist. He received his B.A. from Duke University and Ph.D in History from the Freie Universität, Berlin.

## Camille Crossman

Camille Crossman is a doctoral student in Architecture at the Université de Montréal. She holds a Bachelor and a Master in architectural design. Her research thesis, which is conducted within the framework of the L.E.A.P (Laboratoire d'Étude de l'Architecture Potentielle) under the direction of Prof. Jean-Pierre Chupin, deals with the processes structuring qualitative judgment in the specific context of juries of public architectural competitions.

## Carmela Cucuzzella

Carmela Cucuzzella is an Assistant Professor in the Design and Computation Arts Department of Concordia University. She is also Graduate Program Director of the program Digital Technologies in Design Art Practice. She is scientific director of the Concordia University antenna lab of L.E.A.P (Laboratoire d'étude de l'architecture potentielle), which is based at Université de Montréal. She completed her PhD in 2011, from the Faculté de l'Aménagement of the Université de Montréal. Her research interests are in the domain of design for sustainability, specifically how these new design imperatives have shifted ideals of quality and in turn, the visual language of contemporary architectural and urban space. She teaches history, theory and project courses in Design, as well as a cross-disciplinary course with the Engineering faculty in Innovation and Critical Thinking at Concordia University. She is an associated member of District 3, an incubator space for start-ups at Concordia University. She was a contributing author of the Guidelines for Social Life Cycle Assessment of Products, published in 2009, which was an international collaborative effort. She has published in numerous articles and books on the topics of design, sustainability, judgment, expertise, architectural competitions, and life cycle thinking.

## Françoise Fromonot

Architect by training (studied and graduated from Paris-La Villette between 1986 to1994), Françoise Fromonot dedicates herself to the critique and pedagogy of architecture since 1995. She is the author of several books on contemporary architecture and urbanism, of note: Jørn Utzon et l'Opéra de Sydney (Milan, Paris, Corte Madera, 1998) and Glenn Murcutt (Milan, Paris, Londres, 2003), both of which have received book awards by the Académie d'architecture in Paris, in 1997 and 2004,and of a critical analysis of the last consultation to date for the renovation of the center of Paris, La campagne des Halles-Les nouveaux malheurs de Paris (Paris, 2005). She participated as editor and has regularly contributed to numerous journals, such as, l'Architecture d'Aujourd'hui, le visiteur, Casabella, d'Architectures, and A+ (Brussels). In 2007 she, with 4 other critiques and historians, founded the journal, criticat, where the n°1 appeared in January 2008. (www.criticat.fr). She is a tenured professor at the École nationale supérieur d'architecture (ENSA) de Paris-Belleville (project, history and theory) and has lectured in the Master d'Aménagement Urbain of the school of Ponts et Chaussées, and in the Master of Urbanism of Political Science for many years. She has taught in diverse schools of architecture as invited professor, such as, Berlage Institute (Rotterdam), at the Akademie der Bildenden Künste (Vienna), in the Rome School of Cornell University (Ithaca NY), and at the University of Chengdu (China). She equally participates at the Parisian antenna program of Rice University in Houston since its foundation.

## Bechara Helal

Bechara Helal is a doctoral student in Architecture at the Université de Montréal. He holds a Bachelor in Engineering (École Polytechnique) as well as a Bachelor and a Master in Architectural Design (Université de Montréal). His research thesis, conducted within the L.E.A.P (Laboratoire d'Étude de l'Architecture Potentielle) and directed by Professor Jean-Pierre Chupin, deals with the emergence of the laboratory in architectural theory and practice as a space of research and production of knowledge.

## Thomas Hoffmann-Kuhnt

Thomas Hoffmann-Kuhnt was born in 1944 in Wiesbaden, Germany. He qualified as architectural draftsman and, after evening classes for further education, he studied architecture at the Technische Universität in Munich. While still a student, he founded the publishing company wettbewerbe aktuell in 1971, whose editor and editor-in-chief he is to this day. At the beginning of the 90s the publishing company moved to Freiburg and later on the journal was extended by the wa-online presence and the important wa-special subjects series.

## Antigoni Katsakou

Antigoni Katsakou is an architect and holds a PhD degree from the Swiss Federal Institute of Technology in Lausanne (2011). Following graduate studies at the National Technical University of Athens (1999), she completed a postgraduate Master course at Barcelona Tech (2001). Co-author of the book Concours en Suisse : 2000-2005 (Lausanne: PPUR, 2008 & 2009), she has practiced and lectured in Greece, Switzerland, and the United Kingdom. She has presented her work in many international scientific meetings, and published in several languages with various editing houses. She works on the subject of housing competitions since 2006. From 2011 on, her research focuses on the subject of the architectural design, and studies the use of oblique geometry in plan for to enrich, through the construction of visual sequences, the user's experience in space. She has carried out a postdoctoral research on the subject, as a Visiting Fellow at the Space Group of the Bartlett School of Graduate Studies, University College London (2012-2013). Her work has been supported with numerous grants and funding awards by several Swiss Institutions. She currently lives and works in London, United Kingdom.

## Loïse Lenne

Loïse Lenne is an architect undergoing a PhD about event in architecture at the University Paris-Est. She teaches at the schools of architecture of Marne-la-Vallée and Paris-Malaquais. She is a member of the editorial board of Marne(s). She took part in the writing of La Défense, a Dictionary (Parenthèses, 2012).

## Carlo Menon

Carlo Menon (1981, Italy) is a qualified architect and a researcher. After graduating from La Cambre, Brussels, in 2006, he worked in public service organizing competitions for the Belgian French-speaking government. Since 2012 he has been pursuing postgraduate studies in architectural history and theory at The Bartlett, London. His main field of research is authorship in collaborative ventures such as architectural magazines and competitions, both intended as fields of conflictual representations producing a collective result. He currently lives between London and Brussels, where he participates in various teaching and publishing projects. He is co-founder of a large-format, experimental magazine called Accattone.

## Sofia Paisiou

Sofia Paisiou works as a researcher at the Institut of Architeture at the University of Applied Sciences and Arts of North-western Switzerland (FHNW). Her current research for the project "MWB - Hindernisfreies Wohnen" is a study of the residential building typologies in the canton of Basel-Stadt followed by a detailed analysis and problem solving for representative types. The research gives important answers about the typology of existing buildings stock in Basel-Stadt in regard to Universal design and produces innovative tools that address the Universal design potential of these types. Sofia Paisiou graduated as an architect-engineer from the National Technical University in Athens, Greece and also holds a Master in Urbanism from Technical University of Delft in the Netherlands. In 2008 she began her PhD studies, working on the SNF funded project (SNF No. 120595) 'Design competitions, a procedural analysis' under the supervision of Prof. Joris Van Wezemael at the Dept. of Architecture at ETH Zurich. Sofia Paisiou has worked as an architect and urban designer in architectural offices in Athens, Rotterdam, Vienna and Bern.

## Jan M. Silberberger

Jan M. Silberberger is a Post-Doc researcher at ETH Wohnforum-ETH CASE (Department of Architecture, ETH Zurich). He has studied Architecture and Urban Planning at the University of Stuttgart/Germany and Visual Communication and Fine Arts at the Hochschule fuer bildende Kuenste in Hamburg, Germany. In 2011 he finished his PhD studies at the University of Fribourg's Geography Unit. His research focuses on decision-making within planning processes.

## Susanna Sirefman

Susanna Sirefman brings a number of dimensions to her role as founder and president of Dovetail Design Strategists, but none as essential as her training as an architect, which she received at the renowned Architectural Association School of Architecture, London. Her firm, Dovetail Design Strategists, the leading independent architect selection firm in the United States, provides a comprehensive range of services designed to identify the right architect for a client's building program. Ms. Sirefman's deep knowledge of the field informs her ability to advise on design, synthesize architectural concepts, and make architecture accessible to the general public. Ms. Sirefman is a contributor to the *Wall Street Journal* and has authored five books on contemporary architecture (http://www.dovetailstrategists.com/publications) including *Whereabouts : New Architecture with Local Identities*. For *Whereabouts*, and its accompanying exhibition and symposium, Ms. Sirefman received grants from the National Endowment for the Arts and Graham Foundation for the Fine Arts. Ms. Sirefman has taught on the faculty of Parsons School of Design and City College New York School of Architecture and serves as a popular speaker and visiting critic at architecture and urban design programs across the country. Susanna Sirefman is a Fellow of the Forum for Urban Design; and a member of the Author's Guild

## Fabiano Sobreira

Fabiano Sobreira, architect and urban planner (Federal University of Pernambuco, 1996). Doctor on Urban Development (Federal University of Pernambuco / University College London, 2002). Post-doctoral research at LEAP (Research Laboratory of Potential Architecture), École d´architecture, Université de Montréal (2009). Architect, chief of the Section for Accessibility and Sustainable Design, Brazilian Parliament. Professor at University Uniceub, Brasília. Editor of concursosdeprojeto.org. Architect, associate of MGS - Macedo, Gomes & Sobreira.

## Ignaz Strebel

Ignaz Strebel is a geographer within the research unit ETH Wohnforum – ETH CASE (Centre for Research on Architecture, Society & the Built Environment), Faculty of Architecture, ETH Zurich. He took his PhD at the University of Fribourg in Switzerland in 2003. He was previously a researcher in geography and architecture at the Universities of Glasgow and Edinburgh, and his recent work has focussed on urban transformation accomplished in work settings, such as, among others, building care, research laboratories, and the offices of building administration, planning firms and housing administration.

## David Vanderburgh

David Vanderburgh is an architect and professor of architecture at the University of Louvain, Belgium, where he has taught design theory and history since 1995 and is currently head of the "Engineer-Architect" Bachelor Program. He holds degrees from Harvard College and the University of California, Berkeley. His PhD Thesis (Berkeley, 1992) was entitled "Cultures of Public Architecture: The Reform of French Provincial Prisons, 1830-1880." He has published and lectured on, among other subjects, architectural reform, the discipline of architecture, architectural competitions, and theories of representation. He remains involved in design practice through competitions, small-scale design and exhibitions.

## Joris Van Wezemael

Prof. Dr. Joris Van Wezemael is an associated Professor (Privatdozent) at the Department of Architecture (ETH Zürich) and an investment manager at a private company. He studied Geography with Sociology and Economics at the University of Zurich, where he also did his PhD in Urban Studies and Housing. During his Postdoc period in the UK he worked mostly in the field of spatial planning. He obtained his Habilitation (state doctorate) in Architectural Sociology (ETH Zürich) and was called on a Chair for Human Geography at the Universtity of Fribourg. His interests in research and teaching focus on the metamorphosis of contemporary urban landscapes.

## Jean-Louis Violeau

Sociologist, Jean-Louis Violeau is a professor at ENSA Paris Malaquais. He heads the team called, Architecture-Culture-Society affiliated with CNRS. His work spans the study of architects, the elite, and the multitudes. Specifically, the institutional body of architects, it's history, and the spaces for learning, it's position in the division of labour, and of course the practices that animate the end users or the citizens –depending on the point of view. His thesis on *Les Architects et mai 68* was available in 2005 from the publishers *Recherche*, review launched under the aegis of Felix Guattari and of the CERFI. The continuation of this work, *Les architectes et mai 81*, appeared in 2011 from the same publishers. He has just finished coordinating (with Craig Buckley) the translation in 2011 of an anthology of the journal *Utopie. Texts and Projects, 1967-1978*, supported by the publishers *Semiotexte* and *MIT Press*. He is part of the editorial committee of the Nantes urban journal *Place Publique* et the Parisian journal *Urbanisme*. He regularly collaborates with the magazines *AMC-LE Moniteur* architecture et *d'a / architecture*, as well as the journal *Esprit*.

# Acknowledgments and Credits

This book is the result of a collective endeavour. The editors would like to acknowledge the following authors, individuals and institutions for their invaluable contribution, help and generosity in the preparatory research work, in the organizing of the symposium in 2012 and in the final editing and design of this book in 2014.

At Université de Montréal, both the *Laboratoire d'étude de l'architecture potentielle* and the *Research Chair on Competitions and Contemporary Practices in Architecture* contributed to the initial research work that paved the way for the present book. Both entities organised a symposium, which gathered most contributors to this international inquiry. Entitled "*International Competitions and Architectural Quality in the Planetary Age*" this conference took place at the *Université de Montréal* on March 16th and 17th 2012. (For complete and detailed information on this conference please refer to: *http://www.crc.umontreal.ca/index.php*). The editors would like to thank Mr. Shohei Shigematsu, partner and director of OMA, New York, and Mrs. Line Ouellet, director of Musée National des Beaux-Arts du Québec, for giving the keynote lectures that marked this event and which confirmed the need for an international compendium of expertise. Professors Anne Cormier, Nicolas Roquet, Denis Bilodeau and David Vanderburgh kindly participated in the peered review process and provided necessary orientation.

All authors gathered in this book have generously offered their contributions for a better understanding of the crucial role of international competitions in the shaping of culture and the building of knowledge.

Ange Sauvage, Claude Bédard and Tiphaine Abenia did a wonderful work for the infography and collected information for the index of cited competitions. We would like to thank Konstantina Theodosopoulos, Dale Byrns and Samuel Dubois, for the preliminary translation as well as Tracy Valcourt and Sheena Hoszko, for the extensive work on the translation, editing and proof reading of most chapters.

The editors and publisher would like to express special thanks to Catherine Bisaillon for her fine typographical work and for the graphic layout and design of this new collection and book.

Many thanks to the *Université de Montréal*, through its *Vice-décannat à la recherche à la création et à l'innovation* for its invaluable support to the *Research Chair on Competitions and Contemporary Practices in Architecture*. Successively, Vice-provost Joseph Hubert and Vice-provost Geneviève Tanguay provided a clear direction and financial support for the creation of a unique Research Chair on Competitions at the Université de Montréal. Complementary and substantial funding from *Social Sciences and Humanities Research Council (SSHRC)* of Canada and *Fonds de recherche Société et culture Québec (FRQSC)* allowed for the initial scientific event and for the editing and printing of this book.

## ▬ Illustration Sources
**Please refer to each chapter and each image legend for precise references per author.**

CPSIA information can be obtained
at www.ICGtesting.com
Printed in the USA
LVOW05*2035021017
550882LV00018B/431/P

9 780992 131708